HANDBOOK ON POSTCONSERVATIVE
THEOLOGICAL INTERPRETATION

HANDBOOK ON POSTCONSERVATIVE THEOLOGICAL INTERPRETATION

edited by
RONALD T. MICHENER
MARK A. LAMPORT

prologue by
ROGER E. OLSON

foreword by
MEROLD WESTPHAL

introduction by
JOHN SANDERS

CASCADE *Books* • Eugene, Oregon

HANDBOOK ON POSTCONSERVATIVE THEOLOGICAL INTERPRETATION

Copyright © 2024 Wipf and Stock Publishers. All rights reserved. Except for brief quotations in critical publications or reviews, no part of this book may be reproduced in any manner without prior written permission from the publisher. Write: Permissions, Wipf and Stock Publishers, 199 W. 8th Ave., Suite 3, Eugene, OR 97401.

Cascade Books
An Imprint of Wipf and Stock Publishers
199 W. 8th Ave., Suite 3
Eugene, OR 97401

www.wipfandstock.com

PAPERBACK ISBN: 978-1-6667-4405-7
HARDCOVER ISBN: 978-1-6667-4406-4
EBOOK ISBN: 978-1-6667-4407-1

Cataloguing-in-Publication data:

Names: Michener, Ronald T., editor. | Lamport, Mark A., editor. | Olson, Roger E., prologue. | Westphal, Merold, foreword. | Sanders, John, 1956–, introduction.

Title: Handbook on postconservative theological interpretation / edited by Ronald T. Michener and Mark A. Lamport ; prologue by Roger E. Olson ; foreword by Merold Westphal ; introduction by John Sanders.

Description: Eugene, OR : Cascade Books, 2024 | Includes bibliographical references and index.

Identifiers: ISBN 978-1-6667-4405-7 (paperback) | ISBN 978-1-6667-4406-4 (hardcover) | ISBN 978-1-6667-4407-1 (ebook)

Subjects: LCSH: Bible—Hermeneutics. | Bible—Theology.

Classification: BS476 .H245 2024 (paperback) | BS476 .H245 (ebook)

VERSION NUMBER 10/22/25

From Ron—To Bernie Yorton, my first college Bible professor who expanded my horizons with a pithy dictum on a chalkboard: "The familiar often becomes the true"; and to Stanley J. Grenz, who helped me wrestle with the prospects of postmodern evangelical theology.

From Mark—To my father, D. Keith Lamport, who explained, interpreted, and applied scriptural truth for a generation of young adults; and to his father, my grandfather, Varley H. Lamport, who did the same for a generation of troubled souls at our local city rescue mission. Your descendants have likewise taken up teaching and living kingdom truth in tribute. We owe a great debt to you.

Contents

About the Editors | *xiii*

Acknowledgments | *xvii*

Preface | *xix*
        EDITORS

Prologue: Postconservative Evangelical Theology | *xxiii*
        ROGER E. OLSON

Foreword: Who's Afraid of Interpretation? | *xxvii*
        MEROLD WESTPHAL

Introduction: The Nurturant Values Undergirding Postconservative Theology | *xxxi*
        JOHN SANDERS

SECTION 1   POSTMODERN PHILOSOPHICAL INTERPRETATION

Chapter 1   Phenomenological Hermeneutics | 3
        J. AARON SIMMONS

Chapter 2   Postmodern Hermeneutics | 17
        CHRISTINA M. GSCHWANDTNER

Chapter 3   Deconstructive Hermeneutics | 29
        CARL RASCHKE

Chapter 4   Political Theology and Hermeneutics: The Apocalyptic Paul as Case Study | 44
        WEMIMO JAIYESIMI & JONATHAN TRAN

Chapter 5	Literary Theory and Hermeneutics | 60
	OLIVER PEEL
Chapter 6	Postliberal Hermeneutics | 76
	RONALD T. MICHENER
Chapter 7	The Religious Turn in Postmodern Thought: Caputo and Kearney on Hermeneutics and Faith | 92
	B. KEITH PUTT
Chapter 8	Convictional Hermeneutics: James K. A. Smith on the "Logic of Incarnation" | 108
	FRED P. EDIE
Chapter 9	Hermeneutics and the End of Apologetics | 124
	MYRON BRADLEY PENNER

SECTION 2   DOCTRINAL INTERPRETATION

Chapter 10	Dramatic Hermeneutics | 139
	NIKOLAUS WANDINGER
Chapter 11	Incarnational-Trinitarian Hermeneutics | 155
	JENS ZIMMERMANN
Chapter 12	Sacramental Hermeneutics | 171
	KIRK R. MACGREGOR
Chapter 13	Spirit Hermeneutics: Interpretation as Transformation of Lives and Communities | 186
	HANNAH MATHER
Chapter 14	Creedal Hermeneutics | 203
	MARK MOORE
Chapter 15	Missional Hermeneutics | 218
	GREG MCKINZIE
Chapter 16	Open and Relational Hermeneutics | 235
	CHAD BAHL & THOMAS JAY OORD
Chapter 17	Cruciform Hermeneutics: Finding the Crucified Christ in Scripture's Genocidal Portrait of God | 249
	GREGORY A. BOYD

Chapter 18	Nonviolent Hermeneutics | 265	
	JARED NEUSCH	
Chapter 19	Pentecostal Hermeneutics | 280	
	JACQUELINE N. GREY	
Chapter 20	Holistic Evangelical Hermeneutics | 296	
	STEVEN B. SHERMAN	
Chapter 21	Embodied Hermeneutics | 314	
	BRIAN MACALLAN	
Chapter 22	Ecological Hermeneutics | 329	
	CHERRYL HUNT	

SECTION 3   CONTEXTUAL INTERPRETATION

Chapter 23	Intercultural Hermeneutics | 347
	LARRY W. CALDWELL
Chapter 24	Racial Identity Hermeneutics | 365
	YUNG SUK KIM
Chapter 25	Race and Hermeneutics | 381
	RODOLFO GALVAN ESTRADA III
Chapter 26	Asian Hermeneutics | 397
	K. K. YEO
Chapter 27	African Hermeneutics | 414
	ELIZABETH MBURU
Chapter 28	Indigenous North American/Turtle Island Hermeneutics | 429
	T. CHRISTOPHER HOKLOTUBBE & H. DANIEL ZACHARIAS
Chapter 29	Latinx Hermeneutics | 445
	SAMMY ALFARO
Chapter 30	Black Theology Hermeneutics | 461
	SANDY DWAYNE MARTIN
Chapter 31	Womanist Hermeneutics | 477
	CHERYL A. KIRK-DUGGAN

Chapter 32   Gender and Hermeneutics: Spacious Ambiguities | 494
              KAREN STRAND WINSLOW

Chapter 33   Intersex Hermeneutics | 510
              MEGAN K. DEFRANZA

SECTION 4   SCRIPTURE AND INTERPRETATION

Chapter 34   Deconstruction Hermeneutics and the Old Testament | 527
              PETER ENNS

Chapter 35   Deconstruction Hermeneutics and the New Testament | 541
              CHRIS TILLING

Chapter 36   Ancient Near East Hermeneutics | 557
              JOHN H. WALTON

Chapter 37   Biblical Cosmology Hermeneutics | 572
              ROBIN PARRY

Chapter 38   Penultimate Hermeneutics | 588
              DAVID STUART

Chapter 39   Figural Hermeneutics | 604
              DAVID NEY

Chapter 40   Scapegoat Hermeneutics | 619
              JENNIFER GARCIA BASHAW

Chapter 41   Christ-Shaped Hermeneutics | 633
              JASON BYASSEE

Chapter 42   Memory Studies Hermeneutics | 647
              MEGAN C. ROBERTS

SECTION 5   PASTORAL-APPLICATIONAL INTERPRETATION

Chapter 43   Apprenticeship Hermeneutics | 667
              DAVID STARLING

Chapter 44   Trauma Hermeneutics | 681
              RICHARD RICE

Chapter 45   Disability Hermeneutics | 695
THOMAS E. REYNOLDS

Afterword: The Emergence and Trajectory of Postconservative Thought | 711
JOHN R. FRANKE

Afterword: Do Evangelical Biblical Practices Make Sense? | 721
TELFORD WORK

About the Contributors | 730

Index of Names and Subjects | 737

About the Editors

Ronald T. Michener (Dr. theol., Faculté Universitaire de Théologie Protestante de Bruxelles) is Professor and Chair of the Department of Systematic Theology, Evangelische Theologische Faculteit, Leuven, Belgium. His research focuses broadly on the interplay between postmodern philosophy and evangelical theology. Publications include *Postliberal Theology: A Guide for the Perplexed* (2013); *The Matrix of Christian Ethics: Integrating Philosophy and Moral Theology in a Postmodern Context* (2010, with Patrick Nullens); and *Engaging Deconstructive Theology* (2007).

Mark A. Lamport (PhD, Michigan State University) has been a professor at graduate theological schools in the United States and Europe for 40 years. He is coauthor of *Nurturing Faith: A Practical Theology for Educating Christians;* coeditor of the seven-book series *The Global Story of* Christianity (2022–2204); editor of *Handbook of Philosophy and Religion* (2022); *Handbook of Contemporary Christianity in the United* States (2022); *Christianity in the Middle East* (2020); *Encyclopedia of Christianity in the Global South* (2018); *Encyclopedia of Martin Luther and the Reformation* (2017); *Encyclopedia of Christianity in the United States* (2016). He works from Grand Rapids and Fort Myers.

ABOUT THE INTRODUCERS AND AFTERWORD CONTRIBUTORS

John R. Franke (DPhil, University of Oxford) is theologian-in-residence at Second Presbyterian Church in Indianapolis and affiliate professor of theology at Christian Theological Seminary. A recognized leader in postconservative interpretation, he has published widely in the areas of Christian theology, hermeneutics, and mission.

ABOUT THE EDITORS

Roger E. Olson is Emeritus Professor of Christian Theology of Baylor University's George W. Truett Theological Seminary. Before joining that faculty, he taught theology at Bethel University (Minnesota) and Oral Roberts University. He holds the PhD in Religious Studies from Rice University.

John Sanders (ThD, University of South Africa) is Emeritus Professor of Religious Studies at Hendrix College. His publications include *Embracing Prodigals: Overcoming Authoritative Religion by Embodying Jesus' Nurturing Grace*, *Theology in the Flesh: How Embodiment and Culture Shape the Way We Think About Truth, Morality, and God*, and *The God Who Risks: A Theology of Providence*.

Merold Westphal (PhD, Yale University) is Emeritus Distinguished Professor of Philosophy at Fordham University (New York) and served as editor and scholarly advisor of dozens of top journals and publishing houses. Having published hundreds of articles, essays, and reviews, Westphal has written *Whose Community? Which Interpretation?: Philosophical Hermeneutics for the Church* (Baker Academic, 2009).

Telford Work (PhD, Duke University) is professor of theology at Westmont College, Santa Barbara. His publications include *Jesus—the End and the Beginning*, the *Brazos Theological Commentary on the Bible: Deuteronomy*, *Living and Active: Scripture in the Economy of Salvation*, *What About Evolution?* and courses and lectures on YouTube and telfordwork.net.

ABOUT THE EDITORIAL ADVISORY BOARD

Jennifer Garcia Bashaw (PhD, Fuller Theological Seminary) is Associate Professor of New Testament and Christian Ministry at Campbell University in North Carolina. Her teaching and publications focus on New Testament studies, hermeneutics, and practical theology and she is the author of *Scapegoats: The Gospel through the Eyes of Victims*.

Peter Enns (PhD, Harvard University) is Abram S. Clemens chair of biblical studies at Eastern University, St. Davids, Pennsylvania. His interests include Second Temple hermeneutics, Hebrew Bible, New Testament use of the Hebrew Bible, incarnational conceptions of Scripture, and the impact of science on Christian theology. His publications include *Inspiration and Incarnation*, *The Evolution of Adam*, and *How the Bible Actually Works*.

John R. Franke—see above

ABOUT THE EDITORS

Brian Macallan (ThD, Stellenbosch University, South Africa) is Senior Lecturer in Theology at University of Divinity, Stirling Theological College (Australia). His publications cover areas in process philosophy and theology, teaching and learning, and constructive and autoethnographic approaches to theology.

Sandy Dwayne Martin (PhD, Columbia University/Union Theological Seminary) is Professor of Religion at the University of Georgia specializing in American Religion and Christianity. Among his publications is *Black Baptists and African Missions* (Mercer University Press).

Roger E. Olson—see above

Cynthia Shafer-Elliott (PhD, University of Sheffield) is Associate Professor of Hebrew Bible/Old Testament at Baylor University. Her research emphasizes household archaeology and issues of food, gender, religion, and social memory. Shafer-Elliot is an experienced field archaeologist and is part of the archaeological excavations at Tel Halif and Tel Abel Beth Maacah in Israel.

Fernando F. Segovia (PhD, University of Notre Dame) is the Oberlin Graduate Professor of New Testament and Early Christianity at the Divinity School, Vanderbilt University. His research revolves around such issues as method and theory, ideological criticism (ethnicity-race; empire-postcolonialism; materialism), and contextual interpretation (Global South).

Steven B. Sherman (PhD, Fuller Theological Seminary) is Associate Professor of Philosophy in the College of Theology at Grand Canyon University (Phoenix). His teaching and publications primarily focus on philosophy and ethics, philosophical theology, hermeneutics, philosophy of religion and worldviews.

Acknowledgments

Michael Thomson, senior acquisitions editor at Wipf and Stock, carried our idea full-on (a rather-lengthy, one-volume treatment of this topic) to the editorial board of Wipf & Stock, successfully navigating it through their arduous process. Always the professional, always the cheerleader—your support, Michael, for a long association has been a wonderful part of my (Mark) schooling in publishing.

Thanks also to Baker Publishing for permission for adaptation pertaining to some text by David Starling in his chapter on "apprenticeship hermeneutics" which appears in his 2024 book on aspects of the same topic.

The following were instrumental in shepherding the contents of the book into production-worthy copy—Joshua Erb (senior editorial consultant) as well as a stellar team of indexers: Philip Bustrum, Mel Wilhoit, Heidi Herbruck, Jerry Franz, Jean Van Horn, Kris Mounts, and Jerry Mounts, Jr.

Ron thanks his colleagues at the Evangelische Theologische Faculteit (Leuven, Belgium) for modeling faithfulness to diversity and solidarity in the faith. It's been a joy to work with such fine Christian scholars through the years who truly practice *fides quaerens intellectum* with grace and charity.

Mark begs the readers' toleration for a moment of personal reminiscence. *This book, his 20th since 2015, will be the last.* For forty consecutive years he has published over 200 academic pieces in journals ansd books—a feat *no one* who met him would have ever imagined. Mark suspects he rose to the challenge due to being awarded—unfairly, he still thinks, even after 50 years—a "C" in English composition as a seventeen-year-old university student. He then willed to learn the craft of writing, primarily by studying good writing from phenomenal authors, including fiction and non-fiction, then imitating. Mark wishes to acknowledge mentors and colleagues who have shepherded through the years—George Thomas Kurian, Jim Packer, John Stott, Garrison Keillor, and even the ancient professor who came out of retirement to give him that "C". Mark could not be happier to conclude his publishing career with this fascinating topic of theological interpretation in close association with Ron Michener, a fine scholar and friend.

Finally, a variety of keen-eyed, supremely-hospitable colleagues at Wipf & Stock have improved our book and made the publishing process so much more enjoyable—Charlie Collier, Stephanie Hough, George Callihan, and Calvin Jaffarian.

Preface

RONALD T. MICHENER AND MARK A. LAMPORT

AUTHORITY AND CONTROL

The fundamental themes of Martin Luther's reforms locate the Bible as the ultimate foundation of all Christian belief and practice. But the problem which then emerged (and continues still!) is *"How can one speak of the Bible as having any authority when it is so clearly at the mercy of its interpreters?"*[1] The fundamental problem of theological identity, as Alister McGrath extrapolates, and as other branches within Christianity perceived, was primarily about a certain way of doing theology that could lead to an *uncontrollable diversity of outcomes,* and that's a problem, isn't it? And who would have the definitive prerogative to decide what is orthodox and what is heretical? This was "a dangerous idea" McGrath argues that opened the floodgates to "a torrent of distortion, misunderstanding, and confusion."[2]

So, the two major concepts the editors and contributors of this volume must put in play for the readers' consideration of theological interpretation are *authority* and *control*. When Christianity identifies sacred documents, such as the scriptural texts of the Old and New Testaments, as its ground of the faith, an authoritative stance then rules the content and practices of the faith. And, when a hermeneutical method is installed to interpret this authority, a means of control is exercised to ensure structures and believers have fences to contain rogue interpretation.

Not surprisingly, various tangents within the breadth of the Christian family, namely, denominational branches and even transdenominational wings within these groups, often described as fundamentalist or moderate

1. McGrath, *Dangerous Idea,* 93.
2. McGrath, *Dangerous Idea,* 208–9.

or liberal or Pentecostal, are keen to provide interpretative tools which guide ways of knowing and applying Scripture result in their preferred outcomes. In other words, a fundamentalist hermeneutical stance confirms fundamentalist views, a Pentecostal hermeneutical stance supports its Pentecostal views, and so forth.

Thus, we ask, can there be legitimate means that does not work from the desired results back into the interpretative method, and can cultural, geographical, economic, social, political, governmental, and ethnic values be excluded from incursion into interfering with the words God intends for Christians rather than redirecting God's revelatory intentions through illegitimate grids? Let us start our exploration.

LOCATING POSTCONSERVATIVE THEOLOGY IN A MILIEU OF CHRISTIAN VOICES

Hermeneutics, the academic study of textual interpretation, and this handbook, shines light on various slants, perspectives, presumptions on theological interpretation. Several works have emerged making this project a worthwhile comparative sourcebook to highlight recent trajectories in "postconservative" theological interpretation.

The notion of "postconservative" theology stems from its context in relationship with or response to conservative or traditional evangelicalism, as noted by both John R. Franke's *The Character of Theology: A Postconservative Evangelical Approach* (Baker Academic, 2005) and Roger E. Olson's, *Reformed and Always Reforming: The Postconservative Approach to Evangelical Theology* (Baker Academic, 2007). In its initial context, postconservative theology was expressed as orthodox and biblical, but open to new insights about how to interpret Scripture. But the new insights must be faithful as well as fresh. Postconservative theology is not the same as "progressive theology,"[3] which tends to lean toward indeterminant faith expressions, whereas postconservative allows for particular faith commitments and expressions but understands that the constructive task of theology is never finished. Postconservative is, however, postfundamentalist in the sense that there is, as James K. A. Smith notes, "a recognition of our hermeneutic situatedness—owning up to our finitude and the inescapability of 'traditioning' in

---

3. We think some see both postconservative theology and progressive theology as "liberal." But classical theological liberalism was embedded in and/or reacting to Enlightenment thinking. Progressive theology, on the other hand, is postmodern and hence, post-Enlightenment, but also non-conservative and committed to indeterminacy in faith expression. Postconservative theological expressions are also postmodern (i.e., rejecting modernist, Enlightenment reductionism) but may still express a determinate, local, particular faith commitment and expression.

how we encounter the world and interpret texts . . . the Bible wasn't dropped from the sky" but it was, "handed down to us by communities and traditions of interpretation" that are "contestable."[4] In agreement with Smith, postconservatives acknowledge that we cannot escape our backgrounds and traditions in order to interpret from a standpoint of neutrality. We are always and already embedded within a context.

MISSION AND SCOPE OF THE BOOK

The hermeneutical perspectives expressed in these forty-plus chapters, although overlapping at various junctures, will provide an overview of the breadth and diversity of interpretive perspectives among postconservatives. The essays will highlight the sensibilities, issues, and developments that are influential in contemporary theological interpretation, both in method and focus.

Many books currently used in theological studies present a conservative, grammatical-historical approach toward an evangelical hermeneutic of theological interpretation, but few display the broader landscape of postmodern and/or postconservative perspectives. For example, Cambridge University Press' *Companion to Hermeneutics* (2019); Blackwell's *Companion to Hermeneutics* (2016), and Routledge's *Companion to Hermeneutics* (2017) cover a broader range of issues from philosophical to theological hermeneutics. We wish to focus only on theological interpretation, such as A. K. M. Adam's *Handbook of Postmodern Biblical Interpretation* (Chalice, 2000), which emphasizes alternate theological themes within continental philosophy. Our contents will focus, however, on postconservative (broadly evangelical) theological approaches and themes that are emerging today.

This is not a handbook to argue "for" postconservative theological interpretation. That is, it is not intended to make specific arguments for positions, but rather serve as a *descriptive* handbook.[5] It will serve as a reference highlighting the variety of twenty-first century interpretive lenses, perspectives, that are used in theological and biblical interpretation that stretch the margins of classical, fundamental, or conservative evangelical theology. All labels are of course insufficient, but this is the general idea. It is not a critically evaluative handbook, but a descriptive handbook on many of the currents in our contemporary evangelical and post-evangelical landscape. If there is a better term to use other than "postconservative" so be it, but we cannot think of one at this juncture.

---

4. Smith, *Fall of Interpretation*, 5.

5. Although, some authors may implicitly argue for a particular position within their description.

This volume has enlisted authors that emphasize various interpretive theological lenses used for doing theology among various postconservative theologians, rather than emphasizing the philosophical background to hermeneutical theory present in other works, such as past influential thinkers including Gadamer, Grondin, Ricœur, Heidegger, etc. Our resource could possibly function as a companion to *Evangelical Theological Method: Five Views* (IVP Academic, 2018). This emphasis of the chapters, therefore, will not be on the nuts and bolts of "how to" interpret, but rather on the *theological impulses* that govern various lenses (Bible, cultural context, etc.) for doing theology and the way Scripture functions with respect to the practice of interpretation.

ORGANIZATION OF THE BOOK

After the front-pieces (written by Merold Westphal, Roger Olsen, and John Sanders) have oriented readers to the context and major concepts of postconservative theological interpretation, readers are invited to dip into five discrete thematic units:

- Postmodern Philosophical Interpretation (chapters 1–9)
- Doctrinal Interpretation (chapters 10–22)
- Contextual Interpretation (chapters 23–33)
- Scripture and Interpretation (chapters 34–42)
- Pastoral-Applicational Interpretation (chapter 43–46)

Finally, two scholars at the forefront of ongoing dialogue on postconservative hermeneutics—John Franke and Telford Work—offer "afterwords" as a means of critiquing and reality-testing the chapters and offer a way forward in the conversation.

So, come along and join in. Listen to the embedded assumptions as well as the explicit posits of the chapters. Our task is not agreement, but engagement. If the book challenges your thinking and methods of interpreting the sacred documents of Christianity without sacrificing truth for expediency and merely capitulating to learned theological practices, we have succeeded. Let the fun begin!

BIBLIOGRAPHY

McGrath, Alister. *Christianity's Dangerous Idea: The Protestant Revolution—A History from the Sixteenth Century to the Twenty-First*. San Francisco: HarperOne, 2007.

Smith, James K. A. *The Fall of Interpretation: Philosophical Foundations for a Creational Hermeneutic*. Grand Rapids: Baker Academic, 2012.

Prologue

Postconservative Evangelical Theology

ROGER E. OLSON

The year was 1993, the month was November. I was driving home from a theological conference in Chicago. There some "young Turks" of evangelical theology, including especially my friend Stanley J. Grenz, had presented some new ideas about postfoundationalist evangelical theology. Several of us were excited about discovering an evangelical approach to theology that we be decidedly postfundamentalist but not liberal. We wanted to escape the "left-to-right" "spectrum" of theology in which a person was either conservative or liberal. We were inspired to some extent by the writings of the newly emerging "Yale School of Theology" also known popularly as "postliberal theology." But we were never liberal, so we couldn't call ourselves "postliberal." We were excited about developments in narrative theology, especially Hans Frei's now classic book of hermeneutics entitled *The Eclipse of Biblical Narrative* (1974). We were restless and unsettled, disappointed with the direction in which most notable evangelical theologians seemed to be going, back, for example, to the rationalistic theologies of Charles Hodge and Benjamin Warfield. We sought a new way to be evangelical theologically without being foundationalist or rationalistic.

At the same time, several of us were interested in postmodern thought, especially the musings of Jacques Derrida, John (Jack) Caputo, and Alister McIntyre. We were beginning to look to Stanley Hauerwas as a possible guide into our evangelical future in theology. Most of our conservative colleagues in evangelical theology were foundationalists in epistemology and were seeming to make something called "the evangelical tradition" a kind of shackles on what we could think or write or say. Some among us were thinking and writing about "open theism," the idea that God limits Godself not to know the future in absolute, comprehensive detail. Whereas Calvinism was the norm among leading evangelical theologians, most of us did not consider ourselves that.

As I drove home after that especially exciting and energizing meeting in Chicago I mused about a new label for our emerging, new approach to evangelical theology. Suddenly the term "postconservative" popped into my head. "Postconservative evangelical theology." When I arrived home I almost immediately sat down and in a matter of hours produced an article entitled "Postconservative Evangelicals Greet the Postmodern Age." I submitted it to *Christianity Today* and they rejected it. So, I submitted it to *Christian Century* and they accepted it and published the article in its May 1995 issue. For me, anyway, the rest is history. Later I wrote a full volume about the postconservative approach to evangelical theology entitled "Reformed and Always Reforming: The Postconservative Approach to Evangelical Theology" that was published by Baker Academic in 2007.

Immediately after the appearance of my *Christian Century* article I was called into my college president's office to discuss it. I could tell he had received letters and phone calls objecting to the article and to my presence on his faculty. I was teaching theology then at Bethel College and Seminary, now Bethel University, in suburban St. Paul. The president gently chided me for stirring the evangelical pot, so to speak, and asked me to submit my writings to him before submitting them for publication. I declined and waited for the fallout. But none came. My president supported me, especially after I wrote an "in house paper" explaining that "postconservataive" did *not* mean liberal or even anti-conservative.

In 1996 Stanley Grenz and I were invited to be on a panel together with evangelical theologians Millard Erickson and Bruce Ware at a regional meeting of the Evangelical Theological Society. The meeting was held at Northwestern College in suburban St. Paul, a rather conservative, even "fundamentalish" institution (in my opinion). Stan and I were publicly chided by Erickson and Ware with the latter theologian accusing us of "worshiping at the feet of the goddess of novelty." That stung. I thought it was very unfair. The backlash against my label "postconservative evangelical" was sometimes harsh and often based on misunderstanding if not misinterpretation. Which is why I finally wrote *Reformed and Always Reforming*—to explain in great detail what I meant by "postconservative evangelical theology."

To be honest and forthright, my "model" for a postconservative evangelical theologian was Stanley Grenz, but I also included, at least in my own mind, Clark Pinnock and a few other so-called "progressive evangelical theologians." What did they have in common? Well, at least that all three of us and others who bought into the new label were influenced by evangelical theologian Bernard Ramm who sought to break out of the "mold" of evangelical theology crafted by the likes of Carl F. H. Henry.

After I thought I coined the label "postconservative evangelical" I found out that two theologians had used it before me. One was Jack Rogers, then professor of theology at Fuller Theological Seminary. Years before I had read his little memoir entitled *Confessions of a Conservative Evangelical* (1974) and I resonated with his expressed discomfort with the conservatism of his own Reformed spiritual formation. After I began identifying as a postconservative evangelical it occurred to me that Jack's book's title did not fit the content and message. So I called him and asked him if, perchance, his original title was "Confessions of a Postconservative Evangelical" and the publisher changed it. He affirmed my theory. Then, I realized that Clark Pinnock has used the label "postconservative" for post-Vatican 2 Catholic theology in *Tracking the Maze: Finding Our Way through Modern Theology from an Evangelical Perspective* (1990). So I wasn't the first to use the term as I had originally thought.

So what did—and do—I mean by "postconservative theology?"

First, for me, "postconservative" always modified "evangelical." I used the adjective to distinguish *our* newish approach to evangelical theology from the typical conservative approach which was, and largely still is, foundationalist and prone to giving "the received evangelical tradition" (read Charles Hodge's theology with various minor modifications) binding authority among at least American evangelical theologians.

The key idea was and is that *the constructive task of theology is never finished*. We postconservatives, decidedly evangelical in spirit, believed conservative evangelical theologians considered the constructive and reconstructive tasks of theology completed, perhaps by Charles Hodge, and saw the only real tasks of evangelical theology as critical and re-expressive in new cultural idioms. We postconservative evangelicals believe there is always new light to break forth from fresh and faithful study of God's Word, the Bible. N. T. Wright has written that he considers himself one of us in *Justification* (2016). Richard Bauckham has told me personally that he identifies as a postconservative evangelical theologian.

Second, for me, "postconservative" means *not* considering or treating *traditional belief* as binding even for evangelical Christianity except insofar as it is faithful to God's word. Postconservatives are evangelicals in David Bebbington's sense, but are at the same time open to new insights into Christian doctrine and practice.

Third, and I suppose this is the most specific feature, postconservative evangelicals do not adhere to *biblical inerrancy* as it is usually defined and described by conservative evangelical theologians such as those who wrote "The Chicago Statement on Biblical Inerrancy." We think the word "inerrant" is problematic and would prefer to talk about the Bible as "perfect with respect to purpose." We are not very concerned about harmonizing all seemingly conflicting statements of fact in scripture and we embrace all the genres of scripture as inspiring and authoritative even if they cannot be translated directly into propositional language. Postconservative evangelicals love the Bible, but we do not think of it as, or treat it as, a no-yet-systematized systematic theology. This is what we fear conservative evangelicals do to the Bible. We think of theology as reflection on the meaning and implications of the Bible. We do not reject systematic theologies but our attitude toward them is that of Alfred Lord Tennyson:

> Our little systems have their day;
> They have their day and cease to be.
> They are but broken lights of Thee
> And Thou, O God, art more than they.

I worry that some theologians and students who have adopted my term "postconservative" equate it with progressivism leading in the direction of liberal theology. I and we most definitely did not intend that. We were and are *orthodox Christians* while at the same time remaining open-minded and exploratory about the possibilities of new ways of thinking about God within a broadly evangelical frame of reference.

Foreword

Who's Afraid of Interpretation?

MEROLD WESTPHAL

We see the same Bible differently, depending on where we're standing. As Justo González states, none of us sees the whole landscape, nor do any of us see that landscape 'as it really is.'[1]

Two things to note: *First*, this text calls attention to an obvious and easily observable fact. Whether we are talking about literary classics, the United States Constitution, or the Bible, we find a rich variety of interpretations, often in opposition with one another. *Second*, we are given an equally observable explanation of this fact. We "see" (read, interpret) differently from each other because we are "standing" in different places. In other words, there is, as Paul Ricœur has put it, a "conflict of interpretations" because we never occupy, as Thomas Nagel has put it, "the view from nowhere." We are always somewhere when we read a text.

These "somewheres" or perspectives (metaphors from physical vision) can be identified in many ways: as races, classes, genders, cultures, societal practices, standpoints, prejudices (pre-judgments), gestalts, traditions, language games, or paradigms. Some of these are inherited by nature, some infused by nurture.

We can think of these "places" as homes in which we dwell, as anticipations of experience, as angles of vision. To a significant degree they form our identity, and they shape the way we interpret the world around us, including the textual world. To be more precise, they play an a priori role, since we bring them to experience, and they condition what and how we experience. Of course, they can be strengthened, weakened, or altered in and by experience, but then they play an a priori role in a correspondingly different way.

1. Joel B. Green, on the front cover of *Fuller* magazine, Issue #8, 2017.

We can call the hermeneutical theory implied here perspectival pluralism. It is a pluralist account because these "places" vary from group to group and from individual to individual and in both cases from time to time. It is perspectival because each "place" is somewhere and neither nowhere or everywhere. As our opening quotation puts it, it is because we don't see "the whole landscape" that we don't see it "as it really is."

This is nicely illustrated by the story of the six blind men from Hindustan. They "saw" the elephant with their hands, but only a part and not the whole. Accordingly, they insisted, respectively and dogmatically, that the elephant was like a wall, a spear, a snake, a tree, a fan, and a rope. "Though each was partly in the right they all were in the wrong."[2]

It would seem that the apostle Paul holds to an eschatological version of such a hermeneutics:

> For we know only in part, and we prophecy only in part, but when the complete comes, the partial will come to an end.

After suggesting that in our partiality we are epistemically like children, unaware of our limits, he draws the conclusion that as such we do not grasp reality "as it really is."

> For now we see in a mirror dimly, [through a glass darkly, KJV] but then we will see face to face. Now I know only in part; then I will know fully, even as I have been fully known. (1 Cor 13:9–12 NRSV)

Something of the same metaphor is at work here as when we speak of seeing the world through rose colored glasses. The perceptual conditions that enable us to see at all prevent us from seeing perfectly. That is what is meant above by saying that our perspectives "condition" our perceptions, including our interpretations. They are not unconditioned, absolute, final.

We can image a member of the Corinthian congregation taking Paul to task in a conversation that goes like this.

"But doesn't that imply an 'anything goes' relativism that undermines the gospel?"

"But *we are relative*, human and not divine. The gift of revelation doesn't transubstantiate us into fourth and fifth persons of the trinity. The doctrine of creation and the biblical polemic against idolatry remind us that only God is God. But that didn't keep me from opposing Peter to his face on the question of eating with gentiles. Gal 2:11–14."

---

2. This poem is easily found on the internet and quoted in my *Whose Community?*, 25–26.

"But how can evangelism and missions continue if our interpretations don't grasp reality 'as it really is'"?

"Do you recall any hesitation of timidity in my proclamation when I first came among you? I have risked my life in preaching the gospel, but I try never to forget that 'we have this treasure in clay jars' [earthen vessels, KJV], so that it may be made clear that this extraordinary power belongs to God and does not come from us" (2 Cor 4:7 NRSV).

"So you seek to combine bold preaching with hermeneutical humility?"

"Actually, it's worse than that. If the doctrine of creation insists that we are finite, the doctrine of the fall reminds us that we are fallen and that as sinners (and all have sinned) we 'suppress the truth.' Rom 1:18 NRSV. Our knowledge is not only conditioned by our finitude but also contaminated by our fallenness. We put the limited understanding we are able to gain into the service of our human all too human all too human purposes. Whether these are personal or political we are the Pharisees and the Sadducees."

It seems we are not at home on the (theological and biblical) range. For these are discouraging words, and we are tempted to flee them. We are tempted to deny our hermeneutical relativity by claiming for our interpretations an objectivity free from filtering by our subjectivity, our finitude and our fallenness. The most shameless attempt to do so I have ever come across was in a promotion for a new translation of the Bible. The publishers claimed that it was so accurate and so clear that "no interpretation needed."[3]

Without actually making such a claim, we are easily tempted to think that way by the Reformed doctrine of the perspicuity of scripture and the Catholic teaching that it was only the will and not the intellect that was damaged by the fall. Whatever its source or form, the refusal to take the hermeneutical turn can be called epistemic fundamentalism, noting both that it can occur anywhere on the theological spectrum and that it can and does occur outside of theological interpretation altogether.

Similarly, where does the hermeneutics of humility stand in relation to a (relatively) new tradition (*sic*) of postconservative evangelicalism? It provides firm philosophical support for the first characteristic Roger Olson lists in his introduction to this volume (to follow). Biblical interpretation and theological teaching is never finished and final. There is always new insight to be gained and old misunderstandings to be overcome.

There is also an affinity with a second earmark, the subordination of every tradition to Scripture. But, of course, this does not mean that our traditions are subject to the finitude and fallenness that the hermeneutical

---

3. Jamie Smith called my attention to this. See Smith, *Fall of Interpretation*, 39. This view can be called "naive realism." See *Whose Community?*, 18.

circle and the hermeneutics of suspicion point out while our Scripture is unconditioned and uncontaminated. For we never have the Bible apart from our interpretations of it, and these are not divinely inspired but human, all too human.

In the third place, such an hermeneutical theory helps such a theology to understand why it does not need the doctrine of inerrancy, which all too easily forgets the dialectical unity of divine and human in Scripture (as in the person of Jesus) at the expense of the human, not only in the production but also in the reading of the Bible.

Finally, Olson wants his theology to be orthodox. We have already seen the deep affinity of the hermeneutical turn with the doctrines of Creation and the Fall. I see no tension between these reflections and other dimensions of historic Christian orthodoxy except where (some) church has sought to make its tradition (*sic*) the final, unconditioned version of orthodoxy.

So how do we seek to hear God's voice in the earthen vessels that are our theologies? Joel Green concludes the quotation with which these reflections began by writing, "Taken together, though—by the church across time and round the globe—we are drawn closer to hearing and understanding the big picture of what God is saying and doing through his Word." Perhaps instead of fleeing perspectives we should multiply them. For after all, we *are* relative, and only God is absolute.

BIBLIOGRAPHY

Smith, James K. A. *The Fall of Interpretation: Philosophical Foundations for a Creational Hermeneutic*. Downers Grove, IL: Intervarsity, 2000, 39.

Westphal, Merold. *Whose Community? Which Interpretation? Philosophical Hermeneutics for the Church*. Grand Rapids: Baker Academic, 2009.

Introduction

The Nurturant Values Undergirding Postconservative Theology

JOHN SANDERS

In recent years many thousands of people have left evangelicalism and conservative Catholicism in the United States. This is particularly true of young people. A staggering 59 percent of people aged eighteen to twenty-nine have left the church permanently or for a prolonged period. People give different reasons for their departure. Some say the church is closed-minded and fear based. Some left due to the negative treatment of gays. Others were told that if you are a Christian then you must vote Republican. They believe that if being a Christian means to be fearful of ideas and people who are different from those of your tribe and that you must march lock step with one political party, then to hell with that. Speaking of hell, many of those who leave the church no longer believe that a God who says, "I love you but if you don't live exactly how I say, then I'm going to torture you in hell for all eternity."

Values are at the heart of this exodus and these same values motivate those who affirm postconservative theology. The term "postconservative" refers to those raised in conservative Christianity who see the need to transform some of its beliefs and practices to make it more faithful to the gospel of Jesus. Several of the contributors to this volume have spent much of their lives working to reform conservative Christianity on topics such as what God is like, the nature of the Bible, and how to live out the Christian life. They seek to show those leaving church that there are alternative forms of Christianity that embody their values.

I believe that those leaving the church and postconservatives tend to operate with what social scientists refer to as Nurturant values. These Nurturant Christians seek to reform or break from what I call Authoritative religion.[1] This chapter will explain the differences in values between Nurturants and Authoritatives and show how these values lead to conflicting approaches to the Bible, doctrines, and what psychologists call cognitive styles.[2] Whereas the chapters in this book focus on specific approaches postconservatives use to understand the Christian life, this chapter provides a "big picture" account of what these chapters have in common.

THE CORE VALUES OF NURTURANTS AND AUTHORITATIVES

Nurturants prioritize empathy, cooperation, dialogue, perspective taking, and shared governance. They realize that we live in various communities, so we need to work together. Understanding the situation of others is paramount to facilitate this. They favor shared governance in institutions rather than autocratic leaders. Even when one person has the final responsibility, taking the concerns of others into account is important. People need to be self-reliant as they make their way through life. Encountering new situations may require different actions rather than simply mimicking what others have done in the past. They understand that many situations are complex and require nuance and qualification rather than an all-or-nothing mentality. They tend to have "epistemic humility" in that they make claims to truth but realize there are things they do not know and may have to revise their ideas. When it comes to justice, Nurturants want all people to have a solid opportunity to fulfil their potential in life. Individuals need to work hard, yet we also need vibrant educational and social structures in place to empower people to flourish.

Many of the chapters in this book are about perspective taking—how other groups of Christians make meaning and interpret the Bible. Other chapters discuss the complex nature of knowledge and why we may not be able to arrive at a single agreed upon belief on a given topic. Still others promote the hermeneutics of human flourishing. In short, the postconservative approach to life embraces Nurturant values.

Authoritatives prioritize a very different set of values. Obedience to rules and to those in authority is paramount for both families and churches. Authoritatives view the world as a dangerous place and strictly enforcing the rules is the best way to get people to survive in the struggle against others. Children are seen as morally weak and must be taught individual

---

1. Other names for the Authoritative approach include strict father, authoritarian, and disciplinarian.

2. For documentation and elaboration of the material in this chapter see Sanders, *Embracing Prodigals*.

responsibility by getting them to follow the rules. When people break the rules, harsh punishments are enacted to instill fear of disobedience in the future. Authoritatives prefer an unchanging social order—keeping roles and relationships the way they have been for centuries. Many hold that this means that males should be in charge. In addition, they tend to think in black and white, all-or-nothing, terms. Issues are clear and do not need qualifications. They desire certainty in their claims and moral judgments. They exhibit what psychologists call "cognitive closure" instead of open-mindedness. They define justice as getting what you deserve. If you follow the rules, then you deserve a reward. If you do wrong, then you must pay for it.

When presented with this summary, people find the Nurturant and Authoritative ways of life quite familiar because they have encountered them in parents, teachers, and coaches as well as in films and books. Before we leave this summary, three qualifications are needed. First, it is not the case that Nurturants are never concerned about obedience or that Authoritatives never care about cooperation. Rather, it is a matter of priorities. Authoritatives place little concern on perspective taking and the need for dialogue whereas Nurturants highly promote these. Second, the models are prototypes of these ways of life. Individuals will manifest various degrees of likeness to these ideal types. Third, though social science research focusses on Nurturants and Authoritatives, there are two additional models: Permissive and Disengaged. The four types are based on whether one has high or low expectations of others and whether one is highly affirming of others.[3] The Disengaged do not care how others live and do not offer affirmation to them. Permissives are highly affirming of others but have low expectations for them. They are on your side and tend not to care what you do. Authoritatives have high expectations but are low on affirming. They tend to be the "tough love" coaches, teachers, and parents. Only Nurturants expect a lot from others and provide high affirmation to help them succeed. Jesus practiced a Nurturant way of life.[4] He has high expectations in that he wants people to stop sinning and he lavishes grace and affirmation on people to empower them to change. That the Nurturant approach to life is superior to the Authoritative approach is shown by studies in different countries and cultures around the world.[5] For instance, Nurturants have higher degrees

---

3. The four types are not due to personality traits. Rather, they are based on Diana Baumrind's widely used typology of child rearing. However, for what I call "Authoritative" she uses "Authoritarian" and for what I call "Nurturant" she uses "Authoritative." I follow the lead of most social scientists on this topic in my terminology.

4. See Sanders, *Embracing Prodigals*, chapter 2.

5. See Sanders, *Embracing Prodigals*, 8–9, 41–5, 118, and 125.

of prosocial behavior, greater life satisfaction, higher self-esteem, and less anxiety than Authoritatives. They are more accepting and forgiving towards others. Their communities have lower death rates from natural disasters and infectious diseases.

The core values held by Nurturants and Authoritatives shape what each side finds reasonable and unacceptable in the Christian life. The different values attract them to very different positions on topics such as the nature of the Bible, God, sin, salvation, and hell.

APPROACHING THE BIBLE

Nurturants see the Bible as a key tool that God uses to shape Christian communities. It is an invitation to a way of life, a guide for the pilgrimage, not a list of rules to memorize. Authoritatives hold the Bible as the ultimate rulebook whose detailed instructions are to be followed without question. Many Nurturants believe the Bible contains multiple points of view on many topics and sometimes there is outright disagreement between biblical writers. Authoritatives tend to believe God "wrote" the Bible so there is only one point of view on all topics though it may be challenging to harmonize the texts. Whereas Nurturants believe that the best of what humans learn from the natural sciences, social sciences, and the humanities should be placed in dialogue with biblical teaching, Authoritatives claim that the Bible always trumps "human reasoning." What about biblical texts that teach ideas that go against what we know from science or go against moral standards we now take for granted? What about the texts that depict God performing violence? Can Christians question the Bible and set aside some biblical teachings? Authoritatives say "Absolutely not! You don't question God."

However, Authoritatives do set aside some biblical teachings even though they never admit it. Here are two examples. Joshua 10:13 says, "The sun stood still, and the moon stopped, until the nation took vengeance on their enemies." When I ask Authoritative Christians what the text means they say, "The earth slowed in its rotation." That is, they believe that the earth rotates and revolves around the sun—heliocentrism. Yet, the text declares that it is the sun that moves—geocentrism. Martin Luther and others used this verse to claim that God knew the solar system better than Copernicus or Galileo. Today, Authoritatives believe Galileo was correct and no longer use this verse as divine proof that geocentrism is correct. Another example is Exod 21:20–22. It says that a slave owner can severely beat a slave with a rod so long as the slave does not die that day—if the slave dies the next day, that is okay. Prior to the Civil War a pastor said this verse grants slave owners "divine authority" to beat slaves harshly. He said that those who disagreed with slavery were rejecting God's unchanging moral commandments. Today, most Authoritatives believe slavery is immoral and do not use the Bible to "divinely" sanction slavery. They set aside these biblical teachings while claiming they never set aside God's teachings.

From the beginning of Christianity, people have found various teachings in the Bible troublesome and developed principled ways to pick-and-chose which biblical teachings to follow and which to set aside. The two main ways of doing this are criterial internal to the Bible and criteria external to the Bible. Here are three examples of the internal criteria. First, you take Jesus's principle of love and argue that if another biblical text instructs us to do something unloving, then that text is wrong. A second option distinguishes between commands that were normative before Jesus but are no longer obligatory after Jesus. A third route says to follow the trajectory on a topic in the Bible to see if latter biblical writers challenge oppressive practices sanctioned by earlier writers such as the treatment of women. The following are two examples of the external criteria. First, you hold that anything in the Bible classified as "cultural" is not binding on all Christians for all times and places. For instance, women wearing expensive clothes to church (1 Tim 2:9). A second external criterion is to use the best scientific and moral reasoning to revise traditionally accepted interpretations of texts or to reject the texts outright. This last criterion was used to overturn geocentrism while several of the internal and external criteria were used to overturn the biblical approval of slavery. Today, Nurturants use these criteria in debates involving divine violence texts and same-gender relationships.

GOD

Nurturant Christians believe that Jesus is the model of God and that Jesus lived out Nurturant values. Some religious Authoritatives in Jesus's day took exception to Jesus when he showed grace and hospitality to Jews who did not follow God's rules. Such people did not, for instance, go to synagogue, keep the Sabbath, or eat the right foods. Jesus agrees that these people are not in proper relationship with God, but he says the best way to transform people is to shower them with grace, acceptance, and forgiveness that they do not deserve. That is, you first show affirmation to empower them to change. In addition, Jesus shows grace and acceptance to those outside his in-group when he deals with non-Jews such as Roman military officers and Canaanites.

Nurturants believe God has high expectations for how we should live, and God lavishes love and acceptance on us to empower our lives. Divine hospitality comes before the call to live a new way of life. Divine justice seeks to help all people to flourish and to rehabilitate offenders. Surveys show that when Nurturants are asked to describe what God is like they use the following adjectives: forgiving, merciful, loving, accepting, not controlling, caring, and generous.

Authoritatives have a very different view of God. They hold that God will accept us only after we change. Clean up your act, follow God's rules, and then God will care for you. God cares only for those who follow the rules and hates the outsiders. God is just because God gives people what they deserve. If you follow the rules for how to be a Christian, then God rewards you with heaven. God sends the disobedient to hell. Those who believe in an Authoritative God describe God as critical, punishing, judging, wrathful, disapproving, controlling, strict, and unforgiving.

SIN AND SALVATION

For Nurturants, sin is understood in relational terms—it is about harming relationships. Salvation is about restoring relationships. To accomplish this, God simply forgives and shows grace which empowers people to be transformed and flourish. Nurturants affirm a range of views regarding atonement. The *Christus Victor* theory understands the human situation as one in which God's children have been taken hostage by the forces of evil. Jesus's goes into the stronghold of the powers of evil and is victorious over them via his resurrection, liberating the children to return to God's home. Abelard (twelfth century) put forth the model of love view which says Jesus's life, death, and resurrection demonstrate God's amazing love to us which empowers us to love as Jesus did. The scapegoat theory (see chapter by Bashaw in this book) holds that groups tend to blame individuals or minority groups who do not fit the norm when severe hardships face a community. These people are driven away from the community or punished in some way. By becoming a scapegoat Jesus frees us from this horrible cycle.

For Authoritatives, sin is framed as breaking rules and deserving punishment. Salvation is about paying for the crime. The dominant view of atonement among Authoritatives is called penal substitution and goes like this. Humans have broken God's rules and must be punished so that God's moral accounting books are balanced. God must give people what they deserve and what they deserve for sinning against an infinite being is hell. Salvation is made possible by Jesus who lived a perfect life of obedience to God's laws and did not deserve punishment. God punished Jesus in our place (substitute) and Jesus paid God the price to balance the moral books (penal). It is crucial to note that according to this theory God does not forgive anyone! Rather, Jesus paid God in full. It is like a family with several children and one of them has disobeyed. The parent says the disobedient one must be punished. But then one of the siblings says that they will take the punishment instead and the parent replies that it does not matter who is punished, so long as someone pays the price. In this case the sibling who broke the rules is not forgiven. Rather, someone else was punished in their place. Penal substitution fits hand-in-glove with Authoritative values, but Nurturants find this model of atonement abhorrent.

SAVING NON-CHRISTIANS

If Jesus is the only savior, what about those who never heard of Jesus or those who grow up in other religions? Because Nurturants believe that love includes concern for "outsiders" as well as members of one's own tribe, they are attracted to views that affirm a wider hope. One view is known as inclusivism. It holds that God's spirit is working outside the confines of the church and the saving work of Jesus is applied to those who respond positively to the information they have from God. Others prefer the idea of a postmortem opportunity to encounter Jesus after death.

Authoritatives believe God cares only about the insiders which is why they affirm a view known as Restrictivism. Jesus captains the lifeboat of salvation but it never reaches everyone. Salvation is restricted to those who hear about and exercise trust in Jesus before they die. Since most people in history have died never really hearing about Jesus, most humans are damned in hell.

HELL

For Authoritatives, hell is eternal conscious torment. This is what people deserve for breaking the rules of an infinite God. The gates of hell are locked from the outside by God to keep people from escaping. Nurturants find an eternal torture chamber incompatible with both God's justice and love. What does tormenting people for eternity accomplish except vindictiveness? True justice seeks to transform people (rehabilitation) and death cannot prevent God from seeking God's lost children. Because Nurturants have different understandings of justice and love than Authoritatives, they find other views of hell meaningful. Some prefer the view that hell is remedial (restorative justice) and seeks to rehabilitate those who have locked themselves in hell. Some believe that this will eventually result in universal salvation. Others affirm a view called annihilationism in which the finally impenitent cease to exist.

COGNITIVE STYLES

People from the two models manifest different preferences for how they approach life. They have what psychologists call different "cognitive styles." Nurturants believe it is very important to "walk a mile in the shoes of another" to envision how that person or group experiences a situation. Perspective taking is fostered in families and education. Authoritatives, on the other hand, place little value on perspective taking. Whereas Nurturants believe they may find something beneficial from learning about other views, for many Authoritatives the only reason to learn a position with which they disagree is to show why it is wrong. By way of example, a student of mine once went to the academic dean to criticize the way I was teaching the course on world religions. She did not like that I presented each religion in a positive light. My job, she told the dean, was to show how Christianity is right and every other religion is from the devil.

Nurturants practice a "pilgrim" or quest religion that is on a journey which has not reached its destination. Hence, they adjust plans if necessary and locate better routes as they walk the religious path. They are open to changing their minds about some things. Nurturants may hold a belief with strong conviction, yet they retain humility by acknowledging they do not know everything and so might be wrong. Authoritatives practice a "fortress" religion where all the right ideas and practices are already settled, and one defends them against opponents. Changing one's mind about a topic is a sign of weakness. They tend to hold their beliefs with absolute certainty and make no distinction between what they believe and what God believes. That is why Authoritatives often consider people who affirm different views as guilty of sinful thinking. A pastor did not like what I wrote in one of my books asked me: "Why do you put a question mark where God put a period?" He believed I rejected what God said on the subject, but I explained to him that I was not questioning God, I was questioning his interpretation of the Bible on that topic.

Authoritatives score high on what psychologists call the "defensive theology scale." They think there is only one correct view on a topic, and it is black and white. If you disagree, then you are considered a threat to the community. They like to ask those with a different view, "What if you are wrong?" Authoritatives tend to be fearful of God punishing them if they hold incorrect beliefs. They enforce monopoly religion where everyone must believe the same things, or they must be kicked out of the congregation. A key problem is that they have not been able to agree on the single correct view on topics such as baptism, the Eucharist, spiritual gifts, divorce, the nature of God, the nature of the Bible, the millennium, and the like. They have produced dozens of multi-view books demonstrating that they cannot agree on a host of important topics despite their claim that they have "the clear teaching" of the Bible on their side. Nurturants, on the other hand, are more comfortable with what I call a "constrained pluralism" of views. For example, someone may prefer one view of atonement, say *Christus Victor* over the model of love or the scapegoat theories. Yet, they see legitimacy in the other two views. They acknowledge that Christians hold a range of views on a host of topics. While they believe that not all views are equally good and some should be rejected (such as penal substitution), they are comfortable with more than one view being held by members of the community.

SOCIAL ORDER

Authoritatives favor a stable society. They become anxious when changes occur to roles and traditions such as occurred in the United States when women received the right to vote, the desegregation of schools, and the decriminalizing of interracial marriage. Religious Authoritatives tend to believe that long-standing social conventions are ordained by God rather than created by humans so changing them means going against God. Even today, about half of Authoritatives in America believe that women should return to their "traditional" roles. The majority of religious Authoritatives believe that males must be in charge of churches and the home. Evangelicalism, the Roman Catholic Church, and Mormonism are examples of this mindset. Religious Authoritatives opposed the civil rights movement and today they oppose acceptance of same-gender relations. In addition, they remain upset that state sponsored prayers and plaques of the Ten Commandments were prohibited in public schools. One might think that the Beatitudes of Jesus would be more important to Authoritatives than the Ten Commandments. However, I believe that the Beatitudes embody Nurturant values that seem "wrongheaded" to Authoritatives. The Ten Commandments, on the other hand, symbolize "law and order" which refers to God-given unchanging moral absolutes that result in an unchanging social order. That is why the Ten Commandments have such symbolic value to Authoritatives.

Though Nurturants believe in the need for social order, they tend to see social roles and traditions as human constructions that are never perfect. Thus, reforming them so that everyone can fulfill their potential and flourish is something God wants us to do. This is exemplified when Jesus said that the Sabbath was made to help people rather than people being made to obey the Sabbath (Mark 2:27). For Nurturants, moral rules are guides for what to do in typical situations rather than exceptionless absolutes. When biblical texts on female submission or same-gender relations are put forward by

Authoritatives as divine moral absolutes, Nurturants handle such texts in the ways discussed above in the section on the Bible.

ECONOMICS AND HEALTH CARE

Nurturants and Authoritatives have widely divergent views on many social and political issues.[6] For instance, there is a huge gap in income between the top earners and most workers. In addition, there is a disparity between the total wealth of the few at the top and the majority of the population. Many Nurturants believe that this situation is the result of laws regarding taxes, laws stipulating where people of color could live, and banking policies.

For hundreds of years, sinful systems were put in place that heavily benefited a few people. Religious Nurturants believe that the government should do more to address these problems. Authoritatives, on the other hand, believe life is a level playing field for everyone. If you are poor, it is what you deserve for not working hard enough. Wealth indicates that you played by the rules and worked hard. Authoritatives reject the idea that sinful systems are to blame for these economic inequalities—it is solely the fault of the individuals. Religious Authoritatives, who are poor, believe that God is punishing them for their sins—God gives them what they deserve.

Regarding health care, Nurturants view it as part of the common good. Communities that flourish need good schools, roads, and health care. Everyone should have access to good health care for the overall good of the community. Authoritatives counter that health care is a commodity, like cars and houses. You get what you can afford. If you make lots of money, then you can afford better housing, transportation, and health care. If you do not have the money to pay for good health care, you get what you deserve. Individualism, not the common good, is prioritized in this way of life which is why they dislike the term "social justice."

HOW TO IDENTIFY NURTURANTS AND AUTHORITATIVES

Many social scientists use four questions about characteristics one prefers in children to identify whether someone has Nurturant or Authoritative values.[7] Below are four pairs of traits with two good options in each line. Which do you prefer?

---

6. There are better and worse ways to cognitively "frame" social, economic, and political issues. How to state these in ways that uphold Nurturant values is important. See https://www.topospartnership.com/.

7. See the political science work, *Prius or Pickup?*

- Independence or Respect for Elders
- Good Manners or Curiosity
- Well Behaved or Being Considerate
- Self-Reliance or Obedience

Those who are strongly Nurturant choose independence, curiosity, being considerate, and self-reliance. The strongly Authoritative select respect for elders, good manners, well behaved, and obedience.

Political scientists call these four questions their Rosetta Stone and use them in the American National Election Studies and the World Values Survey in 108 countries representing 90 percent of the world's population.[8] In America, 16 percent select all four Authoritative traits while 26 percent choose three Authoritative traits. Hence, 42 percent of Americans favor Authoritative values. On the Nurturant side, 13 percent select all four Nurturant characteristics while 19 percent select three Nurturant traits. Thus, 32 percent of Americans favor Nurturant values. The remaining 26 percent are "mixed" in that they choose two Nurturant and two Authoritative responses.

People's responses to these questions accurately corelate with preferences ranging from the type of vehicle you drive (small or large), the shows you watch and books you read (those with stereotypical characters versus complex characters), and the kind of beer you drink (light versus craft beers). More significantly, the responses tell us whether you are afraid of outsiders and whether you believe the world is fundamentally a good or dangerous place. The answers people give accurately predict their stances on issues ranging from health care to immigration. I believe the responses also correlate to what people believe about God, sin and salvation, the nature of the Bible, and hell.

HOW TO TALK WITH EACH OTHER

Obviously, there is a huge chasm in values as well as views on different topics between Nurturant and Authoritatives. Each side tends to see the other as immoral. In particular, the cognitive style of Authoritatives makes conversation difficult. Their lack of interest in perspective taking, "fortress" theology, black and white thinking, absolute certainty they are correct, and fear of considering other views, means that it is difficult to persuade them to change their values. Yet, there is hope because even deeply entrenched values and behaviors can change.

8. See *Prius or Pickup?*

First, have patience and be ready for repeated conversations over extended periods of time.[9] If people are a mix of Authoritative and Nurturant, it is easier to persuade them. Though it does happen, it takes much more engagement and repeated reinforcement to transform strong Authoritatives. Changing neural pathways takes time and we can begin to reshape neural pathways in various ways. For instance, Authoritatives believe the world operates best when everyone gets what they deserve. To counter this, bring up memories of when they received something they did not deserve from a parent, teacher, or coach. Activate memories of when they were gracious to another person that did not deserve it. Ask them about instances they are most proud of when they helped someone. Read together passages in the Bible where Jesus and God are gracious, forgiving, and accepting of people warts and all. It is especially important to note the passages where God gives people what they do not deserve. Read stories or watch movies such as *Les Misérables* that depict people acting in ways that contain grace, nurturance, empathy, perspective taking, and the like.

Because religious Authoritatives are fearful of questioning what they have been taught, we need to create a safe place for conversation and thinking. Do not attack them. Rather, show them empathy and invite them to consider what you are saying.

Many Authoritatives are unaware that in Christian history there is more than one view on topics such as atonement or hell. Showing that devout believers have held many different views on such topics and used the Bible to support their views, can begin to open the door to seeing that people with different theological positions are not simply sinners rebelling against God's clear instructions.

Find out what they believe about, for instance, prayer. Do they believe God is concerned and influenced by their prayers or situation in life? If God is open to listening to us, despite our problems, then we should be open to listening to others.

CONCLUSION

Authoritative values and cognitive style are prevalent in conservative churches. Many people are repulsed by the focus on obedience to rules, fear of people outside one's tribe, and the closemindedness they experience in these congregations. Because they were taught that Authoritative religion simply is Christianity and there are no other options, some leave religion

---

9. For general guidelines on how to talk across the political divide see https://www.better-angels.org/talking-across-the-political-divide/?fbclid=IwAR1mibBpS7R49TjJIO8WjWJaqIUhZFHaFH-dggWpooKp-jizbDtKoiDLTVU

completely. Others encounter Christians who are Nurturant and find a form of religion that resonates with their core values. Postconservative theology is quite different from conservative theology in both the views affirmed as well as the cognitive style employed. It provides an alternative to those dissatisfied with conservative religious beliefs and culture. This approach is open minded without saying that anything goes, tends to affirm a range of views even while holding that some ideas are better than others and sees the Christian life as a pilgrimage in which we adjust as we travel towards our destination. Hopefully, you now have a better grasp of the Nurturant values undergirding postconservative theology.

BIBLIOGRAPHY

Hetherington, Marc, and Jonathan Weiler. *Prius or Pickup? How the Answers to Four Simple Questions Explain America's Great Divide*. Boston: Houghton Mifflin Harcourt, 2018.

Sanders, John. *Embracing Prodigals: Overcoming Authoritative Religion by Embodying Jesus' Nurturing Grace*. Eugene, OR: Cascade, 2020.

SECTION 1

Postmodern Philosophical Interpretation

Chapter 1
Phenomenological Hermeneutics
J. AARON SIMMONS

PHILOSOPHY IN THE STREETS

One of the distinctive characteristics of phenomenological hermeneutics is a focus on the everyday first-personal experiences that define existence.[1] However, much of the philosophical work done in this area deploys such a technical vocabulary that it can be difficult to see how it is meant to finds traction in our lives. In order to think about how phenomenological hermeneutics might speak to us today in the context of postconservative interpretation, let's start in the street and then move up to the ivory tower.

Recently, I was walking downtown where I live. People were going into stores, eating at restaurants, riding bikes, driving cars, and sitting on benches. We have all experienced such situations and not given them much thought. Indeed, we often go into stores, grab a bite at our favorite spot, chat with a friend as we navigate the traffic, and keep an eye open for a good spot to sit and enjoy the conversation. It seems that not much could be more ordinary, everyday, commonplace, and philosophically less interesting than walking down the street. And yet, as David Foster Wallace rightly notes, "the most obvious, ubiquitous, important realties are often the ones that are hardest to see and talk about."[2] Wallace offers this comment after telling a little story about some fish:

> There are these two young fish swimming along and they happen to meet an older fish swimming the other way, who nods at them and says, "Morning, boys. How's the water?" And the two

---

1. See Simmons and Benson, *New Phenomenology*.
2. Wallace, *This Is Water*, 8.

young fish swim on for a bit, and then eventually one of them looks over at the other and goes, "What the hell is water?"[3]

Notice that, while swimming, the fish are doing what fish do in similar ways that we do what we do when walking down the city street. In both cases, the world is taken for granted in particular ways as just "there." Like the water for the fish in the story, what we take for granted quickly becomes invisible to us. They didn't understand water because they were too busy swimming in it to pay any attention. Similarly, when we walk down the street, we are so preoccupied with ordering ice-cream, finding a parking spot, and not walking into other people going the opposite direction on the sidewalk that we fail to notice what is going on around us in all sorts of ways.

In Wallace's little book, he suggests that real education, authentic freedom, and profound meaning are all found when we interrogate the way we think things "obviously" are. He encourages us to realize that our way of making sense of the world is not fixed. We can choose to see things differently than we currently do. In order to do this, though, we have to start by realizing that what we initially considered obvious might not be so obvious after all—there are other ways to see things. The point is not that we were wrong in how we understood the world (though we might be), but that we usually live without realizing that we are at every moment constantly choosing how to understand it.

Usually, we tend to assume that we are not assuming anything at all. Our "default setting," as Wallace puts it is that we just go about our business in the "real world" thinking that our experience just "is" the case. In so doing, we forget to attend to our limited perspectives. What the wise old fish understands that the young fish do not is that what we take to be the "real world" is already shaped by our interpretation of what counts as "real." For the old fish, taking the water seriously is a key step in the task of thinking carefully about where he is and where he is going. For the young fish, they are too busy swimming to take account of the idea that there is something like water that makes their swimming possible.

Both Wallace and the old fish highlight the importance of phenomenological hermeneutics.[4] The interpretive frameworks by which things signify as meaningful are made visible when we suspend our assumptions (what phenomenologists call the "natural attitude") in order to think more carefully about the way that the world presents itself to us in our lived experience. Simply put, whether we have ever studied philosophy or not we are always engaged in interpretation and phenomenological hermeneutics

---

3. Wallace, *This Is Water*, 3–4.
4. See Westphal, *Whose Community?*

highlights this fact. Maybe the best way to think of this is that we are always already reading the world as a kind of text. We are piecing it together to try to make sense of it as a coherent story in which we find ourselves. When we take something for granted, or consider it obvious and therefore not worth interrogating, we are not free of interpretive decisions, but simply ignoring the decisions that have been already been made (unconsciously by us, or by others and inherited unconsciously by us). The beginning of the phenomenological hermeneutic task is not simply to make better decisions about how to see things, but instead merely to see that such decisions underlie everything that we "see."

We often hear that "seeing is believing," but when we begin phenomenologically to attend to the pervasive reality of hermeneutics, we better understand that what we already believe opens up what we are able to see as a result. In this way, believing shapes our seeing. Walter Lippman once defined a stereotype as what emerges when we define something before we see it. Yet, folks trafficking in stereotypes rarely think that they are doing so. Instead, they just take themselves to be seeing things "as they are." In therapy and in philosophy, the first step in fixing a problem is admitting that a problem actually exists. Phenomenological hermeneutics is one philosophical name for such an admission.

Consistently, research in sociology and psychology proves that implicit bias impacts what we take to be the case about the world. A concern for truth, then, means that we should be slow to conclude that what we "see" is somehow obviously the case. Instead, we should, as Ludwig Wittgenstein encourages us, "go slowly" and take our time. Wittgenstein's point is basically the same as that of Socrates when, in the *Apology*, he suggests that "the unexamined life is not worth living."[5] Living philosophically, however, is not the same thing as living skeptically. It is instead about living consciously, purposively, attentively. Doing so requires that we own up to the hermeneutic situation in which we are located such that we stop thinking that the goal is to prepare for the "real world" (despite what so many college admissions brochures suggest), and instead try to prepare for the tireless work of being invested in what "world" should be "made real."

As Wallace points out, going slowly can be hard to do given how normal it is for us just to ignore the "water" in which we are swimming. Although phenomenology is often presented as exclusively a descriptive methodology, I think that it is inherently normative in that it is always trying to get us to tell better stories about who, how, and where we are. Indeed, just going with the "obvious" flow dictated by the "real world" is, itself, not

---

5. Plato, *Apology*, 38a.

value neutral. It can often lead to ignorance, arrogance, and dismissiveness to what might really matter. Aaron James even says that it cultivates fertile soil for making us "assholes."[6] Alternatively, when we begin paying attention to the "water," we are better able to cultivate the virtues of humility, hospitality, and gratitude. *Humility* that we don't have it all figured out (best we can tell). *Hospitality* to others with whom we share our contexts of meaning and with whom we navigate what we take to be real. *Gratitude* that freedom is real such that contingency opens onto possibility. Things could be otherwise than they currently are and we have the ability to change the world should we so desire. This is truly an encouraging realization and one that unites Wallace, Wittgenstein, and Socrates in their call for reflective awareness. Wallace thereby concludes with a call to rethink what it means to be educated:

> It is about the real value of a real education, which has nothing to do with grades or degrees and everything to do with simple awareness—awareness of what is so real and essential, so hidden in plain sight all around us, that we have to keep reminding ourselves over and over: "This is water."[7]

Phenomenological hermeneutics is thus about fostering the willingness to pay attention to the "water" of the everyday precisely as we experience ourselves swimming in it.

Nonetheless, there are reasons to be careful here. When it comes to phenomenological hermeneutics it is easy to give in to problematic misunderstandings. The most important thing to keep in mind is that just because hermeneutics is inescapable doesn't mean that everything is just interpretation. Similarly, phenomenology's focus on first-personal experience doesn't mean that solipsism necessarily follows. Admittedly, the technical language of philosophers can lead to misunderstandings on these points. For example, Jacques Derrida's infamous claim "there is nothing outside of the text" might seem to suggest that there is no mind-independent reality at all such that skepticism and solipsism lie just around the corner.[8] Similarly, when Friedrich Nietzsche provocatively claims that there are no facts, only interpretations,[9] one would be forgiven for thinking that he is defending the idea that there is no objectivity, but only subjective opinion. Although I do wish that these thinkers had been a bit more careful about their word

---

6. See James, *Assholes*.
7. Wallace, *This Is Water*, 131–32.
8. Derrida, *Of Grammatology*, 158.
9. Nietzsche, *Portable Nietzsche*, 458.

choice, they are not nearly as radical as they might initially seem. Both Derrida and Nietzsche are simply reminding us that whatever is the case when it comes to mind-independent reality, we are only able to know things from our embodied, finite, human (all too human) perspectives.

Even if x is mind-independently the case, I can only ever know x as it is "given" to me in conscious experience. In this way, Derrida's phenomenology and Nietzsche's hermeneutics both stress the importance of experience to knowing. Broadly speaking, phenomenological hermeneutics follows Immanuel Kant regarding a particular version of anti-realism. Kantian *epistemological* anti-realism is the view that we are unable to get outside of our embodied existence to check whether our account of existence accurately "corresponds" to things as they are independent of my experience of them. Epistemological anti-realism does not require, and must not be confused with, *metaphysical* anti-realism, which is the view that there is nothing that exists independent of human minds. It is, thus, a non-sequitur to suggest that just because I can't know something outside my limited perspective that therefore nothing exists except that perspective.

With these basic qualifiers in place, let's return to the experience of walking down a street. When we, like the old fish, begin to put question marks where everyone else puts periods, and to take seriously what everyone else takes for granted, we can start to see how our interpretations of things reveal themselves in their contingency. What do we "see" (read: assume) as true about other folks when we look at their clothing, their bodies, and their behavior? What do we "see" (read: define) as true about our identity, our community, our religion, and our culture? Asking these questions opens us up to seeing things otherwise. Cultivating a comfort with the hermeneutic dynamics that always accompany our embodied social lives, I believe, can be a resource for overcoming the political division, religious triumphalism, social insularity, and the rampant fear and/or anger that accompany the "culture wars" that so often dictate the "world" in which we live. Indeed, I would go so far as to suggest that getting better at hermeneutics is an important part of resisting the assault on democracy that has marked the rise of populism, Trumpism, and rampant conspiracy-theories.

Realizing that "this is water" is an important step toward realizing that historical differences don't need to continue to define our present reality. Phenomenological hermeneutics shows us that our present economic models, our political structures, and our social priorities could all be improved. Accordingly, broad hermeneutic awareness is perhaps the very condition of social critique. As Miguel de Beistegui so nicely puts it:

> Critique starts from a position of immersion in historical, social, economic contingencies, from which it strives to extract something that exceeds those conditions. It develops a capacity to identify those powers (state power, religious power, economic power, psychiatric or scholastic power, etc.) that want to pull wool over its eyes. It does not allow itself to be taken for a ride. Ultimately critique is constructive as well as personal. It is only because something is inhabited, because a force is thwarted, that critique is required.[10]

Although Beistegui is right to claim that critique and the hermeneutic awareness upon which it depends is a cause for hope in a world so frequently defined by despair, he also appropriately notes that there are strong forces working to keep the "water" invisible so that we continue swimming in the same direction without realizing there are other options. As Michel Foucault argues, what counts as "knowledge" in our social world is always connected to some manifestation of "power."[11] Although getting into the weeds of Foucault's philosophy would take us too far afield here, we can summarize his account as follows: whenever we are considering different ways of making sense of the world (competing hermeneutic frameworks) we should always ask whose interests are benefited by a particular view.

For instance, when we hear that there is continuing racial injustice in our society due to the latent logic of white supremacy operative in our social, legal, political, and economic structures, it is easy to see that such an account does not benefit those currently reaping the rewards of that logic and so they are likely to oppose such a view as "playing the race card," or distract from them by describing Critical Race Theory in perverse and distorted ways and presenting it as the "real" danger, or even by pointing to individual examples of successful people of color as evidence that racism is a thing of the past. Such strategies are not hermeneutically naïve, but instead disingenuous. Similar examples could be offered in a variety of other areas including climate change, immigration, and healthcare.

The strategy of "power," is rarely to meet evidence with evidence internal to a reflective phenomenological appreciation of hermeneutic operations. Power rarely encourages people to be convinced by the best argument. Instead, the typical strategy is to poison the epistemic well such that evidence presented by those with whom one disagrees is immediately assumed to be suspect. Let's term this strategy *hermeneutic foot-stomping*. It basically functions by acting like refutation occurs simply by reiterating one's own view

---

10. De Beistegui, *Thought Under Threat*, 13.
11. See Foucault, *Power/Knowledge*.

of "the real world." Notice that hermeneutic foot-stomping is, nonetheless, a hermeneutic framework. It is not free of interpretation, but simply free of the responsibility that attends admitting interpretation to be functioning in one's belief structure. Additionally, such hermeneutic foot-stomping is antidemocratic because it does not serve to foster the vibrant public discourse in which critique can flourish. Instead, it shuts down critique in the name of reinforcing the social power structure as epistemically unquestionable. As Beistegui explains, resisting hermeneutic critique is antidemocratic because "critique is democratic in that it believes that problems, questions, and even experiments are constructions, and democracy takes place as the dispute around the nature of problems."[12]

Those who benefit from the status quo are invested in making the current state of affairs seem necessary, unchanging, and good. They do not seek to foster deliberative conversation in light of the contingency of hermeneutic perspectives, but instead seek to eliminate an awareness of perspectival difference from the outset. This leads to a binary logic of either being with "us" or being wrong. It might seem that the goal of contemporary democracy would be to get to some sort of overlapping consensus where we all can agree about things, but Beistegui, along with other thinkers such as Chantal Mouffe and Simon Critchley, suggests that when we really grasp the hermeneutic stakes of democratic life we will realize that, "contrary to popular belief, democracy is oriented not toward consensus, but toward *dissensus*."[13] We need each other to push us beyond the straightjacketed assumptions that so often attend our natural attitudes/default settings about the world and our place in it.

OFF THE STREETS AND INTO THE CHURCHES

Of specific relevance to postconservative interpretation theory is the fact that such anti-democratic hermeneutic foot-stomping is especially prominent within conservative religious communities. Whether Christian or not, these groups are largely defined by the hermeneutic foot-stomping often characterizing our natural attitudes insofar as they cultivate communities marked by self-protective theology, social insularity, and a strong opposition to any challenges to the certainty with which they hold their views.[14] Rather than meet questions, doubts, and worries with honest humility about divine mystery, textual complexity, translational ambiguities, and

---

12. De Beistegui, *Thought Under Threat*, 14.
13. De Beistegui, *Thought Under Threat*, 14.
14. For work on the power structures within contemporary white Evangelicalism in the US, see work by Randall Balmer, Kristin Kobes Du Mez, Anthea Butler, and others.

the impact of historical power structures on doctrinal formulations, these religious communities instead frame the doubt and questions as evidence of faithlessness and sin.

Cultivating a general fear of different views as corrupting and dangerous, these communities do not explain to their members that they are operating according to a different hermeneutic framework that makes those views problematic given particular assumptions at work in their particular tradition. Instead, they appeal to the "clarity" of revealed texts, the "certainty" of tradition, and the "obviousness" of their own perspective as not being a perspective at all, but just the way things are. It is exceptionally difficult to engage with such people because the rules of argument are not simply distorted, but entirely rejected as leading to ruin. It should come as no great surprise that such communities work so hard to ignore complaints, cover over scandals, and marginalize their critics. They don't just create an echo-chamber, but they actively foster fear of, animosity toward, and disdain for those who would raise such concerns. It is one thing to encourage members of your community to listen to arguments and then equip them with the tools necessary to distinguish strong from weak claims. It is a very different thing to train the members of your community to view argumentative engagement as dangerous to their salvation and then warn them against training in philosophy as slippery slope toward perdition.

Yet, just like the young fish were raised to ignore the water because of their inherited assumptions about the "real world," it is no wonder that the "Religious Right" in the US has been such a reliable voting block over the past several decades. They have been raised in Sunday School classes, youth groups, and church services that present a very particular (and contingently prominent) political perspective as necessary for Christian social identity. Questions about reproductive rights, gender identity, LGBTQ+ rights, climate change, immigration, health care, or expressions of religion in the public square are rarely able to be considered from a position of good-faith, but instead such questions are immediately described as at odds with what the Bible "clearly" says. Responding that such "clarity" is perhaps a kind of hermeneutic idolatry that might be worth interrogating is rarely met with serious consideration, but instead rejected as an example of dangerous postmodern relativism.[15]

Given the significant influence that conservative religious communities have on American politics, the hermeneutic foot-stomping cultivated in such spaces likely directly impacts the hermeneutic ignorance and epistemic

---

15. Kevin Carnahan and I have argued that this basic epistemic/hermeneutic approach helps to explain the conspiracism within these communities. See Simmons and Carnahan, "It's Much Worse Than You Think."

obstinacy that then characterizes so much of broader social and political discourse. For those of us attempting to cultivate the philosophically aware, hermeneutically sensitive, conscious, responsible adult lives that Wallace calls for, I think phenomenological hermeneutics is a great resource.

Having now done some philosophy in the streets with Wallace, let's now open the door to the ivory tower and have a look around with Heidegger.

HEIDEGGER AS THE WISE OLD FISH

Although Wallace's account of the dangerous that accompany what we take to be "obvious" is an easy entry point into a discussion of phenomenological hermeneutics, his view is basically a (much more accessible) retelling of Martin Heidegger's philosophy. In his influential 1927 book, *Being and Time*, Heidegger opens the text by inviting us to see what we so often take for granted about ourselves and our world. He focuses specifically on the meaning of "being," but for our purposes here what matters is the idea that what is taken for granted as obvious is then ignored as either trivial or forgotten to the point of being no longer visible as a part of one's existential context. Heidegger describes this situation as follows:

> Do we in our time have an answer to the question of what we really mean by the word 'being'? Not at all. So it is fitting that we should raise anew the question of the meaning of being. But are we nowadays even perplexed at our inability to understand the expression 'being'? Not at all. So first of all we must reawaken an understanding for the meaning of this question.[16]

Admittedly this passage is a bit opaque, but we can get at it if we see it unfolding in three hermeneutic steps independent of the specific ontological content with which he is interested. First, Heidegger asks if we understand X. He answers that we don't. Then, second, he says it makes sense, then, to raise to our consciousness, and bring to our attention, that figuring out X is worthwhile. However, he then asks whether we are even aware of the fact that we don't understand X and answers that we are not. Accordingly, third, he suggests that if we ever want to understand X, then we must start by first of all getting people to care about the fact that they aren't even aware that they don't understand it. In this way, Heidegger is like the wise old fish who strives to get the younger fish to grasp what is being asked in the question, "How's the water?" if he ever hopes to get them to attend to the water itself.

Heidegger then goes on to provide three reasons that we aren't even aware of, and certainly not troubled by, the fact that we don't understand

---

16. Heidegger, *Being and Time*, xxix.

the meaning of being—and indeed, don't even grasp why the question about its meaning matters in the first place. His three reasons are all reminiscent of Wallace's point about that which is taken to be obvious is that which remains unquestioned. Notice the similarity:

1. "Being" is the most "universal" concept.
2. The concept of "being" is indefinable.
3. "Being" is the self-evident concept.[17]

All three of these reasons for why we don't understand being appeal to the idea that it is not a failure on our part, but simply the way things are. It is as if Heidegger is asking a first-year college student (or her parents!) why they are majoring in business instead of philosophy and getting the reply, "because I just want to be ready for the real world." The student is not actually giving a reason for her decision, but simply appealing to the way things are as reason enough for not really having to make a decision. If she were to take some philosophy courses, however, she might realize that her appeal to "the way things are" is actually reflective of the way that the world has been handed to her by others. In the same fashion, Heidegger claims that the only way we will be able to catch up to where we are already in terms of our lack of understanding is if we go back and get a better sense of how we got here. Accordingly, he turns to the history of philosophy as a long story about decisions that served to make the question of the meaning of being one that we could no longer recognize as a question worth asking. Just like the first-year student, we all find ourselves already thinking that we know all that we need to know and so don't need to keep asking questions about what we take for granted. Heidegger's name for this mode of thinking that assumes it has everything already figured out is an "average and vague understanding."[18] This average and vague understanding is not singularly a product of our own thought-processes, but instead is "permeated by traditional theories and opinions about being in such a way that these theories, as the sources of the prevailing understanding, remain hidden."[19] It is because we carry with us the inherited history of a story about "the way things are" that we now find ourselves unable to appreciate the contingency of our own conceptions. Heidegger's insight is that hermeneutics is inescapable. Even in our rejection of the need for hermeneutics we are presupposing a variety of other interpretive frames.

17. Heidegger, *Being and Time*, 2–3.
18. Heidegger, *Being and Time*, 4.
19. Heidegger, *Being and Time*, 5.

Suggesting that we must engage in a "destruction of the history of western ontology," in order better to understand the average and vague ontological frameworks that serve to frame our experience of the world, Heidegger turns to the method of phenomenology as the key to such a project. Citing Edmund Husserl's famous adage that phenomenology is simply turning "to the things themselves," Heidegger explains that phenomenology is not about a particular content (a what), but instead about a particular mode of inquiry (a how). The "how" of phenomenology is distinctive in that it sets aside questions of metaphysical actuality (e.g., is such and such the case?) and instead looks at matters of conscious first-personal experience (viz., what is revealed/show/given in my experience?).

Consider the following example. I am now writing this sentence while sitting on my couch looking outside at my backyard. There is a small bunch of pink flowers in front of a tree with white rocks around it. For the phenomenologist, this description is not a statement about the objective existence of flowers, trees, and rocks. Instead, the phenomenologist is interested in the first-personal experience of objects named "flowers," "trees," and "rocks." In order to get at this experiential encounter with the "thing itself," phenomenology rejects the representationalism that was so characteristic of previous idealism. Rather than my experience of the flowers, tree, and rocks being merely a mental representation that prevents me from ever actually knowing the things in themselves (think Kant's phenomena/noumena split), phenomenology develops the idea of intentionality, which is the notion that consciousness is always consciousness of something. In this way, my experience of the white rocks, say, is not a metaphysical assertion regarding the objectivity of rocks, but of the way that a particular object gives itself to my consciousness. I experience the rock, not just a representation of the rock. Nonetheless, the rock can be experienced/given in a variety of "modes." I might be *remembering* the rock that I saw yesterday when I looked out my window. I might be *thinking* about the rock while out for a hike and wonder if the rock on which I just stubbed my toe is the same sort. I might be *desiring* the rock in order to stand on it to get high enough to reach the cups on my top shelf in the kitchen. And the list could go on. The point is that the modes in which I experience the rock doesn't change the rock that I experience (i.e., it is the same rock in every case), but it does change the way in which the rock is presented to my consciousness: as remembered, considered, desired, etc.

Importantly, in order to think about things in this phenomenological way, we have to overcome the temptation simply to see the rock in the "natural attitude" by which we just assume that it is "there." This natural attitude is characterized not only by average and vague understanding, but by a host of theoretical assumptions that go unacknowledged. The natural attitude is our approach when we just take for granted that we already understand things, that they are "obvious" according to the frames of reference that we already have in place. The phenomenological attitude, in contrast, requires us to "bracket" or "suspend" our assumptions about the rock (and everything that might go along with it) in order to attend specifically to our first-personal experience of the rock. By shifting to the phenomenological attitude, we now see that we never see anything unless we see it "as such." I see this particular object-as-rock, I see that one as-flower, and the other one as-tree. My seeing these objects-as-such indicates that I am always enmeshed already in a variety of contexts of meaning such that the objects are not just seen as-objects, but as-already-meaningful.

Consider the flower. If it is my anniversary and I forgot to get my wife some flowers, I might look out my window and see the object not only as-flower, but as-flower-needed-to-make-my-wife-happy. The shift from the natural attitude to the phenomenological attitude is not just that I see it this way, but that I am reflective about seeing it that way as a particular mode in which the flower is presented to me in that moment. For a master gardener, say, the flower might present in the natural attitude as-common-species, but for an infectious disease specialist looking at the way flowers can aid in fighting illness, the flower might present as-possible-cure. The as-such mode of presentation, then, is not the key to phenomenology, but phenomenology is the key to appreciating the as-such mode. Once we enter the phenomenological attitude, having suspended our normal theoretical frameworks and metaphysical assumptions, we can then engage in the task of describing things as they are experienced—when all the socio-cultural baggage that we carry with us is made visible as impacting that experience. Said slightly differently, phenomenology facilitates letting things show themselves as nested in our theories, rather than continuing to allow our theories to dictate how we see things.

For Heidegger, phenomenology is, thus, inherently hermeneutic in that it is a matter of increasing our awareness of how things get constructed as "real" in light of what we have inherited from our histories. He turns to phenomenology in order to restore an awareness of the question of the meaning of being because he thinks that we can't appreciate questions we don't ask unless we see the history that has given rise to why we don't ask them. Again, he is the wise old fish asking us all "how's the water" of our existential conceptions, our ontological commitments, our metaphysical frameworks, and our social arrangements. Phenomenology is not just about putting on glasses to help us see more clearly, but about realizing that we already had glasses on in the first place.

Let's look at one more example to illustrate these main ideas. A couple weeks ago, my family and I went bike riding with a couple friends of ours. I am an avid mountain biker and so had been encouraging our friends to ride with us. They agreed to go and so we had a lovely time until right toward the end of the ride when one of them somehow managed to go off of the paved trail onto the adjacent grass. Now, this was not a big deal because there was no lip on the pavement and she could easily have just ridden back onto the trail, but instead she freaked out, grabbed the brakes with all her strength, and proceeded to flip head-first over the handlebars. She was okay, but in the days that followed she sent numerous pictures of her bruises to my wife and expressed her fear of riding again. Due to that experience, when she looks at bikes she now sees them as-dangerous-in-the-mode-of-fear. Yet, when I see bikes, I see them as-opportunities-for-fun-on-the-trail. Now, you might say that bikes can be both things, which is true, but the phenomenological hermeneutic point is that they are never just neutral objects. They are always already interpreted-as-such relative to our first-personal experience of what we encounter. We could say the same thing about the phenomenon of going off the trail. For my son and I this is what makes riding fun, but for our friend it is what makes it terrifying. So, the same phenomenon is not "given" in the same way/mode due to the experiential context in which it is received. This example speaks to what Heidegger and others will call the "hermeneutic circle." The idea is that our starting points for interpreting things are always opened by other assumed interpretations. Just as Foucault demonstrates that we never get outside of the operations of power, but instead should seek to understand those operations in order not to be naïve or deceived by them, Heidegger demonstrates, via phenomenological hermeneutics, that we never get outside of experiencing the world as meaningful even as we are attentive to the process by which meaning is made.

STREETS, CHURCHES, TOWERS, AND BEYOND

Our consideration of phenomenological hermeneutics started in the street, visited a church along the way, and then moved to the ivory tower, but hopefully it now propels us back into our social, political, and ecclesial contexts with an increased awareness of the importance of paying attention to the "water" in which we swim. Doing so, I believe, is an important step in the direction of restoring stability to our democratic spaces and fostering virtue in our relational interactions. Just as phenomenological hermeneutics highlights the contingency of the way we see things, it can also show the fragility of our response to such contingency. Sadly, Heidegger's brilliant philosophical awareness did not prevent him from being seduced by the vicious temptations of national socialism. Ultimately, phenomenological hermeneutics doesn't guarantee that we become good, but perhaps it can help us to be at least a bit more attentive to the ways that hermeneutic foot-stomping stands as a problem. Insofar as it does that, we are at least more likely to see when our "water" starts getting polluted by ignorance, insularity, and egoism.

BIBLIOGRAPHY

De Beistegui, Miguel. *Thought Under Threat: On Superstition, Spite, and Stupidity*. Chicago and London: University of Chicago Press, 2022.

Derrida, Jacques. *Of Grammatology*. Corrected edition. Trans. Gayatri Chakravorty Spivak. Baltimore: Johns Hopkins University Press, 1998.

Foucault, Michel. *Power/Knowledge: Selected Interviews and Other Writings 1972–1977*. Edited by Colin Gordon and translated by Colin Gordon et al. New York: Pantheon, 1980.

Heidegger, Martin. *Being and Time*. Translated by Joan Stambaugh and revised by Dennis J. Schmidt. Albany and New York: State University of New York Press, 2010.

James, Aaron. *Assholes: A Theory*. New York: Anchor, 2012.

Nietzsche, Friedrich. *The Portable Nietzsche*. Edited and translated by Walter Kaufmann. New York: Penguin, 1954.

Simmons, J. Aaron, and Bruce Ellis Benson. *The New Phenomenology: A Philosophical Introduction*. London: Bloomsbury, 2013.

Simmons, J. Aaron, and Kevin Carnahan. "It's Much Worse Than You Think: The Epistemology of Ignorance, Teflon Hermeneutics, and Social Decay." In *QAnon, Chaos, and the Cross: Christianity and Conspiracy Theories*, edited by Greg Bock and Michael, 84–97. Grand Rapids: Eerdmans, 2023.

Wallace, David Foster. 2009. *This is Water*. New York: Little, Brown, and Company.

Westphal, Merold. 2009. *Whose Community? Which Interpretation?: Philosophical Hermeneutics for the Church*. Grand Rapids: Baker Academic.

Chapter 2
Postmodern Hermeneutics
CHRISTINA M. GSCHWANDTNER

The term "postmodernism" was coined by the French philosopher Jean-François Lyotard who defined it as a disbelief in "big stories" (*grand récits*, often rendered as "metanarratives"). Although this phrase is often interpreted as a rejection of Christianity, deemed to be the quintessential big story, in fact Lyotard concretely indicts rather the grand projects of modernity: capitalism, communism, scientism, belief in unbridled progress, or faith in technology as the unqualified good to solve all ills. Such large, all-encompassing projects, built on a firm, seemingly unassailable foundation, presenting themselves as wholly neutral or without presuppositions, and treated as supremely rational, are no longer convincing today. "Today" for him meant after two atrocious world wars, after the horrors of the Shoah, and later after the demise of communism in the wake of the spectacular disintegration of the Soviet Union. More recently, such belief in grand narratives to explain all of reality from a seemingly neutral and wholly objective perspective, has become untenable in light of the ubiquity of information technologies, the specter of the climate crisis, and the perspectivalism of political fragmentation, often fueled by the all-consuming presence of social media. In contrast to modernity, the postmodern condition is characterized by the proliferation of "little stories," of local narratives, of diverse or even incompatible perspectives, of the apparent inability to communicate or converse across boundary lines between competing discourses. We no longer read the same books, watch the same films, vote for the same parties, sing the same songs, or believe in the same gods: there is no shared worldview that would provide a common horizon of understanding. Increasingly, we find others' perspectives no longer simply unconvincing but often wholly incomprehensible. We do not meet on the same ground and do not operate against a similar horizon of understanding.

Although Lyotard's original notion of postmodernism, or even its broader adoption as a description of contemporary culture, is not usually identified as hermeneutic, it is actually a profoundly hermeneutic claim about the proliferation of "horizons" (in Hans-Georg Gadamer's language) or "worlds" (in Paul Ricœur's terminology). At the same time, it appears to defy something crucial to most previous versions of hermeneutics, namely the possibility to fuse horizons, to enter other worlds of discourse, to converse with each other and to arrive at shared and increased understanding. Is hermeneutics still possible when there are only "phrases in dispute," when an essential "différend" or incompatibility operates between discourses, when any claim to all-encompassing narratives has been abandoned, when all language is always already marked by the injustice of exclusion of all those who do not and cannot speak our language, cannot converse or argue on our terms?

Lyotard's project is carried further by thinkers like Barbara Cassin who argues for the "untranslatability" of discourses—even in the face of the hegemony of "globish" (the bastardized English that has become the apparent new lingua franca)—and who, similar to Lyotard in *Just Gaming*, identifies her own project as "pagan." Is only a new "paganism" possible today in what seems an increasingly secular society? And yet: is our society really so secular? Is it not rather a proliferation of religious discourses in helter-skelter postmodern fashion, according to particular, often highly personal and individual tastes, without hegemony or hierarchy, and without shared doctrinal or creedal authorities? Thinkers like John Caputo and Richard Kearney have argued for a "religion without religion," a "theopoetics" of hospitality, a love or desire that employs the name or the event of "God" rather than insisting on God's existence, returning to "God" after the death of God—and only after passing through atheism or at least agnosticism. Even more confessionally traditional thinkers like the French phenomenologist Jean-Luc Marion think that Nietzsche's "madman's" proclamation of the death of God is to be celebrated rather than mourned, because it constitutes the death of a philosophical idol, an inadequate concept of the divine that we should be happy to discard. Others, like Emmanuel Falque, suggest that a theological hermeneutics can only be recovered starting from the agnostic situation of the human as such (*l'homme tout court*).

This chapter will contend that any viable hermeneutics today—religious or not—must take the postmodern condition as a given. There is no way to return to the modern project with its blind belief in universal rationality, its assumptions that we can find an absolutely certain Archimedean point on which to build all knowledge, or its supreme confidence in the grand narratives of infinite progress. Postmodern hermeneutics instead has to accept the plurality and diversity of "little" narratives, the proliferation of horizons of understanding without hope of a final merger or fusion into one overarching horizon, and the competition, perhaps even incompatibility, of worlds. Acknowledging this contemporary reality need not, however, imply a descent into a complete relativism in which all opinions are equal and no distinctions can be made between better or worse, true or false. Rather, postmodern hermeneutics calls for more vigilance, more wisdom, more discernment, and more careful listening.

HERMENEUTICS IN A UNIVERSE OF LITTLE STORIES

Hermeneutics as a philosophical discipline (rather than a practice of interpreting legal or biblical texts) emerged in the nineteenth century in the effort to develop a general theory of understanding. For Friedrich Schleiermacher and others the goal was to overcome the distance between author and contemporary reader by seeking to ascertain as closely as possible the original meaning of the author in the circling between parts and wholes of a text and context, each illuminating the other. Originally focused on the understanding of texts, hermeneutics expanded to investigate broader psychological and historical horizons in thinkers like Johann Gustav Droysen or Wilhelm Dilthey. Martin Heidegger pushed this even further by speaking of hermeneutic facticity as our fundamental condition, our very way of being in the world. We are thrown into the world and come to understand it, and ourselves within it, only against a horizon of understanding that always already precedes us. The world comes laden with meaning, and understanding can occur only in this situation of discourse.

We reach such understanding, for Hans-Georg Gadamer, not by climbing back into the mind of the author but by the intersection of the horizons of the work (whether literary, artistic, historical, or linguistic) and the horizon of the reader or listener who engages with the work in the continual play of a back-and-forth engagement. Through conversation, we can not only comprehend more but come to genuine understanding of each other. Paul Ricœur, the other main hermeneutic thinker of the twentieth century, suggests that understanding occurs especially through narrative. We find ourselves always in the tension between concordance and discordance: while our lives are fragmented and chaotic, we achieve meaning and identity by narrating the events of our lives and thus endowing them with unity and coherence, albeit always threatened by renewed discordance. Narratives are prefigured in life, which always already has a narratival quality; narratives configure life in the plot of a given story, and then refigure or transfigure the life of the readers who can enter into the narrative or poetic world and there conceive themselves differently. Poetic texts, whether literary, historical, biblical, or otherwise, invite us into their worlds and by appropriating them we can change and give meaning to our own lives.

Thus, while hermeneutics is initially perceived negatively, as dealing with misunderstanding or as bridging the distance between original and contemporary audience, it comes increasingly to denote not lack but possibility: we can enter new narrative worlds, expand horizons of understanding, or conceive ourselves differently in the interaction with new discourses. At the same time, hermeneutic thinkers grow more suspicious of the extent to which radically different worlds can be entered, how fully horizons can merge, or whether complete understanding is possible in any conversation. Translation between discourses contains not only the possibility of opening new worlds but also always involves betrayal. Lyotard seems to deal a death blow to hermeneutics by arguing that there are many situations in which translation is not possible at all, that in the clash of discourses such injustice of untranslatability always already occurs, and that we must abandon the dream of philosophy as the interpretive language between discourses or disciplines. Yet, identifying the suppression of minority voices as an injustice clearly implies that discernment and even judgment are still possible, that some ways of conducting conversations and of listening (or not) are better than others. While there may not be an absolute standard, lodged in some unassailable authority or master discourse, this does not imply that there is no right or wrong, justice or injustice. Rather, discernment, patience, and attentive listening are now needed more than ever.

How, then, might a hermeneutics of many competing and seemingly incompatible "little stories" function today? On the most basic level, we can recognize that even within the destabilizing discordance of our contemporary lives, we still long for concordance, although we tend to be more suspicious of its possibility. People search for identity and meaning, even when they no longer find it in authority, hierarchy, or universal rationality. How are meanings constructed and identities secured in an increasingly chaotic world with its many loudly competing voices? At least three possibilities have emerged, all of which have hermeneutic dimensions while rejecting the hermeneutic project implicitly or explicitly.

When stable meaning seems more and more elusive and whatever identity has been constructed feels increasingly threatened, some opt for fundamentalism: a substitute for the reassuring grand narratives of modernity but on a smaller scale and often in ghetto-like subcultures or alternative communities. If the overarching stories no longer function or can no longer be enforced, then more restricted and more restrictive versions can provide some solace. In this case, there is no longer an attempt to interact with other horizons of understanding or to enter new worlds, but a particular subculture is constructed that features one coherent narrative. Fundamentalism deals with the proliferation of discourses by ignoring or rejecting them all in favor of a carefully calibrated and usually highly restricted vision of the world in its particular corner. The horizon becomes narrowed to such an extent that other horizons cannot even be imagined, much less entered. An alternative private world is fashioned for a small enclave of the elect to which there is often neither entry nor exit. All other worlds—including a shared "public" world—are rejected and spurned. Fundamentalism is an attempt to create a modern or even pre-modern world in a postmodern context by forgoing any claims to universality, neutrality, or pure rationality, but still insisting on the possibility of "absolute" Truth in the framework of narrower horizons. This particular option has obvious religious instantiations, although not all versions of such fundamentalist retrenchment or opting out of broader narratives is religious.

A second possibility is syncretism. Individuals cobble together meaning from fragments of stories, traditions, and practices. They pick and choose among the various possibilities on offer: a bit of this, a bit of that, discard and replace as necessary or desirable. In this way, they stitch together a pastiche or bricolage of symbols, metaphors, rituals, or other meaning-making devices with little concern for their overall coherence, based on the vague criterion of what works for me at this moment in time. Individuals curate images of themselves and of their worlds that are profoundly personal or particular, but at the same time their assembly of bric-a-bracs of ready-made pieces occurs with an eye to how others arrange their presentations of themselves in a paradoxical tension between assimilation to the crowd and assertion of uniqueness. This razor edge between particularity and homogeneity is constantly subject to the threat of oblivion within the incessant flow of the obsessive search for novelty. Of this possibility, too, there are various religious and non-religious instantiations.

A third possibility, which shares some elements with either of the other two, is the "siloing" of opinions, often on political levels, that divides the world into "us" and "them," where no dialogue between the two sides remains a genuine possibility. The horizons have become so divergent that they can no longer meet, much less merge. We effectively live in such different worlds that we become incapable of entering each other's worlds. The public space between worlds has been erased; the two sides no longer share the same universe of discourse. Here meaning and identity is created by a particular "packaged" version where no nuance on any position is possible and any disagreement with the dominant discourse is punished by accusations of betrayal and possible ostracism or shunning. Horizons no longer expand or merge, but become static and fixed. It should be noted that this possibility frequently indulges in strong insistence on justice or morality with the particular "flavor" of the moral outrage determined by the specific horizon of the universe of discourse. Although this option is usually political in orientation, it is certainly also compatible with—and often linked to—particular religious visions of the world.

All of these are postmodern versions of hermeneutics, because their frameworks of understanding and the ways in which meaning is constructed are particular rather than universal, personal rather than neutral or objective, plural or regional rather than cosmopolitan. This applies not simply to texts, but to languages, discourses, metaphors, symbols, broader narratives, visions of the world, frameworks of understanding, and so forth. At the same time, all three in different ways reject hermeneutics at least in the traditional sense. The first version, although it clearly constitutes an interpretation of a particular world, tries to defy hermeneutics by closing down all other horizons of understanding and treating one local horizon as all-encompassing. It thus pretends that its vision of the world is not a matter of interpretation, that its possession of the truth implies complete transparency, and often also that distance to biblical or historical texts and events can be collapsed or at least ignored. The second option, almost diametrically opposed to the first, multiplies horizons and acknowledges the plurality of interpretations, but does not truly seek understanding of other positions in its motley collage of them. Horizons are entirely arbitrary and can be fused or spliced at will without the need to enter them or understand their worlds. The third option acknowledges hermeneutics to an extreme in the sense that it does think that there are two (or more) possible worlds, but it does not believe that these horizons could merge in any form or envision the possibility of learning from another world or understanding its particular horizon. The worlds and horizons remain permanently separate, even as it is admitted that they exist (although often the alternative is condemned as ideology or delusion). None of these positions thinks that genuine conversation across horizons would be possible or that one could enter other worlds and learn from them. The irony of the postmodern situation, then, is that while its perspectivalism is intensely hermeneutic, the main goal and project of hermeneutic understanding has been relinquished or is deemed impossible. In many ways, the internet is the supreme example of this: on the one hand opening the possibility of crossing distances and entering seemingly infinite worlds of interpretation, on the other hand creating echo chambers of increasingly homogenous worlds of particular narrow discourses and images.

HERMENEUTIC HORIZONS IN POSTMODERN WORLDS

How can we enter new horizons in such a diverse yet increasingly "untranslatable" world? Has the hermeneutic possibility of understanding, of stepping into new worlds, or of merging different horizons been closed down definitively? To even begin to answer such questions requires acknowledging fully that there is no longer a universal or absolute foundation of rationality to which we could either return or to which one could appeal on a pragmatic level as a shared ground of knowledge and truth. Regardless of how universal one thinks truth or faith to be, it is the reality of the postmodern situation that such a shared ground is simply no longer available for debate. If the basic presuppositions of rationality are not accepted by all members of the conversation, then they cannot be presupposed. There is no universal backdrop—whether of religious authority, universal scientific truth, or indubitable human rationality—to which one could appeal as final arbiter in dispute.

Yet, this does not mean that no conversation is possible across boundary lines or that one could not negotiate between a variety of positions. It means only that there is no neutral, purely objective measure to which one could appeal because all parties agree to it. Instead, one must work much harder at entering another's world. Horizons are further apart and thus require more significant travel and a more difficult and less secure work of translation. No Rosetta Stone will reveal the equivalence of the languages; there is no master discourse that can negotiate between them. Thus, instead of translating into our own language, we must learn to speak new languages on the terms of those whose native tongues they are, without trying to assimilate them to a discourse deemed superior. In order to bring horizons together across increasingly large chasms, many forms of "detour and return" will be required. The space between discourses must be taken seriously as a distance with its own significance, not simply a gap to be erased. A remainder of untranslatability must always be acknowledged. Indeed, perhaps this must no longer be thought of as a "remainder," but as an essential dimension of any attempt at understanding or translation. We must honor the gap as the creative space that safeguards the potential of each language, horizon, or "world" of discourse to make meaning in radically different ways. The proliferation of discourses raises challenges for understanding, but it also opens new imaginative possibilities in which new ways of being can be explored.

It is crucial to recognize that this is not a complete relativism where all positions are equal, where none can be compared to each other, and in which thus all are equally arbitrary and ultimately equally unreliable. To regard them as equal would require an outside or neutral stance that could provide the weighing of such supposed equality. Rather, discourses are in radical competition with each other, clamoring for space and attention, often trying to top or replace each other. They practically beg for evaluation by continually seeking to entice new listeners. Postmodern philosophy cares deeply about justice—especially in its attention to minority voices previously suppressed by the dominant discourse—and it certainly does not suggest that truth is reducible to personal whim.

In fact, a complete relativism would imply that no conversation is possible at all, because the various universes of discourse would be deemed hermetically sealed against each other and the boundaries between them considered impossible to cross. Acknowledging that worlds of discourse are more radically different than we thought and that no language can be fully translated into another, does not mean that no communication or conversation can occur. We clearly can learn new languages, can move to new places, can appreciate narratives from other cultures and backgrounds, even identify with their characters, can convert to new perspectives or adopt new social or political positions that radically diverge from those with which we began. To relinquish the dream of pure and entirely neutral objectivity is not to give up on truth or justice altogether, but to seek new measures of discernment and to recognize that we cannot step out of all frameworks of understanding altogether in order to regard the world without horizons at all. Without horizons, there are no worlds. Without context, there is no understanding.

Instead, we must negotiate more carefully between islands of meaning, weighing their merits and assessing their fit, as we at least partially dwell within them. No longer can their merit be evaluated on some absolute standard or even on the terms of our own discourse. Rather, discernment will require the difficult labor of traveling between these divergent microcosms, of at least partial entry into the other's world, the effort of living and walking with others for at least part of their way. Such discernment is not simply about 'what works' in the pragmatist sense, because there is no agreement on what the standard would be for judging what works. Rather, it means to try out new garments, to see whether they fit, before we shed our skin. It also means to recognize that garments that do not fit us may well suit someone else very well. This is not just a matter of taste, but involves 'fit' and appropriateness for the situation and person. Does the horizon meet the ground? Does it illuminate and nourish what grows in its soil? Does it allow for dwelling in ways that do not exploit it, in such a way as to render habitation for others—human and nonhuman—impossible? Does the horizon allow for the play of the back-and-forth between artist and audience, such that the audience can become a participant in the performance? Is the world rich in meaning that can sustain complex narrative possibilities? Can it serve as a spacious stage for the tension between concordance and discordance to play itself out with a generous use of myth, symbol, and metaphor?

To discern the hermeneutic possibilities of such horizons they will need to be not only encountered but entered far more fully than in the past. Greater risk is involved in choosing from the proliferation of symbols, narratives, or performances. A wager will always be at work in putting in the difficult labor of learning another language, entering a different world. Learning *this* language means not learning that one. Truly dwelling for some time in *this* world means not making a home in that one. It may also imply the risk of never returning "home" or finding that what was formerly home has now become strange, that one no longer fits into its world, perhaps that one is never truly home anywhere in the sort of self-evident and secure way of earlier forms of dwelling.

What, then, would it mean to communicate across such boundaries, not to remain limited to our own little arbitrary world? It would require engaging in genuine but far more difficult conversations: listening to the particular narratives of others and understanding the ways in which they provide meaning and "concordance" to their lives and communities. It would mean to allow horizons to encounter each other and to overlap to some extent without conflating them or allowing one to subsume and erase the other. Conversation will have to involve the recognition that horizons can be very far apart and thus require suspension of judgment for longer periods of time in order to make genuine listening possible. We have to allot the time and energy it costs to learn the discursive languages of others if we want to understand their perspectives and ensure not only that they can truly interject in or contribute to "our" conversation, but that we could potentially enter theirs. Simple tolerance will no longer be sufficient when the abyss between discourses appears so gaping. Rather, significant humility, generosity, and compassion are required, along with ingenuity and creativity in communicating such different perspectives. Claims to understand others must become more tentative and involve a deeper entry into the others' worlds. Our work of understanding has become much harder. But it is not impossible.

POSTMODERN HERMENEUTICS AND DISCOURSES OF FAITH

For matters of faith, the postmodern condition is actually a great improvement over the situation in modernity. On the basis of absolute—and supposedly neutral—scientific rationality, faith always came up short. Belief in God or miracles seemed incoherent, easily refutable by rigorous thinking or scientific research. In postmodernity, instead, faith may well be a good fit within certain "worlds" or universes of discourse. Many people no longer believe or at least are disenchanted with the overarching stories of scientism, communism, capitalism, or consumerism. Accounts of faith may well offer viable alternatives of meaning. Religious narratives of all backgrounds and confessions can and do now clamor for hearing in the multiform and plurivocal marketplace of conflicting stories.

Yet, this situation of competition also means that religious narratives will only be compelling if they are rich and complex, if they open narrative worlds that seem worth inhabiting and that can provide attractive shelter. In the competition between the many little stories, potential dwellers will only come on shore and start to build homes if the place preserves healthy soils for growing nourishing cultural and intellectual food. If people are left hungry or rendered ill by religious narratives, they will seek more wholesome fare elsewhere. Ritual and symbolism instantiate narrative possibilities in worlds that can be entered if they are sufficiently open and welcoming. Creative imaginative variations allow dialects to flourish within and across languages.

It may also mean holding various aspects of the story more loosely and engaging in broader narrative possibilities. There is no longer a determinate way of telling the story—if there ever was. Instead, the proliferation of media unfurls new creative potential for enacting different elements of the stories, exploring their polyphonic and multivalent character. If the stories can no longer be measured against some absolute neutral standard, if there is not a single overarching story, then new narrative possibilities are opened. New characters can assume new parts in the play, try them on for size and fit. New symbols and metaphors can be explored. New images and new music can set the scene for the stories being performed. Again, that does not mean that all of those options will work or that simply any possibility can be adopted. Rather, various possibilities will have to be tried out for fit and suitability, for their ability to tell the stories in compelling ways, to provide rich narrative worlds that are open for entry rather than closing down the narrative or shutting out the listeners, disabling participation or appropriation.

Kearney insists that this must involve the risk of genuine dialogue with other religious traditions. Novel narrative possibilities emerge only if one listens to other stories and explores their narrative potential. Yet, departing on a fragile vessel to cross unsteady seas in search of new lands and their creative horizons may well mean not to return. Truly learning the language of another faith and genuinely entering the other's world may entail a permanent relocation that neither allows a merger of the horizons nor opens a permanent door between the worlds. This is not simply a threat of losing one's identity or meaning but opens the possibility of shaping identity in new contexts and in conversation with other worlds of meaning. Meaning is no longer a given in a postmodern world but must be constituted creatively and embodied concretely in the context of a plurality of horizons that can neither be wholly merged nor sealed off against each other.

Meaning is not constructed here on the intensely individual levels of the modern project in search of a brave new world. The postmodern projects realize that meaning and identity occur on plural and even communal levels, but that those communities are more fluid and more moveable than they have often been in the past. Narratives are always shared, even if they can be retold in a variety of ways and staged in endlessly imaginative ways. Stories told to no one die a rapid death of oblivion. Not all tellings and stagings are equally compelling, but they always address an infinite number of possible listeners who can choose to take up the story or enter into the proposed world. The telling of the story will be compelling only if such listeners find in the proposed world at least some elements of prefiguration of their own fluctuating stories and if the poetically configured world of the narrative allows for a refiguring of their lives in meaningful but never definitive ways. Such prefiguring and refiguring must be undertaken together with others on at least some level; it is almost impossible to sustain on one's own and it always implies a sharing in others' worlds, even if these are proximate ones.

Religious groups and traditions often have an especially rich reservoir of potential symbols, metaphors, narrative possibilities, and ritual practices. They also permit embodiment and participation in shared meaning in ways that many other stories do only in more transitory fashion. At the same time, they seem to have an almost infinite potential for adopting and adapting new artistic possibilities for creating richer and more compelling worlds of discourse. And given how many competing worlds of meaning are on offer in the postmodern situation, their worlds will only be compelling if they are generous and hospitable rather than restrictive or judgmental. Narratives that are nourishing will be more compelling than those that starve their potential listeners or do not enable meaning and identity to take root and flourish because they suffocate it in unhealthy soils.

In these ways, postmodern hermeneutics opens new possibilities for faith.

BIBLIOGRAPHY

Caputo, John D. *What Would Jesus Deconstruct? The Good News of Postmodernism for the Church*. Grand Rapids: Baker Academic, 2007.

———. *Hermeneutics: Facts and Interpretation in the Age of Information*. London: Penguin, 2018.

Cassin, Barbara. *Sophistical Practice*. New York: Fordham University Press, 2014.

Falque, Emmanuel. *Crossing the Rubicon: The Borderlands Between Philosophy and Theology*. Translated by Reuben Shank. New York: Fordham University Press, 2016.

Kearney, Richard. *Anatheism: Returning to God After God*. New York: Columbia University Press, 2010.

Kearney, Richard, and Brian Treanor, eds. *Carnal Hermeneutics*. New York: Fordham University Press, 2015.

Lyotard, Jean-François. *The Postmodern Condition: A Report on Knowledge*. Translated by Geoff Bennington and Brian Massumi. Minneapolis: University of Minnesota Press, 1984.

———. *Just Gaming*. Translated by Wlad Godzich. Minneapolis: University of Minnesota Press, 1985.

Marion, Jean-Luc. *The Idol and Distance: Five Studies*. Translated by Thomas A. Carlson. New York: Fordham University Press, 2001.

Naas, Michael. "Lyotard Archipelago." In *Minima Memoria: In the Wake of Jean-François Lyotard*, edited by Claire Nouvet et al., 176–96. Stanford: Stanford University Press, 2006.

Ricœur, Paul. "Life in Quest of Narrative." In *On Paul Ricœur: Narrative and Interpretation*, edited by David Wood, 20–33. London: Routledge, 1992.

Smith, James K. A. *Who's Afraid of Postmodernism? Taking Derrida, Lyotard, and Foucault to Church*. Grand Rapids: Baker Academic, 2006.

Westphal, Merold. *Whose Community? Which Interpretation? Philosophical Hermeneutics for the Church*. Grand Rapids: Baker Academic, 2009.

Chapter 3
Deconstructive Hermeneutics
CARL RASCHKE

THE RELATION BETWEEN "DECONSTRUCTION" AND DECONSTRUCTIVE HERMENEUTICS

Deconstructive hermeneutics is a broad-brush, but highly imprecise, term for certain discourses and methodologies in theology and the humanities that have emerged over time from the work of the French philosopher Jacques Derrida (1930–2004). The expression was often employed by both liberal and radical theologians throughout the last decades of the twentieth century to challenge the dominance of rationalist, modernist, or "scientistic" modes of argumentation, focusing on the incapacity of language to "refer" to any kind of objective order in any conclusive sense.

Intimately bound up with the writings in the post-Vietnam era of an upstart group of prominent, younger academic religious thinkers interested in post-structuralist (later termed "postmodernist") philosophy, so-called "deconstructionists" were accused throughout the 1980s and 1990s of all sorts of things from "nihilism" and "relativism" on the right to "mysticism" and "fascism." The latter charge from the Marxist Left was due mainly to the discovery in the early 1980s that one of its key spokespersons, literary critic Paul De Man, had collaborated with the Vichy Government during the Nazi occupation of France during World War II. The general hostility at the time toward "deconstruction" was summed up by celebrated University of Virginia scholar Nathan Scott in his presidential address to the American Academy of Religion in 1986. Scott declared that "deconstruction is itself simply another absolutism which is therefore uncalculated to facilitate any vital dialogue between religious thought and other modes of cultural discourse."[1] Such enmity was amplified in part by the influential writings of Mark C. Taylor, who characterized deconstruction as "the hermeneutics of the death of God." In his writings during that period Taylor sought to conflate deconstruction with the so-called "death of God theology" promoted by Thomas J. J. Altizer.[2]

After the turn of the millennium when deconstruction had gone mainstream in the study of religion, the evangelical world suddenly discovered it through the publication of my own book *The Next Reformation: Why Evangelicals Need to Embrace Postmodernity*. In that work I sought to show how deconstruction gave the lie to the pseudo-rationalist and modernist formulation of biblical hermeneutics found in the 1978 Chicago Statement of evangelical leaders on so-called "inerrancy." The blowback from the religious right was fast and furious, but the term "deconstruction" had a distinct resonance with a new generation of increasingly progressive evangelicals who adopted it as a shibboleth for their growing discomfort with, and anger toward, conservative evangelicalism and its close alliance with the Republican Party. John D. Caputo's *What Would Jesus Deconstruct?* (2007) capitalized on this sentiment and closely identified Derrida's approach with American political progressivism in an effort to revive for the new millennium a form of Walter Rauschenbusch's "social gospel," which at the same time might incorporate the new language of French social theory. Deconstruction, Caputo wrote, "announces the good news about alterity, which it bears to the church. It has prophetic resonances that call for justice to flow like water over the land."[3] Caputo's title was of course a deliberate play on Charles Sheldon's well-known phrase "what would Jesus do?

Today an entirely new generation ("Gen Z") of academics has little or no interest in the kinds of sophisticated academic philosophical or theoretical wrangles that energized their predecessors. Although the word "postmodern" has lost its luster and has well-nigh vanished from the most trendy theological vocabularies, the word "deconstruction" continues to be bandied about in popular postconservative, or post-evangelical , discourse. In fact, it has become a general trope for the crackup of traditional and orthodox beliefs throughout Western society. "Deconstruction" is now used routinely by both pundits and laity as a fancy term in the venerable American self-help tradition of therapeutic examination of one's own prior beliefs, habits, practices, and moral commitments. It has also been deployed by Mennonite

---

1. Scott, "Presidential Address," 3–19 (8).

2. Altizer launched the "death of God" theology movement in the late 1960s with publication of his book *Gospel of Christian Atheism*.

3. Caputo, *What Would Jesus Deconstruct?*, 32.

author and teacher Brad Jersak in what he dubs "The Great Deconstruction," or "the current wave of migration out of previous faith forms into new understandings of God . . . and/or the mass exodus from faith altogether."[4]

Given the promiscuous connotations attached for almost half a century now to the expression, "deconstruction" retains—at least for those scholars who actually take time to peruse the philosophical and theological literature—a certain cachet that distinguishes it from other applications of critical theory to which it bears a distant kinship. Deconstruction is, as Derrida stressed early in his career, *first and foremost about the reading and interpretation of texts*. Thus, the phrase "deconstructive hermeneutics" is in many ways its own kind of pleonasm. Deconstruction is a very special, and highly refined, type of theoretical intervention that is consistent with the long and complex history of both biblical and literary hermeneutics. It is no accident that the so-called "Yale critics"—literary theorists such as de Man and J. Hillis Miller—were the first to introduce Derrida to an American intellectual audience.

Deconstructive hermeneutics differs from the "dialogical" approach of Hans-Georg Gadamer as well as Paul Ricœur's claim that interpretation derives from what he calls the "surplus of meaning" available in the "world of the text" encompassing the richness of human life and experience. For Derrida, the text has no context. Or in his famous, but routinely misunderstood remark, *Il n'y a pas de hors-texte* ("there is no text outside the text"). That is to say, there is no secondary text—no textual "supplement"—to make sense of any given piece of writing. An interpreter cannot make a statement to the effect that "this text x can be interpreted as y," where y functions as the "meaning" of x. There is a tale circulating about the late Harvard philosopher that illustrates this point. According to the legend, which may be of course apocryphal, a brash student once pestered Cavell to explain a difficult point he was elaborating in his lecture. "Professor Cavell," the student gushed, "please tell us what you mean." Cavell then reportedly stopped his lecture, removed his glasses, lowered his head toward the student and replied, "young man, what do you mean by 'what do you mean'?"

Whether this incident actually occurred, the anecdote about Cavell, whose most well-known book was entitled *Must We Mean What We Say?*, exemplifies what Derrida was actually doing with his program of deconstruction. Derrida frequently emphasized that deconstruction is not something *we do* to the text. Deconstruction simply happens as we read and respond to the text. It is what engaging with the text itself does to our understanding of the text. As I frequently remind my students, "deconstruct" is an *intransitive*

---

4. Jersak, *Out of the Embers*.

verb. Contra Caputo, Jesus would not deconstruct anything. It would be impossible. But as all we have and know about Jesus are the texts concerning him (i.e., the Gospels as well as Paul's memorable references to him as "Christ Jesus"), every time we read and seek to interpret these texts not only for ourselves but for the Christian community at large, their meaning is constantly "under deconstruction" and subject to semantic revision. These revisions constitute the basis for the evolution of Christian theology and its understanding of who Jesus is as well as what he "means" over the centuries. A deconstructive hermeneutics on this level would not simply consist in a re-reading of previous interpretations of the Christian textual tradition, but a recognition that the import of the particular texts regarding Jesus—as well as many other matters of faith and doctrine—have a fluidity and historicity that cannot be merely captured in a single and decisive determination of their "meaning."

"THERE IS NOTHING OUTSIDE THE TEXT"

In contrast with modern fundamentalism, there can never be any "plain meaning" or "inerrant" rendering of a given biblical text. Interpretation of the text depends on the historic habits of language and its types of usage shared by any given community of interpreters in any given era. As the old quip goes, God did not actually speak through the biblical authors in the King James English. The meaning of the text "emerges" within the historical and semantic context in which it is encountered and deciphered. Yet it is not strictly a function of a specific *Sitz im Leben* ("situation in life"), as the Germans would say. Again, there is "nothing" outside the text itself that can specify the signification of the text, which is why the familiar charge of "relativism" rarely sticks. For a meaning to be "relative" it must be *relevant* to something other than the text itself.

This distinction between the text and its meaning is at the heart of the philosophical—and by extension theological—problem out of which Derrida's project of deconstruction arises. The history of human thought is by definition an archive of texts in a wide assortment of languages which have been interpreted in various ways over the ages. Theories of interpretation comes down not only to how we read and write about these texts, but how we communicate their meaning in connection with what has already been said about them. Prior to Derrida hermeneutics was often preoccupied with what the text aims to *express*. The meaning of the text, therefore, was assumed to be something "outside," or "other than," the text itself. So-called Romantic hermeneutics, which suffused German thinking throughout much of the nineteenth century, turned on the premise that the meaning of the text was to be found in a moment of cognitive clarity that the philosopher Wilhelm Dilthey dubbed *Verstehen* (literally, "understanding"). The German word has a much richer and nuanced set of connotations than its English counterpart. Dilthey built upon an earlier notion set forth by the German religious thinker Friedrich Schleiermacher that can we can only grasp the implications of a particular text by discerning its relation to the entirety of cultural experience. Vice versa we can only comprehend the significance of the whole through its manifestation in the parts. Schleiermacher called this principle the "hermeneutical circle." For Dilthey, *Verstehen* is this kind of intuitive assemblage of texts and artifacts, which singularly and in concert manifest the depth of knowledge.

Prior to Derrida, the task of hermeneutics amounted mostly to thinking through what is somehow disclosed in the text. The text itself was secondary, and philosophical or theological hermeneutics was primarily concerned ferreting out the treasure trove of independent meaning that supposedly buried in the text. The twentieth century philosopher Martin Heidegger, regarding whom much of the younger Derrida consists in a sustained critique and response, cast the hermeneutical problem in terms of what he named "the destruction of metaphysics" (*die Destruktion der Metaphysik*). According to Heidegger, philosophy since Plato has been "metaphysical" to the extent that what we regard as the objective world is actually a cognitive "frame" (*Gestell*) that conceals Being itself, or at least confuses Being with specific beings. Heidegger called the distinction between Beings and being the "ontological difference." It is the task of philosophy, Heidegger argued, not to think *about* Being, but to think through this difference.

Such a path of thinking Heidegger labelled "hermeneutical," insofar as it recognizes that the classical correspondence theory of language (where "words" and "things" reflect each other) is bound up with the metaphysical framing of the real, and that language itself is indisputably an ongoing process of interpretation that both reveals and conceals what is present within it. Interpretation is not to speak "about" something. Interpretation allows Being itself to speak through language. Heidegger referred to this posture as one of "letting go" (*Gelassenheit*), of allowing "what is" to emerge from concealment by refusing to assign a predetermined meaning to what is said or heard.

Derrida's reading of texts "deconstructively," therefore, derives from Heidegger's paradigm of the "destruction" of the metaphysical attitude toward the text. In Heidegger's words, "language speaks," so that Being may be reveal itself. For Derrida, on the other hand, meaning is never an incidence of revealing or concealing. It is simply a moment in the act of reading and interpreting when we encounter the fact that what we understand now *differs from* what we understood before. Meaning is never given but always *deferred*. In short, we can never determine the precise meaning of a text at any particular moment in the act of reading or interpreting. The meaning shifts with each re-reading or re-interpretation. There is always, according to Derrida, a process of "spacing" *(espacement)* between one interval of signification and the next which exposes the inadequacy of all significations have preceded it. In his early work Derrida plays upon a famous, but contentious, practice in his later work where the latter crossed out the German word for "Being" *(Sein)*) whenever he wrote it. Heidegger's aim was to highlight the point that any capture of the sense of Being in any kind of linguistic or grammatical setting, especially in writing, limits and thereby falsifies its infinite capacity for connotation.

DECONSTRUCTION AS HERMENEUTICS

Derrida makes a similar point when it comes to the practice of textual interpretation. Even the slightest gesture at interpretation of what stands before us in the text puts the previous iteration constantly "under erasure" *(sous rature)*. Because interpretation is a temporal process the meaning that manifests to us at any given point in the activity of reading and writing is erased within the very interval it appears. The ongoing production of "meaning" in interpretation is an interminable process of both the temporal placement of signification and its *displacement*. It is this differential process where both the immediate meaning and the larger context of *meaningful* means by which we might possibly read the text foster what Derrida refers to as a "play signifiers" comparable to a game of hide and seek. Now you see a meaning, now you don't.

A handier approach to Derrida's concept of deconstruction would be to consider what remains his most well-known, and genuinely iconic, illustration. In a 1963 essay entitled "Cogito and the History of Madness," now included in a collection of very early articles published under the title of *Writing and Difference*, Derrida shows the immense philosophical implication of the French word *difference*. The French and English are both spelled the same, but phonetically discrepant. If we pronounce the "e" in the French version, it sounds like an "a" (i.e., as "differance"). Likewise, if we change the spelling of the French word to coincide with how it should be pronounced, it is no longer the same word. Derrida repeatedly cited this anomaly to underscore the difference between speech and writing, and to make the revolutionary claim that the history of philosophy is inseparable from the history of written texts. At the end of his dialogue *Phaedrus* Plato contends that writing distorts and does not faithfully reproduce the meaning of what has been said. But Derrida notes that the written word is all we have at our disposal to decipher the meaning of Plato's dialogues. In fact, Plato himself was reconstructing through his writings what his teacher Socrates was alleged to have said. Since all we have is to work with is written inscriptions along with commentary offering interpretations, except in the magic moment when the spoken word was once spoken (whether it was spoken by God or human beings), the difference that writing makes when it comes to problem of meaning *does make all the difference.* In effect, we cannot experience the original meaning of the text, if there ever was one. All we have is the text itself, which is itself an "interpretation."

The great Jewish rabbi Hillel, whose life overlapped with that of Jesus, famously stressed that the so-called Golden Rule ("that which is hateful unto you, do not do to your neighbor.") was the "whole" of Jewish Revelation or Torah, and that "the rest is commentary." Derrida, an Algerian Jew, may or may not have been influenced by this sentiment, but the sentiment is similar. The meaning of a text is in its extension through language, or commentary. Similarly, all commentary, or interpretation, is at bottom "deconstructive," which does not imply that we reject false readings from the past, but that we learn to assimilate what once seemed adequate but now strikes us as deficient into a richer understanding of both past and present. Hence, we have the now fashionable use of "deconstruction" by those sorts of spiritual seekers who are shedding their fundamentalist or dogmatic beliefs and striving to fill out and enrich their respective world views.

This usage of the term is not necessarily inappropriate, but it has very little to do with the intricate and extremely nuanced function of the locution from the standpoint of hermeneutics. *It implies that deconstruction is something we do to something.* In fact, deconstruction is *what is done to us* through a process in which are already participating. Deconstruction is not some custom intellectual tool we wield in attacking or taking apart a structure of interpretations with which we find fault. In the process of deconstruction we slowly come to realize that what we thought we understood we no longer do, or if we do understand, we do so in an entirely different manner of speaking. Most of us read texts not simply to understand it per se, but in order to situate ourselves as readers and thinkers within the webwork of textual meanings with which we are both familiar and unfamiliar. A deconstructive hermeneuetics, therefore, is one in which textual interpretation invariably entails an ever shifting assemblage of signifying practices involving both interpreter and what is interpreted.

If we pretend to take Derrida seriously, the phrase "deconstructive hermeneutics" is a kind of tautology. Hermeneutics as a whole is the movement of "deconstruction" which happens automatically through the process of interpretation. But few theological thinkers, let alone those who practice biblical interpretation, bother to read Derrida closely. The term "deconstruction" has simply become a stylish word for "taking apart." The reference frame within which the word has come to be commonly deployed remains the nineteenth century Romantic perspective whereby the true "meaning" is dismantle an entire architecture of knowledge and meaning.

DECONSTRUCTION VS. "THE HERMENEUTICS OF SUSPICION"

Ironically, this popular prostitution of the word "deconstruction" goes hand in hand with the modernist assault on meaning. The paradigmatic version of this assault can be found in the famous opening line of Descartes's *Meditations.*" Descrates writes: Several years have now passed since I first realized how numerous were the false opinions that in my youth I had taken to be true, and thus how doubtful were all those that I had subsequently built upon them. And thus I realized that once in my life I had to raze everything to the ground and begin again from the original foundations, if I wanted to establish anything firm and lasting in the sciences."[5] For Descartes, what is left after an extreme bout with what has been termed "hyperbolic doubt" is nothing but the abstract principle of one's own bare self-consciousness. It is what Descartes himself called the *res cogitans*, the "thinking thing," the rational "self." One can rightly argue that modernism itself has crafted this approach and has led, as Derrida once insisted, to a kind of hermeneutical "violence" inflicted when deriving meaning from the text. In his famous early essay entitled "Cogito and the History of Madness" Derrida presses the case that the violence against the text involved with this version of "deconstruction" arises from the *hubris*, or self-inflation, of the *cogito* which presumes a clear and distinct coherence to what we understand in our reading that reflects the rational unity of the reflective subject. The *cogito* constitutes a "structure of exclusion" that gives preferential treatment to those sets of ideas that have already been assigned by inherited passageways for intellectual transmission as the meaning of the text.

Modernist hermeneutics, therefore, amounts to what the twentieth century philosopher Paul Ricœur termed the "hermeneutics of suspicion." Ricœur coined the expression to categorize the methods of the philosophical standard bearers of modernism, including Marx, Nietzsche, and Freud. In his book *Freud and Philosophy* Ricœur traces this hermeneutics directly

---

5. Descartes, *Meditations on First Philosophy*, 59.

back to Descartes.[6] The art of interpretation starts with a skepticism about the contents of what appears to us in consciousness. But it takes this attitude of doubt one step further and treats the very symbols we employ to understand our own conscious experiences as a rebus that must be decrypted. In other words, "meaning" presents itself to us as a code to be cracked through a surrogate set of signs and symbolic operations. The "cipher" that helps us break the code also enables us to compare the "text," or system of signifiers, that constitutes our conventional way of rendering things with an alternate text that serves to inscribe the true meaning. In short, what is routinely taken to be "truth" turns out to be a lie, and the second text that deciphers the first becomes a new "revelation" of meaning that was not apparent to us before. The semantic ledger containing these competing statements is what Derrida describes as a "double session," or the "supplementary double." But unlike modernist hermeneutics, which compels us to choose between a "true" and "false" reading of the text, deconstructive hermeneutics holds the two in suspension and forces us to pursue a meaning, at least provisionally, that seems to waver between both sides of the ledger. There is no "higher" truth squirreled behind the facade of truth we take for granted, no intimation of some obscure, but eminently real meaning stashed away in the corner. Every act of interpretation is not so much a solution as the recognition we are caught on the horns of dilemma, or what Derrida termed an "undecidable."

In one of his most important, albeit obscure and inscrutable, works entitled *Dissemination* Derrida contends that theories of interpretation almost invariably conform to the metaphysical presuppositions of Western philosophy.. The metaphysics of meaning that stalks the Western tradition can be summed up by the Greek locution *mimesis*, from which we derive the English term "imitation." In this tradition "words" mimick, or represent, "things." Derrida also refers to the tradition as one of "logocentrism," which maintains that opposing interpretations can be ultimately resolved into the unity of a single concept. In that respect all interpretations are eminently *decidable*. Derrida writes: "What is it that is decided and maintained in ontology or dialectics throughout all the mutations or revolutions that are entailed? It is precisely the ontological: the presumed possibility of a

---

6. Ricœur writes about these thinkers, whom he dubs "the masters of suspicion," as follows: "If we go back to the intention they had in common, we find in it the decision to look upon the whole of consciousness primarily as 'false' consciousness. They thereby take up again, each in a different manner, the problem of the Cartesian doubt, to carry it to the very heart of the Cartesian stronghold." Ricœur, *Freud and Philosophy*, 33.

discourse about what is, the deciding and decidable *logos* of or about the *on* (being-present)."[7]

So-called "logocentrism," therefore, can be illustrated most precisely through the familiar fallacy of attempting to establish the meaning of a text by discerning the author's intention. This approach is also known as the "intentional fallacy." Most twentieth century literary critics dismissed the notion of authorial intention as a viable hermeneutical principle long before Derrida. But Derrida was in a crucial manner of speaking the first to demonstrate from a linguistic standpoint why the fallacy persists from one generation to the next. The fallacy itself stems from our innate sense that language is, as the philosopher Richard Rorty has put it, a "mirror of nature." Every text must have an author, and that author must have a mind from which the specific text is generated. If we can somehow see into the author's mind, we will also divine what it truly meanings, reproducing the world *as it is* in some fashion. Of course, the tacit metaphor here is a hall of mirrors where world, mind, author, and text reflect each other *ad infinitum*. In the logocentric paradigm the nature of reality is nothing more than a relentless play of mimetic relations which depend on the degree to which we can see clearly the "object" that is supposed to "be present" to us in a determinate fashion.

For Derrida, the presumed mimetic relationship between whatever "is" turns out to be an *oppositional* one instead. The text that serves to "interpret" the text that has gone before it neither muddies nor clarifies an erstwhile meaning. It simply widens the horizon within which the original text can now be comprehended. More importantly, it makes the "texture" of the original text far more porous, opening gaps, lesions, discontinuities, and lacunae that now must be accounted for in ways that were not previously evident. Another way of construing Derrida's notorious dictum that "there is nothing outside the text" is to re-envision hermeneutics as a boundless texture of intertextual linkages rather than a collection of single texts. Glosses or commentaries on texts are just as much a part of this intertextuality as the text itself. The "meaning" of the text lurks in its everpresent ambiguity, or undecidability, which is forever conditioned by possibility of its further interpretation (its "polysemy").

DECONSTRUCTION AND BIBLICAL HERMENEUTICS

"Deconstructive hermeneutics" thus offers immense implications for the interpretation of Scripture, as David Seeley observed as far back as 1994. In

---

7. Derrida, *Dissemination*, 191.

his book *Deconstructing the New Testament*, Seeley asked a very basic question, given the immense prestige of, and interest in, the literary theories of "deconstruction" during that period: "Why employ the thought of Jacques Derrida to read the New Testament?"[8] Seeley remarks that it is the "textuality" of Scripture that not only poses a conceptual problem for contemporaries, but was also the case in biblical times. As Derrida himself repeatedly stresses, textuality—or the phenomenality of inscription as contrasted with the spoken word—distances, or "defers," meaning away from its immediate iteration. Presence is now disclosed as absence. The original signification is "erased." Even the biblical writers themselves struggled with this sort of issue. Both Jesus and Paul quoted Jewish Scriptures that had acquired meanings in their era that varied significantly from their primordial context. The prophet Jeremiah in the sixth century BCE lamented that the Jewish people no longer grasped the import of the original Torah, or Law, inscribed on stone by Yahweh himself on Mount Sinai, and he prophesied that in the age to come it would instead return to the fulness of an immediate presence. "I will put my law in their minds and write it on their hearts" (Jer 31:33 NIV).

According to Seeley, the difference associated with the distance between God's (spoken) word and the written text has bedeviled Christian theology since the first century. Although Protestantism prizes its own foundational tenet that God's written word is also God's direct revelation (i.e., the doctrine of *sola Scriptura*), the history of Christian hermeneutics makes it plainly obvious that the Church of the preceding 1500 years relied for the most part on what it considered to be some imagined "originary voice," as Derrida would call it, that corresponded with Scripture. Augustine's well-known conversion to Christianity, as he recounts in his *Confessions*, on hearing the voice of a child imploring him to "take and read," is a prominent illustration of this attitude. "The basic problem [was] that Scripture, as a written text," Seeley declares, "is simply there, vulnerable to being used (or, from Tertullian's viewpoint, misused) by anyone who comes along for any purpose at all."[9] In that respect the fundamentalist doctrine of the "inerrancy" of Scripture, as codified in the so-called "Chicago Statement" from the late 1970s, is ironically closer to how the early church understood Scripture, although most serious biblical scholars with a grounding in linguistic theory reject—rightly—that view as flawed and self-contradictory. What the early church would *not* have countenanced is the assumption that written Scripture is essentially indistinguishable from the "authorial" voice of God.

---

8. Seeley, *Deconstructing the New Testament*, 1.
9. Seeley, *Deconstructing the New Testament*, 9.

It is this unique tension between what Derrida characterizes as the "phonological" (oral communication) and the "grammatological" (written communication) that uniquely defines the history of Christian hermeneutics. Derrida and deconstruction are "not so foreign to biblical studies as might have been expected," according to Seeley.[10] Regardless of their theological leanings, scholars specializing in biblical interpretation almost universally concur that the Gospels are not the *verbatim speech* of Jesus, but were instead transcriptions from a complex oral tradition that were culled and customized by certain authors for different purposes years after Jesus's death. Hence, the making of the Christian tradition overall involves an intricate and highly nuanced engagement across two millennia with what Derrida regards as the "play" of countless signifiers spun from the tension between different textual readings, all of which claim in some loose fashion to authenticate the *kerygma* of Christ and the apostles, the foundational proclamation of God's salvation. This proclamation is also identified the *evangelion*, which translates into old English as "gospel," or "good news." In Derrida's scheme the *kerygma* constitutes the "phonological" element, which has been lost forever. What we have instead is are texts, and interpretations of texts, which in no way reproduce the phonetic original, but defer its meaning to the open field of hermeneutical interventions that we know as "the tradition." We only have, as the famous nineteenth century German thinker Gottlieb Frege who inaugurated twentieth century linguistic philosophy put it, the "sense" but not the "reference."

If deconstructive hermeneutics is to maintain fidelity to the philosophical insights and innovations Derrida advances, it will raise some major theological issues as well. For example, one of the central implications of deconstructive hermeneutics is that there can be no claim to any kind of "special revelation" outside the text. The primacy which Protestant hermeneutics assigns to the biblical text itself logically entails that Scripture itself is the sole container for such a special revelation, as the Protestant Reformers themselves made clear. Biblical inerrantists, in fact, hold to what might be called a "high" view of the text itself as revelation. But deconstructive hermeneutics tells us that although there is "nothing outside the text" where we might locate God's actual spoken word, there remains the possibility that we might routinely hear divine mutterings in the interstices of textual interpretation as we struggle to receive the true meaning of Scripture as a whole. In ordinary theological terms, therefore, we might infer that deconstructive hermeneutics permits us to allow the Holy Spirit to lead us into new dimensions of understanding and meaning toward which all textual formalisms,

---

10. Seeley, *Deconstructing the New Testament*, 19.

or "fundamentalisms" blind us. The idea that the Holy Spirit "illuminates" us in reading Scripture so that we may apprehend its proper meaning in whatever set of circumstances we find ourselves is essential to many of the Church Fathers, especially Augustine, and it is reinforced regularly in the commentaries of Luther and Calvin.

For a person of faith deconstructive hermeneutics is not at all "nihilistic," as its critics frequently charge because of the dubious impression that it permits us to assign any meaning to the text that might pop up in our minds. The all-too-familiar canard that deconstructive hermeneutics is equivalent to a license to read anything we want into Scripture (the accusation of "relativism") derives from an equally false notion that passages from the Bible are clear and obvious in the same way that the proposition "it is raining now" is clear and obvious (if, in fact, it does happen to be raining). Certain Protestant preachers in the early nineteenth century, as I have argued, confused the dictum of the "plain sense" of Scripture with the idea prevalent at the time that language always "means what it says."

Modern linguistics has forcefully demonstrated that is not at all the case. The "plain sense" of any text always depends on its broader context, and that context itself is shaped by the grammar of the unique idiom which both writer and reader hold in common. The Bible was initially composed in ancient Hebrew as well as *koine* Greek, languages which not only differ from each other, but from English also. So-called "historical-critical" exegesis of biblical texts were pioneered in European universities as early as the late seventeenth century. But it was only with the Enlightenment that certain radical thinkers began to employ such criticism to question the veracity of Scripture itself. Historicizing Scripture, however, does not necessarily relativize it, a "category mistake" that both conservative and progressive routinely make. To point out, for example, that the practice of trial by jury harks all the way back to England at the close of the dark ages says nothing about the validity of such a familiar institution of common law. Similarly, the historical fact that the "revealed" truth of Scripture was first promulgated in Judea, a fractious province of the Roman empire two millennia ago, helps us grapple with the specific context in which it arose, but attests neither for nor against its putative *transhistorical* significance as divine revelation.

Revelation, as the famous theologian H. Richard Niebuhr underscored in an important, but now largely forgotten, book from the early 1940s, is a unique reading—what we might term a "faith reading"—of the meaning of events in human history. Revelation, Niebuhr writes, constitutes something that has "happened which compels our faith and which requires us to seek rationality and unity in the whole of our history." Furthermore, "revelation is like the kingdom of God; if we seek it first all other things are added to us but if we seek it for the sake of these other things we really deny it."[11] The same can be said for the biblical text when we read it from the faith perspective. This exact issue was actually confronted by the Gospel writer Luke, a third-generation Christian, when he set out to explain to his patron Theophilus[12] how to recount the "things" (*logoi*) that have been taught about what Jesus said and did. All the eyewitnesses to Jesus's career were no longer around when Luke composed his Gospel. What the early church had were different "accounts"—some oral, some perhaps already written down—which eventually became the material for the four Gospels. Luke, in fact, had somehow to put together his own "account," which through use of the particular Greek word *diēgēsin* indicates not so much what Niebuhr would term an "external" narrative concerning what takes place but an "internal" one told from the perspective of one who has grasped the meaning of the revelation that is Jesus's death and resurrection as the Jews' long-awaited messiah or "Christ."[13]

Deconstructive hermeneutics compels us to "read between the lines" of a biblical text *as a text* in order to encounter the text itself as the portal to God's revelation through the text which we apprehend through faith and the guidance of the Holy Spirit. The Derridean maxim that "there is nothing outside the text" reinforces Niebuhr's insight that God speaks to through the text only to "insiders," those for whom *sola scriptura* is founded uniquely on *sola fide* ("by faith alone"). That there is nothing outside the text in no way entails there is "nothing to the text." The text comes alive when we read it "deconstructively" to the extent that we are no longer befuddled by what we in our human arrogance presume it means. A genuine deconstructive hermeneutics requires we let God speak in ways we never imagined mere words could ever accomplish.

BIBLIOGRAPHY

Altizer, Thomas J. J. *The Gospel of Christian Atheism*. Philadelphia: Westminster, 1966.

---

11. Niebuhr, *Meaning of Revelation*, 139.

12. "Many have undertaken to draw up an account of the things that have been fulfilled among us, just as they were handed down to us by those who from the first were eyewitnesses and servants of the word. With this in mind, since I myself have carefully investigated everything from the beginning, I too decided to write an orderly account for you, most excellent Theophilus, so that you may know the certainty of the things you have been taught." Luke 1:1–4 NIV.

13. See Moessner, *Luke the Historian of Israel's Legacy*.

———, et al. *Deconstruction and Theology.* New York: Crossroads, 1982.

Caputo, John D. *What Would Jesus Deconstruct?* Grand Rapids: Baker Academic, 2007.

Derrida, Jacques. *Dissemination.* Translated by Barbara Johnson. Chicago: University of Chicago Press, 1981.

———. *Writing and Difference.* Translated by Alan Bass. Chicago: University of Chicago Press, 2107.

Descartes, René. *Meditations on First Philosophy.* Indianapolis: Hackett, 1993.

Gunkel, David J. *Deconstruction.* Cambridge, MA: MIT Press, 2021.

Jersak, Brad. *Out of the Embers: Faith After the Great Deconstruction.* New Kensington, PA: Whitaker, 2022.

Moessner, David Paul. *Luke the Historian of Israel's Legacy, Theologian of Israel's "Christ."* Berlin: Walter de Gruyter, 2016.

Niebuhr, H. Richard. *The Meaning of Revelation.* New York: Harper & Row, 1960.

Raschke, Carl. *The Next Reformation: Why Evangelicals Must Embrace Postmodernity.* Grand Rapids: Baker Academic, 2004.

———. *Postmodern Theology: A Biopic.* Eugene, OR: Cascade, 2017.

Ricœur, Paul. *Freud and Philosophy: An Essay on Interpretation.* Translated by Denis Savage. New Haven, CT: Yale University Press, 1970.

Scott, Nathan A., Jr. "The Presidential Address: The House of Intellect in an Age of Carnival, Some Hermeneutical Reflections." *Journal of the American Academy of Religion* 55 (1987) 3–19.

Seeley, David. *Deconstructing the New Testament.* Leiden: Brill, 1994.

Taylor, Mark C. *Deconstructing Theology.* AAR Studies in Religion 28. New York: Crossroads, 1982.

Vanhoozer, Kevin J. *Is There A Meaning in This Text? The Bible, the Reader, and the Morality of Literary Knowledge.* Grand Rapids: Zondervan, 1998.

Chapter 4
Political Theology and Hermeneutics

The Apocalyptic Paul as Case Study

WEMIMO JAIYESIMI AND JONATHAN TRAN

In the following we examine the political implications of a paradigmatic instance of postconservative biblical interpretation, one that follows the so-called "New Perspective on Paul." The New Perspective is one that seeks to free Pauline literature from certain theological agendas, especially those wedded to Reformation-era theories of atonement. Alternatively, New Perspective hermeneuts seek to return Paul to his own time and place, and by attending to Paul in his context draw forth lessons for our time and place. What makes this perspective "new" is its self-styled effort at dusting off the impositions of a dated theological agenda and allowing Paul to shine by shining on his own terms. One of the contours salvaged once Paul is freed from the impositions is the political character of his writing—say, the fact of his status as both Roman citizen and Roman prisoner—obscured once the heavy-handed atonement-theory reading imposes itself. Under the burden of those impositions, what had always been not only political but obviously so was made narrowly theological, Paul's gospel now morphing into a strangely apolitical set of texts overdetermined by questions of personal salvation. What mattered for Christianity was no longer (taking a rather notorious example from the Protestant Reformation) the political economic meaning of peasant rebellion, but rather the fate of the peasants in heaven or hell. Eventualities like food, poverty, justice, etc. were cast off as distractions from what the Christian gospel really stood for. Downstream, "conservative" or "liberal" named on the one hand competing proposals internal to this narrow theological story (say, ones with wider versus narrower openings into salvation) and on the other "conservative" or "liberal" versions of the already cast-off political considerations, now to be forever distinguished from the theological. By returning Paul to his context and by identifying the essential political contours of that context, Paul could speak for himself, and by extension, us.

Downstream now from the New Perspective we might inquire about the meaning of the political thusly recovered in this postconservative/liberal milieu. That is, once the conceptual blockers have been removed from seeing the political contours of Paul's writings, what ought Christians reading Paul say, see, and do about the political? Offering some answers to this question is what we seek to do in this chapter. We do so by investigating a certain mode of the New Perspective, one keyed to the apocalyptic, "the Apocalyptic Paul." We first summarize its hermeneutic strategy. We then couple that reading strategy with a three-part definition of political theology, hoping that together the three senses can flesh out the apocalyptic interpretive mode and follow out its implications. In doing all this, we offer an account and assessment of a specific instance of postconservative hermeneutics by putting it under the considerable pressures of political theology, concluding with a general appreciation while highlighting a significant problem.

SUMMARIZING THE APOCALYPTIC IMAGINATION

We begin with a summary of some central concerns, argumentative leaps, and overarching visions of the New Testament apocalyptic hermeneutical imagination, especially as it captures Paul and the Pauline corpus, with both looming large in that imagination. The summary presented here will be brief and necessarily less than exhaustive. We only seek to summarize what is necessary for providing backdrop for taking seriously the theo-political entailments of the apocalyptic program.

The Apocalyptic Paul hermeneutic is traceable to the work of number of contemporary New Testament scholars including Douglas A. Campbell, Phillip G. Ziegler, Beverly Roberts Gaventa, Adam Winn, and J. Louis Martyn. Gaventa warns against clustering together these scholars, and others like them, under a "school," preferring instead that they be spoken of as connected by shared "concerns."[1] Indeed, a diversity of emphases characterizes

---

1. Gaventa, "Places of Power in Paul's Letter to the Romans," 295.

the hermeneutical programs of these scholars. So much so that it is not always clear what the "apocalyptic" (variedly invoked by them) names—a programmatic ambiguity we'll return to as a problem later in this summary. Jamie Davies suggests that it serves better to understand the apocalyptic, as used by these scholars, as qualifying a noun (better, that is, to understand them as speaking, for instance, of Paul's eschatology or indeed, his general theological vision as "apocalyptic") rather than the apocalyptic as a noun.[2] So employed, the key claim held by those advancing the concept is not simply that Paul received a revelation, or disclosure (ἀποκάλυψις) from God—which seems straightforward enough, supported almost unambiguously by the New Testament texts that report Paul's vision of the exalted Jesus Christ (Acts 9:1–7, for example). The contention is also not that Paul's writings are akin in form or substance to apocalyptic literatures. Rather, and more pointedly, what apocalyptic scholars of Paul claim in their rendering Paul an apocalyptic figure is that his theology (in its varied respects) turns on a decisive and thoroughgoing apprehension of a paradigmatic disjuncture between a new order (inaugurated by Christ) and a definitively older order that came before the disclosure of God in Christ. Paul, it is argued, envisions the world through an apocalyptic lens (as will be shown, he is said to hold an apocalyptic epistemology) and regards the world viewed by such lights as itself constituting the site of God's apocalyptic intrusion into history (as will be shown, Paul is said to subscribe to an apocalyptic ontology), where the inelegant imagery of rupture and invasion is fully meant.

In the apocalyptic worldview, God's self-revelation in Christ introduces, both at an epistemological and ontological level, a rupture, a complete break with the past. God has broken into the world in the event of the christological unveiling of the Son, unsettling every settlement of past, present, and future, and bringing about something truly new, something without a natural narrative history, defying even the most pious religious expectations of the old covenant. This new reality is only grasped by an epistemological conversion, what Douglas Campbell terms an "apocalyptic epistemology."[3] The term apocalyptic epistemology, so employed, references a novel knowledge regime, a new vantage point from which those "in Christ" are able to know the truth of this apocalypse, this revelation, namely, the reality of the divine new which Christ has ushered in. Campbell sees Paul's statement in 2 Cor 5:16–17—where the apostle declares "from now on, therefore, we regard no one from a human point of view; even though we once knew Christ from a human point of view, we know him no longer in that way. So if

---

2. Davies, *Apocalyptic Paul*, xxvii.
3. Campbell, "Apocalyptic Epistemology," 65–85.

anyone is in Christ, there is a new creation: everything old has passed away; see, everything has become new!" (NRSV)—as precisely suggesting such an apocalyptic epistemology. In this text, for Campbell, Paul's way of viewing himself and others has become radically altered by his encounter with Christ. The apostle no longer regards anyone "from a human point of view." Instead, he has a new epistemological "location," which undergirds his advocacy for a different modality for Christian engagement with the world. His vision of the Risen Lord has cast a light of illumination on things, on the way that he sees the world, and subsequently, engages with it. His glimpse of Christ on the Damascus road forces upon Paul a perspectival reorientation, a paradigm shift of cosmic scale and revolutionary import. The apostle no longer knows "according to the flesh" but now correctly sees things as they truly are. It is in this sense, if one applies the apocalyptic hermeneutic, that Paul is best understood when he talks of having "the mind of Christ" and admonishes others to adopt that mindset (1 Cor 2:10–16; Phil 2:2–7). In the broader context of the second Corinthian epistle, Campbell, drawing from J. Louis Martyn's work on the above quoted text of 2 Cor 5:16–17, highlights Paul's principal contention with the Corinthian Christians to be a concern that they have fallen short of fully grasping the deep orientational change which their being in Christ has or ought to have occasioned in them on these cosmic and revolutionary terms.[4]

But the epistemological transformation within the human self—that is, the new vision of the world which Paul grasps—is itself grounded in the basic fact of the new age inaugurated by Christ's incarnation, ministry, death, and resurrection. As Campbell says, "Paul's actual 'location' participates in a new reality; it has ontological correlates. Indeed, the latter is the basis for the former."[5] In the first place, through Christ, as Beverly Gaventa argues, God decisively has won the cosmic battle which raged between the forces of light and darkness, evil and good, righteousness and sin.[6] This is no small thing, for the stranglehold of these forces had been intent to ruin God's creation, especially by means of the power of sin and death. But in the apocalyptic moment of Christ's death, God's order of righteousness has become established. Paul is thus able to say to the Romans against all reports to the contrary, "sin shall not have dominion over you" (Rom 6:14). Sharpening the point, Philip Ziegler writes, "God inaugurates a new reality in the present through 'creative negation' when, by the cross and resurrection, the vital eschatological future invades the passing age and conquers it from

---

4. Campbell, "Apocalyptic Epistemology," 68.
5. Campbell, "Apocalyptic Epistemology," 75.
6. Gaventa, "Places of Power in Paul's Letter to the Romans."

within."⁷ Consequently, through this gospel God has revealed a new way of understanding power, of what it means to be powerful. Power truthfully perceived—again, against all reports to the contrary—cannot be construed as sheer force over others but instead (subverting the logic of the world) is revealed in weakness. The gospel *is* God's power (Rom 1:16). The cross, hitherto rejected and constituting a scandal to respectable sensibilities, has become a central symbol of God's kingdom and thereby the interpretive key by which one comes to understand Christianity's political character. Paradoxically, by means of the "weakness" of the gospel has God chosen to topple sin's hold over creation, establishing once and for all a new order where sin and death no longer run riot.⁸ The "night has passed" and Christians now "live inside this emergency, bearing 'weapons of light' and clothed with Christ himself (Romans 13:11–14)."⁹ Yet, while this cosmic victory won by Christ is real, believers "in Christ" must remain vigilant "present[ing] their bodies as weapons of Righteousness" (6:13), as the vestiges of the old order remain.[10]

Redemption is therefore imaged within the apocalyptic imagination as rescue, cosmic divine deliverance of creation from the bondage of Sin. Here "Sin" is capitalized to indicate its difference from mere "sins." The capitalized Sin is a deeper heinous force, a kind of animating principle, which "produces sinning."[11] This imagery helps to highlight the radical discontinuities that exist between the epoch before Christ's death and the new era proceeding after it. Campbell sees the incarnation, for instance, as paradigmatic of the discontinuous. As he writes, "prior to the coming of Jesus of Nazareth, neither Paul nor anyone else . . . could have known that Jesus of Nazareth was God incarnate."[12] "The Word become flesh" is a new reality with no antecedents in history. Nothing but Christ anticipates Christ.

Apocalyptic hermeneuts are aware of the tragic legacies of Christian subscription to such radical discontinuity between the Christ moment and human history, especially Jewish history. A notable degree of self-consciousness regarding the horrors of anti-Jewish Christian supersessionism in much of "Christian" Europe and the spectre of the Shoah are discernible in their interpretive projects. For Campbell, the radical discontinuity ushered in by the incarnation must be "appropriately controlled by Christology" in

---

7. Ziegler, *Militant Grace*, 9.
8. Gaventa, "Places of Power in Paul's Letter to the Romans," 301.
9. Gaventa, "Places of Power in Paul's Letter to the Romans," 301.
10. Gaventa, "Places of Power in Paul's Letter to the Romans," 297.
11. Gaventa, "Places of Power in Paul's Letter to the Romans," 296.
12. Campbell, "Apocalyptic Epistemology," 76.

at least the sense that it must be narrated in cruciform manner, and definitely not in the nationalist, triumphalist—and by extension for Campbell, foundationalist—form that the Barth of *The Epistle to the Romans* so rightly opposed.[13] In any case, while the discontinuous is foregrounded, continuities, or at least, aspects of the continuous, as Campbell qualifies, must be acknowledged. God is revealed, with no less integrity, in creation, although it is only now in Christ that the "mystery" of this creation comes fully to be grasped.[14] The event of the incarnate Christ fulfils the promise of Israel's religious longings, serving as climax to history's eschatological horizon.[15] As Gaventa adds, even this apocalyptic moment, which cannot be understood apart from Israel, does not leave Israel behind. God's covenantal commitment remains, even though this owes not to a moral essence inherent in Israel as such but to the faithfulness of God, whose gifts and callings "are unending."[16] The picture here, at least to orthodox Jews themselves, may not pass as an anti-supersessionist understanding of Judaism, but perhaps for the self-conscious Christian apocalyptic interpreter of the New Testament it claims some distance from the malignant expressions of that theology.

The Apocalyptic Paul comes with a commensurately radical Christian vision. The redeemed, saved by God in Christ, now form a new community, the church. Members of this community, established by Christ, in sanctification live in the shadow of the cross. No longer like the unconverted world, whose interrelationships are still circumscribed by the "flesh," the Christian community lives in the power of the Spirit, with believers in this eschatological locality believing that "they each belong to Christ, and through Christ, they belong to one another."[17] The organizing principle of this new community is love, not self-preservation, nor power falsely understood as control of the other; it is service of "brothers and sisters," rather than the self-interested using of the other for the self's profit. The counter ethos of the nascent Christian community in the New Testament surely puts it at odds with its surrounding communities, and indeed, it self-consciously located itself in contradistinction to these communities. Adam Winn sees, in fact, in this new community established by the gospel, an embodied witness against the Roman empire, with its emerging language replete with motifs critical of the imperium's totalizing logic.[18] The very language of gospel (*euange-*

---

13. Campbell, "Apocalyptic Epistemology," 77.
14. Campbell, "Apocalyptic Epistemology," 81.
15. Campbell, "Apocalyptic Epistemology," 81.
16. Gaventa, "Places of Power in Paul's Letter to the Romans," 299.
17. Gaventa, "Places of Power in Paul's Letter to the Romans," 300.
18. Winn, "Striking Back at the Empire," 1–14.

lion)—the same Greek word as that employed in speaking of the emperor's ascension to the throne and his victory in battle—is purposefully co-opted by this new community, put to new ends. As Winn notes, "the 'gospel of Jesus Christ' and the eschatological vision it implied could be heard as a challenge to the 'gospel of Caesar' and the present power of Rome."[19] Although located on the margins of the Roman empire, both socially and politically, this new community "strikes back at empire" through co-opted language articulated in subtle forms of overthrow such as the community's eschatological hope in the consummation of the kingdom when Christ returns—an implicit refusal to grant ultimacy to Rome's prior *euangelion* claims—and its prophetic stance against those who proclaim "peace and security" (i.e., 1 Thess 5:3, which would have been read as an indictment against the Roman empire with its mantra of *"pax et securitas"*).[20] This community also in the organisation of its ritual life undercuts the legitimacy of the empire's way of doing things, as for instance in the way that it reconfigures notions of honour (being lowly is honourable, against the performative magnanimity enjoined by the empire), norms around family life and gender relations (its egalitarianism going against the patriarchal ordering of Roman empire), and its prioritization of the church's competence in settling disputes over that of the Roman courts (thus relativizing the empire's claims to justice).[21]

Having summarized matters, we mention initially and return later to a philosophical problem, and its attending political and programmatic issues, which the apocalyptic imagination presents but its adherents (so far as we know) leave unaddressed. As described, apocalyptic hermeneutics proceeds with an epistemology keyed to an ontology where only some have access to things as they truly are. Christ's apocalypse ushers in a new order, calling time on the older order where sin reigned. Those keyed to the new have available to them possibilities, no matter reports to the contrary, that arrive with liberation from sin and death, while those stuck in the old order remain stuck to its regnant regime, their liberation within reach but closed off by dint of being on the outside of God's revelation. The issue here is not simply the insider/outsider politics on offer. More so it is the philosophical claim underlining those politics. Because the apocalyptic imagination takes as its point of departure radical disjunction and because the radicalness of its Christian vision and the drama of its good-news story depends on maximally maintaining this disjuncture—recall the fully-meant inelegant imagery—it permits of no natural analogues to the truths Christ's apocalypse

---

19. Winn, "Striking Back at the Empire," 6.
20. Winn, "Striking Back at the Empire," 4.
21. Winn, "Striking Back at the Empire," 10.

avails. There is no other way into the world it heralds. Traditionally, Christian theology theorized natural law as at least a type of analogue along these lines, a moral vision that imaged creation shot through with grace, ordering the moral life to God if only indirectly. By the dictates of their claims, such routes of philosophical theorizing are closed off for apocalyptic thinkers since positing creation as always already participating in and disclosive of God's grace would have the effect of pre-empting Christ's apocalypse. Thence does Philip Ziegler decline any "essential continuities of creation" and instead relocates natural law reasoning to the far side of Christ's recapitulation of creation.[22]

This ontology and attending epistemology lead to a deeper problem still. If apocalypse by its nature brooks no antecedents and analogies, then how can its claims be received, much less assessed? Again, this goes deeper than the political insider/outsider issue that comes with suggesting only some in the know, the issue Nietzsche long ago identified as the result of tying together will-to-power and will-to-truth. There is a more basic philosophical problem underlining the political issue. If apocalypse definitionally refuses continuity with what came before, what criteria remain to discern, or even detect, its arrival? This question persists even with Campbell's aforementioned qualification acknowledging continuity through God's revelation in creation, since the meaning of that revelation (according to the logic of Campbell's formulation) has to wait out Christ in order to be fully comprehended—until then, creaturely revelation remains mysterious. Creation cannot itself serve as criterion for adjudicating Christ; in the apocalyptic imagination, Christ alone plays that role. Only Christ explains Christ. Again, consider the counterexample. In natural law reasoning, a moral tradition can turn to its established norms to supply criteria for the adjudication of whatever eventuality befalls it, using its ongoing ethical life to navigate its future. But apocalypse rejects this, imagining itself not only exempt from such prior modes of adjudication but also in proper judgment of them. What makes apocalypse good news is precisely its power to do this, to circumvent the old (where "old" indicates sin and death) by way of the new; the gospel is good in just this way. There remains then no way to decide on apocalypse, no ordinary way to judge it "apocalypse" or "Spirit" or for that matter "Bazabeel."

Purveyors of the Apocalyptic Paul now have to deal with the political issue that comes as an entailment of the philosophical problem: When talking to others, on what can they base their appeal for apocalypse since no court of appeals remains once the claim of apocalypse has been issued?

---

22. Ziegler, "Fate of Natural Law at the Turning of the Ages," 423.

Tradition, ethical life, natural law, the "essential continuities of creation" have all been ruled out, and, again, come under judgment. "Apocalypse" conceptually self-destructs as a function of the cruciform epistemology meant to access it, perhaps saving it from triumphant supersessionism but at the cost of an intractable ontology. It begins to look like a logical absurdity, a concept the meaning of which trucks no criterion of adjudication, reminiscent of Wittgenstein's "private language" thought experiment caricaturing the impossibility of making the inexhaustibly public suddenly and strangely private. For other New Perspective hermeneuts, this spells serious trouble for the apocalyptic program, the philosophical problem issuing in a characteristically programmatic ambiguity:

> Often the word 'apocalyptic' is reduced to a loose, generalized, arm-waving adjective, introduced into sentences to suggest a vague atmosphere of 'cosmic' significance rather than merely private or personal relevance . . . [functioning] as shorthands which those in the know can decode. This then becomes self-referential, with such writers doing what 'apocalyptic' characteristically does, using a private language which initiates can understand, a code for transmitting subversive ideas.[23]

For ease of reference, we call this the Apocalyptic Paul's private-language problem and will return to how it bears on questions of political theology.

APOCALYPTICISM AND THREE SENSE OF THE POLITICAL

In this section, we reflect on connections that might be drawn between apocalyptic hermeneutics (again, as a paradigm instance of postconservative interpretative strategies) and political theology. We begin the discussion by considering what political theology names. Here we find useful, as a baseline of analysis, distinctions noted political theologian Luke Bretherton makes in identifying what the political names in "political theology."[24] Bretherton suggests three distinct senses belonging to political theology. In one sense, the "political" refers to an understanding of politics in terms of statecraft, related to the administration (both in the administrative and charismatic modes) of the state. Within this conception, considerations of sovereignty have been an important theme.[25] This conception of politics, Bretherton notes, follows the influential articulation of political theology offered by Carl Schmitt. In this view of politics an initial interest concerns

---

23. Wright, *Paul and His Recent Interpreters*, 207.
24. Bretherton, "What Is Political Theology? A Testimony."
25. Bretherton, "What Is Political Theology? A Testimony," 3.

how to legitimate the power wielded by the state. Here, power is framed in hierarchical terms, as dominion over others. Or, as Bretherton puts it, in this understanding the "primary concern of politics is the use of unilateral, command and control forms of power and not the fulfilment of moral goods or the cultivation of human flourishing."[26] In the second sense, the political names a more primal, natural, human concern for negotiating life together with others. In this understanding, as Bretherton characterizes it, the political is seen in terms of "common life," as shaped by the ordinary human concerns about coordinating shared goods. These include goods such as the community, the flourishing of one's neighborhood, the environment, security, rights, and other public interests. In this second sense, politics is about the common good, about navigating the mutually constitutive nature of human social existence.[27] In the third sense of the "political," politics, Bretherton notes, is construed in terms of a dualism of "we" against "them," with distinctions starkly drawn between "enemies" and "friends." The "enemy," in this understanding of politics, might be the racialized other, the religious other, the ethnic or national stranger. Such a dualistic conception of politics often sustains, as Bretherton points out, the dehumanizing political projects of such arrangements as chattel slavery, colonization, and, we may add, the inhumane treatments of so-called illegal migrants, so rife in many parts of the world.[28]

Bretherton's three senses of the political offers a baseline for our analysis of the relationship between the New Testament apocalyptic vision and political theology. If the political is understood primarily in terms of power, as is the case in the first sense, then political theology becomes an enterprise of legitimating the "sovereign" power of the state. For Schmitt, the sovereign decides on what constitutes the "state of exception," the occasion when normal legal and bureaucratic arrangements of the state require suspension.[29] It is this capacity for deciding on when a situation requiring "unlimited authority" has come about that, Schmitt thinks, renders politics distinct, beyond being simply about the legal/administrative ordering of society.[30] Political theology in Schmitt becomes an analysis of the way political sovereignty mirrors the nature of the divine; that is, how the political draws upon the theological.[31] Within such an understanding of political theology,

26. Bretherton, "What Is Political Theology? A Testimony," 5.
27. Bretherton, "What Is Political Theology? A Testimony," 5–11.
28. Bretherton, "What Is Political Theology? A Testimony," 13–14.
29. Schmitt, *Political Theology*, 4–15.
30. Schmitt, *Political Theology*, 12,17.
31. Schmitt, *Political Theology*, 37–52.

it is the empirical reality of the state that serves as the critical point of consideration, not revelation, not an apocalypse.

To such an understanding of political theology, with its concomitant conception of power as control, an apocalyptic political theology, oriented as it is to the "sovereign" Lordship of Jesus Christ, will sound a critical, even judgmental note. If power, in the apocalyptic event, as Beverly Gaventa argues, takes on a cruciform existence, no longer as "power over" but as "power with," then an understanding of politics that is organized around control comes, under the relativizing gaze of the apocalyptic imagination, into question. This way of thinking about power would be seen as reflective of the distorted orderings of the "old creation," impossible to reconcile with the new humanity that has been remade, and continues to be remade, in the image of Christ. This new humanity remade "in Christ," as noted earlier, is distinguished by its radical orientation to service rather than to dominion. Power, in the apocalyptic vein, serves a Christology in which the self-giving that Christ (as Paul portrays in Philippians 2) embodies (verses 6–7) is seen as constitutive, given how things actually are, of what it means to be powerful. Similarly, the apocalyptic vision relativises, indeed contravenes, the state's claim of sovereignty. Such claims of sovereignty, we should not forget, tend in actuality toward the necropolitical—evident, not least, in the heinous regime of the Nazi state with which Schmitt was so closely associated. In this respect, the latent critical posture toward secularised conceptions of sovereignty, present in the apocalyptic imagination, should be judged as one of its strengths, if also one of its controversies.

An important aspect of the apocalyptic imagination is its subversive character. Following Adam Winn's argument about the New Testament church's "striking back at empire," Christian communities of the New Testament—seeing themselves as members of a new eschatological reality made possible by Christ—find themselves positioned against the empire's standing authority. In this way, an apocalyptic imagination, as a matter of course given its proclamation of God's lordship over every order of creation, energizes a politics of resistance. One form an apocalyptic resistance might take may be in pushing against all immanent visions of history, whether those that take the form of a cyclical picture of history, in which history is nothing but the repetition of events, or a progressivism that pushes the slow but positive march of history. An apocalyptic worldview can resist this kind of immanentism because of its christological reading of history. In this christological vision of history, something new—authored by Christ and symbolized by the cross as the access point of the meaning of all history—has come into the world, breaking the natural regularity of time.

This christological view of history can also ground expectations of new possibilities open to the world, both in the present and the future. As such, an apocalyptic vision of the world may well provide the best bet for securing a Christian account of hope. Christian hope, as Jürgen Moltmann reminded us, must refuse the temptation toward the kind of "realism" that despairs of the world or, in the opposite direction, a form of optimism that naively fails to reckon with the depth of evil present in the world. Instead, as Moltmann notes, an apocalyptically grounded hope can legitimately claim the realist mantle because, "it alone takes seriously the possibilities with which all reality is fraught."[32] That is, it uniquely sees things as they are, from the vantage point of Christ's rulership over and redemption of all things. The Holy Spirit now instantiates reality, in this new apocalyptic epoch, opening reality up to transcendental vistas beyond the natural—all reports to the contrary be damned. By living into God's time, an apocalyptic imagination refuses to grant ultimacy to the premature closures that vicissitudes of nature impose on the world. Death is not the end. A new world has already come upon the present, "in Christ," and in the end, natural time gives way to the fullness of God's time.

The Apocalyptic Paul proffers resistance not only against certain inducements of time but, given how its spatial imagination of disjunction and discontinuity quite naturally maps onto the struggles of those whose lives already feel left to the wayside, against necropolitical political arrangements and their many material settlements. Here, what is to be highlighted is the way that an apocalyptic imagination can serve to identify, inspire, and empower marginalized groups, the poor "in Christ," in particular, helping them to narrate God as identifying with and enabling the oppressed, and hence their own position on the right side of history even while, like Paul himself, living, and sometimes dying, on the underside of empire. No wonder liberation theologies often take on an air of the apocalyptic. This storying should not be viewed as merely an exercise in meaning-making. Rather, a re-narrating of the world, undergirded by an apocalyptic re-visioning of that world, can support pragmatic endeavours aimed at changing the life-destroying socio-political and economic order. In this regard, attention may be drawn to the book of Acts where the sharing of material wealth with the needy soon came to characterise the early Christian *ekklesia* (Acts 4:32).

---

32. Moltmann, *Theology of Hope*, 25.

APOCALYPTICISM'S PRIVATE LANGUAGE PROBLEM

We now consider some questions that political theology might itself pose to the apocalyptic imagination. To do this we return to the second and third senses of the "political" that Bretherton notes as they bear on the Apocalyptic Paul's private-language problem, which we illustrate using a live example.

With respect to a friend-enemy conception of politics, without necessarily intending to, it is easy to see how in its strong dualism, an apocalyptic imagination can tend toward problematic forms of othering, such that the third sense conspires to bring out the worst of the second sense, weaponizing common life against itself. We have already noted the apocalyptic imagination's "benign" supersessionist tendency, present in the way that it narrates the Christ event as a rupture of time, with no continuity with the past moments preceding it. It is true that, for apocalyptic interpreters, it is God's free grace that grounds the new life "in Christ" which Christians have received, rather than any human self-willing which originates from below.[33] As such those not "in Christ" cannot be seen as "enemies," being themselves objects of God's love. Those not yet in Christ can, too, be engrafted into Christ. There is no boasting "in Christ." Still, even as this is admitted, care must be taken because the spectre of pride, the seduction to see the self, rather than Christ, or, the self's possession of Christ, as the locus of what makes the Christian different from the "world" is a live danger that presents itself to an apocalyptic theology.

As we have already laid out, the political issue of othering some as outsiders to God's revelatory action comes on top of an underlining philosophical problem internal to apocalypticism's strong emphasis on discontinuity and disjunction. Once apocalypse gets tied to an epistemology keyed to an ontological reality into which there are no routes other than apocalypse itself, nothing that can anticipate it or help to discern or detect it, the pride we worry about gets built into the hermeneutic program itself. If the only ones who can interpret a phenomenon happen to be the ones announcing its occurrence, then we are locked in a vicious cycle which cannot help but turn out a politics of othering.

The political context of present-day Nigeria serves well to illustrate the private-language problem. Here, we are thinking specifically of Nigerian Pentecostalism which transmits a dualism strikingly similar to the apocalyptic imagination we have been describing. Indeed, Pentecostalism has long been marked by a rather resolute apocalyptic imagination. Within the Nigerian context, sociological studies such as Ebenezer Obadare's *Pentecostal Republic* find Pentecostalism problematically tending toward the theocratic,

---

33. Ziegler, *Militant Grace*, 151.

exhibiting strong features of hegemony, all of which gets licensed by a self-referential logic cycling between apocalyptic revelation, private interpretation, and political justification.[34] Nigerian Pentecostalism, Obadare reports, has had a penchant for othering, rhetorically and politically demonizing non-Pentecostal, especially Muslim, others. Legitimating itself as responding to perceived threats of an incipient "Islamization" of the country and coopted by a political class intent on power, Pentecostals in Nigeria, Obadare argues, have been prone to valorizing political power, charging the political climate with a suffocating transcendental air (reminiscent of the Schmittian state of exception in that first, sovereign sense of politics) that renders nearly impossible the "rational" dialogic negotiations that are crucial to the flourishing of a democratic polis. We need not endorse, as Obadare does, the propriety of a "separation of church and state"—which he defends as an integral principle of liberal democracy—to take his concerns about Pentecostalism seriously.[35] What Obadare's study highlights—and a lesson to be kept in mind—is the way that a privatized apocalyptic worldview can directly work against the common life that politics might otherwise enliven.

In thinking through this problematic, especially as it instantiates the postconservative philosophical and political milieu in which Christians now read (often quite self-consciously *as* postconservatives) Scripture, we admit that we know no easy way out of the cycle Obadare depicts, which in the final analysis might simply reprise the hermeneutical circle familiar to revelation-focused discourses. We put little confidence in the various schemes that came in the name of Enlightenment liberalism which promised escape by purging the self of the self, turning out in the end to be thinly disguised versions of the same thing. Now on the other side of those pretensions, and in the same old starting place of the hermeneutic cycle, albeit with the self-consciousness of postconservatives, we suggest that a modest posture is perhaps the best posture and propose acknowledgement versus avoidance as a way forward. Perhaps the best that apocalypticism can do is acknowledge the political tendencies that come with its built-in philosophical problem, with the hope that at least admitting the problem might go some ways in mitigating its political effects. We might even submit that such self-consciousness is finally what postconservative hermeneutics comes to as a political theology, acknowledgment as the theological achievement of reading Scripture in light of the apocalyptic God. One would think that a hermeneutical program that not only allows but heralds disruption and judgment would be open to such possibilities—acknowledgment seemingly

---

34. Obadare, *Pentecostal Republic*.
35. Obadare, *Pentecostal Republic*, 165.

part of its hermeneutical DNA. Acknowledgment would then help to direct the Apocalyptic Paul's disruption and judgment as much to the self as to the other, now imagining its own settlements as the site of divine rupture and invasion.

Perhaps a final point is in order. Recall that Philip Ziegler does not give up completely on natural law reasoning—the counterexample we've referenced throughout in hopes of bringing out apocalypticism's own mode of moral reasoning—but instead relocates its mode of appeal not on "essential continuities of creation" but on the far side of Christ's apocalyptic revelation, such that moral judgment might be "secured not by appeal to creation per se, but rather by appeal to the one reality of the one world being remade at the turning of the ages."[36] This makes the Apocalyptic Paul's private-language problem primarily a problem at the start, after which a common life (with its own possibilities for welcoming, or rejecting, the stranger) emerges from the world remade and can serve as a staging ground for subsequent moral reasoning—continuities, criteria, and norms that comprise the church and its witness to apocalypticism's radical Christian vision.

BIBLIOGRAPHY

Bretherton, Luke. "What Is Political Theology? A Testimony." In *What Is Political Theology?*, unpublished manuscript by Luke Bretherton et al., 1–46. New York: Columbia University Press, 2024.

Campbell, Douglas A. "Apocalyptic Epistemology: The Sine Qua Non of Valid Pauline Interpretation." In *Paul and the Apocalyptic Imagination*, edited by Ben C. Blackwell et al., 65–85. Fortress, 2016.

Davies, J. P. *The Apocalyptic Paul: Retrospect and Prospect*. Cascade Library of Pauline Studies. Eugene, OR: Cascade, 2022.

Gaventa, Beverly Roberts. "Places of Power in Paul's Letter to the Romans." *Interpretation* 76 (2022) 293–302.

Moltmann, Jürgen. *Theology of Hope: On the Ground and Implications of a Christian Eschatology*. New York: Harper & Row, 1967.

Obadare, Ebenezer. *Pentecostal Republic: Religion and the Struggle for State Power in Nigeria*. London: Zed, 2018.

Schmitt, Carl. *Political Theology: Four Chapters on the Concept of Sovereignty*. Chicago: University of Chicago Press, 2005.

Winn, Adam. "Striking Back at the Empire: Empire Theory and Responses to Empire in the New Testament." In *An Introduction to Empire in the New Testament*, edited by Adam Winn, 1–14. Atlanta: Society of Biblical Literature, 2016.

---

36. Ziegler, "Fate of Natural," 427.

Wright, N. T. *Paul and His Recent Interpreters: Some Contemporary Debates.* London: SPCK, 2015.

Ziegler, Philip G. "The Fate of Natural Law at the Turning of the Ages: Some Reflections on a Trend in Contemporary Theological Ethics in View of the Work of J. Louis Martyn." *Theology Today* 67 (2011) 419–29.

———. *Militant Grace: The Apocalyptic Turn and the Future of Christian Theology.* Grand Rapids: Baker Academic, 2018.

Chapter 5
Literary Theory and Hermeneutics
OLIVER PEEL

> Now I am here, what thou wilt do with me
> None of my books will show;
> I read, and sigh, and wish I were a tree.
>
> –GEORGE HERBERT, "THE AFFLICTION (I)"

WHAT HAS LITERARY THEORY TO DO WITH THEOLOGY?

The erroneous attribution of the word hermeneutics to the Greek mythological figure Hermes may be a tired analogy with which to begin, but it is still helpful. Not only does that winged messenger convey the words of the gods to humankind; he is also both translator and trickster, relating and obscuring in (almost) equal measure. This draws our attention to the fact that communication and interpretation are fraught activities. And even in itself, the spurious etymology shows us the power and process of the literary imagination, where figures like Hermes dwell as signs, common fountains of meaning and interpretation on which we may draw. We can see how, in the face of an uncertain etymology, a folk etymology emerges that is, in itself, an act of interpretation.

Such an analogy alerts us to the problematic task of theological hermeneutics. The discipline confronts the seeker of meaning with an apparent chasm between the divine Logos and faltering human language. We seek to testify to an infinite and transcendent God who yet dared to make the word understandable, to narrate himself as Immanuel. Christian theology has long been literary in nature. Christ comes to us, according to John's Gospel, as discourse, narrative, speech.

Yet theological hermeneutics and literary hermeneutics, though intimately interwoven, appear as siblings that have drifted apart. One went in search of meaning; the other was perhaps more interested in how meaning is hampered in the act of communication. The reason for this difference, of course, is the radically different perception of their ends. Theology lives or dies by searching out the meaning of God's revelation to us. Literature (or certainly the study of literature that blossomed with twentieth-century literary theory) lives or dies by keeping open the possibility of a text's meaning. In what follows, I will seek to indicate how this differentiation is false and how the two disciplines in fact share many of the same concerns and hold mutually enlightening and enriching tools. So much of literary criticism is concerned with finding meaning and so much of theology is concerned with those moments where language is insufficient to the task of speaking about God.[1]

It would benefit us, then, to keep the relation of these two somewhat estranged disciplines in view. Stephen Prickett calls literary criticism theology's "missing limb," and negotiating its reattachment to the body of Christ is a necessary part of theology.[2] Literary hermeneutics learned from biblical hermeneutics how to approach a text's meaning, possibility, significance, and application. What literary hermeneutics has to offer theology, having developed somewhat separately, is a set of ideas and frameworks for approaching the text in all its rich possibility. As interpreters, we do not have to accept all of these frameworks; we do not even have to accept wholesale any particular framework with which we choose to interact. They are merely tools that augment particular textual aspects, always to the diminution of other aspects. This selectivity is a fact of reading and a necessary part of using any hermeneutical framework. We are never viewing the whole picture; what we need are tools that help us to perceive any given part with greater clarity.

The reader must choose what she cares about when approaching a text, and the Christian's approach to Scripture is no exception to this rule. This pursuit will include a creative approach, interfacing with ideas from outside our denominations and faith communities in order to sharpen a living engagement with a living text. By way of analogy, we might consider the interaction of the polarizing notions of heresy and orthodoxy. Recoiling

---

1. Hereafter, I will mostly refer to literary hermeneutics by its more popular names; either literary criticism (the practice of literary hermeneutics) or literary theory (a collection of frameworks for literary analysis).

2. Prickett, "Narrative, Theology and Literature," 208. This is a limited analogy and is not meant to relegate literary criticism to a lesser discipline. Theology, likewise, could be thought of as a missing limb for literary criticism.

from heresy is not how orthodoxy was formed; rather, it was formed in conversation with heresy, using multivocality as a way of discerning truth. 1 John 4:1 bids us "test" (or scrutinize) the spirits, not silence or ignore them. Hermeneutics demands humility and literary theory can help us in this regard. We might see it as an interpretive community, with various friends kindly reminding us to leave our biases, habits, preferences, and prejudgements at the door.

We may wish to think of theology as a special kind of hermeneutics, concerned specifically with articulating truth; but to separate it entirely from the study of literature is to rob theology of vital questions regarding how we seek, interpret, and proclaim that truth. Perhaps, as with our consideration of Hermes, even an erroneous etymology can fulfil a truthful interpretive purpose. An acute awareness of how we read can prepare us to better engage with God and his revelation to us in Christ, the Word made flesh.

There are numerous excellent introductions both to literary theory and to the interdisciplinary field of theology and literature, so I will not seek to reproduce one here. Rather, I will highlight some key literary theoretical approaches that present significant theological applications. I will then consider if we have moved (or can move) beyond theory in the contemporary interdisciplinary field of literature and theology.

THE HERMENEUTIC CIRCLE OF LIFE

Perhaps the primary fantasy that the discipline of hermeneutics challenges is that of a scientific, objective, and uncomplicated approach to the text. Among Evangelicals, appeals to the direct and simple exegesis of the Reformed tradition may give the impression that all we need to do as hermeneuts is return to the plain sense of text, "the way it used to be." Yet, our retrospective view of the Reformation is somewhat obscured by our modern idea of scrutiny free from bias. In fact, the difficulty of reading and interpreting was vital to the formation of Reformation. Protestantism was sparked by Luther's creative reading of *iustitia* and disseminated through the innovation of the printing press. As Brian Cummings has shown, its genesis was distinctly literary and reliant on the response of an interpretive community.[3] The Reformation, in other words, was a series of complex hermeneutical acts. In turn, the Reformation solidified the vitality of hermeneutics: the theological enfranchisement of the laity meant that the complexity of biblical interpretation was now of immediate, universal importance.

---

3. See Cummings, *Literary Culture of the Reformation*.

To understand hermeneutics as a literary process rather than a direct engagement with plain sense, we must attend to the dynamic communication between author, text, and reader and to the constant interaction of each textual detail with its place in the entire work. It was Martin Heidegger who proposed the concept of the "hermeneutic circle" to describe the process of interpretation.[4] As we read, we move in a circle of expectation, surprise, and revised understanding, as each new single element of the text or context transforms the way we think about the work as a whole. This term distilled the work of Friedrich Schleiermacher (the theologian credited with founding the modern field of hermeneutics) and the philosopher Wilhelm Dilthey on the subject. The hermeneutic circle shows us that we approach a text with our own preconceptions, which are then necessarily challenged by the difficult act of reading itself. We thus return again and again (in a circular fashion) to the moment of interpretation, changed by our interaction with each new detail.

Hans-Georg Gadamer, a student of Heidegger and a key figure in the development of philosophical hermeneutics, makes the point with even greater force. This "projecting" activity of the speaker is inevitable and immediate, and its examination is a necessary part of the hermeneutical journey towards meaning. What thinkers like Gadamer contribute to theology is the realisation that there is no detached, objective way to engage with a text. The idea of achieving a scientific, methodical moment of observation is a fantasy, which greatly problematizes any approach to the text as a collection of data to be interpreted at face value. In Gadamerian hermeneutics, there is no way to escape our own perspective, but the interpretive act is the coming together, the negotiation, and the productive interaction of our "horizon" with the "horizon" of the text.[5]

Though it may be startling to confront the idea that we project our own meaning onto texts and situations, such a recognition is a vital step for theology. Owning projection (rather than apprehension) as immediate and admitting that we cannot escape preliminary thought and historical conditioning in some regard helps us to recognize theology as a process of interpretation that is perpetually unfolding. Perceiving the hermeneutic task as a journey frees us from the illusion of certainty in our vision and perfection in our speech.[6] This in turn frees theological hermeneutics to interact with God's revelation to us from a position of humility.

4. Heidegger, *Being and Time*, 194.
5. Gadamer, *Truth and Method*, 390.
6. I am not arguing against all forms of religious certainty here (for example, with regards to certain core truth claims), but rather against the certainty of our own "vision" and "speech": our interpretation and exposition.

A contemporary theologian and philosopher who has interacted with these ideas is Jens Zimmermann, author of the twelfth chapter in this volume. Zimmermann both expounds and critiques the philosophical hermeneutics of Heidegger and Gadamer in order to propose his theory of incarnational-trinitarian hermeneutics and, more recently, in a project dedicated to retrieving Humanism's religious roots. The latter work, *Humanism and Religion* (2012), reinterprets Heidegger as having pursued many humanist concerns. Zimmermann shows how, for Heidegger, human interaction with transcendent Being is mediated linguistically and poetically. Heidegger "recovers an older theological sense of language as participation in Being," which has been "obscured" by the modern obsession with the author's intention.[7] In fact, language is the medium, the middle, and the "house of Being." Rather than simply conveying factual information, language is performative in theological interpretation: it does not simply *say*, it *does*, a point that draws hermeneutics back to the midrash of Rabbinic interpretation. In this sense, all language that is substantive informs our relation to Being itself.

Returning to where we began this section, then, to restrict interpretation to the plain sense meaning is akin to reducing a novel to a plot summary given in bullet points. To do so is to short-circuit the expansiveness and creativity of theological speech. Everything in life is wrapped up in the act of interpretation and theology is no exception.

THE SIGN, THE SIGNIFIER, AND THE SIGNIFIED

Though semiotics was not originally a literary discipline, part of its influence on theological hermeneutics was through literary theory. The study of signs had a transformative effect on literary theory through the work of Swiss linguist Ferdinand de Saussure (who called his discipline "semiology"). In his *Course in General Linguistics* (1916), Saussure separates what we think of as language into three distinct categories: *langage* (the entire range of linguistic activity), *langue* (a particular language system, e.g., English), and *parole* (individual utterance).[8] His point in doing so is to emphasise that all individual utterance (*parole*) must be viewed within the context of its language system (*langue*). A chess piece in isolation, for example, is devoid of meaning. A knight or rook relies on the context of rules, the chess board, and the other pieces for its meaning.

---

7. Zimmermann, *Humanism and Religion*, 189.
8. See Saussure, *Course in General Linguistics*.

In what was to become one of the most important progressions of twentieth-century linguistics, Saussure (drawing on the work of John Locke) defined the sign as an arbitrary relationship between the signifier (a sound-image that indicates something) and the signified (the something indicated by the sound-image). The learning of a language entails the learning of arbitrary pairings of sounds and their corresponding concepts. For example, there is no significant relationship between the physical qualities of a door and the word door in the English language. A signifier does not derive naturally from the appearance of the signified but rather is created by a community (that shares a common language) and attached arbitrarily to the concept. Together, signifier and signified make up a sign that is significant only within the context and rules of the language that produces it.

Jacques Derrida, the founder of deconstruction (a movement that is the subject of several chapters in this volume), critiqued Saussure's semiotic work and, in particular, his understanding of the relationship between signifier and signified. Derrida argues that the radical difference between signifier and signified should be dissolved and the word "signifier" abandoned as a metaphysical concept.[9] The sign is no longer thought of as a self-contained, stable, scientific object for analysis but rather an unstable, perpetually deferred system of successive signs that modify and supplement each other in the endlessly proliferating act of verbal expression. The binary of signifier and signified is thus broken down and replaced by the process of language as a signifying chain, a pattern of association that has pre-existed our observation and in which we are caught up as participants. By emphasising the ambiguities and contradictions in texts, Derrida and the deconstructionists sought to destabilise and complicate this traditional relationship between signifier and signified and to encourage the "play" (the endless possibility) of *différance*, a concept that combines the ideas of differing (as sign from sign) and deferring (putting off, or constantly modifying meaning).[10]

A contemporary theologian who has engaged with semiotics is Susannah Ticciati. In *A New Apophaticism* (2013), Ticciati demonstrates that the innovation of words as signs lies not with literary theorists but with St. Augustine. Ticciati is concerned with the apophatic tradition of humans as signs of God and seeks to test whether "God-language contributes to the signification of God by way of its contribution to the redemptive transformation of human beings, who thereby themselves become better signs

---

9. Derrida, "Structure, Sign, and Play in the Discourse of the Human Sciences," 917.
10. See also Derrida, "Differance," 932–49.

of God."[11] In Augustinian semiotics, the sign relationship is not a dyadic relationship to observe but a triadic relationship (including "the subject for whom signs signify") to be entered into.[12] Description thus becomes transformation, as the creature is invited into a relationship of signs that God fulfils.

Rather than fixed centers of meaning in themselves, then, humans are signs of God. Thus, doctrine or "God-language" does not point away from humans as signs but rather renders God immanent in language. Ticciati's work is an interesting answer to the reading of signs in both semiotics and deconstruction. Like Derrida, Ticciati is concerned with the breakdown of dichotomies and how that leads to the proliferating possibility of discourse. Furthermore, Ticciati's critique of the human as the center of meaning is similar to that of Derrida's, yet the event that is its replacement is not language itself but the relationship of love and praise that is held within the sign. Working in the apophatic tradition, which emphasizes the difficulty of theological language, Ticciati indicates what for Luke Ferretter is the essential value of deconstruction for theology: insisting on and demonstrating "the proper limits of the function of theological language."[13] By breaking down what to us is automatic, we are aided in approaching the God that both inhabits and is beyond speech.

It is worth noting how selective I am being here in comparing Derrida to Ticciati. When applying literary theory to theology, there is always a risk of cherry-picking or misreading an approach to make it fit a given theological framework. Though apophaticism and deconstruction can certainly be said to have touching points, a wholehearted deconstructive method would ultimately be at odds with Ticciati's constructive approach. To take Derrida more seriously, we may usefully ask, what is it to speak of God if the language of "God" is as much caught up in the chain of signification as any other instance of language? And what can it mean for humans to be the signs of God if this sign is perpetually deferred? A vital part of the hermeneutic discipline is to be precise about how and to what extent we engage with any given theory that lies outside our doctrinal or disciplinary wheelhouse.

DESIRE AND NARRATIVE: PSYCHOANALYTIC CRITICISM

A number of works proceeding from the psychoanalytic tradition have proven interesting interlocutors for biblical hermeneutics due to their

---

11. Ticciati, *New Apophaticism*, 3.

12. Ticciati, *New Apophaticism*, 143. Ticciati is drawing on the work of C. S. Peirce, who inherited and developed this triadic tradition.

13. Ferretter, *Towards a Christian Literary Theory*, 15.

elevation of narrative, story, and plot. "Psychoanalysis," for Sigmund Freud, is "first and foremost an art of interpreting" and so we can see how, in its very conception, this theory of the mind can also be viewed as a theory of the text.[14] For Freud, the mind functions like a text or language and so its interpretation is not just a science but an "art" that deals with the unpredictable psyche and the indefinite border between conscious and unconscious.

Psychoanalytic theory, then, is concerned with the latent and the ambiguous. Psychoanalysis begins with a sense of the subject as divided and proceeds to explore the subject through her desires and their repression and distortion. The analyst, in other words, begins with a complex text (a unity of disunities), then works to understand its mechanisms, or to tell the story of the subject: she must insert herself into the narrative of another in the process of comprehension. In *The Interpretation of Dreams* (1899), Freud asserts that the "dream-thought," which is an unconscious desire or repressed wish, and the "dream-content," which is the distorted manifestation of that desire within the world of the dream, "are presented to us like two versions of the same subject-matter in two different languages."[15] Thus, the disciplines of psychoanalysis and hermeneutics express the same concern with structure and meaning that we found in Saussure and Derrida: their approach is semantic or semiotic in nature.

In *Reading for the Plot* (1984), the Freudian scholar Peter Brooks presents a theory of narrative in which plot is highlighted as the organizing thread that sets boundaries to narrative, making it "possible because finite and comprehensible." Brooks draws on Freud's concept of the death drive to connect plot with desire: "plots are not simply organizing structures, they are also intentional structures, goal-orientated and forward-moving."[16] The narrative—the telling, understanding, and explanation of events—is motivated by a plot that fixes upon an object or destination and compels it toward that unifying end (or death), which will illuminate the whole. As Freud's notion of desire in the divided subject demonstrates, any narrative (whether the story of the self or of the text) is motivated by a tension between two poles. Enlisting the two central tropes of rhetoric that have informed literary theory since the work of Russian linguist Roman Jakobson, Brooks posits the tendency of all plots to present two movements: metaphoric (that which unifies, sums up, and completes) and metonymic (that which strings out the elements one by one in a signifying chain).

---

14. Freud, *Beyond the Pleasure Principle*, 170.
15. Freud, *Interpretation of Dreams*, 131.
16. Brooks, *Reading for the Plot*, 4, 12.

An example may serve to clarify. Consider, for example, the Parable of the Sower:

> And he told them many things in parables, saying: "A sower went out to sow. And as he sowed, some seeds fell along the path, and the birds came and devoured them. Other seeds fell on rocky ground, where they did not have much soil, and immediately they sprang up, since they had no depth of soil, but when the sun rose they were scorched. And since they had no root, they withered away. Other seeds fell among thorns, and the thorns grew up and choked them. Other seeds fell on good soil and produced grain, some a hundredfold, some sixty, some thirty. He who has ears, let him hear."[17]

The very idea of a story is unifying (metaphorical) in itself. When a narrative is begun, it is informed by the promise of an end that will sum up all that has gone before. In the context of this parable, Jesus's story promises a unifying end that transforms the significance of all that is told. The structure of the Bible is ever cognisant of the fact that something with no end is meaningless to finite beings and thus eternity and the Eternal God comes to us (Immanuel) as narrative, as a story with a clear and discernible beginning, middle, and end. We may read the present moments of Scripture only in anticipation of the structuring power of Christ's presence that will (both retroactively and proactively) impose narrative order.

Unity alone, however, cannot produce plot. Plots may progress from and toward unity but the process itself (the middle) tends more towards the stretching out than the pulling in. Metonymy asserts the "signifying chain" (again recalling Saussure and Derrida) of narrative and allows the story to unfold in temporal sequence. Without metonymy, the parable would be rendered thus: "A sower went out to sow and produced grain." For plot to be present, the narrative must display the *process* of sowing: the falling of the seeds "along the path" to be devoured; "on rocky ground" where, rootless, they are "scorched" and "wither"; and "among thorns" to be "choked."

It is in this process that transformation can occur for the reader. This "middle" introduces choice into the ritual of narrative, where the reader is taken through a variety of wrong choices before fixing on the correct one at the narrative's end. The narrative wishes to end but it wishes to end on its own terms: it is seeking the correct death at the correct time. In the context of the parable, the hearing and receiving of the gospel of Christ is the "correct end" for the believer; the narrative, however, delays by fixing upon and understanding the "wrong choices" that illustrate resistance toward the

17. Matt 13:3–9 (ESV).

gospel. The "mastering" (a kind of therapeutic overcoming) of these "wrong choices" through repetition finally leads the hearer toward a correct end in Christ.

Such a theory of plot is not only significant for the biblical text but also for Christian theology as a whole. Patristic texts like Augustine's are enlivened by the connection between narrative, death, and desire: "our heart is restless until it rests in you."[18] Psychoanalytic criticism also encourages theology to engage with the latent and ambiguous aspect of its texts as art. The theopoetics of Hans Urs von Balthasar, the narrative theology of Hans Frei or Stanley Hauerwas, or the theological engagement with poetics in the work of Vittorio Montemaggi or Elizabeth S. Dodd may be of interest to readers wanting to explore creative approaches to theological texts. Those wishing to explore further the work of psychoanalytic thinkers like Freud, Jacques Lacan, and Slavoj Žižek, and their influence on theology might consult Tad Delay's *God Is Unconscious: Psychoanalysis and Theology* (2015).

THE POLITICS OF THE TEXT

There is a wealth of political approaches to the text, yet the Marxist critique remains one of the most challenging and revolutionary. I will therefore use a Marxist thinker as a way to introduce a small section of the great variety of social perspectives on literature and the possibilities they open up for theology. As with all the other concepts mentioned in this chapter, political approaches have significance well beyond textual considerations, but we will restrict ourselves mainly to the aesthetic. Those wishing to consider Marxist thought more broadly from a theological standpoint, including the Marxist critique of religion, might consult Luke Ferretter's *Towards a Christian Literary Theory*.

The ideas of literary theorist and philosopher György Lukács (1885–1971), regarded as one of the founders of Western Marxism', are exemplary of Marxism's significant influence on theories of interpretation. Though not fully converted to Marxism until 1918, Lukács's early aesthetic work demonstrates a keen social and political engagement. Lukács negotiates between "form" and "life," arguing for form as the most fundamentally social aspect of literature. (Lukács takes this idea from Marx's analysis of commodity fetishism, an idea to which we will return shortly, via the work of Georg Simmel.) Form is defined as that which unifies the disparate events of life (that which never ends) into a meaningful structure.[19] The dilemma of life is

---

18. Augustine, *Confessions*, 60.
19. We might observe Lukács's influence on Brooks here.

whether to acquiesce to the formless waves of life or to impose a form from without, with the risk of living an inauthentic yet legible life.

In "Reification and the Consciousness of the Proletariat" (1923), Lukács draws on Marx to formulate a critique of what he calls "reification," a consequence of capitalism in which human life is instrumentalized and fragmented. The human experience is thus characterized by division and passivity. We are no longer unified wholes but disposable objects:

> [the individual's] qualities and abilities are no longer an organic part of his personality, they are things which he can 'own' or 'dispose of' like the various objects of the external world. And there is no natural form in which human relations can be cast, no way in which man can bring his physical and psychic 'qualities' into play without their being subjected increasingly to this reifying process.[20]

This capitalist process isolates the individual from society and isolates each of the individual's qualities as its own discreet commodity, defined by its commercial value.

A theologian that may be seen to have learned from Lukács's aesthetics is Catherine Keller. Drawing together feminist, ecocritical, and deconstructive methodologies to uncover how dynamics of power have silenced the marginalized and oppressed, Keller's *The Face of the Deep* (2002) argues that what appears disorderly with respect to some hegemonic order is often treated as a threatening other and is thus suppressed or even crushed. Furthermore (and here Lukács's aesthetics comes firmly into view) what is other may appear chaotic precisely because oppression has distorted its expression in a variety of ways. A form has been imposed from outside, drawing an inauthentic expression of life. Keller's perspective reveals that our linguistic leveraging of words like "chaos" is frequently weaponized by those who hold power in society. A sincere cry of the marginalized can be outlawed by branding it "chaotic"; evil, conversely, can hide behind our tried and tested traditions.

It could be argued that Keller goes too far in branding the accepted order of things as always negative. We may want to maintain the liberating nature of God's order. Yet we would do well to take seriously the heart of Keller's thesis: that a great deal of productive theology can be done in the space where we resist the easy resolution of imposing our order too quickly. Our systematic impulse to neaten what feels messy to us may come naturally but it is not necessarily a godly impulse. God does instill order, but

---

20. Lukács, *History and Class Consciousness*, 100.

we should not assume that our order is God's order. Keller's prophetic voice challenges those moments of conflation.

A theologian whose work might illuminate Lukács's reification theory is Willie James Jennings. Jennings's work is an example of liberation theology, a Christian school of thought influenced by Marxism and dedicated to the political liberation of the marginalized and oppressed. In *The Christian Imagination* (2010), Jennings challenges our settled ideas of order and power by presenting racism as a Christian idea that leverages the doctrines of creation and providence specifically to create a theology that serves settlers and not indigenous people groups. Dislocation and displacement of story lead to the comparison of bodies (on an imposed scale of Black to white). It also leads to "enclosure": encasing the body in race and enclosing the land in ownership. The settlers overthrow the idea of *being owned by* the land and set up a Western framework of *owning* the land. Thus, as in Lukács, we have fragmentation and commercialisation coming hand in hand.

Jennings suggests that, in answer to this, Christians must relearn the message of the incarnation: that we must cherish the importance of adopting other people's ways of life. Our submission to God's presence will move us away from control and guide us out of comfort towards those to whom we may rather not be joined. Christian discipleship, for Jennings, does not allow us to control the other but rather binds us to the other in love.

DO YOU BELIEVE IN LIFE AFTER THEORY?

Some have argued that we have come to the end of the road: that we either have moved or should move beyond the tired preoccupations of "high theory." Two dissenting voices towards the end of the twentieth century were the neopragmatists Steven Knapp and Walter Ben Michaels, whose "Against Theory" (1982) attacked "not a particular way of doing theory but the idea of doing theory at all."[21] Their argument is that theory constitutes "nothing else but the attempt to escape practice" and that we should leave theory behind, along with its attempt to "govern practice from without."[22]

Yet, more recent work bearing titles that seem to suggest a posttheoretical age in fact describe not an end to theory but rather a change in theoretical concerns. In *Theory after 'Theory'* (2011), Jane Elliott and Derek Attridge argue that theory "continues to thrive" but has undergone a shift "'from one type of content (linguistic, discursive and cultural) to another (material, biological and expressly political)" and from one canon

---

21. Knapp and Michaels, "Against Theory," 723.
22. Knapp and Michaels, "Against Theory," 741–42.

of thinkers to another. The sense is of a need for radical ways of thinking that do not suit the priorities or modes of yesterday's theory.[23] For Terry Eagleton, this is because we are living in a "post-collectivist and post-individualist" age, lacking the idealistic cohesion and touchpoints that gave rise to the intellectual foment of twentieth-century literary theory. Eagleton prompts us to recognize this "vacuum" as an opportunity to imagine new and multiple "forms of belonging."[24] The point is that we must go forward. There is no way back to "an age of pre-theoretical innocence" where we may simply enthuse over a text, unhampered by the latent and ambiguous tissues of its possibility.

To live *after* is not to ignore the voices of those who have gone before but to recognize their valuable contribution to the ongoing conversation around meaning. We continue to live in an intellectual climate shaped by the hermeneutical methods of the past. Though we may extend "beyond" them in terms of foci, theme, or canon, the conversation is never simply over. We may feel like we have moved into the age of the "material, biological and expressly political" but this is necessarily conditioned by our understanding of the "linguistic, discursive and cultural."

Yet, what Knapp and Michaels prophesied is, in one particular aspect, indicative of the current state of the interdisciplinary field of theology and literature. In some senses, we have moved from a century enamoured with theory to a century that is far more enamoured with practice and with the text itself (ignoring, for now, the troublesome idea of separating theory from practice). As Rita Felski encourages in *The Limits of Critique* (2015), we must not allow a "hermeneutics of suspicion" to obscure our true object of study. What we can take from a "high" theoretical age is a wealth of tools that disabuse us of a naïve, unmediated, plain-sense approach to the text. But that does not mean that we should police the text—endlessly trying to "interrogate, unmask, expose, subvert, unravel, demystify, destabilize, take issue, and take umbrage"—to the neglect of the literature in front of us.[25] The *primary* material should remain just that. Yet, it is worth noting that Felski's argument might fall prey to some of the assumptions that "high theory" helps to deconstruct. We may consider, for example, how post-critiques such as Felski's could overlook the vital part suspicion has to play in our love for the text itself.

Those wishing to explore the current interdisciplinary field might consult two journals: *Literature and Theology* (Oxford University Press)

---

23. Elliott and Attridge, *Theory after 'Theory,'* 2.
24. Eagleton, *After Theory*, 21.
25. Felski, *Limits of Critique*, 5.

and *Religion and Literature* (University of Notre Dame). Two editions of the latter (41.2 and 46.2–3), in particular, are dedicated to discussing opportunities, questions, and problems facing those working at the intersection between these two disciplines. Such concerns include whether Religion and Literature can be called a field or discipline, classical literary questions (such as historicity, canonicity, form, and genre) and their significance for theology, and possible pedagogical approaches. Yet perhaps the most fundamental question that arises is the place of religious conviction in the academy and its tension with what we may (problematically) call scholarly, secular neutrality. As Susana Monta asks:

> to what extent does taking religion seriously involve taking it, in Stanley Fish's words, not only as a "phenomenon to be analyzed at arm's length" but as "a candidate for the truth"? [. . .] may the area function, as Susan Felch proposes, as a "contact zone" in which scholars' religious commitments are fully engaged, allowed to inform the totality of scholarly perspective brought to any analytical task?[26]

The presumption of an objective, academic perspective (including its possibility and its desirability) is one that the interdisciplinary conversation is uniquely positioned to deconstruct. One of the primary issues at stake here is the inclusion not just of the whole text but of the whole person in academic endeavour. Felski has noted our need to champion a direct engagement with the primary text itself; alongside this, we must regard the primacy of faith, "what it is to think, feel, and believe."[27]

As David Jasper puts it in *Literature and Theology as a Grammar of Assents* (2016), "things began to go wrong in our enterprise when, with the turn to theory [. . .] we became too philosophical and started asking the wrong questions."[28] Jasper's suggestion is that (1) we approach "things of greatest sanctity and importance" in a literary register that preserves "their mystery as an act of acknowledgement" and (2) that we content ourselves with the "less fashionable" place in the academy that nevertheless champions the importance of confessional thought and practice.[29] In conclusion, then, we might focus less on the *and* of these interdisciplinary conversations and more on the intimate connection that already exists between the two disciplines that should perhaps never have been separated: we might consider the extent to which literature *is* theology and theology *is* literary.

26. Monta, "Introduction," 3–4.
27. Monta, "Introduction: Religion, Literature, and the Academy," 3.
28. Jasper, *Literature and Theology as a Grammar of Assent*, 227.
29. Jasper, *Literature and Theology as a Grammar of Assent*, 227, 233.

Though literary and theological approaches will continue to proliferate in number and shift in foci, the importance of twentieth-century literary theory remains for the way it complicates and enriches the discourse that constitutes the very theological act itself.

BIBLIOGRAPHY

Augustine. *Confessions*. Translated by Henry Chadwick. Oxford: Oxford University Press, 1998.

Brooks, Peter. *Reading for the Plot: Design and Intention in Narrative*. Oxford: Clarendon, 1984.

Cummings, Brian. *The Literary Culture of the Reformation: Grammar and Grace*. Oxford: Oxford University Press, 2002.

Delay, Tad. *God Is Unconscious: Psychoanalysis and Theology*. Eugene, OR: Wipf & Stock, 2015.

Elliott, Jane, and Derek Attridge. *Theory after 'Theory.'* London: Routledge, 2011.

Eagleton, Terry. *After Theory*. New York: Basic, 2003.

Felski, Rita. *The Limits of Critique*. Chicago: University of Chicago Press, 2015.

Ferretter, Luke. *Towards a Christian Literary Theory*. London: Palgrave Macmillan, 2003.

Gadamer, Hans-Georg. *Truth and Method*. London: Continuum, 1975.

Heidegger, Martin,. *Being and Time*. Translated by John Macquarrie and Edward Robinson. London: Blackwell, 1962.

Jasper, David. *Literature and Theology as a Grammar of Assent*. London: Routledge, 2016.

Jennings, Willie James. *The Christian Imagination: Theology and the Origins of Race*. New Haven, CT: Yale University Press, 2010.

Keller, Catherine. *Face of the Deep: A Theology of Becoming*. London: Routledge, 2003.

Knapp, Steven, and Walter Ben Michaels. "Against Theory." *Critical Inquiry* 8 (1982) 723–42.

Lukàcs, György. *History and Class Consciousness: Studies in Marxist Dialectics*. Translated by Rodney Livingstone. Cambridge, MA: MIT Press, 1971.

Monta, Susannah Brietz. "Introduction." *Religion and Literature* 41 (2009) 3–4.

———. "Introduction: Religion, Literature, and the Academy." *Religion and Literature* 46 (2016) 3.

Richter, David H. *The Critical Tradition: Classic Texts and Contemporary Trends* 3rd ed. Boston: St. Martins, 2007.

Rivkin, Julie and Michael Ryan, eds. *Literary Theory: An Anthology*. Malden, MA: Blackwell, 1998.

Saussure, Ferdinand de. *Course in General Linguistics*. Translated by Wade Baskin, NY: Columbia University Press, 2011.

Ticciati, Susannah. *A New Apophaticism: Augustine and the Redemption of Signs*. Leiden: Brill, 2013.

Zimmermann, Jens. *Humanism and Religion: A Call for the Renewal of Western Culture*. Oxford: Oxford University Press, 2012.

Chapter 6
Postliberal Hermeneutics
RONALD T. MICHENER

Postliberal theological interpretation begins from an ecclesial context. It is "post–" liberal because it makes no pretense about eschewing modern liberal epistemological frameworks steeped in reason and historical-critical analysis. It is not trying to provide an "unbiased," "neutral," or "objective" reading of Scripture or doctrine. Postliberal hermeneutics is intentionally and straightforwardly biased and fully immersed in the particularity and grammar of Christian tradition. Postliberal theology is also postconservative, as it moves beyond the foundationalist and biblicistic literalism often associated with conservative (especially, fundamentalist) evangelicals. Postconservative theological interpretation, the focus of this handbook, emphasizes the ongoing constructive work of theological and biblical hermeneutics. To use the popular Reformed dictum and title of Roger Olson's book, postconservative theology is "Reformed and Always Reforming."[1] But this raises the question: If postliberal theology is expressed from its embeddedness within a doctrinal tradition, how can it also be committed to "always reforming" as it participates in interpretation?

Postconservative theological interpretation is committed to ongoing reform because it intentionally recognizes the fallibility and contextual nature of all interpretation. Similarly, postliberal theology is straightforwardly committed to the contextuality or "grammar" of a confessional Christian community when doing hermeneutics, rather than to an overarching,

---

1. Olson, *Reformed and Always Reforming*. Of course, the phrase is simply an English rendition of the historical and widely used Latin phrase, *Ecclesia semper reformanda*.

presupposed, objective religious truth.² That is, rather than looking toward external, objective criteria by which to interpret theological or biblical texts, it is "intratextual" in its approach—looking toward its own narrative and community framework for interpretation.

Before summarizing some overall themes significant for postliberal hermeneutics, this article will first summarize the influence of two major figures in postliberal theology: Hans Frei and George Lindbeck, with a particular emphasis placed on Lindbeck. There are various possible trajectories to take on describing postliberal theology, but summarizing the positions of these two major figures will set the overall agenda and frame the overall sensibilities that govern postliberal theological interpretation. We will begin with some general comments on Hans Frei, Lindbeck's friend and Yale colleague, to whom Lindbeck credits giving him his primary understanding of the place of narrative in Scripture.³ Indeed, Frei was one of the earliest representatives for the development of a postliberal theological sensibility.

KEY FIGURES
HANS FREI (1922–1988)

Frei was born in Germany to secular Jewish parents, although he was baptized a Lutheran. With the rise of Nazi anti-Semitism, in 1935 he was sent to England to attend a Quaker school. It was here where Frei had a conversion experience to Christianity. In 1938, he moved with his parents to the United States and eventually ended up at Yale Divinity School, studying with H. Richard Niebuhr, finishing a doctoral degree in theology in 1956.⁴

For Frei, Christian theology is primarily about "Christian self-description" rather than existential correlation as seen, for example, in Paul Tillich's theological method of correlation. Seeking existential correlation is a method that is immersed in modernity and the human quest for "ultimate meaning."⁵ Frei was arguably the first theologian to use the term "postliberal" (in his doctoral dissertation)—at least in theological sense to which we are referring in this article.⁶ In Frei's major and most well-known work, *The Eclipse of Biblical Narrative* (1974) he argues that many biblical narratives have a "history-like" feature that shaped Christian belief, but this feature was

---

2. See Lindbeck et al., "Panel Discussion," 247.
3. Lindbeck, *Church in a Postliberal Age*, 119.
4. Higton, *Christ, Providence and History*, 16–8.
5. Frei, "Eberhard Busch's Biography of Karl Barth," 103, quoted in Placher, *Unapologetic Theology*, 19.
6. This is pointed out by Hunsinger, "Postliberal Theology," 5.

"eclipsed" or neglected in the eighteenth and nineteenth centuries, being overshadowed by an emphasis on grammatical-historical-verbal interpretation. As a result, the historical referents in the text became more important than the "history-like" narratives that are critical for the identification of Jesus in the Gospels. The questions of literal, historical factuality took precedence over the literary nature of the text.[7] That is, supposed factual claims from the Bible became subject to modern, external tests of veracity apart from the Bible's self-attesting authority. Frei calls this the "great reversal," where interpretation moved to fitting the story of the Bible into another world narrative, instead of fitting an outside world narrative into the biblical story. That is, with Frei's postliberal vision, outside world narratives are written into the narrative of the Bible, so that the narrative of the Bible becomes our narrative and reality.[8]

The empirical and rational methods of inquiry characteristic of the Enlightenment shaped both liberal and conservative impulses in biblical interpretation, both of which were mistaken. Conservatives took an apologetic tone, making efforts to prove the factual content of the Christian narrative without adequately considering its literary character. Liberals, however, neglected the historical elements of the narrative, focusing instead on its existential and ethical implications. In both cases, for Frei, the significance of the reality of the biblical narrative is neglected.[9] Instead, for Frei, we must recover the "history-like" narrative of the text without resorting to conservative literalism or reducing the text to a mere literary existential form. Frei draws from the work Eric Auerbach, claiming that the Bible is a "realistic narrative," where the form of a text and its meaning are connected, and this connection must be maintained when reading. Modern, liberal theological interpretation attempts to draw out the ethical meaning or transcendent reality from its encasement in a particular narrative, which for Frei, is wrong headed. The Bible has its own narrative integrity and must not be simply used for reconstructing historical events on one hand or used for creating universal myths or symbols for humanity, on the other. Frei is not abandoning historical reference; however, he is rather reworking how it is portrayed.[10] As James Fodor puts it: "Frei promotes habits of textual fidelity that reeducate and retrain Christians to think of the Bible less a source to

---

7. Frei, *Eclipse of Biblical Narrative*, 9–10, 223; Higton, "Hans Frei," 221–23.

8. Frei, *Eclipse of Biblical Narrative*, 18, 130; Cf. Fodor, "Postliberal Theology," 235; and Loughlin, "Postmodern Scripture," 316.

9. Michener, *Postliberal Theology*, 51–52.

10. Higton, "Hans Frei," 221–34; Fodor, "Postliberal Theology," 234–35.

be used and more as a text to be indwelt."[11] We are not simply neutral, objective observers of a biblical text to be analyzed, but we are active participants within the narrative itself.

GEORGE LINDBECK (1923–2018)

Hans Frei certainly manifested postliberal sensibilities, but George Lindback brought such perspectives to the forefront of theological reflection with the publication of *The Nature of Doctrine* (1984). Born in Luoyang, China to Lutheran missionary parents, Lindbeck had a great respect for Chinese people and Chinese culture. Unfortunately, due to frequent illness as a young person, he did not learn to speak Chinese proficiently. Lindbeck developed four convictions based on his time in China that shaped his perspectives on culture. First, our communal context is more important than our own self-development. Second, characteristics of being human are similar across cultures. Third, along with these common human characteristics, cultural differences still create difficulties in communication. Fourth, communities that are "book sustained," create stable thoughts and practices that are maintained in the face of various oppositional forces.[12]

Growing up in China, Lindbeck noticed various Protestant missionaries from different denominational backgrounds, many of whom were theologically conservative. Yet, even with their differences, they worked and shared with each other cooperatively. He noticed the same cooperative spirit at his Christian boarding school, even though it was not intentionally ecumenical. This is not to say that the school was absent of theological disagreements, but their unity in Christ trumped their differences. Lindbeck's perspectives of Roman Catholics, however, was marked by suspicion at this time, as Protestants and Catholics did not commonly meet together in China, and the Chinese government considered them as different religions.[13]

At the age of 17, Lindbeck began university studies in the United States. He eventually studied theology at Yale, followed by time at the Pontifical Institute of Medieval Studies in Toronto, and the École Pratique de Hautes Études in Paris. He completely a PhD at Yale on the theologian Duns Scotus. With Lindbeck's work in medieval theology, he was invited to attend Vatican II as a Lutheran representative, which was greatly influential to his ongoing ecumenical engagement. Throughout his education, Lindbeck became more aware of his Lutheran theological roots, eventually becoming

---

11. Fodor, "Postliberal Theology," 235.

12. Lindbeck, "Interview with George Lindbeck," 28–35; Michener, *Postlberal Theology*, 63–64; Brown, *George Lindbeck*, 9–10.

13. Brown, *George Lindbeck*, 11–12.

confessionally Reformed in his commitments. He understood the Reformation as a corrective movement within Catholicism, hence thinking Lutheranism was helpful in bridging the gap between Protestants and Roman Catholics.[14] Shaun Brown insightfully summarizes Lindbeck's position: "Lindbeck argues that the Reformation emphasis upon the solas did not replace the previous tradition, but instead provided a corrective that stands in continuity with the catholic tradition. So instead of seeing the Reformation emphasis upon justification by faith as constitutive of a new type of Christianity, movement Lutherans argue that every doctrine is susceptible to abuse and corruption, and therefore may be in need of reform."[15]

Lindbeck suggests that the postliberal research agenda attempts to retrieve a premodern, pre-foundational interpretation of Scripture for today.[16] Like Frei, he called for a perspective that understands Scripture as an overarching narrative that shapes the world, rather than the world shaping the narrative of Scripture. Lindbeck is most known for his book, *The Nature of Doctrine* (1984) that suggests three theories on how doctrines function. The cognitive-propositional approach emphasizes the informational aspects of doctrine and its truth claims. This approach is noticed in neo-scholastic theological approaches and also in conservative evangelical systematic theologies that focus on doctrinal assertions drawn out from a series of biblical proof texts. The experience-expressivist approach focuses on the emotive or affective aspects of doctrine, typical of liberal and existentially focused theology (e.g., Schleiermacher, Tillich). A third approach, often taken by Roman Catholics, is a combination of the previous two approaches, where both doctrinal propositions and experiential, symbolic elements of doctrine are significant. For Lindbeck, it seems impossible to reconcile these different doctrinal positions without giving up one's own perspective.[17]

Therefore, Lindbeck proposed another approach that he called the cultural-linguistic perspective. He insisted that doctrines do not function as either truth claims or symbolic expressions, but rather as rules, or a grammar, that governs discourse in the church. This is a perspective that Lindbeck argues is not completely unique, but is found, at least in part, in the *regulae fidei* of the early church. But commitment to one's own rules or doctrines within one's faith commitment does not negate the need to express them with fluidity or lucidity. Further, one must not be compelled

---

14. Michener, *Postliberal Theology*, 64; Brown, *George Lindbeck*, 13–14.
15. Brown, *George Lindbeck*, 16.
16. Lindbeck et al., "Panel Discussion," 246. Cf. also Brown, *George Lindbeck*, 125.
17. Lindbeck, *Nature of Doctrine*, loc. 897, 908; Veeneman, *Introducing Theological Method*, 63–64.

to simply utter one's doctrinal beliefs in mere repetition, without updating their formulations. Doctrinal formulations are always human formulations, hence always in need of reconsideration and possible revision[18]

Lindbeck's cognitive-linguistic proposal makes a distinction between doctrine and theology. Doctrines are particular beliefs within a faith community, whereas theology is more extensive in its description of Christian beliefs. Doctrine and theology are indeed related, but the relation is not a necessary relation. Christians may generally agree on doctrinal commitments but disagree on how to interpret the doctrines, as one may see, for example, with differences between Roman Catholics and Protestants on church sacraments.[19]

Additionally, Lindbeck submits that there is a "taxonomy of doctrines." There are "unconditionally necessary" doctrines that are always applicable, "conditionally essential" doctrines (which may be permanent or temporary), and "accidentally necessary" doctrines that have been established by historically embedded practices in the church (such as church liturgical practices on Sunday). The "law of love," for Lindbeck, is unconditionally necessary for Christians since it is to be applied at all times and in all cultures, whereas pacifism has been understood as conditionally essential, depending on one's convictions and historical context. Further, temporary conditionally essential doctrines may be reversible or irreversible. Lindbeck provides the example of the prohibition of slavery as a conditional, now irreversible teaching. By "conditional" this does not mean, for Lindbeck, that slavery was at one point a correct moral activity, he is rather making the point of how this moral injunction operates in practice, historically speaking. Lindbeck is careful to say that the purpose of his taxonomy does not give exhaustive answers to the nature of specific doctrines, but it does show the "formal possibilities" for ongoing discussion.[20]

Now that we have summarized the position of these two foundational figures for the advent of postliberal theology, we will now consider two primary themes in postliberal theological interpretation: Intratextuality and ecumenicity. We will begin with its particular focus on intratextuality, the governing theme for the practice of postliberal hermeneutics, followed by a look at its background influences.

---

18. Veeneman, *Introducing Theological Method*, 68; Cf. Lindbeck, *Nature of Doctrine*, loc. 929–53, 2362.

19. Lindbeck, *Nature of Doctrine*, loc. 2425–99; See also, Veeneman, *Introducing Theological Method*, 67.

20. Lindbeck, *Nature of Doctrine*, loc. 2425–24; See also, Veeneman, *Introducing Theological Method*, 69–71.

IMPORTANT THEMES IN POSTLIBERAL THEOLOGICAL INTERPRETATION: INTRATEXTUALITY AND ECUMENICITY

INTRATEXTUALITY

As mentioned above, postliberal theological interpretation is committed to intratextuality. Intratextuality looks within its own particular faith grammar and context to provide theological meaning rather than a particular faith tradition looking to external sources for its meaning or justification for meaning. As Lindbeck puts it, "meaning is immanent . . . constituted by the uses of a specific language rather than being distinguishable from it."[21] We have often acquired the notion that for theological commitments to be justified as true, they must submit to modernist tests of objectivity and neutrality. That is, our beliefs must square with external criteria or extratextual sources, in order to be counted as true or meaningful. Such modernist extratextual presuppositions are significant for propositional or experiential-expressivist approaches to theology. But for Lindbeck's postliberal cultural-linguistic perspective, one is not compelled to look beyond one's own contextual framework for some sort of objective approval.

This is not to say, however, that the perspective and practice of postliberal intratextuality is without notable influences; it is in fact indebted to background influences from literary studies philosophy, cultural anthropology and sociology, and theology. Due to the importance of these sources as background theological impulses to postliberal hermeneutics, it is beneficial to briefly highlight several of the primary figures under these categories of influence.

INFLUENTIAL SOURCES

Eric Auerbach (1892–1957)

The literary critic Eric Auerbach's work, *Mimesis*, was influential in the formation of postliberal theology. For Auerbach, the Hebrew Scriptures functioned to overcome the reality of its readers, surpassing its mere historicity. The Bible is utterly unique in its claims, and all other overarching frameworks constructed for understanding reality must be encompassed in the world of the biblical text. The Bible requires interpretation that relates all human history to Jesus Christ as the comprehensive plan of God.[22]

---

21. Lindbeck, *Nature of Doctrinee*, loc. 3070. Cf. Veeneman, *Introducing Theological Method*, 72.

22. Springs, *Toward a Generous Orthodoxy*, 46, 69; Goh, *Christian Tradition Today*, 158–59.

Ludwig Wittgenstein (1889–1951)

A philosopher of key influence on the postliberal notion of intratextuality is Ludwig Wittgenstein. His first philosophical inclinations were focused on logical positivism and the one-to-one correspondence of words with facts. The later Wittgenstein, however, was known for "language games," a term referring to the complexities of language and how it is used in everyday life. The use of language is rich, varied, and expansive. Among its uses, it consists of asking questions, giving orders, making requests, and describing events in the present and past, among others. Language is not a "one-size, fits all" tool that uncovers and displays objective, unbiased reality. Scientists, philosophers, physicians, poets, and theologians, all have particular ways of using language for their particular purposes of communication; language games are "played" within particular communicative contexts. This does not mean that one language game within one context is better or truer than another, it is simply a way of explaining how language works. Likewise, it would be improper for physician to impose her use of language within a medical context upon a poet, and vice-versa.[23] When an atheistic astrophysicist claims that God does not exist because of lack of evidence within his scientific discipline, then he already presupposes what properties God must have (and display) if God were to exist. This also would be a transgression of language games, imposing one language game (that of astrophysics) upon that of theology. Instead, as with postliberal theological interpretation, meaning is communicated through a particular intratextual grammar of faith, rather than through some external description of reality or presupposed position of neutrality that adjudicates truth from reality.

Gilbert Ryle (1900–1976)

Hans Frei, in particular, credits the influence of philosopher Gilbert Ryle on his thinking. We see this in Frei's appropriation of Ryle's use of "intention-action-description" to Jesus. Jesus's actions are not pointers to his identity, but they manifest his identity. That is, Jesus's actions *are* his identity.[24] Justin Springs notes that Frei's application of Ryle in this regard is not foolproof, but it does emphasize that to understand essential character and meaning of the story of Jesus cannot be separated from nor made external from the

---

23. See Michener, *Postliberal Theology*, 20–21; Cf. also Wittgenstein, *Lectures and Conversations on Aesthetics, Psychology and Religious Belief*, 57–59.

24. Springs, *Toward a Generous Orthodoxy*, 34.

story itself. Hermeneutics then, is not theory, but it is the practice and priority of reading the story itself.[25]

Thomas Kuhn (1922–1996)

Widely known by his coined phrase "paradigm shift" that appeared in his book, *The Structure of Scientific Revolutions* (1962, 4th edition, 2012), philosopher of science, Thomas Kuhn, explains how historic landmark shifts in scientific understanding have been radically influenced by social factors. As Wittgenstein revealed that incommensurable language games appear in various practices and disciplines of life, so Kuhn uncovers similar patterns of incommensurability through the years of scientific exploration. Drawing from both Wittgenstein and Kuhn, Lindbeck submits that our criteria for what is esteemed as reasonable are too expansive and nuanced to be restricted to any particular theory of reasonability. Our evaluative norms for our faith commitments would be different from those of scientific disciplines. Moreover, the "credibility" of our religious beliefs come from their skillful practice rather than from some external criteria.[26]

Alisdair MacIntyre (1929–)

Moral philosopher, Alisdair MacIntyre, like Wittgenstein and Kuhn, also discusses contextual applications and incommensurability, but in his case, with ethics. Ethics and virtues are not inherently neutral and do not operate independent of the particularity of communities and traditions. In similar epistemological fashion, postliberal theological interpretation focuses on the interpretive tradition of the Christian faith rather than attempting to somehow get outside the faith community to some sort of objective reference.[27]

Clifford Geertz (1926–2006)

Postliberal theology also draws upon the work of cultural anthropologist, Clifford Geertz (1926–2006), who in turn draws from Gilbert Ryle's concept of "thick description" and applies it to ethnographies of human culture. In

---

25. Springs, *Toward a Generous Orthodoxy*, 35, 36. Also see 37–38, 46–51 for further explanation on Frei's use of Ryle.

26. Michener, *Postliberal Theology*, 30–32; Lindbeck, *Nature of Doctrine*, loc. 3439, 3451.

27. Lindbeck et al., "Panel Discussion," 252. Cf. also Michener, *Postliberal Theology*, 27–30.

particular, when discussing religious perspectives, he observes that such perspectives are not put to the test in an empirical manner, but they are considered in view of their teleology and convictions that arise through ritualistic religious practices. Although his citation of Wittgenstein is infrequent, Geertz is clearly influenced by Wittgenstein's notion of language games and how life practices are connected to one's particular context and culture.[28]

Peter L. Berger (1929–2017) and Thomas Luckmann (1927–2016)

Sociologists Peter L. Berger and Thomas Luckmann observed that sociological factors shape one's understanding of reality within particular cultures. Even everyday conceptions of the external, physical world are shaped by cultural perspectives and the transmission of that which is accepted and understood as knowledge in a particular culture. For instance, the Tibetan monk's understanding of reality will vary from that of a business executive in New York City. The job of the sociologist, then, is to describe these differences among various cultures. The influence of Berger and Luckmann on the development of postliberal theological interpretation may be apparent at this point. As we have noticed with postliberal theology, the *description* of a community's theological practices is vitally important to understand how doctrine works in the theology of that community's faith tradition.[29]

Thomas Aquinas (1225–1274)

With Lindbeck's background in medieval theology, it is not surprising that Thomas Aquinas would in some way have an impact on his postliberal theological sensibilities. At one point, he even called himself a "Wittgensteinian Thomistic Lutheran." And indeed, the influence of Thomas on Lindbeck is clear. True knowledge of God, for Aquinas, comes in the context of the community of faith. For Lindbeck and postliberal theology, a Christian's concept of God will not be the same as that of an unbeliever since the context of truth is different. Likewise, for postliberal theology, the world of Scripture is itself the interpretative framework for understanding reality; truth is an internal, intratextual reality of the Christian from within that interpretive framework. But the interpretive framework is not simply reduced to propositions or assent to certain beliefs, but it is the practical outworking of that faith in the context of the Christian faith community.[30]

---

28. Michener, *Postliberal Theology*, 32–36.

29. Michener, *Postliberal Theology*, 36–40.

30. Marshall, "Aquinas as Postliberal Theologian," *Thomist: A Speculative Quarterly Review*, 384–86, 401; Michener, *Postliberal Theology*, 43; Lindbeck, *Nature of Doctrine*, loc. 3134–48.

Karl Barth (1886–1968)

Perhaps the most significant theological influence on postliberal theological interpretation is that of Karl Barth. Barth is known for his unwillingness to allow theological liberalism to determine theological understanding. With Barth's liberal theological mentors, general revelation and an accompanying understanding of natural theology were used to justify National Socialism, which highlighted the perversion of the attempt of human efforts to seek God. God is beyond all human rationality or understanding; God is only known via God's own initiative to reveal Godself in and through Jesus Christ. One may never reason from a position outside of faith (a faith only granted and bestowed by God) to faith.[31]

CRITERIA FOR INTRATEXTUAL INTERPRETATION

It is important to note that with the various influences on postliberal theological interpretation, none of the disciplines and their representatives are used to legitimize or justify belief claims made by postliberal theology. Rather, they are presented to show how multiple disciplines of thought and research point to the reductionist inadequacy of modernist empiricism and rationalism and point to the sensibility behind the postliberal embrace of an intratextual, community-shaped grammar for expressing the reality of Christian faith. With this in mind, what then would be criteria for postliberal intratextual interpretation?

Jeffrey Goh submits six "rules" for intratextual reading of the Bible, derived from Lindbeck. First, the Bible must be understood as unique and untranslatable to the modern world. That is, it is the interpretive community must remain true to the culture and world of the Bible. Culture is interpreted from the vantage point of the Bible, not vice-versa. Second, the canon of the Bible provides the unity of its narrative from the story of Israel through Jesus's ministry, death, and resurrection. Third, our grammatical faith discourse stems from our particular faith community (whether tacitly or intentionally) from which our interpretation will take place. Fourth, we must remain true to the stories of the Bible as they are in their narrative, realistic, particularity. Although the Bible certainly contains different genres of literature, this does not change the interpretive task of respecting the Bible's broad, all-encompassing framework. Fifth, "figural interpretation" must be respected, keeping in mind the unity of the canon. Reading typologically allows readers, for example, to understand Jesus Christ in view of the Hebrew

---

31. Michener, *Postlberal Theology*, 43–6.

Bible and see Israel's story as the basis for Christianity. Maintaining this interpretative continuity through the Bible's overall narrative is essential for postliberal, intratextual hermeneutics. Sixth, intratextual interpreters always read, as we have emphasized above, from the Bible to realities external to the Bible, rather than vice-versa. Intratextual interpretation understands reality from within the context of the Christian community and remains faithful to that community context.[32]

It may seem ironic that it is the intratextuality of postliberal theological interpretation with its emphasis on the narrative continuity of the biblical text and the grammar of particular Christian faith community expressions that are significant for building ecumenical bridges.[33] It is this second key feature of ecumenicity to which we now turn.

ECUMENICITY

The importance of ecumenicity for postliberal theological interpretation may not seem obvious at first, as one may easily conclude that due to its emphasis on intratextuality that postliberal theology may lead to insularity or sectarianism. However, this is not the case. In fact, it is just the opposite. In fact, the focus on ecumenical hospitality is the driving force behind much of Lindbeck's work. A term used to describe this ecumenical hospitality, borrowed from Hans Frei, is "generous orthodoxy." A generous, hospitable perspective on Christian orthodoxy does not dilute differences, but acknowledges the breadth of the biblical story in which Christians locate themselves, while at the same time remaining committed to practicing their faith within a distinctive faith tradition. A robust postliberal theological perspective desires to affirm the particularity of one's faith community and its theological grammar and ecclesiological convictions. Further, it is essential to identify such "grammatical" differences among various communities of faith in order have respectful, conciliatory ecumenical dialogue. Rather than watering down our beliefs, when we recognize the particularity of our convictions in comparison with, or in contrast to, those from another tradition, we have substantial areas on which to pursue discussion. This same charitable sensibility of recognizing and respecting differences in the faith community of the other, may also be applied to interreligious dialogue, even though the overarching story of Christian faith would not be the common ground of discussion.[34]

---

32. Goh, *Christian Tradition Today*, 187–202.
33. Michener, "George Lindbeck," 72.
34. Michener, *Postlberal Theology*, 9; Michener, "George Lindbeck," 66–67; 73–75.

PROMISE AND POTENTIAL OF POSTLIBERAL INTERPRETATION

As we have seen, postliberal theological interpretation is postconservative but it is by no means theologically liberal. It embraces the narrative of Scripture but does not succumb to the reductionistic mindset of modernity that is overly dependent upon historical evidence and rationality. Furthermore, in its embrace of, and embeddedness in, the story of Scripture as the descriptive impetus to Christian faith, it also does not succumb to the literalism of evangelical fundamentalist forms of interpretation.

There are a number of additional theologians not mentioned nor cited in this article that may be characterized as postliberal theological interpreters, even though not all of these would claim such a title. A sampling of such authors would include, but not limited to, Stanley Hauerwas, Paul Holmer, George Hunsinger, David Kelsey, Kathryn Tanner, and Ronald Thiemann. Additionally, there are three others I wish to briefly mention that provide insights for a critical appropriation and/or adaptation of postliberal theological interpretative sensibilities today.

JAMES K. A. SMITH—PRAGMATIC COMMUNITY RELATIVISM

Drawing upon the philosopher, Richard Brandom, James K. A. Smith suggests that his book, *Who's Afraid of Relativism?*, may be considered a "prequel" to Lindbeck's *The Nature of Doctrine*, making a more explicit theoretical, philosophical link between church practice and doctrine. What we do in our community faith practices, precedes what we think in our doctrinal expressions. This is not to discount doctrinal propositions, but it restructures its priority by looking first to the descriptive, relative character of community that is situated within a particular faith tradition. Relativism does not mean arbitrary in this context, but "relative to" a particular Christian context. For example, the Nicene Creed and the doctrines therein, express the content of the practices of the early church at this stage in Christian history, which allow the Christian community to discern the norms that represent faithfulness to that community. For today, Smith submits that Christian communities must revitalize their faithfulness to Christian practices in their communities to be effective witnesses of the gospel for the world.[35]

---

35. Smith, *Who's Afraid of Relativism*, 20, 151–52, 160–64, 177.

MARK RANDALL JAMES—POSTLIBERAL INTERPRETIVE WISDOM

As we noticed for Smith, understanding the reality of Christian truth is made manifest in the practice of the interpretive Christian community. Mark Randall James, however, desires to link the postliberal theological interpretive vision to the practice of ancient biblical wisdom, nurtured by the reading of Scripture in Christian community. In his desire to eschew the excesses of reason, Smith's perspective may downplay the use of reason in wisdom without warrant. James argues that postliberal interpretation submits that rational, religious commitments are embedded and embodied in our linguistic learning practices as individuals and in our communities of faith. Rather than seeing the world of the Bible as an isolated, semiotic world unto itself, James emphasizes that the language and practice of the Bible is an ongoing, interrelated process of learning, using, and putting our learning to the test, all which require nurturing through wisdom.[36] If we understand our times to reflect a crisis in hermeneutics, rather than looking to a new interpretive theory, James advise us "to renew a practice of formative scripture reading" in wisdom, beginning with the common sensical wisdom of the book of Proverbs.[37]

KEVIN J. VANHOOZER—DRAMATIC, CANONICAL, AND LINGUISTIC THEO-DRAMA

Drawing resources from Hans Urs von Balthasar, and speech-act theory, Kevin J. Vanhoozer proposes what he calls a "canonical-linguistic" theology. He critiques Lindbeck's postliberal theology while at the same time reformulating it, in an effort to preserve the importance of propositions in evangelical theology, which he thinks Lindbeck downplays in his own cultural-linguistic approach. Vanhoozer's postconservative approach emphasizes the rich diversity of language expressed in propositions in the Bible that include, among others, facts, commands, promises, and words of comfort. Interpretation must not be reduced that which operates only within the context and purview of our community of faith but must be done in view of the context of the entire canon of Scripture. Scripture is the dramatic script that we, those acting out God's narrative ("theo-drama") through the church, must perform with the guidance of the Holy Spirit. Vanhoozer then maintains the postliberal emphasis upon the story of our

---

36. James, "Beginning of Wisdom," 1–2, 14–15.
37. James, "Beginning of Wisdom," 19–20.

faith in community but especially highlights the importance of propositions practiced and performed while looking to the divine playwright.[38]

CONCLUSION

The observations we have made of Smith, James, and Vanhoozer are only three of a number of possible trajectories illustrating the promise and potential of postliberal hermeneutics. As we have seen, postliberal interpretation offers postconservative theological sensibilities that move beyond the reductionisms of Enlightenment that paved the way for liberal, theologically thin impulses of relevance. Rather than seeking existential relevance, postliberal theology seeks commitment to the story of the Bible within the commitment to Christian communities of faith, and the particular expressions and formations of those communities in the practice of and reading of the Bible. This is not to say that postliberal interpretation is without relevance for today, but it is a relevance that stems from finding Christian faith within the all-encompassing story of the Bible in which we are invited by God to participate.

BIBLIOGRAPHY

Brown, Shaun C. *George Lindbeck: A Biographical and Theological Introduction*. Eugene, OR: Cascade, 2022.

Fodor, James. "Postliberal Theology." In *The Modern Theologians: An Introduction to Christian Theology since 1918*, edited by David F. Ford with Rachel Muers, 229–48. Malden, MA: Blackwell, 2005.

Frei, Hans W. *The Eclipse of Biblical Narrative: A Study in Eighteenth and Nineteenth Century Hermeneutics*. New Haven, CT: Yale University Press, 1974.

Goh, Jeffrey C. K. *Christian Tradition Today: A Postliberal Vision of Church and World*. Louvain Theological and Pastoral Monographs 28. Leuven: Peeters, 2000.

Higton, Mike. *Christ, Providence and History*. London: T. & T. Clark, 2004.

———. "Hans Frei." In *Christian Theologies of Scripture: A Comparative Introduction*, edited by Justin S. Holcomb, 220–39. New York: New York University Press, 2006.

Hunsinger, George. "Postliberal Theology." In *The Cambridge Companion to Postmodern Theology*, edited by Kevin J. Vanhoozer, 42–57. Cambridge: Cambridge University Press, 2003.

---

38. Vanhoozer, *Drama of Doctrine*, 37–50, 278–79; See also, Michener, *Postliberal Theology*, 137–39.

James, Mark Randall. "The Beginning of Wisdom: On the Postliberal Interpretation of Scripture." *Modern Theology* 33 (2017) 9–30.

Lindbeck, George A. *The Church in a Postliberal Age*, edited by James J. Buckley. London: SCM Press, 2002.

———. "An Interview with George Lindbeck: Performing the Faith." *Christian Century* (November 28, 2006) 28–35.

———. *The Nature of Doctrine: Religion and Theology in a Postliberal Age*. 25th Anniversary ed. Louisville, KY: Westminster John Knox Press, 2009. Originally published in 1984.

Lindbeck, George, et al. "A Panel Discussion: Lindbeck, Hunsinger, McGrath & Fackre." In *The Nature of Confession: Evangelicals and Postliberals in Conversation*, edited by Timothy R. Phillips and Dennis L. Okholm, 246–53. Downers Grove, IL: InterVarsity, 1996.

Loughlin, Gerard. "Postmodern Scripture." In *Christian Theologies of Scripture: A Comparative Introduction*, edited by Justin S. Holcomb, 300–22. New York: New York University Press, 2006.

Marshall, Bruce. "Aquinas as Postliberal Theologian." *Thomist: A Speculative Quarterly Review* 53 (1989) 353–402.

Michener, Ronald T. "George Lindbeck: Ecumenical Unity through Ecclesial Particularity." In *Generous Orthodoxies: Essays on the History and Future of Ecumenical Theology*, edited by Paul Silas Peterson, 57–77. Eugene, OR: Pickwick, 2020.

———. *Postliberal Theology: A Guide for the Perplexed*. London: Bloomsbury/T. & T. Clark, 2013.

Olson, Roger E. *Reformed and Always Reforming: The Postconservative Approach to Evangelical Theology*. Grand Rapids: Baker Academic, 2007.

Placher, William C. *Unapologetic Theology: A Christian Voice in a Pluralistic Conversation*. Louisville, KY: Westminster John Knox, 1989.

Smith, James K. A. *Who's Afraid of Relativism: Community, Contingency, and Creaturehood*. Grand Rapids: Baker Academic, 2014.

Springs, Jason A. *Toward a Generous Orthodoxy: Prospects for Hans Frei's Postliberal Theology*. Eugene, OR: Wipf & Stock, 2010.

Vanhoozer, Kevin J. *The Drama of Doctrine: A Canonical–Linguistic Approach to Christian Theology*. Louisville, KY: Westminster John Knox, 2005.

Veeneman, Mary M. *Introducing Theological Method: A Survey of Contemporary Theologians and Approaches*. Grand Rapids: Baker Academic, 2017.

Wittgenstein, Ludwig. *Lectures and Conversations on Aesthetics, Psychology and Religious Belief*, edited by Cyril Barrett. Berkeley: University of California Press, 1972.

Chapter 7

The Religious Turn in Postmodern Thought

Caputo and Kearney on Hermeneutics and Faith

B. KEITH PUTT

Stephen Fry characterizes him as "the most extraordinarily pert and precocious baby that ever drew breath," a commentary with which I entirely agree, considering the various fascinating accounts of his birth.[1] I do question, however, Fry's later reference to the baby as an "infant," since the etymology of that term, *in fari*, literally means "one who cannot speak."[2] Indeed, a significant aspect of the baby's precocious character is his having been born with a full command of language, evidenced by his immediately conversing with his mother Maia, the eldest of the Pleiades, in rather sophisticated logical discourse. Furthermore, this loquacious offspring began life as a neonatal cattle rustler, undoubtedly one with extraordinary courage, since he chose to steal the beautiful white cattle belonging to the god Apollo. Amazingly, he got away with the theft through the sheer use of wit and cleverness, striking a deal with the god—who was his half-brother by the way—thereby establishing himself as also quite adept at using persuasive language as a potent rhetorical tool. He further developed his skill in using—or misusing—language in order to become equally proficient at lying and dissimulating.

---

1. Fry, *Mythos*, 100.
2. Shipley, *Origins of English Words*, 25.

Ultimately, and not surprisingly, his precocious verbal character results in his being labeled a trickster, a thief, and a magician later in adulthood![3]

Who exactly was this "pert and precocious baby," and what did he develop into as an adult? Well, his mother named him Hermes, and he eventually morphed into the divine herald; that is, his father Zeus tasked him with being the messenger god in the Greek pantheon. Given his skill with language, no one should be surprised at his being made the official mediator of information between the gods and humans, acting as the conduit of revelation, ensuring that humans properly receive all divine communications directed at them from Mt. Olympus. Of course, if Hermes delivers pertinent information from the gods, that information must be heard or read and then deciphered, since supernatural expressions remain ineffective if they cannot be understood. Consequently, in bearing Olympian messages, Hermes creates contexts in which human beings must strive to comprehend and appropriate the meaning inherent in the various divine dispatches. In other words, in announcing proclamations from the gods, he provokes ongoing processes of interpretation. Perhaps that is why one etymological theory derives the word "hermeneutics," meaning the "science of interpretation," from the Greek words *hermeneuein*, "to interpret," and *hermeneia*, "interpretation," which, in turn, emerge from the name "Hermes." Richard Palmer certainly accepts this etymology and contends that since Hermes took what transcended human conceptuality—the thoughts of the gods—and transformed it into a form that humans could comprehend, hermeneutics, from its very inception, overtly focused on the issue of producing a clarity of understanding.[4] As a result, to interpret means to act as another "Hermes" and to mediate a proper understanding of meaning.

Of course, the issue of understanding foundationally concentrates on semiotics, the science of signs, on the necessity to discern what, if anything, signs, symbols, events, phenomena, and experiences may signify or "mean." Since this concentration consistently defaults to linguistic signs, that is, to oral and written language as expressions of discourse, the German philosopher Hans-Georg Gadamer insists that, "all understanding is interpretation and all interpretation takes place in the medium of a language."[5] That interpretive "fact" further indicates that hermeneutics is a universal issue, a necessary action that human beings can never avoid, since we never extricate ourselves from linguistic contexts.[6] Yet, as noted above, the uni-

---

3. Brown, *Hermes the Thief*, 17–18.
4. Palmer, *Hermeneutics*, 12–13.
5. Gadamer, *Truth and Method*, 350.
6. Gadamer, *Philosophical Hermeneutics*, 3–17.

versality of the hermeneutical ambition to understand exceeds the limits of discourse and involves any semiotic attempt to discover or create meaning, to comprehend a "why" or "what" regarding the very fabric of our lives. In other words, not only do we seek to understand oral and written language, but we also seek to understand historical events and existential encounters. As David Tracy contends, whenever "we act, deliberate, judge, understand, or even experience, we are interpreting."[7] As a result, whenever we relate to another individual, express an opinion about an event, decide to act in a particular manner, explain why a work of art inspires us, or even seek the comfort of some theory that pretends to rationalize an enigmatic moment, we rely on the influence of Hermes and hope to "make some sense" of the resulting situation.

THE ENTANGLEMENT OF HERMENEUTICS AND RELIGION

Given the etymological connection of "hermeneutics" with Hermes, who is, again, a god, one should not be surprised that hermeneutics perpetuates an undeniably direct connection to religion and theology, so much so that even when it is extended past overtly theological texts and religious experiences, for example, to instances of secular literature or to common life occurrences, the mythological core of hermeneutics remains operative in every endeavor to understand potential meaning. In the most secular, non-religious, or anti-theological applications of interpretation theory, remnants of the sacred and the "divine" persist. As such, the religious cannot efface the hermeneutical, and the hermeneutical cannot deny its religious genealogy. Indeed, one may find in various philosophers of language arguments confirming the symbiotic semiotic relationship between religion/theology and interpretation theories. For example, the French philosopher Paul Ricœur considers the history of hermeneutics to be a disclosure of something of the "essence" of the religious itself. In other words, he claims that "religious faith may be identified through its language, or, to speak more accurately, as a kind of discourse." If that is true, however, then one can only comprehend religion through a hermeneutical approach.[8] He argues that the approach must be viewed as a series of circles. One is religious because one enters into the circle of a "founding word," then into the circle of "mediating texts," and finally into the circle of "traditions of interpretation."[9] He alleges that the significance of these circles cannot be diminished precisely because

---

7. Tracy, *Plurality and Ambiguity*, 9.
8. Ricœur, *Figuring the Sacred*, 35.
9. Ricœur, *Critique and Conviction*, 145.

religious sensibilities "would remain mute if [they] did not receive the power of the word of interpretation."[10] Consequently, he offers a compelling case for acknowledging that one cannot study a religion without paying close attention to the originary language that established that religion, the secondary language that established the various traditions of interpretations of that religion, and the contemporary language utilized to express that religion's current status.

Another, somewhat complementary, confirmation of the connection between interpretation theory and religion may be found in the deconstructive hermeneutics of Jacques Derrida. Whereas Ricœur demonstrates that one cannot engage religion without a close investigation into its language, Derrida professes that one cannot engage language without acceding to its systemic religious and theological implications. In other words, no matter how language is used or in what context, at least two theological inclinations remain operational. First, Derrida argues that no interpretation of language avoids the potential contamination of absolute meaning. When establishing the sense or meaning of any discourse, an interpreter may be deceived into concluding that *the* meaning of a word, sentence, or text can be established, which, in turn, would result in authenticating *the* absolute legislating interpretation of a statement or text. He refers to this as a totalizing of linguistic meaning predicated upon the belief in a "transcendental signified," that is, a belief that something or someone transcendent to the hermeneutical process determines what every sign or combination of signs signifies. He declares that, traditionally, the "transcendental signified" denotes God as the supreme interpreter who prescribes the one true meaning, with this denotation being so potent that one assumes the "age of the sign is essentially theological" in that the birth of the sign is the birth of divinity.[11] Consequently, no language ever escapes the "theological" intimation that one might overcome linguistic uncertainty without remainder and, in doing so, distinguish the indubitability of some discrete meaning.

Second, since Derrida does not embrace the notion of a "transcendental signified," he must maintain the reality of hermeneutics as always open to risk, specifically, the risk of misinterpretation. In other words, a residual uncertainty qualifies every interpretation to the point that the interpreter should avoid the arrogance of believing that misinterpretation may not occur. It always may. Derrida believes that this hermeneutical risk characterizes all language, which means that uncertainty, the suspicion of the negative, and the "essential" weakness of discourse to capture meaning

---

10. Ricœur, *Critique and Conviction*, 47.
11. Derrida, *Of Grammatology*, 13–4, 20; Derrida, *Writing and Difference*, 280–81.

absolutely culminate in a quality inherent in all signs, symbols, and texts quite similar to traditional "negative theology."[12] Negative, or apophatic, theology emerges from the belief that the transcendence and alterity of God are such that human beings can never comprehend the divine character or never be absolutely certain that their theological interpretations are valid or true. In other words, in every theological claim about God, there always remains a residue of systemic non-knowing, a negativity that can never be canceled, which frustrates every attempt to know God clearly and with certainty. Yet, Derrida does not reduce this negative understanding of language just to the overtly theological. He argues that, even in the most secular and anti-religious text, a residual negative theology operates, precisely because no language ever totally encompasses either the world or meaning.[13] Furthermore, he contends that no one can escape these limitations, since language always starts "without us, in us and before us." He continues, "This is what theology calls God, and it is necessary, it will have been necessary, to speak."[14] This necessity, "*il faut*" in French, literally means "lack" or that which is "wanting."[15] Consequently, for Derrida, it is another expression of the apophatic that haunts every oral and written communication, thereby affirming, yet again, that hermeneutics and theology endure in an interpretive entanglement.

UNDECIDABILITY AND THE HERMENEUTICAL RISK

In the contemporary context, John D. Caputo and Richard Kearney are two of the most prolific and creative thinkers who attempt to annotate the interpretive entanglement expressed by Ricœur and Derrida. Their various hypotheses regarding comprehending and appropriating meaning inherent within religious and theological texts and traditions represent some of the most provocative and penetrating explorations into how to recover the "sacred" and the "divine" in a post-metaphysical world, a world in which religion and God are often diminished, ignored, or attacked as objects of quaint, superstitious, or irrational beliefs. Of course, Caputo and Kearney most definitely embrace much of the modern suspicion of divine transcendence and certainly do not wish to resurrect the dogmatic and obscurantist doctrines of an earlier Christendom. Nevertheless, they also refuse to resign from the game and forfeit a victory to the cultured despisers of religion

12. Derrida, "How to Avoid Speaking," 76.
13. Derrida, *On the Name*, 69.
14. Derrida, "How to Avoid Speaking," 99.
15. Derrida, *On the Name*, 76.

who, in ghettoizing sanctity and hermeneutical subtlety, fail to realize the ethical and social implications of interpreting what appears to be a tenacious "mystical element" in existence, an element that cannot be understood reductively through the structures of logic or science. Consequently, both thinkers choose to establish variant hermeneutical approaches that affirm science and critical historiography, yet without simultaneously affirming those approaches as totalized or absolute in their interpretations.

Even a succinct survey of Caputo's and Kearney's various hermeneutical theologies will indicate profound and productive similarities between their analyses, while also noting a few areas where they significantly disagree. Indeed, one of the legislating similarities between the two involves their shared infatuation with God. Caputo claims that Kearney is "a man filled with God, driven by a passion for God"; yet, so, too, is Caputo. Both men are consumed with *le désir de Dieu* ("the desire for God"), something of an Augustinian restlessness or obsession to discover God.[16] Caputo alleges that Kearney's "diacritical hermeneutics" and his own "radical hermeneutics" present two paths that constantly converge before eventually diverging into two different destinations, likening their work to the transcontinental railroad that was begun at two different ends and finally connected in the middle.[17] Kearney certainly concurs with this correlation of their hermeneutics, referring to Caputo as "the archi-evangelist of American deconstruction," who is today "more prolific, provoking, inspiring, and engaging than ever."[18] He admits to the preponderance of agreement over disagreement throughout the broader extent of their theories and identifies that tension as a mark of good dialogue, insisting that their difference "may be one of emphasis rather than of kind" and most often "appears to be no more than a hairline nuance."[19]

Caputo adopts as an axiom of his radical hermeneutics the principle that "interpretation goes all the way down, to the root," which, of course, explains why he refers to his hermeneutics as radical (*radix*, "root"), as a hermeneutics consistently acknowledging that one never escapes the necessity for interpretation because that necessity is rooted in the very structures of human existence.[20] On the one hand, this rootedness illustrates the finitude of life, the reality that human beings are not God and cannot attain total knowledge and absolute certainty. Søren Kierkegaard famously made this

---

16. Caputo, "Kearney's Enthusiasm," 309.
17. Caputo, "Diacritical Hermeneutics," 57.
18. Kearney, "Game of Jacks," 570.
19. Kearney, "Kingdom," 129.
20. Caputo, "Where Is Richard Kearney," 561.

exact point when he declared that existence cannot be a system for humans, precisely because individuals can never pull themselves out of space and time in order to reach an Archimedean point from which they can transparently survey every aspect of reality.[21] This in turn requires that every human decision occurs within the context of a functional non-knowing, that is, depends upon a "leap of faith" that cannot be secured as relying on an unshakable foundation. On the other hand, given this lack of potential closure to the process of interpretation, radical hermeneutics constantly adopts a critical attitude toward every prescribed meaning or explanation offered by any person or community. In other words, taking the movement of understanding to its roots results in accepting the difficulty of life, of realizing that one lives consistently in a state of "fear and trembling." Caputo clearly testifies that one cannot avoid an element of mystery or non-knowing in every claim to know and that that unavoidable "coefficient of uncertainty" empowers a perpetual commitment to critique and suspicion.[22]

Kearney, too, insists that the risk of uncertainty qualifies every act of interpretation and does so by using the same linguistic imagery as Caputo, stating that interpretation "goes all the way down. Nothing is exempt."[23] Not surprisingly, therefore, Kearney considers the concept of the "wager" to be an essential trait of every hermeneutics since one must constantly risk taking a leap of faith and anticipating the validity of any interpretive conclusion.[24] He predicates that risk on what he calls "negative capability," a phrase he borrows from John Keats.[25] The phrase translates the idea of non-knowing or Derrida's emphasis on negative theology or Kierkegaard's idea of fear and trembling. One might even connect it to both Ricœur's premise that one's first approach to any text relies on making a preliminary guess as to its meaning[26] and also his *de jure* statement that one must choose between hermeneutics or absolute knowledge, since the former cannot supply the latter and the latter cannot be attained through the former.[27] Kearney clearly concurs here with Ricœur when he concedes that "the absolute can never be understood *absolutely* by any single person or religion."[28]

---

21. Kierkegaard, *Fear and Trembling*, 7.
22. Caputo, *On Religion*, 20.
23. Kearney, *Anatheism*, xv.
24. Kearney, *Anatheism*, 81.
25. Kearney, "Across Oceans," 324–25.
26. Ricœur, "Hermeneutics and the Human Sciences," 137.
27. Ricœur, *Essays on Biblical Hermeneutics*, 153.
28. Kearney, *Anatheism*, 16.

Now Caputo adds to the above discussion one of the most common and most crucial concepts for summarizing the inherent risk that constitutes hermeneutics, the Derridean concept of "undecidability." That concept absorbs both Derrida's concern about premature claims that absolute meaning has been established ("transcendental signified") as well as his concern that one might refuse to accede to the negative theological trait qualifying all language. Yet, Caputo persistently warns that one should never confuse undecidability with indecisiveness, a confusion that occurs far too often among readers of both Derrida and Caputo. Indeed, for several years, Caputo accused Kearney of just such a confusion, designating that misreading as one of the primary differences between their theories.[29] That accusation did genuinely once have merit, but not any longer,[30] because Kearney has now recognized undecidability to be as Caputo claims, the "*condition of possibility* of a decision."[31] Without undecidability, no decision would be activated, at least not in the genuine sense of that term. Deciding means to deliberate among alternatives, to confront the uncertainties of conclusions, or, one might say, to take the Kierkegaardian leap of faith. If one did not have to do make these moves, then a choice would not be a choice but a necessity, since the outcome could be programmed and predicted merely by using some objective algorithm. In other words, the "decision" would be programmed, would ensue as the simple output of a coded system that worked mathematically toward a foregone position or action.[32] Both Caputo and Kearney reject that possibility precisely on hermeneutical grounds, since, again, all attempts to comprehend existence must occur within the ambiguities of finite experience and the promise of language. That situation accounts for the inescapable anxiety of cognitive dissonance, which incites the question "have I made the correct decision or not?" That uncertainty means that I can never—never—be absolutely sure, because decision depends on hermeneutics and hermeneutics depends on the potentiality for misinterpretation and on the reality that one can never exhaust the implications of meaning.

INTERPRETING A GOD WHO PERHAPS MAY BE

Of course, given the discussion above, one must ask the obvious questions: How then am I to proceed? Upon what exactly must I rely in the insecure,

---

29. Caputo, "Abyssus Abyssum Invocat," 123–24.
30. Kearney, *Strangers, Gods, and Monsters*, 201.
31. Caputo, "Where Is Richard Kearney," 562.
32. Kearney and Caputo, "Anatheism and Radical Hermeneutics," 215.

finite, hermeneutical contexts in which all of life takes place? Apparently, one must rely on the leap of faith. "Faith" becomes the only recourse, with "only" not being taken in a reductive or Stoic sense of "relenting." Faith is not settling on a response; it is not a subordinate or depleted acquiescence. For both Caputo and Kearney, it is, instead, a passion, a significant commitment to remaining open to the future of productive meaning, a hoping against hope that something new, unexpected, and, yes, even impossible may happen. Yet, this relationship between undecidability and faith intensifies the strong bond between hermeneutics and religion. Most assuredly, the passion for trusting in the possibility of the impossible as a source of possible meaning and purpose not yet fully known, not even imaginatively conceivable, motivates one to maintain a certain hospitality toward the future, an openness to unending questions, expectations, and dissatisfactions with the *status quo*. For Caputo, that passion may be expressed as a love for God, which means, of course, that one can never separate theology and hermeneutics.[33] For Kearney, that passion may be expressed as an eschatological hope predicated upon the lure of a loving God—which means, of course, that one can never separate theology and hermeneutics![34] Yet, one must never ignore the hermeneutical inevitability of "fear and trembling," since every exercise of faith reveals again and again the risk, the mystery, and the lack of assurance that faith portends. Indeed, if those mysteries did not remain, then faith would be knowledge and not faith. Consequently, hermeneutics disallows the believer any absolute certainty that the hope subsisting within faith will be fulfilled. It might, but then again, it might not. Faith and hope could lead to a redemptive end, but maybe not. There are no guarantees that one can genuinely rise above a consistent hermeneutical "maybe."

Not surprisingly, Caputo confesses that since his radical hermeneutics concedes to the obligatory "maybe," it must lead to a theology of the "perhaps," with "perhaps" acting as a synonym for the risk, undecidability, and apophatic nature of language and comprehension—or one might say, as a synonym for "maybe."[35] In his most recent work, *Specters of God*, he has a brief section entitled "A Theology of Perhaps," in which he claims that when we reference the name of God, we reference something unconditional, something that does not exist as a literal being and, therefore, cannot be properly understood in literal terms through scientific or mathematically logical discourse. Instead, God must be approached poetically through the

---

33. Caputo, "Possibility of the Impossible," 144–45.
34. Kearney, *God Who May Be*, 37; Kearney, *Poétique du Possible*, 229.
35. Caputo, "Diacritical Hermeneutics of God," 57.

dynamics of symbols, parables, metaphors, and linguistic/artistic representations.[36] As a result, theological hermeneutics must be a hermeneutics of the poetic. Furthermore, he asserts that "a poetics is always a grammar of the 'perhaps,' which is the prime modality of the event."[37] Consequently, Caputo claims that interpreting God within the context of a theopoetics seeks to avoid the various traditions of metaphysical theology with their confusion of God and Being and focus on a more radical theology of the event, with "event" denoting an unprogrammed breaking out (*e-venire*) of an unexpected occurrence.[38]

Since one cannot directly experience the event as a mere happening in some phenomenological manner, it intimates the non-knowing mystery that cannot be confined within the conceptual idolatry of discrete concepts or disclosed unambiguously in existential or historical occurrences. This means that one can never claim to have identified a discrete referent to the name of "God." Instead, the name of "God," which remains open to constant substitution and affected by the undecidability between the constructive and the deconstructive, effects a "messianic" attitude of aspiration toward what is "to come."[39] Of course, what is "to come" may be a deliverance or a disaster. As one struggles again with the risk of interpretation and hopes against hope for a redemptive meaning, one concludes that the name of "God" operates in every current context as an interruptive and constructive critique of the *status quo* and as the reminder that one can never transcend the coefficient of uncertainty infecting the desire to know, which, of course, leads inevitably back to faith.

Still, questions remain. For example, if one has faith, in what or whom does one trust? Does one simply have faith without some object as if confidence and expectation were devoid of intentionality, that is, lacking an object of the preposition—confidence *in* ___ or expectation *of* ___? Does Caputo's "God" of the perhaps, his apophatic "deity" that never escapes the limitations of negative theology while ostensibly intervening in reality as a disruptive, messianic dynamic, genuinely "exist" in any sense of that term? When Caputo asks, "What do I love when I love my God?," what answer does he find most believable and most therapeutic?[40] Well, that answer must certainly not pander to metaphysics and fuse or confuse "God" with Being or a being. In other words, Caputo insists that one should not refer to God

---

36. Caputo, *Specters of God*, 255–58; Caputo, *Folly of God*, 104.
37. Caputo, *Weakness of God*, 105.
38. Caputo, *Weakness of God*, 3–6.
39. Caputo, *Deconstruction in a Nutshell*, 156.
40. Caputo, *On Religion*, 6.

as "existing." Instead, he insists that one should speak about the "insistence" of God, of God as "insisting" in reality as a call, a summons to hospitality, to love, to justice, to concern for those that Jesus called the "least of these."[41] Caputo, therefore, loves a God who does not coerce or dominate, a God who does not possess omnipotence or magically manipulates reality, but a God who is immanent in the world as the lure of an invocation to individuals, summoning them to acts of mercy and justice. He loves a God that one does not explicitly pray *to* but prays *for* or prays *that* in the sense that one yearns for God's insistence to become incarnate within the structures of existence; that is, one prays for God to become immanent in the world, prays that there will be a God "acting" redemptively and ethically. Surprisingly, Caputo proclaims that such a God also prays, yearning to become active in denouncing oppression, hatred, and injustice.[42] This means that Caputo rejects any interpretation of God "as some super-being who out-knows, out-wills, out-does, out-powers, and out-exists every entity here below."[43] On the contrary, Caputo's God does not exist; there is no God there. God only insists as that tenacious and mysterious call to love the neighbor and the enemy, and the insisting God only exists when human beings respond to that call. There is no God but the God that enters history through the ethical acts of hospitality and mercy committed by people who seek to instantiate God and God's kingdom as an alternative reality and moral hermeneutics over against the oppressive and uncaring institutions of the world and their dehumanizing hermeneutics. Of course, that means for Caputo that God's "presence" may or may not appear. People may refuse to respond to the divine call or may simply fail to transcend the socio-political impotence that forbids them from transforming oppressive networks. Those potentialities stimulate the question "will God be revealed in reality?" The answer must always remain, "perhaps, but perhaps not."

Kearney would agree with much of Caputo's radical theology detailed above. Although he certainly does not want to detach theology completely from categories of Being, he refuses to promote the traditional metaphysical approach of classical theism in which God acts as a hyper-being with total sovereign control of every aspect of reality. Instead, he, likewise, embraces a theopoetic perspective to interpretation and concludes that the proper manner for doing theology depends fundamentally on the creative categories of symbols, metaphors, and narratives, along with the imaginative potential

---

41. Caputo, *Insistence of God*, 15–16.
42. Caputo, *Insistence of God*, 31–33.
43. Caputo, *Weakness of God*, 39.

inherent in the visual arts, dance, and music.[44] In other words, although Kearney functionally adheres to the death of the metaphysical God, he does not conclude that one can no longer acknowledge the veracity of faith in a reinterpreted God. Indeed, Kearney confesses that he promotes a passionate hermeneutical return to God through interpreting a poetic God that comes "after" one renounces interpretations of the metaphysical God. He denotes this "after" perspective with the Greek word "ana," a concept that means "after" or "again." He confesses that the term requires that one endeavors to "do" God through a process of "retrieving, revisiting, reiterating, [and] repeating."[45] He seeks to come back to the God who remains after the God of metaphysics has been abandoned. This "after" God enjoins an "after" faith, a reinterpretation of what it means to believe, a faith that comes after the propositional, rationalistic faith one so often discovers in fundamentalist, dogmatic, and categorically orthodox hermeneutics.

Kearney condenses "after" God and "after" faith in the term "anatheism," which practically depends on Paul Ricœur's notion of the "second naivete."[46] Ricœur contends the faith must sustain a critical motif, that is, never separate itself from some creatively analytical expression of doubt. When one investigates faith critically, one always encounters the efficacy of risk or the redemptive dynamic of questioning. Such an analytical viewpoint effects a deconstructive phase that clears the space for a reexamination and rearticulation of faith. Obviously, it can also produce a loss of faith, actually convince "believers" of the invalidity of their doctrine; however, that is never a necessary outcome of the process. The deconstructive phase may well ensue in a deeper and more convincing faith by establishing a renewed commitment to God under a different set of hermeneutical conclusions. Again, Ricœur calls this faith after faith a "second naivete," and this phrase is precisely equivalent to Kearney's idea of anatheism. Yet, anatheism cannot be reduced to just another doctrinaire interpretation of God and faith. On the contrary, anatheism may well establish a belief in God without God, since Kearney confesses that "God" may be synonymized by other names, such as "mystery," "depth," or "ultimate meaning."[47] One may well be a traditional atheist and still be an anatheist, if one adheres to the primary "sacred" morality that Kearney believes "names" his God after God, a morality

---

44. Cf. Kearney and Clemente, *Art of Anatheism*.
45. Kearney and Zimmerman, *Reimagining the Sacred*, 8.
46. Kearney, "Epiphanies of the Everyday," 7.
47. Van Troostwijk and Clemente, *Richard Kearney's Anatheistic Wager*, 64.

inclusive of hospitality, a concern for "widows and orphans," and a desire for *agape* as divine love.[48]

Even so, how should an anatheist, especially a theistic anatheist, interpret God after the traditional God of metaphysics has been relinquished? Not surprisingly, Kearney responds biblically by giving a distinctive reading to Exod 3:14, the verse that became the foundation for the confusion of God and Being. When God tells Moses that "I am who I am," does God not confirm beyond doubt that the divine and the ground of Being are indistinguishable? Kearney responds with an emphatic "No," because he translates God's self-disclosure in the future tense as "I will be who I will be."[49] That translation leads him to interpret God as a "God who may be," a God who will be "God" but only in the future, only after engaging relationally with human beings. The God "who may be" calls to humanity, as God did to Moses, and summons them to a life of *imago Dei*, to a life lived in the "image of God," which is an image of love, grace, and hospitality to the stranger. Only if and when humans respond to God affirmatively, accept their sabbatical vocation to join God in the evolving creation of the world, will there be a chance that God will be who God desires to be.[50]

Naturally, humans may not always respond appropriately, thereby leaving God chronically vulnerable to not becoming who God yearns to be. God, therefore, may be the God who may *not* be who God envisions God to be. Stated otherwise, one could claim that such a God may be—but only maybe. That "maybe" signals something quite profound and quite complementary to Caputo's theology of the perhaps. Since "maybe" is a synonym for "perhaps," Kearney's anatheistic hermeneutic of faith echoes Caputo's radical hermeneutic of faith and, accordingly, testifies to the possibility that God, as a God of the perhaps, will perhaps be God. Perhaps there will have been a God in some future perfect "future," some eschatological, messianic "to come."[51] But maybe not, perhaps not. One can never evade the risk or the need for faith and hope. One may always be after God, perhaps, and after a God of the perhaps. Strictly speaking, however, one cannot elude hermeneutics and claim shelter in the absolute. For this reason, in both hermeneutics and theology, one continually walks in faith and not by sight, in uncertainty and not by the absolute.

---

48. Kearney, *Anatheism*, 48; Kearney, *Poétique du Possible*, 240.
49. Kearney, *God Who May Be*, 22, 38.
50. Kearney, *Wake of the Imagination*, 50.
51. Caputo, *Cross and Cosmos*, 272.

BIBLIOGRAPHY

Brown, Norman Oliver. *Hermes The Thief: The Evolution of a Myth*. Spain: Barakaldo, 2022.

Caputo, John D. "Abyssus Abyssum Invocat: A Response to Kearney." In *A Passion for the Impossible: John D. Caputo in Focus*, edited by Mark Dooley, 123–27. New York: State University of New York Press, 2003.

———. *Cross and Cosmos: A Theology of Difficult Glory*. Bloomington: Indiana University Press 2019.

———. *Deconstruction in a Nutshell: A Conversation with Jacques Derrida*. New York: Fordham University Press, 1997.

———. *The Folly of God: A Theology of the Unconditional*. Salem, OR: Polebridge, 2016.

———. "God, Perhaps: The Diacritical Hermeneutics of God in the Work of Richard Kearney." *Philosophy Today* 55 Supplement (2011) 56–64.

———. *The Insistence of God: A Theology of Perhaps*. Bloomington: Indiana University Press, 2013.

———. *On Religion*. 2nd ed. New York: Routledge, 2019.

———. "The Possibility of the Impossible: A Response to Kearney." In *Cross and Khôra: Deconstruction and Christianity in the Work of John D. Caputo*, edited by Marko Zlomislić and Neal DeRoo, 140–50. Eugene, OR: Pickwick, 2010.

———. "Richard Kearney's Enthusiasm." In *After God: Richard Kearney and theReligious Turn in Continental Philosophy*, ed. John Panteleimon Manoussakis. NewYork: Fordham University Press, 2006.

———. *Specters of God: An Anatomy of the Apophatic Imagination*. Bloomington: Indiana University Press, 2022.

———. *The Weakness of God: A Theology of the Event*. Bloomington: Indiana University Press, 2006.

———. "Where is Richard Kearney Coming From? Hospitality, Anatheism, and Ana-deconstruction." *Philosophy and Social Criticism* 47.5 (2021).

Derrida, Jacques. "How to Avoid Speaking: Denials." In *Derrida and Negative Theology*, edited by Harold Coward and Toby Foshay, 73–142. Albany: State University of New York Press, 1992.

———. *Of Grammatology*. Translated by Gayatri Chakravorty Spivak. Baltimore: Johns Hopkins University Press, 1976.

———. *On the Name*. Translated by David Wood et al. Stanford: Stanford University Press, 1995.

———. *Writing and Difference*. Translated by Alan Bass. Chicago: University of ChicagoPress, 1978.

Fry, Stephen. *Mythos: The Greek Myths Reimagined*. San Francisco: Chronicle, 2019.

Gadamer, Hans-Georg. *Philosophical Hermeneutics*. Translated and edited by David E. Lange. Berkeley: University of California Press, 1977.

———. *Truth and Method*. New York: Crossroads Publishing Company, 1982.

Kearney, Richard. "Across Oceans: A Conversation on Otherness, Hospitality and Welcoming a Strange God." In *Debating Otherness with Richard Kearney: Perspectives from South Africa*, edited by Daniël P. Veldsman and Yolande Steenkamp, 307–42. Cape Town, SA: Aosis, 2018.

———. *Anatheism: Returning to God After God*. New York: Columbia University Press, 2010.

———. "Epiphanies of the Everyday: Toward a Micro-Eschatology." In *After God: Richard Kearney and the Religious Turn in Continental Philosophy*, edited by John Panteleimon Manoussakis, 3–20. New York: Fordham University Press, 2006.

———. "A Game of Jacks: Review Essay of John D. Caputo's Recent Works." *Philosophy Today* 55 Supplement (2011) 570–86.

———. *The God Who May Be: A Hermeneutic of Religion*. Bloomington: Indiana University Press, 2001.

———. "The Kingdom: Possible and Impossible." In *Cross and Khôra: Deconstruction and Christianity in the Work of John D. Caputo*, edited by Marko Zlomislić and Neal DeRoo, 118–39. Eugene, OR: Pickwick, 2010.

———. *Poétique Du Possible: Phénoménologie Herméneutique de la Figuration*. Paris: Beauchesne, 1984.

———. *Strangers, Gods, and Monsters: Ideas of Otherness*. New York: Routledge, 2002.

———. *The Wake of Imagination: Toward a Postmodern Culture*. London: Routledge, 1994.

Kearney, Richard, and John D. Caputo. "Anatheism and Radical Hermeneutics: Dialogue With John D. Caputo." In *Reimagining the Sacred: Richard Kearney Debates God*, edited by Richard Kearney and Jens Zimmerman, 193–218. New York: Columbia University Press, 2016.

Kearney, Richard, and Matthew Clemente, eds. *The Art of Anatheism*. London: Rowman &Littlefield, 2018.

Kearney, Richard, and Jens Zimmerman, eds. *Reimagining the Sacred: Richard Kearney Debates God*. New York: Columbia University Press, 2016.

Kierkegaard, Søren. *Fear and Trembling/Repetition*. Edited and translated by Howard V. Hong and Edna H. Hong. Princeton: Princeton University Press, 1983.

Palmer, Richard E. *Hermeneutics*. Evanston: Northwestern University Press, 1969.

Ricœur, Paul. *Critique and Conviction: Conversations with François Azouvi and Marc de Launay*. Translated by Kathleen Blamey. New York: Columbia University Press, 1998.

———. *Essays on Biblical Interpretation*. Edited by Lewis S. Mudge. Philadelphia: Fortress, 1980.

———. *Figuring the Sacred: Religion, Narrative, and Imagination*. Translated by David Pellauer and edited by Mark I. Wallace. Minneapolis: Fortress, 1995.

———. *Hermeneutics and the Human Sciences: Essays on Language, Action, andInterpretation*. Edited and translated by John B. Thompson. New York: Cambridge University Press, 1981.

Shipley, Joseph T. *The Origins of English Words: A Discursive Dictionary of Indo-European Roots*. Baltimore: Johns Hopkins University Press, 1984.

Tracy, David. *Plurality and Ambiguity: Hermeneutics, Religion, Hope*. San Francisco: Harper &Row, 1987.

Van Troostwijk, et al., eds. *Richard Kearney's Anatheistic Wager: Philosophy, Theology, Poetics*. Bloomington: Indiana University Press, 2018.

Chapter 8
Convictional Hermeneutics
James K. A. Smith on the "Logic of Incarnation"
FRED P. EDIE

James K. A. Smith is a prolific scholar of religion and an influential voice in postconservative circles. He is sometimes described as a "hermeneuticist" not only for his careful interpretation of various streams of thought but also because he offers an account featuring *interpretation itself* as the fulcrum of human existence. His take on interpretation follows what he calls the "logic of incarnation" wherein he proposes to make space again for transcendence in a modern world flattened to immanence and also to celebrate (not lament) multiple and multivalent interpretations of texts, persons, and Christian life as gifts from the God who "loves difference and loves differently."[1] Smith, who answers to professional descriptions of "philosopher of religion" and "philosophical theologian," names a variety of diverse formational influences upon his scholarly vocation and Christian character. These include strict (even fundamentalist) Protestantism, graduate level studies and teaching in Roman Catholic institutions, participation and ministerial leadership within faith communities including Pentecostal ones, and a long and happy tenure at Calvin University, a Reformed institution with ties to Dutch-flavored Calvinism. Perhaps due to this breadth of formation, Smith's scholarly projects range equally far and wide, crossing disciplinary borders with the speed and ease of a EurRail bullet train. This chapter attends to Smith's phenomenological analysis of religion[2] while also

1. Smith, *Fall of Interpretation*, 2012, 20.
2. Phenomenology seeks to understand human experience as it unfolds in all its

showing his efforts to transform it by introducing Christian theology to the conversation. In addition, it seeks to highlight how, to the great benefit of the church, Smith is no less passionately devoted to "translation scholarship" including attention to the practices of worship and discipleship formation in faith communities all while discerning the cultural impacts of technology, secularism, and consumerist capitalism upon Christian life.[3]

THE DESCENT TO MODERNITY

Imagine viewing three framed paintings of the same scene (say, a wind and wave-swept coastal headland), one by a premodern artist, the other by a modernist, and the third whose painter is influenced by postmodernism. If observers from these different eras were to gather and view these three paintings side by side, they might recognize that they envisage the same scene, each one depicting elements of water, rock, wind and sky. Upon closer inspection, however, viewers will also perceive subtle (or radical!) dissimilarities. For example, the artists may highlight some features of the scene and mute others; each may make different use of color, light, and perspective. Further, each painting is likely to employ its technique and style to signal underlying meanings—the artists' intimations of reality, value, purpose, truth and more—themselves indicative of a host of underlying philosophical (and, as Smith will demonstrate, *theological*) assumptions shaping their respective eras. Assuming that the artists and their viewers from the different periods could conceive of the paintings unfamiliar to them as *art*, they might still argue vigorously over them. How would they decide which painting is most "true" to the scene, for example? (At play here is the philosophical concern called "epistemology," or knowledge pertaining to truth.) Which painting best depicts reality? (This is the question of "ontology," the dimensions of existence.) And which capacities should viewers of the paintings call upon—their visual senses, imaginations, minds, hearts, or souls—to make sense of them? (Here philosophy considers the issue of "anthropology," what makes humans *human* and how they engage the world.) Making matters even more complicated, these differing conceptions of epistemology, ontology, and anthropology are entrenched in differing cultural practices and "social imaginaries," ways of imagining so deeply internalized by members of a culture that they find them difficult to consciously identify,

---

complexity. As a branch of philosophy, it is less interested in thinking and reflecting upon ideas and more concerned with pre-theoretical, moment to moment, lived experience as a driver of human existence.

3. Smith, *Nicene Option*, 7. See paragraph two for a list of translational titles.

articulate, or even summon to awareness.[4] Because of their immersion in premodern, modern, or postmodern imaginaries, viewers of the paintings may not even be able put a finger on the dissonance their experience of the unfamiliar paintings evokes.

Throughout his writings, Smith effectively brings the contrasting and conflicting assumptions of these three eras to light, this for the purpose of critiquing modern sensibilities and proposing alternatives (both pre- and postmodern) he deems more suitable.[5] As readers know, "Modernity" is the name for an historical era in the west beginning, depending upon whom you ask, somewhere between the thirteenth and sixteenth centuries. It featured the emergence of nation states, gradual (and limited) political shifts from imperial rule to democracy, and the transition from rural, agricultural economies to urban, industrial ones. Of primary interest for this chapter, modernity also describes an intellectual sensibility and a social imaginary characterized by unique takes on the aforementioned philosophical categories. Smith highlights three features of modernism:

An ontological shift to "immanent" reality framed within the limits of human experience and knowledge and to the exclusion of premodern belief in transcendence, wherein reality is understood to participate in and depend upon the transcendent realm.[6]

An epistemological emphasis upon self-justifying reason and the "facts" of scientific evidence for establishing truth in the form of "ideas" in place of faith, pre-rational belief and trust, originating beyond and surpassing what humans could know through their own efforts.

An anthropological portrait of human beings as disembodied, self-constructing, wholly rational, self-interested thinkers replacing the premodern portrait of persons as embodied, relational, and practicing creatures compelled by their desires to love others including God.

Modernism holds important implications for Smith's account of the meaning and status of hermeneutics (the art or science of interpretation). First, in contrast to pre-modernity where knowledge is received as a gift from a transcendent source, moderns imagine themselves as its exclusive creators. This stance sets the stage for the rejection of dependence upon or even consideration of transcendence and leaving only flat immanence,

---

4. According to Charles Taylor, a social imaginary is "the way ordinary people 'imagine' their social surroundings," less in "theoretical terms" and more often "carried in images, stories, and legends, etc." See *Secular Age*, 171–72.

5. Smith emphasizes that the relations between pre-modernity, modernity, and postmodernity include continuity as well as discontinuity. However, he often criticizes postmodern scholarship for not sufficiently distancing itself from modern assumptions.

6. Smith, *Introducing Radical Orthodoxy*, 87–122.

a "what you see is what you get" depiction of being in the world. Second, modernity imagines truthful knowledge to be universalizable, freed from contextual limits and biases. Pre-modern *stories* purporting to explain how the leopard got its spots or, for that matter, how a dusty, provincial Jew saves the world ring too fanciful (unscientific) and idiosyncratic (not rationally universalizable) to sound truth to modern ears. Modernity insists its knowledge be distilled from all that cultural baggage: folkways may work for folks; traditions for traditionalists, or religion for religionists; but science and reason work for everyone, everywhere, every time. Modern knowing purports to free us from fancy and to deliver the fullness of reality. Third, because the modern knowledge regime built by science and reason represents itself as unbiased, objective, and comprehensive in its knowing, it insinuates deliverance from the need for interpretation. Reason and science deliver full and immediate access to reality is it *really* is. Fourth, even as modernity promised blue sky transparency—limitless unmediated knowing in a world of entirely fathomable immanence—it stealthily eliminated from consideration what it was incapable of seeing or preferred not to fathom. In addition to ruling out transcendence, modernity eliminated from consideration extra-rational dimensions of human experience—aesthetic wonder, desires of the heart, embodied habits—that might otherwise have disclosed a mysterious and beckoning surplus, an ontology and epistemology stretching beyond the filters of reductive modern accounts.

POSTMODERN CORRECTIVES TO MODERNITY

This brief trip to Modernity Land positions us to appreciate Smith's constructive philosophical and theological dialogue with postmodern thought in light of its (and Smith's) efforts to see a way past the pitfalls of modernity. In this effort, Smith offers a mostly appreciative "*two* cheers for postmodernism"[7] for its re-assertion of much of what modernity had banished: the possibility of transcendence, the significance of human embodiment for being and knowing, and the appreciation for difference over universality including the irreducible situatedness of human experience of the world. All of this supports his wider project to establish the constitutive nature of interpretation at the heart of human existence.

Smith is aware that continental philosophy with its "deconstructive" tag has not conducted effective public relations especially in North America. It is blamed for everything from the death of God to relentless relativism; hence Smith's careful translation of this scholarship and its claims to a

---

7. Smith, *Nicene Option*, 65.

skeptical audience. With each conversation partner, he shows how continental scholars "deconstruct" a pillar of modernity which Smith then cheers (modestly and not without critique) for the possibilities it opens.

LYOTARD ON METANARRATIVES

Jean-Francois Lyotard, to the extent that he is known across the Global North, is feared as the wrecker of "metanarratives," grand stories purporting to provide exhaustive accounts of reality. At first glance, Christians would seem to have just cause to be alarmed, for whose narrative could be more "meta" than one claiming to account for everything from the origin of the cosmos to its final consummation? But Smith points out that Lyotard's target isn't religious or cultural stories so much as totalizing modern accounts (sociobiology, for example) claiming, as we've seen, to be self-justifying through "appeals to universal reason."[8] Lyotard is especially vexed by modernist failures to recognize that its science, reason, technical rationalism, etc. are, in fact, *stories themselves*—elaborate just-so stories whose explanatory power depends upon both the specific contextual niches from which they emerge and faith in their epistemic premises.[9] By drawing back the curtain on science/reason's overreach to universality, Lyotard gives Smith reasons to cheer. First, scientific claims to epistemological omniscience are tempered, and second, a leveling space is opened where other stories (including the Christian story) with its alternative claims to reality, truth, and human purpose (rooted in *love* more than simplistic facts) may present their visions without apology.

FOUCAULT ON THE FORMATIVE POWER OF PRACTICES

Michel Foucault, on the other hand, is recognized for his critical insight into the exercise of power in modern communities and institutions. He contends that whereas power was once enacted through external means—the fashioning of legal codes enforced by policing and punishment—modern power regimes discipline mostly through surveillance and repression. In gist, because power is embedded within the entire "disciplinary society," and not exercised exclusively at the city jail, all members of a society are formed into compliance—even with unjust regimes.[10] Foucault contends that these hidden dynamics can subvert the good intentions of helping institutions like schools and medical facilities, and, as Smith adds, congregations. With

---

8. Smith, *Who's Afraid of Postmodernism?*, 65.
9. Smith, *Who's Afraid of Postmodernism?*, 67.
10. Smith, *Who's Afraid of Postmodernism?*, 90.

regard to remedies, Foucault is pointedly less interested in reestablishing (modern) ideas or ideals of justice and focused instead upon excavating hidden institutional *practices* of disciplinary power. Smith accepts Foucault's critical insight into the discipline exercised through practices but, in place of an anti-institutional hermeneutics of suspicion, he urges the promotion of good institutions exercising their disciplinary power through just practices of hospitality, reconciliation, forgiveness, and peacemaking.

DERRIDA AND THE IMPACT OF CONTEXTS UPON KNOWING

Smith allows that Christians are also inclined to shudder at Jacques Derrida's declaration: "There is nothing outside the text."[11] Is he signaling there is no God behind the Bible? Will he drown us all in a sea of relativism? Can language (spoken or written) ever hope to point to any referent beyond itself? As with Lyotard and Foucault, Smith patiently seeks to disentangle the good Doctor D. from the monster of popular imagination. He explains that for Derrida "language is the necessary filter through which the world comes to us."[12] Put differently, Derrida is claiming that human beings don't possess direct, unmediated access to reality, they necessarily employ language to interpret their experience of it. What Derrida "really means" by "nothing outside the text," therefore, is "there is nothing outside of *context*."[13] Contrary to modern claims to universalizable knowledge, Derrida posits that humans are finite, linguistic beings situated in cultures and, therefore, are not afforded a pure, all-seeing view from nowhere. Instead, our takes on reality are housed in culturally mediated linguistic forms which we can't escape. So, for Smith, Derrida is not the postmodern Boogeyman permanently scaring off truth or transcendence. He is simply pointing out that truth claims are always clothed in hermeneutical garb. For humanity, truth is always interpreted truth, and interpretation goes all the way down.

SMITH'S HERMENEUTICAL KEY: THE LOGIC OF INCARNATION

Smith is appreciative of postmodern efforts to restore narratively-embedded ways of knowing, the formative efficacy of communal practices over the transmission of ideas, and the inevitability of interpretation as a constitutive feature of human life. Each of these sensibilities provides an antidote to modernism's assertions of universal, unmediated knowledge through

---

11. Smith, *Who's Afraid of Postmodernism?*, 21.
12. Smith, *Who's Afraid of Postmodernism?*, 34.
13. Derrida quoted in Smith, *Jacques Derrida*, 62.

science and reason and its false construal of humans as disembodied cognizing beings. In this section we seek to appreciate better Smith's contention that not only is hermeneutics inevitable, it is a divinely-given gift to finite, diverse creatures.

THE GOODNESS OF INTERPRETATION

I'm aware that this treatment of hermeneutics can appear to be so much abstraction. Allow me to illustrate what's at stake. My denomination, *United* Methodism, recently dis-united over issues related to human sexuality. Each side accused the other of false interpretations, including of Scripture. By all accounts, differing interpretations of reality and truth were not received as good gifts, they merely served to cast difference into stark opposition that dehumanized opponents, all of whom are baptized members of Christ's Body. It seems Professor Smith will need to unwrap this "gift" a bit more.

Smith traces his own awakening to the significance of interpretation to his college studies. There he discovered the biblical literalism of his upbringing could be compared and contrasted with, say, an Augustinian biblical interpretation or a Lutheran one. Smith traces the history of literalist (non-) interpretation of Scripture to scientific and rationalist threats to the credibility of religious belief. In response to these, some conservative nineteenth- and twentieth-century theologians promoted a vision of Edenic existence prior to the Fall as a space of immediate (unmediated) access to God's presence, power, and vision for their lives. They contended that Adam and Eve existed happily, transparently, *nakedly* in uninterrupted communion with God. As a result of their fall into sin, however, the original humans were forced out of the garden and away from God's immediate presence. Life that had been so good and so transparently full of meaning became muddled. It's at this point that interpretation makes its unfortunate entrance. Sinful human beings, no longer knowing God intimately, are consigned to trying to discern from a distance who God is and what God requires. But biblical literalists solve this problem (the problem of the fall to interpretation) by declaring that God's redemption in Christ restores clear-sighted immediacy. God-given insight to the (singular) meaning of Scripture spares fundamentalist readers from struggling to interpret it or the God who authors it; the redeemed simply read, understand, and live faithfully once again in Edenic immediacy—no interpretation required. In light of this stance, readers can appreciate how in the case of Methodist V. Methodist, where one party conceded its stance as an interpretation of Scripture while the other claimed its reading of the same yielded unmediated access to the divine will diminished prospects for reconciliation.

But Smith contends there's no such thing as direct access. He points out how decidedly *modern* fundamentalist claims to non-interpretation are in their promises to deliver the full, unvarnished truth just as science and reason claim to do. Equally problematic, he contends, this literalist "hermeneutic of immediacy" makes a theological mistake.[14] Citing Gen 1:31—God's declaration of the goodness of creation—Smith argues that creatureliness, by definition, entails *finitude* (only the Creator is beyond limit) and therefore insists that partial knowing requiring ongoing interpretation is not a consequence of fallenness but a "constitutive aspect of human existence . . . impossible to overcome (without our becoming gods)."[15] Further, this recognition of the ubiquity of interpretation means that multiple views will proliferate, even conflict with one another. Instead of despairing, however, Smith rejoices, declaring his hermeneutic "Pentecostal," that is, one that creates a "space where there is room for a plurality of God's creatures to speak, sing, and dance in a multivalent chorus of tongues."[16] For Smith, interpretation, including multivalent interpretation, including multivalent *biblical* interpretation, is a sustaining gift from God, a constitutively good feature of creaturely diversity.

Smith discovers a similar modernist version of hermeneutics as "fallen" operating covertly in continental philosophical hermeneutics. Derrida, for example, as a non-practicing Jew, would appear to have no dog in the fight over the hermeneutical consequences of a *theology* of creation and fall. Contrary to fundamentalists of all stripes, he readily allows that: "In the beginning is hermeneutics."[17] In other words, there is no aspect of our "experience—that interpretive way in which we navigate our being-in-the-world—that escapes the play of signifiers or the conditioning of difference."[18] But unlike Smith, Derrida does not feel blessed by this state of affairs, because, he states, interpretation can never fully overcome the "harsh law of spacing," the distance—the gap—between interpreter and the other being interpreted.[19] Language employed to interpret (to bridge that gap) therefore always partially *misinterprets*. Thus, to interpret is to do violence; to participate in the "fatal necessity of going astray" which falsely misconstrues the

---

14. Smith, *Fall of Interpretation*, 4.
15. Smith, *Fall of Interpretation*, 89–90.
16. Smith, *Fall of Interpretation*, 20.
17. Derrida quoted in Smith, *Fall of Interpretation*, 119.
18. Smith, *Jacques Derrida*, 44.
19. Derrida quoted in Smith, *Fall of Interpretation*, 124.

other.[20] For Derrida, this is an unavoidable state of affairs, not the result of a mythos of the fall, but an "original violence" that is a condition of existence.

Smith cheers Derrida's insistence that interpretation is a constitutive feature of human life, and, due to the law of spacing (the lack of immediacy), that it is never exhaustive, but rejects his conclusion that it is always, inevitably violent. Asking rhetorically whether the interpretive act of naming a child is a violent act, Smith suggests that Derrida has fallen back into modern philosophical wishful thinking for the immediacy of knowing. He says "only if one is looking for immediacy and full presence [will] the finitude of interpreting [be] considered a lack, a fall, an impurity."[21] Instead, Smith insists that "interpretation is not a violation of purity but rather a way of connection, a way of *being—with* that is essential to be(com)ing human. Rather than being the first violence, to be named is to be loved, is to be part of a community."[22]

INTERPRETATION AND RE-AWAKENING TO TRANSCENDENCE

Smith carries this concern for hermeneutics into phenomenological efforts to speak of God. Remember, Derrida's law of spacing presumes I don't have immediate or complete access to other persons, other cultures, or anything else I experience, which forces me to fill in the gap by way of belief-full interpretation. There are, for example, depths to my spouse I can't fathom (though her long-suffering is evident to all). Despite my interpretive efforts, she remains at least partly a stranger to me even after forty years. This strangeness eludes my power to fully know her; she *transcends* my experience of her. Yet even while I can't possibly circumscribe her mystery, "I *believe* [my spouse] to be an ego" who is there for me as I am for her.[23]

Smith welcomes these phenomenological baby steps toward transcendence but deems them insufficient because they fail to follow through, to "persist," in their postmodern impulses. Derrida, for example, voices his preference for a quintessentially modernist "religion without religion," and a "messianicity without messiah."[24] Why these generalizing qualifications? Readers will appreciate he is here seeking to avoid committing interpretive violence. He presumes that to name God in a particular fashion—"the God of Israel," for example—violates the condition of God's transcendence—for he assumes God must be above all names or otherwise fail to be

20. Derrida quoted in Smith, *Fall of Interpretation*, 123.
21. Smith, *Fall of Interpretation*, 133.
22. Smith, *Fall of Interpretation*, 133.
23. Smith, *Speech and Theology*, 24.
24. Smith, *Jacques Derrida*, 115.

transcendent. In addition, he is convinced that naming the "God of Israel" inexorably leads to naming those outside of Israel *godless*. This, in turn, subjects them to religious violence. Consider for a moment past and present Christian persecution of Jews and Muslims and you sense his point. Or consider my Methodists and me, people of "open hearts, open doors, open minds," casting aspersions upon one another in the name (of our particular interpretations) of God.

THE LOGIC OF INCARNATION

Smith counters, however, that in the effort to avoid the religious violence, Derrida has uncritically accepted modernity's erasure of context, particularity and difference which he has otherwise rightly insisted upon displaying in every other domain except for religion. Smith's constructive counterproposal is for a more "persistent postmodernism which relinquishes the very *requirements* of universality and purity as constitutive of knowledge . . . ."[25] Drawing upon Christian doctrine, he proposes a hermeneutics operating out of the "logic of incarnation, a kind of 'genius' given to thought by the Incarnation" and a way of speaking and conceiving that welcomes particularizing (religious) accounts of transcendence without succumbing to interpretive violence.[26]

Incarnation, as Christians know, is the dogmatic claim for Jesus as fully God and fully human—transcendent Divinity indwelling very particular, very immanent flesh—with neither humanity nor divinity subsumed by the other. For Smith, incarnation dignifies, even enchants, the ordinary stuff of humanity and, indeed, all of material existence. In addition, incarnation bears an iconic quality, pointing beyond itself to make "knowledge of transcendence possible."[27] Yet even as the transcendent God is incarnate in the Son, "the incarnation signals a connection with transcendence that "does not violate or reduce such transcendence, but neither does it leave it in a realm of utter alterity without appearance."[28]

We can immediately sense the potential in this logic for overcoming modern ontological divisions and dualisms. In place of the modern frame where transcendence and immanence are divided from each other or situated oppositionally and hierarchically with one dominating or denying the other, Smith proposes incarnation as the space "wherein the transcendent

---

25. Smith, *Nicene Option*, 68.
26. Smith, *Nicene Option*, 70.
27. Smith, *Speech and Theology*, 123.
28. Smith, *Speech and Theology*, 126.

inhabits the immanent without loss."[29] Put differently, through incarnation, transcendence may *participate* in immanence and vice-versa.[30] Contra modernism, through incarnation an indwelling, a sharing, and an overcoming of dualistic either/or divisions is possible.

Transcendence indwelling immanence "without loss" also addresses the postmodern concern to prevent interpretive violence. If incarnation is sufficiently capacious to welcome the dwelling of transcendence in immanence, it can certainly mingle the hermeneutically familiar together with the strange in peaceful communion. Incarnation, as it welcomes creaturely participation in transcendence without extinguishing transcendent mystery, bestows the gift of deep hermeneutical humility and unceasing interpretive charity. By simultaneously revealing and concealing, incarnation gently proposes, instead of a monological, reductionist, and potentially violent being and knowing, multiple and multivalent truthful interpretations bearing particular insights born of differing contexts for the good of particular peoples situated within specific historical eras and social locations.[31] In other words, if my Methodists and I were better formed into an incarnational hermeneutic, we might have imagined our denomination as opening a shared space to welcome diverse, even divergent, interpretations of human sexuality. Having escaped the (crumbling) modernist artifice pretending to pronounce absolute, singular, universal truth, we might have found the patience and hospitality to remain in communion with one another and to wonder (in the sense of *praise!*) at the difference in our midst.

TAKING INCARNATION TO CHURCH
INCARNATIONAL WORSHIP

If Incarnational hermeneutics is key to both philosophical and theological coherence, where and how may we hope to find it? How may we participate in transcendence-in-immanence? Smith's simple answer is to worship—though the longer one consumes at least four full books and parts of several others. Communal worship, for Smith, turns out to be a primary venue for the incarnate God to appear and to act and for human creatures to respond in praise, thanksgiving, and service. In turn, he contends, these creaturely doxologies—songs and signs and gestures of praise—con*form* persons ever more deeply to the likeness of the Three-in-One they laud. The manner of

---

29. Smith, *Radical Orthodoxy*, 226.

30. Smith, *Radical Orthodoxy*, 75.

31. Neither Smith nor even Derrida favors endlessly indeterminate interpretation. See Smith, *Jacques Derrida*, 63–64.

this formation is of special interest to Smith, because it contrasts with modern assumptions that the best way to make disciples requires filling them with Christian ideas. In contrast, Smith homes in on the formative efficacy of worshipful *practices*. His primary interest here is not only worship in a general sense but in *liturgies*, communal ritual enactments of the Christian Story repeated together over time. Smith supports his depiction of liturgical formation with a compelling philosophical anthropology both as means to explain why the modern account is wrong, and, constructively, how and why we humans are so susceptible to (or, perhaps better, *created for*) formation through liturgical practice.

Grounded in the principle of incarnation, Christian worship presumes to participate in transcendence made immanent. Worship focused upon the Father revealed in and through the Son by the power of the Spirit should, by definition, be deeply incarnational. But Smith rejects the notion that we encounter incarnation through concepts and definitions. Instead, incarnation first makes its way to us in a predictably incarnational manner—through our ways of worship. When we raise our God-given arms in praise or sink to our occasionally creaky knees in contrition, when we taste rich bread and wine, when we swim in baptismal waters, "behind and under this is a core conviction, an implicit understanding that God inhabits all this earthy stuff, that we meet God in [these] material realities . . . , that God embraces our embodiment, embraces *us* in our embodiment."[32] In other words, we learn incarnation by performing it; we acquire a "feel" for incarnation in our bodies, even our "guts" as we sacramentalize ordinary creaturely gestures, symbols and even ourselves—in these liturgical rites.

A PORTRAIT OF LITURGICAL ANIMALS

We will return to liturgical practices below, but, for now, we attend to Smith's anthropological "portrait" of human beings, creatures he describes as "liturgical animals"—created for and (re-)created through their worship.[33] How is this possible? Building upon the work of Martin Heidegger and Augustine, Smith's first answer is to suggest that we humans are fundamentally affective beings, "lovers" more than thinkers, who are beckoned, allured, and propelled through life by our desires.[34] Smith notes that even as these initial brushstrokes of portrait may seem strange, they are at least as old as Christianity. The "heart" appears in the Scriptures as the center of human value, character and motivation. Augustine famously confesses to a heart

---

32. Smith, *Desiring the Kingdom*, 140.
33. Smith, *Nicene Option*, 38.
34. Smith, *Desiring the Kingdom*, 39.

that remains restless until it finds its proper rest in God. In addition, according to Smith, whether its end is God or golden idols, the heart's desires effectively fashion an implicit vision of the good life (a "kingdom") and draw us toward its realization. Motivations of the heart are so powerful that they compel Smith to repeatedly quote the Pascalian dictum: "The heart has reasons of which reason knows nothing."[35]

For Smith, the best way to appeal to the heart is through aesthetics, including the abundant harvests of human creativity—architectural projects, visual and performing arts, literature, and others. We Christians find ourselves literally *moved* by our participation in the aesthetic realm: awed by the soaring heights of a cathedral drawing our eyes heavenward, overjoyed by music calling us to dance, exultant as our hearts are *lifted up* in hymns of praise to God. Smith also calls attention to the poetic features of language; metaphors and other figures of speech—God as "mother hen," for example—which evoke transcendence by way of earthy imagery, a form of poetic indirection which refuses to grasp what it names. (Note the logic of incarnation at work!). Then there is literature's power to draw us into the lives of characters by way of appealing to our own storied nature. In life as in stories, desire drives the plot.

Drawing upon the work of Maurice Merleau-Ponty and others, Smith names this affective/aesthetic/analogical register "imagination" but quickly signals he intends something other than the basic dictionary definition—that which appears in the mind but not to the senses. Instead, he is keen to stress that this imaginative sensibility registers far less in the mind than on the plane of the body-in-action. It is pre-theoretical, not yet (or ever) congealed into categories of thought and mostly tacit and therefore not rising to the level of consciousness. Again, the significance (and signification) desire registers within us on this non-conscious, non-cognitive, non-linguistic plane. In this case, it is the *body* that imagines.[36]

Because this imagination is a feature of the body that propels us through life, it is linked to action, to practice. Our affectively-embodied imagination drives/summons us toward our own desired ends, kingdoms of one sort or another, be they gated consumerist castles or God's house on a hill with room for all. Curiously, this imagination not only leads to practice, it is also inscribed in and through repeated practice, even micro-practices. Smith describes how the injunction to "sit up straight" reiterated on a thousand different occasions not only leads to improved posture, it disposes one to desire and therefore *intend* the world as a space of uprightness. In other

---

35. Smith, *Speech and Theology*, 43.
36. Smith, *Imagining the Kingdom*. See chapter 1.

words, practices become the means to evoke and habituate desires toward certain ends. Our embodied imagination is "built up as habits carried in the body," and, in this way, it carries us through life.[37] Put differently, in our bodily imaginations we develop a "feel for the game," an under-the-radar sense of how life works and how we will lean into it.[38] In still other words, our bodies are continually engaged in a hermeneutical enterprise. They may not tell us what they're up to, but always and everywhere they offer moment-to-moment *interpretations* of our progress toward the kingdom of our dreams.

Note how starkly this portrait of human being contrasts with its modern antecedent. In Smith's account, and unlike Descartes's, humans do not think up an idea of the good life, perform a cost benefit analysis on the pros and cons of their concept, then decide based on reason whether or not to pursue their ideal. Instead, in Smith's view, humans, propelled by their hearts, tacitly, *bodily* navigate this nexus of desires, practices, and habits toward a mostly implicit vision, one that intends their lives and the life of the world in certain ways. To be clear, Smith would *not* say that cognitive thought or the capacity to stand back and reflect on unfolding experience is irrelevant, only that when it comes to seeking ultimate ends, the conscious, deliberative mind is not driving the bus.

LITURGICAL FORMATION

At this point we make our way back to Christian liturgy. It turns out that human beings are perfectly tuned to liturgy's capacity to awaken and allure human hearts to the ends for which they are created. As we've seen, liturgy, as a set of practices, places bodies in motion. In the regular repetition of bodily gestures—sharing and receiving Christ's peace through handshakes and hugs, cupping our palms to receive consecrated bread, joining hands and receiving the benedictory "Go forth to serve the Lord!"—the imagination is evoked and oriented toward God's kingdom. As Smith says, worship involves us in the affectively laden "poetics" of God's biblical story of salvation from creation to promised consummation, centered upon the life, death, and resurrection of Jesus. In this story, we "sense" God's love and grace (*God's* desires) meeting and beckoning our desires. This storied involvement comes by way of a liturgical "kinesthetics," however, where through ritually enacted symbols, shared gestures, and the patterning of time the worshiping

---

37. Smith, *Imagining the Kingdom*, 44.

38. Smith, *Imagining the Kingdom*, 86. Following Pierre Bourdieu, Smith describes how communities socialize the bodily imagination. See also Smith, *How Not to Be Secular*.

assembly *performs* the gospel.³⁹ The gift, for Smith, is twofold. Not only has the church received this incarnational means of liturgical formation—the practice of ordinary materiality whereby transcendence acts upon and within earthly and human bodily immanence, it is also the space where the transcendent God inhabiting Jesus the Christ is present and active in the midst of this assembly—the gift of Incarnation itself.

CULTURAL LITURGIES

Yet all is not well in Liturgy Land. While this account of liturgy and liturgical animals affirms the redemptive efficacy of *Christian* liturgy, unfortunately, in North America at present, the church is not alone in its worship, and "the devil has had all the best liturgies."⁴⁰ Smith famously diagnoses a number of "cultural liturgies"—shopping at the mall as a liturgy of the consumerist kingdom, the fighter-jet flyover of the giant American flag-draped football field as liturgized adulation of the nationalist "military-entertainment complex," even the self-aggrandizing imaginary conjured by the "wedding industry"—as competing against Christian liturgies and vying for the imaginations of worshipers.⁴¹ In other words, just as with Christian worship, these, too, are liturgies of "ultimate concern" operating mostly beneath the radar of human consciousness while demanding our loyalties.⁴² Smith's answer is for faith communities to double down on historic Christian liturgy, to replace cultural liturgies (and, for that matter, entertaining (consumerist) Christian worship "experiences") with the nourishing food that only the Christian practices of book, bath, table, and its patterning of time can provide.

CONCLUSION

Smith has devoted his scholarly life to constructing a "logic of incarnation" for hermeneutics, then to sharing its implications across a number of fields. In its reassertion of the possibility of transcendence, incarnation provides the means to resist the modern (philosophical and theological) descent to nihilistic immanence. At the same time, and in response to continental philosophy, Smith shows that appeals to transcendence, even God, are not doomed to violence, because, by way of incarnation, transcendence is revealed, but its mystery remains profound. Interpretation persists, therefore,

---

39. Smith, *Imagining the Kingdom*, 16–21.
40. Smith, *Imagining the Kingdom*, 40.
41. Smith, *You Are What You Love*, chapters 2 and 5.
42. Smith, *Nicene Option*, 41.

as a feature of God's good creation; its multivalent pluriformity leading to the praise of the One who remains infinitely fathomable.

Smith also extends the logic of incarnation beyond the realm of thought to include an affectively embodied imagination, a "know-how" tacitly operative in human bodies as well as throughout the social body. This imagining by the body-in-action provides an implicit, peripheral, a-perception of more-than-immanence. Christian liturgical worship evokes this imagination and draws worshipers into the liturgical practice of the saving work of the God through the performance of God's story. In this way, humble bodily beings are made to be God-bearers. But for Smith and for all of us, the real miracle is Incarnation itself—God made manifest in human form for the life of the world.

BIBLIOGRAPHY

Smith, James K. A. *Desiring the Kingdom: Worship, Worldview, and Cultural Formation*. Grand Rapids: Baker Academic, 2009.

———. *The Fall of Interpretation: Philosophical Foundations for a Creational Hermeneutic*. Grand Rapids: Baker Academic, 2012.

———. *How Not to Be Secular: Reading Charles Taylor*. Grand Rapids: Eerdmans, 2014.

———. *Imagining the Kingdom: How Worship Works*. Grand Rapids: Baker Academic, 2013.

———. *Introducing Radical Orthodoxy: Mapping a Post-Secular Age*. Grand Rapids: Baker Academic, 2004.

———. *Jacques Derrida: Live Theory*. London: Bloomsbury, 2005.

———. *The Nicene Option: An Incarnational Phenomenology*. Waco, TX: Baylor University Press, 2021.

———. *Speech and Theology: Language and the Logic of Incarnation*. London: Taylor & Francis, 2002.

———. *Who's Afraid of Postmodernism?: Taking Derrida, Lyotard, and Foucault to Church*. Grand Rapids: Baker Academic, 2006.

———. *You Are What You Love: The Spiritual Power of Habit*. Grand Rapids: Brazos, 2016.

Taylor, Charles. *A Secular Age*. Cambridge, MA: Harvard University Press, 2007.

Chapter 9

Hermeneutics and the End of Apologetics

MYRON BRADLEY PENNER

The God who lets us live in the world without the working hypothesis of God is the God before whom we stand continually. Before God and with God we live without God. God lets himself be pushed out of the world [and] on to the cross. He is weak and powerless in the world and that is precisely the way, the *only* way in which he is with us and helps us. . . . The Bible directs [humans] to God's powerlessness and suffering; only the suffering of God can help. To that extent the development of *the world's coming of age* . . . which *has done away with a false conception of God, opens up a way of seeing the God of the Bible*, who wins power and space in the world by his weakness.[1]

DIETRICH BONHOEFFER

Imagine with me a future (perhaps not so distant) in which a ferociously anti-science social and political movement has gained such sway across the globe that scientific institutions of learning and research—even the very practice of science itself—are so thoroughly distrusted, despised, and maligned, that the pursuit of science is halted and the knowledge it brings has fallen into such disrepute that no one values it anymore.[2] A

---

1. *Letters and Papers from Prison*, 360–61 (my italics).

2. I am adapting Alastair MacIntyre's "Disquieting Suggestion," in MacIntyre, *After Virtue*, 1ff. I use version of this thought-experiment in Penner, *End of Apologetics*, 1ff.,

massive and violent global uprising against the scientific establishment has targeted laboratories, instruments, and technology in order to wipe out all vestiges of scientific concepts, theories, and practices. A world government now controls all sources of information and knowledge—digital and otherwise—and bans any reference to science, and all perspectives that value it, from being taught, carried out, or even discussed. Eventually there are no scientists left. All those trained in the theory and practice of the scientific approach to knowledge are either dead or have abandoned it. Science as we know it effectively is erased from human civilization.

Now further imagine that after a while—perhaps decades—some people, remembering the incredible advantages that science had produced for human society, start to wonder again. And so there emerges a reactionary movement to the anti-science crusade. An underground society forms to gather what knowledge of science it can. What they can retrieve, however, is only fragmentary: they possess only bits and pieces of theories, chapters in books, partial articles, miscellaneous scientific instruments and equipment, and all of it is disassociated from the overall scientific worldview from which they originally came, and the wider practices and theoretical underpinnings in which they originally made sense. But within this society people begin again to speak of "science." They resurrect scientific terminology—like neutron, aliphatic hydrocarbon, and ribonucleic acid (etc.)—and use them in systematic and interrelated ways; yet also in ways completely *different* to how those terms formerly were used. No one even seems to notice that this is not at all what once was called—what *we* now call—science.

In many respects this scenario describes our situation today with respect to Christian faith after the modern European Enlightenment.[3] And, more to the point, it provides an important context for understanding a postconservative approach to Christian theology. I do not mean, of course, that our views of science are all wrong. But this scenario illustrates the kind of transformation Western society has experienced. It shows how the Enlightenment had both a dramatic and comprehensive effect on how we in Western societies think and act and understand ourselves and our world—and especially *God* (faith). Like the people in our thought-experiment, who experienced a sweeping alteration to how they see and experience the world,

---

and the argument that follows here is an adaptation the argument made there at book length.

3. MacIntyre makes a similar suggestion in, *After Virtue*, 1ff. Also note that I am using the terms modern, modernism, modernity, and the Enlightenment, as roughly (and somewhat inaccurately) synonymous, to reference the radical upheaval in sixteenth century Europe, which continued through the nineteenth century and affected all aspects of thought and life in the global West.

we too have undergone a violent upheaval that affects all our concepts and perceptions. We are modern. Or postmodern. And what is more, we seem not even to realize that our view of the world—and correspondingly, how we live in it—has fundamentally changed from former times.

With this in mind, I propose that a postconservative theological approach is best framed in terms of at least two things: first, it is *against apologetics*;[4] and therefore it is also, second, *hermeneutical* in its approach to Christian belief. That is to say, I believe that we can get at the core issue of a postconservative hermeneutics through a critique of *modern* apologetics—the sort of engagement with Christian faith that emerges in and as a result of the modern Western Enlightenment.

So the question (or cluster of questions) I have is this: What happens to the discipline of Christian apologetics in a postconservative, postmodern approach to Christian theology—that is, once one understands that something like the situation of our thought-experiment above is our actual situation with regard to Christian faith? How do we still speak about, think of, and practice Christian faith *then*? What would a "postconservative apologetics" look like? Apologetics, after all, is an inherently conservative project—that of *conserving* belief, maintaining Christian doxastic commitments in the face of modern innovations. So how does one approach faith be *after* or *other* than its conservative, apologetic emphasis in modernity? What does Christian witness look like in a postconservative, postmodern context?

These questions cannot be addressed fully here, of course, but in brief: my suggestion is that at least one way of being postconservative involves looking for and to the *end of apologetics*. This postconservative approach is fundamentally opposed to the basic paradigm of modern theology, which rests on foundations set for it by modern theories about how and why we know things to be true (epistemology). Apologetics takes center stage in modern theology as it attempts to meet Enlightenment challenges to Christian belief head-on by understanding and recommending Christian belief in terms set out for it by modern science and the modern way of thinking about the world. Over and against this, the postconservative approach to theology I recommend understands Christian belief and witness in terms of a hermeneutical approach that negotiates faith in reference to the texts and

---

4. By "apologetics," here, I refer to the *modern* Enlightenment project that attempts to establish the rational foundations for Christian faith/belief. This definition of apologetics is important as it refers to a particular species of apologetics. Generally, the term apologetics refers to the reasoned defense of the Christian faith. In this chapter I am focused on how apologetics is usually practiced today and I am suggesting that contemporary apologetics is conditioned by its relationship to the modern Enlightenment.

traditions thorough which Christians have heard (and continue to hear) the voice of God through the apostles and prophets. So, in what follows I begin by situating a postconservative approach according to our current cultural location in relation to modernity—the great "disaster" that erased our cultural and intellectual memory. This context is, as Bonhoeffer notes above, "the world come of age," which I explain in reference to modernism and postmodernism. I then critically engage the epistemological paradigm of modern apologetic project to show that it is doubly self-defeating: it is bad philosophy and bad theology. And so I argue that Christian faith should instead be approached in terms of a hermeneutics. I conclude that the *end*, or goal, of this sort of postconservative approach is rooted in our Christian confession of Jesus Christ as Lord.

THE POSTCONSERVATIVE CONTEXT: POSTMODERNISM AND "THE WORLD'S COMING OF AGE" (BONHOEFFER)

The postconservative condition I describe bears a striking and critical resemblance to the *postmodern* condition.[5] I am not suggesting that the two terms are equivalent or that postconservatives are necessarily "postmodernists," but there is an important relationship between them. I will explain.

To get a sense of what I am speaking about, one must grasp what Charles Taylor means when he refers to the Enlightenment as "the Great Disembedding."[6] Modernity, here, fundamentally involves a societal shift— in terms of how Western people think, but also in terms of how we live, the practices that structure our daily lives and give them meaning. To be modern in this sense involves two critical moves. First, it is to leave behind, erase, renounce, the *enchanted* premodern "world of spirits, demons, and moral forces which our ancestors lived in,"[7] in order to correct and overcome the biases and superstitions of the premodern world that blinded them in the pursuit of truth and hindered them from the establishment of rational societies of peace and prosperity. The premodern mind accepts that God and the world (with all its beings) are part of the same reality, and that human reason functions in conformity to the *logos* (Greek: word, reason) of the universe. Modernity, however, disenchants the world and reimagines it so reason is assumed to be *internal* to human beings and the human person (more or less) is a disembodied mind and the free and unencumbered

---

5. However fruitfully they might be differentiated for other purposes, here the terms "postmodern," "postmodernism," and "postmodernity" are used as synonyms as indicating a singular intellectual and social milieu.

6. Cf. Taylor, *Secular Age*, 146ff.

7. Taylor, *Secular Age*, 26.

center of rational thought. And so, secondly, the modern world is imagined more like a machine. The task of reason in modernity principally is epistemological: its function is to measure, categorize, and exercise intellectual mastery and control over an otherwise brute and irrational universe that does not necessarily have a purpose or a center or even a unifying principle. Modern philosophy, then, shifts its focus to establishing rationally certain foundations from which to erect a body of beliefs that is true and justified (i.e., knowledge). And what it discovers in this pursuit is incredible explanatory power over a range of natural phenomena; namely, empirical science.[8]

As such, the modern Enlightenment is experienced as *progress* by those who undergo it. It leaves behind and strips away the superstition and (on its terms) the irrationality of premodern belief in and dependence on God, religion, and faith as sources for belief and gets at the way things *really* are. And so modern progress leaves us in a condition of *secularity* in which it becomes possible for us to imagine that the existence of God, or any religious sense of a realm beyond or deeper than the world examined through empirical science, is optional. Not only is belief in God rare in our secular condition, it is counter-intuitive. The modern shift, then, is more of an eradication of a world than an adjustment to some theories about the world. The remarkable thing is that once we are installed in modernity, it seems to us as intuitive and "natural"; it is, as Taylor notes, "the only possible [mindset] that makes sense" to us.[9] We are prone, therefore, to entertain a quite distorted view of the process by which we became embedded in modern categories, and, like our fictional characters above, do not even realize that our discourse and perceptions are radically altered. Moderns tend not to know that they are *modern*; they merely see themselves as being reasonable. So there is an important sense in which *being modern entails or amounts to a critical blindness about being modern.*

This is why I prefer to think of postmodernism as the awareness of ourselves *as modern*. Postmoderns are those who understand the modern turn, not as progress (social and intellectual) per se, but as a contingent force that shapes how we see the world and live in it—and then attempts to cope with and move *through* the modern disembedding that defines their world. I see the postmodern, then, less as a congealed set of propositions or a defined philosophical/theological "position," and more as an *ethos*.[10]

---

8. It is important to remember that natural science was practiced prior to modernity, and that modern empirical science is not the only way natural science has been (or can be) practiced.

9. Taylor, *Modern Social Imaginaries*, 17.

10. Note that this usage entails that the casual and often repeated dismissals of "postmodernism" as mere relativism (the belief that truth is "relative") and sheer

It is a mindset or basic response to a set of material and discursive conditions; it is a way of seeing things and being in the world. In the condition of postmodernity, all the certainties of modernity are up for grabs, so to speak, and negotiable.

So what does all this have to do with postconservative theology and apologetics? To appreciate the connection, we first need to recognize that in modernity theology, too, undergoes the same pressures of modernity's disembedding, and subsequently becomes almost unavoidably apologetic (defensive). Modern theology, in a sense, carries on its own Enlightenment project that congeals into two basic streams: liberal and conservative. Both the liberal and conservative apologetic projects imagine the world in roughly the same modern way, particularly in terms of the norms and standards of rationality. However, they differ in their relationship to traditional (orthodox) belief. Whereas modern liberal theology *accommodates* Christian belief to modern science and culture in its apologetic efforts, modern conservative theology uses apologetics defensively to *preserve* the reasonability of more traditional Christian belief. To grossly oversimplify, liberal theology tailors Christian belief to the claims and challenges of modern scientific rationality; conservative theology uses modern scientific rationality to demonstrate that there is no inherent conflict between Christian belief and the claims of modernity. And they each are largely unaware of themselves as modern.

A *post*conservative, then, is someone who knows the contingency of modernism and understands it as our basic context, and yet for this reason is not willing engage in the modern liberal theological project of revising Christian belief either. So there is a sense in which the essays in this volume, insofar as they are "postconservative," concern the "coming of age" not only of conservative theological movements but, as Bonhoeffer describes in the epigraph above, of humanity in general. When Bonhoeffer writes these words he is awaiting execution in a Nazi prison camp—perhaps the most horrific symbol of modernity's "progress." And while the ideas he expresses in these writings are the subject of much debate amongst scholars, when he speaks of his social-cultural situation in the mid-twentieth century as humanity's "coming of age" and of its "false conception of God," Bonhoeffer clearly is referring to the effect that modern progress has on our total view of the world and how we live in it. Something has happened. Bonhoeffer *sees* it, he acknowledges it, and tries to account for it. He recognizes that something like a Great Disembedding has occurred and that it challenges and changes all our Christian concepts and how they shape our lives, beginning

---

nihilism (the belief that there is no inherent meaning or value in human life) are utterly simplistic and entirely unhelpful.

with our concept of God. And his response is to conserve Christian belief, to point back to the biblical text and to faith in Jesus Christ. But *not*, it is important to note, in modern apologetic terms. He does not double-down on modernity and attempt to demonstrate the reasonableness of Christian belief or accommodate faith to modern categories. He takes note of our situation and searches for a way to cope with it. This is what makes Bonhoeffer postmodern in the sense described here, as well as a prime example of a postconservative approach to Christian theology. So being postconservative involves our awareness of ourselves *as modern, as* those who have gone through the Enlightenment; as those who live in a world in which (at least functionally) God does not exist; as those who, in Bonhoeffer's words, have laboured under "a false conception of God."

MODERN THEOLOGY AND THE END OF APOLOGETICS

Perhaps at this point you find yourself asking what, exactly, is the problem with modernity—and, by extension, modern apologetics. Has not the Enlightenment brought monumental gains in science and knowledge? And what is more obvious that the value of Christian apologetics—making Christian belief rationally defensible? How can that be bad?

These are important questions. But note that they also come from *within* the modern paradigm and therefore beg the central question at issue: namely, the necessity or legitimacy or inherent value of making the modern turn. In other words, they are asked from a position that assumes that the modern disembedding was inevitable and/or necessary and unequivocally marked a moment of progress for humans. I am not so sure about that. And what is more, these questions orient the issues of Christian faith around the values and categories of modernity and not the Good News of Jesus Christ. What these sorts of questions belie is that modern apologetic challenges to faith are driven by their embeddedness in the modern way of imagining the world insofar as they require that (1) God's existence is not intuitively plausible, (2) each individual person is responsible to justify her beliefs rationally for herself, (3) their arguments are imagined to take place in a neutral space outside of political power, and (4) truth, reason, and faith are construed solely in terms of the modern epistemological paradigm.

So my response to the questions above is to ask a different question—one that seeks to reorient the issue around the Christian message, not modern values: Is the Christian witness a genius or an apostle?[11] At the heart of this question, this distinction between a genius and an apostle,

---

11. See Søren Kierkegaard's essay, "On the Difference Between A Genius and an Apostle," in the appendix of Kierkegaard, *Book On Adler*.

is an insistence that Christian speech about God first and foremost is an instance of Christian *witness*—a *confession* before others of the truth one has encountered in Jesus Christ. This question also functions to highlight the central issue of the modern turn highlighted above, namely the issue of *authority*.

Søren Kierkegaard,[12] in his criticism of modern theology, raises this distinction to highlight the fact the Christian basis for belief is essentially different from that required by the norms of modern epistemology. In modernity, Kierkegaard thinks, the highest possible authority for our beliefs and practices rest on genius: in a world imagined on modern terms, the only possible source of authority lies with those who possess superior rational capabilities. The Great Disembedding of modernism initiated a crisis of authority: it had stripped away all the traditional sources and norms for belief (religion, tradition, culture, family, etc.). In its place, moderns turned to its new, internal, conception of human reason, which is imagined as a timeless, universal human capacity that remains unaffected by its concrete circumstances. The genius, as one who is *more* brilliant, intelligent, rational, etc., than others, is thereby more *authoritative*—even if we cannot quite understand them or personally access their evidence and arguments. The genius says, "Trust me, I'm smarter than you and I can tell you that this is the most reasonable thing to believe." In the modern world, genius (as the embodiment and expression of modern reason) is the only possible source of authority left.

Apostles, however, stand in stark contrast to geniuses and, as I see it, are much more appropriate models for the Christian witness. The apostle does *not* appeal to reason, but to *revelation*. They may or may not be more rational or brilliant or intelligent than anyone else—that is entirely beside the point. The apostle is *called by God* and given a word to speak. The apostle is authoritative, then, because they speak the word of God, and *not* because of their intellectual capabilities. In the Christian Scriptures, God's good news in Jesus Christ, the gospel announced by the apostles, is not something cleverly devised or philosophically deduced; it is a wisdom of God revealed to them through Jesus Christ by the power of the Holy Spirit.[13] The apostle says: "Here is the word of God—listen to it!" However much human reason might be necessary to *understand* the apostolic proclamation, insofar as it qualifies as revelation, reason has no role to play whatsoever in

---

12. Kierkegaard was a Danish philosopher and theologian who lived from 1813–1855.

13. Cf. 1 Corinthians 1–2, especially 1:22–29 and 2:6–11; and 2 Pet 1:16–21.

grounding the apostle's claims. Therefore the apostolic message cannot be made legitimate or illegitimate by demonstrations of its rational status.

The upshot of the genius/apostle distinction, then, is that the degree to which a Christian witness appeals to their genius for their authority is also the degree to which their witness fails to be *Christian*. And remarkably, what one finds often with apologetic efforts is that what is defended is not the gospel but *modern philosophy*.[14] Regularly the core message of the Christian gospel is so closely identified with modernism by Christian apologists that challenging modern philosophy itself is construed as blasphemous and a rejection of the Christian message. The problem with this is that, philosophically it makes the truth of the Christian gospel as tenuous as modern philosophy, while theologically it flirts with conceptual idolatry by making human reason the standard by which the truthfulness of God's gospel revealed in Jesus Christ is measured. And so a postconservative who wants to think and speak of God in ways other than modernity is against apologetics and will call for the end of apologetics precisely in order to preserve the true *end* (as in goal or purpose) of apologetics.

FALLIBILISM AND HERMENEUTICS

The Kierkegaardian distinction between a genius and an apostle provides not only a substantial critique of the modern apologetic paradigm but also suggests an alternative to it. The insistence on the utterly transcendent source of the apostle's call indicates two further features of a postconservative approach to Christian theology after modernity.

First, human reason is limited and fallible. Implied in the genius/apostle distinction is the idea that reason is historically situated (within time) and contextual and not, as modernity imagines it, a capacity that operates timelessly as a universal or unbiased judge that is unaffected by actual circumstances. Here human reason does not occupy a transcendent or neutral perspective but operates from within the everyday entanglements of human life. It is not able to apprehend every moment nor is it capable of grounding its truth-claims absolutely. A word from God may be transcendent but human perspectives are not. A postconservative understands that when we try to justify truths by appealing to a modern conception of human reason, in actual fact we always do so from some contingent, particular point of view that is shaped in large part by some particular group's perspective. What counts for us as a justification is part and parcel of the social practices in which we engage. This is because the concepts and language we use to do

---

14. This claim is developed in Penner, *End of Apologetics*, 42.

so (and in which we think) are deeply embedded in our social practices. In the end genius collapses back on itself and has no authority, originality, or proficiency, that does not come from the court of public opinion. There is no other way for genius to ground itself.

Second, the transcendence of the apostle's call means that the postconservative operates more easily within a *hermeneutical* framework than the epistemological paradigm of modernity. Hermeneutics, of course, concerns interpretation, and when we begin with God's transcendent call we are placed in what might be called an irremediably hermeneutical situation. We have been addressed. We have received a word. This is where our knowledge and understanding begins, as we wrestle with the meaning of the word we have heard; as we interpret it. And human reason cannot epistemically master the apostolic message nor can it improve upon it or assimilate it into a wider theory of anything. God announces his and it is ours to *understand* and *interpret*, but not to justify or rationalize directly in the sense of establishing its legitimacy. Of course, questions about legitimacy inevitably arise as one wrestles with intellectual and existential difficulties encountered in life, but these are questions that occur *within* the context of the received revelation and not wider questions of justification.

What marks off my postconservative hermeneutical paradigm from the modern epistemological one is its emphasis on the embodied, contextual nature of human reasoning and understanding. If the modern epistemological paradigm is focused on the question, "Is it (belief about the world/reality) true and justified?" the hermeneutical paradigm suggested here replaces it with the question, "Is it *intelligible* and *meaningful*?" The pressing issue is not solving an abstract set of theoretical problems but interpreting the symbols and texts of a received tradition on order to understand their meaning and significance in relation to a concrete set of problems and exigencies that we encounter. A hermeneutical approach is not driven by a desire for mastery and control, but by a desire for dialogue and shared meaning. To be sure, there will be arguments, logic, evidence, and so on that are crucial parts of the process of arriving at conclusions within interpretive traditions, but these are invitations for response from differing points of view rather than an attempt to foreclose on them. These alternate points of view that emerge through dialogue are not barriers to understanding but enable us to gain greater insight into the text (as well as ourselves, our world and others) as we submit our interpretations to critical tests that are free and open to critique and response.

Historically Christian faith has always embodied (or at very least sits quite comfortably with) the insight that "we can believe only by interpreting."[15] The Hebrew-Christian tradition has *always* and *essentially* been hermeneutical in both its literary and philosophical senses. The Hebrew-Christian tradition has always been *textual* in the rather straight-forward literary sense that it is focused on interpreting a received set of texts (God's word) within a community that receives them. Interpretation of the word of/from God is the primary intellectual activity of the Hebrew and Christian traditions. Hebrew-Christian reflection always begins with a received body of texts and speech-acts through which God has spoken. And the Hebrew-Christian tradition is also hermeneutical in the philosophical sense which emphasizes that human knowledge and understanding begins in the middle of life's experiences. It has its origins in *revelation*—with an event expressed in language (text) that is interpreted within the tradition. It does not begin with philosophical speculation. The biblical God is the One-who-*speaks* and *reveals*. So the first moment of critical reflection is to wait and listen—to *hear* from God. Subsequently, the Hebrew-Christian *logos* (word, reason) is one that always exhausts human reason and comes to us from the outside. It is never a word (a reason) that rests on human rational capacities and displays the circular relation between believing and understanding.

CONCLUSION

So, how do we understand and think about Christian faith once we recognize that our view of the world (God, self, and others) and the way we inhabit it is caught up within the categories and practices of modernity—once we realize that the way we imagine the world and live in it is profoundly shaped by Enlightenment ideals and values (and to that degree partial and distorted)? The answer, I insist, is not to double-down on the modern worldview and mount an apologetic offensive to establish the rational foundations of Christian belief. The postconservative answer I propose is to look for *the end* of that apologetic paradigm and to approach Christian belief and witness in terms of a hermeneutical approach that negotiates the faith through the texts and communal practices in and through which God has spoken (and still speaks) to us by way of the apostles and prophets.

I began by showing how the modern apologetic paradigm undercuts the very gospel it wishes to defend and doubly "deconstructs" itself: not only does modern apologetics suffer the same challenges in establishing rational foundations for belief as modern philosophy, but it ends up treating human

---

15. Ricœur, *Symbolism and Evil*, 352.

reason as the source and ground of its discourse. The problem theologically, then, is that the modern apologetic paradigm makes an idol out of human reason and operates as if God does not, in fact, exist. Over and against the paradigm of modern apologetics, I juxtapose a postconservative hermeneutical approach that brings us to the end of apologetics—it acknowledges both the fruitlessness (spiritually, intellectually) of modern apologetic epistemological paradigm and calls Christian witness back to itself, its (true) *end*: the confession of Jesus Christ. So what we find is that a postconservative hermeneutical paradigm of the sort I recommend does at least three things: 1.) It focuses on hearing God speak in the context of the community of the faithful; 2.) it accepts human limitations and the multiple layers of meaning in any speech situation that produce a conflict of interpretations; and, finally, 3.) it understands that human reason is no longer its own ground but is caught up in the faith-commitments of network of perspectives and relationships that provides for us the basic context in which we think and act and believe. Reason, for my sort of postconservative, finds its sphere of operations within the space made within human understanding by the word of God to and through the community of God's people addressed in Jesus Christ.

To be postconservative in some respects is caught between the rock of modernity and the hard place of the premodern worldview. On the one hand, we cannot simply recollect ourselves back into premodern forms of Christian faith, with their hierarchical universe and naïve picture of the world. And yet, on the other hand, we are far too aware of problems of the modern paradigm to find its programme tenable. A shift to a hermeneutical approach to Christian faith like the kind that I propose carefully negotiates faith in reference to the texts and traditions out of which we hear the apostles and prophets speak. It acknowledges that hearing God speak is an event that occurs in the context of a faithful community and requires careful and rigorous interpretation. And it also accepts the fact that sometimes we get it wrong and that there are often multiple layers of meanings at work which produce a conflict of interpretations. These differing viewpoints must be worked out with fear and trembling, as there is no absolute zero-point from which we may judge once-and-for-all the right- or wrongness of our perspectives. However, adopting a hermeneutical paradigm, does not leave us shiftless and rootless. In fact, there is a sense in which a hermeneutical approach leaves us much *more* rooted—in a community, in oneself, in God—but without the (illusory) modern appeal to the authority of the genius.

BIBLIOGRAPHY

Bonhoeffer, Dietrich. *Letter and Papers from Prison*. Translated and edited by Eberhard Bethge. London, UK: SCM, 1997.

Kierkegaard, Søren Aabye. *Concluding Unscientific Postscript to Philosophical Fragments, Two Volumes*. Translated and edited by Howard V. Hong and Edna H. Hong. Princeton: Princeton University Press, 1992.

———. *The Book On Adler*. Translated and edited by Howard V. Hong and Edna H. Hong. Princeton: Princeton University Press, 2009.

Gregor, Brian, and Jens Zimmermann, eds. *Bonhoeffer and Continental Thought: Cruciform Philosophy*. Bloomington: Indiana University Press, 2009.

Grenz, Stanley J., and John R. Franke. *Beyond Foundationalism: Shaping Theology in a Postmodern Context*. Louisville, KY: Westminster John Knox, 2001.

MacIntyre, Alastair. *After Virtue: A Study in Moral Theory*. 2nd ed. Notre Dame, IN: University of Notre Dame Press, 1984.

Penner, Myron Bradley. *The End of Apologetics: Christian Witness in a Postmodern Context*. Grand Rapids: Baker Academic, 2011.

Ricœur, Paul. *The Symbolism of Evil*. Translated by Emerson Buchanan. Boston: Beacon, 1967.

Taylor, Charles. *A Secular Age*. Cambridge, MA: Harvard Belknap Press, 2007.

———. *Modern Social Imaginaries*. Durham, NC: Duke University Press, 2004.

SECTION 2

Doctrinal Interpretation

Chapter 10
Dramatic Hermeneutics
NIKOLAUS WANDINGER

ORIGIN OF THE APPROACH

I should disclose at the beginning that I am about to introduce the readers to a particular type of dramatic hermeneutics, namely to one that originated with the Swiss Jesuit Raymund Schwager (1935–2014), who was professor of dogmatic theology at the Catholic-Theological Faculty of the University of Innsbruck, Austria. However, his hermeneutics is not a one-man show. A larger group of Dramatic Theologians has developed in his wake, and the approach has grown beyond the German-speaking world. Schwager's approach stands in a broader tradition of Dramatic Theology, whose most important representative certainly is Hans Urs von Balthasar (1905–1988) with his *Theo-Drama*.[1] Schwager was inspired by Balthasar's theology, yet placed the emphases in his Dramatic hermeneutics differently.[2] I will therefore concentrate on Schwager's approach and will try to explain it in a systematic manner, which entails that I will begin by his fully developed hermeneutics and will work my way back chronologically to its beginning.

RESOLVING CONTRADICTIONS IN INTERPRETING THE HISTORY OF JESUS

Schwager's dramatic hermeneutics did not spring up from a philosophical interest but from concrete problems in interpreting the Christian Bible and consequent difficulties for the ideas on salvation, also known as soteriology.

1. See Balthasar, *Theo-Drama*.
2. See Schwager, "Balthasar" and Schwager, "Briefwechsel mit Hans Urs von Balthasar."

CONFLICTING IMAGES OF GOD AND ITS CONSEQUENCES FOR IDEAS ON SALVATION

The two most important problems treated by Schwager were the apparent contradiction in the image of God even within the New Testament; and the seemingly different, sometimes contradictory, soteriologies, in the NT and throughout the history of Christianity.

The conflicting images God emerge when comparing various parables that the New Testament places in Jesus of Nazareth's words. One of the most striking examples of a parable that emphasizes God's limitless capacity for forgiveness is the parable of the prodigal son or of the merciful father (Luke 15:11–32). It tells of a father who is willing to pay his younger son the inheritance that would be his only after the father's demise, then he receives the son back after he has squandered the inheritance and has sunk to the lowest possible position. Not only does this father receive the son back, he even "ran" (!) towards him, "embraced him and kissed him" (Luke 15:20)[3] and ordered a feast to celebrate the return of his found-again son. His older son meanwhile has worked all his life for his father and when he realizes that a feast in honor of his younger brother is given, he becomes angry and refuses to join. Again, the "father came out and entreated him" (Luke 15:28). This father, who stands for Jesus's divine Father, literally runs and walks out of his way to welcome his prodigal son and assuage the anger of his resentful son. For this reason, some exegetes have taken him to show an image of God that is all-merciful and unconditionally forgiving. Schwager agrees with them that with Jesus "salvation and repentance exchanged places, and he offered the sinner God's forgiveness, irrespective of whether the sinner was willing to repent or unprepared to do so."[4]

The judgment parables, however, evoke a different image of God. A perfect example is the parable of the unforgiving servant (Matt 18:23–35). Here, a master at first demands the repayment of an unimaginable sum of money (200,000 years' wages!) from his servant, and when the servant cannot deliver, the master threatens to sell him with family to make up for the loss. The servant begs the master for patience, and the master forgives the whole sum. Afterwards, the servant meets a colleague of his, who owes him about 4 months' wages. Again, the debtor asks for patience, but the creditor denies that and has his colleague jailed. When the master hears of this, he retracts his forgiveness and has the hard-hearted, servant delivered to the jailers. The chapter ends by Jesus summing up: "So also my heavenly Father

---

3. All Bible quotations from the English Standard Version.
4. Schwager, *Jesus in the Drama*, 55.

will do to every one of you, if you do not forgive your brother from your heart" (Matt 18:35).

The question arises: If God is like the merciful father of the first parable, can he also be like the master in the second parable? It seems contradictory to say so. The problem is exacerbated when two different soteriologies come into play, for both of which we find evidence in the New Testament. What was termed Jesus's message of the imminent kingdom of God seemed to imply salvation by unconditional proactive divine forgiveness. The ideas voiced in Paul's writings but also in the last supper narratives seem to say that salvation is somehow conditioned on Christ's salvific death on the cross.

The exegetical question here might be somewhat dated, but the larger problem behind it, whether the New Testament message about God and in its wake also the soteriologies of Christian churches, are contradictory, seems timeless.[5] One answer, sometimes given is that the attempt to conform God to the precepts of human logic is presumptuous. Since God is the unfathomable mystery, paradoxes in God-talk are not only permitted but necessary. Schwager did not object to that. Yet, he argued that paradoxes may not amount to outright contradictions. He supported this argument not with formal logic but with the praxis of faith and with lived spirituality: If Christian belief were satisfied with contradictory notions of God, claims about God would become arbitrary. If an idea and its exact contradictory opposite were allowed to be posited of God, then anything could be said of God—and this would eventually make religious speech futile.[6] And it would make faith and trust in such a God impossible. Therefore, while paradoxes will remain and tensions may exist, outright contradictions would nullify theological thinking and belief.

RESOLVING THE CONFLICT: THE DRAMA OF JESUS

Schwager found a solution by interpreting the New Testament Witness of Jesus's life as a drama in five acts,[7] which I will summarize.

Each act is formally defined by the person(s) who have the initiative and thereby produce the context for everything that happens in the act; the context is essential for correctly interpreting the content, which is the material element of the act.

Act I is initiated by Jesus's proclamation of the unrestrained forgiveness and nonviolence of God and contains Jesus's announcement of the

---

5. See: Schwager, *Der wunderbare Tausch*; Jersak and Hardin, *Stricken by God?*; Heim, *Saved from Sacrifice*.

6. Cf. Schwager, *Jesus in the Drama*, 1.

7. See Schwager, *Jesus in the Drama*, 29–158.

kingdom of God, the *Basileia*; by this he aspires to gather Israel anew. This message aims at acceptance. The announcement of the kingdom is not to be viewed as the prognosis of a miraculous appearance of said kingdom out of nowhere. Instead it is a prophetic act of announcement. The announced kingdom is already present in the person of Jesus, yet it only fully materializes if and when the people of Israel accept it. This acceptance would consist in their readiness to forgive, as the heavenly Father has forgiven them.

Act II is initiated by the public rejection of this message. While a small group tried to follow Jesus, the leaders of the people rejected his message, objected to it and opposed him. Act II contains Jesus's reaction to this rejection of this message: a proclamation of judgment in parables of judgment and even of hell. At this stage, we have the situation that was described in the parable of the unforgiving servant: he had been forgiven but did not accept this and refused to emulate his master.

A first attempt at avoiding the contradiction between the merciful father and the vindictive master would be to say: the situation is different. The merciful father forgives his repentant son, while the vindictive master punishes an obstinate refusenik, who was already given his chance but declined to accept it.

This is partly true, but it does not solve the problem because it would still mean that divine forgiveness was not as unconditional as it had appeared. Moreover, it suggests that when humans failed to emulate God in the way they should, God would invert the structure of imitation and emulate the negative human behavior he had criticized before. This seems strange, to say the least. It looks more like a human logic of retribution than a wise divine decision.

Schwager draws a different conclusion: He views the fact that in the parable God emulates bad human behavior as an indication that Jesus here is not explaining his vision of his divine Father; rather he is mirroring his opponents' misguided view of God: they envision God as vindictive and judgmental and because of that, they act among each other in the same way. They therefore pronounce a human self-judgment over each other and wrongly believe that this is a divine judgment. Nevertheless, the message of Act II is very serious: Jesus does not retract God's offer of forgiveness but he warns against the human self-judgment that will ensue, when this offer is rejected. It is not that God judges and punishes but humans do that among themselves. Still, God permits this self-judgment to occur without any intervention. By that Jesus makes clear that human decisions are relevant for human salvation. Condemnation—and the violence connected to it—does not originate from God, but it is nevertheless the real, necessary consequence if and when people reject Jesus's message. Does that solve the problem? Not really, Schwager, explains:

> [. . .] does it make a difference whether an angry God damns people or whether a 'kind' God looks on as his creatures damn themselves [. . .]? The result is the same. So the pressing question faces us: is Jesus' message of salvation after all really a message of salvation?[8]

Yet, we are not yet at the end of the drama. Act III commences with the authorities' initiative to annihilate Jesus. In this act, Jesus himself is judged, convicted and put to death. He becomes his adversaries' victim. They act in complete accordance with the image of God depicted in the judgment parables, and they judge with the assumption of judging in God's place. Jesus, however, responds not with vengeance and vindictiveness. Rather he refuses to be defended by the sword (Matt 26:51–52), clearly states the injustice of the action against him (John 18:23), yet takes it upon himself as God's will (Matt 26:53–55); he even prays for his persecutors (Luke 23:34). In short, he acts completely consonant with the image of the merciful father he had proclaimed in the first act, living the love of enemies he had preached then (Matt 5:44–45) to the last. The act ends with Jesus's death, and thus also with an open question: who in the end, acted in the right way, as both he and his adversaries claimed to act in the name of God but espoused opposing images of him?

The answer is given in Act IV, which is initiated by the person who so far has been the object of the dispute: God, the Heavenly Father. His intervention comes when all human action has come to an end. According to the gospel witness, he raised Jesus from the dead. Thus, he makes a final ruling in the dispute between Jesus and his adversaries. By raising Jesus, God rules in Jesus's favor, vindicating Jesus's image of God. This entails, however, also a ruling in favor of the son's prayer for his adversaries. Thus God's verdict of the resurrection is a clear rejection of Jesus's adversaries' image of God and at the same time a clear acceptance of Jesus's prayer for them to be forgiven. The persecutors' "theo-logy" is refuted, their possibility for salvation is re-instated.

Thus, in the appearances of the risen Lord, the tensions between the previous acts are resolved and a decision between the two opposing images of God reached. The disciples also gain a new perspective on Scripture (our Old Testament): a christological criterion for interpreting them emerges. This is densely narrated in the story of the way to Emmaus. Here the risen

---

8. Schwager, *Jesus in the Drama*, 81.

Lord explains to the disciples: "'Was it not necessary that the Christ should suffer these things and enter into his glory?' And beginning with Moses and all the Prophets, he interpreted to them in all the Scriptures the things concerning himself" (Luke 24:26–27). As "Christ" is the translation of "Messiah," this is the beginning of a specifically Christian understanding of the term, as for Judaism (from the time of Jesus until today) the Messiah certainly is not to suffer to enter his glory. This is a Christian interpretation, which can only be sustained by identifying Christ with the Suffering Servant of the book of Isaiah (Isa 42:1–7; 49:1–9; 50:4–9; 52:13—53:12) and with many whose suffering and victimization have been depicted in the Hebrew Bible, especially in Psalms of Lamentation, the most important one being Psalm 22, whose beginning Jesus prayed on the cross (Matt 27:46; Mark 15:34). So here, according to the Dramatic Hermeneutics of Schwager, the New Testament institutes its own hermeneutics for what Christians have called the Old Testament, a hermeneutics that gives these writings a center and a certain thrust (we will return to this later).

Finally, Act V is initiated by the coming of the Holy Spirit. He continues Jesus's movement of gathering throughout the world on two levels: in the growing community of believers, the visible church; but also beyond the visible church throughout humanity. The fifth Act has no end before the end of times and it contains all other acts like a hologram.

Let us now analyze what Schwager has actually done here.

DRAMATIC HERMENEUTICS— METHODOLOGICAL ANALYSIS

ACTS AS THE TRANSFORMATION AND PURIFICATION OF THE IMAGE OF GOD

By moving through these acts, Schwager develops a consistent image of God free from contradiction, and free from violence. The non-violent, proactively forgiving, unconditionally merciful image of God introduced in the first act remains true but it is transformed and enhanced: In the second act it is added that God will not redeem his subjects by "cheap grace"[9] but respects their freedom and asks their acceptance of his offer. When they refuse, they expose themselves to a self-judgment, which they experience as divine judgment. Acts III and IV transform this yet again, as Jesus himself voluntarily undergoes that human self-judgment and thus shows that human resistance to divine forgiveness has to be viewed on a much deeper than a merely moral level. Jesus's recognition that his persecutors did not

---

9. A term coined by Bonhoeffer, *Cost of Discipleship*, 43–44; 223–304.

know what they were doing, recasts the distinction between "sheep" and "goats" (cf. Matt 25:31–46) not as separation between different people but as a rift cutting through each and every person—and finally the development of the doctrine of original sin tries to capture this insight.

Viewed in that perspective, the seeming contradiction between redemption by unconditional proactive divine forgiveness and redemption through the cross, is also overcome. The dramatic reading shows that proactive divine forgiveness turns into salvation through the cross, if and when humans reject unconditional forgiveness. The cross is not a precondition that God erects for his forgiveness, it is the condition that humans erect when they reject the kingdom and that God then uses to overcome their resistance by his son taking on the human self-judgment in substitution. This is also the meaning of numerous sayings that explain that Christ "had to suffer." This necessity did not originate from a divine command to suffer but from a divine call to faithfully stay true to the message of the all-forgiving God, even in the face of lethal resistance against it.[10]

In Schwager's dramatic hermeneutics, the passion and resurrection necessitate a transformation of all judgment parables. That can be exemplified by the parable of the Evil Tenants (cf. Mark 12:1–12 / Matt 21:33–36). The parable clearly alludes to the story of the people of Israel, the persecution of many prophets, and the killing of Jesus. The similarity ends, however, with the son's death. In the parable the son's father avenges his son, kills his murderers and takes the vineyard from them. The aftermath of Jesus's killing is described in a fundamentally different way, though: It follows the resurrection of the killed son, his return with a message of peace to the disciples who had abandoned him (cf. John 20:20–21), and after Pentecost the disciples' announcing that same message to the inhabitants of Jerusalem, although they deem them guilty of Jesus's death (Acts 2:22–24.37–41).[11] In a similar way, all judgment parables have to be transformed: God's leaving humans to their self-judgment is not the end of the drama. The end of the drama is the message of peace by the one who underwent this judgment voluntarily in place of guilty humans.

By employing this dramatic hermeneutics of transformation, two extremes are avoided: The conflicting images of God are not seen as equally true but a clear decision is effected. Yet none of the texts becomes irrelevant. They first emphasize the importance of human freedom, and then, in another dramatic move, show how God can still work his salvation by undermining human resistance from within. A similar transformation must also

---

10. See Wandinger, "Salvation."
11. Cf. Schwager, *Jesus in the Drama*, 135–36.

occur in the understanding of the cross,[12] of judgment,[13] of sacrifice,[14] and of holiness.[15]

INTERDEPENDENT AGENTS

A drama enacts on stage an important feature of real life: the back and forth between interdependent agents. In real life, no one can simply act on their own: one can set an initiative and then has to wait how others will react to that, and depending on their response, one will again react to them. Schwager applied this to his reading of the New Testament and used it to distinguish his five acts. Thus, he envisioned Jesus as really interwoven into human interaction. The divinity accorded to him by Christian faith does not preclude that, his true humanity, however, demands it. Schwager does not apply this only to Jesus's interaction with other human beings but also to Jesus's filial relationship with his divine Father. One should not

> assume a priori that his [Jesus'] message and his self-understanding remained in all points unaltered during his ministry. If he was really determined by what was to happen in the dawning kingdom of God and knew himself for certain to be sent by the Father, then the deepest and most inaccessible point of his identity must lie in his current, new experience of God [. . .].[16]

Schwager's hermeneutics supposes that this analogously pertains to all human relationships with God: If and when God enters into a relationship with humans through revelation and salvation, he does it in a dramatic way, meaning that God allows himself to be drawn into interdependency with humans, and by that he becomes an agent who not only initiates chains of action but also reacts to the responses that humans give.

Surprisingly K. Rahner, who is not usually counted among Dramatic theologians, espoused a dramatic understanding of revelation corresponding well to Schwager's dramatic hermeneutics:

> God's acting throughout the history of salvation is not like a monologue that God performs with Himself, but a long dramatic dialogue between God and His creatures, in which God offers the human person the possibility to really respond to His word and thus in fact makes His own future word dependent

---

12. See Wandinger, "Salvation."
13. See Niewiadomski, "Opfer-Täter-Verhängnis."
14. See Moosbrugger, "René Girard and Raymund Schwager on Religion."
15. See Palaver, *Transforming the Sacred*.
16. Schwager, *Jesus in the Drama*, 52.

on the free response of the human person. [. . .] History is not just a play that God enacts for Himself in which creatures would only be His puppets, but the creature is a real co-actor in this divine-human drama of history[. . .][17]

One might object that here God's independence from human action, his sovereignty—to say nothing about his traditional attributes of omniscience and immutability—cannot be sustained. God would become one player among many. To respond to this possible objection, we will have to deal with the relationship between the divine author of the drama and the agents within it.

AUTHOR AND AGENTS

Notwithstanding the fact that the biblical writings have a complicated history of human authorship, dramatic hermeneutics wants to bring the divine authorship of Scripture into focus. Put more exactly, it is not divine authorship of Scripture but divine authorship of the drama of salvation history condensed in the drama contained in Scripture.

As with human dramatists, so in the biblical drama the author himself is beyond the universe of the story (he is transcendent) and yet everything that happens within the story is his word. However, because in the drama of salvation the human agents are real authors themselves and act out of their own—more or less—free will and their own—good or bad—decisions, this does not mean that the author determines every facet of the drama. And certainly not everything said about the author (God) in that drama must be seen as direct revelation. In a literary drama, several characters may voice quite different, even contradictory, opinions. The author of the drama does not hold all these opinions, they just want to display the whole range of different convictions that drive the action. Whether we can gauge the conviction of the author, is far from certain. In the same way, the drama of revelation has different roles that voice different, even contradictory, opinions. By going through Schwager's dramatic interpretation, we realized that they cannot all be true, but we came to the recognition of God's message through interpreting the resurrection as vindication of Jesus's message and refutation of his adversaries'. This, of course, rests on the truth of the belief in Jesus's resurrection and in his special role as the Son of God.

If one accepts these tenets of faith, however, one can gain from them, what may be called a christological criterion for discerning direct revelation from indirect revelation. It accepts that the divine author—in contrast to

---

17. Rahner, "Theos im Neuen Testament," 373, my translation.

human dramatists—has put a character into the play that represents him completely: Jesus Christ the ultimate revealer. For a Christian dramatic hermeneutics, Christ is the key for unlocking the mystery of the drama of salvation history. He is the ultimate representative of the divine author, though not in the role of author. His acts are conditioned by the limitations and the perspectives of a character within the drama, but this character acts in perfect harmony with the author of the drama, who is the Lord of history. Therefore he can be history's key. The divine author may well be omniscient, but as he is transcendent to the play, none of the agents, not even the Son, are (cf. Mark 13:32).

This dramatic hermeneutics allows us to view the whole Bible and all of its parts as authored by God, while accepting at the same time that the human agents and human co-authors of the story have added their distinct understandings and misunderstandings in a way that makes them an inseparable part of divine revelation. However, inseparable does not mean indistinguishable. The christological criterion allows us to distinguish between direct and indirect revelation, the latter could also be called revelation *sub contrario*, i.e., between God's undistorted image and human projections and misunderstandings.

CHARACTERS AND PERSONS

Another important aspect of dramatic theology is the relationship between the real, historical persons in the biblical stories and what should be called the characters they enact. The nature of biblical revelation requires that the important characters are not fictitious but real persons. Yet, since the discovery of historical-critical method, we have learned that it is not necessary that every detail be historically accurate. The New Testament interprets real events and narrates them to posterity to reveal the deeper meaning of these events.

For our dramatic hermeneutics this means that the characters in the biblical drama do not in the first place represent themselves as individuals, but they play a revelatory role in salvation history. In Jesus the two completely coincide: his person is his character, which means that there is no difference between what he depicts in the drama and what pertains to his person. In all other agents the two partly or even completely fall apart. An example for the latter is Judas, the traitor. He was called to be one of the Twelve, so the role envisioned for him by Jesus would have been similar to what the other apostles were called to. Yet, he decided on a different path and played the part of the traitor dying in isolation and desperation. Thus, Judas embodies a person who falls into utmost delusion, sin, despair, and in the end, he commits himself into hell. The distinction between person and character permits us, however, to leave the question about the historical Judas's salvation open, as we cannot know about that. Our dramatic hermeneutics allow for the possibility to distinguish between the role a person plays in the drama and their salvation as a real person.

APPLICATIONS BEYOND THE HISTORY OF JESUS

What I related so far, might let it appear that this dramatic hermeneutics has a very limited range of application, namely the New Testament accounts of Jesus of Nazareth's life and death. This would be a misinterpretation, though. I decided to introduce this hermeneutics in the form of its fullest development first, and will now add other applications.

DRAMATIC HERMENEUTICS OF THE OLD TESTAMENT

Even before Schwager developed the five act model for the New Testament, he already employed dramatic hermeneutics to elucidate Old Testament writings. Here, we have no unified story and therefore no acts. Still, some aspects of the dramatic hermeneutics are instrumental, above all the distinction between author and agents, which has to be further clarified.

Again, the divine author is beyond the action, he is transcendent; and we do not have a character who completely embodies the author in the play. Instead, we have several agents who speak and act for the author. Among those are certainly the prophets. In contrast to Jesus in the New Testament, they do not represent the author completely; they are oftentimes passionately emotional, sometimes even vindictive, and their image of God is an amalgamation of mercy and wrath. Yet, Schwager discerns in the Old Testament "the condensation of a process of learning,"[18] which leads to a progressive revelation of the God's true nature, which turns out to be non-violent.

This might surprise, as some Old Testament passages depict God quite to the contrary as violent. The development that Schwager attests here, is not a linear, continuous progression but it occurs in leaps and bounds and is interrupted by many backlashes. It is "dramatic" in this sense. In retrospect, however, there can be seen a "common basic structure"[19] that removes God more and more from violence and reveals that violence's origin is with humans, not with God. Schwager sorts OT-passages that depict God's relationship to violence into four categories: very few that depict an arbitrarily violent deity; quite a few that show divine violence in defense of the

---

18. Peter, "Die Bibelhermeneutik," 379, my translation.
19. Schwager, *Must There Be Scapegoats?*, 43.

downtrodden or as punishment for human sin; passages where God himself is not violent but uses human violence as an instrument to punish evil-doers; and finally, God withdrawing his presence from his people in response to their sinfulness and leaving them to their own self-judgment[20]—the latter being the link to Jesus's judgment parables.

A central point of reference for this reading of the Old Testament are, again, the texts from the book of Isaiah, known as the Songs of the Suffering Servant, which we encountered already. The central message of these texts is that a servant guided by God is persecuted by a group of people who are convinced that this man is rejected by God and that they are doing God's will when they kill him. But in reality, God is on the side of this servant, and the mob acts against God's will. God helps the servant not by violently protecting or by later avenging him, but by strengthening him to endure his lot in faithfulness. What is really amazing, however, is that the misguided persecutors overcome their ignorance and come to see the truth (see Isa 53:3–5). For Schwager, this conversion epitomizes the conversion that the Old Testament as a whole wants to bring about. It consists in two elements: God is on the side of the persecuted victim; this occurs in a non-violent, non-intrusive manner.

For Schwager, the texts of the Suffering Servants are the center from which Old Testament revelation should be understood. Yet, he readily admits that this cannot be concluded from within the Old Testament, as the relevant texts do not occupy a central place and their central role cannot be discovered from the Old Testament alone but in retrospect from the New Testament. He argues:

> By themselves the Old Testament writings can therefore not be brought together under a common denominator. Different tendencies remain standing side by side. At most, a real center can be found only when all the writings are interpreted anew in the light of the fate of Jesus. Such a new interpretation is legitimate, since the Old Testament itself is a history of constant reinterpretations.[21]

Thus, he employs a specific Christian understanding of these texts, already using what I have called the christological criterion.[22] Schwager therefore views Old Testament texts as "mixed texts"[23] that contain direct and indirect revelation: i.e., revelation of the true God but also mythological

20. Cf. Schwager, *Must There Be Scapegoats?*, 61–62.
21. Schwager, *Must There Be Scapegoats?*, 135.
22. For a Jewish perspective, see Goodhart, "Jewish-Christian Dialogue."
23. Schwager, "Biblische Texte als »Mischtexte«."

misunderstandings that confuse the holy with the sacred.[24] The two kinds of texts cannot be separated from one another but must be discerned.

Therefore, we have to look at one more aspect of the relationship between author and agents. In some passages of the Old Testament God appears as an agent when he talks to people or is described as acting in a certain way. Is this then to be taken as the author himself entering into the drama? This would be quite a breach in our dramatic hermeneutics, in which the christological criterion determines the stance of the author. When God appears to become an actor in the play, we must interpret that as a character in the play claiming to speak as the author; the interpretation and discernment of elements in that character that constitute a direct revelation of God and elements that are amalgamations with human misrepresentation and misunderstanding does not depend on whether the character is named "God" but on the closeness of his message and action to Christ's. This corresponds to the mainstream Christian tradition having accepted the Old Testament as canonical and divinely inspired but at the same time insisting that it was a preparation for Christ and had to be interpreted through this lens.

In the end, however, the problem of mixed texts between direct revelation and the amalgamation with human misunderstandings is not a problem of the Old Testament alone. The reason for it is the human propensity to ever again project own misunderstandings into divine revelation.

> Every Old and New Testament saying requires [...] a process of discernment and new interpretation. As the new interpretation can be misunderstood again, this process never comes to an end. Every generation and every individual has to conduct it anew. Consequently, the true God discloses Himself only through a way of faith, on which the images that are construed all the time, have to be discerned ever again.[25]

DRAMATIC HERMENEUTICS OF HISTORY AND DOCTRINAL DEVELOPMENT

Finally, it should be noted that this dramatic hermeneutics has also been applied to the history of doctrinal development of the first millennium, especially the great christological debates and their resolution.[26] Here I can only summarize the most important insights: As in the Bible, so also

---

24. See Palaver, *Transforming the Sacred*; Girard, "Evangelical Subversion of Myth"; Girard, *I See Satan Fall*, xiii–iv, 62–70.

25. Schwager, "Biblische Texte als »Mischtexte«," 366, my translation.

26. See Schwager, *Dogma und dramatische Geschichte*.

in the church, conflicts existed and they were driven partly by legitimate differences, partly by sinful stubbornness. Formulations became candidates for dogmatization, i.e., for being declared valid authoritative expressions of the faith of the church, only when those who formulated them incorporated their opponents' legitimate concerns.[27]

The background for this insight seems to be Schwager's earliest idea of dramatic interaction, which he got from St. Ignatius of Loyola, namely that the Holy Spirit might in fact move different persons to opposing positions, not because the Spirit would contradict himself but because the human task is to discern the will of God by a dramatic process of working out the potential for mutual correction and complementarity of the differing viewpoints.[28] I suggest that many of today's conflicts in ecclesial communities could be moved towards a solution with this kind of dramatic hermeneutics as well.

CONCLUSION: REVELATION AS DRAMATIC INTER-ACTION

In conclusion, I want to admit that what I have tried to summarize here this is not just a dramatic hermeneutics, it is a dramatic theology of revelation that takes Rahner's idea of a real interaction between God and humans very seriously. What distinguishes this dramatic theology from other types of theology is that it makes this insight the linchpin of its theologizing. As a consequence, no theological topic can be adequately dealt with without taking this dramatic nature of revelation into account.

BIBLIOGRAPHY

Balthasar, Hans Urs von. *Theo-Drama. 5 Vols.* Translated by Graham Harrison. San Francisco: Ignatius, 1988–1998.

Bonhoeffer, Dietrich. *The Cost of Discipleship.* New York: Touchstone, 1937.

Girard, René. "The Evangelical Subversion of Myth." In *Politics and Apocalypse*, edited by Robert G. Hamerton-Kelly, 29–49. East Lansing, MI: Michigan State University Press, 2007.

———. *I See Satan Fall Like Lightning.* Translated by James G. Williams. Maryknoll, NY: Orbis, 2001.

Goodhart, Sandor. "A Jewish-Christian Dialogue." In *The Prophetic Law*, 33–55. East Lansing, MI: Michigan State University Press, 2014.

---

27. Niewiadomski and Moosbrugger, "Dogma und dramatische Geschichte," 28–29.
28. See Schwager, "Das dramatische Kirchenverständnis," 182–84.

Heim, S. Mark. *Saved from Sacrifice: A Theology of the Cross*. Grand Rapids: Eerdmans, 2006.

Jersak, Brad, and Michael Hardin, eds. *Stricken by God? Nonviolent Identification and the Victory of Christ*. Grand Rapids: Eerdmans, 2007.

Moosbrugger, Mathias. "René Girard and Raymund Schwager on Religion, Violence, and Sacrifice. New Insights from Their Correspondence." *Journal of Religion and Violence* 1 (2013) 147–66.

Niewiadomski, Józef. "Das Opfer-Täter-Verhängnis Und Die Frage Nach Dem Letzten Gericht." In *Erben Der Gewalt. Zum Umgang Mit Unrecht, Leid Und Krieg*, edited by Jörg Ernesti et al., 101–16. Weger, Brixen, 2015.

Niewiadomski, Józef, and Mathias Moosbrugger. "*Dogma Und Dramatische Geschichte* Als Versuch Der Rehabilitierung Des Kirchlichen Dogmas." In *Dogma und dramatische Geschichte. Christologie im Kontext von Judentum, Islam und moderner Marktkultur*, edited by Józef Niewiadomski and Mathias Moosbrugger. Gesammelte Schriften, 17–37. Freiburg i. Br.: Herder, 2014.

Palaver, Wolfgang. *Transforming the Sacred into Saintliness. Reflecting on Violence and Religion with René Girard*. Elements in Religion and Violence. Cambridge: Cambridge University Press, 2020.

Peter, Karin. "Die Bibelhermeneutik Von Raymund Schwager Als Inspiration Und Spezifische Aufmerksamkeitslenkung Für Die Bibeldidaktik." *ZKTh* 142 (2020) 378–95.

Rahner, Karl. "Theos Im Neuen Testament." In *Sämtliche Werke*, 346–403. Freiburg: Herder, 1997.

Schwager, Raymund. "Biblische Texte Als »Mischtexte«. Das Hermeneutisch-Spirituelle Programm Der ›Entmischung‹." In *Kirchliche, politische und theologische Zeitgenossenschaft*, edited by Mathias Moosbrugger, 360–67. Freiburg i. Br.: Herder, 2017.

———. "Briefwechsel Mit Hans Urs Von Balthasar." In *Kirchliche, politische und theologische Zeitgenossenschaft*, edited by Mathias Moosbrugger, 451–71. Freiburg i. Br.: Herder, 2017.

———. *Dogma Und Dramatische Geschichte. Christologie Im Kontext Von Judentum, Islam Und Moderner Marktkultur*. Edited by Józef Niewiadomski and Mathias Moosbrugger. Gesammelte Schriften. Freiburg i. Br.: Herder, 2014.

———. "Das Dramatische Kirchenverständnis Bei Ignatius Von Loyola. Historisch-Pastoraltheologische Studie Über Die Stellung Der Kirche in Den Exerzitien Und Im Leben Des Ignatius." In *Frühe Hauptwerke*, edited by Mathias Moosbrugger, 37–256. Freiburg i. Br.: Herder, 2016.

———. *Jesus in the Drama of Salvation: Toward a Biblical Doctrine of Redemption*. Translated by James G. Williams and Paul Haddon. New York: Crossroad, 1999.

———. *Must There Be Scapegoats? Violence and Redemption in the Bible*. Translated by M. L. Assad. 2nd ed. New York: Crossroad, 2000.

———. "Der Sohn Gottes Und Die Weltsünde. Zur Erlösungslehre Von Hans Urs Von Balthasar." In *Der wunderbare Tausch. Zur Geschichte und Deutung der Erlösungslehre*, edited by Nikolaus Wandinger, 448–511. Freiburg i. Br.: Herder, 2015.

———. *Der Wunderbare Tausch. Zur Geschichte Und Deutung Der Erlösungslehre*. Gesammelte Schriften. Edited by Józef Niewiadomski. Edited by Nikolaus Wandinger. Freiburg i. Br.: Herder, 2015.

Wandinger, Nikolaus. "Salvation through Forgiveness or through the Cross? Raymund Schwager's Dramatic Solution to a False Alternative." In *Mimesis and Atonement: René Girard and the Doctrine of Salvation*, edited by Michael Kirwan and Sheelah Treflé Hidden, 95–114. New York: Bloomsbury, 2017.

Chapter 11
Incarnational-Trinitarian Hermeneutics
JENS ZIMMERMANN

This chapter shows that Christians should relate to the world and others through an incarnational-Trinitarian interpretive framework. They should do so because the Bible and the Christian tradition teach that the world is created out of nothing by a God who became human to perfect and glorify his creation, and that this ultimately incomprehensible God revealed himself as the unified relation of three "persons" recorded in the Scriptures as Father, Son, and Spirit.

Three main assumptions ground this claim. First, I use the terms "interpretation" or "hermeneutics" in the sense established by the tradition of philosophical hermeneutics beginning with Martin Heidegger and further refined by Hans-Georg Gadamer and Paul Ricœur. For them, interpretation is an essential part of being human; human knowing is essentially interpretive. And, as we will see, the incarnation itself reveals the hermeneutic nature of truth because here the transcendent truth of God is mediated through temporal, linguistic, and cultural media of first-century Jewish-Palestinian culture. Moreover, embracing the fundamentally interpretive nature of human knowing liberates us from the tenaciously persistent misconception that religious truth claims are less true or rational than scientific assertions.

Second, Christians ought to embrace a realist view of reality in contrast to our presently pervasive anti-realist cultural mindset. Realism means that material and spiritual realities are not *essentially* socially constructed but rather are discovered. Christians *must* be metaphysical realists because they believe not in an impersonal, scientific construct called "nature" but in a creation endowed with intelligibility and order by a personal creator God. In contrast to a certain scientific definition of "nature," creation is not a strictly immanent, materialist realm governed by the more or less mathematically determined laws of physics. Even though quantum physics since the mid-twentieth century has revolutionized this static, self-enclosed view of nature,[1] much current science and popular culture nevertheless refuses to admit the intersection of materiality and spirituality. Realists hold to (and respectfully appropriate) the givenness or *giftedness* of naturally ordered life, and to creational dynamics in conformity to which humans flourish. Some call this realist view of interpretation "critical realism" to capture our immersion in an intelligible, objective world that is nevertheless accessible only through the historical, social, and linguistic structuring of human consciousness.

Third, an incarnational-Trinitarian hermeneutics assumes a biblical anthropology. However we may explain human origins, human beings are made by God for communion with God. As those created in God's image (more on this below), human beings are *persons*. Persons reflect the Trinitarian mystery insofar as they are irreducible to any analysis and are structured according to the Word (*Logos*) in their constitutive freedom, sociality, and desire for transcendence. The incarnation has revealed the goal of personal existence as becoming *Christlike*. By "putting on Christ," as the apostle Paul says (Rom 13:14), persons fulfill their destiny to be transformed into his likeness (2 Cor 3:17–18).

These three basic assumptions—a creational realist cosmology, hermeneutic epistemology, and biblical personalist anthropology—provide guiding principles for the Christian tradition's incarnational-Trinitarian interpretive framework. We will now sketch some practical implications of this hermeneutic for the Christian life by answering three questions: Who is the interpreter? What is the reality within which we interpret? And, toward what end do we interpret?

WHO IS THE INTERPRETER? TRINITARIAN-INCARNATIONAL ANTHROPOLOGY

To respond to the question "who interprets?", we start with the incarnation. The Christian tradition holds that the image and likeness of God in which human beings were created (Gen 1:26–7) is Christ (Col 1:15), into whose image we are to be transformed (Col 3:10) by putting on his new humanity (Rom 13:14; Col 4:24). Christ shows us what true humanity looks like and at the same time enables everyone who believes in him to become like him

---

1. See, for example, Heisenberg, *Physics and Philosophy*; and Borella and Smith, *Rediscovering the Integral Cosmos*.

through direct participation in his human-divine life. Briefly put, Christ reveals who human interpreters are in the first place (those made in his image), who they are to become, and therefore toward what end we interpret the Scriptures and the world alike. In short, for Christians, all interpretation is dedicated to humanizing all our relationships by allowing Christ to take shape in us. Paradoxically, the more we become like Christ, the more we become our true, God-intended, particular selves.[2] The Christian interpreter is a finite creature who shares in the new humanity of God and interprets reality in general and the Scriptures in particular in order to become shaped into Christlikeness. To become Christlike is to love one another with the same love God displays for humanity and to become immortal by the power of his grace.[3]

Human knowledge itself follows the pattern of the incarnation. God's becoming human is the becoming flesh, in time and space, of God's transcendent being. God's truth is mediated through the materiality of human culture, tradition, and language. In contrast to Platonism, for which the truth of ultimate reality could only be refracted through matter as a distorted copy, the incarnation assures us that just as Jesus renders truly present God the Father (John 1:18), so is God's truth—indeed, God himself—conveyed without essential loss within history through the materiality of language, tradition, and culture. Yet we must also remember that we are fallible human interpreters of God's perfect self-interpretation; even if in Christ "all the fulness of God was pleased to dwell" (Col 1:19), this does not mean we can exhaustively interpret and thereby "capture" that fulness with our limited interpretive abilities.

Dietrich Bonhoeffer clearly grasped this incarnationally rooted, hermeneutic quality of our knowledge of God:

> Just as the reality of God has entered the reality of the world in Christ, what is Christian cannot be had otherwise than in what is worldly, the "supernatural" only in the natural, the holy only

---

2. The reason Christ indwelling us does not produce mere clones but shapes each person into his or her unique personality lies in God's non-competitive relation to creation. God is not merely one Person among others, not simply "another Thou" who stands over against us like any human other, only bigger or more knowledgeable. God is rather the very creator of our personhood, the one who created all things out of nothing and is the very ground and sustaining power of the person. Because this creator has, in his incomparable love, freed the human other to be remade into God's image, we perceive him as another "Thou." However, we only are persons because God loves us and recognizes our uniqueness. It is because of this special creator-creature relation that Christ's indwelling cultivates our unique personal selves. See Guardini, *Welt und Person*, 42.

3. See, e.g., Athanasius, *On the Incarnation*, §44 (p. 147).

> in the profane, the revelational only in the rational. The unity of the reality of God and the reality of the world established in Christ . . . realizes itself again and again in human beings. Still, that which is Christian is not identical with the worldly, the natural with the supernatural, the revelational with the rational. Rather, the unity that exists between them is given only in the Christ-reality, and that means only as accepted by faith in this ultimate reality. This unity is preserved by the fact that the worldly and the Christian, etc., mutually prohibit every static independence of the one over against the other, that they behave toward each other polemically, and precisely therein witness to their common reality, their unity in the Christ-reality.[4]

Bonhoeffer sums up for us the Christian's interpretive stance within a meaningful creational order. In Christ, the unity of all things in the creator God has been revealed. We now know that Christ came, as Athanasius put it, "to fill all things with the knowledge of Himself."[5] Yet Christ also shows us a tension between the fallen created order and the new creation he inaugurates. As Bonhoeffer puts it, the ultimate word of the renewed creation and the penultimate fallen creation are in "polemical" (i.e., war-like) tension. Indeed, Christ shows fallen creation what it was really meant to be, yet this transformation that already occurred in his deified humanity will only happen at his second coming. Christians live in the old humanity, the old world, but are already sharing in the new. Therefore, our reality is opaque to us. The creative, interpretive task of the Christian and of the church, then, is to discern God's ultimate reality within the penultimate and fallen—yet *reconciled*—creation that awaits final renewal.

THE INCARNATIONAL-TRINITARIAN BASIS OF REALITY

All interpreters, especially Christians, must also account for the fact that who we are and how we understand truth depends on our intuitive understanding about the nature of being as such. Everyone thinks and acts, whether consciously or subconsciously, based on some understanding of ultimate reality that frames how one integrates life experience into a meaningful whole. In this sense, all human knowledge proceeds on a fundamental trust or *faith* in the nature of reality. To this extent, then, all human knowing is equally a matter of faith. Christians differ only, albeit radically, in their belief that "God alone is the ultimate reality."[6] As Bonhoeffer explains, "That

---

4. Bonhoeffer, *Ethics*, 59.
5. Athanasius, *On the Incarnation*, §45 (p. 151).
6. Bonhoeffer, *Ethics*, 48.

God alone is the ultimate reality is, however, not an idea meant to sublimate the actual world, nor is it the religious perfection of a profane worldview. It is rather a faithful Yes to God's self-witness, God's self-revelation."[7]

Moreover, on account of the incarnation, Christian interpretation must always be christological. Bonhoeffer puts this christological emphasis as follows:

With what reality will we reckon in our life? With the reality of God's revelatory word or with the so-called realities of life? With divine grace or with earthly inadequacies? With the resurrection or with death? This question itself, which none can answer by his own choice without answering it falsely, already presupposes a given answer: that God, however we decide, has already spoken the revelatory word and that we, even in our false reality, can live no other way than from the true reality of the word of God. The question about ultimate reality places us in such an embrace by its answer that there is no way we can escape from it. This answer carries us into the reality of God's revelation in Jesus Christ from which it comes.[8]

Bonhoeffer's point is that everyone should be conscious of the interpretive framework one inhabits because it shapes our expectations and guides our actions. As we have seen, for Christians this framework is God's self-revelation in Christ and is therefore, as I will show, Trinitarian. Yet there are many possible ways of thinking about ultimate reality: materialist or naturalist conceptions that deny any transcendent reality, general notions of transcendence or spiritual dimensions, or concrete, non-Christian traditions religious or otherwise. It is worth emphasizing that no neutral vantage point for engaging reality exists; everyone, no matter of what philosophical, intellectual, or cultural persuasion, trusts—indeed, has *faith* in—some interpretive framework of ultimately *metaphysical* assumptions not verifiable by the empirical, scientific means. Natural science itself, for example, relies on the metaphysical assumptions of the cosmos' intelligibility and human rationality. Hence there is no privileged access to reality, even though natural science often claims this for itself.

The distinctly Christian view of reality, as we have seen, is determined by the church's confession that "Jesus is Lord" (John 20:28; Rev 17:14), and therefore by the confession of a *Triune God*. Jesus's claim that "I and the Father are one" (John 10:30), and the New Testament's equation of the God's Spirit with Christ (Rom 8:9) required a Trinitarian understanding of God, as also indicated by the church's primordial practice of baptizing in the name of Father, Son, and Holy Spirit. Major Christian creeds like the Apostle's

---

7. Bonhoeffer, *Ethics*, 49.
8. Bonhoeffer, *Ethics*, 49.

creed or the Niceno-Constantinopolian creed serve to remind Christians of this biblical view of reality. We confess our hermeneutical framework every time we profess to believe "in one God, the Father almighty, maker of heaven and earth, of all things visible and invisible," in "one Lord Jesus Christ, the son of God" who is "begotten and not created," and in "one Holy Spirit, the Lord, the Giver of Life."

This Trinitarian framework enables Christians, for instance, to appreciate our irreducibly corporeal existence. Early theologians like Irenaeus (c. 130–c. 202) upheld a Trinitarian understanding of creation against gnostic religions that opposed matter to spirit and consequently rejected both God's enfleshment and the bodily resurrection of the dead. For Irenaeus, however, God creates humanity out of matter *and* spirit with his two hands, the Son and the Spirit.[9] As he puts it: "for through all these things God reveals himself as Father, [a process] wherein the Spirit works, the Son truly administers, and the father truly approves, [and in which] the human being, however, is truly completed unto salvation."[10] And more generally with respect to this interpretive frame, according to Augustine anyone who accesses truth, believer or not, does so by the power of God's Spirit. God's Spirit illumines *all* truth through God's "inner light of truth (*interiore luce veritatis*)," the things God "manifests internally."[11] And the wisdom that the Spirit illumines in our use of reason is itself "Christ, that is, God's unchangeable power and eternal wisdom."[12] We therefore cannot rigorously divide the truth of the church and of the world into mutually exclusive categories.

This incarnational-Trinitarian view of creation has several other consequences for a Christian hermeneutic, three of which we note here. First, Christians hold that there is one creator God who created all things out of nothing. Irenaeus already lists this belief as part of Christianity's basic doctrinal framework (the rule of faith): "The rule of truth which we hold, is, that there is one God Almighty, who made all things by His Word, and fashioned and formed, out of that which had no existence, all things that exist."[13] As Simon Oliver has pointed out, this belief significantly shapes our understanding of reality. God as creator is beyond creation, and therefore *not* another being or object, not even the greatest or most powerful, among other beings or objects. God is rather the sustaining ground of all being, that

---

9. Irenaeus, *Adversus Haereses*, IV.Preface.4.
10. Irenaeus, *Adversus Haereses*, IV.20.6.
11. Augustinus, *De Magistro—der Lehrer*, 12.40.
12. Augustinus, *De Magistro—der Lehrer*, 11.38.
13. Irenaeus, *Adversus Haereses*, I.xxii.1; trans. *ANF* 1:347.

which makes life, being, and our very thinking about being possible.[14] In this way, *creatio ex nihilo* invalidates competitive relations between God and creation.[15] More of God's presence or activity in creation, that is to say, does not mean less of human freedom. In fact, as Oliver notes, true freedom only becomes possible on account of creation out of nothing.[16] Only a God who is himself entirely self-sufficient can grant the relative autonomy of creation and of the human creature who reflects God's own character of freedom. If critics of Christianity fully grasped this classic teaching, they could turn from a rather worn-out and misapplied complaint that the traditional view of God constitutes *onto-theology* (i.e., that God is reduced to a being among other beings) to more interesting grievances.

Moreover, the doctrine of creation rules out the opposition of science and theology. Being in all its original aspects was called into existence and is sustained by one creator God. Hence, however we think of physics, human origins, or the nature of the universe, natural science and other discourses, like theology, cannot ultimately be in conflict since all things visible and invisible have the same author. Furthermore, creation out of nothing establishes the nature of being as *gift*. Creation is the gift of God, made and sustained by him. Human beings are creatures, dependent on God's sustaining grace, and they receive creation not to master it but to tend, cultivate, and guard it as God's gift.

Only a modern scientific understanding of nature as a self-contained material mechanism void of any spiritual or mental dimensions could, philosophically speaking, permit the forcible manipulation of the environment and/or human nature. This misconception of "nature" as mere raw material lies at the root of many current social issues, including environmental exploitation, the growing transgender ideology, and the reinterpretation of biological life as information or data. Whether we believe that the body is a foreign object that should conform to my subjective desires or sense of identity; or whether we describe ourselves in computational terms as biological hardware that can be programmed by upgradable software programs, the root cause of the dehumanizing and ultimately self-destructive tendencies is our erroneous view of creation. Many modern critics from Martin Heidegger and Hans-Georg Gadamer to Jacques Maritain, C. S. Lewis, or George Grant (and, more recently, Charles Taylor) have pointed out this fateful shift from the premodern idea of a higher natural order to which

---

14. Oliver, "Every Good and Perfect Gift is from Above," 33.
15. Tanner, *Jesus, Humanity and the Trinity*, 2.
16. Oliver, "Every Good and Perfect Gift is from Above," 35.

human thinking and acting should conform to the constructivist view that we are masters of nature and of ourselves.

The second important consequence of an incarnational-Trinitarian frame is the nature of God as *personal*. The Trinity establishes personal relationality as the ontological core of being. Even before Christ's coming, the utterly transcendent God of the Hebrew faith established an I-Thou relation at the heart of reality, which the Jewish scholar Martin Buber famously described in his 1923 book *I and Thou*. "I-Thou," Buber writes, is "the foundational word" of relationality that can only be spoke with one's whole being.[17] Buber also recognized the gift-nature of reality and the importance of *encountering* reality rather than constructing it.[18] The experience of art gripping us and speaking to us, for example, is based on this idea of encounter. Nonetheless, encountering the world of things—tables, trees, etc.—is an I-it relation that is secondary to the fundamental I-Thou relation based on God's presence in all things.[19] And it is only in encountering another limit to myself, another person or "Thou," that our personal being is confirmed as "I."[20]

It was not, however, until the incarnation that the full extent of reality's personal structure was revealed and the creative wisdom and word of God was equated with the incarnate Christ. As Paul puts it:

> He is the image of the invisible God, the first-born of all creation; for in him all things were created, in heaven and on earth, visible and invisible, whether thrones or dominions or principalities or authorities—all things were created through him and for him. He is before all things, and in him all things hold together. He is the head of the body, the church; he is the beginning, the first-born from the dead, that in everything he might be pre-eminent. For in him all the fulness of God was pleased to dwell, and through him to reconcile to himself all things,

---

17. Buber, *Ich und Du*, 39.

18. "Die Welt als Erfahrung gehört dem Grundwort Ich-Es zu. Das Grundwort Ich-Du stiftet die Welt der Beziehung." Buber, *Ich und Du*, 41. Buber stipulates three spheres within which this world of personal relation arises: life with nature; life with other human beings; and life with "mental entities" (geistigen Wesenheiten), which is also a reflection of personal life but without the dimension of uttered language.

19. The Hebrew Bible also personifies God's creative and sustaining power of the cosmos in the figure of wisdom, who was with God when he laid the foundations of the earth. See Prov 8:22–31.

20. "Der Mensch wird am Du zum Ich." Buber, *Ich und Du*, 55. For Buber, higher animals, when addressed by humans, can be on the verge of consciousness, but even then they remain selves without proper egos.

whether on earth or in heaven, making peace by the blood of his cross. (Col 1:15–20)

The reconciliation and glorification of creation to God through the perfect humanity of Christ had important implications for Christian Scripture, cosmology, and anthropology. Early Christian theologians re-interpreted all of Scripture and God's purpose for creation in light of Christ's becoming human, crucifixion, resurrection, and ascension. For Christ was interpreted as the second Adam (a term standing for humanity as a whole rather than for an individual male) who completed the task of uniting creation with God its creator—a task in which the first Adam had failed. The incarnation showed, to use Irenaeus's favorite term taken from Eph 1:10, that Adam had failed to *recapitulate* creation in himself in order to draw it into communion with God. It is through Christ that this task is finally completed so that all creation is saved through humanity. Through the humanity of God, creation itself "will be set free from its bondage to decay and obtain the glorious liberty of the children of God" (Rom 8:21).

Early Christian theologians like the Cappadocian fathers[21] and, later, Maximus the Confessor (580–662) held that Christ, God incarnate, completed the task originally assigned to human beings to recapitulate and glorify God's creation as a conscious and personal praise of the creator. In human beings, who combine in themselves matter and spirit, the cosmos was meant to respond in love to God. The Greek philosopher and theologian Christos Yannaras argues that the incarnation, God's becoming flesh, shows us that the purpose of creation itself is to become transformed into the personal:

> The incarnation of the Logos does not mean that God becomes the world and the world becomes God. It means that the world's personal potentialities and their universal recapitulation in the human person, the unisimilar existential truth of personal universality towards which every form of existence tends dynamically, reaches its natural 'end' in the theantropic person of Christ, in the unconfused, immutable, undivided and unseparated unity of the divine and human natures—of God and the world—in one person and one hypostasis.[22]

---

21. The Cappadocian fathers include Basil of Caesarea (330–379), also known as Basil the Great; Gregory of Nazianzus (329–390), the second of three church fathers in Eastern Christian tradition given the title "the Theologian" along with the author of John and Symeon the New Theologian; and Gregory of Nyssa (335–395), Basil's younger brother and recognized as "the father of fathers" at the Second Council of Nicea in 787.

22. Yannaras, *Person and Eros*, 151.

This christological interpretation of reality accomplishes two important things. First, through Christ, all aspects of reality are interconnected, and any false dichotomy between matter and spirit or mind is eradicated. An incarnational-Trinitarian hermeneutic countenances neither the ancient gnostics whom Irenaeus already battled with the incarnation, nor modern transhumanist gnostics who dream of leaving the body behind in order to achieve immortality through the digitization of the flesh. Christian belief in the resurrection of the dead evidences the great value the tradition places on the body. And, the embodied, personal existence that flows from a Christian worldview thus defines the *historicity* of human being and knowing. We are addressed and known by God as unique, embodied persons, whose knowledge, shaped within time by our historical circumstances while yet striving to transcend them toward universal insights into the human condition, we call "wisdom."

Secondly, Christ the *Logos*' union and maintenance of the cosmos prohibits the opposition of faith and reason. This logos, is, however, not that of the Greeks nor the propositional, quasi-scientific knowledge favoured by analytic philosophers or cognitive scientists who reduce mind to algorithmic codes. The Christian logos is fundamentally that of a person who addresses us.

The German Lutheran theologian Oswald Bayer has argued that this emphasis on the personal could possibly be too narrow. He attributes such a reduction to Karl Barth's dialectical theology, the shortcoming of which lies "in its lack of attention to the constitutive mediation of God's address through the world. Misled by its personalism, [dialectical theology] insisted almost absolutely on [God's] address and truth as 'purely' personal encounter. *The world's presence paled by comparison.*"[23] Bayer's judgment parallels Bonhoeffer's analysis that not only the Reformed Barth but also Lutheran theologians obscured Christian's ability to reason based on God's creation. As Bonhoeffer explained:

> The concept of the natural has fallen into disrepute in Protestant ethics. For some theologians it was completely lost in the darkness of general sinfulness, whereas for others it took on the brightness of the primal creation. Both were grave misuses that led to the complete elimination of the category of the natural from Protestant thought [. . .] The significance of the natural for the gospel was obscured, and the Protestant church lost the ability to give clear guidance on the burning questions of natural life. Thereby it left numerous people without answers or help in

---

23. Bayer, *Schöpfung als Anrede*, 3 (italics added).

> vital decisions, and fell more and more into a static proclamation of divine grace. Confronted by the light of grace, everything human and natural sank into the night of sin, so one no longer dared pay attention to the relative differences within the human and the natural, for fear that grace would lose its character as grace.... The results of this loss were grievous and far-reaching. If there were no longer any relative differences within a fallen creation, then the way was clear for any kind of arbitrariness and disorder, and natural life, with its concrete decisions and orders, could no longer be considered responsible to God.[24]

Bonhoeffer tries to reverse Protestantism's lack of attention to the Book of Nature, as it is called, by recovering natural reasoning about human dignity and rights. The later Barth tried to counter the same gap between revelation and nature in his *Church Dogmatics* with a christological reconstruction of reality, yet, as Bayer argues once again, Barth never succeeded. He was unable to maintain a natural theology, on the one hand, and distinguish clearly between God's presence in the world and his saving address through special revelation, on the other.[25]

Bonhoeffer's lament is motivated by an ethical problem: the inability of Protestants to oppose evil practices like the Nazi euthanasia program on general, rational grounds that, while not contradicting the teachings of Scripture, do not require Christian confessional allegiance. Ethics, however, is not the only interpretive area affected by the refusal of natural theology. What about aesthetics, for example? What about more general knowledge about God and the human condition we find in art, poetry, literature, and music?

The key task is to close the gap between God's transcendence and immanence in creation without leveling everything to our subjective whims, whims that can find (and have found) brutally destructive expressions in political, dehumanizing mass movements. (Barth, after all, was correct to worry about this danger.) The Catholic theologian Hans Urs von Balthasar argues that the experience of the *beautiful* can combine immanence and transcendence. In fact, for Balthasar, the human experience of beauty is analogous to encountering a personal other and, ultimately, to the gracious, loving address of God. When we encounter beauty, whether in a work of art or in the self-less, gracious actions of other people, we are confronted with something that we did not construct or control. We encounter something that draws us out, something that demands our respect, attention, and

---

24. Bonhoeffer, *Ethics*, 171–73.
25. Bayer, *Schöpfung als Anrede*, 3.

reciprocation. The phenomena of the personal (as address) and the beautiful (as encounter) thus converge in *love*.[26] It is only finally God's love, as revealed in Jesus Christ, that underlie both beauty and the power of the personal.[27]

Moreover, love is something that, unless I want to distort or ignore it, requires my self-denial and utter attention to another. This is already so in our human relations, but all the more so in God's love for us. When we encounter God's love, he reveals our lack of love and the unconditional, gracious offer of his love so crassly that our only possible reaction is worship.[28] In Christ the *Logos*, God's love as grace reveals the glory (*doxa*) and therefore the splendor or beauty of God.

Finally, the third crucial consequence of an incarnational-Trinitarian interpretive framework is the centrality of language for human knowledge. Early Christian theologians, following John's Gospel, held that Christ, as "true God," is also "God, the Word and Power of God."[29] In the beginning, as the Gospel of John tells us, "was the Word." In God's creation, all things exist through the Word (πάντα δι' αὐτοῦ ἐγένετο), and in him toward God (πρὸς τὸν θεόν, John 1:1–3). Creation came into being and exists through God's speech. The Bible thus affirms the Word-Character of creation and therefore the linguistic nature of understanding. As the Catholic philosopher Romano Guardini explains, "the fact that the World exists in the form of [God's] speech is the reason why there is language in the first place." The world itself is "wordlike (*worthaft*) [that is], it proceeds from speech and exists as spoken." This linguistic structure of creation "explains the human possibility of language and the objective world's disclosure of meaning through language."[30]

An incarnational-Trinitarian view of creation thus yields the following interpretive framework: as creatures, we inhabit an already meaningful cosmos. The word "cosmos" means "order," a rational-moral order of things built into God's creation for us to discover and to which we can conform. Going against this grain of the universe will have detrimental repercussions. Deciding, for example, that we can ignore biology as the basis of our sexuality will inevitably turn out to be destructive of our humanity. Moreover, the incarnation reveals that in Christ all aspects of reality are unified, and that the beautiful (or aesthetics) and the personal are indeed fundamental categories of truth. Hence, not only natural science but (much more

---

26. See, e.g., Balthasar, *Glory of the Lord*, vol. 1.
27. Bayer, *Schöpfung als Anrede*, 92–94.
28. Balthasar, *Glaubhaft ist nur Liebe*, 36–37.
29. Athanasius, *On the Incarnation*, §55 (p. 108).
30. Guardini, *Welt und Person*, 141–42.

profoundly) art, literature, poetry, and related humanities disciplines that speak the personal language of God's cosmos contribute to our understanding of the human condition.

And yet, as Christ's renewing work through the incarnation demonstrates, creation and human creatures are not as they should be: they require the renewal that is already present in Christ the firstborn of the new creation. It is from his new humanity that we must discern what truly human action and a humane society look like. The task of the church, Paul tell us, is to reflect this new humanity in unity and peace for the world to see (Eph 2:14–16).

INTERPRETATION AS CHRIST FORMATION

Given this framework, we must ask: to what end to we interpret? In other words, what is the purpose of the Christian life? The Christian life, as we indicated above, is the pattern for *all* human life, namely fulfilling the purpose of our creation to become like Christ by being drawn through the power of the Spirit "into the very triune life of God."[31] The Eastern tradition, along with Western theologians like Jerome, Augustine, and Aquinas, describe this transformative process as *deification*, by which they mean *Christification*: becoming like Christ and therefore becoming a human being in the most complete possible sense. I conclude by briefly reflecting on the significance of Christification within a Trinitarian-incarnational hermeneutic.

First, in an ecclesial context, interpretation is Christformation through the reading of the Scriptures, participation in worship and the sacraments, and the practice of virtue. As modern Christians, we are wont to say that these practices immerse us in God's story. Let us remember, however, that we mean by this not listening to mere fiction but our participation in a *reality* that has a narrative structure. The sacrament of baptism truly initiates us into a new life and reality that Christ won for us, and the sacrament of communion is not a mere commemoration but is the true feeding on Christ's person that strengthens our participation in the humanity of God. The church's liturgy draws believers into salvation history and unites them with the presence of all the saints. Finally, our reading of the Scriptures is a similar encounter, for the Scriptures, too, are "a sacrament of God's presence."[32] They are a part of fallible creation through which God elects to make himself present to us. This approach to the Bible does not do away with careful historical-grammatical exegesis, but it makes such reading subservient to

---

31. Torrance, *Worship, Community and the Triune God of Grace*, 18.
32. Sonderegger, *Systematic Theology*, 2:69.

encounter with Christ, who is the heart of the biblical text. We must read the Bible, as Bonhoeffer puts it, as the book of the Christian church through the lens of Christ, who is the new creation, "the beginning, the new, the end of our entire world."[33]

If the purpose of reading the Scriptures is transformation into Christlikeness, then biblical interpretation serves virtue formation. Christians should read the Scriptures not principally to satisfy curiosity or to nail down "what really happened" but to enter into God's presence and, just so, to become changed into Christlikeness. The Western tradition had termed such transformative reading *Lectio divina*, a prayerful contemplative "mastication" of the text focused on communion with God and the transformative work of the Holy Spirit. In the early and medieval churches, such reading was accompanied by ascetic practices of abstaining from bodily pleasures like food and sex to subordinate the bodily passions, thus directing the whole human person back to communion with God.[34] Without denying the potential excesses of such practices, I believe Christians would do well to recover this deeply embodied reading practice in service of virtue formation. Habituation to life practices in Christlikeness are the only effective measure for countering the currently fashionable assimilation of Christian life to many follies of contemporary culture.

Second, interpretation as Christformation is not limited to personal bible study nor even the church community but also pertains to the so-called "secular" realm. Not only does a Christian's life within the various overlapping spheres of life, including secular, civic life, contribute to formation into Christlikeness; the Christian also has a responsibility toward the secular world. While the church is not the world, *all human beings* are called to communion with God so that they may experience true freedom and liberation from the fear of death. As we stated earlier, from a Trinitarian-incarnational point of view, the Christian life is about becoming most fully human. Christ has modelled the perfect human life in service to others in his dedication to freedom, responsibility, justice, and peaceful communion.

A Christian hermeneutic should thus be dedicated to humanizing culture and work within its institutions, including politics, toward these ends.[35] The aim of such humanization is not to create heaven on earth

---

33. Bonhoeffer, *Creation and Fall*, 22.

34. For a brief yet comprehensive description of asceticism as valuation rather than denigration of the body, see Larchet, *Theology of the Body*.

35. This humanization of culture entails the establishment and maintenance of laws and institutions commensurate with human persons in their uniqueness, freedom, mutual responsibility, but it may also require resisting unjust, inhuman institutional structures or social practices through argument or civil disobedience.

but to reflect, wherever possible, the new humanity inaugurated by Christ: we ought to work for peace, unity, justice, and equality while at the same time respecting the integrity of God's natural order as it currently exists until Christ returns. This is not an easy task. It requires both the embodied reading practice and sacramental church life in service of Christformation we mentioned earlier, *and* the disciplined discernment of reality based on the best possible knowledge in the relevant areas for a proposed action. Nonetheless, it is on the basis of this Trinitarian-incarnational hermeneutic that Christians should work together with all other willing parties, whether secular or of other religions, who are dedicated to human flourishing.

BIBLIOGRAPHY

Athanasius of Alexandria. *On the Incarnation: Greek Original and English Translation*, Translated by John Behr. Yonkers, NY: St. Vladimir's Seminary, 2011.

Augustine. *De Magistro—der Lehrer*, Eds. Peter Schulthess and Rudolf Rohrbach. Paderborn: Schöningh, 2002.

Bayer, Oswald. *Schöpfung als Anrede. Zu einer Hermeneutik der Schöpfung.* Tübingen: J. C. B. Mohr (Paul Siebeck), 1986.

Bonhoeffer, Dietrich. *Creation and Fall: A Theological Exposition of Genesis 1–3.* Edited by Martin Rüter and Ilse Tödt (German ed.) and John W. De Gruchy (English ed.). Translated by Douglas Steven Bax. Minneapolis: Fortress, 1996.

———. *Ethics.* Edited by Ilse Tödt et al. and translated by Reinhard Krauss et al. Dietrich Bonhoeffer Works 6. Minneapolis: Fortress, 2005.

Borella, Jean, and Wolfgang Smith. *Rediscovering the Integral Cosmos.* Brooklyn: Angelico, 2018.

Buber, Martin. *Ich und Du.* Martin Buber Werkausgabe 4: Schriften über das dialogische Prinzip. Gütersloh: Gütersloher Verlaghaus, 2019.

———. *I and Thou.* Translated by Walter Kaufmann. New York: Free, 2023.

Guardini, Romano. *Welt und Person: Versuche zur christlichen Lehre vom Menschen.* Paderborn: Matthias Grünewald Verlag, 1988.

Heisenberg, Werner. *Physics and Philosophy: The Revolution in Modern Science.* New York: HarperPerennial, 2007.

Irenaeus of Lyons. *Adversus Haereses = Gegen Die Häresien.* Fontes Christiani. Latin-German edition. Edited by Norbert Brox et al. 5 vols. Freiburg; New York: Herder, 1993.

———. "Against Heresies." In *Ante-Nicene Fathers: The Writings of the Fathers Down to A. D. 325*, edited by Alexander Roberts et al. and translated by

Alexander Roberts and William Rambaut, 1:309–567. Edinburgh: T. & T. Clark, 1885.

Larchet, Jean-Claude. *Theology of the Body.* Yonkers, NY: St. Vladimir's Seminary, 2017.

Oliver, Simon. "Every Good and Perfect Gift is from Above." In *Knowing Creation: Perspectives from Theology, Philosophy, and Science,* edited by Andrew B. Torrance and Thomas H. McCall, 27–47. Grand Rapids: Zondervan, 2018.

Sonderegger, Katherine. *Systematic Theology,* Volume 2: *The Doctrine of the Holy Trinity: Processions and Persons.* Minneapolis: Fortress, 2020.

Tanner, Kathryn. *Jesus, Humanity and the Trinity: A Brief Systematic Theology.* Minneapolis: Fortress, 2001.

Torrance, James. *Worship, Community and the Triune God of Grace.* Downers Grove, IL: InterVarsity, 1996.

Balthasar, Hans Urs von. *Glaubhaft ist nur Liebe.* Einsiedeln: Johannis Verlag, 1963.

———. *The Glory of the Lord: A Theological Aesthetics,* Volume 1: *Seeing the Form.* Edited by John Riches and translated by Erasmo Leiva-Merikakis. San Francisco: Ignatius, 2009.

———. *Love Alone Is Credible.* Translated by D. C. Schindler. San Francisco: Ignatius, 2004.

Yannaras, Christos. *Person and Eros.* Brooklyn, MA: Holy Cross Orthodox Church, 2007.

Chapter 12
Sacramental Hermeneutics
KIRK R. MACGREGOR

Sacramental hermeneutics is the style of biblical interpretation which holds that Jesus is really present in all of Scripture—namely, that the essence or nature of Scripture is the Second Person of the Trinity—and responds to Jesus's presence in the various ways that befit him. Thus Old and New Testaments alike have Jesus as their center, and the exegesis of Scripture is the disclosure of Jesus himself in all of his fullness. When interpreters approach Scripture, they come as directly to Jesus as they would if traveling with him through first-century Palestine. Just as Jesus is truly the Logos shrouded in flesh, so Scripture is truly the Logos shrouded in text. Through Scripture, all persons are made, in a Kierkegaardian vein, contemporaneous with the original eyewitnesses. Interpreters ought to receive Scripture precisely as they would receive Jesus. Though infrequently discussed as a formal category until recent times, sacramental hermeneutics has been practiced throughout the history of the church. In his four-volume *Exégèse médiévale: Les quatre sens de l'écriture* (1959–1964), Henri de Lubac showed how sacramental hermeneutics reached its high watermark in the Middle Ages via the quadriga, i.e., the literal, allegorical, tropological, and anagogical senses of Scripture.[1] Today major advocates of sacramental hermeneutics include Catholic theologian Matthew Levering and Protestant theologian Hans Boersma.

---

1. Lubac, *Exégèse médiévale*.

SACRAMENTAL THEORY OF SCRIPTURE

The sacramental theory of Scripture resembles transubstantiation in that the substance of the Old and New Testaments is the eternal Word of God, who manifests himself under the accidents of the written word of God. But unlike transubstantiation, in which the substances of bread and wine are transformed into the body and blood of Christ only when the words of consecration are spoken over them, there is never a time at which Scripture is not, in substance, the Logos. Such a theory is ontological in that it describes the permanent nature of Scripture, standing in contrast to Karl Barth's instrumental theory of biblical inspiration in which Scripture is not intrinsically the word of God but becomes the word of God only when God chooses to use it to effectuate personal encounter with an individual.[2] The sacramental theory carries profound implications for the meaning of Scripture, which assumes a twofold quality. Every passage of Scripture possesses a divine authorial intent and human authorial intent, which may or may not converge. Typically what Christ, the divine author, intends to convey by Scripture surpasses what the human author intended to convey. The human author gives the types or shadows, pointing toward the ultimately real meanings determined by Christ. A paradigm example is found in ante-Nicene patristic interpretation of the book of Joshua. When the human author intends to convey Israel's defeat of the Canaanites through divine empowerment, this intent points to what Christ intends to convey, namely spiritual Israel's defeat of the spiritual Canaanites, or the triumph of the righteous over the wicked, through the empowerment of Christ's life, death, and resurrection. Following modern biblical criticism, one may believe that God never commanded Israel to slaughter the Canaanites; however, God used this shadow to communicate the final victory of good over evil that Christ facilitates. It is therefore possible in theory for a sacramental theorist to maintain that Scripture is inerrant, verbally and plenarily, in terms of what Christ intended to convey by its words while errant in terms of what its human authors intended to convey by its words. However, a sacramental theorist does not need to take this route (and most theorists do not).

But now the question arises: how it is possible for God to ensure the communication of infallible truth through the medium of potentially fallible human words? The answer, in my judgment, may be readily found in the doctrine of divine middle knowledge and its application to the question of biblical inspiration. The doctrine of divine middle knowledge holds that, logically prior to God's decision to create the world, God knew the truth-value of all hypothetical conditionals, or statements of the form "if

---

2. Barth, *CD*, I/1:109–10.

such-and-such were the case, then so-and-so would be the case." Such knowledge is known as middle knowledge. Hence the second person of the Trinity middle-knew that if he were to create Peter and Peter found himself in a particular set of circumstances, then Peter would freely write words that serve as vehicles and even repositories for timeless truths that the Logos wished to convey. The Logos also middle-knew whether any other possible persons, if instantiated in various circumstances, would freely do the same. Apprised of this knowledge, the Logos then providentially creates a world in which just the right people find themselves in just the right circumstances for their free production of a sacramentally inerrant Scripture. This scenario resonates with the *Catechism of the Catholic Church*: "To compose the sacred books, God chose certain [humans] who, all the while he employed them in this task, made full use of their own faculties and powers so that, though he acted in them and by them, it was as true authors that they consigned to writing whatever he wanted written, and no more."[3]

Sacramental hermeneutics gained prominence through the *nouvelle théologie*, a French Catholic school of thought launched in the mid-twentieth century that attempted to retrieve the insights of the early church fathers for the *ressourcement*, or renewal, of the Catholic faith. The sacramental theory of Scripture was expounded by movement leader Jean Daniélou in his 1950 *Sacramentum futuri: études sur les origines de la typologie biblique*.[4] The theory quickly gained traction among Protestant theologians as well for the renewal of their own tradition. Since it is far less obvious that Christ is the essence of the Old Testament than that he is the essence of the New Testament, the bulk of scholarship on sacramental hermeneutics has dedicated itself to the art and science of finding Christ in the former set of covenantal writings. Boersma therefore urges the examination of "the Old Testament as a sacrament (*sacramentum*) that *already contains* the New Testament reality (*res*) of Christ."[5]

THE IMPORTANCE OF INTERPRETIVE PARTICIPATION

Sacramental hermeneutics stresses the importance of the interpreter's growth in sanctification as central to the interpretive task. The essential feature of temporal reality that makes this growth possible is its sharing in the life of God the Trinity.[6] Levering notes how this sharing was presupposed by

---

3. John Paul II, *Catechism*, 36 [1.106], quoting Paul VI, *Dei Verbum*, sec. 11. The gender-inclusive "humans" replaces the original term "men."

4. Daniélou, *Sacramentum futuri*.

5. Boersma, *Real Presence*, xv; emphasis in original.

6. Levering, *Participatory Biblical Exegesis*, 1.

Christian metaphysics until the advent of late medieval nominalism: "The standard patristic-medieval account explained creatures in terms of finite participation in divine being, and grace as a radical christological-pneumatological deepening of this participation."[7] Following the Logos Christology that dominated patristic theology, the Logos, or pre-incarnate Christ, is the divine mind, the divine rationality, and the supreme ordering principle governing and upholding the universe. Insofar as the interpreter is renewing their mind and so manifesting the purpose of reason, the interpreter is participating in the Logos. The repletive presence of the eternal word which fills the temporal dimension of life with meaning can be consumed as spiritual food by sitting down at the table of the written word (John 6:53–58). By eating this spiritual food, our souls will never die, or suffer spiritual separation from God (John 6:51, 58). All Scripture is ultimately written for our instruction (1 Cor 10:6), specifically to tutor us in righteousness so that we may be prepared to undertake every virtuous act (2 Tim 3:16–17). Yet such undertaking is not ultimately our own accomplishment, but Christ's power working through us (1 Cor 15:10). When we learn from the school of Scripture, we sit at the feet of Christ the master teacher; when we act on Scripture's teaching, we morally, not ontologically, share in God's nature (2 Pet 1:4).

Sacramental hermeneutics approaches biblical texts as an opportunity to take in knowledge from and of Christ, the master teacher and ultimate author of the texts. Such knowledge discloses the most profound meaning of Scripture itself. Studying Scripture is, in Levering's words, "a conversation with God mediated by the texts' *participatory* historicity that unites 'hermeneutical discipline' with 'spiritual discipline.'"[8] Thus exegesis is mainly "a participation in the Teacher, Jesus Christ, in and through participation in the realities that Christ, by the Holy Spirit, communicates to his Church."[9] Following Augustine (354–430), Levering furnishes a hermeneutical rubric that conjoins "God's teaching, the human author's teaching, and the interpretive teaching of the doctrinal tradition of the Church as well as that of the tradition of ecclesial exegesis."[10] In this schema, God's instruction via the words of human authors may well transcend the instruction intended by those human authors. The interpretation of Scripture is therefore not a dispassionate analysis of documents but a progressively intense communion

---

7. Levering, *Participatory Biblical Exegesis*, 3.

8. Levering, *Participatory Biblical Exegesis*, 63; emphasis in original. Levering quotes the terms "hermeneutical discipline" and "spiritual discipline" from Reno, *Ruins*, 180.

9. Levering, *Participatory Biblical Exegesis*, 63.

10. Levering, *Participatory Biblical Exegesis*, 70.

with Christ via the documents and the community of believers who share in the life of Christ.[11] The Bible possesses "efficacious authority," as it, "unlike other texts, commands and obtains the response of faith . . . When one recognizes that in and through Scripture God is teaching, one must believe Scripture's teachings. God is truth, perfect wisdom, and his words are not merely offered to us."[12] This authority took center stage in the writings of the Anabaptist theologian Balthasar Hubmaier (1480–1528). Hubmaier distinguished between merely human writings and the holy Scriptures on the grounds that the former lack efficacious authority while the latter possess it:

> This is exactly the difference between a man's [w]ord and God's [W]ord, for a man's word does not give the strength to perform what it commands, as for example, Pharaoh's magicians were unable to imitate Moses' signs and wonders. They were defeated because their words were human words, Exod. 8. But whatever God commands, he gives power and strength to those who believe and who will it, that we may do it without compulsion, for therein is the finger of God, Exod. 8, that all things are possible to the believer, Mark 9:23.[13]

God's overarching aim for the Bible is to facilitate and nurture fellowship with his adopted human children, who manifest the theological virtues of faith, hope, and love. This aim gives the Bible its unity.[14]

DIMENSIONS OF SACRAMENTAL HERMENEUTICS

Boersma argues that sacramental hermeneutics includes, but is not limited to, the following modes of reception: hospitable, incarnational, harmonious, doctrinal, nuptial, prophetic, and beatific.[15] Hospitable reception charitably welcomes Christ as Christ draws near to us in the text of Scripture.[16] This reception is evidenced in the way early church fathers such as Justin Martyr (c. 100–c. 165), Irenaeus (c. 130–c. 202), Tertullian (c. 155–c. 220), Origen (c. 185–c. 253), and John Chrysostom (c. 347–407) interpreted Genesis 18 as a theophany of Christ, accompanied by two angels, to Abraham.[17] It may be grounded, as I have argued elsewhere, in Jesus's own interpretation

---

11. Levering, *Participatory Biblical Exegesis*, 70.
12. Levering, *Participatory Biblical Exegesis*, 73.
13. Hubmaier, *Theologian*, 553.
14. Levering, *Participatory Biblical Exegesis*, 73.
15. Boersma, *Real Presence*, vii–ix.
16. Boersma, *Real Presence*, 56.
17. MacGregor, *John's Gospel*, 169–74; Boersma, *Real Presence*, 56–80.

of Genesis 18 (John 8:31–59), displayed in his observation that the Jewish leaders, unlike Abraham, sought to kill him (John 8:39). Indeed, the Jewish leaders understood Jesus to be claiming that he had met Abraham (John 8:57). Based on the linguistic evidence, I contend that the only plausible Old Testament referent to Abraham's having the seeming opportunity to kill Jesus but not attempting to do so is Genesis 18.[18] For Origen, Genesis 18 reveals that purity of life is a prerequisite for meeting Jesus, based on the fact that Abraham and all males in his household were circumcised prior to the theophanic encounter (Gen 17:23–27). This circumcision Origen took to mean "circumcision of the ears, of the lips, of the flesh, and of the heart."[19] By contrast, Lot, ostensibly uncircumcised in these ways, could only receive the two angels but not the preincarnate Christ.[20] When Christ condescends to us and accommodates his own divine being to us in the sacred text, the interpreter is called to respond with the reverse of xenophobia, namely a *philoxenia* in which the stranger becomes a friend.[21]

Chrysostom employed the exegesis of Genesis 18 as a case study of a *media via* between an exclusively literal and an exclusively allegorical approach. This *media via* constitutes a hermeneutical precision which accurately perceives what Christ communicates in each text of Scripture, both Old and New Testaments. Chrysostom also stressed that a necessary condition for hermeneutical precision is other-centered relational virtue.[22] Accordingly, if the interpreter does not show *agapē* to other human beings, the interpreter cannot accurately decipher Scripture. Boersma explains that, for Chrysostom, "Abraham does *not* know who his visitors are, and it is precisely this lack of knowledge that makes his virtue stand out . . . In other words, Abraham's hospitality functions not at the vertical level, as something offered to God—though that is the serendipitous side effect—but it functions first and foremost at the horizontal level: it is offered to unknown, needy strangers."[23] Chrysostom's reading is reminiscent of the parable of the sheep and the goats (Matt 25:31–46), in which Jesus remarks that what is done to the least of these is done to him (Matt 25:40).

Incarnational reception claims that Christ and the New Testament principles he established are seeds already implanted in all Old Testament

---

18. MacGregor, *John's Gospel*, 159–68.
19. Boersma, *Real Presence*, 67.
20. Boersma, *Real Presence*, 65–6.
21. Boersma, *Real Presence*, 58.
22. Boersma, *Real Presence*, 70, 72–73.
23. Boersma, *Real Presence*, 74; emphasis in original.

events, even those that shock our moral sensibilities.[24] As a case in point, Boersma calls attention to Origen's largely allegorical exegesis of the Conquest narratives in Joshua.[25] There is scholarly disagreement about whether Origen believed the battles depicted in Joshua actually occurred.[26] As Mark Chenoweth points out, "Surprising as it may be to the modern reader of Joshua, Origen never deals at length with the question of whether God *did* order Joshua the son of Nun to destroy so many people . . . Given that Origen does not believe that every event in scripture had to occur, we are left somewhat in the dark as to what he thought God did and did not command Joshua the sun of Nun to actually do."[27] Regardless, Origen thought the true value of these events lay in their typological rather than historical character. In modern philosophical terminology, Origen held that any Old Testament text that portrayed God as something other than the greatest conceivable being must be understood primarily if not exclusively in an allegorical way. Commenting on God's ordering Joshua to circumcise the Israelites a second time (Josh 5:2), Origen posited, based on the literal impossibility of anyone being circumcised twice, that the second circumcision refers to the circumcision of the heart described by Paul (Rom 2:28–29), performed by the Holy Spirit at the moment of regeneration. He accused the Jews and gnostics of his day as interpreting Joshua in a literal and thus exclusively violent manner, leading the former to assert the moral legitimacy of divinely ordained violence and leading the latter to claim that the God of the Old Testament was an evil demiurge opposed to the God of love who became incarnate in Jesus.[28]

Following the Platonic theory of forms mediated through Philo (c. 20 BCE–c. 50 CE) and Clement of Alexandria (c. 150–c. 215), Origen maintained that Joshua presents us with shadows that find their reality in heavenly entities.[29] According to Origen, the Israelites' passing through the Jordan River symbolizes baptism, as Christians forsake the earthly kingdom foreshadowed by Egypt and the wilderness and enter the heavenly kingdom foreshadowed by the promised land. The leader of the earthly expedition,

24. Boersma, *Real Presence*, 112–13.

25. Boersma, *Real Presence*, 105–30.

26. Daniélou, *From Shadows to Reality*, 238; Lubac, *History and Spirit*, 122; and Jacobsen, "Allegorical Interpretation," 290 argue that Origen believed in the historicity of the Conquest narratives, while Beal, *Joshua*, 68–69, 141; Farber, *Images*, 313–23; and Franke, "Introduction," xxii appear to argue that Origen disbelieved in the historicity of the Conquest narratives. I find myself sympathetic to the latter option.

27. Chenoweth, "Origen's Interpretation," 106; emphasis in original.

28. Boersma, *Real Presence*, 108–11.

29. Boersma, *Real Presence*, 108–9.

Joshua (*Yeshua* or LXX *Iēsous*), shares by providential design the name of Jesus, leader of the heavenly expedition. The book's figures of physical warfare against rulers, soldiers, and noncombatants under the command of Joshua represent the Christian's spiritual warfare against Satan, the demons, and the wiles of the flesh under the command of Jesus.[30] Purging the promised land of the Canaanites symbolically depicts purging our bodies of its lusts. The earthly purge's resulting in Joshua's allotment of the promised land to the Israelite tribes illustrates how the spiritual purge results in Jesus's allotment of eternal life to Christians. The Israelite tribes' experiencing rest from war (Josh 14:15) finds its fulfillment in Christians experiencing the true Sabbath rest provided by Jesus (Matt 11:28–30; Heb 4:9–11). In sum, Origen located in Joshua a roadmap from spiritual infancy to spiritual maturity.[31]

Harmonious reception occurs when we allow Christ to encounter us through the music of the Psalms and other melodic passages of the Old Testament in order to cultivate harmony among the faculties of the soul.[32] To see how Old Testament music can play this role, Aquinas's contention that any artwork participates in the divine ideal or ideals that it symbolizes proves instructive. Every ideal is found in Christ, the ultimate art of God.[33] The Psalms therefore serve as a channel through which Christ allows the ideals to flow from the heavenly realm into the Christian's soul. These ideals bring into proper balance the soul's faculties. Therefore, reflection on and meditatively singing the Psalms enables Christians to achieve balance between memory, will, and reason and so exhibit the sound mind Paul exhorts Christians to display (Rom 12:2). Harmonious reception also views the Psalms as spoken to, about, and by Christ, a theme highlighted by Augustine. Boersma remarks: "This christological focus of Augustine makes clear that it is not just music and virtue that can unite us to the eternal harmony of God, but that a christological reading of the psalms does much the same thing."[34] Augustine, and the church fathers before him, saw psalms that addressed God as addressing Jesus. They also regarded the psalms in general, and not simply psalms that the New Testament identified as prophecies of Jesus (e.g., Ps 22; 110), as about Jesus. When Ps 1:1 states, "Blessed is the one who does not walk in step with the wicked or stand in the way that sinners take or sit in the company of mockers,"[35] Augustine interpreted

---

30. Chenoweth, "Origen's Interpretation," 99–104.
31. Chenoweth, "Origen's Interpretation," 100.
32. Boersma, *Real Presence*, 132–37.
33. MacGregor, "Aquinas," 242–43.
34. Boersma, *Real Presence*, 148.
35. All biblical quotations in this chapter are from the NIV.

"the one" as the *theanthrōpos*, namely Jesus. Augustine contended that Jesus is here implicitly being contrasted with Adam, who did walk, stand, and sit in the manner described by obeying the voice of Satan in distrust and disregard of the voice of God, specifically Christ, in the Garden of Eden.[36] One could also read Psalm 24 as a prophecy of Jesus's triumphal entry into Jerusalem: "Lift up your heads, you gates; lift them up, you ancient doors, that the King of glory may come in. Who is he, this King of glory? The Lord Almighty—he is the King of glory" (vv. 9–10). Further, many of the psalms were seen as spoken by Christ through the human author. Just as Psalm 22 was viewed as Jesus addressing God the Father from the cross, so Psalm 26 was interpreted as Jesus asking God the Father to vindicate his sinless life by resurrecting him from the dead. Such interpretation is known as prosopological exegesis, since it asks for the identity of the person (*prosōpon*) uttering the psalm.[37]

Doctrinal reception is the reading of the Old Testament through which Christian doctrine is formulated. In Pauline fashion (2 Cor 3:6), such interpretation "always moves from the letter to the spirit."[38] Boersma illustrates this style of reading through third to fifth century patristic interpretation of Proverbs 8, which typically but not exclusively regarded God's wisdom as the Logos. Thus Origen, perceiving that God could never lack his wisdom, understood Prov 8:22, "The Lord brought me forth as the first of his works, before his deeds of old," as referring to the Logos' eternal generation from God the Father.[39] However, such eternal generation runs the risk of making the Logos subordinate in being to the Father. Athanasius (c. 296–373) avoided this implication by stressing that the proverbs expressed truth in figurative language and, in Boersma's words, "serve as sacramental containers for a reality that comes fully into the open when God reveals himself in the incarnation of Jesus Christ."[40] Likewise, Athanasius differentiated between the economic Trinity and the immanent Trinity. The economic Trinity is God as revealed in his administrative operations towards humanity, while the immanent Trinity is God in his own being. Thus Prov 8:22 refers to the incarnation of the Logos rather than the Logos' origination.[41] By contrast, Gregory of Nyssa distanced Proverbs 8 entirely from subordinationist implications by claiming that the text refers primarily to the *ordo*

---

36. Boesma, *Real Presence*, 148–49.
37. Boersma, *Real Presence*, 152.
38. Boersma, *Real Presence*, 159.
39. Boersma, *Real Presence*, 159–64.
40. Boersma, *Real Presence*, 168.
41. Boersma, *Real Presence*, 171–73.

salutis. This reading was accomplished by reading Proverbs 8 through the lenses of the New Testament, viewing disputed terms in the chapter as clues which found their solution in those terms' New Testament usage. Employing Eph 4:24, Gregory of Nyssa read Prov 8:22 as claiming that, via the virginal conception, God fashioned the incarnate Jesus as the start of the works of salvation. Employing 1 Cor 3:10–11, Gregory of Nyssa interpreted Prov 8:30, "Then I was the artisan at his side,"[42] as a reference to Paul, the expert builder who laid the ecclesial foundation of Jesus. Employing 1 Corinthians 12, Gregory of Nyssa interpreted the "rich inheritance on those who love me" (Prov 8:21; cf. 8:35) as the gifts of the Spirit dispensed throughout the earthly body of Christ.[43]

Nuptial reception embraces the analogy of spiritual marriage with God found throughout both the Old and New Testaments to aid believer and church in fulfilling their salvific pledge of life, love, allegiance, and fidelity to God and in experiencing spiritual communion with God. Throughout the Christian tradition, the *locus classicus* for nuptial reception is the exegesis of the Song of Songs. Boersma argues, in controversial fashion, that several early church fathers allegorized the Song of Songs not because they viewed sex as evil and were scandalized by the book's overt eroticism but because they saw sex as good both for the physical pleasure it provides and for its pointing beyond itself to the believer's and the church's spiritual intimacy with God.[44] I concur with his argument and would extend it to Bernard of Clairvaux's (1090–1153) interpretation of the Song which characterized Cistercian spirituality. As Jean Leclercq comments on Bernard's understanding of Song 1:2, "Let him kiss me with the kisses of his mouth,"

> The kiss of the Father and the Son is the Holy Spirit. Christ gives the kiss to his spouse, or bride, whom he fills with his Spirit. The Spirit, in turn, unites the bride to the Father through the Son. Mystical union is the extension of the relationship of love that exists among and unites the three divine Persons. The bride, who is actually the Church and the soul, hopes that this mystery of charity will be fulfilled in her. The fulfillment can take place only through the working of the Holy Spirit, who enables the bride to experience mystical knowledge in which love becomes understanding.[45]

---

42. Here I follow the NIV's first marginal reading.
43. Boersma, *Real Presence*, 181–82.
44. Boersma, *Real Presence*, 189.
45. Leclercq, "Introduction," 47.

Here Bernard used the Song as a vehicle which allows Christians individually and collectively to enter into the *agapē* that characterizes the intertrinitarian relationships, as their personal commitment to the three trinitarian persons enables them to experience mystical union with God. The Song, like Origen's interpretation of the book of Joshua, furnishes a manual for Christian spiritual progress. When Christians gradually grow in their reliance upon Christ, they move from drawing near his feet (just after conversion) to drawing near his hands (at the midpoint of the journey toward sanctification) to drawing near his lips to receive the kiss (at the moment one achieves entire sanctification), which results in spiritual ecstasy.[46]

I have argued elsewhere that John intends his depiction of the wedding at Cana in which Jesus turns water into wine as a double entendre for his disciples entering into a spiritual marriage with him.[47] At the beginning of the pericope when one would expect the people getting married to be named, Jesus and his disciples are named instead (John 2:2). Where one would expect the mother of the groom to be mentioned, Mary is mentioned instead (John 2:1). It was the groom's responsibility in a first-century Mediterranean wedding to provide the wine, but when the wine runs out, Mary, as the true mother of the groom, comes to Jesus, the true groom, to provide the wine (John 2:3–5). When the wine is furnished, the master of ceremonies praises the earthly groom, not realizing that he has praised the incorrect groom (John 2:9–10). When one would expect the bride to pledge her life to the groom, we find that "his disciples believed in him (*episteusan eis auton*)" (John 2:11). The phrase *pisteuō eis auton*, I contend, is carefully crafted by John to denote the type of commitment that characterizes a marriage.[48] The analogy of spiritual marriage was not lost on the Protestant Reformers. Using the analogy of common property in marriage, Martin Luther (1483–1546) explained how faith weds us to Christ and accomplishes salvation, entailing both the forgiveness of sins and the imputation of righteousness:

> [An] incomparable benefit of faith is that it unites the soul with Christ as a bride is united with her bridegroom. By this mystery, as the Apostle teaches, Christ and the soul become one flesh [Eph. 5:31–32]. And if they are one flesh and there is between them a true marriage . . . it follows that everything they have they hold in common, the good as well as the evil. Accordingly the believing soul can boast of and glory in whatever Christ has as though it were its own, and whatever the soul has Christ

---

46. Leclercq, "Introduction," 47.
47. MacGregor, *John's Gospel*, 110.
48. MacGregor, *John's Gospel*, 111–2; the argument is furthered in 113–17.

claims as his own. Let us compare these and we shall see inestimable benefits. Christ is full of grace, life, and salvation. The soul is full of sins, death, and damnation. Now let faith come between them and sins, death, and damnation will be Christ's, while grace, life, and salvation will be the soul's; for if Christ is a bridegroom, he must take upon himself the things which are his bride's and bestow upon her the things that are his.[49]

Luther substantiated this argument by citing the Song of Songs and the book of Hosea, which employs the marriage between Hosea and Gomer to illustrate the marriage between God and his people.[50]

Prophetic reception views prophecy and its fulfillment as joined via a sacramental link that cannot be reduced merely to predicting a future event. It rather sees the fulfillment as the prototype, preexistent in the mind of God, on which the prophecy was modeled. The book of Isaiah, and the servant songs in particular, functioned in the mind of Jesus, the New Testament writers, and the early church fathers as providentially containing the mystery of Jesus's birth, kingdom ministry, death for the sins of the world, and resurrection.[51] N. T. Wright has demonstrated that Jesus took Isaiah as foundational to his messianic identity. Regarding Isaiah 53, two major lines of Jewish interpretation existed in Jesus's day: one seeing the servant as the messiah but not having the servant suffer, and the other having the servant, depicting the nation of Israel, suffer without being the messiah. It is probable that Jesus wove together portions of these two interpretive trends in giving shape to his self-understanding and the meaning of his crucifixion, as displayed at the Last Supper.[52] Indeed, at the very beginning of his ministry, Jesus identified himself as the anointed one about whom Isaiah 61 spoke (Luke 4:16–21). Peter and Philip recognized Jesus as the figure described in Isaiah 53 (1 Pet 2:22–25; Acts 8:32–35), and Matthew saw Jesus's virginal conception as the reality underlying Isa 7:14 (Matt 1:22–23).[53] Significantly, Origen, in commenting on "a Lamb, looking as if it had been slain" (Rev 5:6), stated not that Jesus's sacrifice was patterned after the Old Testament animal sacrifices, but that the Old Testament animal sacrifices were patterned after Jesus's sacrifice.[54]

---

49. Luther, *Selections*, 60.
50. Luther, *Selections*, 61.
51. Boersma, *Real Presence*, 219–31.
52. Wright, *Jesus*, prog. 4 (17:44–19:35, 7:19–12:36). Wright describes only the first line of interpretation I present.
53. Boersma, *Real Presence*, 227, 224.
54. Boersma, *Real Presence*, 229.

Prophetic reception is also marked by intertextuality. For instance, Cyril of Alexandria (c. 376–444) interpreted the "polished arrow" of Isaiah 49:2 by turning to Ephesians: "the 'arrow' chosen above all is Christ, hidden in a 'quiver' as I have said by the Father's foreknowledge. He was known before the world's foundation (cf. Eph: 1:4) and he appeared among us when the whole world was on the verge of destruction."[55] This move from Isaiah to Ephesians was facilitated by the verbal connections Cyril saw between the two texts. They both contain "hiding" language ("in the shadow of his hand he hid me" in Isa 49:2 and "this mystery, which for ages past was kept hidden in God" in Eph 3:9) and "choosing" language ("the Holy One of Israel, who has chosen you" in Isa 49:7 and "for he chose us in him" in Eph 1:4). Cyril then moves from the stunning effect of the arrow to the bride "faint with love" in Song 2:5.[56] Boersma unpacks Cyril's thinking at this juncture: "in Isaiah 49 Christ is the 'chosen arrow' proclaiming the mystery once hidden in God's providence, while in Song 2:5 he is the groom creating a piercing wound of love in the beloved. Christ, it would appear, is both the archer and the arrow, wounding the beloved by placing himself within her heart."[57] Hence prophetic reception interweaves the threads of Scripture into a coherent whole.

Beatific reception translates the gospel message of the New Testament into the lives of believers.[58] Boersma spotlights the attempts of Gregory of Nyssa (c. 335–c. 394), Augustine, and Leo the Great (c. 400–461) to translate the Beatitudes into the praxis of their own lives and those under their spiritual care.[59] An early modern example can be found in the writings of Hubmaier, who located in the Beatitudes the necessary traits of those who live out the gospel and practice true spirituality. True spirituality, for Hubmaier, lies in accepting the entire cross that Jesus has given his followers to bear as opposed to fragments thereof:

> All who desire to live a godly life in Christ Jesus will be persecuted, 2 Tim. 3:12. For where Christ is and dwells, there he brings the cross with him on his back from which he gives every Christian his own small cross and if it comes accept it with joy and patience, and not pick and choose our own chips and bits of wood in false spirituality, selecting and gathering them up without divine understanding . . . Who are these people? . . . The

---

55. Quoted in Boersma, *Real Presence*, 243.
56. Boersma, *Real Presence*, 243–44.
57. Boersma, *Real Presence*, 244.
58. Boersma, *Real Presence*, 251.
59. Boersma, *Real Presence*, 249–72.

poor in spirit. Those that mourn. Those who are meek. Those who hunger and thirst after righteousness. The merciful. The pure in heart. The peacemakers. Those who are persecuted for righteousness' sake. Those who are reviled and despised on account of Christ's name. Also those against whom much evil is spoken falsely for Christ's sake, Matt. 5:3ff.[60]

Following the Beatitudes, in Hubmaier's reckoning, guarantees full embrace of the cross that we must bear as Jesus's followers.

CONCLUSION

Sacramental hermeneutics constitutes a multidimensional interpretive program rooted in a provocative sacramental theory of Scripture and participatory praxis in Scripture. By maintaining that Jesus is the eternal substance of the Bible under the accidents of text, this program shines fresh light on how the Bible, "living and active," is "sharper than any double-edged sword . . . penetrat[ing] even to dividing soul and spirit" (Heb 4:12). For it is, in essence, the "sharp sword" (Rev 19:15) issuing forth from the mouth of Jesus, "the Word of God" (Rev 19:13). Moreover, this program enhances the practice of *lectio divina* by revealing the study of Scripture to be an invitation into the presence of the living Lord.

BIBLIOGRAPHY

Barth, Karl. *Church Dogmatics*. 4 vols. Edited by G. W. Bromiley and Thomas F. Torrance. Translated by G. T. Thomson and Harold Knight. Edinburgh: T. & T. Clark, 1956–1975.

Beal, Lissa M. Wray. *Joshua*. Edited by Tremper Longman III and Scot McKnight. The Story of God Bible Commentary 6. Grand Rapids: Zondervan Academic, 2019.

Boersma, Hans. *Scripture as Real Presence: Sacramental Exegesis in the Early Church*. Grand Rapids: Baker Academic, 2018.

Chenoweth, Mark. "Origen's Interpretation of Violence in the Book of Joshua." *The Christian Libertarian Review* 2 (2019) 91–115.

Daniélou, Jean. *From Shadows to Reality: Studies in the Biblical Typology of the Fathers*. Translated by Wulstan Hibberd. New York: Burns and Oates, 1960.

_____. *Sacramentum futuri: études sur les origines de la typologie biblique*. Paris: Beauchesne, 1950.

---

60. Hubmaier, *Theologian*, 364–65.

Farber, Zev. *Images of Joshua in the Bible and Their Reception*. Berlin: de Gruyter, 2016.

Franke, John R. "Introduction to Joshua Through 2 Samuel." In *Joshua, Judges, Ruth, 1–2 Samuel*, edited by John R. Franke and Thomas C. Oden, xvii–xxxi. Downers Grove, IL: IVP Academic, 2019.

Hubmaier, Balthasar. *Balthasar Hubmaier: Theologian of Anabaptism*. Translated and edited by H. Wayne Pipkin and John H. Yoder. Scottdale, PA: Herald, 1989.

Jacobsen, Anders-Christian. "Allegorical Interpretation of Geography in Origen's Homilies on the Book of Joshua." *Religion and Theology* 17 (2010) 289–301.

John Paul II, Pope. *Catechism of the Catholic Church*. 2nd ed. New York: Doubleday, 1997.

Leclercq, Jean. "Introduction." In *Bernard of Clairvaux: Selected Works*, translated by G. R. Evans, 13–57. New York: Paulist, 1987.

Levering, Matthew. *Participatory Biblical Exegesis: A Theology of Biblical Interpretation*. Notre Dame, IN: University of Notre Dame Press, 2008.

Lubac, Henri de. *Exégèse médiévale: Les quatre sens de l'écriture*. Paris: Cerf, 1959–1964.

———. *History and Spirit: The Understanding of Scripture according to Origen*. Translated by Anne Englund Nash. San Francisco: Ignatius, 2007.

Luther, Martin. *Martin Luther: Selections from His Writings*. Edited by John Dillenberger. New York: Anchor, 1962.

MacGregor, Kirk R. "Aquinas, Christology, and Art." *Bridges: An Interdisciplinary Journal of Theology, Philosophy, History, and Science* 14 (2007) 233–50.

———. *A Historical and Theological Investigation of John's Gospel*. Cham, Switzerland: Palgrave Macmillan, 2020.

Paul VI, Pope. *Dei Verbum*. The Holy See. November 18, 1965. https://www.vatican.va/archive/hist_councils/ii_vatican_council/documents/vat-ii_const_19651118_dei-verbum_en.html.

Reno, R. R. *In the Ruins of the Church: Sustaining Faith in an Age of Diminished Christianity*. Grand Rapids: Brazos, 2002.

Wright, N. T. *Jesus: The New Way*. DVD containing 6 programs. Worcester, PA: Christian History Institute, 1998.

Chapter 13
Spirit Hermeneutics
Interpretation as Transformation of Lives and Communities

HANNAH MATHER

What happens when we read Scripture in relationship with the triune God? More specifically, what does the Holy Spirit do? When we start to consider this, we begin to appreciate that reading Scripture in relationship with the Spirit is much more than cognitively interpreting the Bible's words. These are words that, through the activity of God the Spirit—and in relationship with God the Father, God the Son, *and us*—impact our mind, emotions, and actions, reaching out from the pages and into our lives. This is also an interpretive process that can work in reverse whereby the Spirit, in constant unbreakable communion with the Father and the Son, communicates with us as we go about our lives in ways that leads us back to truths contained in Scripture. From this hermeneutical perspective, interpretation with the Spirit involves transformation of lives and communities. Scripture is central but interpreting Scripture with the Spirit; or *the Spirit interpreting us* and in that process leading us to Scripture; extends beyond the written words.

PRACTICALITIES
NOTE ON HERMENEUTICS

We might understand hermeneutics as the science of interpretation or the approaches, methods, and principles of understanding that lie behind the interpretive act. The term has typically been used in relation to Scripture[1], but hermeneutics relates to all of life and not just texts. Depending on our audience, it is sometimes simpler to use *interpretation* as more people understand the term.

What is being offered here is a hermeneutical (or *interpretive*) *perspective*, not an approach to biblical interpretation. An *approach* conveys something a person does whereas the emphasis here is on *seeking to understand what the Spirit of God does, or seeks to do, when a person reads or hears Scripture*. Once we begin to understand even a small part of this work, we are better placed to engage in partnership with this activity.

NATURE AND CHARACTER OF GOD

Humans are fallible, capable of wrong-doing, and with finite knowledge. This means we are flawed and limited in ability and capacity to fully *know* the ways of God. We will never *fully* understand the Spirit's ways (for example, John 3:8; Isa 55:8)[2] but why is this the case? An answer lies with the nature and character of God.

God as Father, Son, and Spirit, is both invisible *and* incarnate. In other words, the triune God is unseen and unknowable—and yet paradoxically—*also* seen, known, and expressed. God's communication follows God's nature and character. Therefore, the Spirit interprets Scripture to us in ways that are transformative and holistic, visible, known, and reachable, *and yet* at the same time, utterly and always tantalizingly beyond our grasp. In our earthly lifetimes, we will only ever know in part (1 Cor 13:9). This chapter is offered for the furthering of understanding concerning the Spirit's role in the interpretation of Scripture and with this foundational appreciation.

WHAT AND WHO ARE YOU READING FOR?

If you are reading this, you probably have an interest in this topic and a level of theological[3] understanding. You might be a student wanting to learn more about pneumatic interpretation (I will explain this term). Perhaps you

---

1. Scripture: sacred writings of Judaism and Christianity in the Christian Bible considered God's self-revelation in written form and inspired and authoritative for Christian faith and practice.

2. All Scripture quotations are taken from the Holy Bible, New International Version, 2011.

3. The word *theology* broken down is *theo* (God) and *ology* (study of). In Greek, *theo* is God, whilst *ology* is an adaption of *logia*, meaning to speak of or to tell. Amidst the variety of approaches, disciplines, and nuances, theology, at its center, is the study of God and God's relationship with the world.

are not studying in the formal academic sense but enjoy thinking and learning. You may be retired, in full-time Christian ministry, or a committed Christian with a career outside the church. Whoever you are, I hope to write for you in simple ways that engage and further your understanding without too much theological jargon. However, this is a complex topic and so quite the task.[4]

Prevenient Spirit

This chapter is written assuming that those reading this believe that Jesus Christ is the way, the truth, and the life (John 14:6). However, if you consider yourself atheist, agnostic, or of another faith, you are also very welcome here. This chapter places relationship with the triune God as a central component of interpreting Scripture with the Spirit but it also appreciates that God is on some level working to reconcile all things and people to him (for example, Col 1:20; Acts 17:25–28). In writing this, I reflect on John Wesley's understanding of prevenient grace as a drawing grace of God working in all people's lives without exception, beckoning a person towards faith in Christ. Prevenient grace, justifying grace, and sanctifying grace are all inner workings of the Holy Spirit at different stages of a person's initiation journey: pre-conversion, at conversion, post-conversation; drawing, forgiving, and transforming. In a sense we might understand that by each stage, the Spirit works to draw or reconcile a person ever closer into fulfilment of life in Christ. The Spirit is sometimes described as the reconciler and this reconciliationary process may start whilst a person is still a distance away. Perhaps that person will always remain a distance away. The Christian God is a patient God, loving all people where they are, always inviting and never demanding.[5]

Back to What and Who

To you, the reader: what and who are you here for? What reasons do you have for wanting to think more about the Spirit's role in the interpretation of Scripture, and *for whom* are you ultimately reading this chapter for? The times when we read, study, and learn are often more inner-focused, solitary activities but their output is always external for what we learn in these times

---

4. The theological task is twofold: to understand the complex but communicate it in ways that draw people into understanding. Simplifying the complex is hard but it is a necessary discipline if we are serious about connecting with and not confounding others.

5. For more on prevenient grace, see Lane, *Sin and Grace*, 73–80.

impacts our interactions with others. On one level or another, all people learn in order to apply their freshly-gained insights and understandings to how they live and work in relationship with those around them. Whether we realize it or not, for better or worse, relationship with others and the communities in which we live and work are central to everyone's learning purposes. Relationship and community are also central to understanding the Spirit's purposes in the interpretation of Scripture but unlike us in our flawed fallibility, the Spirit's purposes and outputs are always pure and good.

PERSONAL CONTEXT AND PERSPECTIVES

This chapter appreciates that context is important for understanding. Therefore, I offer my own brief personal context. I am a British scholar located within the context and perspective of the Pentecostal and charismatic traditions. I value belonging to a range of church traditions including the more conservative reformed tradition in Scotland where I live. After years within explicitly Christian and academic environments, I spend much of my time within broader secular contexts and with people who do not have strong faith commitments.

Some years ago I reconnected with a faith that had been present with me since childhood but never explored in depth. This reconnection happened through a church course which had a combination of simply communicated theological teaching grounded in Scripture and spaces of time with opportunity to meet with God through encounter with the Holy Spirit.[6] During one such time, I experienced a powerful but intimate connection with the Spirit that convinced me that God was real and wanted a personal relationship with me. The biblical-theological teaching and Spiritual experience were both integral but neither were enough without the other.

Like many other Christians, I read Scripture to meet God in the words. When I open the pages of the Bible and seek to read devotionally and prayerfully, I expect that God by the Spirit will meet me through the passages in ways that show me more about who God is, who I am, and guide me in how I live, work, and interact with others around me. Conversely, I also expect that the Spirit will meet me as I live and work and, in doing so, lead me back to truths contained in Scripture.

---

6. Giving space in church services to experientially encounter the Holy Spirit alongside worship and teaching is common practice in charismatic and Pentecostal churches..

FOCUS AND DEFINITIONS

This chapter considers the interconnections between the Spirit, Scripture, and us (and our surrounding *contexts*) to offer thoughts concerning ways the Holy Spirit interprets Scripture to us as we read and hear it (and as we live and work and encounter situations that lead us back to the truths contained in the pages of the Bible). Included are examples to indicate where the interpreting Spirit might have been at work. I use the word *might* intentionally: the Spirit's communication follows God's nature and character; invisible and yet also incarnate, unseen and yet at the same time, seen. To the best of our limited understanding, we can *believe* this was the Spirit speaking to us through this passage of Scripture—or working in our lives in ways that lead us to it—but can we ever declare that we definitively know this? The English language has limitations: we know and at the same time we do not know. The truth the Spirit brings is grasped by faith and not by sight. This side of heaven we will only ever know in part.

First, some definitions: *Pneumatic interpretation is* the conscious or subconscious perception, discernment, or reception of truth brought by the Spirit through the interpretation of Scripture. *Pneumatic appropriation* is an act of communication brought by the Spirit through our engagement with Scripture. This communication is to personal and contemporary contexts and coheres with the original passage and its surrounding passage in some way. These definitions are the same as used in my book, *The Interpreting Spirit* (2020). They will be used over Spirit hermeneutics, the term arguably made popular by Craig Keener's, *Spirit Hermeneutics* (2018).[7]

Affectively, ethically, and cognitively are three ways that the Spirit communicates with us as we engage with Scripture. In simple terms, affect, ethics, and cognition might be understood as emotions, actions, and the mind but their meaning is a little more nuanced. *Affect* is a disposition that evokes feeling of fondness and connectedness to someone or something. Particular affections are wide-ranging and include love, joy, desire, sorrow,

---

7. Other terms that have been used in relation to the Spirit's role in the interpretive process include *pneumatic hermeneutics, pneumatic exegesis, charismatic exegesis, renewal hermeneutics,* and *pentecostal hermeneutics* (small "p"). *Pentecostal hermeneutics* (capital "P") is an adjoining discussion area inhabited by scholars discussing charismatic and Pentecostal approaches to interpretation (in the ecclesial sense). Within this area are implicit and explicit discussions about the Spirit's role. Most scholars who have written on pneumatic interpretation in the modern era (1970s onwards) are from the charismatic and Pentecostal traditions so there is cross-over between these two research areas. For more on Pentecostal hermeneutics, see the chapter in this handbook. See Mather, *Interpreting Spirit* for an historical analysis of thought from Pentecostal and charismatic scholars writing in this area.

compassion etc.[8] *Ethics*, moral principles or values held by an individual or group which influence behavior, is here used specifically in relation to action and conduct. *Cognition* is "the mental act or process by which knowledge is acquired, including perception, intuition, and reasoning" (Collins English Dictionary).

As the title of this chapter suggests, the focus here is one of interpretation as transformation: the written words of Scripture taking practical shape in our lives through the interpreting work of the Spirit. When approached from this vantage point, a vista emerges that the Spirit does not *just* cognitively interpret Scripture to us—the Spirit, through our interaction with the written words and truths in Scripture and in relationship with God, affectively, ethically, and cognitively and simultaneously personally and communally *interprets (transforms) us*.

INTERPRETATION AS TRANSFORMATION

Basing judgements solely on reason and knowledge reduces interpretation to an activity we do with our minds but the Holy Spirit is interested in much more than just our minds, working to holistically interpret and transform us in ways that include but extend beyond our minds. The Enlightenment, the intellectual movement that swept Europe in the seventeenth and eighteenth centuries has had a long-lasting, and arguably detrimental and rationalistic, influence on Christian scholarship.[9] Read Pentecostal scholar, Scott Ellington's thoughts on why this is relevant to how scholars (particularly those in the West) have been approaching their interpretive methods:

> A predominantly rationalistic worldview unnecessarily restricts both our approach to Scripture and the ways in which we make ourselves available to hear from God. By excluding the supernatural and focusing instead exclusively on the rational, much more scholarship has become impoverished in the way it understands God to be present and has distanced itself from that which millions of Christians experience as an important part of their faith.[10]

---

8. Pentecostal scholar, Lee Roy Martin, has written extensively on affective interpretation, e.g., *Spirit of the* Psalms. For an historical work, see Edwards, *Religious Affections* (1746).

9. For opinions, see Francis Martin, "Spirit and Flesh in the Doing of Theology," 3–31; Ellington, "Pentecostalism and the Authority of Scripture," 16–38; Wright, "Challenge of the Enlightenment," 52–63.

10. Ellington, "Pentecostalism and the Authority of Scripture," 36.

Consequentially, satisfactorily considering the Spirit's role in the interpretation of Scripture requires placing the relational presence and activity of God centrally and considering unseen, supernatural, experiential, and faith-based elements alongside those rational, evidenced and seen.[11] In other words, including factors that more traditional evangelical scholarship have traditionally left out of their hermeneutical considerations. Let's consider a few of these "interpretation as transformation" factors before looking at examples from two people's lives.

THROUGH AND BEYOND THE WRITTEN WORDS

As we read Scripture, the Spirit communicates *through* but also *beyond* the written words interpreting and appropriating scriptural truth to our lives and situations in ways that cohere in some way with the narrative and its surrounding framework. This appropriation to personal contexts is what I have described as pneumatic appropriation, and the *through and beyond* aspect of the Spirit's interpretive activity pervades much of the concepts presented here.

AFFECTIVE, ETHICAL, AND COGNITIVE INTERPRETATION

The Spirit communicates truths contained in Scripture holistically and transformatively *to us*, *in us*, and *through us*. Affect, ethics, and cognition are central to this. The biblical writers, and especially those who wrote the Hebrew Bible, recognized the heart as the integrative center from which all understanding stemmed (for example, Solomon's prayer, 1 Kgs 3:9, "Give your servant a discerning heart to govern your people and to discern between right and wrong").[12] When we view the heart as the center-point for understanding instead of the mind, affective and ethical factors start emerging as interlinking parts of the interpretive process alongside the cognitive. *All* understanding, regardless of whether it is Spirit-given, involves the interrelation of a person's affections, ethical actions, and cognitive faculties. So too pneumatic interpretation: as a person engages with Scripture in knowing relationship with God or in such a manner that invites the relational activity of God, the Spirit works in, with, and through that person *holistically*, transforming their affections and ethical actions, as well their cognitive faculties.

---

11. I hesitate to call this an 'interpretive method' because pneumatic interpretation is something the Spirit does in relationship with us as we engage with Scripture, not something we do ourselves.

12. See Mather, *Interpreting Spirit*, 9, 133–34 for discussion regarding the heart as the center of discernment.

CREATIONAL AND REDEMPTIVE INTERPRETATION

Ellington highlighted the importance of integrating the experiential, unseen, and relational alongside the rational and evidenced and this is especially pertinent when considering the Spirit's role.[13] Expounding this further, could it be that aside from—but perhaps also within and certainly through—the written content of Scripture, *another content* or *material* is communicated to us by the Spirit as we interact with it? And if there is another content or material, what is it? Could it be that this other (or extra) material contains certain life-giving biographical hallmarks that carry and reveal the triune God's relational nature? And could it be that as we engage with Scripture in a manner that seeks to know God more, the Spirit works to holistically interpret this extra biographical material to us?

Three particulars of God's nature are the creational (Father), redemptive (Son), and reconciliational (Spirit). It therefore follows that the *biographical material* interpreted to us by the Spirit (as we read or hear Scripture) is creational, redemptive, and reconciliational in nature, revealing and interpreting the Father, Son, and Spirit to us holistically as we read or hear it. Let's think about these aspects in more detail.

Creational

The Holy Spirit is the bringer of life (Rom 8:2; 2 Cor 3:6). Life-bringing is part of the Spirit's nature and a hallmark of the Spirit's communication. As we read Scripture—and provided God is present within that interpretive activity—the Spirit works to bring the written words of Scripture to life in our lives in ways that are extra to the written content.[14] In this way, the Spirit communicates through Scripture in manners that support and honor its content and meaning and which extends biographically into our lives.

The relationship between the Spirit and Scripture been likened to a marriage partnership with the Spirit and Scripture being mutually supporting but fulfilling different roles.[15] If a role of the Spirit's in this Spirit–Scripture partnership is bringing the written words to life in ways that align with the Spirit's life-giving nature, then the Spirit's appropriation of Scripture to us will naturally extend *through* but also *beyond* the written words interpreting

---

13. Remember, we are seeking to understand an interpretive perspective here, not seeking to develop an interpretive method.

14. Moltmann described this as verbal and non-verbal expressions. Moltmann, *Spirit of Life*, 3.

15. See discussion about this in *Interpreting Spirit*, 54–59, drawing on Moltmann, Steven Land, and Clark Pinnock. Land and Pinnock both described the Spirit-Scripture relationship as a marriage.

its truth holistically (affectively, ethically, and cognitively) within our lives. This is *a creational act*. The following words from German systematic theologian, Jürgen Moltmann, may help to draw these concepts out further:

> The Spirit is the subject of determining the Word, not just the operation of that Word. The efficacies of the Spirit reach beyond the Word. Nor do the experiences of the Spirit find expression in words alone. They are as multifarious and protean as sensory reality itself. The Spirit has its non-verbal expressions too. The indwelling of the Spirit "in our hearts" goes deeper than the conscious level in us. It rouses all our senses, permeates the unconscious too, and quickens the body, giving it new life (1 Cor. 6:19f). A new energy for living proceeds from the Spirit. To bind the Spirit solely to the Word is one-sided, and represses these dimensions. The non-verbal dimensions for their part show that the Word is bound to the Spirit, but that the Spirit is not bound to the Word, and the Spirit and Word belong in a mutual relationship which must not be conceived exclusively, or in merely intellectual terms.[16]

Redemptive

Following God's triune nature, this pneumatic–creational interpretation is triune. In other words, if a particular role of the Spirit's in the Spirit–Scripture partnership is to bring life to the words we read or hear, then the Spirit's activity must also be characteristic of the nature of the three-in-one God. Therefore, whilst the creational, life-giving nature of pneumatic interpretation especially illustrates the Spirit's relationship with the Creator–Father who created the world and gave life to all things, it also illustrates and points to the Redeemer–Son.[17] The Spirit is the Spirit of the Father who created the world and gives humankind the redemptive opportunity of fullness of life through Jesus the Son. The Spirit *is also* the Spirit of the Son who, given by the Father, redeemed and continues to redeem all creation. Therefore, the Spirit is the source of life through the Father *creationally* and the Son *redemptively*. Consequently, the Spirit cannot just illuminate parts of Scripture to our minds as we read and hear them, but must *also* create and redeem in that action because creating and redeeming is central to God's nature. However, this activity also requires our participation; relationship

---

16. Moltmann, *Spirit of Life*, 3.

17. E.g., Genesis 1 and 2. Cf. Rom 8:11, the Spirit of God who raised Jesus from the dead living in us and giving life to us.

with God and the creational and redemptive work that happens through it is a partnership.

This means that the Spirit's interpretive efforts *must* extend beyond what happens in our minds as we read Scripture, transforming our affections and decision-making in respect of our ethics. In other words, the life-bringing creational and redemptive work brought by the Spirit through Scripture as we engage with it extends biographically into our lives, carrying with it hallmarks of the triune God's nature and character.[18]

SIMULTANEOUSLY PERSONAL AND COMMUNAL INTERPRETATION

No person is an island; we exist in relational systems. The things that impact us will, to one extent or another, impact the people, systems, and structures around us. Our thoughts and feelings influence our actions and interactions: cognition and affection informs ethical action.

God as Father, Son, and Spirit is divine community and the Spirit interprets Scripture to us in ways that are consistent with the nature and character of God. Having considered the creational and redemptive aspects of pneumatic interpretation, another characteristic is the simultaneously personal and communal. God is community so part of the Spirit's nature is also community. Consequently, the Spirit interprets Scripture to us in ways that are uniquely special to us individually but are also always communally, community, and relationship oriented. Pneumatic interpretation is always simultaneously personal and communal.

We might experience a deeply personal and transformative work but if it really is the Spirit interpreting Scripture to us, there will always be an outward-focused communal intent, consistent with God's nature and character, and requiring our ethical partnership. Whilst we might not ever be able to say for certain, "this was definitely the Spirit showing me that passage of Scripture (see Orientation section)," the simultaneously personal and communal aspect alongside other aspects of God's nature and character such as the creational and redemptive are indicators that this is the Spirit's interpretive work.

RECONCILIATIONAL INTERPRETATION

Whilst God is three-in-one and so the Father and the Son also carry this characteristic, the reconconciliational aspect points to a special characteristic

---

18. Also on the Spirit-Father creational element of pneumatic interpretation was Stanley Grenz who suggested that the Spirit uses Scripture as an instrument for personal communication, creating eschatologically according to God's creational purposes. See *Interpreting Spirit*, 105 and Grenz, "Spirit and the Word," 365.

of the Spirit's as the reconciler and overall *bringer-into-relationship*. As we engage with Scripture, the Spirit works to reconcile, drawing us into relationship with and understanding of God as Father, Son, and Spirit, and with those around us.[19]

Consequently, another indicator of the Spirit's interpretive presence is if what we read or hear leads towards bringing about reconciliation of understanding and reconciliation with others. When this happens, we would experience changes to our thinking and affection that transform our ethical decisions and actions. This could take a few short moments or a longer process of change over a period of time. Again, however, this pneumatic-reconciliational activity also requires our active partnership. The paradox is that when we are the most affectively receptive to God we are also the most ethically willing to make room for the Spirit by modifying behavior, and to be in a state of passive reception, active behavior is also required. This interaction between affect and ethics—and the passive and active aspects within both components—impacts cognition, facilitating pneumatic interpretation.[20]

SUMMARY

The Spirit interprets Scripture to us holistically. As we engage with it, the Spirit works through and beyond the written words, interpreting Scripture to us affectively, ethically, and cognitively, in ways that are personal and individual but which also always have a larger communal intention requiring a person's ethical partnership. Whilst the Spirit *is* God, the Spirit also (self)-interprets God to us through the written words of Scripture. These words carry certain life-giving biographical hallmarks such as the creative, redemptive, and reconciliational, once again extending beyond the written, rational, and cognitive, and into that person's life and the world that surrounds them. Because God is invisible and yet also incarnate, the Sprit's communication carries that same quality. Pneumatic interpretation, therefore, is both interpretable and yet somehow also always beyond interpretation.

---

19. See Mather, *Interpreting Spirit*, 100–104 for further detail.

20. I developed this concept in *Interpreting Spirit*, calling it the affective-ethical paradox and drawing on Hans Urs von Balathasar's pneumatology in "Preliminary Remarks," 340–46.

PRACTICAL EXAMPLES: JENNY AND WILLIAM

The pneumatic-hermeneutical theology we have just explored has not been simple so here are examples from two people's lives to help bring this into practical shape. After each one, I offer thoughts about ways the Spirit may have interpreting Scripture to them and interpreting and transforming them and their situation in the process.

As you read, allow yourself to think and reflect. Note down anything you find especially interesting or disagree with and think constructively about your reasons for this. Refer back if it is helpful. You may also want to reflect on instances from your own life where pneumatic interpretation may have been happening. Take your thoughts and develop them for yourself and the communities of people who surround you.

JENNY: 1 CORINTHIANS 10:13

"And God is faithful; he will not let you be tempted beyond what you can bear. But when you are tempted, he will also provide a way out so that you can endure it."

Jenny's husband had a progressive and long-term health complication. She was part of a small group of churchgoers who met regularly in each other's homes for companionship, Bible study and prayer. Knowing about Jenny's situation, at one gathering, Jenny shared that there were certain practical and emotional elements that were becoming more difficult for them to manage. Concerned about this, she asked the group to pray with her about it. Although she did not use these words, Jenny needed to find a way through this difficult time.

As the group prayed together, a thought about "a way out" came into David's imagination.[21] He shared this with the others, also sharing that it reminded him of the words in 1 Cor 10:13. As they talked and prayed about it, an idea began to germinate amongst them about whether meeting with a therapist might give Jenny breathing space and help her (and her husband) to navigate this challenging time. Jenny felt peaceful and hopeful when she thought about this and the idea remained with her as she travelled home.

Jenny did connect with a therapist and went on to meet with her regularly. These times gave her much-needed space in her week where she could talk freely in a trusted environment with someone who could support her. Unlike the people of Israel referred to in 1 Corinthians 10, Jenny was not struggling with idolatry per se, but she was in a situation that was becoming

---

21. For a valuable but dense consideration of the Spirit's interaction with our imagination, see Yong, "Pneumatological Imagination," 119–218.

increasingly difficult for her to bear and this follows a broader interpretation of the verses.[22] Jenny's times with her therapist, prompted by a prayer-triggered thought that led the group to this verse, provided a way out for her, helping her to endure her situation.[23]

If this *was* pneumatic interpretation—and various indicators suggest that it was—this is where the Spirit was holistically interpreting Scripture to her, working to transform Jenny and her situation:

As the group prayed together, the Spirit brought words to David's imagination that reminded them of the words in 1 Cor 10:13. Jenny's meetings with the therapist were a tangible manifestation of the realities of that verse for her and an example of God's faithfulness to her personally. The Spirit, therefore, spoke through and beyond the written words of 1 Cor 10:13, appropriating them for her personally and providing a way out that had potential to nourish and support Jenny and her husband.

Within this were simultaneously communal aspects alongside the personal. The thought about a way out—that led to 1 Cor 10:13—that led to the idea of a therapist—started with one person and ended with group discussion and discernment. This communal discernment process aligns with the decision-making process outlined in Acts 15 undertaken by the apostles and elders during the council at Jerusalem and the Spirit's involvement with the process (v. 28, "it seemed good to the Holy Spirit and to us").[24] Moreover, whilst the pneumatic interpretation/transformation concerned Jenny most directly, it would also have impacted her husband too. The potential impact on their relationship indicates the likelihood of redeeming and reconciling activity at work also, suggesting the presence of the biographical content revealing the nature and character of God spoken of earlier, namely the Redeemer-Son and the Reconciler-Spirit.

Finally, the affective, ethical, and cognitive aspects of pneumatic interpretation could have been present in that the Spirit brought the passage to David's imagination as he prayed, impacting his cognition, and also worked communally in the group's concurrence with that thought and their developing the idea for forward route for Jenny. The Spirit could have worked ethically with David's decision to share his thought with the others and in Jenny's decision to find a therapist. Finally, the Spirit's affective

---

22. For example, Morris, *I Corinthians*, 144: "*Temptation* here may be used in the sense of temptation to sin, but it seems to have the broader sense of 'testing,' and to include trials of every kind."

23. Names have been changed.

24. For perspective on Acts 15 in relation to (Pentecostal) community discernment, see Thomas, "Women, Pentecostals and the Bible," 41–56. For further analysis, see Mather, *Interpreting Spirit*, 77–79, 84.

interpretation may have been present in the peace and hope Jenny experienced when thinking about the idea, and was potentially also present in the (affective) compassion the home group showed for Jenny and her situation.

WILLIAM: THE PAIN OF UKRAINE AND THE CROSS AND RESURRECTION.

William is an artist and retired vicar.[25] He experienced what may have been pneumatic interpretation in February 2022.

Watching the news during the week that Russia invaded the Ukraine, William was struck by "the awfulness of . . . an early image of a block of flats hit by a missile causing death, destruction, and a gaping hole" in its side.[26] The following Sunday at church, William began thinking about and praying over this image. As he did, "a reminder of Jesus on the cross and a gaping hole in his side from the soldier's sword" came to mind. The image from the news and the reminder of Jesus on the cross came together in William's imagination and an idea for a painting was born. It depicts a dying Jesus in front of a bombed block of flats which are painted in the colors of the Ukraine flag (it is not intended to be comfortable viewing). William's painting has since been used as a tool for prayer and meditation in churches and seminaries in the UK and US.

If this was pneumatic interpretation—and again, various indicators suggest that it was—this is where the Spirit was at work:

William's experience could be an example of the Spirit communicating with us as we live and work in ways that leads us back to truths contained in Scripture. Whilst no specific Bible passage came to his mind, broader biblical-theological concepts did[27] and in the words written to accompany the painting, William stated:

> The Christian teaching is that Jesus died on the cross for our sin. None of us is blameless, not least the soldier with the spear or the Russians with the missile. But the poignant promise through the pain—even the pain of Ukraine—is that the message of the

---

25. Church of England clergy. Reverend William Mather is also my father.

26. Quotations are taken from the words William wrote to accompany the Pain of Ukraine painting in February 2023 on the year anniversary of the invasion. Available on request.

27. Some relevant Scriptures here are the soldier piercing Jesus's side with a spear in John 19:34 and the suffering servant in Isa 53:4–5, "Surely he took up our pain and bore our suffering . . . But he was pierced for our transgressions, he was crushed for our iniquities; the punishment that brought us peace was on him, and by his wounds we are healed."

cross is more powerful than any tyrant. Through it comes peace in the heart that lasts forever.

A year later the conflict has widened and deepened. Thousands more flats, homes and businesses have been hit. Cities have been devastated. Millions have become refugees or been internally displaced.

But the power of the cross brings resurrection hope. It also brings energy to pray even in the worst of times that there will be peace and there will be new life.

The Spirit, it seems, connected with William in his life, leading him towards particular theological concepts within Scripture that William brought to detail in a painting and its accompanying words.

The painting's continuing use as a teaching tool and aid for meditation and prayer resonates with the simultaneously personal and communal aspects of pneumatic interpretation. Additionally, Its use as tool to pray for change in the situation in Ukraine together with meditation on the message of hope achieved only through Christ's death and resurrection, suggests the presence of redemptive and reconciliational aspects of pneumatic interpretation, showing the Redeemer-Son and the Reconciler-Spirit to us.

Finally, as was the case with Jenny and 1 Cor 10:13, the Spirit appears to have worked holistically and transformatively, bringing the image of the flats back to William's mind in a church service and triggering the idea for a painting that was subsequently used as a meditation, prayer, and teaching aid. In both Jenny and her friends and William's cases, Spirit invited them to participate and enter into a particular route of (interpretive and transformational) activity that aligned with the verse and/or biblical-theological concept in some way. By this route, the Spirit interpreted Scripture *to* them *but* in this manner, the Spirit *also* worked to interpret and transform them personally *and* those people and situations around them.

PARTNERSHIP AND RELATIONSHIP

Jenny and William's stories[28] show how the Spirit can holistically and transformatively interpret truths contained in the Bible to us. These truths align with the written content or biblical-theological concepts in some way and bear unique personal relevance to our own lives and surrounding communities. Through this process, the Spirit works in affective, ethical, and

---

28. For more practical examples of pneumatic interpretation, see *Interpreting Spirit*, 68–69 (Rickie Moore), 108–9 (Gordon Fee), 122n493 (Frank Macchia), 148 (Craig Keener), 165–66 (Daisy Wilkins).

cognitive partnership with us to transform *our* lives *and* the lives of the people and communities around us.

Pneumatic interpretation is affective, ethical, and cognitive; creative, redemptive, and reconciliational; and simultaneously personal and communal. It is interpretation from the Holy Spirit of God through the words of Scripture working in transformational partnership with us. In other words, the Spirit moves us out from the written word and into society, changing us (interpreting and transforming) and changing (interpreting and transforming) the lives and situations of those around us. The Spirit will always do this in ways that (self)-interpret God as Father, Son, and Spirit to us and which point us back to Scripture.

In William's situation, the communities concerned were not just those communities who could see and prayerfully reflect on the painting, but *also* the people of Ukraine for whom the painting was intended to inspire prayer for. Also illustrated by William's story is that the Spirit can work in reverse,[29] highlighting certain things to us as we carry out our lives that lead us back to the truths contained in Scripture.

As a final word, relationship with God is central to pneumatic interpretation. The paradox is that the all-powerful Spirit of God, the ultimate "drawer-er into relationship" also requires our affective, ethical, and cognitive participation. Moral integrity, humility, and openness before God *really matters* for those of us who are serious about interpreting Scripture with the Spirit and being interpreted *by* the Spirit, not just for our own sake, but for the sake of the communities around us.

BIBLIOGRAPHY

Balthasar, Hans Urs von. "Preliminary Remarks on the Discernment of Spirits." In *Explorations in Theology IV: Spirit and Institution*, translated by Edward T. Oakes, 337–51. San Francisco: Ignatius, 1995.

Edwards, Jonathan. *The Religious Affections*. Reprint with slight variations. Edinburgh: Banner of Truth, 2014.

Ellington, Scott A. "Pentecostalism and the Authority of Scripture." *Journal of Pentecostal Theology* 9 (1996) 16–38.

Grenz, Stanley J. "The Spirit and the Word: The World-Creating Functions of the Text." *Theology Today* 57 (2000) 357–74.

---

29. Another example is Frank Macchia, watching a show in Las Vegas and becoming deeply impacted by the symbolism of live and death within it. For his description, see Macchia, "Resurrection: A Dance of Life," 223–24. For analysis in relation to pneumatic interpretation, see Mather, *Interpreting Spirit*, 122n493.

Keener, Craig S. *Spirit Hermeneutics: Reading Scripture in Light of Pentecost*. Grand Rapids: Eerdmans, 2016.

Lane, Tony. *Sin and Grace: Evangelical Soteriology in Historical Perspective*. London: APOLLOS, 2020.

Macchia, Frank D. "Resurrection: A Dance of Life." *Pneuma* 27 (2005) 223–24.

Martin, Francis. "Spirit and Flesh in the Doing of Theology." *Journal of Pentecostal Theology* 18 (2001) 3–31.

Martin, Lee Roy. *The Spirit of the Psalms: Rhetorical Analysis, Affectivity, and Pentecostal Spirituality*. Cleveland: CPT Press, 2018.

Mather, Hannah R. K. *The Interpreting Spirit: Spirit, Scripture, and Interpretation in the Renewal Tradition*. Eugene, OR: Pickwick, 2020.

Moltmann, Jürgen. *The Spirit of Life: A Universal Affirmation*. Translated by Margaret Kohl. London: SCM, 1991.

Morris, Leon. *I Corinthians: An Introduction and Commentary*. London: Tyndale, 1971.

Thomas, John Christopher. "Women, Pentecostals and the Bible: An Experiment in Pentecostal Hermeneutics." *JPT* 5 (1994) 41–56.

Wright, N. T. "The Challenge of the Enlightenment." In *Scripture and the Authority of God*, 52–63. 2nd ed. London: SPCK, 2013.

Yong, Amos. "The Pneumatological Imagination: Epistemology in Triadic Perspective." In *Spirit-Word-Community: Theological Hermeneutics in Trinitarian Perspective*, 119–218. Eugene, OR: OR: Wipf & Stock, 2002.

Chapter 14
Creedal Hermeneutics
MARK MOORE

At first glance, a chapter on creedal hermeneutics might seem ill-fitting for a book on postconservative theological interpretation. After all, are not the creeds the penultimate representation of orthodoxy and conservative theology. It is important to remember, however, that postconservative is not anti-tradition. It is a theological framework that is open to new developments in theology which build on the traditional foundation of the faith. This chapter will not approach the creeds as the final answers in theology, but rather as a starting point of a much longer conversation that has spanned two millenia. Some basic questions that this chapter seeks to answer are: how do the creeds, particularly the Apostles' Creed and the Nicene Creed, help us read and apply Scripture, what does the developmental process of the creeds teach us about the nature of theology and hermeneutics, how do the creeds free us to explore theological frontiers rather than confine us to the past? In order to answer these questions this chapter will briefly describe the creedal process and some of the main voices that guided the development of these foundational declarations. It will also propose that the creedal process provides a model for postconservative theological interpretation that is both grounded and free.

CREEDAL HERMENEUTICS DEFINED

Creedal hermeneutics, simply defined, is a form of biblical and theological interpretation that is modeled after the creedal process, a process of identifying key theological ideas in Scripture and providing short, collective summaries of those ideas. Christopher Hall understands creedal hermeneutics as a way of learning to read and interpret Scripture as the church fathers did.[1] It is not so much the content of the creeds but the creedal process of interpreting Scripture in a holistic manner that is key here. The creeds were never intended to replace Scripture but rather draw out what Scripture was saying about the nature of God, the person of Jesus, and the roles of the Holy Spirit and the church. Athanasius stressed that the members of the council of Nicaea sought to develop a creed from "the acknowledged words of Scripture."[2] The creedal process of reading Scripture sought to define the essential claims of what Christians believed about God. In this way, early creedal statements stood as essential identity markers for Christian theology which guided further theological interpretation. The creedal process did not result in final answers for the vast questions about God. Rather, it guided the church into a faithful articulation of the revelation of God in Scripture. In many ways, the creeds served as fenceposts defining the basic tenets of Christianity as found in Scripture. Stanley Hauerwas suggests that the boundaries defined via the creedal process represent a faithful reading of Scripture.

While the use of terms like boundaries and fenceposts might appear restrictive, the creedal process provides a strong foundation for further exploration of theological truths. Tertullian, writing about the Rule of Faith, which serves as a sort of protocreed during the early apostolic period, noted, "Provided the essence of the Rule is not disturbed, you may seek and discuss as much as you like. You may give full rein to your itching curiosity where any point seems unsettled and ambiguous or dark and obscure."[3] The creedal process is not meant to be constrictive but rather constructive, allowing the church to build further theological reflection upon the strong foundation of core biblical truths.

The creeds were also developed to guard against misreadings of Scripture. Michael Bird stresses the importance of creedal statements in shaping and directing theological interpretation. He states that in creeds, "you are saying: this is the stuff that really matters. You are declaring: this is where the boundaries of the faith need to be drawn. You are suggesting: this is what brings us together in one faith."[4] Bird especially emphasizes the importance of creeds for certain anti-creedal strands of evangelicalism, noting that creeds are first and foremost biblical and carry on biblical traditions as

---

1. See Hall, *Reading Scripture with the Church Fathers*.
2. See Blaising, "Creedal Formation as Hermeneutic Development."
3. Tertullian, *Prescriptions Against Heretics*, 14.
4. Bird, *What Christians Ought to Believe*, 18.

well as defend the faith from heretical views. Carl Trueman also warns anti-creedal traditions. For Trueman, the creeds provide a superior reflection on the overall testimony of Scripture and the creedal process finds its roots in Scripture itself. Referencing 2 Tim 1:13–14, ("What you heard from me, keep as the pattern of sound teaching, with faith and love in Christ Jesus. Guard the good deposit that was entrusted to you—guard it with the help of the Holy Spirit who lives in us.") Trueman states, "the Bible itself seems to demand that we have forms of sound words [patterns of sound teaching], and that's what creeds are."[5]

Theological interpretation is dialectic in nature, a series of conversations throughout the history of the church. Creedal hermeneutics provides a model that guides this conversation. It is a model that develops a strong theological foundation to ground further theological reflection. In light of the postconservative theological tradition, creedal hermeneutics opens the door to further theological exploration while providing steady footing for the journey. It will be helpful now to provide a brief summary of the creedal process by looking as the development of both the Apostles' Creed and the Nicene Creed. The development of both creeds provides the clearest understanding of the creedal process and its role in understanding creedal hermeneutics.

Nearly two millennia of Christian theology have given rise to numerous theological voices. These voices are often contradictory to one another. Augustine held a particular view while Luther held another. Wesley opposed Calvin. Barth eluded both liberal and conservative viewpoints in some areas. While these voices have immensely enhanced the church's understanding of certain complexities of Christian theology, they have the potential of leaving the average student of theology or Christian in a haze of confusion, wondering what exactly Christians believe about anything. This confusion has led to what may be considered a form of theological agnosticism, when one is unsure if anyone can know anything definite about God.

At times, it is important to reaffirm the essential claims of Christian theology, to define the parameters once again. The unique aspect of creedal hermeneutics is that it uses the creedal process, the process of identifying and articulating essential claims of theology, as a way of fostering further theological reflection from a place of agreement. The creedal process allows the church to continually reenter the theological conversation while reexamining past proclamations. For Khaled Anatolios, the creedal process demonstrates that hermeneutics always precedes theology.[6]

---

5. Trueman, *Creedal Imperative*, 75–76.
6. Antolios, *Retrieving Nicaea*, 111.

Creedal hermeneutics also helps guide each new generation as it attempts to understand the handed-down proclamations of the church while also breaking new ground. Barth stressed the vital importance of keeping theology and the creeds together for just this purpose: "Because the Church must again and again understand its Confession anew and because it is again and again confronted with the necessity of confessing anew, it requires Dogmatics alongside the Confession."[7] Each new generation should therefore engage in theological interpretation that is guided by the creedal process and yet free to explore the vast area beyond creedal proclamations.

CREEDAL DEVELOPMENT

THE APOSTLES' CREED

Tracing the development of the Apostles' Creed proves to be an arduous and complicated task. The first appearances of the Apostles' Creed in its current form date to the eighth century with the final Latin formula, what is known as the Textus Receptus, dating even later, to the sixteenth century. The creed undoubtedly bears a connection with creedal formulations of an early time, resembling some of the earliest Christian confessions of the Western church and so stands as both a representation of the later development of the creedal process and one of the earliest expressions of the church. While the theory that the Apostles' Creed can be traced back to the original Apostles has been thoroughly rejected, a great number of scholars draw a connection between the current Apostles' Creed and the baptismal formulation known as the Old Roman Symbol. To accept the Apostles' Creed as only an eighth century or later creation of the church would be a failure to recognize its theological and creedal development. The Apostles' Creed did not simply appear in the eighth century, but the line tracing its development from the Old Roman Symbol is not straight and often blurred.

The final Latin formulation of the Apostles' Creed, the exact form that is still used by many today, is drawn from the writings of Melchior Hittorp, the canon of Cologne, published in 1568. The text of this final formulation reads as follows:

> I believe in God the Father almighty,
> creator of heaven and earth;
> I believe in Jesus Christ, His only Son, our Lord,
> Who was conceived by the Holy Spirit, born of the Virgin Mary,
> Suffered under Pontius Pilate, was crucified dead and buried,

---

7. Barth, *Credo*, 4.

He descended into hell, the third day he rose again from the dead;
He ascended into heaven and sits at the right hand of God the Father almighty;
from thence he will judge the living and the dead;
I believe in the Holy Spirit,
the holy Catholic Church,
the communion of saints,
the remission of sins,
the resurrection of the flesh,
and eternal life. Amen.

This final formulation represents the full and complete development of the Apostles' Creed, but little about the true origin of the creed can be known by this final form. This text will be used, though, as a starting point to then work backward toward earlier formulations of the initial centuries of Christianity.

As noted above, while this sixteenth-century version represents the complete and final Latin formulation of the text, the first fully developed version of the Apostles' Creed to be comparably representative of its current form appears in the eighth century in the writings of Saint Priminius, particularly his missionary manual, *de Singulis Libris Canonicis Scarapsus*. Saint Priminius was the founder and first abbot of the monastery of Reichenau, Germany, and later the abbot of the monastery at Hornbach. In his writings, Priminius referenced the Apostles' Creed by reminding his readers of their baptism experience and the liturgy used. In this liturgy, we find an interrogatory confession; a clear outline of the Apostles' Creed is seen in the questions asked by the priest. While this reference gives us the Apostles' Creed in its final recognized form, it clearly hints at a prior formulation and prior use. Priminius does not take credit for the formation of the interrogatory sequence he depicts, which indicates that this practice clearly precedes his writing and one could assert the eighth century as well. The clear baptismal function represented here underscores one of the main functions of the Apostles' Creed.

When dealing with both the sixteenth- and eighth-century formulations of the Apostles' Creed, JND Kelly clearly notes a connection to what is known as the Old Roman Symbol.[8] The fourth century serves as a bridge between the Old Roman Symbol and the Apostles' Creed, particularly the writings of Rufinus (c. 390) and Marcellus (336–341). It is also in the fourth century when one first sees the linguistic combination of symbol and apostle, Symbolum Apostolorum, written in a letter from the council of Milan to

---

8. Kelly, *Early Christian Creeds*, 399–400.

Pope Siricius, most likely composed by Saint Ambrose. In examining these three references to the Old Roman Symbol, it is clear that the belief that this tradition can be traced back to the original twelve apostles is alive and well at this time. Rufinus provides a detailed narrative as to how this tradition was passed down from the Apostolic period, but again this theory has been thoroughly rejected by modern scholarship for good and evident reasons. The text of the Old Roman Symbol from Rufinus does prove helpful in tracing the origins of the creed, though. In his commentary on the creed, what Rufinus notes as the Old Roman Symbol can be reconstructed as follows:

> I believe in God the Father almighty.
> And in Jesus Christ, his only Son, our Lord;
> Who was born by the Holy Spirit of the Virgin Mary;
> Was crucified under Pontius Pilate and was buried;
> The third day he rose from the dead;
> He ascended into heaven; and sits on the right hand of the Father;
> From thence he will come to judge the quick and the dead.
> And in the Holy Spirit,
> The Holy Church,
> the remission of sins,
> the resurrection of the flesh.

Compared with the Textus Receptus above, the modifications are minimal but evident. Marcellus, the bishop of Ancyra in Cappadocia records a similar version of the symbol in Greek some sixty years before Rufinus, showing that this pattern was well-established before Rufinus.

The basic structure for the Old Roman Symbol can be traced back even further when one notes the similarities between Rufinus's version and the interrogatory baptismal creed found in the work *Apostolic Tradition* by Hippolytus dating to the early third century (c. 215) and written in Greek. When tracing the historical and theological development of the Apostles' Creed from its foundation in the Old Roman Symbol, it is also important to note prior theological and creedal developments leading up to the Symbol itself. The main bridge between the Apostolic teachings found in the New Testament and the Old Roman Symbol is the Rule of Faith. The Rule of Faith represents the core of the early patristic tradition and teachings, offering insight into how they read and interpreted essential elements of the biblical message. The Rule of Faith was not viewed as a competitor with Scripture but was rather drawn from and founded on the biblical message. Bryan Litfin observes that while the Rule was initially used as a catechetical summary for baptismal preparation it was always viewed as "a convenient summary of catholic orthodoxy."[9] Among three conclusions that Litfin makes regarding the patristic understanding of the Rule of Faith, he notes that the Rule was used to emphasize "unchanging, absolute truths" regarding the primary affirmations of Scripture.

Two main patristic writers who utilized the Rule in argumentation and theological development were Irenaeus of Lyons and Tertullian. Irenaeus identified the Rule with the overarching narrative of Scripture and considered it the logic of Scripture, while Tertullian also understood the Rule as the reason or order of Scripture. Litfin asserts that for Tertullian and Irenaeus the elements of the Rule form the greater Christian metanarrative. This metanarrative is at the heart of creedal hermeneutics.

While the primary function of the Apostles' Creed in its earliest form was baptismal preparation, the formative elements of the creed reveal the way the earliest voices in the church read and interpreted Scripture. For many in the patristic period, Scripture was read as an overarching story. The metanarrative of Scripture guided further theological interpretation of specific passages. The creedal process evidenced in the development of the Apostles' Creed reveals that the creed was not meant to be the sum total of theology or the only affirmation of the catechumen. It was, rather, a foundational guide for a much larger theological conversation.

THE NICENE CREED

Comparatively, tracing the historical development of the Nicene Creed is a bit clearer and provides defined time periods and key figures involved in the process. The creedal process involved in the formation of the Nicene Creed also presents greater clarity on how the Church Fathers read and interpreted Scripture, giving us a clearer understanding of the function of creedal hermeneutics. While the Apostles' Creed has clear baptismal and catechetical roots, the Nicene Creed emerges to address theological concerns. The core theological questions that guided the Council of Nicaea had been swirling around the early church since the time of the Apostles and generally revolved around the person and nature of Jesus Christ himself. Who was Jesus in relation to God? How should the phrase Son of God be understood? How did Scripture answer these questions? The early creeds and symbols were clearly Trinitarian, but the exact relationship between the Father, Son, and the Holy Spirit was not always clearly defined. Christian theologians in the second and third centuries offered a variety of explanations.

The pre-Nicene theological landscape of the second century displays a boom in the number of voices coming together to answer these questions

9. Litfin, "Learning from Patristic Use of the Rule of Faith."

about the exact nature of Jesus in relation to Father. John Meyendorff notes that the second-century church was faced with a "profusion of doctrinal and mystical claims," most coming from gnostic sentiments.[10] Many of the second-century attempts to answer these questions were rightly guided by a desire to protect the strong monotheism that they saw in the narrative of Scripture. Often their answers failed to express the equality with God that Jesus possesses in Scripture as well. Those who attempted to protect the oneness of God at all costs could be labeled Monarchists. In this view, God the Father alone is regarded as God and therefore the human Jesus was either "adopted" as the Son of God or was simply a vessel for God to inhabit for a brief time. The Son had no distinction within the Godhead. Other second-century writers rejected these two views but still failed to fully grasp the nature of equality and distinction. Most notably, Origen taught that Jesus was to be considered God along with the Father but he insisted on the distinct subsistence of the Son. In some ways Origen foreshadows themes later picked up by Arius like his stress on the distinct subsistence of three divine hypostases, his rejection of the term homoousios, and his avoidance of imagery describing the Son as emanating from the Father or being begotten. Yet Origen also insisted on the eternal existence of the Son and that God has always been Father, which paved the way for several key points at Nicaea.

Origen's beliefs would be carried on by some of his pupils in Alexandria but also challenged by Western leaders like Dionysius of Rome. The church in the West had in many ways settled on the consubstantiality of the Trinity, which Tertullian developed in the latter part of the second century. Tertullian taught that the Son and the Spirit were of the same substance, or homoousios, as the Father. Those in Alexandria, following Origen's lead, were at first uncomfortable using this type of phrasing, but eventually adopted it to differentiate Jesus from other created beings.

While the church in the West had seemingly accepted the equality of the Son and the Father, there were still those who sought to save a strong monotheistic view of God. The most famous guardian of monotheism at the turn of the fourth century was Arius. Arius was a priest at the church of Baucalis and sought to protect the oneness of the God of Christianity. Kelly provides us with the strong words of Arius as presented to Bishop Alexander: "We acknowledge one God, Who is alone unbegotten, alone eternal, alone without beginning, alone true, alone possessing immortality, alone wise, alone good, alone ruler, alone judge of all, etc."[11] Arius asserted that the divine essence of God could not be shared with the Son; therefore the

---

10. Meyendorff, "Nicene Creed," 8.
11. Kelly, *Early Christian Creeds*, 231.

Son and the Spirit were not of the same substance as the Father. He stressed that they were created beings, emphatically asserting that there was a time when both were not. Kelly sums up the Arian point of view contested by Athanasius in this way: "The net result was the Trinity, or divine Trias, was described, in speciously Origenistic language, as consisting of three Persons. But the three Persons were three utterly different beings, and did not share in any way the same substance or essence as each other."[12]

Arius's main opponent during this time was Athanasius. Athanasius stressed that if the Son and Spirit were created beings, even if they were created before the beginning of the world, then human beings would have no real contact with God through them. Athanasius also stressed that if the Son were a finite creature he would not be able to comprehend the infinite nature of God. The Son would not truly know the Father and therefore could not fully reveal the Father to humanity.

The Council of Nicaea, which was assembled by Constantine to provide unity for the church in the spring of 325, provided a definitive answer and resolution for this debate by developing a formal creed refuting the claims of Arianism. While the exact details of the council are lost to history since no official transcripts of the meetings were ever released, the text of the creed that was produced by this council exists and its very particular wording is telling of the events of the proceedings. The ecumenical nature of the council affirms that the Nicene Creed stands as the first ecumenical creed of the church, marking a new stage in creedal development. It would be incorrect, though, to assert that the Council of Nicaea created the famous creed out of nothing. It clearly resembles the baptismal creeds that have been shown to be common since at least the early second century. Scholars have suggested that either the baptismal creed of Palestinian Caesarea or the creed of Jerusalem most likely served as the basis for the creed formulated at Nicaea.

Between the Council of Nicaea and the current form of the Nicene Creed lies another important step, the Council of Constantinople in 381. The earlier version of the creed was further refined at this council. It will be helpful to compare the texts of each creed to note the significant additions. The text of the Council of Nicaea's creed is as follows:

> We believe in one God, the Father Almighty, Maker of all things visible and invisible.
>
> And in one Lord Jesus Christ , the Son of God, begotten of the Father [the only-begotten; that is, of the essence of the Father, God of God], Light of Light, very God of very God,

---

12. Kelly, *Early Christian Creeds*, 232.

begotten, not made, being of one substance (homoousion) with the Father; by whom all things were made [both in heaven and on earth]; who for us men, and for our salvation, came down and was incarnate and was made man; he suffered, and the third day he rose again, ascended into heaven; from thence he shall come to judge the quick and the dead.

And in the Holy Ghost.

The text of the Constantinopolitan Creed is as follows:

We believe in one God, the Father Almighty, Maker of heaven and earth, and of all things visible and invisible.

And in one Lord Jesus Christ, the only-begotten Son of God, begotten of the Father before all worlds (æons), Light of Light, very God of very God, begotten, not made, being of one substance with the Father; by whom all things were made; who for us men, and for our salvation, came down from heaven, and was incarnate by the Holy Ghost of the Virgin Mary, and was made man; he was crucified for us under Pontius Pilate, and suffered, and was buried, and the third day he rose again, according to the Scriptures, and ascended into heaven, and sitteth on the right hand of the Father; from thence he shall come again, with glory, to judge the quick and the dead; whose kingdom shall have no end.

And in the Holy Ghost, the Lord and Giver of life, who proceedeth from the Father, who with the Father and the Son together is worshiped and glorified, who spake by the prophets. In one holy catholic and apostolic Church; we acknowledge one baptism for the remission of sins; we look for the resurrection of the dead, and the life of the world to come. Amen.

As one can see, the later Constantinopolitan Creed further develops several key points in the creed. Most notably, this version develops the understanding of the Holy Spirit from one line to several lines that give further detail to essential affirmations concerning the person of the Holy Spirit. The Constantinopolitan version of the creed represents the current form of what is considered the Nicene Creed and was officially affirmed at the Council of Chalcedon in 451. At Chalcedon, the Nicene Creed was accepted by both the church in the West and the church in the East, marking its unique status as an ecumenical statement of belief. While the addition of *et filioque* in 589 caused division between the East and the West, it does not negate the ecumenical nature of the creed.

It is clear from the historical origins of the Nicene Creed that its formulation carried with it a particular task or function, that is, to serve as a test for orthodoxy. Kelly observes that the Nicene Creed and others that would follow during the fourth century "were put forth not merely as epitomes of the beliefs of their promulgators, but as test of orthodoxy of Christians in general."[13] This function marked a transition from the localized baptismal creeds that preceded the Nicene period. The formulation of the Nicene Creed served as a statement to those, like Arius, who taught other views on the nature of Jesus and the Holy Spirit. The use of the term substance (ousia) twice displayed a clear rebuke of Arian thought. The particular language used displayed the need felt by those present at Nicaea to further develop the theological language used to talk about God. The simple baptismal formulas of the past simply would not work against the likes of Arius. Further clarification as to the precise relationship of the Father to the Son was needed to fully grasp the conception of God presented in Scripture.

Another function of the Nicene Creed, as evidenced by the formation of the Council in Nicaea, was ecumenical unity. The creed was designed to bring the church universal together in agreement over the key essentials of Christian belief. This unity did not occur at once though, but rather over a fifty-year period after the council while the creed was debated and examined further. With the affirmation of the creed by the Council of Constantinople, an apparent ecumenical unity was achieved. The ecumenical unity noted here is not meant to disregard further debates or controversies but rather to underscore the achievement of the creed as a lasting summation of essential elements of the biblical narrative.

The creedal process involved in the development of both the Apostles' Creed and the Nicene Creed reveal to us key ways in which the early church read and interpreted Scripture. First, the later, formal creeds of the Christian church have roots in the creedal material found in Scripture. They cannot be seen as mere inventions of the second- through fourth-century church. Second, the creedal statements in Scripture and the later conciliar creeds took into account the totality of the biblical message to clearly identify the God whom Christians worship and serve. This identification of God also distinguished Christianity from other religions. Finally, the overarching primary function of the creedal process was to identify and articulate essential elements of the Christian message in Scripture.

KEY MARKS OF CREEDAL HERMENEUTICS

The beauty of creedal hermeneutics is found in both its rich historical foundation and in the model it provides for interpreting and applying Scripture.

---

13. Kelly, *Early Christian Creeds*, 205.

Creedal hermeneutics is not the only approach to biblical and theological interpretation, but in it we find an approach to theological interpretation that builds upon the complete message of Scripture, instead of relying on a sample of proof-texts. The creedal process also provides a way of articulating the comprehensive message of Scripture and reflecting on that articulation. With this articulation and reflection in balance, the theological interpreter is given freedom to explore the continual questions of theology while standing on a firm base of theological affirmations. This objectivity and freedom allows theological interpretation to respond to ongoing shifts in the cultural landscape and remain faithful to the core beliefs of the biblical message. The creedal process also stresses ecumenical unity, a unity often devoid in theology. The simplicity of the creeds unites varying theological voices around core affirmations of Scripture, developing a strong and diverse bond. This final section will explore several key marks of creedal hermeneutics and examine the benefits of this approach to postconservative theological interpretation.

THE TOTALITY OF SCRIPTURE

The creedal process examined in this chapter highlights a main emphasis of creedal hermeneutics, the desire to faithfully represent the complete message of Scripture. During the Arian controversy of the fourth century, Arius and his followers used several prooftexts to support their view that the Son was entirely separate from the Father. Athanasius and others asserted that Arius and his followers were selectively using texts while ignoring the totality of the biblical message regarding the Son.[14] Athanasius and others involved in the creedal process of Nicaea collected a more comprehensive list of biblical passages that helped them highlight the core affirmations of the nature of the Son and how to best articulate those affirmations in a biblically faithful manner. Creedal hermeneutics, then, provides us with a model of postconservative theological interpretation that takes into account the totality of Scripture.

ARTICULATION AND REFLECTION

Definitions of theology are numerous. Etymologically, the term refers to words about God. Barth describes theology as a free science. It is a science in that it is a discipline of study and discovery, but yet it is fundamentally different in regard to the relationship between the student and the object of study. According to Barth, "Theology is a free science because it is based on

14. See Blaising, "Creedal Formation."

and determined by the kingly freedom of the word of God."[15] The theologian does not have control over the object of study the way a biological scientist does while examining the dissected remains of a cadaver. Since God is free the theologian must humbly pursue theological interpretation. Still, two core functions of theology emerge: articulation and reflection. Theology is meant to say something about God, but we must also continually reflect on our own articulations and measure them by the core affirmations of the biblical message. Theology is not simply a reiteration of what has been said about God but rather a dialectic of articulation and reflection.

In mirroring the creedal process, creedal hermeneutics best performs both functions of theology. The primary function of creedal hermeneutics is the articulation of primary affirmations of the biblical narrative. This articulation guides the theological conversation into greater reflection and investigation. If theology is only articulation, then the conversation is cut short. If theology is only reflection, it becomes too ethereal and enigmatic. Theology, then, offers no real answers and loses its influence in the real world, remaining primarily a thought experiment for theologians. Theology needs both the substance of articulation and the freedom of reflection.

OBJECTIVITY WITH FREEDOM

Another key mark of creedal hermeneutics is that it offers objectivity with freedom. Theological interpretation is neither unguided nor purely subjective. One can know certain core affirmations of the biblical narrative that have been recognized and proclaimed by the church. One can proclaim them again for new generations as they examine and reflect on the proclamations of the past. Objectivity grounds the process of reflection and removes the fear of exploring new ideas. By holding onto core affirmations, one need not fear getting it "wrong" theologically. In the absence of this fear, the theologian is truly free to explore deeper mysteries and take more chances.

Freedom is a necessary part of the theological process because it allows each new generation to ask their own unique questions and seek relevant answers. Theological freedom also allows for differences of interpretation. Diverse theological voices are given the freedom to explore and ask questions as long as they remain faithful to the biblical message.

---

15. Barth, *Evangelical Theology*, 9.

ECUMENICAL UNITY

By focusing on the essentials, creedal hermeneutics provides a foundation for greater ecumenical unity. The desire for unity among the diverse churches of the first three centuries of Christianity served as a primary impetus for early creedal formulations. The unifying nature of creedal formulations can be particularly seen in the writings of Paul. Often when Paul refers to an earlier creedal formulation he does so to note a unity of belief between himself and the church or person he is writing to. In the opening lines of the book of Romans, as Paul introduces himself to a church to which he has not traveled, he references a brief creedal statement that serves as the core of the gospel of Jesus (Rom 1:3–4). While the origin and authorship of the creedal statement is debated, it is clear that Paul references key essential identity markers of the Christian faith that both he and the church in Rome hold. In this shared belief Paul establishes unity with the Romans before he proceeds with his letter. In his letter to the Philippians Paul also uses an earlier creedal formulation to remind the church of her core beliefs and establish unity within the church (Phil 2:5–11).

The later conciliar creeds also provided a foundation for greater ecumenical unity. As summaries of the core beliefs of the Christian faith, they unified the developing and evolving church around a core narrative. The model provided by creedal hermeneutics seeks to provide a common ground for all sides of the conversation surrounding any given doctrine. While some disagree on the nuances of varying views they can find unity in core affirmations. This unity should also provide cause for charity toward those who hold opposing views noting that essential beliefs are affirmed. Creedal hermeneutics sheds light on the complex nature of certain doctrines and provides the adequate grounds for diversity and unity.

ASSESSMENT OF CULTURAL INFLUENCE

Theology is a contextual discipline. Theology does not happen in a vacuum but rather is shaped by its particular cultural context. The cultural context of the fourth century and the growth of alternative expressions of Christianity led to the formation of the conciliar creeds. The culture of the church in the sixteenth century led to the Reformation, and so on. Without the proper core affirmations of Scripture it can be difficult to gauge whether the advancements within theology due to cultural influence are beneficial, though. Establishing clear core affirmations which remain stable in the flux of cultural tides, provides a way of assessing theological advancement and the influence of culture.

Creedal hermeneutics seeks to understand a middle ground between liberal and conservative theology. Likewise, postconservative theological interpretation notes that not all claims of modern thought can or should be accepted without modification, and neither are all of the claims of traditional thought so fixed that new insight cannot shape greater understanding of certain doctrines.

Affording both foundation and freedom, creedal hermeneutics reveals itself to be a helpful ally in postconservative theological interpretation. The creedal process reaffirms core affirmations of the complete biblical message while providing theologians with the freedom to reflect on past articulations and change course when necessary.

BIBLIOGRAPHY

Anatolios, Khaled. *Retrieving Nicaea: The Development and Meaning of Trinitarian Doctrine*. Grand Rapids: Baker, 2018.

Barth, Karl. *Credo*. New York: Charles Scribner, 1962.

——— . *Evangelical Theology: An Introduction*. Translated by Grover Foley. Holt, Rinehart, and Winston, 1963.

Bird, Michael F. *What Christians Ought to Believe: An Introduction to Christian Doctrine through the Apostles' Creed*. Grand Rapids: Zondervan, 2016.

Blaising, Craig A. "Creedal Development as Hermeneutical Development: A Reexamination of Nicaea." *Pro Ecclesia* 19 (2010) 371–88.

Hall, Christopher A. *Reading Scripture with the Church Fathers*. Downers Grove, IL: InterVarsity, 1998.

Kelly, J. N. D. *Early Christian Creeds*. 2nd ed. New York: D. McKay, 1961.

Litfin, Bryan M. *Getting to Know the Church Fathers: An Evangelical Introduction*. Grand Rapids: Brazos, 2007.

Meyendorff, John. "The Nicene Creed: Uniting or Dividing Confession." In *Faith to Creed: Ecumenical Perspectives on the Affirmation of the Apostolic Faith in the Fourth Century: Papers of the Faith to Creed Consultation, Commission on Faith and Order, NCCCUSA, October 25–27, 1989—Waltham, Massachusetts*, edited by S. Mark Heim. Grand Rapids: Eerdmans for Commission on Faith and Order, National Council of the Churches of Christ in the U.S.A., 1991.

Tertullian. *Prescriptions Against Heretics*. In *A Journey Through Christian Theology: With Texts From the First to the Twenty-first Century*, by William P. Anderson and Richard L. Diesslin. Minneapolis: Fortress, 2010.

Trueman, Carl R. *The Creedal Imperative*. Wheaton, IL: Crossway, 2012.

Chapter 15
Missional Hermeneutics
GREG McKINZIE

Missional hermeneutics is an approach to Scripture that begins with a theological commitment to the church's participation in God's mission. In this approach, the church reads the Bible as (1) a narrative rendition of God's mission, (2) a collection of case studies in missiological contextualization, (3) a source of equipping for participation in God's mission, and (4) an ongoing narrative that the church reads through the experience of participation in God's mission. The commitment to participation in God's mission begins with missional theology and issues in missional praxis, which circles back to a theological interpretation of Scripture that informs ongoing practice.

Missional hermeneutics includes ecumenical and evangelical approaches to Scripture. Among ecumenical perspectives, the emphasis falls on God's work in the word, to which the church's biblical interpretation *may* serve as a witness. Among evangelical perspectives, the emphasis falls on God's work *through* the church's biblical interpretation. Both prioritize God's mission—the purposes of God in the world. Between the two emphases, the hinge is a theological conception of the church's agency in God's mission. The bent of missional hermeneutics, therefore, varies depending on the theology and ecclesiology one presumes.

The following account of missional hermeneutics begins with a historical survey of missional theology and proceeds to an exploration of the interpretive interests that emerge from it. A typology of missional hermeneutics gives way to the contributions of missiological hermeneutics and the theological interpretation of Scripture. Altogether, missional hermeneutics holds together distinctive emphases on text and reader, combining a vision of the biblical narrative that bears witness to the Triune God's mission with the formation of Christian communities that participate contextually in God's ongoing work in the world.

MISSIONAL THEOLOGY

GOD'S MISSION

Missional theology emerged in the twentieth century from early manifestations of a postcolonial reality, a critique of missiological ecclesiocentrism, and a theological focus on the kingdom of God. Together, these pressures pushed the world Christian movement toward a new understanding of God's mission in which the church is a participant in God's purposes. The Latin phrase *missio Dei* (God's mission) became a token of monumental theological shifts and a field of contest between two visions of ecclesial participation in those purposes.

The 1952 meeting of the International Missionary Council at Willingen, Germany, was a watershed event at which the disorientation and self-critique infusing mid-twentieth-century Christian mission came to expression. Chief among the concerns that animated the gathering was the faltering of colonial models of missions. Following closely on the heels of Mao Tse-tung's closure of communist China in 1949, Willingen was marked by a keen awareness of the limits of Western influence on the global stage. No longer could the church presume the access, much less the legitimacy, that Western colonialism has once granted.

Among Willingen participants, the primary response to this new global landscape was *a critique of ecclesiocentrism*. Historically, missions had been conceived of as the work of the church. Now, there arose a theological prioritization of the work of God in places where the Western church had limited access or influence. Naturally, this raised sharp questions about the role of the church in God's purposes.

For some, labeled "Christocentric," the church's proclamation of Christ is a sine qua non of mission. According to this perspective, the church's witness is essential for understanding the meaning of God's redemptive work in the world, and there is hope in the *eventual* eschatological significance of this witness despite the church's absence in closed fields. For others, labeled "theocentric," the *present* eschatological significance of God's work in the world is primary, thus where justice and human flourishing prevail through the revolutionary movements of history, the church may participate.

A critical tension, therefore, becomes clear at Willingen: the church's participation in God's mission is neither irrelevant nor essential. The primary question, however, was the nature not of the church's work but God's. Only by capturing a theological vision of God's activity in the world could Willingen's diverse constituency begin to stipulate the church's relation to it.

For this reason, an emphasis on the kingdom of God emerged from Willingen as a vital component of the theology of mission in the latter half of the twentieth century. As a biblical concept, "the kingdom of God" provided a terminological handle on the debate. For those who prioritized the church's participation in mission, God works *through* the church until the consummation of God's kingdom as the revelation of Christ's reign. For those who prioritized God's work in the world apart from the church, God's work manifests the kingdom in the present through the realization of justice and human well-being, in which the church *may* participate.

The Willingen conference can be seen as the point of departure for the rift in the world Christian movement that resulted in disjunctive ecumenical and evangelical approaches to mission and, therefore, to later missional theology and hermeneutics. Nonetheless, the pressures of the looming postcolonial reality produced a consensus regarding the priority of the *missio Dei*.[1] The most urgent problem with this consensus was the vagueness of the Trinitarian lineaments of *missio Dei* theology.

TRINITARIAN ADVANCES AND SETBACKS

Karl Barth articulated the first modern connection between the classical Trinitarian notion of *missio* and the theology of mission.[2] Though Barth's early argument (1932) does not develop a Trinitarian missiology, it emphasizes the point that God is the subject of mission. By 1952, his Trinitarianism had shaped the theological discourse within which Willingen would construe mission in distinction from the faltering endeavors of the colonialist church. The discussion as a whole is framed by the Barthian idea that God's Triune mission is distinct from the church's mission, reflecting the *diastasis* between God and humanity on which Barth's theology of witness depends.[3]

In turn, Lesslie Newbigin's thought was especially influential on Willingen's presumptive *missio Dei* consensus. He authored the conference's official statement, which includes the following key passage:

---

1. See Bosch, *Transforming*, 392–93.

2. Barth, "*Die Theologie und die Mission in der Gegenwart.*"

3. Karl Hartenstein, in particular, mediated dialectical theology to Willingen. See Schwarz, "Legacy of Karl Hartenstein," 126.

We who have been chosen in Christ, reconciled to God through Him, made members of His Body, sharers in His Spirit, and heirs through hope of His Kingdom, are by these very facts committed to full participation in His redeeming mission. There is no participation in Christ without participation in His mission to the world. That by which the Church receives its existence is that by which it is also given its world-mission. "As the Father hath sent me, even so send I you."[4]

His subsequent work develops this confession through a Trinitarian ecclesiology: "The life of the Church is a real participation in the life of the triune God, wherein all life and all glory consist of self-giving, a *koinonia*."[5] Yet, Newbigin's Trinitarianism remained general, specifying neither how the church's witness is participation in the Triune life, nor in what sense the church's work in history amid the tides of culture relates to the Triune mission.[6]

The great chronicler of mission theology, David Bosch, argues that Willingen produced a definitive conclusion: "The classical doctrine on the *missio Dei* as God the Father sending the Son, and God the Father and the Son sending the Spirit was expanded to include yet another 'movement': Father, Son, and Holy Spirit sending the church into the world."[7] Following Willingen, however, two perspectives prevailed, neither of which made much of the conference's Trinitarian concerns. The ecumenical perspective conceived of the church as a mere consequence of God's mission, a contingent instrument of God's work in the world. The evangelical perspective conceived of the church as an essential agent of God's mission, an indispensable witness to God's saving work.[8] Neither side needed Trinitarian theology to marshal its arguments. This was, perhaps, a natural consequence of the combination of Barth's influence and Willingen's vagueness. For if infinite qualitative difference stands between the Triune *missio Dei* and ecclesial witness, and we can specify nothing more about what the church's "participation" in the life of the Triune God might entail, little is left but to argue about the relative instrumentality of ecclesial missions.[9] Ultimately,

---

4. "Statement on the Missionary Calling of the Church," 190.
5. Newbigin, *Household of God*, 129.
6. See Newbigin, *Trinitarian Doctrine for Today's Mission*, 33.
7. Bosch, *Transforming Mission*, 390
8. See Hoekendijk, *Church Inside Out*; McGavran, *Conciliar-Evangelical Debate*.
9. Notably, John Stott, the chair of the authoring committee of The Lausanne Movement's First International Congress on World Evangelization in 1974, reframed the regnant Great Commission paradigm of evangelical mission with a Johannine theology (John 17:18; 20:21), establishing a Trinitarian evangelical understanding of mission.

however, the concept of participation in the Triune life would provide a theological bridge between God's work and the church's. This bridging gave rise to missional theology and the hermeneutics that pertains to it.

MISSIONAL ECCLESIOLOGY

In 1992, Newbigin led the first meeting of The Gospel and Our Culture initiative in Britain, but it was not until the launch of the Gospel and Our Culture Network (GOCN) book series in the United States that his influence began to turn the tide. In 1998, the publication of *Missional Church: A Vision for the Sending of the Church in North America*, edited by Darrell Guder, launched the "missional church" conversation into the mainstream.[10]

With Newbigin and the Vatican II document *Ad Gentes*, Bosch had declared that a key entailment of the *missio Dei* is that the church is *missionary by nature*.[11] Bosch's summary of the *missio Dei* is *Missional Church*'s point of departure, which "necessarily shifts all the accents of our ecclesiology."[12] The authors of *Missional Church* include biblical interpretation among these shifts: "our disciplined use of a missional hermeneutic should shape and guide the continuing formation of the church in our changing society."[13] They continue: "We urgently need biblical scholarship that will probe the scriptural record, using a missiological hermeneutic, to enable the church in North America to structure itself in radical obedience to God's mandate to be Christ's witnesses. If we read the biblical witness missionally, we will not fall prey to the naïve and unfaithful notion that the goal lies simply in replicating some particular New Testament church."[14] For the early GOCN, the Trinitarian understanding of God's mission was definitive for reading Scripture as a missional church. Yet, the hermeneutical implications of missional ecclesiology remained to be developed.

To this end, in 2002, the GOCN established its regular meeting, The Forum on Missional Hermeneutics, at the annual meeting of the Society of Biblical Literature. The Forum has generated a variety of proposals (see below) and hosted many of the major voices in the broader missional

---

But this served to promote a more holistic view of what God sends the church to do, in distinction from the ecumenical vision of the church's participation in what God does in the world. See Stott and Wright, *Christian Mission in the Modern World*, 22.

10. Guder, *Missional Church*.

11. Bosch, *Transforming Mission*, 9, 390, 519; see Newbigin, *Open Secret*, 1; *Ad Gentes* 2.

12. Bosch, *Transforming Mission*, 5.

13. Guder, *Missional Church*, 227.

14. Guder, *Missional Church*, 228.

hermeneutics discourse. At this juncture, however, the point is the Forum's connection to the missional ecclesiology movement whose roots are in the tensive theology of Willingen mediated through Newbigin. Just as the conference had done a half-century earlier, the proponents of missional ecclesiology appealed to the doctrine of the *missio Dei* in response to widespread cultural crisis. Now, however, the crisis had come home. At the turn of the twenty-first century, it was evident that the churches of the West needed to re-envision their relationship to their home cultures. Mission could no longer be conceived of as merely a "sending" activity directed toward foreign contexts. Instead, churches must understand their nature as participants in God's mission "at home," amid the waning credibility and influence of traditional ecclesiologies.

MISSIONAL THEOLOGY

Across the theological disciplines, a swell of publications highlighted the theological significance of God's mission following *Missional Church*. Within a decade, diverse, sometimes divergent theological viewpoints had rallied to the neologism *missional*. Biblical, constructive, and practical theology, as well as missiology, each contributed to the framework within which missional hermeneutics developed.

Craig Van Gelder and Dwight Zscheile's 2011 volume *The Missional Church in Perspective* captured the complexity of emergent missional theology with a thoroughgoing "mapping" of the alternatives. Their analysis is incisive:

> The key issue, comprised of two closely related questions, is: to what extent are we simply dealing with human agency, and to what extent is God's agency operative and discernible within human choices? This issue represents a significant distinction that allows us to discern several branches of the missional conversation. The dividing line between branches revolves around the extent to which one starts with the mission of the church and the extent to which one starts with the mission of God; when starting with the mission of God, it also has to do with how robust the trinitarian theology is.[15]

The question of the church's agency in relation to God's mission, bound inseparably to the Trinitarian theologies (or lack thereof) that frame the missional language game, remains primary a decade later. Nonetheless, the contours of missional theology are solidly established. Like the banks of a

---

15. Van Gelder and Zscheile, *Missional Church in Perspective*, 70.

river, *missio Dei* (the Triune God's eschatological purposes) and *missiones ecclesiae* (the church's particular, contextual participation in God's mission) channel the flow of missional theological reflection on Scripture, tradition, context, and practice.

A TYPOLOGY OF MISSIONAL HERMENEUTICS

Distinctive approaches to missional hermeneutics flow between the banks of missional theology. Reflecting the dichotomy between *missio Dei* and *missiones ecclesiae*, two primary currents emphasize the biblical text and the reading community respectively. Although the distinction between text and reader is commonplace in hermeneutics, it is important to recognize its unique valence in missional hermeneutics. On the one hand, Scripture is the revelation of God's ongoing mission in narrative form, including a record of how God's people engaged biblical texts as participants in God's mission at various points in the story. On the other hand, reading Scripture forms the church for contextual participation in God's mission, which in turn forms the church for interpretation.

FOUR STREAMS

Missiologist George Hunsberger synthesized the early years of the Forum's presentations into four "streams of emphasis" in missional hermeneutics. The first stream is *the missional direction of the story*: "The *framework* for biblical interpretation is the story it tells of the mission of God and the formation of a community sent to participate in it."[16] Here, missional hermeneutics emphasizes a shift from biblical interpretation that justifies and explains church missions to a biblical theology that understands God's mission as its narrative logic. The second stream is *the missional purpose of the writings*: "The *aim* of biblical interpretation is to fulfill the equipping purpose of the biblical writings."[17] Missional hermeneutics, therefore, attends to the function of Scripture in relation to the missional nature of the church. Biblical interpretation forms the reading community for witness. The third stream is *the missional locatedness of readers*: "The *approach* required for a faithful reading of the Bible is from the missional location of the Christian community."[18] From this angle, missional hermeneutics happens when the church reads Scripture as participants in God's mission. Missional reading requires contextual engagement with the biblical text in response to the

---

16. Hunsberger, "Mapping the Missional Hermeneutics Conversation," 50.
17. Hunsberger, "Mapping the Missional Hermeneutics Conversation," 53.
18. Hunsberger, "Mapping the Missional Hermeneutics Conversation," 55.

local church's faithfulness to its particular calling. The fourth stream is *the missional engagement with cultures*: "The gospel functions as the interpretive *matrix* within which the received biblical tradition is brought into critical conversation with a particular human context."[19] The universality of God's saving purposes in the work of Christ regulates biblical interpretation. In particular, the New Testament writers' paradigmatic interpretation of Israel's Scripture demonstrates how the gospel guides missional hermeneutics through the interaction of biblical text and cultural context.

The identification of these four streams has proven generative for the ensuing discourse on missional hermeneutics. Nonetheless, subsequent developments contribute to a fuller typology ordered to the heuristic distinction between text-centered and reader-centered approaches. On the text-centered end of the dichotomy are *narrative theology* and *gospel lenses*. (1) Missional narrative theology includes both (1.1) a theological engagement with the story of the Triune *missio Dei* narrativized in Scripture and (1.2) the identification of God's mission as the center of that narrative in biblical-theological terms. (2) Reading Scripture through gospel lenses includes both (2.1) a hermeneutical prioritization of the gospel (the revelation of God's universal saving purposes in the life, death, and resurrection of Jesus) and (2.2) an appreciation for how New Testament authors exemplify such readings. On the reader-centered end of the dichotomy are *Scripture's function* and *social location*. (3) Scripture's function includes both (3.1) the formation of the reading community's identity as a missional community and (3.2) the equipping of the community for practical engagement in God's mission. (4) Social location includes both (4.1) the hermeneutical practices of contextualization and (4.2) the hermeneutically formative effects of missional participation. The following table captures these key dimensions of missional hermeneutics:

A Typology of Missional Hermeneutics	
Text-Centered: The Story of God's Mission	
1. Narrative Theology	
1.1. Trinitarian Origins	The biblical narrative as an expression of the *missio Dei*
1.2. The Plot of Scripture	Mission as the center of biblical theology
2. Gospel Lenses	

---

19. Hunsberger, "Mapping the Missional Hermeneutics Conversation," 59.

2.1. *The Gospel Matrix*	The universality of the *kerygma* as interpretive discrimen
2.2. *Interpretive Paradigms*	Apostolic interpretation as exemplary missional reading
Reader-Centered: The Formation of God's People for Mission	
3. Scripture's Function	
3.1. *Identity Formation*	Reading for the formation of missional ecclesiology
3.2. *Equipping for Mission*	Reading for practical engagement in missional participation
4. Social Location	
4.1. *Contextualization*	Reading in dialogue with local, cultural contexts
4.2. *Participation in Mission*	Reading in light of missional experience

Of these dimensions, the two that pertain to social location connect the Forum on Missional Hermeneutics discourse to major contributions from other fields of study. The practices of missiological hermeneutics developed in the last sixty years are indispensable to missional interpretation. Likewise, the interdisciplinary discourse known as theological interpretation of Scripture enriches missional hermeneutics.

MISSIOLOGICAL HERMENEUTICS

There is a nontrivial overlap between the missional hermeneutics articulated by Forum interlocutors and the missiological study of cultural contextualization. Still, missional theology has developed in relative isolation from academic missiology. A full accounting of the reasons for this separation is beyond the scope of the present discussion. Suffice it to note that evangelical missiology's acute interest in global evangelism in the last seventy years, particularly in regard to the contextual interpretation of the Bible, produced a hermeneutical focus on cultural anthropology that has been of little account to missional theologians focused on the renewal of Western churches in their home contexts.[20]

Contextextualization encompasses a diverse set of perspectives and practices. Among those, the most consequential contribution to missional

---

20. This too-brief analysis is not meant to minimize the considerable contributions of the broader missiological community. The energy and influence of evangelical missiology is, however, undeniable, and the evangelical fixation on the nature and use of the Bible has generated major hermeneutical contributions in the movement's missiological literature.

hermeneutics is attention to the role of worldview in biblical interpretation. Worldview analysis is a tool of missiological anthropology that seeks to lay bare the cultural systems that both cross-cultural missionaries and indigenous readers bring to the biblical text. A second major contribution of missiological hermeneutics comes from the discourse called intercultural hermeneutics. This approach adds to worldview analysis a methodological commitment to mutuality in both cultural and textual interpretation.

WORLDVIEW AND CONTEXTUALIZATION

Anthropologist Clifford Geertz is the best representative of the conceptualization of *worldview* that has shaped missiology.[21] Evangelical missiologists Paul Hiebert and Charles Kraft developed missiological models of worldview over the course of their careers, culminating in two important volumes.[22] Their models establish four dimensions of the missiological conception of worldview:

1. *Worldview analysis serves God's mission*. It is participatory in nature—developed only by engagement with others' worldviews for a dialogical participation in others' lives. The missiological conception of worldview is not designed for purely descriptive purposes but overtly raises the question of how worldviews change (mutually), in order to read Scripture and participate more wisely in God's transforming work in the world.

2. *Worldviews are human, socio-cultural phenomena*. They are a feature of humanity, not a choice. The anthropological elaboration of the concept proceeds through rigorous ethnography. It is concerned with the way people actually make meaning in cultural contexts.

3. *Worldviews are pretheoretical, implicit, and explicable*. A worldview is a model not of *what* a cultural group thinks but of what they think *with*. It is a tacit, pretheoretical dimension of culture. Yet, worldview can be made explicit. An explicated worldview tends to take the propositional form of a "belief" or "core value," but this is deceptive because an explicated worldview tends to ignore the implicit aspects of the worldview that determines its explication.

4. *Worldviews are commensurable*. Translatability is the fundamental assumption of the missiological conception of worldview. The rigor of

---

21. See, e.g., his essay, Geertz, "Ethos, World View, and the Analysis of Sacred Symbols."

22. Hiebert, *Transforming Worldviews*; Kraft, *Worldview for Christian Witness*.

worldview analysis is motivated by the experience of radical difference and misunderstanding. Yet, the presumption of a critical realism makes a triangulation between God, world, and worldviews feasible for missiological contextualization.

In summary, vulnerable engagement in mutual transformation, rigorous ethnographic observation, dialogical explication of tacit cultural phenomena, and a functional critical realism in the midst of deep difference designate the contours of a missiological theory of worldview.

Worldview theory lies at the heart of the missiological practice of contextualization. The essential issue is how a reader's worldview interacts with Scripture, producing contextual interpretations. This interaction depends on the anthropological analysis of text and reader, therefore both are subject to questions about the worldviews of those who do such analysis.

Among some advocates of missional hermeneutics, a worldview can be distilled through five questions: (1) Who am I? (2) Where am I? (3) What's wrong? and (4) What is the remedy?[23] These questions purportedly get at the narrative core of worldview, thereby facilitating a hermeneutical encounter between the biblical worldview's answers and those of the reader's worldview.[24] Attention to worldview marks a productive linkage between the anthropological approach of missiology and the process of readerly formation in missional hermeneutics. Worldview analysis, therefore, offers a vital resource for the contextualization of the biblical narrative of God's mission in the lives of reading communities that do not experience cultural transformation merely by virtue of understanding the broad contours of the biblical narrative in missional terms.

INTERCULTURAL HERMENEUTICS AND RECONTEXTUALIZATION

The complexity of worldview theory requires a high degree of technical competency, which tends to make its hermeneutical contributions monological. At the same time, the rise of world Christianity and the emergence of global postcolonial theologies demand the revisioning of missiological contextualization in intercultural terms. In a robustly intercultural hermeneutics, biblical interpreters of one culture engage in coequal dialogue with those of another culture.

In order to explain intercultural hermeneutics, German missiologist Henning Wrogemann adds to Geertz's semiotic analysis of culture the commitments of discourse theory, which insists on a dialogical negotiation of

---

23. Walsh and Middleton, *Transforming Vision*, 35, formulated these questions.
24. See, e.g., Goheen and Bartholomew, *Living at the Crossroads*, 24.

power, status, and identity between and within cultural configurations. The key issues that discourse theory raises are *agency* (Who interprets culture?), *uniformity* (Is a culture homogenous?), *objectivity* (Which commitments inform cultural interpretation?), and *dynamism* (How does cultural change inform interpretation?). Thus, discourse theory funds the postcolonial critique of cultural interpretation in which semiotic analysis attempts to describe a culture as a static whole from an expert's neutral perspective. For Wrogemann, the combination of semiotic analysis and discourse theory produces a conception of intercultural hermeneutics in which "cultures are to a certain extent delimitable spheres containing those things taken for granted within one's own lifeworld; yet at the same time, they are conceptual formations of social cohesion oriented toward certain publicly communicated identity markers."[25] Both the anthropological analysis of these delimitable spheres and the public negotiation of socially determined formations are essential. From this combination, a missiological vision of contextual theologies emerges.

John Franke extends the notion of intercultural hermeneutics to biblical interpretation:

> Contextuality is inherent in the process of understanding and communicating. From this perspective, biblical interpretation, meaning, and communication always involve the recontextualization of texts and their particular appropriations in a variety of social and historical settings. The ongoing activity of recontextualization in and for a diversity of cultural settings is the essence of intercultural hermeneutics. Hence, intercultural hermeneutics has an inherently relational dimension that involves seeking to understand the social contexts of other interpreters.[26]

Franke's "recontextualization" language contrasts with the typical "contextualization" of evangelical missiology. Because the gospel is not a predetermined quantum that needs only to be fitted into the cultural semiotics of the other determined by the foreign missionary's anthropological analysis, intercultural hermeneutics endeavors to engage in deeper interpretive mutuality. Hence, "one way to understand this process is to think of each of the participants in a conversation as a missionary to the other."[27] The theological affirmation of the participation of the other in God's mission entails a rejection of foundationalist, totalizing interpretations of Scripture. Instead, intercultural hermeneutics is a genuinely dialogical *reading with*.

25. Wrogemann, *Intercultural Hermeneutics*, 155.
26. Franke, "Intercultural Hermeneutics and the Shape of Missional Theology," 90.
27. Franke, "Intercultural Hermeneutics and the Shape of Missional Theology,"

MISSIONAL INTERPRETATION OF SCRIPTURE

The emergence of a missional approach to the theological interpretation of Scripture is another major development in missional hermeneutics. Theological interpretation of Scripture, a discourse that seeks to bridge the academically siloed disciplines of biblical studies and systematic theology, predates missional hermeneutics. It emphasizes the significance of theological commitments for the careful exegesis of biblical texts. Rooted in debates about the biblical theology movement, theological interpretation has an essential point of contact with missional hermeneutics through narrative theology (see Hunsberger's first stream above) and shares a basic interest in the theological formation of the reading community. Missional interpretation of Scripture, then, represents the reorientation of missional hermeneutics toward a more theologically grounded vision of both the biblical narrative and readerly formation.

READING SCRIPTURE MISSIONALLY

Theological interpretation is a set of practices meant to cultivate (1) perceptions of the subject matter of Scripture as God's revelation, (2) approaches to the text of Scripture as canon, and (3) dispositions in readers of Scripture as the church.[28] The perceptions, approaches, and dispositions of theological interpretation can together be abbreviated as faith—faith in the God who speaks, through the canon, to the church. For missional hermeneutics, the God who speaks in and through Scripture is the Father who sends the Son, who in turn with the Father sends the Spirit and the church in the power of the Spirit. The canonical narrative of God's redemptive purposes is *the story of God's mission*, into which the church is drawn. The formation of the church is *purposive*—the ecclesial community's transformation is for participation in God's mission.

Among the leading lights of theological interpretation of Scripture, New Testament scholar Michael Gorman has most prominently engaged with missional hermeneutics. His 2015 volume in the GOCN series, *Becoming the Gospel: Paul, Participation, and Mission*, advances his understanding of Pauline *theōsis* (the doctrine of human participation in the divine life[29]) through the theme of mission, arguing that "Spirit-enabled transformative participation in the life and character of God revealed in the crucified and resurrected Messiah Jesus—is the starting point of mission and is, in fact,

---

28. These three components reflect the summary of three approaches to theological interpretation in Vanhoozer, "Introduction," 23.

29. See Gorman, *Cruciformity*; Gorman, *Inhabiting the Cruciform God*.

its proper theological framework."[30] The upshot is: *"To participate in Christ is both to benefit from God's mission of liberation and reconciliation and to bear witness to this divine mission—thus furthering it—by becoming a faithful embodiment of it."*[31] All Christians are ambassadors of Christ, not because all are evangelists but because all participate in *theōsis*, which entails the church's embodiment of the gospel. Reminiscent of Newbigin's Willingen statement, to participate in Christ just is to participate in God's mission.

Gorman's work focuses on the textual side of missional hermeneutics. By exploring Paul's theology, he offers a missional reading of the biblical narrative and an exploration of Paul's exemplary missional interpretations. But the practice of theological interpretation of Scripture also invites attention to the formation of readers.

READERLY FORMATION

Theological interpretation of Scripture includes the affirmation that certain practices cultivate the perceptions, approaches, and dispositions that should characterize the Christian reading community. Among these practices are the formative use of the Rule of Faith, prayer and worship, canonical readings, attentiveness to Christian tradition, and reading Scripture as an ecclesial community with conscious interests. Together, these practices produce distinctive *theological commitments* (convictions, customs, and concerns), *narrative configurations* (embodied construals of the biblical story in readers' lives), and *hermeneutical virtues* (characteristics and capacities of the reading community).

Adapting Umberto Eco's "model reader," Joel Green represents the concern for readerly formation. He ponders "what sorts of communities are open and able to hear the words of Scripture as God's word addressed to them."[32] The question behind the question, however, is: what *makes* the sorts of readers who are able to hear? This highlights the relationship between two hermeneutical concerns regarding readerly formation. On the one hand, how does Scripture form readers? On the other hand, what formation does a reader need in order to read Scripture well? It is no surprise that these two form a circle. A certain readerly disposition is necessary for Scripture to do its formative work; Scripture's formative work is necessary to cultivate that disposition. Model readers are both generated by the text and approach the text with dispositions of openness. But the question remains: what disposes readers to such shaping?

30. Gorman, *Becoming the Gospel*, 4.
31. Gorman, *Becoming the Gospel*, 36; emphasis original.
32. Green, *Practicing Theological Interpretation*, 9.

Many advocates of theological interpretation understand the biblical narrative in implicitly missional terms because narrative is inherently teleological, and Scripture's plot is that of God's purposes. What, then, disposes readers to the story's formative work? Participation in the story—in God's mission. Yet, missional hermeneutics also considers the relationship between theological interpretation and Christian formation: the purpose of the story is *formation*, this formation is *for mission*, participation in mission *is* readerly formation, and in this way Scripture makes readers *capable* of hearing its message. The ideal reader is a participant in God's mission.

Missional hermeneutics, thus, entails a reorientation of theological interpretation's formative practices in terms of the *missio Dei*. The consequence of this reorientation is that a hermeneutical circulation characterizes all three aspects of readerly formation—between the Scripture that engenders commitments and the commitments that direct interpretation, between the narrativity of Scripture and the narrativity of readers, and between the virtues that Scripture cultivates and the virtues with which the church reads. Participation in God's mission is the commitment that Scripture should engender and with which the church should read, the narrative of God's mission is the narrative of Scripture in which readers' narrativity should participate, and the virtues that Scripture cultivates are for the participation in God's mission through which the church reads virtuously.

The hermeneutical spiral that comes into view holds readerly formation in the tension between text and reader. While the nature of the text (the missional commitments it engenders, the missional narrative it presents, the missional virtues it cultivates) is one half of the issue, the question of readerly formation shifts the accent to the experiential dimensions of interpretation. For missional hermeneutics, well-formed readers are constituted as an interpretive community through participation in the ongoing *missio Dei*.

CONCLUSION

Missional hermeneutics flows from missional theology. The turbulent theological reframing of mission that Willingen generated highlights the critical relationship between God's agency and the church's. Accordingly, biblical interpretation follows from readers' Trinitarian and ecclesiological assumptions. In missional hermeneutics, the dichotomy of text and reader reflects this insight. The Triune God works through Scripture, bearing witness to the story of God's universal saving purposes; the church, formed by Scripture for participation in God's work, reads through the experiences of mission.

Participation in the Triune life is the crux of missional hermeneutics. Between the narration of God's mission (including the exemplary interpretations of participants in the biblical story) and the formation of God's people (including the effects of participation in God's ongoing work) missional hermeneutics concerns itself with the union of the church's agency with God's, in Christ, through the Holy Spirit, to the glory of the Father. Missional interpretation expresses this concern by attending to God's formation of readers for and through participation in the Triune *missio Dei*.

BIBLIOGRAPHY

Barth, Karl. "Die Theologie und die Mission in der Gegenwart." In *Theologische Fragen und Antworten*, 100–126. Zolikon, Switzerland: Evangelischer Verlag, 1957.

Bosch, David J. *Transforming Mission: Paradigm Shifts in Theology of Mission*. American Society of Missiology Series 16. Maryknoll, NY: Orbis, 1991.

Ad Gentes. "Decree on the Mission Activity of the Church." http://www.vatican.va/archive/hist_councils/ii_vatican_council/documents/vat-ii_decree_19651207_ad-gentes_en.html.

Franke, John R. "Intercultural Hermeneutics and the Shape of Missional Theology." In *Reading the Bible Missionally*, edited by Michael W. Goheen, 86–103. Grand Rapids: Eerdmans, 2016.

Geertz, Clifford. "Ethos, World View, and the Analysis of Sacred Symbols." *The Antioch Review* 17 (1957) 421–37.

Goheen, Michael W., and Craig G. Bartholomew. *Living at the Crossroads: An Introduction to Christian Worldview*. Grand Rapids: Baker Academic, 2008.

Gorman, Michael J. *Becoming the Gospel: Paul, Participation, and Mission*. GOCS. Grand Rapids: Eerdmans, 2015.

———. *Inhabiting the Cruciform God: Kenosis, Justification, and Theosis in Paul's Narrative Soteriology*. Grand Rapids: Eerdmans, 2009.

Green, Joel B. *Practicing Theological Interpretation: Engaging Biblical Texts for Faith and Formation*. Theological Explorations for the Church Catholic. Grand Rapids: Baker Academic, 2011.

Guder, Darrell L., ed. *Missional Church: A Vision for the Sending of the Church in North America*. The Gospel and Our Culture Series. Grand Rapids: Eerdmans, 1998.

Hiebert, Paul G. *Transforming Worldviews: An Anthropological Understanding of How People Change*. Grand Rapids: Baker Academic, 2008.

Hoekendijk, J. C. *The Church Inside Out*. Edited by L. A. Hoedemaker and Pieter Tijmes and translated by Isaac C. Rottenberg. Philadelphia: Westminster, 1966.

Hunsberger, George R. "Mapping the Missional Hermeneutics Conversation." In *Reading the Bible Missionally*, edited by Michael W. Goheen, 45–67. The Gospel and Our Culture Series. Grand Rapids: Eerdmans, 2016.

Kraft, Charles H. *Worldview for Christian Witness*. Pasadena, CA: William Carey Library, 2008.

McGavran, Donald, ed. *The Conciliar-Evangelical Debate: The Crucial Documents, 1964–1976*. Pasadena, CA: William Carey Library, 1977.

Newbigin, Lesslie. *The Household of God: Lectures on the Nature of the Church*. Eugene, OR: Wipf & Stock, 2008.

———. *The Open Secret: An Introduction to the Theology of Mission*. Rev. ed. Grand Rapids: Eerdmans, 1995.

———. *Trinitarian Doctrine for Today's Mission*. Eugene, OR: Wipf & Stock, 2006.

Schwarz, Gerold. "The Legacy of Karl Hartenstein," *International Bulletin of Mission Research* 8 (1984) 125–31.

"A Statement on the Missionary Calling of the Church." In *Missions under the Cross: Addresses Delivered at the Enlarged Meeting of the Committee of the International Missionary Council at Willingen, in Germany, 1952; with Statements Issued by the Meeting*, edited by Norman Goodall, 188–92. New York: Friendship, 1953.

Stott, John, and Christopher J. H. Wright. *Christian Mission in the Modern World*. Updated and exp. ed. Downers Grove, IL: InterVarsity, 2015.

Van Gelder, Craig, and Dwight J. Zscheile. *The Missional Church in Perspective: Mapping Trends and Shaping the Conversation*. The Missional Network. Grand Rapids: Baker Academic, 2011.

Vanhoozer, Kevin J. "Introduction: What Is Theological Interpretation of the Bible?" In *Dictionary for Theological Interpretation of the Bible*, edited by Kevin J. Vanhoozer, 19–25. Grand Rapids: Baker Academic, 2005.

Walsh, Brian J., and J. Richard Middleton. *The Transforming Vision: Shaping a Christian World View*. Downers Grove, IL: IVP Academic, 1984.

Wrogemann, Henning. *Intercultural Hermeneutics*, Volume 1, *Intercultural Theology*. Translated by Karl E. Böhmer. Missiological Engagements. Downers Grove, IL: IVP Academic, 2016.

Chapter 16
Open and Relational Hermeneutics
CHAD BAHL AND THOMAS JAY OORD[1]

Open and Relational Theology (ORT) addresses key questions about biblical inspiration, interpretation, inerrancy, authority, and more through a particular theological lens. In this essay, we explore those questions. We cannot account for every opinion of those who rightly fit within the ORT camp. But we identify common themes to shed light on the promise of this approach to biblical issues.[2] We believe ORT provides plausible and livable approaches to Scripture, and Christians would do well to adopt this theological framework.

BASIC IDEAS IN OPEN AND RELATIONAL THEOLOGY

Open and Relational Theology (ORT) represents a wide umbrella of diverse perspectives. Those under that umbrella share at least two ideas, corresponding with the label with which they identify:

Open—God experiences time sequentially, moment by moment. The future is open.

Relational—God and creation relate by giving and receiving. God is relational.[3]

---

1. The authors thank Brian Felushko for his help in writing this essay.

2. Most open and relational thinkers identify as Christian, and ORT thinkers represent various denominations in Christianity. Others identify as Jewish, Muslim, with other religions, or no tradition. Other labels common among ORT thinkers include "open," "relational," "evangelical," "post-evangelical," "process," "feminist," "neo-classical," "postmodern," "theopoetic," etc.

3. For an accessible introduction to open and relational theology, see Oord, *Open*

These two ideas capture what ORT thinkers believe correlates with the general way biblical writers talk about who God is and how God acts.[4] They also fit our experience of reality, because we experience existence as open and relational. But they stand at odds with traditional theologies that characterize God as timeless and impersonal, which makes a difference when considering Scripture.

Augustine, Thomas Aquinas, Anselm, Martin Luther, and John Calvin are among the influential theologians who believed God to be nonrelational and timeless. They thought creatures and creation do not affect or influence God. They also believed God does not respond emotionally to creatures. Anselm, for instance, said God was compassionate only when considered from the human perspective. But God is not compassionate as God actually *is*. Anselm adopts the classic view of impassibility, because compassion would involve God being emotionally influenced by those who suffer.

ORT, in contrast, says God both affects creation and creation affects God. God really suffers when we suffer and rejoices when we rejoice. This view fits the general witness of Scripture, which portrays God as emotionally engaged. ORT takes as straightforward biblical claims about God responding to what creatures do, including becoming angry, sad, happy, or proud of creatures, depending on their actions. Creatures partner with their Creator, which means they influence God and help decide outcomes.

Biblical writers describe God as an experiential agent who experiences time moment by moment. Rather than timeless or "outside time," God is everlastingly timefull or "inside time." Some in the ORT community say God has everlastingly been creating. They embrace the biblically supported view that God creates from chaos. Other ORT thinkers say God related timefully in Trinity prior to creating the universe out of nothing (*creatio ex nihilo*).

Further, ORT rejects the idea God predestined everything from all eternity. And it rejects the notion God exhaustively foreknows the future. After all, the future could only be known with certainty if it was already settled. We find this ORT perspective illustrated when God expresses regret and disappointment over how things turned out,[5] and when the biblical writers portray God as surprised,[6] and uncertain whether Israel will remain faithful.[7] The Bible witnesses to this point of view when it shows God as hav-

---

and Relational Theology.

4. Manuel Schmid criticizes open theists who claim the biblical text *perfectly* aligns with their position. The more sober claim is that Scripture aligns better with open theism than alternative theologies. See Schmid, *God in Motion.*

5. E.g., Gen 6:5–6; 1 Sam 15:10, 35; Ezek 22:29–31.

6. E.g., Isa 5:3–7; Jer 3:6–7; 19–20.

7. E.g., Gen 22:12; Exod 16:4; Deut 8:2; 13:1–3; Judg 2:20–3:5; 2 Chr 32:31.

ing a change of mind, often because of our prayers.[8] And ORT is exemplified by passages that portray God as laying out possibilities of what may or may not happen, depending on what creatures choose.[9]

Those in the ORT tradition resist claims that history is a prerecorded album, simply playing over time. They affirm rather that it's an improvisation, an in-the-moment composition with no specific predetermined outcome. Existence is an open-ended adventure, and God has goals for the flourishing and beauty of creation. God has plans but does not control creatures. The Bible, in general, supports this view.

AN OPEN AND RELATIONAL FRAMEWORK

It is easy to see how the premises of ORT can aid in establishing a helpful hermeneutical framework. Below we suggest four key principles that embody Open and Relational biblical interpretation: *love as primary, Jesus as paragon, God as uncontrolling,* and *inspiration as dynamic.* Later, we put these themes to the test as we explore a passage of Scripture traditionally considered difficult for an Open and Relational perspective.

LOVE AS PRIMARY

Critical to most ORT thinkers are claims about God's love and God's desire that creatures love in return. These claims come from the Bible where love towers as a theme, being directly addressed 686 times. No biblical writer gives a more succinct argument for the centrality of love within the divine than the apostle John when he states: "God is love" (1 John 4:8,16). The Open and Relational thinker sees the accounting of God's love as Scripture's fundamental aim and takes seriously the primacy it receives throughout the biblical narrative.[10] ORT rejects classical theism's proclivity to minimize love in lieu of other attributes, such as sovereignty and control. ORT advocates often start with love when thinking about who God is and what God desires.

ORT supporters often say Scripture's fundamental theme is love. The description of God as loving recurs often: "The Lord, the Lord, a God merciful and gracious, slow to anger, and abounding in steadfast love and faithfulness, keeping steadfast love for thousands, forgiving iniquity and transgression and sin . . . " (Exod 34:6–7). Indeed: "Though the mountains

---

8. E.g., Exod 32:14; Num 14:12–20; Deut 9:13–14, 18–20, 25; 1 Sam 2:27–36; 2 Kgs 20:1–7; 1 Chr 21:15; Jer 26:19; Ezek 20:5–22; Amos 7:1–6; Jonah 1:2; 3:2, 4–10.

9. E.g., Exod 3:18–4:9; 13:17; Jer 38:17–18, 20–21, 23; Ezek 12:1–3.

10. Oord, *Pluriform Love,* 28. Oord defines love as "acting intentionally, in relational response to God and others, to promote overall well-being."

be shaken, and the hills be removed, yet my unfailing love for you will not be shaken nor my covenant of peace be removed" (Isa 54:10). This depiction occurs more often in the Old Testament than any other description of God, although it takes various forms.[11] ORT scholar Richard Rice concludes, "Love is the essence of divine reality, the basic source from which all of God's attributes arise."[12]

While the broad biblical witness points to a God who loves relentlessly, ORT scholars admit some passages do not portray God as loving. They take various approaches to claim Scripture is authoritative, without claiming the Bible is a systematic theology or inerrant. A common interpretive move says the general drift of Scripture and the revelation of God in Jesus points to a God who loves persistently, even though a minority of passages might say otherwise.[13]

JESUS AS PARAGON

The revelation of God in Jesus Christ plays an important role in how ORT Christians interpret the Bible. Many build from claims like Jesus is "the image of the invisible God," and the one in whom "all the fullness" of God dwells (Col 1:15,19). The writer of Hebrews echoes this sentiment when saying Jesus is "the exact representation of [God's] being" (1:3). And Jesus declares, "I and the Father are one" (John 10:30).[14]

According to most ORT thinkers, Jesus's love best reveals God's nature. Jesus healed the sick (John 9:1–7), cared for the poor (Matt 25:41–43), loved those difficult to love (John 4:1–26), and fought against injustice (Matt 7:3–5). He was more concerned with serving than being served (John 13:1–17). And He would much rather suffer with others than wield power over them (Luke 22:47–53). ORT thinkers are reluctant to assign any action to God inconsistent with the love witnessed to in Jesus.

When interpreting biblical passages pertaining to divine providence, classical theists typically start with a view of sovereignty that says God ordains or permits all that occurs. This starting point makes it difficult to account for biblical stories that portray God as violent. After all, in more

---

11. Fretheim, *Suffering of God*, 25. For other occurrences of this phrase, see Exod 20:6; Num 14:18; Deut 5:9–10; 7:9; 1 Kgs 3:6; 2 Chr 30:9; Neh 9:17, 31; Ps 86:15; 103:8, 17; 106:45; 111:4; 112:4; 145:8; Jer 30:11; 32:18–19; Lam 3:32; Dan 9:4; Joel 2:13; Jonah 4:2; Nahum 1:3.

12. Rice, "Biblical Support for a New Perspective," 21.

13. Oord, *Pluriform Love*, chs. 1–2.

14. Jersak, *More Christlike God*; Young, *Unblaming God*. Many ORT thinkers note how Jesus of Nazareth differs from God, such as not being omnipresent, being able to die, and not knowing all things.

than a thousand passages, notes biblical scholar Eric Seibert, "God drowns humanity, sends plagues, hardens hearts, annihilates 'sinners,' instigates wars, and even commands genocide. By the time you reach the end of the Old Testament," says Seibert, "God has killed (or sanctioned the killing of) nearly 2.5 million people."[15]

When ORT thinkers address biblical violence, they begin by believing God is loving. This prompts them to question biblical accounts that portray God as cruel, vengeful, or ruthless. Such a view of God fits better with the revelation found in Jesus and our deepest moral intuitions. The result is a vision that fits the repeated biblical portrayals of God as a loving parent, friend, leader, or partner. An ORT model "takes Scripture very seriously," says Clark Pinnock, "especially the dynamic, personal metaphors."[16]

GOD AS UNCONTROLLING

Another key idea in ORT says creatures have real agency. Complex creatures like humans have genuine but limited freedom. Love seems to require a degree of freedom, and those who love do not take away freedom from others. Because God loves creatures and creation, God does not overpower or control. Instead, God calls, empowers, and offers creatures the possibility to engage in creative partnership.

The relationship between God's power and creaturely power has been an ongoing discussion in Christian history. If "divine omnipotence" means God exerts all power or always controls, ORT rejects it.[17] But ORT thinkers do not say God is powerless. Rather than controlling like a dictator tries to do, God works persuasively and responsively like a loving parent. In an Open and Relational accounting of providence, perfect power is persuasive power. God guides creatures of diverse complexities toward what is good, even in the most desperate situations. ORT thinkers sometimes argue that it takes more power to love than to control by fiat.

Traditional theologies claim God governs creatures by direct or indirect control. One tradition says everything is predetermined as part of a timeless master plan. Other traditions say God allows or permits genuinely evil events, even though God could stop them. In these theologies, God is a controlling Architect working from a predetermined blueprint, or a Fixer singlehandedly producing outcomes. Traditional theologian R. C. Sproul captures this view: "The movement of every molecule, the actions of every planet, the falling of every star, the choices of every volitional creature, all of

15. Seibert, "Reimagining God in the Old Testament," 132.
16. Pinnock, *Most Moved Mover*, 62.
17. Oord, *Death of Omnipotence and Birth of Amipotence*.

these are subject to His sovereign will. No maverick molecules run loose in the universe . . . if such a molecule existed, it could be the critical fly in the eternal ointment."[18] ORT advocates would disagree.

Some ORT thinkers say God could have created a universe in which there was no free will. "God is a superior power who does not cling to his right to dominate and control," says Clark Pinnock, "but who voluntarily gives creatures room to flourish."[19] This approach says free creatures cause evil using the freedom God voluntarily gives them. "If God genuinely gives an agent the ability to freely choose," argues Gregory Boyd, "God must allow the agent to go [her own way] regardless of how much God might want the agent to choose otherwise."[20]

Other ORT thinkers say God *must* give freedom and *cannot* control. They make this claim, in part, because they believe a God who allows evil is morally responsible for failing to stop it. For them, God's self-giving, others-empowering love is essential to who God is.[21] Thomas Jay Oord makes this argument: "God cannot control people, other creatures, or circumstances that cause evil. Because God always loves and God's love is uncontrolling, God cannot control anyone or anything."[22] In other words, God's love is uncontrolling by nature.

Whether voluntarily or essentially, ORT affirms the existence of a freedom-granting, relational God. This view helps when ORT thinkers account for evil and, as we will see, when they think about biblical inspiration and interpretation. And it stands in stark contrast to theologies that say God directly or indirectly controls all creation.

INSPIRATION AS DYNAMIC

Most Christians believe God inspired the Bible. But what inspiration means varies widely among believers. Some speak as if biblical writers acted as passive vessels through which the Holy Spirit imposed revelation with perfect accuracy. Inspiration so understood is often called "dictation" and considered an act of overpowering omnipotence. Those who endorse this view believe God can guarantee the Bible to be without error through its writing, preservation, canonization, and translation.

At the other end of the spectrum are those who consider the Bible a work by humans alone. In this scheme, God creates and sustains creation

18. Sproul, *What Is Reformed Theology*, 175.
19. Sanders, *God Who Risks*.
20. Boyd, *Inspired Imperfection*, 121.
21. Oord, *Uncontrolling Love of God*, 94–95.
22. Oord, *God Can't*, 28.

but does not communicate to biblical writers nor otherwise relate in history. This God is unengaged and aloof.

ORT advocates affirm a symbiotic view of biblical inspiration. God communicates, and humans respond. Because God's action is uncontrolling, however, biblical texts may not faithfully reveal God's intentions or actions. Biblical writers may sometimes misunderstand. Their worldviews also influenced them, which means the texts reflect their beliefs about science, history, and more.

The writers of Scripture may attune themselves well to God's communication, however. When they do, the Bible provides truths about who God is and what God wants. Because God communicates in an uncontrolling way, we and others must discern and interpret.[23]

Some in the ORT community believe God voluntarily communicated through fallible humans. Gregory Boyd affirms this perspective. In what Boyd calls "the Cruciform Model of Inspiration," God uses imperfect humans and an imperfect text. These imperfections are redeemed through Jesus's death. "When viewed through the lens of the cross," argues Boyd, "all the errors, contradictions, inaccuracies, and morally offensive material in Scripture point to the God who is definitively revealed on the cross."[24] God willingly accepts the errors we find in Scripture in the same way God takes on sin in the passion narrative.

Others in the ORT community argue God does not choose whether to reveal perfectly or guarantee a perfect Bible. After all, a God who *could* communicate perfectly and guarantee an inerrant text bears responsibility for errors and miscommunication. "If God is allowing the ancient Hebrews who wrote the Bible to misunderstand him to be a warrior god that commands genocide," Gabriel Gordon wonders, "doesn't that presuppose God has the ability to share a more accurate view of himself so that the ancient Israelites don't slaughter their enemies?"[25] Gordon and others argue that God's revealing is inherently uncontrolling. This means God did not *allow* the Bible's mistakes and inaccuracies as if God could have prevented them.

INERRANCY AND INTERPRETATION—FURTHER NOTES

Especially in the modern era, some Christians consider the Bible to be error free or infallible. They want a fully trustworthy Scripture, free from any mistake. Because the Bible has mistakes and inconsistencies, however, some

23. Gordon, *God Speaks*.
24. Boyd, *Inspired Imperfection*, 153.
25. Gordon, *God Speaks*, 55.

people will appeal to the original writings as inerrant. But no one can verify this claim, and it is useless when reading the Scriptures we actually have.

Christian ORT thinkers consider the Bible a primary source for understanding God and living well. But they don't consider it inerrant in the strict sense. It's not a word-for-word recitation from God put to paper. ORT thinkers do not say God controlled the writers, the canonization process, the translation processes, or interpretations. While traditional approaches to Scripture have attempted to frame all passages as internally consistent and all claims divinely decreed, ORT thinkers are free of such assumptions.

Such an approach to the Bible allows ORT thinkers to criticize biblical stories that, for instance, depict God as sanctioning violence. It helps them account for unfulfilled divine prophecies and contradictory narratives. This method takes seriously cultural ideas from ancient times at odds with contemporary sensibilities. But ORT advocates do not question the reliability of God when the reliability of the biblical text is questioned.[26] "Unless one adopts a problematic view of biblical inspiration that disallows any real participation of the human mind in writing the biblical texts," says Terence Fretheim, "one must be open to the possibility that sinful and finite writers did not always get theology straight. Not all biblical portrayals of God are accurate."[27]

The principle that ORT advocates use to reject the idea that the original autographs or current Bibles are inerrant also helps them resolve discrepancies of interpretation. One need not be in the Christian community for very long to discover that biblical texts are afforded to a wide variety of viable expositions. This diversity increases as the diversity of the readers increases. It leads some people to wonder, "Who has *the right* interpretation?"

ORT proponents see Scripture as a flexible and dynamic text that can be understood in various ways, depending on the context and experience of the analyst. "Many different interpreters in many different, specific contexts represent many different interests are at work on textual (theological) interpretation," says Walter Brueggemann. "Interpretive voices and their very different readings of the texts come from many cultures in all parts of the globe, and from many subcultures, even in Western culture." The Bible, therefore, is not a rigid document; the readings are remarkably supple, open, and varied.[28] ORT advocates delight in this diversity, because they recognize that readers have differing biologies, histories, cultures, ethnicities, and concerns. They are open to new interpretations. And ORT advocates are

---

26. Pinnock, *Scripture Principle*, 100–105; Pinnock, *Most Moved Mover*, 50–51.
27. Fretheim, "Bible in a Postmodern Age," 140.
28. Brueggemann, *Theology of the Old Testament*, 61–62.

committed to using all available tools (including scientific developments, textual criticism, experience, sound reasoning, tradition, and more) to mine for truth and seek appropriate applications of the text.

While ORT advocates care about what the biblical texts may have meant in their original contexts, what the authors may have intended, what genres are at play, and more, they also wonder how the Spirit may call readers to respond to the text today. The lived experience of contemporary people matters when questions of biblical interpretation are asked. After all, the meaning of the text "is open-ended," says Ronald Farmer, "evolving with the creative advance of the world."[29] This means that "the biblical text is more a source for fresh proposals for imagining what is and what might be than it is a repository of static teachings."[30]

THE OPEN AND RELATIONAL FRAMEWORK APPLIED

To illustrate an ORT approach to a difficult biblical story, let's look at a passage from Numbers 15. We'll compare this approach with more traditional views of the same passage. We've chosen a brief passage for our purposes.

> While the Israelites were in the wilderness, a man was found gathering wood on the Sabbath Day. Those who found him gathering wood brought him to Moses and Aaron and the whole assembly, and they kept him in custody because it was not clear what should be done to him. Then the Lord said to Moses, "The man must die. The whole assembly must stone him outside the camp." So the assembly took him outside the camp and stoned him to death, as the Lord commanded Moses. (Num 15:32–35)

CONTEXT OF THE PASSAGE

Sound interpretation is necessarily contextual. Numbers is the fourth book of the Pentateuch, and this collection tells us Israel's origin story as a nation. In Genesis, God promises Israel's patriarch, Abraham, and his descendants the land of Canaan. All that bless Israel will be blessed, and all that curse Israel will be cursed. In Exodus, we find the growing nation of Israel enslaved by the rulers of Egypt. God sends Moses, who speaks to both Israel and Egypt; through Moses (and a few choice plagues), Israel is freed from slavery. In Numbers, the story of the forty years Israel spent in the wilderness between Mt. Sinai and the promised land of Canaan unfolds.

---

29. Farmer, *Process Theology and Biblical Interpretation*, 22.
30. Farmer, *Process Theology and Biblical Interpretation*, 23.

A trip on foot from Mt. Sinai to Canaan should take about two weeks. Instead, we see the story play out over approximately forty years. Why is this? In Numbers 13, we read that after Israel makes it halfway through the wilderness, the Lord commands Moses to send spies into Canaan to scout out their future home. When the group comes back, they are terrified. The inhabitants of the land, they report, are powerful and their cities are large and fortified. While the faithful do not see this as a deterrent, the majority are frightened into paralysis. This both disappoints Moses and angers God, who asks, "How long will these people treat me with contempt?" (14:11) Then God threatens, "I will strike them down with a plague and destroy them" (14:12). Moses intervenes; God relents. But God declares, "Not one of you will enter the land I swore with uplifted hand to make your home" (14:30). And the spies sent into Canaan were "struck down and died of a plague before the Lord" (14:37).

Numbers 15 begins benignly, with instructions given to Israel to prepare for conquering Canaan. Nestled between these commands, however, we find the story of the Sabbath-breaker.

TRADITIONAL INTERPRETATION

The retributive actions ascribed to God in Numbers are troublesome. They do not form a picture of a loving God. They do not comport with the vision of God we find revealed in Jesus, nor our moral intuitions about fairness and flourishing.

Old Testament scholar Gordon J. Wenham offers an interpretation typical of traditional approaches. "This incident demonstrates how highhanded sinners were dealt with when caught in the act," he says.[31] Wenham believes divine justice is at play. He believes the passage is consistent with Exod 31:15, which states, "Whoever does any work on the Sabbath is to be put to death." The only question for Wenham seems to be confirming whether the gathering of sticks was considered "work." In Exod 35:3, the kindling of fire on the Sabbath is prohibited. But there is no explicit instruction on whether preparations warranted a similar punishment. Wenham suggests the man's motivations were enough to justify execution. "By collecting sticks," Wenham says, "the man was demonstrating his clear intention of lighting a fire on the Sabbath."[32]

In the traditional reading, harsh judgments are consistent with God's character and sovereignty. God could have killed everyone in the desert because everyone rebels. God is gracious, believes Wenham, because only

---

31. Wenham, *Numbers*, 131.
32. Wenham, *Numbers*, 132.

some are killed. According to some traditional theologies, God would have predestined these rebellious activities. And God must have good reasons for killing some, because God foreknows all things. A sovereign God works from an eternal blueprint, and stoning people for picking up sticks is justified in that blueprint.

AN OPEN A RELATIONAL ALTERNATIVE

ORT advocates build from a view of divine love and the moral intuitions of most readers. If God's solution for disobedience includes stoning, we cannot make good sense of the forgiving God we find elsewhere in the Bible. If God always loves, we should *not* believe God wants people stoned for picking up sticks. After all, God's love is covenantal (*hesed*), affectionate (*ahavah*), and unconditional (*agape*). Numbers 15 should not be used to justify the killing of those who disobey God.

ORT thinkers resist attributing to God actions inconsistent with Jesus's love. Using what he calls a "Christocentric hermeneutic," Eric Seibert distinguishes between the God of the text and who God actually is. "Old Testament portrayals that do not correspond to the God Jesus reveals," he says, "should be regarded as untrustworthy and distortions." After all, Seibert argues, God's character is most clearly and completely revealed in Jesus. He points to words attributed to Jesus: "Anyone who has seen me has seen the Father. How can you say, 'Show us the Father'? Don't you believe that I am in the Father and that the Father is in me? The words I say to you I do not speak on my own authority. Rather, it is the Father, living in me, who is doing his work" (John 14:9–10).

Seibert argues that God's loving character is immutably consistent. While God may act differently at different times in various situations, God's eternal attribute of love does not change. God will not vacillate between mercifulness and maliciousness, because God is steadfastly loving.[33] Thomas Jay Oord calls this God's essence-experience binate, which says God's essence of love is unchanging, but God's loving experience changes depending on the circumstances.[34]

Seibert believes Numbers 15 is an example of human writers portraying God as they envisioned deity rather than as God truly is. Their experiences and worldview affected their interpretive lenses. To illustrate, Seibert offers a hypothetical scenario: Suppose a woman suddenly feels tenderness in her neck. She thinks nothing of it until she notices a nagging cough and a light case of the sweats. She takes her temperature and finds she has a fever. The

---

33. Seibert, *Disturbing Divine Behavior*, 185–86.
34. Oord, *Pluriform Love*, 120.

woman would likely think a virus, perhaps influenza, had infected her. She might take medication, rest, and put herself in the best position to recover.

Now consider the same scenario having occurred in a world that lacked knowledge of microscopic viruses or modern medicine. In this world, the woman may have been taught her ailment resulted from a practitioner of dark medicine. She might conclude that she had offended god (or the gods). In the same way, Seibert says the writers who knew nothing of the revelation of divine love we find in Jesus might think a controlling God killed a man picking up sticks. This view might prevail in ancient times and even today among those who think God punishes disobedience with death. Such ancient and contemporary people might believe God sanctions warfare and genocide (1 Sam 15:3). In fact, they might believe God is the sole causal agent for all things, good and bad (Isa 45:7).

ORT proponents not only point to a God who loves consistently, but also to a God who does not control the interpretations of events. So if Moses thought he heard God commanding the stoning of the man who picked up sticks, ORT advocates can say Moses failed to interpret well God's communication. Some may say God *voluntarily* gave humans interpretive freedom, which led to this error. Others say God's uncontrolling nature means God *can't* control interpreters and prevent their erroneous interpretations. In either case, ORT thinkers consider decrees involving retribution to be misunderstandings.

The Open and Relational thinker does not make the claim that fallible beliefs negate the validity of the overall story of the Old Testament. ORT advocates point to passages such as 2 Tim 3:16, in which the author states, "All Scripture is God-breathed and useful for teaching, rebuking, correcting and training in righteousness." But God did not *breathe* directly onto parchment paper. Instead, God metaphorically breathed into humans, who sometimes got things right and sometimes missed the mark. And the point of this passage is the usefulness of Scripture for living a good life, not that the Scriptures are inerrant.

God doesn't reveal the truths in Scripture and life in a crystal-clear manner. Our particular perspectives shape how we interpret the biblical texts. When we construct theology in light of tensions in the Bible, we are presented with three possibilities. We can . . .

1. Pick among texts that portray God according to our own likes and dislikes or in terms of a religious tradition.
2. Insist that biblical differences be consolidated or glossed over to present a single picture of God.

3. Seek a unified portrayal of God, but understand that some biblical texts will not fit.[35]

Most ORT advocates opt for the last option. They believe the general biblical witness portrays God as loving, relational, open, and uncontrolling. But they don't claim *every* passage or story portrays God this way.

CONCLUSION

In this introductory essay, we have proposed four key hermeneutic principles that most ORT thinkers accept: *love as primary, Jesus as paragon, God as uncontrolling,* and *inspiration as dynamic.* We tested these precepts and explored a passage often seen as troublesome. An ORT perspective offers a compelling model of God and a way to approach the Bible that makes sense.

The picture of God presented by Open and Relational Theology (ORT) arises from the general drift of Scripture. It's a picture that makes sense of our experience and makes a difference in how we live our lives. A God who is open and relational, who loves and does not control, also helps us answer questions Christians ask. For these reasons, we invite readers to consider adopting an ORT approach to Scripture.

BIBLIOGRAPHY

Boyd, Gregory. *Inspired Imperfection: How the Bible's Problems Enhance its Divine Authority*. Minneapolis: Fortress, 2020.

Brueggemann, Walter. *Theology of the Old Testament: Testimony, Dispute, Advocacy*. Minneapolis: Fortress, 2005.

Farmer, Ronald L. *Process Theology and Biblical Interpretation*. Gonzalez, FL: Energion, 2021.

Fisher, Christopher, *God is Open: Examining the Open Theism of the Biblical Authors*. Createspace, 2017.

Fretheim, Terence. "The Bible in a Postmodern Age." In *Rethinking the Bible: Inerrancy, Preaching, Inspiration, Authority, Formation, Archaeology, Postmodernism and More*, edited by Thomas Jay Oord and Robert P. Thompson, 105–20. Grasmere, ID: SacraSage, 2018.

———. *God and the World in the Old Testament*. Nashville: Abingdon, 2005.

Gordon, Gabriel. *God Speaks: A Participatory Theology of Inspiration*. Glen Oak, CA: Quoir, 2021.

Jersak, Bradley. *A More Christlike God*. New Kensington, PA: Whitaker, 2001.

---

35. Fretheim, "Bible in a Postmodern Age," 152.

Oord, Thomas Jay, *Open and Relational Theology: An Introduction to Life-Changing Ideas*. Grasmere, ID: SacraSage, 2021.

———. *Pluriform Love: An Open and Relational Theology of Well-Being*. Grasmere, ID: SacraSage, 2022.

———. *The Uncontrolling Love of God: An Open and Relational Account of Providence*. Grasmere, ID: SacraSage, 2015.

Pinnock, Clark. *Most Moved Mover*. Grand Rapids: Baker, 2000.

———. *The Scripture Principle: Reclaiming the Full Authority of the Bible*. 2nd ed. Grand Rapids: Baker Academic, 2006.

Rice, Richard. "Biblical Support for a New Perspective." In *The Openness of God: A Biblical Challenge to the Traditional Understanding of God*, 11–58. Downers Grove, IL: Intervarsity, 1994.

Sanders, John. *The God Who Risks: A Theology of Providence*. Downers Grove, IL: Intervarsity Academic, 2007.

Schmid, Manuel. *God in Motion: A Critical Exploration of the Open Theism Debate*. Waco, TX: Baylor University Press, 2021.

Seibert, Eric A. *Disturbing Divine Behavior: Troubling Old Testament Images of God*. Minneapolis: Fortress, 2009.

———. "Reimagining God in the Old Testament." In *Deconstructing Hell: Open and Relational Responses to the Doctrine of Eternal Conscious Torment*, edited by Chad Bahl, 129–40 Grasmere, ID, SacraSage, 2023.

Sproul, R. C. *What is Reformed Theology*. Grand Rapids: Baker, 2005.

Young, Deanna. *Unblaming God*. Grasmere, ID: SacraSage, 2023.

Chapter 17
Cruciform Hermeneutics
Finding the Crucified Christ in Scripture's Genocidal Portrait of God

GREGORY A. BOYD

In this chapter I argue that all Scripture, including its violent or otherwise troubling portraits of God, should be interpreted through the lens of Jesus's sin-bearing and self-sacrificial death on the cross.[1] I call this "the Cruciform Hermeneutic," and my central claim is that this cross-centered way of interpreting the Old Testament's (OT) sub-Christ-like depictions of God enables us to discern how these portraits, as violent and ugly as they may appear on the surface, actually anticipate and bear witness to the love of God that was most perfectly revealed in Jesus's self-sacrificial death.[2]

Before proceeding, however, I would like it to be clear that when I henceforth refer to "Jesus's death," "the cross," "the crucifixion," or "the crucified Christ," I am not referring to Jesus's death *in contrast to* his life and teachings or *in contrast to* his resurrection and ascension. In agreement with Thomas Torrance, I rather believe we must understand Jesus's life, ministry, death, and resurrection "as one dynamic event from incarnation to

---

1. By "sub-Christlike," I mean any literary representation of God that ascribes to God character that falls short of the other-oriented loving character that Jesus taught and modeled. I should also note that this essay should be considered a cursory introduction to the Cruciform Hermeneutic. For a fuller unpacking, see Boyd, *Cross Vision*, and Boyd, *Crucifixion of the Warrior God* (henceforth, *CWG*).

2. Space does not permit a discussion of problematic depictions of God in the NT. On this see Neufeld, *Killing Enmity*, 2011.

ascension."³ Yet, I shall contend that it is Jesus's sacrificial, sin-bearing death that should constitute the interpretive centerpiece of the "one dynamic event" that constitutes Jesus's distinctive revelation of the Father.

Hence, whenever I refer to "the cross," or some equivalent, please remember that I'm referring to Jesus's death as the *summation* and *culmination* of everything Jesus was about. It is the throughline that weave's all the various aspects of the "one dynamic event" that comprises the revelation and work of Jesus Christ. And, as will become clear shortly, I embrace this conclusion because I believe it is grounded in the New Testament (NT).

A CONFLICT OF COMMITMENTS

The Cruciform Hermeneutic arises out of an apparent conflict of commitments. On the one hand, followers of Jesus are called to completely trust the character of God that was fully displayed in Jesus's cross-centered life and ministry. John sums up this revelation when he says, "God is love," and then defines love by pointing us to the cross (1 John 4:8; cf. 1 John 3:16). We are thus called to trust that God is perfect love.

On the other hand, the historic-orthodox church has always taught "the plenary (complete) inspiration of scripture," and I have good reason for believing that this traditional conviction is both true and important. This creates a conundrum, however, for while most depictions of Yahweh in the OT reflect the same loving God who is revealed in Christ, it also cannot be denied that the OT contains certain depictions of God that do not seem very loving. For example, God wipes out most life on earth with a flood (Gen 6–8); incinerates entire cities (Gen 19), slays thousands of grumblers by fire, plague and an apparent earthquake (Num 16); causes parents and children to cannibalize one another (Lev 26:28–29; Jer 19:7, 9; Lam 2:20; Ezek 5:9–10), and causes fetuses to be ripped out of their mother's wombs (Hos 13:16).⁴ If this sort of activity reflects God's perfect love, I am at a loss as to what "perfect love" might mean.

Yet, arguably the least-Christlike portrait of Yahweh in the Bible is found in story of Israel acquiring the land Yahweh had promised them. On the eve of their invasion, the Lord is depicted as giving the Israelites the following instructions:

> When the Lord your God gives [the people of Canaan] over to you and you defeat them, then you must utterly destroy (*herēm*)

---

3. Torrance, *Incarnation*, 37, cf. 183–88.

4. For a comprehensive overview of Scripture's violent depictions of God, see *CWG*, 1:286–333.

them. Make no covenant with them and show them no mercy. (Deut 7:2)

Herēm means "to utterly destroy," but it also carries a religious connotation. To engage in *herēm* is to utterly destroy a population *as act of devotion*.[5] Hence, these passages depict Yahweh commanding his people to annihilate "everything that breathes"(Deut 20:16–17)—men, women, children, infants, and even the animals—in certain regions of Canaan, and to do this as an expression or worship! And to top it off, Yahweh makes a point of insisting that, as his people carry out this horrifically violent worship, they are to "show no mercy"—something we can easily imagine some Israelite soldiers were tempted to do as they heard doomed mothers desperately pleading for the lives of their babies.

While some Christian scholars object to this label, I frankly do not know what to call the *herēm* command except *divinely sanctioned genocide*. If any other group of people believed their god had commanded them to wipe an entire population of people off the face of the earth, for any reason, I doubt anyone would hesitate to label it "genocide." For this reason, it would feel disingenuous for me to refrain from applying this label to the *herēm* command simply because it appears in the book I happen to believe is divinely inspired.

Because I consider this the most challenging portrait of God, I will largely focus my attention on it, using it as a stand-in for all of Scripture's sub-Christlike depictions of God. And the problem that this and other sub-Christlike depictions of God pose for us is this: How can we fully trust Jesus's cross-centered revelation that God is perfect, other-oriented love while at the same time trusting that the whole Bible, including its genocidal depiction of God, is divinely inspired?

DEFENDING THE GENOCIDAL PORTRAIT OF GOD

For all who hold to the plenary inspiration of Scripture, there really only two possible ways of responding to this conundrum. First, we could trust that the genocidal depiction of God is accurate and then try to demonstrate how this portrait of God can be made to look more consistent with the God of perfect love revealed in the crucified Christ. Defenders of this perspective thus argue, for example, that God had good, just and even loving reasons for uttering this macabre command. Many also try to reduce the amount

---

5. On *herēm*, see *CWG*, 1:302–5. This command is repeated and/or carried out *thirty-seven times* in the OT.

of violence presumed in the text by arguing that the *herēm* command was perhaps intended hyperbolically.[6]

I deeply respect the commitment to Scripture that motivates these people to defend this and every other portrait of Yahweh in the OT. But while I once was persuaded by many of the arguments these scholars use, I confess that I no find them compelling.[7] Moreover, I at some point came to consider it a self-evident truth that genocide can never be justified. But most importantly, I at some point came to the realization that Jesus not only endorsed the OT as the inspired story of God, he taught that all Scripture was divinely inspired for the ultimate purpose of bearing witness to him, and more particularly, to his suffering, death, and resurrection.

For example, despite the fact that Jesus had taught his disciples three separate times that he was going to Jerusalem to suffer and die, when this actually happened, his disciples were despondent (Matt 16:21–22; 17:21–22; 20:17–19). After his resurrection, Jesus appeared to two of these distraught disciples and said:

> Oh, how foolish you are and how slow of heart to believe all that the prophets have declared! Was it not necessary that the Messiah should suffer these things and then enter into his glory?

To this Luke adds: "Then beginning with Moses and all the prophets, he interpreted to them the things about himself in all the scriptures" (Luke 24: 25–27; cf. 44–46).

From this and other relevant Scriptures, it became apparent to me that the exegetical challenge we face is not merely to disclose how disturbing depictions of God can be made to look less monstrous, and perhaps a bit more consistent with the revelation of God in the crucified Christ. The task is rather to disclose how Scripture's genocidal portrait bears witness to Jesus's sacrificial death and resurrection. And *that* is a much more formidable challenging than trying to put the best possible spin on the genocidal portrait of God. Which brings me to our second option . . .

LOOKING FOR A DEEPER MEANING

Scripture's genocidal portrait of Yahweh was deeply disturbing to a number of early Christian leaders such as Origen, Gregory of Nyssa and John Cassian. These thinkers held fast to their commitment to the inspiration of all Scripture, but they also considered it obvious that the depiction of Yahweh

---

6. E.g., Copan, *Is God a Moral Monster?*, 163–65, 175–76.
7. For my critique, see *CWG*, 1:379–414.

giving the *herēm* command couldn't be taken at face value. It contradicts our moral sensibilities, and, more importantly, it contradicts Jesus's cross-centered revelation of God as perfect love.[8] But for these authors, if this depiction of God wasn't inspired to be accurate, then it must have been inspired *to be inaccurate*. And in their view, the Spirit-intended purpose for this inspired inaccuracy, and for all sub-Christlike depictions of God, was to encourage devoted readers to grow by compelling them to dig for a deeper meaning to these divine portraits, a meaning "more worthy of God," as Origen frequently put it.[9] If we continue to patiently and humbly dig, Origen contends, we will invariable find "a treasure" buried beneath the surface of the text, a "treasure" that will disclose the Christ-centered meaning that these inaccurate depictions of God were inspired to have.[10]

Now, the particular way Origen and other early church leaders unearthed the "treasure" beneath the surface of Scripture's sub-Christlike divine portraits was by using allegory. Origen, for example, interpreted the various populations of people whom Yahweh commanded to be slaughtered to be allegorical references to various kinds of sin that God wants his people to slay.[11] While this method of interpreting ancient texts was widely respected in Origen's day, it is so no longer, and for a number of very cogent reasons. Allegory will thus play no role within the Cruciform Hermeneutic.

At the same time, I believe that the claim of these early church theologians that the God-intended meaning of Scripture's genocidal portrait of Yahweh is found not on it's obvious surface-meaning but in its depth is insightful and profoundly important. I consider it a tragedy that the project of looking for a deeper, Christ-centered meaning in Scripture's disturbing divine portraits was brought to an abrupt halt in the fourth and fifth centuries. Once the church became a politically powerful institution, Scripture's disturbing portraits of God ceased being *problematic* and actually became *advantageous*. For whenever church leaders needed to rally the Christian troops to rise up in arms against a foe, they could appeal to the precedent set by God's violent actions and commands in the OT—which, sadly, has been the primary role Scripture's violent depictions of God have played throughout history. The church thus stopped wanting to find a deeper meaning within these violent divine portraits.

---

8. For a fuller discussion of the early church's search for a deeper meaning with a focus on Origen, see *CWG*, 1:417–61.

9. Origen, *First Principles*, 4.2.9. On inspired imperfections in the Bible, see Boyd, *Inspired Imperfection*.

10. Origen, *First Principles*, 4.2.1; 4.2, 8–9 ; Origen, *Homilies on Joshua*, 8.1, 7; 10:2; 12:3.

11. See e.g., Origen, *Homilies on Joshua*, 12.1, cf. 13.3, 15.1, 15.6, 17.1.

Especially in light of our heightened sensitivity to religious violence today, I am convinced that the time is long-passed due to recover the early church's search for hidden treasures beneath the surface of Scripture's sub-Christlike divine portraits. But whereas early church thinkers interpreted these portraits through the lens of the allegory, I will now contend that the NT itself suggests that we should interpret this and similar sub-Christlike depictions of God in Scripture through the lens of the cross.

THE CENTRALITY OF THE CROSS

What follows are the eight most important considerations that have led me to adopt a cross-centered approach to Scripture.[12]

1. *The Necessity of Messiah's Suffering.* We've already seen that Jesus explicitly taught his disciples to interpret Scripture in a way that discloses the necessity of the Messiah's suffering, death and exaltation. I'll now add that Paul reflects a similar conviction when he passes on an ancient confession to the Corinthians that includes the claim that Jesus "was buried and . . . raised on the third day in accordance with the scripture" (1 Cor 15:4). As N. T. Wright has forcefully argued, when Paul says, "in accordance with scripture," he is not merely claiming that there are several passages in the OT that predict Jesus's death and resurrection. Rather, as Jesus himself had done, Paul was claiming that the entire biblical narrative bears witness to the necessity of Jesus's death.[13]

    If the ultimate God-inspired purpose of all Scripture is to bear witness to Jesus's crucifixion and resurrection, doesn't it make sense to interpret all Scripture in light of Jesus's death and resurrection?

2. *The Cross-Centered Gospel.* The cross lies at the center of the gospel the early church preached. We find the cross at the heart of virtually every sermon or speech in the book of Acts.[14] Along the same lines, NT scholars have identified a number of "mini-Gospels" in Paul's writings, places where he succinctly sums up his gospel message. And in every single one, Jesus's sacrificial death, confirmed by the resurrection, is the centerpiece.[15]

---

12. For a fuller account of the centrality of the cross in the *NT*, see *CWG*, 1:173–228.
13. Wright, *Day Revolution Began*, 229–30, 280. See also 1 Pet 1:11; Luke 24: 44–46.
14. E.g., Acts 2:23, 3:13–15, 18, 26; 4:10–11; 27, 30; 5:30.
15. E.g., Gal 1:4; 2:19–20; 3:13–14, 26–28; 4:3–6 . See Gorman, *Cruciformity*, 2001, 75–94; Wright, *Day the Revolution Began*, 229–33.

Indeed, so central is the cross to Paul's understanding of the gospel that he uses "the gospel" and "the message of the cross" interchangeably (1 Cor 1:17–18). Similarly, Paul refers to those who oppose the gospel simply as "enemies of the cross," and when Christians are persecuted, Paul claims "they are being . . . persecuted for the cross of Christ" (Phil 3:18; Gal 6:12). This identification of the "gospel" with "the message of the cross" explains how Paul could say to the Corinthians that he "resolved to know nothing while I was among you, except Jesus Christ, and him crucified" (1 Cor 2:2). Paul could only make such a comment if he assumed that everything he has to teach the Corinthians is contained in "Jesus Christ, and him crucified."

3. *Extended Passion Narratives.* While the disciples remained oblivious to what was going on, the flow of each of the Gospels moves inexorably in the direction of Jesus's crucifixion from the start. The great nineteenth-century NT scholar, Martin Kähler, was hardly overstating the matter when he famously declared, "One could call the Gospels passion narratives with extended introductions."[16] Since Jesus's passion is the focal point of each Gospel, I submit that it makes sense to interpret Jesus's life and teaching, and ultimately the whole of Scripture, from this vantage point.

4. *The Hour Jesus Glorifies the Father.* Not only is John's Gospel oriented toward the cross from the very start, but throughout this Gospel Jesus holds up his impending crucifixion as "the hour" in which he would "glorify" the Father's "name," and here it is important to remember that one's "name" in ancient Semitic thought refers to their character (John 12:28).[17] Of course, Jesus was always glorifying his Father, and when Jesus told Philip, "Whoever has seen me has seen the Father," he was speaking a truth that characterized Jesus's entire life (John 14:9). Yet, Jesus highlights his sacrificial death as the "hour" when the Father's true character would be most unambiguously put on display.

5. *The Cruciform Power of God.* One of the most spectacular ways Paul reflects the centrality of the cross for his understanding of the gospel is that he allows the cross to completely transform his understanding of God's power. While the "message of the cross" sounds "weak" to the natural mind, "to those of us who are being saved," Paul says, " [the cross] is . . . the power of God" (1 Cor 1:18, 24, 30). Contrary to the coercion-kind of power that people have uniformly ascribed to gods

---

16. Kähler, *So-Called Historical Jesus*, 80.
17. Cf. John 7:30; 8:20; 12: 31-33; 13:31-32; 17:1.

throughout history, Paul dares to claim that the true nature of God's power is only fully revealed in Jesus's weak-appearing, self-sacrificial death. God's power, in short, is the power of his perfect, other-oriented, self-sacrificial love.

If we accept Paul's radical reconceptualization of God's power—something I submit most theologians throughout church history have found challenging—it only makes sense to interpret all Scripture, including its troubling sub-Christ-like depictions of God, with the awareness that God's power is the power of his influential, self-sacrificial, weak-looking love. And when we read Scripture in this light, my claim is that it radically changes what we find to be revelatory about all sub-Christlike depictions of God in Scripture.

6. *Cruciform Discipleship.* The centrality of the cross in Paul's thinking is evident in the fact that the cross completely shapes his understanding of discipleship, as Michael Gorman has demonstrated extensively.[18] For Paul, the call to follow Jesus is a call to *actually follow Jesus*, which means, to cultivate a cruciform mindset and lifestyle (e.g., Phil 2:3–9). It is, most fundamentally, a commitment to "[b]e imitators of God" by "living in love, as Christ loved us and gave himself for us" (Eph 5:1–2). Everything followers of Jesus do is to be done in a way that reflects the other-oriented love of the cross, and Paul took care to ensure that his own ministry reflected the humility and weakness of the cross.[19] Moreover, in following this call, Paul and other NT authors taught believers to expect to share in Jesus's suffering.[20]

This cruciform model of discipleship permeates Jesus's ministry as well. This is perhaps nowhere more powerfully expressed than when Jesus instructs his disciples to no longer demand "an eye for an eye" when wronged, as the OT had three times commanded, but to instead choose to "not resist an evildoer."[21] The term "resist" (*antistemi*) forbids responding i*n kind* to an aggressor, as when one violently retaliates against someone. While we may, and we must, do everything within our power to disrupt "an evildoer," we are not permitted to respond to them with the kind of aggression they've exhibited toward us. To the contrary, Jesus says:

---

18. Gorman, *Cruciformity*; and Gorman, *Apostle of the Crucified Lord.*

19. E.g., 1 Cor 1:17; 2:3; 2 Cor 11:7, 30; 12: 5, 6–9; Phil 3:6–9; 1 Cor 16:14.

20. E.g., Acts 5:41; 9:16; Rom 8:17, 36; 2 Cor 1:5; 11:23; Phil 1:29; 3:10; Jas 5:10; 1 Pet 4:13–16; Gal 2:19–20.

21. Matt 5:39, cf. Exod 21:24; Lev 24:19–20; Deut 19:21.

... love your enemies, and pray for those who mistreat you, that you may be children of your Father in heaven. For he causes his sun to shine on the righteous and the wicked and his rain to fall on the righteous and the wicked. (Matt 5:44–45; cf. Luke 6:27–36.)

Jesus is instructing his disciples to adopt the same posture toward enemies that he would later demonstrate when he was arrested, beaten, and crucified. Jesus could have called legions of angels to fight on his behalf, and his disciples, with their triumphalist conception of the messiah, were more than willing to do so. Yet, Jesus instead chose to demonstrate God's love toward his enemies by offering up his life on their behalf. This is the response to "enemies" that Jesus as well as Paul call us to imitate (Rom 12:14–21; cf. 1 Pet 2:21; cf. 1 Cor 11:1).

It is important to notice what Jesus bases his enemy-love command on. It has nothing to do with the character of the "enemy" before us, but everything to do with the character of our heavenly Father. We are to love, bless, pray for, and do good to our enemies *because this is the way our heavenly Father loves*. God loves the way the sun shines and the way the rain falls: *indiscriminately* and *unconditionally*. And since this is how our Father loves, Jesus teaches that this is how we are to love all others if we wish to be considered "children of [our] Father in heaven."

All of this anticipates the revelation of God's character and will for us on the cross. And this further confirms the appropriateness of placing Jesus's sacrificial, sin-bearing death at the center of our approach to Scripture.

7. *The Cross and Salvation.* The dimension of the NT that centralizes the cross concerns the NT's conception of salvation. In the magnificent hymn that is found in Paul's letter to the Colossians, Christ is first exalted as the Creator of all, the sustainer of all, and the redeemer of all (Col 1:15–18). Paul then declares that, "in [Christ] all the fullness of God was pleased to dwell, and through him God was pleased to reconcile to himself all things, whether on earth or in heaven, by making peace through the blood of his cross" (Col 1:19–20). Paul's reference to "the blood of the cross" is a simply another way of referring to Jesus's sacrificial death. Paul is thus declaring that the self-sacrificial love of God disclosed on the cross is now working in every human heart and throughout the cosmos to reconcile all things to himself and to one another.

God's ultimate goal of bring universal reconciliation "by the blood of the cross" encompasses everything else that the NT has to say about salvation. For example, the cross frees humans and the whole creation from the rebel powers that oppressed us for ages (1 Cor 2:6–8; Col 2:14–15; cf. John 12:31). Moreover, it is by means of the cross that we receive forgiveness of sin and find healing for our souls, our bodies and our communities (e.g., 1 Pet 2:24; Eph 2:11–16). And it is by means of the cross that we are given a new standing "in Christ," by which we inherit "every spiritual blessing in the heavenly realms" (Eph 1:7, cf. 1:3–14).

If the cross lies at the heart of everything the NT has to say about salvation, and if all Scripture is intended to bear witness to Jesus and the salvation he brings, I submit that it only makes sense to interpret all Scripture through the lens of the cross.

8. *The Cross in the Christian Tradition.* The final consideration that compels me to regard the cross as the centerpiece of everything Jesus was about, and thus the centerpiece of all Scripture, concerns the authority of church tradition. The strong emphasis I place on the revelation of God in the crucified Christ should not be considered novel. For while it has been applied in widely different ways and with varying degrees of consistency, according to Henri de Lubac, the cross has always been at the center of the church's hermeneutic, theology and practice.[22] The very fact that the two ordinances that all branches of Christianity have always agreed upon—communion and baptism—both have Jesus's death and resurrection as their focal point confirms de Lubac's point.

Yet, as is generally recognized, no one in church history centralized the significance of the cross more passionately than "the theologian of the cross," Martin Luther."[23] According to Luther, the cross is "the key hermeneutical principle in understanding Scripture."[24] Indeed, Luther went so far as claim to "see nothing in Scripture except Christ crucified."[25]

Unfortunately, while Luther claimed he could see "nothing . . . except Christ crucified," he never explained how he sees "nothing except Christ crucified" in the depiction of Yahweh commanding Israelites to "show no mercy" as they slaughter "everything that breathes"

---

22. Lubac, *Scripture in the Tradition*, 1969. See CWG, 1:251–59.
23. McGrath, *Luther's Theology of the Cross.*
24. Tomlin, *Power of the Cross*, 173.
25. Weimarer Ausgabe 4:153, quoted in Wood, *Captive to the Word*, 171.

in certain regions of Canaan. The Cruciform Hermeneutic aims to correct this serious omission.

THE CRUCIFORM HERMENEUTIC

Having established the foundation of the Cruciform Hermeneutic, it is now time to flesh out precisely how this hermeneutic works.

THE UGLY CROSS REVEALS A BEAUTIFUL GOD

I first began to see how the inaccurate genocidal depiction of God in Scripture bears witness to the cross when I asked the question: *How does cross reveal the beautiful nature of God?*

When an unbeliever considers Jesus's crucifixion from "the natural point of view," as Paul once did, the crucified Christ appears as nothing more than one of a vast multitude of criminals and troublemakers that Rome crucified in Jesus's day (2 Cor 5:16). And, not surprisingly, it is horrifically ugly, for crucifixion was intended by the Romans to be an instrument of terror.

Our perception of the cross changes radically, however, when we embrace "the message of the cross," which is the belief that God was in the crucified Christ, bearing the sin of the world to reconcile the world to himself (2 Cor 5:18–19). In other words, the cross becomes the full revelation of God when we by faith look *through* the ugly surface-appearance of this first-century crucified troublemaker to behold God stooping an unsurpassable distance to become this first-century crucified troublemaker and to bear our sin. And note this: it is the unsurpassable *distance* that God was willing to cross, and the unsurpassable *sacrifice* that God was willing to make, that reveals the unsurpassable *love* of God to us. But only those who believe "the message of the cross" are able to see this revelatory event going on beneath this surface of this horrifically ugly crucified troublemaker.

At the same time, when we by faith look through the ugly surface-appearance to see God stooping out of love to bear our sin, the ugliness of the cross takes on a whole new meaning. For now we understand that this ugliness reflects not just the vicious cruelty and injustice of the Roman empire: it reflects the ugly sin that Christ was bearing.

This is why the cross is simultaneously horrifically ugly and supremely beautiful for believers. The horrific ugliness of the cross reflects the ugliness of the sin Christ bore. Yet, when we believe "the message of the cross" and accept that the Lord of creation stooped an unsurpassable distance to become our sin (2 Cor 5:21), the cross becomes supremely beautiful. For again, the unsurpassable extremity to which God was willing to go on our behalf reflects the unsurpassable love that God eternally has for us and the unsurpassable love that God eternally is. And that, we can all agree, is supremely beautiful.

THE CROSS AND DIVINE ACCOMMODATIONS

If the cross reveals what God is *truly* like, it reveals what God has *always* been like. God didn't start being altogether perfect love when he became a human and gave his life for us on the cross. Rather, if we trust "the message of the cross," we must conclude that God has always been the kind of God who has been willing to stoop as far as is necessary to bear the ugly sin of his people and to therefore take on an appearance that reflects the ugliness of the sin that God is bearing.

We actually find God stooping to accommodate peoples sin quite a lot throughout the biblical narrative. For example, God's idea for marriage was for people to have one partner for life (Gen 2; 22–25; Matt 19:4–6). But like all other ANE nations, the Israelites at some point began to practice polygamy, and there came a time when God decided to stoop to accommodate this practice, presumably because it was beneficial to women and children whose husbands and fathers had died in war. And note that, once Yahweh stoops to accommodate this non-ideal practice, he bears the sin of a polygamy-approving deity by taking on an appearance in the biblical narrative of a deity who approves of, and even blesses men with, multiple wives (e.g., 2 Sam 12:8).

Similarly, it is clear in Scripture that Yahweh never wanted the Israelites to have a king, for he wanted Israel to model for the nations of the world what it would look like for a people to trust God to be their King and warrior instead of a man and his army. Yet, as threatening nations loomed on the horizon, there came a time when the fearful Israelites insisted on having a human king to raise up an army and fight for them (1 Sam 8:4–22). Though Yahweh told Samuel that this meant "they have rejected me as king," he nevertheless stooped to accommodate the Israelite's demand (1 Sam 8:7). And we must again note that, as soon as God relinquished his ideal in order to stoop to accommodate the Israelite's demand, he takes on an appearance within the biblical narrative of a rather typical ANE deity whose relationship with his people is mediated through a king[26]

In each of these cases, we can see that God was doing in a pen-ultimate way what he does in a supreme and ultimate way on the cross. God was stooping to bear the sin of his people and to thereby take on an appearance

---

26. On the importance of kingship in the theology that permeated the ANE, see *CWG*, 2:852–62.

that reflects the ugliness of that sin. And in both examples, we must notice that it is not the accommodating surface-appearance of God in the biblical narrative that reveals God's true character and will to us, for this ugly appearance reflects the sin God is bearing. What rather reveals God's true character to us is when we, with eyes of faith, believe "the message of the cross" and can therefore look through the ugly surface-appearance of these portraits to see God mercifully stooping to bear the sin of his covenant people. And this, I submit, is how these accommodating depictions of God bear witness to the definitive revelation of God on the cross.

LITERARY CRUCIFIXES

In my estimation, this is precisely how we should interpret the genocidal portrait of Yahweh along with all other sub-Christlike depictions of God. When we find God commanding his people to "show no mercy" and to slaughter "everything that breathes," we shouldn't consider the surface-meaning of this ugly depiction to be an accurate reflection of God's character or will, for our call is to fully trust the character of God revealed in Christ. Rather, the ugliness of the surface-appearance of the genocidal portrait of God reflects the ugliness of the sinful conception of Yahweh that God was, out of love, stooping to bear.

What reveals God's true character to us in this macabre divine portrait is the simple fact that God was willing to stoop to remain in covenantal solidarity with his people and to bear the sin of his people's fallen and culturally conditioned view of him.

When we interpret disturbing canonical portraits of God through the lens of the cross, we might say they become *literary crucifixes*. The ugliness of these portraits anticipates the ugliness of the cross, while the beautiful fact that God was willing to stoop to accommodate his people's fallen and culturally conditioned views of him anticipates the beauty of the cross. These literary crucifixions thus bear witness to the truth that, what God did in an ultimate way on the cross, God has been doing in pen-ultimate ways throughout history. They each disclose the truth that "Jesus Christ is the same yesterday and today and forever" (Heb 13:8).

CONFIRMATIONS OF THE CRUCIFORM INTERPRETATION

Trusting Yahweh to Fight. Some might at this point be wondering: if Yahweh didn't want the Israelites to slaughter the indigenous people of Canaan, why didn't he just intervene and tell them, "When you enter the land I've promised you, I don't want anyone doing any killing"!?

Fair question. To which I respond, *he did . . . numerous times.* There are dozens of canonical passages in Scripture in which Yahweh tells the Israelites that, if they would simply trust him, he would go ahead of them and drive their enemies off the land and they would never need to rely on swords.[27] This is precisely why Yahweh originally didn't want the Israelites to have a king or an army, and its why he continually reminded his people that he hates war and is always working for peace.[28] In this light, doesn't the very fact that the Israelites relied on swords when they took possession of their promised land already suggest that they were *not* fully trusting Yahweh and were thus *not* operating in accordance with God's expressed will?

What is more, in certain passages Yahweh actually shares various plans as to how he might drive the indigenous people off the land, without resorting to violence and without needing any assistance from the Israelites. For example, at one point while the children of Israel were wandering in the wilderness, the Lord declared that his plan was to "make your enemies turn their backs and run." And then Yahweh adds:

> I will send the hornet ahead of you to drive the Hivites, Canaanites and Hittites out of your way. But I will not drive them out in a single year, because the land would become desolate and the wild animals too numerous for you. Little by little I will drive them out before you, until you have increased enough to take possession of the land.[29]

While pesky insects may be unpleasant, this gradual plan for relocating the indigenous population strikes me as a good bit more Christ-like than the plan to "utterly destroy . . . everything that breathes." What happened to this non-violent plan? I can only conclude that Yahweh's non-violent plans fell on deaf ears, and for the same reason Jesus's teachings to his disciples about the need for him to suffer fell on deaf ears.

Nor is this terribly surprising when you consider the broader ANE context. Throughout the ANE, *what it meant* for a deity to promise his people new territory was that this deity would help his people conquer, slaughter and/or enslave the inhabitants of that territory. No one in the ANE ever dreamed of a deity who could give his people new territory without

---

27. E.g., Josh 24:11–13, 16–19; Judg 6:7–10; Ps 20:6–8; 44:3; 146:3–6; Isa 11:1; 30:1–4; 42: 25; Hos 10: 13–14; Isa 31:1; Ezek 33:26.

28. E.g., Ps 46:9–10; Ps 140:2; Isa 2:5; 11:1–9; Hos 2:18; Mic 4:3.

29. Exod 23: 27–30. For another non-violent plan, see Lev 18:25–27.

his people needing to engage in fighting.[30] And in this light, it isn't hard to imagine Yahweh saying to his people, "I will give you the promised land by driving out your enemies," but what his people heard was, "I will give you the promised land by *helping you* drive out your enemies," for this is how any ANE person would likely have "heard" this promise and command.

GOD'S OPTIONS

Now, one might suppose that God could have simply taken control of his peoples' thinking to coerce them into hearing him correctly and believing only true things about him. But we've already seen that the cross reveals that God's power is the power of his other-oriented love, and this kind of love never forces people to conform to one's will (1 Cor 13:4–7). As Irenaeus put it, "there is no coercion with God, but a good will is present with Him continually."[31]

Alternatively, one might suppose that Yahweh could have responded to Israel's failure to trust him by simply giving up on them and starting over with someone else. There were certain times when Yahweh wanted to do that very thing (Exod 32:7–13). What stopped him, however, was the promise he made to Abraham that all the families of the world would be blessed through his descendants (Gen 12:1–3; 15:1–6).

So, if God will neither coerce his people into hearing him correctly nor abandon his people because they cannot hear him correctly, God's only remaining option is to remain in covenantal solidarity with his people by stooping to accommodate their fallen and culturally-conditioned beliefs about him. Anticipating his full self-revelation on the cross, God stooped to bear the sin of his people and to thereby take on an appearance that reflects the ugliness of that sin.

Yet, we will only discern this beautiful revelation if we exercise faith to look through the ugly surface-appearance of the sin-bearing genocidal divine portrait to find a treasure buried beneath its surface. And the treasure we discover in the depths of this ugly, sin-bearing divine portrait anticipates and reflects the same treasure we find in the depths of the ugly, sin-bearing cross. It is the beauty of a humble, stooping, sin-bearing God of perfect love.

---

30. For references to discussions surrounding the ANE concept of "holy war" and the manner in which this concept is reflected in Israel's campaign against the Israelites, see *CWG*, 1:302–5.

31. Irenaeus, *Against Heresies*, ANF 1:518. Similarly, another early author notes, "Coercion is no attribute of God" (*Epistle to Diognetus*, 7:4, 545). On the importance of morally responsible free will in the early post-apostolic church, see Boyd, *Satan and the Problem*, 39–49.

BIBLIOGRAPHY

Boyd, Gregory. *Cross Vision: How Jesus' Crucifixion Makes Sense of Old Testament Violence,* Minneapolis: Fortress, 2018.

———. *The Crucifixion of the Warrior God: Interpreting the Old Testament's Violent Portraits of God in Light of the Cross.* Minneapolis: Fortress, 2018.

———. *Inspired Imperfection: How the Bible's "Problems" Enhance Its Divine Authority.* Minneapolis: Fortress, 2018.

———. *Satan and the Problem of Evil: Constructing a Trinitarian Warfare Theodicy.* Downers Grove, IL: InterVarsity, 2001.

Copan, Paul. *Is God a Moral Monster? Making Sense of the God of the Old Testament.* Grand Rapids: Baker, 2011.

Epistle to Diognetus, 7:4. In *Apostolic Fathers: Greek Texts and English Translations of Their Writings,* edited and translated by J. B. Lightfoot and J. R. Harmer and edited and revised by Michael Holms. Grand Rapids: Baker, 1992.

Gorman, Michael J. *Apostle of the Crucified Lord: A Theological Introduction to Paul and His Letters.* Grand Rapids: Eerdmans, 2004.

Gorman, Michael J. *Cruciformity: Paul's Narrative Spirituality of the Cross.* Grand Rapids: Eerdmans, 2001.

Irenaeus. *Against Heresies.* Repr. Pickering, OH: Beloved, 2014.

Kähler, Martin. *The So-Called Historical Jesus and the Historic Biblical Christ.* Translated by Carl E. Braatan. Philadelphia: Fortress, 1964.

Lubac, Henri de. *Scripture in the Tradition.* Translated by Luke O'Neill, New York: Herder and Herder, 1969.

McGrath, Alister E. *Luther's Theology of the Cross: Martin Luther's Theological Breakthrough,* New York: Blackwell, 1985.

Neufeld, Thomas R. Yoder. *Killing Enmity: Violence and the New Testament,* Grand Rapid Baker Academic, 2011.

Origen. *First Principles.* Translated by G. W. Butterworth. Gloucester, MA: Peter Smith, 1973.

Tomlin, Graham. *The Power of the Cross: Theology and the Death of Christ in Paul, Luther and Pascal.* Eugene, OR: Wipf & Stock, 2007.

Torrance, Thomas. *Incarnation: The Person and Life of Christ.* Edited by Robert T. Walker. Downers Grove, IL: IVP Academic, 2008.

Wood, A. Skevington. *Captive to the Word: Martin Luther, Doctor of Sacred Scripture.* Milton Keynes: Paternoster, 1969.

Wright, N. T. *The Day the Revolution Began: Reconsidering the Meaning of Jesus's Crucifixion.* New York: Harper One, 2016.

Chapter 18
Nonviolent Hermeneutics
JARED NEUSCH

In 1917, a few days before US President Wilson would declare war on Germany, he addressed Congress in preparation for their vote on participating in what we now know as World War I. In his inspiring speech, besides making use of language from New Testament letters like 1 Peter and Hebrews, he states that America must fight to "bring peace and safety to all nations and make the world itself at last free." Readers may also recognize much of this objective more prominently as Jesus's job description.

Nearly three decades later President Roosevelt broadcast a famous prayer over the radio to 100 million Americans as the events of Normandy unfolded. The religious language and biblical allusions used to sanctify America's war efforts in this transmission were innumerable. On the other side of the Atlantic, Germany deployed the first few verses of Romans 13 to garner support for Hitler and his militaristic exploits. This was an interpretive move Germany had been exercising for over a decade since one of their theologians first invoked it in 1933 on Potsdam Day. Unfortunately, no single country or regime has acquired a monopoly on this reading of Romans 13. Its language of "governing authorities," "every person be subject," and "instituted by God" (coincidentally removed from its context) is a slam dunk for catalyzing religious patriotism and mobilizing Bible-believing citizens.[1]

The wielding of such a hermeneutic is a tale as old as time, and it remains alive and well today. In 2003 the US Secretary of Defense arranged Bible verses on the cover page of his intelligence briefings to President Bush

---

1. All biblical quotations are from the NRSV Updated Edition (2021).

for the invasion of Iraq. These included, for example, Isa 26:2, "Open the gates, so that the righteous nation that maintains faithfulness may enter in"; and Isa 6:8, "Then I heard the voice of the Lord saying, 'Whom shall I send, and who will go for us?' And I said, 'Here am I; send me!'" Even more recently in a crowded pro-war rally in Moscow, Russian President Putin borrows language from Jesus in John 15:13 to galvanize the crowd towards support for his invasion of Ukraine, proclaiming, "There is no greater love than if someone gives his soul for his friends."

Today, when we set out to interpret the Scriptures, we do not do so in a vacuum. There is already, especially in current or post-empire nations, a strong current of a biblical hermeneutic of violence fueled by exceptionalism and triumphalism. Indeed, the Scriptures have been weaponized by those who profess to follow Jesus to endorse their own violence and war.[2] For lack of a better metaphor, a war has been waged on hermeneutics, and we are faced with the task of discovering how the revelation of God in Christ through his Spirit compels us to read the Scriptures quite differently.

KEY TERMS

This chapter aims to be a modest proposal for a biblical hermeneutic of Christian nonviolence. It will come as no surprise that in an effort to achieve maximum clarity, along the way we must define our load-bearing terms. First, because of the nature of this volume, it would seem an extended definition of hermeneutics is unnecessary. Here, I simply mean a method or theory of interpretation. So, in this case, I am proposing a reading of the Scriptures through the interpretive lens of Christian nonviolence.[3]

Our second, and considerably more complicated, term is "violence." In my experience, too much quibbling over what is meant by "violence" can evolve into a red herring. A slew of hypothetical scenarios and questions are proffered resulting in needless diversions. Is violence *any* kind of use of physical force, or only physical force that results in pain or physical harm? What about boxing? Ju-jitsu? Is a surgeon slicing into her patient technically violence? For most, the term conjures up images of street fights, guns, and war. Others look beyond physical force and point to verbal, emotional, ecological, and economic violence; even with faulty exegesis, it may

---

2. There is no shortage of examples here. Cf. Lapina and Morton, *Uses of the Bible in Crusader Sources*; Byrd, *Sacred Scripture, Sacred War*; Prior, *Bible and Colonialism*.

3. In this essay I propose a hermeneutic of *Christian* nonviolence. There is, however, a rich history of nonviolent action not overtly or at least consciously connected to Jesus. See for example some of the history of nonviolent action in Sharp, *Politics of Nonviolent Action*.

be said that violence is being done to the text! But, if in this chapter we include all such applications, the boundaries of the hermeneutic become so strained that, ultimately, they snap, resulting in the general condemnation of all things evil.[4] And while noble explorations for another setting, we need greater precision for the task at hand: to propose a particular hermeneutic of nonviolence that squelches the aforementioned hermeneutic of violence used to justify atrocities like war, genocide, and capital punishment.

In this essay the use of the term, violence, will be in reference first and foremost to lethal violence. This clear distinction, I have found, produces a useful clarity so that the discussion is not hamstrung through ambiguity. Secondarily, I refer to the intentional, non-lethal, physical harm of another human. And again, while matters such as the cruel treatment of wildlife, or verbal violence towards humans are critical matters, these will not be the focus of this chapter.

WHY NOT A POSITIVE HERMENEUTIC?

It must now be considered, why an apophatic hermeneutic (not-X) instead of a positive/cataphatic hermeneutic (Y)? In other words, why establish a nonviolent hermeneutic rather than, for example, a hermeneutic of love, peace, or a Christ-centered hermeneutic? In defense of a hermeneutic of Christian non-violence (not-X), each of the above cataphatic hermeneutics merit addressing.

First, a hermeneutic of love. In Matt 5:43–44, Jesus proclaims, "You have heard that it was said, 'You shall love your neighbor and hate your enemy.' But I say to you: Love your enemies and pray for those who persecute you." It is commonly misconceived that Jesus is challenging an Old Testament command to love your neighbor and hate your enemy. This, however, is not the case. Although the Old Testament is rife with the killing of enemies, there is no accompanying command to hate them. The Lord speaks to Moses in Lev 19:18 and says, "You shall not take vengeance or bear a grudge against any of your people, but *you shall love your neighbor* as yourself: I am the Lord." Over time scribes and Pharisees took interpretive license and settled on a narrow definition of "neighbor." Naturally, the saying evolved into, "love your neighbor, and hate your enemy." This is why Jesus needed to re-clarify with a command that removed some of the interpretive latitude: "love your *enemies*."

---

4. Bufacchi, for example, presents a useful distinction between two different ways of defining violence. The first (the Minimalist Conception) is the intentional use of physical force for pain or harm. The second (Comprehensive Conception) is more broadly in reference to a violation of personhood or rights. "Two Concepts of Violence," 193–204.

Two-thousand years on, the meaning of "enemies," remains relatively clear. Therefore, in "love your enemies," we have located the remaining candidate for interpretive elasticity: Jesus's verb choice, ἀγαπάω. Thankfully, Jesus issues a useful definition for ἀγαπάω and its noun cognate. In a sister command, Jesus says, "This is my commandment, that you ἀγαπάω one another as I have ἀγαπάω-ed you. No one has greater ἀγάπη than this, to lay down one's life for one's friends" (John 15:12–13). Here, Jesus provides imagery well beyond a general respect, warm feelings, or thoughts and prayers. He is explicit that the kind of ἀγαπάω he commands is active and self-sacrificial at its core. In Matthew, although Jesus does not then offer a definition for ἀγαπάω, the command is immediately preceded by instruction on self-sacrificial acts towards the enemy, and then followed by how God ἀγαπάω-s both the good *and* evil by giving the gift of sunshine and rain—the necessary elements for their flourishment. And yet, even with these contextual indicators, the command, "ἀγαπάω your enemies," is commonly (mis)interpreted to mean "hope for their repentance, but if necessary, kill for the greater good." And it is because of our proven commitment to such semantic ambiguity on "love," that we cannot be trusted with the lack of specificity in such a hermeneutic.

Why not, then, a "hermeneutic of peace"? In short, this is because the vast majority of swords are drawn in the name of peace. Peace is the ideological carrot dangled before society to justify war after war after war. It is always just beyond the horizon of one more necessary death or invasion. Energizing this line of thinking is what has been famously coined as "the myth of redemptive violence."[5] So it goes that the right measure of violence aimed at the right people will bring about the solution or redemption desired. While an appealing and arguably pragmatic notion, this is, crucially, in contradiction to both the life and teachings of Jesus. It could have been, and indeed *was*, argued that what Israel needed was the destruction of its oppressors. Surely this would bring peace to Israel. Instead, Jesus's fellow Jews had to witness the torture and murder of their Messiah, their hope (by their oppressors no less) all while he forgave them *and* their subjugators. A simple hermeneutic of peace is, therefore, too easily employed in a reading of both the love and destruction of enemies.

Finally, why not more generally opt for a Christ-centered hermeneutic? Such a hermeneutic has immense value, and in fact, may be found in this volume. However, as with a hermeneutic of love or peace, there is a similar need for clarity. We should not assume that behind a Christ-centered hermeneutic, there is consensus on *what Christ is like*. While, yes, this

---

5. Wink, *Powers that Be*.

hermeneutic is what followers of Jesus can and *should* be employing, sadly, we must then ask: which Christ? There is, for example, on one end of a spectrum, the view represented in this chapter, which reads the texts about Jesus, and finds him to be wholly nonviolent, self-sacrificially loving his enemies. Near the other end of the spectrum is a famous claim from a celebrity pastor that in the book of Revelation, Jesus is depicted as a prize-fighter. He follows this up with asserting he could never worship someone he could beat up. This pastor and I may prefer different Bible translations for our study, but we certainly read the same New Testament canon. The name "Jesus Christ" has been the wind in the sails of violent crusades, all the while energizing the movement of enemy-loving martyrs. Unfortunately, even with four different New Testament authors telling the story of Jesus, we cannot simply propose a Christ-shaped hermeneutic and expect to see the Scriptures interpreted with reasonable consistency. This helps to expose the main thrust of this chapter. I am proposing that rereading in light of Christ *is* reading with a commitment of nonviolent love towards enemies. And while this is not the only hermeneutical commitment that stems from Jesus, it *is* critical, especially for followers of Jesus living in war-dependent nations.[6]

GOD'S DEFINITIVE SELF-REVELATION IN CHRIST

Even *if* we arrive at the conclusion that the life and teachings of Jesus, most climactically the cross and resurrection, present him as nonviolent, what justification do we have for rereading the Scriptures through this particular interpretive lens? To answer this, we must begin with the knowledge that God has definitively revealed God's self in Christ. Hebrews 1:1–3 states:

> 1 Long ago God spoke to our ancestors in many and various ways by the prophets, 2 but in these last days he has spoken to us by a Son, whom he appointed heir of all things, through whom he also created the worlds. 3 He is the reflection of God's glory and the exact imprint of God's very being, and he sustains all things by his powerful word.

We can know with confidence what God is like because, in an act of grace, God has gifted this self-revelation through the incarnation of the Son by the Spirit. The Word of God taking on flesh exists as the supremely reliable representation of God. As the author of Hebrews states, what we see in Jesus Christ of Nazareth is *the exact imprint* of God's very being. Jesus then proclaims that he, himself, is the truth (John 14:6). This is the case in a

---

6. See, for example, Hauerwas's examination of the relationship between America's identity and war, *War and the American Difference*.

broader sense, but more specifically for our purposes here, Jesus is the truth *about God*. Douglas Campbell explains, "to look at Jesus and to see what he is like is to look at God and to see what he is like. God is not reducible to Jesus, but if Jesus is God and God is one . . . then the rest of God will not be fundamentally different from Jesus."[7]

To begin his Gospel, John states, "In the beginning was the Word, and the Word was with God, and the Word was God" (1:1). Continuing reference to the arrival and revelation of God, the Word, he would go on to write, "No one has ever seen God. It is the only Son, himself God, who is close to the Father's heart, who has made him known" (1:8). Despite numerous Old Testament texts documenting humanity's interaction with and *seeing* God in various forms and ways, John declares that prior to the incarnation *no one has seen God*. One can imagine Moses, for example, taking issue with John's seemingly brash assertion. It is not as though, in making this claim, John has temporarily forgotten the stories of Adam and Eve with God in the garden (Genesis 2–3), Moses speaking with God "face to face" (Num 12:8), or Isaiah glimpsing God on the throne (Isa 6:1). He is well-aware of the biblical tradition here. And this, I would argue, is precisely the point. It is no accident that John begins his *bioi* of Jesus Christ, the incarnation of God, with the claim that, thus far, no one has seen God. John is wielding a double-edged sword. Not only is he making a case for the absolute clarity and trustworthiness of the image of God found in the incarnation. He is also drawing attention to the inferiority of all other images of God.

In comparing depictions or revelations of God, John is not making an argument of quantity, but quality. Yes, the Scriptures suggest that others have in fact seen God. But the *qualitative* difference is of such severity that John can deny this. In other words, to claim that Jesus Christ is the definitive revelation of God, is to simultaneously claim that all other depictions of God are non-definitive. This, I argue, is to say that they are less reliable, lower-resolution images. There are varying levels of blurriness in these images, and only in Christ are the contours of God and God's character truly and clearly seen. This means that Christ does not only complete incomplete images of God. The revelation of God in Christ *corrects* misconceptions about God and what God is like. The incarnation functions as a living breathing "you've heard it said about God, but I say to you . . . "

If we had, in fact, always known what God is like, we should wonder why the repeated emphasis from Jesus on showing us the Father. When Jesus makes claims like, "If you know me, you will know my Father also. From now on you do know him and have seen him" (John 14:7), the subtext

---

7. Campbell, *Pauline Dogmatics*, 15.

appears to be that apparently our theology (our God-talk and God-thought) needed altering. And so, this is not to say that the Scriptures have had it "wrong" per se. The Bible is a faithful witness, but sometimes it witnesses to our evolving understanding of God. To speak absolute truth about God, the Scriptures must be reread through the revelation of God in Christ. Again, as John said in 1:8, prior to the magnificent clarity of the incarnation, it is as though we had *never* seen God.

To make the claim that Jesus Christ, the Word of God, is the definitive or supreme revelation of God, we must take seriously the subsequent biblical and theological implications. Put simply, this is not a hollow trope; this must mean something! We must, and this is difficult for some to swallow, read the Scriptures as though, in qualitative comparison to the incarnation (John 1), God has yet to be seen. Traditionally, it is a commitment to the doctrine of the inerrancy and inspiration of Scripture that fetters this claim. But this, I argue, is a fundamental misunderstanding of the nature and function of the Scriptures. I cannot dedicate the space in this chapter to address issues of inerrancy, infallibility, and inspiration.[8] But I can, in short, assert that Jesus is the key for understanding the Scriptures. We cheapen the notion of a Christ-centered hermeneutic when we reduce it to noticing pre-incarnational Christophanies. It is indeed enjoyable to observe shadows of Christ in Daniel descending into certain death in the lions' den, and yet emerging. Or Jonah's journey into the belly of the fish, and ascending three days later offering forgiveness to sinful humanity. And again, although delightful, we must take a Christ-centered hermeneutic further than discovering these Easter eggs, and instead explore where Christ is *correcting* non-incarnational (or we might say anti-Christ) depictions of God. And this interpretive task may only be done, of course, by consulting the incarnation.

Barth states, "Every question concerning the Word which is directed away from Jesus of Nazareth, the human being of Christ, is necessarily and wholly directed away from Himself, the Word, and therefore from God Himself, because the Word, and therefore God Himself, does not exist for us apart from the human being of Christ."[9] In other words, any theologizing and/or biblical interpretation we do, any musing about the nature and ways of God, *must* occur at the foot of the incarnate Word. Similarly, and in terms of this essay, any interpretation of texts about God *must* be done here as well.

---

8. For a helpful investigation into the notion of the inspiration of Scripture that allows for both a human and divine element, see Enns, *Inspiration and Incarnation*.

9. Barth, *Church Dogmatics*, I/2:166.

To base truth claims about God outside of God's Word, the Son, is to commit the error of Foundationalism.[10] Douglas Campbell explains that to adopt truth criteria about God outside of the self-authenticating self-revelation of God in Christ "denotes here our provision of a different foundation for truth from the one that God has laid for us in Jesus, and hence a structure that we ultimately build for ourselves."[11] The questions to be asked are, upon what foundation do we evaluate truths or falsities about God? And subsequently, through what cipher then do we interpret texts about God? Our resounding answer must be: God's definitive self-revelation of the Son by the Spirit. Karl Barth, speaking of Jesus, the Word, writes:

> For in the Word of God it is decided that the knowledge of God cannot let itself be called in question, or call itself in question, from any other position outside itself. The Word of God will not let it move from its own place into another. And even if it wanted to, there is no other place from which somebody or something can compete with the Word of God which establishes the knowledge of God. . . . It must refuse to let its reality be debated from any position, and must start out by establishing its own reality.[12]

So, to return to our question: what right do we have to read the sacred Scriptures through the interpretive lens of the revelation of God in Christ? Every right. It is not merely a *permissible* or *justified* interpretive ethic; it is the *supreme* and *mandatory* hermeneutic for understanding God.

THE ROAD TO THE EMMAUS HERMENEUTIC

We can now affirm that we know what God is like with confidence because God has provided the exact imprint of his nature in his Word, the Son. We do not know or understand *all* of God, but we do know what God *is like*. His vastness is beyond our comprehension, but his character is not. Therefore, as was raised above, the question remains, is "violent" an attribute of the Son, subsequently revealing the Father as violent? There is an abundance of Old Testament texts that show God as both enacting and endorsing violence. But now that God has provided the most authoritative truth about himself in Jesus, we must cross-check our past thoughts and speech about God with the Word of God. While we certainly have gotten many things right, our

---

10. Campbell has coined and developed this term in his works, for example, *Pauline Dogmatics*.
11. Campell, *Pauline Dogmatics*, 37.
12. Barth, *Church Dogmatics*, II/1:4.

only assurance of theological accuracy stems from God as revealed in Jesus Christ.

To return to the question of violence in the Father, not only is there a staggering lack of a gospel witness to any form of violence in Jesus, but, to the contrary, there is a clear condemnation of violence any time it is proffered to advance his kingdom. Satan, Roman soldiers, and even his disciples invite Jesus to drink from the cup of violence, and Jesus maintained absolutely consistency in his rejection of this approach. Beyond this, we are provided with overt instruction on how to treat those we would most wish violence upon. Do not resist them, but instead, ἀγαπάω them and pray for them. Why? Because this is also the way the Father operates (Matt 5:43–45). Any of the above texts could be used to make a sufficient case for the nonviolence of Jesus. It may be argued, however, that the most poignant and most decisive evidence on the matter is what we learn about God through the cross and resurrection.[13]

Rather than looking at the crucifixion texts across the Gospels, I want to approach this somewhat obliquely through a story in Luke occurring shortly after the resurrection. In Luke 24, two of Jesus's disciples are on a seven-mile walk from Jerusalem to Emmaus. As they exit Jerusalem where their teacher, leader, and their hope was crucified by their oppressors, one can imagine quite a range of emotions in these travellers: despair, fear, loneliness. And with the report of the empty tomb earlier that morning from Mary Magdalene, Joanna, Mary the mother of James, and the other women, there may yet have been seedlings of hope and expectancy. As they discussed the recent happenings, Jesus, somehow unrecognizable, appeared and joined them on their walk. Projecting ignorance, he asks them what events had just taken place in Jerusalem. Still unaware of his identity, they responded:

> The things about Jesus of Nazareth, who was a prophet mighty in deed and word before God and all the people, [20] and how our chief priests and leaders handed him over to be condemned to death and crucified him. [21] But we had hoped that he was the one to redeem Israel. Yes, and besides all this, it is now the third day since these things took place. [22] Moreover, some women of our group astounded us. They were at the tomb early this morning, [23] and when they did not find his body there they came back and told us that they had indeed seen a vision of angels who said that he was alive. (Luke 24:19–23).

---

13. See, for example, Boyd, *Crucifixion of the Warrior God.*

Jesus, still unrecognizable, issues a rebuke: "'Oh, how foolish you are and how slow of heart to believe all that the prophets have declared! Was it not necessary that the Messiah should suffer these things and then enter into his glory?' Then beginning with Moses and all the prophets, he interpreted to them the things about himself in all the scriptures" (Luke 24:25–27).

This progression resulting in Jesus's hermeneutics lesson is of central importance. First, in light of Jesus's quite strong rebuke, we must consider the disciples' version of events. They describe Jesus as a prophet who was mighty in both word and deed. This is true. They explain that the chief priests and leaders turned him over to be crucified. This is true. They then express their hopes that Jesus was going to redeem Israel. This was prophesied. And finally, they allude to their amazement at the women's report of the empty tomb this morning. This is reasonable. Nevertheless, Jesus's response is to pronounce them as foolish and slow to believe what the prophets had declared.

We must then pay special attention to verse 26 where Jesus offers the reason for their chiding. This reveals not only what was wrong with the disciples' version of events, but subsequently the interpretive ethic Jesus would go on to employ. "Was it not necessary that the Messiah should suffer these things and then enter into his glory?" The Scriptures did not just proclaim that the Messiah would be mighty in word and deed. Nor did the text simply predict that he would redeem Israel. The issue Jesus is raising is *how* this Messiah, a prophet mighty in word and deed, would redeem Israel. The method of redemption and glorification was the error in their biblical hermeneutic and, at least in part, the reason why these disciples were not awaiting the resurrection in a crowd outside the tomb on Easter morning.

The Gospels bombard us with the idea, both overtly and subtextually, that those around Jesus hoped he would overcome evil and bring about salvation in a typical worldly fashion. Rome would be brought to their knees via the sword, and at long last, Israel would rule the roost. And yet, one could hardly script a more antithetical series of events as they would occur. As we know, the one who was meant to put his boot on the throat of Rome, was shamefully tortured and crucified, *by their oppressors* no less. This, according to Jesus, is what the prophets had declared (not to mention Jesus's own predictions).

Suffering, itself, has no particular intrinsic value. God finds no delight in pain or suffering for the sake of suffering—quite the contrary. In a violent world, however, suffering is a near inevitability for those committed to loving all people (friends *and* enemies). This is why it was said that the Messiah must suffer and enter into his glory this way. What the disciples had failed to capture is that their Messiah, Jesus, was the kind of Messiah who would overcome evil through suffering *because* of his nonviolent, self-sacrificial enemy-love. Jesus, revealing the Father, shows them that God is one who deals with evil and injustice by dying for the oppressor and the oppressed alike, all while forgiving his own killers. This is how God overcomes evil and brings about redemption and justice: nonviolent enemy-love and forgiveness. This is the way of the Christ and his followers—to take up their cross, a symbol of self-sacrificial love and forgiveness. And it is with this theological correction that Jesus opens up the Scriptures to teach the disciples how to interpret them. In other words, although they had been familiar with the Scriptures, they were failing to read them through the lens of a Messiah who would overcome evil in *this* way.

Before transitioning to what this means for us now, we should note that it is not only his life, his teaching, his suffering, and his death that were nonviolent. The resurrection demonstrates this as well. One might expect that if a King or a leader of a revolution were murdered by the occupying powers and then somehow returns to life, a bloodbath of vengeance would ensue. Instead, when Jesus resurrects, rather than exacting vengeance or inciting violence in his followers, he peacefully commissions his disciples to spread the good news, and welcome all into the family. Further, he opts to remain in his crucified body, so that his peaceful absorption of our violence remains permanently on display.

A QUESTION OF METHOD

And so, now, as readers of Luke 24, we are faced with the task of rereading the Scriptures with the knowledge of the God who suffers, because he loves and forgives his enemies. To fail to read with such a hermeneutic is biblical interpretation doomed from the outset—or in Jesus's words, "foolish." It is, however, one thing to know *what* interpretive ethic we are meant to adopt in our reading, and quite another to know precisely *how* this is employed. The New Testament writers express that the Old Testament is meant to be read in the light of Jesus Christ, but they stop short of providing a detailed "how-to" manual. Because of this, we are exposed to a wide range of contemporary hermeneutical techniques trying to properly account for the interpretive impact of Christ on the text. It is no surprise, then, that the main variation in these approaches is in how they engage with texts of divinely commanded, endorsed, or enacted violence.[14]

14. Lynch, for example, provides a useful overview of eight different interpretive approaches to the "texts of terror" in the Old Testament (adapted from Roger Olson). There is a wide range of scholars who embody a hermeneutic either neatly found on this list, or some combination of a few. Lynch, for example, admits his approach combines

In a chapter of this length there is insufficient space to engage with other approaches with any real rigor. However, I believe it will be useful to briefly compare two relatively recent publications that demonstrate a thoughtful and careful engagement with the text. The first is Gregory A. Boyd in his two-volume work, *The Crucifixion of the Warrior God: Interpreting the Old Testament's Violent Portraits of God in Light of the Cross*. Not unlike my own proposal, he bears the conviction that Jesus was nonviolent in his life, death, and teaching, *and* that this serves as a revelation of the Father. Further, for Boyd, it is not the whole career of Jesus, but specifically *the cross* that serves as *the* key for interpreting the Scriptures. Thus, he argues that "the NT reflects a crucicentric, rather than merely a Christocentric, orientation."[15] And therefore, he employs what he calls a "cruciform hermeneutic" in his rereading of the Old Testament.

For Boyd, when Christ was willing to bear our sin and take on the image of a criminal on the cross, this was not an isolated, unique engagement with humanity. He argues that God, in various ways, has always been willing to take on our ugliness. So, in Old Testament texts where God is depicted as violent (anti-cruciform), this is divine accommodation, demonstrating a merciful willingness to be portrayed in this way. Boyd carefully lays out these premises and works through a number of Old Testament texts to demonstrate how one executes this hermeneutic. Such a brief summary does not do the complexity and thoroughness of Boyd's book justice. However, the primary criticism of Boyd's work is that his hermeneutic is a bit too totalizing in its interaction with the Old Testament. Is this approach to the text too blunt of an interpretive tool? In other words, are the nuances and complexities of these layered Old Testament narratives squashed with one drop of the cruciform mallet?

This is some of what Matthew Lynch argues in his book, *Flood and Fury: Old Testament Violence and the Shalom of God*. In contrast to Boyd's approach, Lynch is committed to the idea that within the Old Testament text itself, we can understand God and his character in relation to these "texts of terror" where God appears to be either carrying out, commanding, or endorsing extreme violence, even apparent genocide. We need not run to the cross to be rescued from these texts; instead, a more careful and informed look at the Old Testament will help alleviate at least some of our concerns on divine violence. There is much to be celebrated in Lynch's book. He has masterfully demonstrated that with reading "along the grain" of the text, Genesis, for example, condemns violence much more strongly than is

---

four different approaches from his register. *Flood and Fury*, 19–25.

15. Boyd, *Crucifixion*, 1:142.

usually grasped. And his attentiveness to dual accounts (minority report vs. majority report) in the violent conquest narratives often demonstrates a very different reading than the true eradication of all forms of life.[16] These (and much more) are indeed valuable insights for approaching the Old Testament, and without them, we risk over-solving issues that are in fact less severe than typically portrayed.

However, despite his major contributions to this interpretive conversation, certain issues remain. For Lynch, to understand these texts of terror (here specifically the flood and the conquest narratives), we must begin with the first page of the Bible. "Genesis 1 focuses our reading of Genesis 1–11, and really of the whole Bible. The Old Testament offers this challenge: 'Read the whole thrust of Scripture *this* way, by looking through the lens of Genesis 1, which sits first in the canon because it anticipates the whole.'"[17] And while I agree with Lynch that Genesis 1 is necessary interpretive context for interpreting, for example, Genesis 7, this *first* must be read through the interpretive frame of God's self-revelation in Christ. In other words, it is indeed hermeneutically responsible to carefully attend to the wider context and grain of the text in Genesis. But *more importantly*, one must not come to conclusions about God, God's character, and God's actions without having God's self-revelation in Christ situated as the closest lens to the eye of the reader.

One other major concern worth noting at this point is the absence of a clear criteria for determining whether an act of violence is holy, benign, or sinful. Lynch appears to acknowledge that violence is destructive. Violence is, in Genesis, what "tears at the goodness of creation, bringing it to a point of collapse and destruction."[18] And yet, employing pottery as one of his metaphors for creation, he explains that God was unable to make an adjustment to redeem the pot. He simply had to start over. "Violence had rotted creation's core. Demolition was the only option if creation was to have a future. God didn't come to this decision out of anger. In fact, the flood story never mentions divine anger. Instead, God's grief takes center stage."[19] In other words, violence had knocked creation off course, and only an act of greater violence could make things right again. But as mentioned, it is unclear how one is able to make the distinction between sacred and profane acts of mass violence. Is it, as Lynch has signalled, whether violence is accompanied by the appropriate emotion (e.g., anger or grief)? Or, as he

16. Lynch, *Flood and Fury*, 117. A phrase borrowed from his colleague, Brad Jersak.
17. Lynch, *Flood and Fury*, 27.
18. Lynch, *Flood and Fury*, 65.
19. Lynch, *Flood and Fury*, 69.

would go on to argue, is this corporate drowning sanctified because it facilitates the "possibility of renewal"?[20] In this model, this is no small matter as it would help develop criteria for how mass acts of violence are assessed today.

Concerns notwithstanding, the christocentric interpreter needs many of Lynch's insights. Often, these Old Testament depictions of God being reinterpreted in light of Christ lack Lynch's textual precision and awareness. That said, I do find his approach to be christologically under-informed. While he *does* uncover Genesis's semi-condemnation of violence, he does not allow Jesus's wholesale rejection of violence and cruciform approach to evil to query whether God attempted to curb the damages of violence through an act of divine violence. And this is where the commitment to letting Christ function as the definitive image of God for our interpretation becomes crucial.

I hold that with the non-violent, enemy-loving Christ as our dominant interpretive ethic, paired with certain useful insights from approaches like Boyd's and Lynch's, we are well equipped to approach the text. And so, again, although the New Testament confirms that we must reread the Scriptures in light of Christ, it stops short of communicating precisely how this is done. While we are fortunate to have small pockets of Christocentric interpretation demonstrated by New Testament authors, these are only glimpses that revisit a mere fraction of the Old Testament. Rather than the limited data being a source of discouragement, I believe the lack of detailed hermeneutical instruction to be an invitation—an interpretive adventure. At times along the journey we will miss the mark, and other times we will discover truth. There really is no other way to operate with a Christ-centered hermeneutic, one that bears witness to a nonviolent enemy-loving God, than in communion with the Spirit of Christ, the truth, who then leads us into all truth.

BIBLIOGRAPHY

Barth, Karl. *Church Dogmatics the Doctrine of God, Volume 2, Part 1: The Knowledge of God; the Reality of God*. London: Bloomsbury, 2004.

———. *Church Dogmatics the Doctrine of the Word of God, Volume 1, Part 2: The Revelation of God; Holy Scripture: the Proclamation of the Church*. London: Bloomsbury, 2004.

Boyd, Greg. *Crucifixion of the Warrior God: Interpreting the Old Testament's Violent Portraits of God in Light of the Cross*. 2 vols. Minneapolis: Fortress, 2017.

---

20. Lynch, *Flood and Fury*, 70.

Bufacchi, Vittorio. "Two Concepts of Violence." *Political Studies Review* 3 (2005) 193–204.

Byrd, James P. *Sacred Scripture, Sacred War: The Bible and the American Revolution.* Oxford: Oxford University Press, 2013.

Campbell, Douglas. *Pauline Dogmatics: The Triumph of God's Love.* London: SPCK, 2020.

Enns, Pete. *Inspiration and Incarnation: Evangelicals and the Problem of the Old Testament.* Grand Rapids: Baker Academic, 2005.

Hauerwas, Stanley. *War and the American Difference: Theological Reflections on Violence and National Identity.* Grand Rapids: Baker Academic, 2011.

Lapina, Elizabeth, and Nicholas Morton, eds. *The Uses of the Bible in Crusader Sources.* Leiden: Brill, 2017.

Lynch, Matthew. *Flood and Fury: Old Testament Violence and the Shalom of God.* Downers Grove, IL: IVP Academic, 2023.

Prior, Michael. *The Bible and Colonialism: A Moral Critique.* Sheffield: Sheffield Academic, 1997.

Sharp, Gene. *The Politics of Nonviolent Action.* Boston: Porter Sargent, 1973.

Wink, Walter. *The Powers that Be: Theology for a New Millennium.* New York: Bantam Doubleday Dell, 2000.

Chapter 19
Pentecostal Hermeneutics
JACQUELINE N. GREY

This chapter explores the nature and task of the interpretation of Scripture in the Pentecostal tradition. Pentecostalism began as a restorationist movement in the late nineteenth and early twentieth centuries. Seeking to retrieve the primitivist impulse of the early church, particularly as described in the book of Acts, early Pentecostals emphasized the empowering experience of the Holy Spirit. These origins have influenced both prioritization of biblical texts and the methods by which the community interprets them. Yet, as Pentecostalism has grown during the last century and spread across countries and cultures, the glue that binds this increasingly disparate movement has become difficult to identify. Scholars now refer to global pentecostal-*isms* rather than a singular community. However, while there is great diversity among its global expressions, what commonly unites Pentecostalism is not doctrine but an experience. That is, there is a family resemblance among Pentecostals worldwide that emphasizes the experience of God's Spirit and subsequent manifestations, including the gifts of the Spirit such as speaking in tongues. This common experience unites Pentecostals more than mere doctrine, though doctrine is important. It is also this common experience of the Holy Spirit in the interpretive process that is at the heart of a Pentecostal hermeneutic.

To explore the development of Pentecostal hermeneutics we will first briefly review the historic debate pertaining to how the Pentecostal community reads and interprets Scripture. This summary will highlight the concern for what Simon Chan calls a "traditioning process" within Pentecostal scholarship.[1] The goal of this process is to maintain the ethos of the early movement while dynamically renewing the methods and emphases of interpretation to meet the needs of the present communities. In general, this process has been aided by the identification of three core elements of a Pentecostal hermeneutic, which are: the Holy Spirit, Scripture, and Community. Subsequently, second, the revelatory role of the Spirit in the reading process will be discussed. Pentecostals express a deep value for the experience of the Holy Spirit while holding to a high view of Scripture. Third, Pentecostal attitudes to Scripture will be examined. The narrative of the Acts of the Apostles provides the framework and interpretative lens for reading Scripture. The community anticipates the experiences of the Spirit described in Scripture to be evidenced in their world today. Therefore, fourth, the role of the community will be examined, recognizing that this community comprises a plethora of grassroots congregations across global contexts. We will conclude with some reflections on the future of Pentecostal hermeneutics.

THE HISTORY OF PENTECOSTAL HERMENEUTICS

The development of the Pentecostal movement and the composition of its community has shaped the way they read the Bible. Early Pentecostalism developed in a context of premillennial fever and burgeoning expectation for an end-time revival in those "latter days" to usher in the return of Jesus Christ. Pentecostalism also tended to take root in communities of the poor and marginalized, though there were some exceptions.[2] This led to an anti-intellectualism of the early communities and their suspicion of higher criticism.[3] Kenneth Archer has highlighted the adoption of the text-proof method, particularly in the USA, that would allow the early communities to look beyond the plain meaning of Scripture to find greater meaning in its words and phrases.[4] The meaning of Scripture was not considered tied to the intention of the author, as per the historical-grammatical method, but found in encounter with the Holy Spirit. There is little evidence of critical reflection by early Pentecostals regarding their comprehension and interpretation of Scripture, instead, as Gordon Fee surmises, the nascent community simply obeyed what could be taken literally and spiritualized the

---

1. Chan, *Pentecostal Theology and the Christian Spiritual Tradition*, 2.

2. Australian Pentecostalism is one example of an exception, with its early adherents primarily from rural and lower-middle class groups. See Chant, "Spirit of Pentecost: The Origins and Development of the Pentecostal Movement in Australia, 187–1939," 66.

3. Grey, *Three's a Crowd*, 20.

4. Archer, "Early Pentecostal Biblical Interpretation," 65.

rest.[5] Instead, it would be their children and grandchildren who would begin the process of reflection on their reading practices.

Like most conservative Christian groups, Pentecostals throughout its history has upheld the authority and reliability of the Bible. This emphasis caused them to align with Evangelicalism in the fundamentalist/modernist debate in the USA during the 1920s and the following decades. Despite rejecting the cessationist claims attached to these conservative groups, second generation Pentecostal scholars (or "Pentecostal Scholastics" as Jacobsen and Oliverio call them)[6] in the 1950s onwards, began to reflect on their theology and made early attempts to systemize their beliefs, usually based on categories borrowed from Evangelicalism. Yet, it was an uneasy alliance. Pentecostals did not fit in either category of conservative nor liberal and were mostly rejected by both. As Cheryl Bridges Johns notes, "Fundamentalists saw Pentecostals as a dangerous sect. Mainline Protestants viewed them primarily through the lens of the social sciences, defining them as people who, uprooted from agrarian soil, sought solace in ecstatic religion."[7] Ironically, it was the increased entry of Pentecostal students into the halls of higher learning and supposedly liberal theological institutions in the 1970s and 1980s that led to a re-thinking of their former alliances and identity, particularly in the emerging quest to define a Pentecostal hermeneutic.

Two key scholars that emerged as proponents of an evangelical approach to Pentecostal hermeneutics were Robert Menzies and Gordon Fee. Driven by a high view of Scripture and nervousness over the slippery boundaries of postmodernity, these scholars promoted a hermeneutic based on the bedrock of the authorial intention of the biblical authors. Their argument was, in essence, that since Pentecostals were evangelicals due to their common affirmation of the authority of Scripture then they should adopt evangelical approaches to reading Scripture.[8] As Oliverio observes, "This affirmation of inerrancy continues a belief in the singularity of the voice of God in Scripture."[9] Therefore, for Menzies, the singular historical context anchors the text to a singular meaning which provides the basis for evaluating other interpretations and keeping our own prejudices "from obliterating the text."[10] In this approach, there cannot be multiple meanings but only multiple applications.

5. Fee, *Gospel and Spirit*, 86.
6. Oliverio, *Theological Hermeneutics in the Classical Pentecostal Tradition*, 116.
7. Johns, *Re-Enchanting the Text*, 20.
8. For an overview of this debate see Oliverio, *Theological Hermeneutics*.
9. Oliverio, *Theological Hermeneutics*, 141.
10. Menzies, "Jumping Off the Postmodern Bandwagon," 117.

In opposition to this view, various Pentecostal scholars, including Timothy Cargal and Mark McLean, argued for approaches that tended to be more aligned with postmodern sensibilities, yet having the goal of maintaining the Pentecostal tradition of reliance on the Holy Spirit. These scholars developed what Oliverio calls a "contextual-Pentecostal" approach, highlighting the role of the reader in the interpretive process.[11] Scholars who developed this approach often utilized the philosophical ideas of Hans-Georg Gadamer and Paul Ricœur, particularly to demonstrate the impossibility of the objectivity of the reader. For example, Dempster argued that a Pentecostal hermeneutic went beyond the explanation of the historical context of the text to "activate the reader's participation" in the narrative world of the text. Yet, as Dempster argued in the 1990s, this subjective impulse must be constrained to ensure the reader does not uncritically impose their experience onto the text.[12] So while allowing the possibility of multiple meanings, the range of meanings was not without boundary.

The concern of such scholars was that an evangelical approach undermined Pentecostal distinctives and experiences as "nice but not necessary."[13] Instead, they argued that the Spirit who authored the Scriptures should be able to inspire or illuminate its meaning, regardless of a reconstructed intention of the author (assuming this can even be known). Yet, at the center of this debate concerning Pentecostal adoption of an evangelical or postmodern approach was the question of identity. What was required was a third approach that upheld the high view of Scripture of early Pentecostalism, while recognizing the dynamic role of the Holy Spirit in the interpretive process. This alternative approach evolved primarily from the work of scholars identified with the "Cleveland School": Rickie D. Moore, J. Christopher Thomas, and Kenneth Archer. The model they developed was based on the influencing factors of the Spirit, Scripture, and community.

Arguably the most influential work in the development of the model of Spirit-Word-Community, was the 1994 article by Thomas that utilized the Council of Jerusalem (Acts 15) as a model for a Pentecostal hermeneutic.[14] In his article, Thomas examined the process of how the early church community interpreted the Scripture of Amos 9:11–12 in light of their experience of the Holy Spirit working amidst the gentiles in order to discern God's guidance for the inclusion of the gentiles. The Council's concluding decision to indeed include the gentiles "seemed good to the Holy Spirit and

11. Oliverio, *Theological Hermeneutics*, 185.
12. Dempster, "Paradigm Shifts," 129–31.
13. McLean, "Toward a Pentecostal Hermeneutic," 37.
14. Thomas, "Women, Pentecostalism, and the Bible."

to us" (Acts 15:28). In his "experiment," Thomas then applied this model to the contemporary issue of women in ministry. This approach by Thomas highlighted the Pentecostal propensity towards primitivism and pragmatism captured by Dayton, "Pentecostals read the account of Pentecost in Acts and insist that the general pattern of the early church's reception of the Spirit . . . must be replicated in the life of the individual believer."[15]

Following this, much of the development of Pentecostal hermeneutics has focused on exploring in more specificity the elements of the model of Spirit-Word-Community. Yet, from this concern to stay consistent with the distinctives and values of the early Pentecostal community there has developed among more recent scholarship an emphasis on retrieval. That is, as part of the traditioning process, Pentecostals scholars have sought to examine the reading approaches of the earlier community to enhance the hermeneutic of the contemporary community. This, in many ways, is part of the legacy of Steven J. Land and his landmark monograph *Pentecostal Spirituality: A Passion for the Kingdom*.[16] Land provided a significant contribution in orienting scholarship on Pentecostal theology to the tradition's embedding of its theology in its lived spirituality—in its many songs, tongues, dances, fervent prayers, practices of faith, habits of Christian life.[17] In particular, Land focused on the first ten years of the Pentecostal movement as this represented for him the heart of Pentecostal spirituality. More recently, scholars have continued Land's project to examine early Pentecostal readings using methods such as *Wirkungsgeschichte*, the history of effects. Utilized by Pentecostal scholars such as Melisssa Archer, this method seeks to understand the influence of a text on the community.[18] In the very least, considering the ways the earlier Pentecostal community interpreted Scripture can inspire new and creative readings for the present community.

With this in mind, we turn to the first key element of a Pentecostal hermeneutic: the experience of the Spirit. However, while the Spirit is prioritized in this sequential discussion, this trialectical framework of Spirit-Word-Community is relational and dynamic. As observed by Amos Yong, as all three elements intersect and mutually inform each other within the matrix.[19] The intersection of the three elements is captured by Melissa Archer's observation:

---

15. Dayton, *Theological Roots of Pentecostalism*, 23.
16. Land, *Pentecostal Spirituality*.
17. Oliverio, *Theological Hermeneutics*, xii.
18. Archer, *I Was in the Spirit on the Lord's Day*, 62.
19. Yong, *Spirit-Word-Community*, 23.

The goal of Pentecostal hermeneutics, however, is not just to understand a certain biblical text cognitively; rather, the goal is both to understand and be transformed by the biblical text. Such an encounter with the Scripture is best done within the Pentecostal community under the direction of the Holy Spirit.[20]

Therefore, we turn to the role of the Holy Spirit as the first element in the framework of Spirit-Word-Community.

SPIRIT

From the outset, it must be acknowledged that the ordering of these central elements of a Pentecostal hermeneutic are not haphazard. The Holy Spirit is *primus inter pares* of these components because the Spirit existed prior to Scripture and the church community. Scripture is invested with authority by the Holy Spirit; without the breath of the Spirit the biblical text is powerless.[21] As Scott Ellington asserts, "Without the Spirit there would have been no Word, incarnate or written; without the Word, no church."[22] Therefore, the pneumatological starting point affirms that it is the Spirit of Christ who has and continues to transform the ordinary words of the Word into an extraordinary encounter with the triune God to build the community of faith.

Yet, the precise role of the Spirit in the process of interpretation is challenging to identify and articulate. Pentecostals affirm the Spirit as not only inspiring the production of Scripture but also its interpretation. Therefore, despite the diversity of global Pentecostalism, the movement shares a common concern to nurture and value the Spirit's role in their reading experience. That is, Pentecostals value both the experience of the Spirit in the act of reading as a pneumatically inspired revelation, as well as the influence of prior experiences of the Spirit in the interpretative process.

Johnny Kumar notes that "For Pentecostals, the Spirit can illuminate passages of Scripture in new ways."[23] The experience of a pneumatically inspired and fresh revelation when reading a biblical text is valued and sought by the Pentecostal community. It is not pursued as a novelty but as part of a vibrant relationship with the Spirit of Christ. The moment of inspiration during the act of reading of Scripture is colloquially known as the "aha" moment; when a new understanding is awakened, particularly if the revelation did not come from formal study of the text. Cheryl Bridges

---

20. Archer, *I Was in the Spirit on the Lord's Day*, 52.
21. Nel, "Attempting to Define a Pentecostal Hermeneutics," 10.
22. Ellington, "Pentecostalism and the Authority of Scripture," 24.
23. Kumar, "Between Conviction and Critique," 233.

Johns prefers to use the Hebrew term *yada* to capture such "knowing" that is received in this revelatory experience.[24] Therefore, in this *yada* moment, the reader claims to have had an insight or a deeper comprehension of the text revealed to them by the Holy Spirit. Sometimes this insight is linked to prophetic revelation due to the convicting nature of the knowledge by which "the secrets of their hearts are laid bare" (1 Cor 14:25 NIV). In this way, the Spirit reads the reader as they read the Scriptures.[25] However, this requires the heart of the reader to be quieted so they can hear the Spirit speak to them through the text.[26] Yet, as Yong notes, it is the role of the Spirit "to expand, illuminate, apply, and communicate the truth which is embodied in Jesus."[27] This requires the reader to be open to the inbreaking of the Spirit as they read, both in their mind and heart. The purpose for this insight is not just for cognitive information about God, but for the transformation of the whole person and their community.[28] The reader is changed by this pneumatically inspired revelatory encounter with the text. For Pentecostals, encounters with the Spirit are considered radically transformative.

Pentecostal readers also undoubtedly bring their pneumatic experiences to the process of interpreting a text.[29] Craig Keener refers to this as the triggering of an association by the reader between a previous experience of God and the text presently being read.[30] That is, meaning is produced when the world of the text and the world of the reader collides and fuses (as per Gadamer).[31] This approach aligns with the model of Chris Thomas based on Acts 15, where the testimony and experience of the Spirit at work among the gentiles influenced the Council's selection and interpretation of Amos 9. For Pentecostals, pneumatic encounters are not limited to Scripture but could arguably occur anywhere—including during worship, hiking in nature, or other unexpected places—since the Spirit is everywhere. However, as Neumann notes, such experiences of the Spirit would not be understood by Pentecostals as simply a generic "religious experience." Rather, Pentecostal experience of the Spirit is quite tied to the revelation of Jesus based on the Christian Scriptures.[32] That is, while the Holy Spirit's voice is not

---

24. Johns, *Re-Enchanting the Text*, 133.
25. See Mather, *Interpreting Spirit*.
26. Philemon, *Pneumatic Hermeneutics*, 80.
27. Yong, *Spirit-Word-Community*, 41.
28. Philemon, *Pneumatic Hermeneutics*, 46.
29. Nel, "Attempting to Define a Pentecostal Hermeneutics," 15–16.
30. Keener, *Spirit Hermeneutics*, 34.
31. Dempster, "Paradigm Shifts," 133.
32. Neumann, *Pentecostal Experience*, 331–32.

reduced to or equated with Scripture,[33] there is a special connectedness to the word which reveals the Word (Jesus). As Cheryl Bridges Johns observes, it is in the activity of engaging with the Scriptures that the pneumatic voice thrives.[34] This observation highlights once again the interconnectedness of the trialectical elements of Spirit-Word-Community in a Pentecostal hermeneutic.

In a descriptive study of grassroots readers within the Australian Pentecostal community, Jacqueline Grey observed the interplay between Scripture and pneumatic experience. That is, "Readers often began with a spiritual experience and sought the Scriptures to find resonances with, and understanding of, their parallel pneumatic encounter."[35] Yet, this initial experience was usually informed by an event or experience described in Scripture—the narrative into which the reader entered and sought to replicate. It reflects a dynamic interaction that is mutually informing: Scripture informs contemporary experience and experience informs the reading of Scripture. Grey asserts, "This cycle is grounded in the Pentecostal impetus to recover, restore, and experience the activity of the Spirit for the present day in continuity with the narrative of Scripture."[36] Similarly, the Pentecostal reader often utilized imagery and events from Scripture to articulate their ineffable encounter with God. In this way, Scripture functions as a model for both experience and the interpretation of experience. Of course, this does not give the reader permission to make the text say what they want. Nor does it legitimize the reader uncritically reading their experience on to the text.[37] However, it acknowledges that the pneumatic experiences of the Pentecostal community undeniably shape their interpretation of the text.[38]

According to Mark Cartledge, such divine encounters are mediated through the particularities and expectations of the Pentecostal community. That is, pneumatic experience is generally shaped and guided by the interpretative grid of community expectations.[39] This includes revelatory experiences when reading Scripture. Peter Neumann refers to these interpretive grids as "mediated immediacy," to both reflect this reality but still allow for the transcendence of God.[40] These communal expectations

---

33. Archer, *Pentecostal Hermeneutic for the Twenty-First Century*, 132.
34. Johns, *Re-Enchanting the Text*, 144.
35. Grey, *Three's a Crowd*, 136.
36. Grey, *Three's a Crowd*, 136.
37. Oliverio, *Theological Hermeneutics*, 191.
38. Ellington, "Hearing and Speaking," 217.
39. Cartledge, *Mediation of the Spirit*, 66.
40. Neumann, *Pentecostal Experience*, 31.

for how and when God is encountered do have a socializing impact on the community as they read Scripture. These expectations are modeled and reinforced through preaching, testimonies of *yada* moments when reading Scripture narrated by community members, and through worship songs. It is the community that nurtures and shapes the pneumatic experience of the individual. As Cartledge explains, "The community share in and shape the experience together; individuals do not experience the Spirit in isolation from the social dynamics of the corporate event."[41]

This work of the Spirit also reinforces its nuanced role in this trialectical framework of Pentecostal hermeneutics. Despite the recognition that it is the Spirit who invests Scripture with authority, it is by reading Scripture that Pentecostals seek to encounter God for themselves and then validate their experience as from God by its resonances with the narrative of Scripture. It is a somewhat circular process, as the Pentecostal community determines that a revelation and experience have pneumatic origins based on its association with the ideas and experiences found in the Bible. Knowledge and experiences that claim to be from the Spirit must be discerned by the Pentecostal community as valid. This validation process then is usually determined by the alignment of the experience with Scripture.

SCRIPTURE

As noted above, it was and is the work of the Spirit that makes the words of the human writers of Scripture holy and fit for divine service.[42] The focus of this section is understanding the attitude of Pentecostals towards Scripture. Kumar writes "Pentecostals note three areas where the Holy Spirit is believed to be active concerning Scripture. First, in the inspired production of the text; second, in the transmission of the text; and third, in the interpretive process."[43] Pentecostals consider the Bible to be the "Living Word" through the enlivening process of the Spirit at work in and through the reading of the text. As Johns writes:

> In the power of Spirit-Word, the materiality of the biblical text abounds with real presence. It is a space that offers potential for re-orienting existence; it is transforming space, alive and radiating by the Holy Spirit. Scriptural space offers a truth that seizes and captures us in its holy power.[44]

---

41. Cartledge, *Mediation of the Spirit*, 68–69.
42. Johns, *Re-Enchanting the Text*, 134.
43. Kumar, "Between Conviction and Critique," 233.
44. Johns, *Re-Enchanting the Text*, 140.

Pentecostals, therefore, focus on the final form of the Scriptures. The concerns of higher criticism and the historical development of the text are not as important to Pentecostals as the life within the text.[45] The Bible is considered God's revelation in written form, and God continues to reveal his purposes through this text to the present community.

While holding to a high view of Scripture, the Pentecostal community approaches the text as an overall narrative which provides the record of God at work in the world. This is particularly evident regarding the prioritization of the narrative of Acts, the text on which Pentecostals base their emphasis of Spirit baptism. As the early church encountered the Holy Spirit at Pentecost, so the Pentecostal community seeks to emulate this transformative experience described in the biblical text. Pentecostals immerse themselves in the text, seeking not just to understand it but to participate in the narrative. Their motivation for reading the Bible is to meet with and encounter God, and thereby interpret it accordingly. Scripture has a formative role for Pentecostals. Autero refers to this as *lectura creyente* or "believing reading" in which the reader it open to receiving a message from God through any text and any time.[46]

Therefore, for Pentecostals, the book of Acts did not end with the Apostles. Instead, believers join the story and continue the acts of the Apostles today. This does not mean that Pentecostals have an open canon—Scripture is still considered the ultimate authority in doctrine and arguably in practice—but they are open to God moving today as described in the canon. The text is not an end in itself but a mechanism to know God. Pentecostals look to the biblical text not only for doctrine, but more importantly as an authoritative model to inform their experience. Seeing their own experiences in the biblical narrative they declare like Peter on the Day of Pentecost: "this is that." Highlighting this attitude towards Scripture, Craig Keener writes:

> In the global Pentecostal approach to Scripture, the supernatural God of the Bible is the God of the present, real world. The line between salvation history in the biblical narrative and continuing salvation today is thin, so that readers approach the text as a model for life and ideally expect God to continue to act as he acted in Scripture.[47]

Therefore, a Pentecostal attitude to Scripture highlights it as a powerful, living, and immediate text by which readers come to know—relationally and experientially—the God it reveals.

45. Archer, *I Was in the Spirit on the Lord's Day*, 53.
46. Autero, *Reading the Bible Across Contexts*, 333.
47. Keener, *Spirit Hermeneutics*, 28.

However, the emphasis on experience means that Pentecostals often interpret Scripture *ahistorically*, divorcing the text from its historical and cultural context in favor of an immediate application to the life of the reader. The grassroots Pentecostal reader has little interest in the author's intention or even the content of the text, reducing the distance between themselves and the historical horizon of the text.[48] It is this weakness in the Pentecostal reading practice that scholars such as Grey seek to address through proposing principles for interpretation that encourages the community to recognize their historical distance from the text while maintaining an experiential dynamic.[49] Such approaches emphasize that the historical and cultural context of the text is important because it values the situation in which God spoke to, and was at work within, earlier communities. If Pentecostals affirm that God speaks to the community in the present, then it is essential they also respect the situation and context in which God spoke to individuals and communities in the past, including the biblical writers. Yet, while encouraging readers to be faithful to the historical and social context of the Bible, Pentecostal scholars also highlight the role of the reader in the interpretive process. The renewed emphasis on the role of the reader in the development of a Pentecostal hermeneutic raises the question of where meaning resides. Clearly, Pentecostals undeniably recognize that the Bible can speak meaningfully across manifold contexts beyond authorial intention or its original setting. This acknowledgment then leads us to consider the authoritative role of the community in this trialectical framework.

COMMUNITY

Some aspects of the element of community in a Pentecostal hermeneutic have already been identified in this chapter, including the socializing role of the community that guides the interpretation of experience, and the role of community discernment. This brief section on the role of the community then will focus primarily on the question of defining the community in light of global Pentecostalism, and why this recognition of context is important for the development of a Pentecostal hermeneutic.

As the scholarly discussion of Pentecostal hermeneutics has evolved, it is arguably the role of community that has become the most debated element in the last two decades. Initially, the discussion on hermeneutics tended to present the idea of community as a generic, universal concept. The community was presented by earlier scholars, such as Thomas and Archer,

---

48. Grey, *Three's a Crowd*, 119.
49. See Grey, *Them, Us, and Me*.

as an ideal community of how readers should approach the hermeneutical task, rather than reflecting how real readers in the Pentecostal community interpret Scripture. Scholars such as Grey and Autero began to challenge this idealism by exploring the processes and outcomes of grassroots readings, that of "ordinary readers" in Australia and Bolivia, respectively. Readers are not ideal but are real people in specific communities. Their contexts influence the outcome of their interpretations.

More recently Pentecostal scholars have begun to explore deeply the contextual nature and identity of the community in the trialectical framework of Spirit-Word-Community. This includes the impact of the reader's location in the interpretive process. The horizon of the Pentecostal communities reading Scripture is not singular but diverse, it is particular rather than universal.[50] Rodolfo Estrada asks: "Does the community's contextual identity necessarily have a place within a pentecostal reading strategy given that pentecostalism is a global movement that is ethnically and culturally diverse?"[51] The role of community in a global Pentecostal hermeneutic must include recognition of its diversity of locations, cultures, contexts, and identities. It must reflect the "many tongues" of the Pentecost event in Acts 2. Our identity as readers is not context-free. The subjectivity of the Pentecostal reader is not solely due to the influence of their pneumatic experiences, but also their contextual location. Therefore, Estrada asserts, "The contextualized identity of the interpreter is the future of a pentecostal hermeneutic."[52]

This recognition of the diverse nature of the reading community can be seen as consistent with the ecclesial structure of most Pentecostal groups and its identity as a grassroots movement. Many denominations within Classical Pentecostalism are organized as a network of local churches united for common purposes, such as ministry training and overseas mission work. Therefore, the contextual identity of such grassroots reading communities cannot be ignored as a significant factor in the interpretive process. This suggests that Pentecostal readers not only make associations between the text and their pneumatic experience, but that they also make self-critical associations between the text and their contextual experience.[53] Such relevance seeking orientation is not unique to Pentecostal readers but is a dynamic that certainly forms part of the disposition of the Pentecostal community. For example, Estrada noted that Chicanos who identify as

---

50. Grey, *Three's a Crowd*, 137.
51. Estrada, "Is a Contextualized Hermeneutic," 343.
52. Estrada, "Is a Contextualized Hermeneutic," 349.
53. While this topic has many resonances also with reader-response approaches to Scripture, it is beyond the scope of the chapter to explore the connections.

resident aliens in the US tend to be drawn to characters and texts in Scripture that exist in the margins.[54] Autero's study of Bolivian reading communities observed how the socio-economic status of the two groups influenced their reading of the biblical texts.[55]

Yet, while recognizing the diversity of cultures and situations in which global Pentecostalism exists, there are arguably some shared commonalities that do unite the disparate communities, including a mutual emphasis on relationality. Even readers who exist in the rampant individualism of Western Pentecostalism cannot encounter God in the text without recognizes the role of their community and their engagement with the community. Reading Scripture is a relational experience since it cannot be isolated from multiple communities, both divine and human.[56] The role of community highlights how the human community provides the interpretative grid by which the reader's pneumatic experiences and situational context is both shaped and understood. The reader develops this grid from their participation in, and shared identity with, the local Pentecostal community in its context.

A consequence of a reader's participation in community is that the local, grassroots congregation can and should provide the boundaries for discernment. The community guides the reader to discern the validity of their pneumatic experience. As Thomas's example of the Council of Jerusalem in Acts 15 exemplifies, when the community of believers needed to determine whether the gentiles should be integrated into their ecclesia, they called for a Council and discerned together. During the Council meeting they heard the testimonies of the work of the Holy Spirit and sought Scripture together. It required humility to listen to one another despite the conflict and disagreements that led up to the meeting. They submitted to one another in the process of corporate discernment. The Pentecostal reader today must also engage in the process of corporate discernment in their contextualized community. Similarly, Pentecostal communities should also be willing to hear the voice, and engage with, the broader Christian community as they seek to live out their readings of Scripture.

CONCLUSION: LOOKING TO THE FUTURE

In conclusion, the three key components of Spirit-Word-Community intertwine and intersect as they inform the outworking of a Pentecostal

---

54. Estrada, "Is a Contextualized Hermeneutic," 353.
55. Autero, *Reading the Bible Across Contexts*.
56. Yong, *Spirit-Word-Community*, 192–93.

hermeneutic. The Holy Spirit is considered essential in every step of the interpretive process. However, it is the dynamic experience of the Spirit—both providing revelatory insight of a text, and as a source for associations for the reader of Scripture—that is particularly noteworthy in a Pentecostal approach to interpreting Scripture. The text itself is considered a narrative that Pentecostals join and continue today. The community in their diverse contexts provides the interpretive grid by which pneumatic experiences are mediated and discerned.

While each of these elements of Spirit-Word-Community continue to be developed and deepened by Pentecostal scholars, there are new lands of exploration being opened. Key areas of future research include ecumenical and philosophical engagement in hermeneutics. Despite some initial forays into these fields,[57] Pentecostal scholars are presently beginning to experience the benefits of philosophical theories and frameworks as new tongues to articulate their distinctives. Similarly, Pentecostal scholars engaging in ecumenical spaces are also discovering synergies with other Christian traditions that provides rich material for Pentecostals to continue their traditioning process to meet the hermeneutical needs of future communities.

BIBLIOGRAPHY

Archer, Kenneth J. "Early Pentecostal Biblical Interpretation." *Journal of Pentecostal Theology* 9 (2001) 32–70.

———. *A Pentecostal Hermeneutic for the Twenty-First Century: Spirit, Scripture and Community.* London: T. & T. Clark, 2004.

Archer, Melissa L. *I Was in the Spirit on the Lord's Day: A Pentecostal Engagement with Worship in the Apocalypse.* Cleveland, TN: CPT, 2015.

Autero, Esa. *Reading the Bible Across Contexts.* Leiden: Brill, 2016.

Cartledge, Mark. *The Mediation of the Spirit: Interventions in Practical Theology.* Grand Rapids: Eerdmans, 2015.

Chan, Simon. *Pentecostal Theology and the Christian Spiritual Tradition.* Sheffield: Sheffield Academic Press, 2000.

Chant, Barry. "The Spirit of Pentecost: The Origins and Development of the Pentecostal Movement in Australia, 187–1939." PhD thesis, Macquarie University, 1999.

Davies, Andrew. "What Does It Mean to Read the Bible as a Pentecostal?" *Journal of Pentecostal Theology* 18 (2009) 216–29.

Dayton, Donald W. *Theological Roots of Pentecostalism.* Grand Rapids: Baker Academic, 2011.

---

57. Oliverio, *Theological Hermeneutics*, 253–310.

Dempster, Murray W. "Paradigm Shifts and Hermeneutics: Confronting Issues Old and New." *Pneuma* 15 (1993) 129–53.

Ellington, Scott A. "Hearing and Speaking: Exploring the Dialogue between Author and Reader in a Pentecostal Hermeneutic." *Journal of Pentecostal Theology* 28 (2019) 215–27.

———. "Pentecostalism and the Authority of Scripture." *Journal of Pentecostal Theology* 4 (1996) 16–38.

Estrada, Rodolfo G., III. "Is a Contextualized Hermeneutic the Future of Pentecostal Readings?: The Implications of a Pentecostal Hermeneutic for a Chicano/Latino Community." *Pneuma* 37 (2015) 341–55.

Fee, Gordon D. *Gospel and Spirit: Issues in New Testament Hermeneutics.* Peabody, MA: Hendrickson, 1991.

Grey, Jacqueline. *Them, Us, and Me: How the Old Testament Speaks to People Today.* Sydney, NSW: APS, 2008.

———. *Three's a Crowd: Pentecostalism, Hermeneutics, and the Old Testament.* Eugene, OR: Pickwick, 2011.

Johns, Cheryl Bridges. *Re-Enchanting the Text: Discovering the Bible as Sacred, Dangerous, and Mysterious.* Grand Rapids: Baker Academic, 2023.

Keener, Craig S. *Spirit Hermeneutics: Reading Scripture in Light of Pentecost.* Grand Rapids: Eerdmans, 2016.

Kumar, Johnny. "Between Conviction and Critique: A Hermeneutical Exploration of the Nexus between Academic and Ecclesial Praxis within the Australian Pentecostal Community." PhD thesis, Australian Catholic University, 2022.

Land, Steven J. *Pentecostal Spirituality: A Passion for the Kingdom.* Cleveland, TN: CPT, 2010.

Menzies, Robert P. "Jumping Off the Postmodern Bandwagon." *Pneuma* 16 (1994) 115–20.

Mather, Hannah R. K. *The Interpreting Spirit: Spirit, Scripture, and Interpretation in the Renewal Tradition.* Eugene, OR: Wipf & Stock, 2020.

McLean, Mark D. "Toward a Pentecostal Hermeneutic." *Pneuma* 6 (1984) 35–56.

Nel, Marius. "Attempting to Define a Pentecostal Hermeneutics." *Scriptura* 114 (2015) 1–21.

Neumann, Peter D. *Pentecostal Experience: An Ecumenical Encounter.* Eugene, OR: Pickwick, 2012.

Oliverio L. William, Jr. *Theological Hermeneutics in the Classical Pentecostal Tradition: A Typological Account.* Leiden: Brill, 2015.

Philemon, Leulseged. *Pneumatic Hermeneutics: The Role of the Holy Spirit in the Theological Interpretation of Scripture.* Cleveland, TN: CPT Press, 2019.

Purdy, Harlyn Graydon. *A Distinct Twenty-First-Century Pentecostal Hermeneutic.* Eugene, OR: Wipf & Stock, 2015.

Thomas, John Christopher. "Women, Pentecostalism, and the Bible: An Experiment in Pentecostal Hermeneutics." *Journal of Pentecostal Theology* 5 (1994) 41–56.

Yong, Amos. *Spirit-Word-Community: Theological Hermeneutics in Trinitarian Perspective.* Eugene, OR: Wipf and Stock, 2002.

Chapter 20
Holistic Evangelical Hermeneutics
STEVEN B. SHERMAN

Twice a week, students file into my class to discuss theology, philosophy, and hermeneutics. Expectations and goals differ as much as meal choices before and after class. Most try to listen, process, and understand claims, arguments, and evidence—whether presented by me or their peers. Everyone assesses two things: the presenter's (a) *interpretation* of things and (b) *character*. We must. Humans are born interpreters and evaluators—making impassioned and meaningful learning possible, and fun![1]

I'll call this classroom interaction "hermeneutical heralding, heterogeneity, and hospitality." *Hermeneutics* happens as we *participate* in trying to interpret and understand something. *Heralding* happens as we *profess* something to be important, meaningful, or true about the subject-matter. *Heterogeneity* happens as we *process* the subject matter from diverse standpoints. *Hospitality* happens as the classroom environment becomes a *pleasant place* to share and dialogue about views and interpretations of things.[2] So, how do these classroom experiences fit with this chapter's topic: holistic evangelical hermeneutics? What relevance might this hermeneutical approach have for your own life? Just as class enthusiasm excels when heralding, heterogeneity,

---

1. Nevertheless, sometimes class is far from perfect; tech-related distractions and sleep-deprivation are two pesky flies in the academic learning-environment ointment!

2. A hospitable spirit is challenging to maintain since everyone carries particular presuppositions about the meaning of *terms*, including those in this chapter (e.g., "holistic" and "evangelical"). We need to define our terms carefully so that we don't "speak past" one other, but instead, communicate with the same meaning (i.e., "commensurably"). *Absolute* commensurability may be beyond reach, but often our language *adequately* allows us to share meaning and understanding.

and hospitality occur, so holistic evangelical hermeneutics excels when the same three ingredients mix. My thesis is that this approach, at its best, offers beneficial hermeneutical flavor, delivering faithful, flexible, and fitting interpretations and understandings of things to be understood—"texts"—along with answers to the important practical question, *What does this have to do with my life and why does it matter?* We have good reasons—academic and practical—for considering holistic evangelical hermeneutics as a viable way of approaching texts—and living well in light of them.

This chapter's outline is simple. Part 1 clarifies the three principal terms that comprise our topic (holistic, evangelical, hermeneutics), examines the meaning of those terms *combined*, and discusses what to expect when utilizing the compound term in interpreting and understanding texts. Part 2 considers how holistic evangelical hermeneutics approaches texts in these four arenas: biblical, theological, philosophical, and cultural/intercultural, comparing and contrasting this approach with some alternatives. Part 3 offers practical insights and further responses to the concern, "What does this have to do with my life, and why does it matter?"

PART 1—SETTING THE STAGE: KEY WORDS, TERMS, AND EXPLANATIONS

Words we use get misunderstood or misinterpreted—by family, friends, and foes. Good storytelling benefits from this and the unintended consequences encountered in those narrative situations—particularly comedies and tragedies. But misunderstanding and misinterpretation irritates us when we're trying to communicate something accurately. We *expect* what we share to be *rightly* interpreted and understood. That's why we care about using appropriate words and phrases—to get our point across. Understanding is at the *heart* of hermeneutics.

The *terms*—i.e., the *meaning* of words we use—are more important than the specific words themselves—even though the terms depend on and emerge from those words. Terms involve the specific definition, explanation, and/or meaning of words and phrases used in a given context. For example, *love* is a word but there are many different terms (or meanings) associated with it. How someone *uses* the word in a specific *context* and for a specific *purpose* makes all the difference. Saying you love smoothies, your cat, your family, a friend, a film, baseball, or the Lord will signify something different in each instance. It's important that we clearly and properly explain the meaning and intention behind the words and sentences we construct. A famous saying sums up why: "A text without a context is a pretext."

Speaking of words, three key ones constitute this chapter's title: holistic, evangelical, hermeneutics. Each word contains many potential terms (*or* meanings), depending on context, worldview, presuppositions, experience, and more. I hope to clarify these principal words and their terms—first individually and then when combined.

KEY TERM #1: HERMENEUTICS

Hermeneutics is a word with *many* meanings, including the following:[3] It is the science and art (or theory and practice) of interpretation. It is the process of understanding "texts"—particular subjects to be understood. It involves "the effort to understand how humans understand, especially 'texts' . . ."[4] It "explores *the conditions and criteria* that operate to try to ensure responsible, valid, fruitful or appropriate interpretation."[5] These conditions and criteria include aspects like worldview, assumptions, knowledge, experience, practices, and context, which impact our understanding of texts: whether biblical, theological, philosophical, cultural/intercultural, or otherwise.

Hermeneutics extends beyond *individual* interpretation. We inhabit hermeneutical *communities* that maintain worldviews, assumptions, knowledge, experience, and practices. For example, different academic communities possess divergent social, political, and religious interpretations and understandings. Each community constructs and broadcasts its "message"—communication intending to persuade its audience to understand things the way that community does.[6] Such messages work like "scripts," presenting a narrative (story) or vision of how things are—or ought to be. These narratives comprise worldviews: ways of looking at the world (i.e., reality).

Hermeneutics involves discerning what is being communicated and why. Becoming good interpreters requires gaining knowledge of "the hermeneutical world" and skills necessary for understanding things well. Some

---

3. No comprehensive consensus exists among scholars on the definition, explanation, and meaning of these words (hermeneutics, evangelical, holistic). Nevertheless, we can progress in determining some aspects characterizing each word, seeking the most plausible explanations and considering how they're used. For instance, when using *evangelical* in "holistic evangelical hermeneutics," the term/meaning in that context carries a particular fitting connotation that, in a different context, it might not.

4. Treier and Sweeney, *Hearing and Doing the Word*, 1.

5. Thiselton, *Hermeneutics*, 4.

6. Differences in hermeneutical communities are found in virtually every industry/domain in society; for instance, business, politics, government, law, education, churches, and media/social media.

hermeneuticians believe that *speech-act theory* is a valuable linguistic tool for interpreting and understanding communication—spoken and written.[7] The three main parts of speech-acts include "locution" (the articulating of certain words), "illocution" (some act performed *in* articulating something, typically having an intended purpose), and perlocution (the effect/response brought about in the hearer/reader). While messages or scripts may carry all three speech-act parts, the hermeneutical *goal* typically involves bringing about a particular activity or behavior.

Besides "general hermeneutics" (described above), "special hermeneutics" recognizes and proceeds from a distinctly *theological* grounding, often associated with "biblical" or "theological" hermeneutics. Utilizing *both* general and special hermeneutical approaches makes sense for this chapter; each contributes to the interpretive process and for how we understand texts—including various assumptions, beliefs, and practices we bring to the hermeneutical table.[8]

KEY TERM #2: HOLISTIC

In relation to hermeneutics, "holistic" denotes an expansive, multifaceted approach to interpreting and understanding texts. The concept of holistic presumes a broader, total system approach in contrast to (over)simplified interpretive procedures focused exclusively on, say, an author's intention, word studies, or subjective application—although it may include these as part of a multilayered hermeneutic.[9] It comprises at least the following important elements for interpreting and understanding texts:[10]

- Considering multiple interpretive factors (like presuppositions)
- Integrating various disciplines (theology, philosophy, psychology, social/cultural, and others)
- Embracing interpretive fallibility and need for humility (given human imperfection)
- Integrating speech-act theory

---

7. See Briggs, "Speech-Acts Theory," 763–66.

8. "General hermeneutics" considers standard/universal theories and/or approaches to interpreting and understanding texts. "Special hermeneutics" embraces a *theological* basis as essential for properly interpreting/understanding texts.

9. I'm using the singular construction, "hermeneutic," as a rough equivalent to "interpretive principle or process."

10. For this "Holistic" section, I am indebted to Westphal, *Whose Community*, 66–68.

- Ideally seeking coherent harmony of perspectives (rather than eliminating all but one)[11]
- Acknowledging the "hermeneutical circle" or spiral (biblical texts inform our theological commitments, and vice versa; interpretations carry presuppositions)
- Accepting multiple sources of knowledge
- Ideally aiming for the highest degree of objectivity and quality "reproduction" and "production"[12]
- Appreciating better "translations" or "interpretations"
- Carrying on conversations with "epistemic humility" with others that see the text differently[13]

This multilayered, holistic approach provides increasing probability of better interpreting and understanding texts.

KEY TERM #3: EVANGELICAL

At its most basic level, "evangelical" has to do with the *evangel*—the gospel (good news) of God's kingdom, chiefly imparted through Jesus Christ. Beyond this general description, many diverse and divergent explanations persist.[14] For our purposes, we'll maintain focus on theological and hermeneutical meanings of evangelical.

Theologically, evangelical is often associated with particular core doctrines—central teachings preeminently connected with the gospel (*evangel*). Dialogue and debate persist about the specific number and content of these doctrines. Lists typically include at least the following:

- Divine inspiration and authority of Holy Scripture (the Bible), "the word of God" in human words
- Centrality of the life, death, and resurrection of the incarnate Son of God, Jesus the Messiah (i.e., Christ)
- Christ's effectual atoning (saving) sacrifice for human sin

---

11. See Westphal, *Whose Community*, 66.
12. See H2o example in Westphal, *Whose Community*, 112.
13. See Westphal, *Whose Community*, 115–18, 129.
14. For instance, in popular culture, a spectrum of attitudes exists towards *evangelicals*. Sometimes the term in its plural form is said to convey certain political or social positions (such as the "religious right," "evangelical left," or "traditional morality"), whether such associations are viewed as positive or negative.

- Triune nature of God (Father, Son, and Spirit = Trinity)
- Need for conversion (turning away from idols and toward God) and placing trust (faith) in God's saving work on one's behalf
- Growing in the grace and knowledge of God, seeking to love God with one's whole being and loving others as oneself, enabled by continually being filled with the power of the Holy Spirit
- Gathering regularly for worship and fellowship with like-minded Christ-followers
- Teaching others the good news and making disciples (followers) of Jesus

Evangelical may include other features or modifiers—some scholars omit these; others insist on them. For instance, most evangelicals hold to a "high view" of Scripture and add terms to denote this such as "Word of God," "infallible" (at least in what it teaches), "inerrant" (no errors in the original writings, called autographs, although copies of those are what exist today), and/or "verbal, plenary inspiration" (usually touching each text or unit of meaning throughout the whole text/Bible). Other scholars choose different terms like "trustworthy" or "faithful" to connote their view; some reject most or all these for a more general sense of inspiration and authority.

For *every* core doctrine, the same multiple descriptions, qualifiers, and modifiers apply, depending on theological assumptions and commitments. This *should* be expected since diverse factors influence our interpretations and understandings. Nevertheless, the *broadest* schema above also reveals this unity: at least *some* important theological beliefs and moral practices *are shared* by virtually everyone who falls within a broad evangelical spectrum.

Evangelicalism is a large tent (spectrum); it's neither a denomination nor a stream. Evangelical theologians and practitioners (in the broad, core sense outlined above) inhabit all major Christian "streams" today: Protestant, Catholic, Eastern Orthodox, Anglican, and Pentecostal.[15] A higher percentage of evangelicals likely inhabit Protestant and Pentecostal streams based on those group's particular histories/heritages and expressions of faith.

Let's now bring the three key words together to form "holistic evangelical hermeneutics" and see what happens when we apply it to biblical, theological, philosophical, and cultural/intercultural arenas—and the difference it might make to our individual lives.

---

15. Although scholars do not unanimously affirm these divisions, I find these five streams a helpful heuristic device for general distinctions.

COMPOSITE TERM: HOLISTIC EVANGELICAL HERMENEUTICS

Holistic evangelical hermeneutics may be described as a broad-ranging approach to interpreting and understanding texts from a distinctly Christian worldview grounded in Scripture, preeminently centered in the good news of the triune God's kingdom/rule and embodied in the identity/person and mission/work of Jesus Christ. The Holy Spirit enables, inspires, and illuminates the interpretation, understanding, and practice of texts, especially among those seeking to love and serve God.

Many *alternative* ways exist for interpreting and understanding texts; most provide important discoveries and insights about reality (e.g., philosophical, scientific, psychological, and sociological). Still, holistic evangelical hermeneutics—with its strong *faith-seeking-understanding* approach—makes room for important biblical claims and theological commitments. Hermeneutical models with contrasting worldviews (e.g., atheistic or pantheistic) or assumptions (e.g., a low view of Jesus) typically lack room for such commitments. Consequently, we see contrasting interpretations on crucial subject like Scripture, faith, moral problems and solutions, our place in the world, and the meaning and purpose of life. What about *alternative Christian* hermeneutical schools of thought—*non*-evangelical or *non*-holistic approaches? These do tend to share *some* interpretive overlap with evangelical commitments; for example, assuming God's existence, divine creation (*contra* evolutionary naturalism), God's relationship with humanity, and Jesus Christ's unique life, death, and resurrection. Even so, evangelical approaches typically focus more on central theological doctrines (noted under "Evangelical" heading), and on other key aspects like discipleship and evangelism.[16]

Besides important *general* holistic elements for interpreting and understanding texts (see components under "Holistic" above)—vital *evangelical* holistic elements exist and include:

- Recognizing multiple sources of knowledge (e.g., Scripture, the Spirit, tradition, community, wisdom, reason/reasoning, perception, creation, culture)
- Appreciating God speaking through texts (both then and now)
- Valuing the continuing work, and all the gifts, of the Spirit (continuationism)

---

16. Among evangelical hermeneuticians, debate occurs over what are primary, secondary, or tertiary doctrines—plus how much interpretive influence should accompany each division. My focus remains more on *primary* territory when operating from a holistic evangelical hermeneutic.

- Recognizing both "Word and Spirit" as essential to understanding Scripture[17]
- Practicing wisdom (*phronesis*) and making meaning concrete in the current context, seeing application and embodiment in parallel when done correctly and well[18]

Fusing these distinct evangelical elements with a general holistic approach provides a beneficial horizon for *further increasing* the probability for better interpreting and understanding texts.

In Part 2, we'll consider how this hermeneutical approach works within four important arenas: biblical, theological, philosophical, and cultural/intercultural. The method I'll employ will include (1) providing background information and hermeneutical questions/concerns related to the domain, (2) concisely analyzing the text of each domain (and/or specific texts within it), (3) briefly considering and evaluating competing hermeneutical approaches to the particular text, and (4) conveying the outcomes of holistic evangelical hermeneutics for interpreting and understanding these texts.

PART 2—HOLISTIC EVANGELICAL HERMENEUTICS: INTERPRETING AND UNDERSTANDING TEXTS IN FOUR HERMENEUTICAL ARENAS

INTERPRETING BIBLICAL TEXTS VIA HOLISTIC EVANGELICAL HERMENEUTICS

Why do people interpret the Bible in so many different ways?[19] Family and upbringing, friends and social circles, knowledge and learning levels, assumptions and beliefs—comprise some reasons for differing attitudes and approaches. Even among holistic evangelical hermeneuticians, backgrounds and ideas and experiences distinctly shape theological views. This includes views of the Bible: its origin, history, doctrines/teachings, stories (narratives), purposes, and inspiration. Perhaps the central issue concerns *meaning*: What does the Bible *communicate* for its readers to know, understand, and do? That's a great *hermeneutical* question!

Other big questions need careful consideration: Who or what determines *ultimate* authority in giving meaning to the text? Is it the author, the text itself, or its reader/s? How do we *determine* which should have priority?

17. See Westphal, *Whose Community,* 148–49.
18. See Westphal, *Whose Community,* 108–10.
19. While diverse views on the Bible exist among other (non-Christian) theists, pantheists, and atheists, I'll focus mainly on Christian scholars who seek to understand the Bible *as Scripture*.

What matters *most* when seeking to understand Scripture? Is it the background or history of the text itself (terms, language, sentences, context)? Is it the intention, purpose, or communication action of the author? Is it the theological or moral teaching? Is it the application (if any) for today? Is it the personal/subjective message the reader gets from the text? Is it the meaning/message for the Christian community (church) today? Is it the Spirit's illumination and/or use of the text for believers throughout history? It's complicated! Yet, these questions—and diverse responses—help explain why biblical interpretations often contrast, which leads to this related query: Is there a *best* method for understanding the text, or at least some approaches better than others? Or is it just a free-for-all pluralism with every approach equally valid or invalid? Judicious responses are needed.

While various hermeneutical models contribute some valuable, tangible insights for understanding biblical texts, a holistic evangelical approach seems unique in that it combines (a) gospel-centeredness; (b) core theological commitments; (c) crucial textual background and biblical languages tools; (d) historical-traditional interpretation materials; (e) reasonable reflection and integration re additional knowledge sources; and (f) inspiration and wisdom from the Spirit. Admittedly, evangelical history sometimes displays deficiencies and errors in interpretation and comprehension for anti-intellectual, social-political, rationalistic, scientific, and other reasons. Yet, since the closing decades of the twentieth century, academic, intellectual, and hermeneutical flourishing has increased exponentially among scholars committed to the *evangel*—many welcoming more holistic approaches to biblical (and/or theological) hermeneutics.[20]

It may be helpful to say what holistic evangelical hermeneutics does *not* look like in the biblical arena. First, it doesn't focus *exclusively* on considering the biblical text/s from a single angle—be it historical, grammatical, functional, ethical, scientific, etc. While these aspects shed important light on biblical texts, unidirectional attention effectively eliminates all but one "tool" in the hermeneutician's toolbox![21]

Second, holistic evangelical hermeneutics does not get sidetracked with peripheral matters that distract and undermining concentration on understanding biblical texts. Still, paying *appropriate* attention to *all* relevant (including secondary) issues matters: for instance, the cultural context.

---

20. For example, Kenneth Archer, Craig Bartholomew, Stephen Fowl, Joel Green, Craig Keener, Grant Osborne, Anthony Thiselton, Daniel Treier, Kevin Vanhoozer, Merold Westphal, and Amos Yong, among many others.

21. Hammers and screwdrivers have their distinct functions; using a screwdriver to hammer nails (or vice versa) works against the tool's design—the same applies to not using *hermeneutical* tools properly.

Third, a holistic evangelical hermeneutic does not assume—or seek—some "neutral" way to understand texts. The Bible itself assumes its readers are *not* neutral—whether it is addressing the people of God, particular Christ-followers, or others. Moreover, evangelical is *not* a neutral term; it connotes faith/trust in the Good News and action in light of it. Consider the many New Testament passages that focus on the resurrection of Jesus Christ and the important implications for humankind (e.g., see 1 Corinthians 15). A holistic evangelical approach begins with affirming this Good News, grounded in underlying theological commitments arising from the Spirit-inspired word of God (in human words), as well as various supporting sources and/or evidences (e.g., eyewitness testimonies, conversion experiences, miracles, fulfilled prophecies). Virtually any hermeneutic that denies the possibility of supernaturalism (in general) or miracles (in particular), as atheism does, will interpret *as false* biblical texts containing these claims. Resurrection passages, then, must be interpreted in a naturalistic/materialist way. Conversely, a consistent pantheistic approach will interpret these same texts in a supernaturalistic/immaterialist way, while necessarily denying the reality or importance of the physical/material aspects involved (e.g., Jesus's body, post-Resurrection appearances involving touch, taste, and other senses).

Ultimately, then, a holistic evangelical approach to the text/s of the Bible presupposes and proceeds from core theological commitments while utilizing scholarly and pastoral interpretation tools with hermeneutical wisdom. This promising hermeneutic offers beneficial and inspiring ways of interpreting and understanding the biblical text/s.

INTERPRETING THEOLOGICAL TEXTS VIA HOLISTIC EVANGELICAL HERMENEUTICS

Theology encompasses a massive discipline. Numerous scholars devote lifetimes exploring *theological* topics, questions, claims, and responses. Amid the extensive subject-matter and perspectives, a holistic evangelical hermeneutic may be distinguished from alternative models while bringing to bear several resources for "theologizing" (i.e., doing theology). Consider a topic/text like the Doctrine of Human Beings (Anthropology). Where do we begin in terms of study, interpretation, or understanding? The "entry point" may depend on particular academic disciplines (biology, psychology, sociology, theology), special interests (political, economic, existential), presuppositions (naturalism and supernaturalism), etc. From a holistic evangelical worldview, *ultimate* authority rests in what the Scriptures communicate *as a whole* on any particular theological subject-matter. Secondarily, one then investigates what other authoritative have to tell us.[22]

Theological texts arise from *reflection* on what Scripture, along with other key sources, communicate about God, Jesus Christ, humankind, creation, etc.—including particular attributes and relationships. For example, consider the topic/text, "the knowledge of God" (i.e., theological knowledge). Evangelical scholars generally affirm Holy Scripture as the most indispensable source for theological knowledge. The Bible repeatedly makes claims and gives evidence for God's self-revealing to human beings, and being known by them. Examples are ubiquitous.[23] Views differ, though, as to the authority or use of utilizing sources beyond the Bible for knowledge of God. For scholars who appeal to additional sources, the question becomes *which* to include and why, and how to prioritize/rank them. These sources may include Church tradition/Christian community, creation, perception of God, the Spirit and manifestational gifts, divine wisdom, virtue, reason, and culture. Agreement/disagreement over prioritizing these sources will depend on hermeneutical dynamics like academic environments, preunderstandings and presuppositions, spiritual life and experience, and colleagues and influencers.

Materialistic approaches to theological knowledge will radically contrast with an evangelical hermeneutic. For instance, a scientism worldview ("matters is all there is") will eschew the idea of knowledge of God since an *immaterial* God cannot exist in an exclusively *material* world. Pantheism, though, agrees (in part) with an evangelical worldview since each view affirms that immaterial reality exists. However, pantheism disagrees with an evangelical worldview by denying real or substantive material aspects of the world. Ultimately, pantheism's concept of God and theological knowledge radically diverges from a holistic evangelical approach—a hermeneutic that recognizes multiple ways the triune God may be known and is known—personally and corporately—as demonstrated in the biblical text, Christian history, and existential experiences.

INTERPRETING PHILOSOPHICAL TEXTS VIA HOLISTIC EVANGELICAL HERMENEUTICS

Philosophical texts generally include deep thinking about major questions and issues of life, such as: Does God exist? What's real? What's true? What's right and wrong? What and how can I know? What/who am I? Are humans

---

22. Primary and secondary sources have to do with *priority* of authority for knowledge, truth, meaning, etc.

23. For instance, 2 Cor 2:14–15. See Sherman, *Revitalizing Theological Epistemology*.

free or determined? What's the meaning or purpose of life? Multiple hermeneutical responses accompany these crucial questions and issues. Not surprisingly, worldview assumptions *guide the potential criteria* for interpreting or explaining things. The question is, Which offers the *best* explanation? This process of *reasoning or inferring to the best explanation* is well-known to philosophers and other academicians. In brief, it comprises several (typically six or seven) important categories: for instance, *explanatory scope*. By considering factors based on each category, one reasons or infers about which explanatory framework better answers a wider variety of issues. Remember, though, there is no "neutral" starting point from which everyone begins to consider theological questions; rather, provisional understandings and presuppositions are unavoidable. Recognizing this may help humble myopic, absolutist, and triumphalist explanations.[24]

Let's briefly explore the "Problem of Evil," employing inference to the best explanation to see which explanation may provide the best answer to this conundrum. Space constrains limit this to three perspectives—atheism, pantheism, and (Christian) theism—related to the *empirical* Problem: the claim that there is too much evil in the world for God to exist and/or to justify belief in God.[25] This position contains several underlying assumptions. First, it assumes human beings somehow can know or understand (perhaps even calculate?) the amount or quantity of evil in the world—apparently compared to the same amount or quantity of good. But we need to ask, How could this be possible, considering the substantial *limitations* of human knowledge and understanding? What does it take to know, quantify, and assess *every* instance of evil and good—fully and accurately? Who could or should decide how to measure this or determine who has the final say over whether this determination rules God "out of existence"? Even if there were some standard measure for weighing total good and total evil in the world (say, some AI-based calculation), how could this include all *thoughts, feelings, intentions, situations/contexts,* and other factors *beyond the mere acts of evil and good?* This seems impossible—*unless* there is some all-knowing (omniscient) Being who possesses all would-be necessary attributes like perfect understanding, truth, justice, and wisdom. Exactly *why* such a God would allow evil raises other philosophical and theological questions. Theists primarily respond with "defenses" concerned with demonstrating

---

24. See Moreland and Craig, *Philosophical Foundations for a Christian Worldview,* 61–63, for a summary of categories and elements comprising inference to the best explanation.

25. Other primary approaches to the Problems of Evil include the logical and the existential. The logical is based on an *a priori* or rational focus; the existential, on an *a posteriori* or experiential perspective.

the *possibility* of God and evil coexisting, or with "theodicies" concerned with explaining *why* God and evil coexist, details of which we must leave to others.[26]

Intellectual atheists committed to reasonable and truthful efforts to support their claims may be commended for engaging the challenging Problem of Evil. Dialogue and debate on this issue provide opportunities to think through worldviews, hermeneutical approaches, and potential solutions. Even so, it seems to me that trying to understand the Problem by beginning with *ruling out* a divine Being, other immaterial beings (e.g., angels), and all supernatural possibilities and attestations is unhelpful. Ultimately, this hermeneutic asks limited, fallible humans to shoulder the entire weight for accurately knowing and judging *everything* about evil, as well as good—thus, closing the door on a potential divine Being without such limitations.[27]

What, then, about intellectual pantheism? It does seem to *simplify* the Problem by eliminating the reality of—or at least substantial differences between—good and evil. Some pantheists opt for reckoning good and evil as not being real or different things, but rather opposing principles. The Problem, then, somehow "disappears" or is "harmonized" into a oneness. But the question for pantheism is, How *reasonable* is a hermeneutical approach that ultimately denies what appears to be well-attested and confirmed by *billions* of people throughout history (for instance, the evil of Hitler and the Nazi "Final Solution": the Holocaust)?

It appears neither atheistic nor pantheistic approaches provide a sufficiently compelling answer to the Problem. Let's consider if a theistic worldview—enacting a holistic evangelical hermeneutic—answers the Problem of Evil more convincingly.

A holistic evangelical approach recognizes that since this is a supernatural world, and since the Bible speaks authoritatively and quite clearly on matters of evil and good, God may be heard speaking in the text (God's word in human words). Ultimately, then, a *divine* author—rather than merely human authors—addresses the Problem by speaking-for-a-purpose, which involves speech-acts: locutions (words and sentences), illocutions (desired responses) and perlocutions (enacted outcomes). Through the hermeneutical circle (or spiral) process of biblical texts informing our theological commitments and vice versa, we're called to listen especially to the incarnate Word—Jesus Christ. As the *fully divine and fully human* member

---

26. For instance, see Plantinga, "Free Will Defense"; and Adams, *Horrendous Evils and the Goodness of God*.

27. It appears that atheists bear the burden of demonstrating the *impossibility* that God exists—in this *actual* world or in any *possible* world.

of the Trinity, Christ takes center stage with his authoritative explanations and interpretations of the Problem, and all else! Later church writings, along with Christian theology, philosophy, experience, and testimony via church history, plus various non-Christian sources across world history (e.g., Aristotle), may also contribute to a holistic evangelical hermeneutics endeavor: pride of place remaining with the Good News (*evangel*).

INTERPRETING CULTURAL/INTERCULTURAL TEXTS VIA HOLISTIC EVANGELICAL HERMENEUTICS

It seems to me there's probably no better—at least no more relevant—text to consider for cultural/intercultural hermeneutics than social media. Chances are virtually everyone reading this chapter knows what social media is, uses it regularly or occasionally, has strong opinions about it, and may welcome guidance for better interpreting and understanding it. If social media is anything—and it is *many* things—it's enormously wide-ranging with numerous elements/aspects. Simplistic statements like, "Social media is horrible" (or "awesome") don't help us analyze or understand this increasingly ubiquitous technology.[28] Perhaps utilizing holistic evangelical hermeneutics may help enhance reading this text. Two alternative approaches also will be considered: subjective relativism and conventionalism (or cultural relativism). First, though, let's work on a few important definitions.

"Cultural texts" are things created or done by humans that may be interpreted.[29] Just what culture *is* or *encompasses* needs interpretation itself!

Social media is a type of cultural text or "artifact"—developed by humans for various purposes. There is no standardized or shared definition of social media. Still, aspects generally include a broad-ranging category of online (Internet-based) interactive technologies that facilitate for user and virtual-community communication, particularly websites and apps that involve sharing of profiles, messages, digital photos and videos, and other types of information. These may involve social networks and organizations, accessible via computer desktops, laptops, and mobile devices (e.g., smartphones). Most government, business, political, law enforcement, non-profit, religious, and other organizations heavily invest in and utilize social media.

---

28. Not everyone uses or has access to social media; currently, the percentage of users is roughly 60 percent (4.8 billion) of the world's population (see https://datareportal.com/social-media-users). Many don't have access to the Internet or social media due to factors like government restrictions, economic hardship, and infrastructure problems.

29. I'm limiting discussion to "cultural" (and not "intercultural") aspects due to space constraints.

Unarguably, using social media impacts our identity and self-perception.[30] That's why our social "networks" matter; they strongly shape our interpretation and understanding of self and others, including God. Correspondingly, a holistic evangelical approach to social media begins with considering how social media contributes to or detracts from the Good News. Can or does social media facilitate for *God's priorities*—above all, loving the Lord with all we are, and others as ourselves? Of course, the problem with this and related crucial questions is that *it depends*. It depends on *what, which, and how* social media users engage with diverse online materials, and how social media providers engage with users. Consequently, a holistic evangelical hermeneutic avoids polarizing, simplistic, all-or-nothing generalizations. Instead, it must consider social media's beneficial and/or redeemable qualities—as well as unbeneficial and irredeemable aspects—including specific user and provider attitudes and activities.

Again, underlying worldview commitments ultimately fuel our interpretations and understandings. Therefore, evangelical theological commitments take center stage—even as one navigates the social-media sea of religious pluralism, spiritualities, and "Christian" heterodoxies.[31]

Many online organizations and individuals are kingdom-focused, servant-agents of gospel-centered transformation. Other online groups and persons appear primarily motivated by and focused on particular products, services, interests, or ideas. The *holistic* facet of evangelical hermeneutics prompts consideration of potential and/or actual values, virtues, benefits, purposes, and goodness involving social media; this includes filtering, interpreting, and understanding the text/s of social media via ultimate (theological) and secondary (e.g., scientific, sociological, psychological) authority sources.

In contrast, a *subjectivist* hermeneutic approaches social media exclusively from the individual user, or particular provider, perspective. Desires, goals, emotions, and values reside entirely *within* (internal to) the persons involved; no external entity—divine or human—possesses ultimate authority or communicates what "ought to be" the case. Instead, what "is" is all there is; moral goods or oughts beyond one's own internal feelings or sense

---

30. This lends support to a *relational ontology* metaphysical view (i.e., our identity as humans has virtually everything to do with our relationships with others).

31. Heterodoxies include unorthodox positions/beliefs considered heretical by virtually the whole Christian church (e.g., Jesus as merely human or not human, salvation achieved by oneself rather than by Christ's atoning sacrifice for sin, the Holy Spirit as an impersonal force rather than divine member/person of the Trinity).

do *not* exist. A subjectivist motto might be, "I assume what I believe is true even though I have never questioned the basis for my many beliefs."[32]

Logically, subjectivism insists social media user's or provider's motives or activities *cannot* be evaluated/judged since everything is merely a matter of personal preference—regardless the content or activity involved (e.g., whether this includes videos of children freed from human trafficking, or instead, videos of child pornography). Subjectivism allows no greater basis for interpreting or understanding than oneself. Practically (and fortunately), most reject this hermeneutic. However, many embrace conventionalism (or cultural relativism).

A *conventionalist* hermeneutic approaches social media wholly from a particular *cultural* or societal perspective; thus, it's *sociocentric*. Users' and providers' desires, goals, and values toward social media are compelled by particular social group/s viewed as the *ultimate external authority*—"authorizing" what encompasses social media oughts (goods) and ought nots (evils). A conventionalist motto might be, "I assume that the dominant beliefs of the groups to which I belong are true even though I have never questioned the basis for those beliefs."[33] Groups range widely from family to friends to employers to social-media "influencers" to multiple others. While these groups provide guidance or support, they often hold *contrasting* perspectives and give *contradictory* interpretations/views of social media. It seems one is left with no more than a current cultural relativism,[34] lacking an anchor or objective source for evaluating or understanding social media.[35]

PART 3—CONCLUSION OF THE MATTER: WHAT THIS HAS TO DO WITH MY LIFE AND WHY IT MATTERS

Our journey through holistic evangelical hermeneutics has brought us to a final, eminently practical question: "What does this have to do with my life, and why does it matter?" At least four responses may help justify the personal value this hermeneutical approach offers.[36]

---

32. Paul and Elder, *Miniature Guide to Critical Thinking*, 21.

33. Paul and Elder, *Miniature Guide to Critical Thinking*, 21.

34. Cultural relativism becomes more complex and confusing when considering *intercultural* aspects (e.g., involving different languages, terms, approaches, and assumptions).

35. Cultural "trending" entails the absence of any core universal/objective basis from which to interpret and understand texts.

36. Review Parts 1 and 2 for additional responses.

First, holistic evangelical hermeneutics provides one with a *coherent worldview and theological grounding* that serve as both lifeline and anchor from which to interpret and understand texts. The underlying worldview story (metanarrative) invites all to enter in, connect their own narrative/story, and discover personal belonging and identity. Core doctrines—such as God's attributes (e.g., Trinitarian nature, love, justice, truth), revealed Word (preeminently Jesus Christ and Scripture), atonement and redemption (through Christ), way of life (morality), and Spirit empowerment and presence—serve to instruct, shape, correct, and guide followers in hermeneutical wholeness and hospitality.

Second, the *holistic* aspect of this approach may benefit one's life in several ways. It can help counteract unreflective, popular, and/or myopic interpretation and understanding. Also, by seriously pursuing a broad-based and objective (universally-true) understanding of things, one may judiciously integrate discovered truth and wisdom wherever found (since all truth is from God).

Third, the Spirit—ultimate interpreter and knower of all things—is also the divine comforter and truth-bearer amid the cultural cacophony. The interpretive Spirit—hermeneutically active throughout history—continues to communicate communally and personally, primarily within and through Christian community gathered around Jesus Christ. The Spirit's interpretive activity works in conjunction with conscientious study, collegial learning, worship and fellowship gatherings, and prayer and contemplation.[37]

Fourth, because a holistic evangelical approach is *public*—the Good News being on display for all to examine—one may benefit from opportunities to share and learn with others at the "hermeneutical table." This table provides access to shared listening, learning, and expressing one's interpretation and understanding of texts (versus provincial, "privatized," or insular-group methods). Controversy, challenges, disputation, and new ideas are welcomed. While an evangelicals hermeneutic will preserve its core theological commitments, such commitments are public and open to all: contrasted with secretive or elitist approaches.

Our journey into holistic evangelical hermeneutics ends where our story began—in the classroom: but wider still, *the classroom of life*. How one approaches biblical, theological, philosophical, cultural/intercultural, and other texts matters greatly. The heralding, heterogeneity, and hospitality of holistic evangelical hermeneutics—at its best—offers advocates and

---

37. Jesus's greatest commandment includes terms (heart, soul, mind, strength) that, together, infer the whole self matters in loving the Lord your God (Luke 10:27a). Undervaluing any aspect undermines one's call and ability to love God fully.

practitioners a theologically-grounded, holistically-oriented, and practical way forward for interpreting and understanding texts.

BIBLIOGRAPHY

Adams, Marilyn McCord. *Horrendous Evils and the Goodness of God*. Ithaca, NY: Cornell University Press, 2000.

Bartholomew, Craig G. *Introducing Biblical Hermeneutics: A Comprehensive Framework for Hearing God in Scripture*. Grand Rapids: Baker Academic, 2015.

Keener, Craig S. *Spirit Hermeneutics: Reading Scripture in Light of Pentecost*. Grand Rapids: Eerdmans, 2016.

Klein, William W., et al. *Introduction to Biblical Interpretation*. 3rd ed. Grand Rapids: Zondervan, 2017.

Moreland, J. P., and William Lane Craig, *Philosophical Foundations for a Christian Worldview*. 2nd. ed. Downers Grove, IL: InterVarsity, 2017.

Paul, Richard, and Linda Elder. *The Miniature Guide to Critical Thinking: Concepts and Tools*. 6th ed. Dillon Beach, CA: Foundation for Critical Thinking, 2009.

Plantinga, Alvin. "The Free Will Defense." In *God, Freedom, and Evil*, 29–34. Grand Rapids: Eerdmans, 1977.

Sherman, Steven B. *Revitalizing Theological Epistemology: Holistic Evangelical Approaches to the Knowledge of God*. Eugene, OR: Pickwick, 2008.

Thiselton, Anthony C. *Hermeneutics: An Introduction*. Grand Rapids: Eerdmans, 2009.

Treier, Daniel J., and Douglas A. Sweeney. *Hearing and Doing the Word: The Drama of Evangelical Hermeneutics in Honor of Kevin J. Vanhoozer*. New York: T. & T. Clark, 2021.

Vanhoozer, Kevin J., ed. *Dictionary of Theological Interpretation of the Bible*. Grand Rapids: Baker Academic, 2005.

Vanhoozer, Kevin J., et al., eds. *Everyday Theology: How to Read Cultural Texts and Interpret Trends*. Grand Rapids: Baker Academic, 2007.

Westphal, Merold. *Whose Community: Which Interpretation?: Philosophical Hermeneutics for the Church*. Grand Rapids: Baker Academic, 2009.

Yong, Amos. *The Hermeneutical Spirit: Theological Interpretation and Scriptural Imagination for the 21st Century*. Eugene, OR: Cascade, 2017.

Chapter 21
Embodied Hermeneutics
BRIAN MACALLAN

The last century has seen a shifting landscape in terms of where the Christian faith is located globally, as well as where its current areas of growth and decline are being manifested. As the center of gravity shifts towards the Global South in areas like South America, Africa, and Asia, so does its theological outlook. Various post-colonial theologies are part of the critique of inherited Christian theological positions. Current challenges abound with ecological and political uncertainty being at the forefront. Despite the potential of this global diversity, and its ability to speak contextually to the numerous cultural challenges, at times our Christian tradition stumbles and splinters in its response. Conservative theologies, while not necessarily intending to do so, remain insular and reactionary. A post conservative theology seeks to be faithful to the Christian tradition yet engages meaningfully with its context, realizing that Scripture itself can function critically to reform and reshape the tradition itself.

With these sensibilities in mind, this chapter seeks to offer an embodied hermeneutic that returns to Scripture and tradition, as well as other cultural and philosophical resources, to provide a constructive theological proposal that attempts to address some of the ecological and political challenges we face globally.

An embodied hermeneutic is one which seeks to ground what we think ecologically and politically in the body, with all the ethical implications that this entails. It is hoped that this post conservative proposal is one that would find traction across the different Christian traditions (intentionally plural). The quest is for a hermeneutical nexus in which Scripture, tradition, and context seek to find embodiment. Therefore, the hermeneutical task in this chapter involves the interpretation of these various sources, while also demonstrating how that task contributes to an ethical framework.

CHRISTIAN TRADITION AND THE BODY

Christian tradition and the role of the body have been subjects of dialogue and critique for over two thousand years. This extensive period offers numerous examples where Christian's views on the body have been influenced by prevailing concerns and philosophical outlooks governed by unique contextual factors. I acknowledge that my own critique may also be subject to these factors. Hermeneutically, by exploring and interpreting the Christian tradition concerning the body, an alternate approach to these historical challenges in relation to our current context can be articulated.

In the early centuries of the church, as it grew within the Roman Empire, two tendencies emerged among early Christians. On one side, there was a strong ascetic inclination that viewed the body as inherently negative, necessitating its subjugation through neglect or engaging in physically demanding tasks (such as the case of Simon the Stylite). On the other side, which was more commonly found within certain gnostic circles, there was a tendency to consider the body as irrelevant. Despite differences, both tendencies shared a common belief: the body was considered of lesser value compared to what was referred to as the soul. As such, it was either to be disregarded or actively resisted.

The existence of the soul (spirit will be used interchangeably throughout) has been a timeless question that has captivated the minds of philosophers and theologians. It continues to be a subject of profound contemplation today. At its core, this inquiry raises existential concerns about what it means to be human and the possibility of life beyond physical death. The heart of the matter lies in the inherent duality embraced by certain traditional perspectives on the soul, which often clashes with scientific viewpoints denying its existence. However, focusing solely on these opposing positions obscures the vast array of other perspectives that exist within the debate.

Nancey Murphey argues that the understanding of the soul and its relationship to the body has varied over time. Ancient philosophy and studies of Scripture and theology offer diverse opinions on the subject. Pinpointing the exact origin of the belief that our soul is a distinct aspect of ourselves, separate from the physical body, remains elusive. However, evidence from various burial practices, including those observed in Neanderthal cultures, indicates a belief in the continuity of existence beyond death. This is exemplified by the inclusion of specific items in burials, symbolizing the individuals' aspirations to carry them into the afterlife. Whether it be the pharaohs of ancient Egypt, or individuals from enslaved backgrounds, this pattern of belief persists across different societies and historical periods.

Research suggests that belief in the existence of a soul is commonly held by most people, while it is less prevalent within the scientific community.[1] The AWARE study, conducted to explore various dimensions of near-death experiences (NDEs), including the existence of the soul, yielded inconclusive results.[2] Their hypothesis suggests, however, that if individuals who are clinically dead undergo experiences outside of their physical bodies during cardiac arrest, it becomes more plausible to consider the existence of a soul-like entity. However, confirming this scientifically seems to be a distant goal.

In the Christian tradition, as well as in other religious traditions, there is a desire to affirm the presence of an entity related to the body but distinct from it. This indicates that the question of the soul, its nature, and its historical conceptualization remains diverse and unresolved. Within the context of the book where her article appears, Murphey aimed to make sense of the philosophical, theological, biblical, ethical, and scientific development surrounding the question, "Whatever happened to the soul?"[3] She suggests that any understanding of the soul should satisfy these disciplines to be considered truly Christian. Broadly speaking, her stance is that a Christian conception of the soul should be connected to a non-reductive physicalism, perceiving the soul as an embodied reality while not reducing it to the functions of the body.

Theological and biblical perspectives exhibit diversity, with both dualistic and more holistic understandings of the relationship between the body and the soul in the offing. Her exploration of philosophy and science reveals a similar diversity, yet ultimately affirms the interdependence of the mind on physical processes, as indicated by biology, neuroscience, and cognitive science. These disciplines shed light on specific faculties historically attributed to the soul. Hence, the proposal offered in this chapter is in sympathy with affirmations of the embodied nature of soul (spirit) within

---

1. Barrett, *Born Believers*.
2. Parnia et al., "*Aware Study,*" 1799–1805.
3. The oft touted difference between Greek dualist and Hebrew holistic perspectives is also fraught. Murphey suggests, "So it is clear that recent theological and biblical scholarship has not conclusively settled the issue. Biblical scholars are closer to consensus than theologians, but the dichotomy "Greek dualism versus Hebraic holism" is an oversimplification, and the typical method used to address this issue-studies of word usage-is now recognized to be inadequate." See, Murphey, "Human Nature," 1–29.

the body, where there is a dynamic interplay between the two. This view is, therefore, connected to certain emergent perspectives where spirit/soul/mind are emergent from the body but have levels of downward causation and become a location for divine/human engagement. I argue that a hermeneutical task that takes seriously our soul/spirit as embodied, and not a distinct ontological substance, offers practical and theoretical perspectives helpful for an embodied hermeneutic that is ethically informed. It is one that moves beyond the early gnostic and acetic alternatives, while also moving beyond reductive materialism or dualism. It places a high value on the body which can be supplemented by certain theological concepts which can further ground an embodied ethic.

There is a strong tradition of the body as a form of ethical and political protest across religious traditions. One can think of Martin Luther King, and those at the Edmund Pettus bridge, who place their bodies in the way of injustice. The other powerful image, regardless of one's particular view of the action, is seen in the self-immolation of a Buddhist monk made famous in Vietnam. The dominant paradigm in psychology today also emphasizes the importance of seeing the human being as a connected whole that is biological, sociological and psychological (the Bio-Psycho-Social model). This interconnection notes that psychological concepts and thoughts can influence the body. Changes in one's social environment can change ones genetic outlook (the role of epigenetics). The better aspects of the acetic tradition remind us that bodily adjustments can shape our psychological and spiritual experiences.

The argument I would like to make is that Christians are well placed to make the hermeneutical move to affirm the validity of seeking to embody our ethics in the decisions we make about our body. We can choose to eat certain products that embody God's dream for the world. A Christian embodied hermeneutic can draw on a rich theological heritage that can speak to and ground such an ethic.

EMBODIED HERMENEUTIC

There are numerous theological concepts and doctrines well suited for developing an embodied hermeneutic that takes the ethical task seriously. How we interpret and engage with these are crucial to hermeneutics generally, and the interpretive task being undertaken here specifically. The incarnation is the most obvious (and often the most cited). The embodied nature of God is affirmed in the view that "God was in Christ." This doctrine has the potential to emphasize the sacredness of the physical world and human bodies. It underscores the value of our embodied lives and provides a theological basis for recognizing the importance of our bodies in ethical decision-making and engagement with the world. The idea of being created in the image of God, or more traditionally, *The Imago Dei*, suggests that human beings are created in the image and likeness of God. As Pannenberg has suggested, there are a range of options as to how this has been understood within the Christian tradition.[4] Some have wanted to suggest it says something about who we are in relation to God, while others that it focusses more on our task as representatives of God on earth, or perhaps a combination of the two. Regardless of one's theological proclivities on this issue, the doctrine itself can contribute to an embodied theological ethic by affirming the inherent worth, dignity, and equality of all human beings. It affirms the sacredness of human bodies while simultaneously calling for the recognition of God's connection to each person.

Embracing an embodied theological ethic aligns with this incarnational thinking by affirming the physical nature of human existence. Further, it can promote justice, equality, and respect for all individuals as being stewards of God's good earth. The image of God is directly related to this in affirming God's involvement with the world, and as one who partners with humanity in the responsible care of the earth and its resources. It calls for an ecological awareness, a quest for sustainability, along with the protection of the natural world. I believe an embodied theological ethic can draw from this in recognizing the interconnectedness between human beings and their environment, and by advocating for environmental justice. The concept of the kingdom of God (while noting certain problematics with its masculine features) also speaks to the vision of a just and compassionate society, characterized by love, peace, and the well-being of all (features of kingdom living). By emphasizing the transformative nature of God's involvement on Earth, it can lead to an active engagement in building a more equitable, just, and inclusive world.

An embodied theological ethic, that takes seriously the hermeneutical challenge, aligns with this vision, I suggest, by advocating for social justice, challenging oppressive systems, and working towards the realization of kingdom values in the here and now (more of this to come). These theological ideas, or lenses, that I have briefly touched on, provide a framework for understanding the significance of our bodies, the interconnectedness of all beings, our responsibility as stewards of creation, and the pursuit of justice and compassion. Hermeneutically, by engaging in these theological concepts, an embodied theological ethic can find theological grounding and

---

4. Pannenberg, *Anthropology*, 47–50.

inspiration for its principles and practices. Broadly though, before delving into specifics, what would the implications of this hermeneutical endeavour?

One such implication, I suggest, is that an embodied theological ethic recognizes the profound significance of our physical bodies in our spiritual and moral lives. Hermeneutics does not happen in a vacuum but can have bodily consequences. It acknowledges that our bodies are not mere vessels for our consciousness, or souls, but are integral to our existence and engagement with the world. This perspective validates that our bodies are locations for both experiencing and expressing our beliefs, values, and ethical choices. It emphasizes the unity of body and soul/spirit, and the interconnectedness between our physicality and our moral agency. This will become apparent when I offer an example and framework for what an embodied ethic might look like that demonstrates the importance of an embodied hermeneutic more generally.

An embodied theological ethic also calls for the integration of faith and action, noting that our beliefs and values should be reflected in *how we live* our how our lives engage with the world (think of the example offered earlier with the protest at the Edmund Pettus bridge). It challenges us to align our ethical choices, and behaviors, with the principles and teachings with the best of our religious or spiritual traditions. In my opinion, this integration involves a commitment to social justice, compassion, and the pursuit of the common good. It encourages us to be actively involved in addressing systemic injustices, promoting inclusivity, and advocating for the well-being and flourishing of all people, particularly the marginalized and vulnerable. I will offer a practical example of this later with the SHE (sustainability, health, ethics) acronym and how this might function to achieve these goals. The body *is not* merely a vessel for the soul but an integral aspect of our being. Our physical experiences and interactions shape our moral choices and how we choose to relate to each other and the world around us. Along with these theological offerings, panentheism, as a philosophy of religion idea, can further ground an embodied hermeneutic and its ethical task.

PANENTHEISM AND EMBODIED HERMENEUTICS

There are different interpretive traditions when wrestling with the God/World relationship. Panentheism is one such tradition that I believe is important when considering an embodied hermeneutic from a theological and philosophical standpoint. Panentheism asserts that God is both immanent within the world and yet transcendent.[5] All things are in God and God

5. Culp, "Panentheism."

is in all things.[6] God is, therefore, intimately present in every aspect of creation while simultaneously surpassing it. This understanding provides a framework that has the potential to inform and enrich our reflection on an embodied hermeneutic.

Panentheism does not seek to create an unbridgeable gap between reality and God but rather attempts to affirm both the inherent sacredness and interconnectedness of existence. The thinking goes, that if God is immanently present in every aspect of creation, including the physical realm, then our bodies too, as part of that creation, hold inherent value. This recognition challenges any inclination to devalue or neglect the body (as we noted has happened historically within the Christian tradition). It further emphasizes the significance of our ethical considerations that honor and care for our physical self, along with the embodied experiences of others. Crucially, thinking panentheistically, has the potential to encourage an ecological awareness and a holistic approach to ethics. By recognizing God's presence in the natural world, panentheism calls for us to be stewards of that world, promoting both sustainable practices and responsible care for the environment. Is this not a good outcome for our hermeneutical explorations?

Panentheism also fosters a relational understanding of ethics. If God is intimately present within each person and the world, our ethical actions extend beyond our own narrow individualistic concerns. An embodied hermeneutic, shaped by panentheism, invites us to consider the impact of our choices on others. Perhaps controversially for some, it encourages us to recognize that God can never be totally separate from others, suggesting a solidarity that transcends boundaries, affirming the inherent worth of every person. Panentheism can also challenge our dualistic thinking by noting the interconnectedness of the spiritual and the physical aspects of reality. It rejects the notion of a rigid separation between the sacred and the secular, inviting us to integrate our spiritual beliefs and values with our embodied existence (no easy task). This integration fosters a more holistic and authentic approach to ethics, as our spiritual convictions are not detached from our everyday lives, but rather are woven into the fabric of our actions and our engagement with the world.

The emphasis on the soul/spirit as embodied, along with several of the theological doctrines explored to date, including the affirmation of Panentheism, provides the grounding for a hermeneutical journey that culminates in embodiment. I suspect this is hardly controversial. In the second part of this chapter, I will now ground the previous hermeneutical undertaking by using these theological concepts and reflections for an embodied ethics.

---

6. Clayton, "Varieties of Panpsychism."

One that takes seriously our current and contextual challenges. I intend to further provide a practical example of what an embodied theological might then look like, which I believe is the natural outcome of taking seriously an embodied hermeneutic.

ECOLOGY, EMBODIED HERMENEUTICS AND ETHICS

Climate change is a deeply polarizing issue in many countries around the world. Christians remain divided on human-driven climate change but have tended to take conservative positions on this and related issues. The difficulty with climate change is the difficulty in understanding its effects. We can understand the result of acid rain in nearby environments, and pollution in our creek, making the connection between cause and effect more visible. This is more difficult, although not impossible, with climate change. The retort by climate sceptics that climate change has always taken place, and is always happening, is certainly true. What is often overlooked though is that the amount of carbon we are emitting into the atmosphere has been significantly above normal carbon emissions historically.[7] The scientific community is unanimous in its assessment that humans are contributing decisively to this increase of carbon into the atmosphere.[8] One of the challenges we face is our ability as a species to make sacrifices for future generations when we might not see those benefits ourselves. Evolution has shown that we often make short-term decisions based on survival instincts. One could, however, make a strong evolutionary argument that if we don't do something about climate change our offspring will have no place to live and our "line" will die out. The example of an embodied ethics, still to be discussed, seeks to address some of these challenges. I believe this is important as human-driven climate change is the most serious existential threat we have faced as a species since we made that trek out of Africa to populate the earth.[9] Even putting climate change aside, our economic practices have resulted in significant damage to the environment and our food chain. Often Christians, by emphasizing an escapist eschatology, find themselves unable to meaningfully address these issues. An escapist eschatology is diametrically opposed to the quest for a Christian embodied hermeneutic.

---

7. Redfern, *Earth*.
8. IPCC, *Summary for Policymakers*.
9. Chomsky, "Prophet of Dystopia," 43.

CLIMATE CHANGE AND ESCAPIST ESCHATOLOGY[10]

In the contemporary Christian landscape, there is a noticeable shift away from liberal interpretations of the tradition. The prevailing inclination now leans towards a supernaturalist perspective, placing great emphasis on healing and prophecy, which often aligns with fundamentalist tendencies. Fundamentalism, a term with a complex history and contextual variations, has historically been closely linked to apocalyptic eschatology. However, it is important to recognize that while the majority of Christians believe in the concept of the second coming, there exist diverse understandings regarding its unfolding. Fundamentalist thinking places significant importance on the prediction of end times, even prompting James Barr in the 1970s to acknowledge its potential to exert a far-reaching influence on conservative evangelicalism.[11]

During the 1970s and 1980s, a notable alignment of apocalyptic reasoning with the political agenda of the Republican party emerged in the United States.[12] The Christian right in America has transcended passive waiting and actively engages in shaping the future to bring about a millennial era. This particular view of the end times has become deeply ingrained within evangelical thinking. As Clark explains, Pentecostals, fundamentalists, and evangelicals share the belief that the battle between God and Satan will unfold during the end times.[13] Fundamentalists, in particular, perceive this ongoing battle as manifesting on Earth itself.

Regretfully, this perspective on the future carries a catastrophic undertone, envisioning the destruction of the Earth rather than its renewal. It suggests that heaven serves as an escape from this world, where believers are called to ascend into the clouds. Žižek notes that fundamentalists tend to interpret the apocalypse in a strictly literalistic manner, grounded solely in biblical terms.[14] However, Keller encourages us not to concede the concept of apocalypse solely to fundamentalists.[15] Instead, she invites us to envision an alternative future, challenging the notion of a final, all-powerful intervention from above. An escapist eschatology, works against the theological concepts of incarnation, stewardship, *The Imago Dei* and the kingdom of God. It doesn't mesh well panentheism or the embodied nature of thinking about the body and soul. In opposition to an escapist eschatology

---

10. This section is informed from Macallan, *Counter Apocalyptic*.
11. Barr, *Fundamentalism*, 191.
12. McDowell and Kirkland, *Eschatology*, 20–21.
13. Clark, *From Angels to Aliens*.
14. Žižek, *Living in the End Times*, 336.
15. Keller, *God and Power*, 4.

I would now like to propose an example of an embodied hermeneutic that is informed by our discussion to date, and one that addresses several of the challenges already highlighted.

SHE: A FRAMEWORK FOR AN EMBODIED ETHIC[16]

I have published two articles focussing on this framework as an embodied ethic. What follows is a shortened version which functions to illustrate an outworking of several of the theological and philosophical claims made earlier in this chapter arguing for an embodied hermeneutic. Crucially, it seeks to respond to current challenges and move beyond an escapist eschatology.

John O'Donahue suggests that the body is our sole dwelling in the vast expanse of the universe. We have one body and one life. To actively participate, to the best of our abilities, in the realization of God's vision for the world, we can strive to maintain the health of our bodies for as long as possible. Of course, as our discussion demonstrated earlier, our bodies are not solely vehicles to achieve goals and be good stewards. Our bodies have intrinsic value as being made in God's image.

Yet, a deeper layer unfolds when we consider how changes in our dietary choices, and our perceptions thereof, can catalyze personal and societal transformations. By embodying specific values through our food choices, we can embrace an embodied ethic that not only transforms ourselves but also affects the world around us in sympathy with an embodied hermeneutic and the theological proposals offered earlier. I therefore propose an acronym, SHE (Sustainability, Health, and Ethics), as a framework for an embodied ethic. Opting for sustainable, healthy, and ethical eating not only reshapes our individual lives but also carries the potential to reshape the world towards justice. This approach encapsulates the interconnected and relational nature of reality advocated by earlier, underscoring our shared journey in life and our collective responsibility for its stewardship. Our Christian tradition possesses the power to directly contribute to a brighter future for our planet. Adopting a SHE approach to food enables us to actively participate in shaping an alternative outcome, countering the current trajectory. It embodies an ethical commitment in a tangible way.

SUSTAINABILITY

Meat consumption has traditionally been the norm for the human species, and the notion of abstaining from meat appears challenging for many.

16. This section is drawn from two previous articles I have published in this area. See Macallan, *SHE*; Macallan, *Eating as Partnering*.

However, it is imperative, at the very least, to reject unsustainable and ecologically detrimental meat production practices, substantially reducing our meat intake. The beef industry alone accounts for approximately 30 percent of carbon emissions fuelling climate change. This stems from various factors, including the energy expended on growing livestock feed and the logistical processes involved in the industry. With the world's population projected to surpass 10 billion in the coming years, sustaining the entire planet on a meat-based diet is simply untenable.[17] Additionally, studies have demonstrated the incomparable calorie generation capacity of plant-based diets compared to meat-based ones.[18] Efficient and sustainable land use becomes crucial when considering the ethical value of ensuring food access for the least privileged among us. By reducing our meat consumption, we actively participate in realizing values that promote a more just and sustainable world, three times a day. This truly embodies an ethic that can transform the world through seemingly small actions.

Addressing climate change through dietary choices represents only a fraction of our potential impact. We also possess the opportunity to reduce carbon reliance in our homes, such as through the installation of solar energy systems whenever feasible. Although seemingly small, collective acts can initiate significant change. By embracing small, individual turnings like installing solar panels in our homes or workplaces, we actively engage in God's desire for the world. When faced with bewildering challenges and uncertain paths, embracing these small changes becomes a source of hope and progress. Returning to the topic of meat consumption, reducing our reliance on it becomes a tangible way to embody our ethics, even if it comes at a personal and social cost. Often, friends and family may struggle to understand the shift towards a plant-based diet, but the potential positive impact on sustainability, health, and ethics cannot be understated.

HEALTH

This brings us to the second element of the SHE acronym: health. The contemporary dietary landscape is fraught with debates and controversies, often characterized as "diet wars." While it is important to acknowledge the negative aspects of society's fixation on health and youth, we must not discount the fundamental importance of health for our overall well-being, both physically and mentally. Just because some individuals develop an unhealthy obsession with health does not negate the significance of prioritizing

---

17. Clark et al., "Which Diet?," 4110.
18. Pimentel, "Sustainability of Meat-Based and Plant-Based Diets and the Environment," 660–63.

our well-being. It is akin to acknowledging that overeating exists but does not negate the necessity of nourishing our bodies.

Applying the SHE grid to red meat consumption led me to the conclusion that reducing, if not eliminating its intake, aligns with sustainability, health, and ethics. However, the same evaluation does not universally apply to fish, as numerous studies highlight the significant health benefits associated with its consumption. Nevertheless, ethical considerations arise regarding the sustainability of fishing practices and the ecological consequences affecting our oceans.

ETHICAL CONSIDERATIONS

Ethics takes center stage in the final component of the SHE acronym, and perhaps most relevant to the theological affirmations concerning the kingdom of God and stewardship. Here we explore the questions surrounding the killing of animals. In relation to this, philosopher Dan Dombrowski prompts us to question the ethical fairness of killing sentient beings solely for the pleasure of eating them when there is no inherent necessity to do so.[19] This question may unsettle many individuals raised in a meat-consuming society. Dombrowski suggests that if there is a genuine need to consume meat due to hunger or health concerns, it can be ethically justified. However, within our present contexts, where plant-based diets can provide sufficient nutrients while being more sustainable and healthier, the ethical argument for meat consumption weakens. People draw the line differently when determining the threshold of sentient life, with some feeling comfortable consuming fish while others, like Peter Singer, revising their views on crustaceans.[20] Even if one believes it is ethically permissible to kill animals for consumption, it is crucial to reflect on the methods employed and the extent of suffering animals endure for our dietary preferences. Scientific research increasingly reveals the remarkable intelligence and emotional complexity exhibited by animals, including pigs, cuttlefish, octopuses, and squid. Separating lambs from their mothers for slaughter inflicts emotional trauma upon both, while factory farming causes considerable anxiety among cows and pigs. It is imperative to consider consuming animals that have been treated well, both in terms of their environment and the food they receive. An embodied ethic affirms the interconnected nature of all things.

In summary, by using the SHE framework, we can evaluate which foods align with sustainability, health, and ethics as embodied ethic. For me

19. Dombrowski, *Philosophy of Vegetarianism*.
20. Singer, *Animal Liberation*.

personally, the beef industry and red meat consumption fail to meet these criteria. However, in my research, I have found that consuming free-range organic eggs does pass the SHE test. It is important to continue exploring ethical dimensions and questioning our choices, as this fosters a deeper understanding of our interconnectedness with the world and its inhabitants.

Rejecting the notion that longstanding practices should remain unchanged, we recognize that we have continually evolved socially and must adapt accordingly. The SHE framework not only serves as a tool for personal decision-making but also enables the actualization of religious values in the world, thereby embracing an embodied ethic. By rejecting the cattle industry and reducing meat consumption, we contribute to the reduction of greenhouse emissions and the preservation of our environment. Additionally, we free up land and water for more efficient food production, catering to the needs of the world's poor. Prioritizing our health allows us to affirm our bodies as the only homes we have in the universe, enabling us to experience and explore the richness of life while actively participating in the creation of a better world. Taking ethics seriously means embracing and valuing all aspects of life, acknowledging the place of our fellow creatures within it. While we may not be able to eliminate all animal suffering, we can take solace in the fact that our conscious choices reduce the mental and emotional anguish they endure.

As science continues to advance, our understanding of animal intelligence and emotional complexity grows. This knowledge extends beyond mammals to encompass birds and cephalopods. Each person must reflect on their own moral boundaries and consider the treatment of animals before making dietary choices. The SHE acronym provides a guiding light in navigating the complexities of sustainability, health, and ethics, hopefully providing an example of a Christian embodied hermeneutic.

CONCLUSION

A Christian embodied hermeneutic is informed by theological, philosophical, and scientific perspectives seen as crucial to the hermeneutical task. The constructive proposal I have offered seeks to ground it in several of these perspectives in conversation with current challenges. The SHE acronym is offered as an example of this ethic, and how it might be applied. As a postconservative perspective, it moves beyond escapist eschatology to one that affirms the body and its relationship with, and as part of, the world.

BIBLIOGRAPHY

Barrett, Justin, *Born Believers: The Science of Children's Religious Belief.* New York: Free, 2012.

Chai, Clark B., et al. "Which Diet Has the Least Environmental Impact on Our Planet? A Systematic Review of Vegan, Vegetarian and Omnivorous Diets." *Sustainability* 11 (2019) 4110.

Chomsky, Noam. "*The Prophet of Dystopia.*" Interview with George Yancy. *New York Times,* April 17, 2017.

Clark, Lynn Schofield. *From Angels to Aliens: Teenagers, the Media, and the Supernatural,* Oxford: Oxford University Press, 2005.

Clayton, Philip. "Varieties of Panpsychism." In *Panentheism and Panpsychism,* 191–203. Leiden: Brill, 2020.

Culp, John. "Panentheism." In *The Stanford Encyclopedia of Philosophy,* edited by Edward N. Zalta. https://plato.stanford.edu/archives/fall2020/entries/panentheism/.

Dombrowski, Daniel. *Philosophy of Vegetarianism.* Amherst, MA: Massachusetts University Press, 1984.

Keller, Catherine. *God and Power: Counter Apocalyptic Journeys.* Minneapolis: Fortress, 2004.

Intergovernmental Panel on Climate Change (IPCC). "Summary for Policymakers." In *Global warming of 1.5°C. An IPCC Special Report on the impacts of global warming of 1.5°C above pre-industrial levels and related global greenhouse gas emission pathways, in the context of strengthening the global response to the threat of climate change, sustainable development, and efforts to eradicate poverty,* 1–32. 2018.

Macallan, Brian. "Eating as Partnering with God's Dream for the World." In *Partnering with God: Exploring Collaboration in Open and Relational Theology,* edited by Tim Reddish et al., 121–38. Grasmere, ID: SacraSage, 2021.

Macallan, Brian. "SHE (Sustainability, Health, Ethics)—A Grid for an Embodied Ethic." *Philosophies* 7 (2020) 1–12.

Macallan, Brian. "A Process Theology of Hope: The Counter Apocalyptic Vision of Catherine Keller." *Religions* 10 (2019) 584.

McDowell, John C., and Scott A. Kirkland. *Eschatology.* Grand Rapids: Eerdmans, 2018.

Murphey, Nancey. "Human Nature: Historical, Scientific, and Religious Issues." In *Whatever Happened to the Soul?: Scientific and Theological Portraits of Human Nature,* edited by Warren Brown et al., 1–29. Minneapolis: Fortress, 1998.

Pannenberg, Wolfhart. *Anthropology in Theological Perspective.* Edinburgh: T. & T. Clark.

Parnia, Sam, et al. "Aware-awareness During Resuscitation-a Prospective Study." *Resuscitation* 85 (2014) 1799–805.

Pimentel, David, and Pimentel, Marcia. "Sustainability of Meat-Based and Plant-Based Diets and the Environment." *American Journal of Clinical Nutrition* 78 (2003) 660–63.

Redfern, Martin. *The Earth: A Very Short History.* Oxford: Oxford University Press, 2003.

Singer, Peter. *Animal Liberation.* London: Vintage, 2015.

Žižek, Slavoj. *Living in the End Times.* London: Verso, 2010.

Chapter 22
Ecological Hermeneutics
CHERRYL HUNT

WHAT ARE ECOLOGICAL HERMENEUTICS?

In 2008, ecological biblical criticism was described as "a recent but growing interest in reading biblical texts in the light of the environmental and ecological challenges that face us in the twenty-first century."[1] Since then the need for such reflection on the biblical texts has become even more obvious; with academic studies and popular writings both providing ample evidence of ecological problems, this chapter will not attempt to explain the wider global context of such biblical studies or justify their value. In response to growing awareness of ecological crisis a large number of studies related to this topic are continuing to emerge. Consequently, there is no room here for consideration of non-biblical ecological hermeneutics or combination approaches such as eco-feminist hermeneutics.[2]

Like other "advocacy" readings of the Bible, ecological hermeneutics has a self-declared viewpoint, in this case to read the texts in light of the ecological situation; implicit in all these readings is a desired goal, to see what they might contribute to Christian ecotheological reflection. To this end, some approaches seek to show that the whole Bible has a positive orientation towards non-human creation while others are open to the possibility that parts of the Bible may be problematic in this regard.

Many studies of this type include rebuttals of claims that the Judeo-Christian tradition bears much responsibility for the exploitative attitudes and technologies that led to our present precarious position—what Lynn

---

1. Gooder, *Searching for Meaning*, 192.
2. For a range of different approaches see Marlow and Harris, *Oxford Handbook of the Bible and Ecology*.

White Jr. called an "ecologic crisis." Although he did not quote them specifically, White read the creation accounts in Genesis, describing humans being made in the image of God, as justifying a human right to "dominance" over animals. Consequently, he claimed Christianity, especially in the West, "is the most anthropocentric religion the world has seen"; it "not only established a dualism of man and nature but also insisted that it is God's will that man exploit nature for his proper ends."[3] White's paper has been cited over and over again in Christian responses to the ecological crises over the past few decades; these responses have included a range of scriptural readings which, while they each ascribe value to the Bible, and all read it in light of the ecological crises we face, differ in how they approach and engage with the texts. Trying to classify or group these diverse responses is, to some extent, artificial since there is a deal of overlap between different writers in the field. However, we will consider some examples here which might be said to represent three somewhat different angles of approach to the biblical texts. For each type of approach we shall focus especially on their readings of the texts of creation, on Jesus, and about "the End" (eschatology).

"THE BIBLE IS GREEN" APPROACH

Readings which could be grouped under this heading specifically challenge White's claims regarding dominance and anthropocentrism; they do this not only by presenting other, "greener" readings of the Genesis creation texts but also by seeking to present other parts of the canon as examples of a "green" attitude within biblical texts as a whole. This approach thus argues that the Christian Scriptures present an ecologically-promoting world-view; the Bible is really green. Whatever the history of the texts' use in justifying human dominance, if read aright, the Bible is really ecologically positive in its view of humanity's role and responsibilities *vis-à-vis* other creatures, and in ascribing intrinsic value to non-human creation. If it has been used to justify exploitation or careless use of creation in the past, that was due to a misreading. This perception of the eco-positive orientation of the overall biblical narrative, as we shall see, sometimes involves reinterpreting, or ignoring, passages that appear to be less eco-positive. This type of engagement with the biblical texts I am calling "the Bible is Green" approach.

FINDING THE WHOLE BIBLE TO BE GREEN

The Green Bible itself, published in 2008, is one just example of this hermeneutical approach; this is the text of the NRSV but with some passages

---

3. White, "Historical Roots of our Ecologic Crisis," 1205.

printed in green—those the editors deem relevant to creation as a whole, and humanity's relationship with it. Accompanying the biblical text is a set of supporting documents some of which are essays by different contributors, including Pope John Paul II on peace with creation, Ellen Bernstein presenting a Jewish perspective and N. T. Wright considering eschatological aspects; some of these other documents help illustrate the hermeneutical stance being taken in this project. For example, chronicling his own growing awareness of how the Bible could speak into ecological issues, Dave Bookless speaks of previously reading the texts as if he was wearing glasses that filtered out anything that didn't concern humans and their relationship with God; a similar metaphor appears in Calvin DeWitt's essay title: "Reading the Bible through a Green Lens."[4] The use of the lens metaphor raises an important question: is this approach characterized by the removal of a pre-existing lens which distorted or obscured ecotheologically relevant passages, that were always there but not noticed before—or is the greenness an artefact of what the contributors are looking for and *through*? Or might it perhaps be both?

The Preface of *The Green Bible* notes how this green lens is constructed: text printed green denotes "passages speaking directly to the project's core mission."[5] Noting that more passages could have been colored green, the Preface continues:

> . . . but the strongest and most direct passages were selected based on how well they demonstrate:
>
> - how God and Jesus interact with, care for, and are intimately involved with all of creation
> - how all the elements of creation—land, water, air, plants, animals, humans—are interdependent
> - how nature responds to God
> - how we are all called to care for creation[6]

Expressed slightly differently, a series of Bible studies within *The Green Bible* picks up "six green themes that appear throughout the biblical narrative": the goodness of creation, God's presence in and interaction with creation, humanity's interconnectedness with God and the whole of creation (including the claim that human beings are called to be "stewards of creation"), the link between creation care and social justice, the impact of human sin on

---

4. *Green Bible*, I-17, I-25–I-34.
5. *Green Bible*, I-15.
6. *Green Bible*, I-16.

creation, and the restoration and renewal (not the passing away) of creation as new heaven and new earth.[7]

Bookless sums up this approach well: "in the end it's not the colour of the ink that makes this a 'Green Bible'; it's the questions you ask as you read it."[8] This recognizes that the new ecologically related questions we bring to the biblical texts are shaping what we find there. Once people have seen passages as having relevance to the natural world, and humanity's relationship with it, they may appear obvious and self-evident but, in fact, generations of Christians may not have seen them because they did not bring to the texts the context and questions we have today. An effect of this strategy is that, often, ethical applications or broader claims are drawn directly from the biblical texts, again on the assumption that they are obvious; a few worked examples will illustrate this interaction of text with context.

ACCOUNTS OF CREATION: "SUBDUE" AND "HAVE DOMINION"

The central text lying behind White's arguments about Christianity, although not cited explicitly, is Gen 1:26–28, especially God's instruction to "fill the earth and subdue it; and have dominion" over all living creatures, on the land, or in the sea or air.[9] This injunction is generally seen as consequent upon, or closely associated with, the distinctive feature of humanity being made in the image of God, and therefore key to human self-understanding with regard to the rest of creation. How might this passage be read with a green lens? (Gen 1:1—2:12 are all printed in green.)

Rather than reading these verses as White does, as mandating "dominance" over and an instrumental attitude towards, non-human life forms, the "Green Bible Trail Guide" rather bluntly simply re-interprets this language of "subdue" (*kabash* in Hebrew) and "have dominion" (*radah*); acknowledging the two creation accounts in Genesis it states that "[b]oth are very clear that human beings were created to be the caretakers of the earth and to live in harmony with everything else God made."[10] More nuanced interpreters may note that the call of Gen 1:28 *precedes* the disobedience of the first human pair, and that the call to have dominion should be understood more as a "dominion of love," a ruling over the rest of the creation in the same manner as God rules;[11] in other words humans are called to support and care for creation as God is spoken of doing (as, for example, in Ps 84:3; 104:10–22;

---

7. *Green Bible*, 1221–35.
8. *Green Bible*, I-23.
9. Similar language is found in Ps 8:6.
10. *Green Bible*, 1226.
11. *Green Bible*, I-86–I-90.

Matt 6:26). Richard Bauckham supports this understanding of "dominion" in Gen 1:26–29 by reference to Ezek 34:2–4; here the harsh dominion of the "shepherds" of the people of Israel is contrasted with the way they should have ruled the people—by feeding and caring for them.[12] He also suggests that the call to "subdue" is not necessarily related to humanity being made in the image of God, as dominion is; *kabash* is only used regarding the land, not its inhabitants. So "subdue" may refer to agriculture, a necessary corollary to the multiplication of human numbers; it is consequent upon the need for the development of agriculture and the cultivation of land as the human population expanded in response to the injunction to "multiply" (Gen 1:28). Furthermore, Gen 2:15 speaks of Adam "tilling" the earth and "keeping" it, suggesting a more cooperative and intimate relationship than the harsh attitudes discussed by White. Arguments of this kind support the concept of humans having been given a positive role and responsibility of having to care for, nurture, and promote the flourishing of the land and of other living creatures, rather than to dominate and exploit them.[13] They often lie, unspoken, behind the blunter claims that the Bible is "clear that" or "says that" humans are meant to be caring for creation.

STEWARDSHIP

One key and influential development of these alternative, gentler readings of "subdue" and "dominion" has been the notion of humans being called to act as stewards over God's creation, with responsibility to manage it, to "exercise rule *on behalf of* God, not *instead of* God."[14]

While the concept of stewardship was very popular in some early eco-theological debates (for instance within Catholic and Anglican documents of the late 1980s/early 1990s), a number of serious drawbacks to it have been noted and it has not featured so prominently in more recent church reflections.[15] Firstly, there is the problem that the Genesis texts themselves do not refer to humanity as "stewards" of other-than-human creation; the claim that the Bible "teaches" us that we are called to be stewards of creation is based on an *interpretation* of the language of "subdue," "dominion" (Gen 1) and "till" (Gen 2) as discussed above. The references to stewards elsewhere in the Bible portray them as household or estate managers of their master's assets (for example, Gen 43:16 and some parables of Jesus including Luke 16:1–8) or, within the church, as stewards of "God's mysteries" (1

12. Bauckham, *Bible and Ecology*, 18.
13. Bauckham, *Bible and Ecology*, 17–19, 21–22.
14. Bauckham, *Bible and Ecology*, 30, emphasis original.
15. See, for example, Pope Francis, *Laudato Si'*.

Cor 4:1). There is no explicit description of humans as stewards of God's creation anywhere in the Scriptures.

Secondly, thinking of humanity as God's stewards is not an especially promising model for ecotheological reflection as it still places humanity in a position of authority and power over the rest of creation. This leads on into questions of how much control it would ever be possible for humans to exert over the natural world, and if creation actually needs managing at all, even if we could do so. (While human activity has certainly had a profound effect upon the earth and its ecosystems, we cannot control many natural processes and ecosystems will continue developing and changing with or without us.)

Thirdly, the whole notion of humanity being stewards casts God as an absent landlord who has left creation in our care—a notion which contrasts sharply with a number of biblical images of God/Jesus continuing to uphold the universe and providing support for all creatures (for example, Ps 104; Matt 6:26; 10:29; Col 1:17). It could also be argued that some biblical passages portray a relationship between God and the natural world in its own right, with no apparent "management," or even appearance, by humans; for instance, consider God's covenant with "every living creature of all flesh" following the account of the Flood (Gen 9:9–17) and read Job 38–41.[16]

GREEN JESUS

For Christian believers, called upon to imitate Christ in their lives, it is of great interest to see how the New Testament might contribute to ecological reflection. Some have pointed out that many of Jesus's parables or teaching illustrations employ images or examples from the other-than-human creation, and some affirm God's care for birds (Matt 6:26 // Luke 12:24 [green in *The Green Bible*]) and the obligations on humans to care for domestic animals (Matt 12:11 [in green]; Luke 13:15 [in black]). Such passages might reflect Jesus's awareness and appreciation of the natural world, although they may simply illustrate his use of images and metaphors familiar to both himself and his audience.

Unsurprisingly, given the approach as outlined in the Preface and the "green themes" noted above, *The Green Bible* has the cursing of the fig tree (Matt 21:18–19 // Mark 11:12–14, 20–21) in black ink. More curiously, the drowning of the Gadarene swine is green in Matthew's account (8:30–32) but black in the other two Synoptic Gospels (Mark 5:11–13; Luke 8:32–33). However, there is no direct engagement with these and other passages which potentially challenge any straightforward sweeping claims that the Bible is

---

16. For an early and more detailed examination of the problems with stewardship, see Palmer, "Stewardship."

green. Aside from such inconsistencies, a simple coloring of text may suggest that ecologically positive passages litter the pages of our bibles but it does not in itself promote a more critical or contextual interaction with the content. For example, the teachings noted above, that speak of God's caring for humble creatures like birds and flowers, do so in the context of counteracting *human* worries about the future: Jesus's conclusion is that, if God cares for humble creatures how much *more* will God care for his worrying audience. And they do not appear to generate any direct guidance on how humans should relate to other elements of creation.

ESCHATOLOGY

One final aspect of the "Bible is Green" approach is the way in which it handles biblical passages which speak of God bringing about "new heavens and new earth" (Isa 65:17–25 [a mix of green and black verses]; 2 Pet 3:13 [black]; Rev 21:1[green]). This is a particularly pressing question regarding passages that also speak of this heaven and earth passing away (e.g., Rev 21:1; see also Mark 13:31) and 2 Pet 3:12's call to believers to lead lives "waiting for and hastening [or earnestly desiring] the coming of the day of God." If these passages are understood to teach the replacement of the present world with a brand new one this might support an attitude towards ecological issues which Wright sums up as "Why wallpaper the house if it's going to be knocked down tomorrow?"[17] (Such attitudes are found among some Christian traditions.[18]) These texts might appear to contradict any notion of the biblical narrative as a whole being green.

A common response, among those working with a type of 'Bible is Green' approach, is to note the existence of passages that imply a greater degree of continuity between this creation and the future. Drawing on texts such as Rom 8:18–23 the argument is that God's overall redemptive project includes not just humans but all of creation, and that this involves not a brand new, replacement planet to which believers shall be taken but a renewed and restored creation that has a clear degree of continuity with the present. Rather than devalue the present world because it will eventually be destroyed anyway "we are called to bring real and effective signs of God's renewed creation to birth even in the midst of the present age"; we have a

---

17. *Green Bible*, I-73.

18. The argument that ecological concern is not a priority for Christians is a feature of some strands within American evangelical thought. See Lowe "Climate Skepticism," especially 436.

mandate to promote the flourishing of the current creation however one might envisage God acting to restore it fully at the end.[19]

EVALUATING THE BIBLE FOR AND FROM EARTH'S PERSPECTIVE: THE EARTH BIBLE

If the "Bible is Green" approach finds the Bible as a whole to be ecologically positive, the next type of reading takes a more nuanced and analytical approach to its texts. Adopting a hermeneutics of suspicion, identification and retrieval the texts are first read with the suspicion that they are, as written, biased towards humanity and not centered on Earth, and/or they have been traditionally interpreted by anthropocentric readers. Then, an attempt is made to break away from this anthropocentrism and read them while identifying with, or as if from the perspective of, Earth and its community, (rather than focus on human beings); this identification allows one to try and retrieve the "voices" of Earth and its components, sometimes from passages where they are not apparent. In this process, some texts are found to be unhelpful or inadequate in resourcing a positive approach towards the Earth and these "grey" texts may have to be omitted from ecotheological deliberations. On the other hand, "green" texts which are found to illustrate one or more principles of "ecojustice" may help in funding "a radical re-orientation towards our planet."[20]

This approach to ecological hermeneutics was pioneered by the Earth Bible Project, originating among Australian scholars led by Norman Habel. This project sought to explore and evaluate different biblical texts in terms of a pre-established set of "ecojustice principles" that were formulated in dialogue between ecologists and biblical scholars:

- *The Principle of Intrinsic Worth*: the universe, Earth and all its components have intrinsic worth/value.
- *The Principle of Interconnectedness*: Earth is a community of interconnected living things that are mutually dependent on each other for life and survival.
- *The Principle of Voice*: Earth is a subject capable of raising its voice in celebration and against injustice.
- *The Principle of Purpose*: the universe, Earth and all its components are part of a dynamic cosmic design within which each piece has a place in the overall goal of that design.

---

19. Wright's essay, *Green Bible*, I-72–I-85, quoted at I-85. See also Bauckham, *Bible and Ecology*, 164–8 on the kingdom as renewal of creation.

20. Habel, *Inconvenient Text*, xvii.

- *The Principle of Mutual Custodianship*: Earth is a balanced and diverse domain in which responsible custodians can function as partners, rather than rulers, to sustain a balanced and diverse Earth community.

- *The Principle of Resistance:* Earth and its components not only suffer from injustices at the hands of humans, but actively resist them in the struggle for justice.[21]

Biblical texts may then be evaluated against whichever principle(s) seem appropriate to their content. The project initially generated a series of volumes of articles covering different texts within both Testaments, and has now produced other books including a new series of Earth Bible Commentaries. We will explore this approach, as the previous one, under the three headings of creation, Jesus, and eschatology.

CREATION

Habel examines the "Earth Story" in Gen 1 with reference to the intrinsic worth of earth. He finds that the story of human origins dominates an account that otherwise has Earth at its center and that, until the advent of humans, clearly affirms Earth as having intrinsic value. Habel disagrees with the "greener" interpretations of "subdue" and "have dominion" put forward by others (see above); he understands the language of Gen 1:26–28 to be that of "harsh control" and calls for us to re-read the creation texts from the perspective of Earth in order to recognize its intrinsic worth.[22] Doing so, Habel finds a story of Earth in Gen 1:1–25 that is interrupted and disrupted by the appearance of humans in verse 26.

Elsewhere, identifying with Earth and its community, Habel speaks of Earth as God's "partner in the creation process" until the "horrible intrusion" of a different, anthropocentric narration at which point Earth becomes "a slave prostrate at the feet of human royals."[23] Moving onto Gen 2, Habel finds an alternative story, one where humans are part of a community of creatures and are called upon to serve and preserve the land (his translation of Gen 2:15).[24] Rejecting the possibility of harmonizing the different accounts—the "grey" one in Gen 1 and the "green" one of Gen 2—Habel suggests that Jesus's teaching offers a means to set aside the former; Jesus's teaching and modeling of a life of service to others, as the servant messiah,

---

21. Habel, *Inconvenient*, 61.
22. Habel, "Geophany," 46.
23. Habel, *Inconvenient*, 67.
24. Habel, *Inconvenient*, 69.

"supersedes the mandate to dominate."[25] Thus, Habel trumps what he finds to be a grey Old Testament text with a christological understanding of power as service.

JESUS'S TEACHING

In other Earth Bible publications, there is detailed analysis and exploration of the possible presence of ecojustice principles in the Gospels, such as an examination of Matthew's account of Jesus's teaching against worry (Matt 25:25–33). Stressing the background to the Sermon on the Mount in the Hebrew Scriptures' teaching on features of the rule of God, Adrian Leske associates the coming of the kingdom with a deliverance characterized by sufficient food, drink and clothes to wear (*contra* the covenant curses in Deut 28:48). Those in the kingdom can rely on God's provision just as do the birds who trust in God's goodness. However, Leske sees this as more than a simple argument that there is no need for human anxiety. Noting the Old Testament links between the flourishing of humans and that of the Land with its other inhabitants, (for example Hos 4:1–3), he suggests that the coming of the kingdom of God transforms the whole Earth community. This implies the intrinsic value and interconnectedness of every element of creation. While he does not use the terminology himself, Leske's treatment would thus appear to declare this passage "green." Despite its being presented as an argument to assuage human anxiety, consideration of its Old Testament backdrop allows us to see how it may be read from the perspective of Earth and retrieved for ecotheological reflection.[26]

ESCHATOLOGY

While other contributors to the Earth Bible volumes differ in the degree to which they apply the ecojustice principles, and not all conclude by critiquing texts that are suspected of being complicit in humanity's mistreatment of the Earth community, the suspicion and retrieval (or non-retrieval) process can be clearly seen in another Earth Bible essay. This considers the passage noted above, 2 Pet 3:7–13, about "waiting for and hastening" the day when the elements of the cosmos melt away, and the heavens burn prior to the appearance of new heavens and earth (vv. 12–13). As might be anticipated from the tenor of this passage, the Earth Bible approach suggests that this

---

25. Habel, *Inconvenient*, 76.
26. Leske, "Matthew 6.25–34."

"presents insurmountable problems for a retrieval of the text from the perspective of Earth."[27]

Taking different passages through the process of suspicion of anthropocentrism, identification with the viewpoint of Earth and its community and, when possible, retrieval, has brought out a number of interesting and thought-provoking readings of the biblical texts. Some of these produce green readings and others grey; of the latter, some may be retrieved through identification with Earth, qualified by other texts, or understood as superseded by the New Testament portrayal of Christ. Others may be irretrievably "grey" but may be of value in alerting us to the cries of creation. With the pressing need for responses to the ecological crises that face us, we can "choose the green rather than the grey texts as guides for life."[28] In either case, a close analysis and picking over of the texts is required and the acid test is one of adherence to one or more of the principles of ecojustice.

FOCUSING ON, AND WITH, ECO-RELEVANT BIBLICAL THEMES: THE EXETER PROJECT

If the first approach sees the whole Bible as providing ecologically-positive grounds for theological reflection, and the second suggests a critical examination is needed to distinguish valuable green texts from potentially damaging grey ones, then the third approach starts by assuming that the biblical materials do not, as they are, directly provide material for such reflection and do not provide ready-to-use ethical guidelines. A creative process of constructive re-reading is needed in light of the ecological circumstances we face.

It is helpful at this point to remind ourselves that a number of issues over the ages have been the subject of much dispute *within and among* churches and believers, because different texts may be used to support opposing theological and ethical stances. For instance, the campaign against slavery was supported *and* opposed using a wide range of biblical texts. Even accompanied by detailed exegesis and considerations of historical context, some texts remain open to more than one reading and therefore, on their own, do not necessarily offer directly usable clear contributions towards modern discussions. We construct meaning as our contemporary context interacts with our understanding of the text in its original context, shaped also by the history of its reception within the Christian tradition.[29]

---

27. Dyer, "When Is the End Not the End?," 55.
28. Habel, *Inconvenient*, 77.
29. Horrell, *Bible and the Environment*, 119–27.

At the same time, for many within the Christian tradition, their understanding of biblical authority does not allow them simply to set aside texts that fail to appear valuable when read in the light of ecojustice principles, even if many of those principles can be seen to be consonant with biblical concepts. How can we retain the sense of value in the texts while at the same time acknowledging that there is little direct guidance there on how to conduct ourselves within an ecological crisis of human making? How can we give the Bible a central role in re-thinking our theology to make it fit for purpose in our current situation without overly simplistic use of proof texts or what might seem a cavalier attitude towards those passages we find hostile to Earth and its communities?

The Exeter Project[30] assumes that texts across the canon need to be considered together, in light of one another and of scientific knowledge, in order to form an ecotheological "doctrinal lens." Considering the biblical texts more widely, through this lens, allows us to find themes conducive to ecotheological reflection, and to suggest a number of biblically-rooted ethical stances, *without claiming that they are simply being read off the page.* This approach by our team, led by David Horrell, recognizes that the Bible is composed of ancient texts from a time when ecological damage was localized and limited to instances of mining waste or soil degradation from overuse; the biblical authors were not dealing with the issues which we bring to the texts, so we need to take care when seeking guidance on questions they were not addressing. Rather than assume "green" texts are there to be found, we need to acknowledge that a process of construction is needed to "make" readings that can contribute towards ecotheological reflection.

CREATION—AND "THE END"

As with the two other approaches, texts were subject to careful exegesis, but we sought to self-consciously re-view the texts in a way shaped by the Christian tradition but also by contemporary scientific contexts and information.

Firstly, we examined closely the two New Testament passages most often cited in Christian explorations of ecological issues: Rom 8:19–23 and Col 1:15–20. Having considered both contemporary analyses of these texts from the Pauline corpus and a range of historical understandings of them, we concluded that both passages were based around a "story" about creation: the other-than-human elements of creation (Rom 8) or the whole cosmos (Col 1). Both of these stories, which have their bases within Old Testament texts, imply that, in some ill-defined way, all of creation, and not

---

30. For an accessible but longer account of this see Horrell, *Bible and the Environment*, 117–44.

just humanity, is included in God's reconciling, liberating work. Rom 8:21 speaks of creation anticipating freedom and Col 1:20 of "all things" being made at peace with God. Both also indicate human involvement in this process but neither offer off-the-peg ecotheological applications.

We then attempted to construct what we called an ecotheologically-informed "lens" taking account not only of biblical scholarship and ecotheology, but also of science. For instance, we recognized that we were only looking in this way due to the pressing scientific evidence for ecological crisis and the advisability of formulating a response consonant with what could be shown to be traditional Christian teaching. In the light of evolutionary and genetic sciences we eliminated any understanding of these texts which indicated the "decay" of Rom 8:21 was a direct result of human sin; there is evidence of death, suffering and extinction since life has been in existence and long before humans evolved. And we acknowledged the difficulty in understanding in what manner non-human creatures needed or would experience, reconciliation to their Creator. However, this construal of the creation story may be seen to suggest a general ethical imperative: for Christians to promote peace and reconciliation between all creatures, not just humanity.

To put some ethical meat on this bare bone, we proceeded to examine other Pauline texts in light of our "lens"; this brought into sharper focus other texts which seemed likely to contribute to the formation of ethical frameworks relevant to ecological crises, including believers' participation in Christ, the present-but-not-yet-fully-present new creation, and Paul's inaugurated eschatology. These all appear in 2 Cor 5:14–21 together with reconciliation.

A WIDER BIBLICAL APPROACH

Horrell then widens this approach, listing a total of six traditional biblical themes that might be brought together to shape our reading of the biblical texts as a whole and that might contribute fruitfully towards scientifically-informed ecotheological reflection: the goodness of creation; the position of humanity firmly within the creation community, even if human beings do have a special role (a dependency and relatedness which is supported by studies of biology and ecology); an interconnectedness, for good or bad, between humans and the land/Earth (such as the ramifications of changes within ecosystems); God's covenant with *all* creation and the theocentric nature of all relationships; creation's call to praise God (scientific and theological accounts of life can both evoke wonder); God's redemptive project being concerned with the eschatological liberation and reconciliation of *all things*. While Horrell admits that many of these themes can be seen to parallel the Earth Bible principles, (for example, the call to praise God is similar to the principle of voice), the suggestion is that a formulation rooted within traditional Christian theological categories will be more persuasive to those within the Christian community than the idea of weighing up the value of Scripture against less explicitly connected ecojustice principles.

These themes, or "doctrinal lenses" might then shape our reading of the biblical texts to allow us to re-view our traditional understandings of, for example, the scope of God's concern in redemption. As Horrell emphasizes, using them "does not imply any pretence that this is simply what the Bible teaches, nor does it deny that there are plenty of other currents in the biblical tradition."[31] It attempts to re-read ancient texts in a consciously constructive new way to find therein resources for contemporary situations, but it also attempts to draw relevant ethical principles from this re-reading exercise. For example, one might argue that the New Testament promotion of an imitation of Christ's self-giving for others (e.g., Phil 2:4–11) could be extended towards other living creatures. In the same way as the Corinthians are asked to give out of their surplus to ensure others have enough (2 Cor 8:8–15), Christians might consider a restriction in their desire for more, in order to free up space and resources on the planet for other species to flourish. While it is still hard to see clear ethical imperatives within the pages of the Bible, adopting vegetarianism might be seen as a move towards promoting peace among all creatures.[32] More specific strategies would rely on input from the sciences although the motivation for them would be based firmly within these readings of the Christian texts and traditions.

THE PURPOSE OF ECOTHEOLOGICAL HERMENEUTICS: MOVING TOWARDS AN ETHICAL RESPONSE

Studies of biblical texts are not undertaken without purpose; as the earth and its inhabitants face a huge anthropogenic period of change and upheaval we turn to the Christian Scriptures for guidance and bases for decision-making. In such situations our hermeneutics are inevitably ethically-driven but it is important to acknowledge that we are not simply reading off instructions from the texts. A number of different approaches may be viable—some may find stewardship a useful concept to generate ethical guidelines—but we must seek to remember that we are doing something to the texts in order to construct this motif. We are not *just* reading but *making a* reading,

---

31. Horrell, *Bible and the Environment*, 136.
32. Horrell, *Bible and the Environment*, 140–43.

constructing meaning in ways inevitably shaped by our context and concerns, and the process of working with other Bible readers to face ecological challenges will be easier if we each acknowledge the different ways in which we are approaching these ancient texts.

BIBLIOGRAPHY

Bauckham, Richard. *Bible and Ecology: Rediscovering the Community of Creation*. London: Darton, Longman & Todd, 2010.

Dyer, Keith D. "When Is the End Not the End? The Fate of Earth in Biblical Eschatology (Mark 13)." In *The Earth Story in the New Testament*, edited by Norman C. Habel and Vicky Balabanski, 44–56. London: Sheffield Academic, 2002.

Gooder, Paula. *Searching for Meaning: An Introduction to Interpreting the New Testament*. London: SPCK, 2008.

The Green Bible. London: HarperCollins, 2008.

Habel, Norman C. "Geophany: The Earth Story in Genesis 1." In *The Earth Story in Genesis*, edited by Norman C. Habel and Shirley Wurst, 34–48. Sheffield: Sheffield Academic, 2000.

———. *An Inconvenient Text: Is a Green Reading of the Bible Possible?* Hindmarsh, SA: Australasian Theological Forum, 2009.

Horrell, David G. *The Bible and the Environment: Towards a Critical Ecological Biblical Theology*. Edited by John Rogerson. Biblical Challenges in the Contemporary World. 2nd ed. London: Routledge, 2014.

Leske, Adrian M. "Matthew 6.25–34: Human Anxiety and the Natural World." In *The Earth Story in the New Testament*, edited by Norman C. Habel and Vicky Balabanski, 15–27. London: Sheffield Academic, 2002.

Lowe, Benjamin S., et al. "Climate Skepticism, Politics, and the Bible." In *The Oxford Handbook of the Bible and Ecology*, edited by Hilary Marlow and Mark Harris, 425–44. Oxford: Oxford University Press, 2022.

Marlow, Hilary, and Mark Harris. *The Oxford Handbook of the Bible and Ecology*. Oxford: Oxford University Press, 2022.

Palmer, Clare. "Stewardship: A Case Study in Environmental Ethics." In *The Earth Beneath: A Critical Guide to Green Theology*, edited by Ian Ball et al., 67–86. London: SPCK, 1992.

Francis, Pope. *Laudato Si'*. Vatican City: Holy See, 2015.

White, Lynn, Jr. "The Historical Roots of Our Ecologic Crisis." *Science* 155 (1967) 1203–7.

SECTION 3

Contextual Interpretation

Chapter 23
Intercultural Hermeneutics
LARRY W. CALDWELL

Intercultural hermeneutics is the study of the theory and practice of interpretation between cultures (in our case, involving the Bible).[1] There are two important components to intercultural hermeneutics and the Bible. First, intercultural hermeneutics involves using culturally appropriate understandings, customs, and behaviors to best communicate the truths of the Bible within a culture. Second, intercultural hermeneutics uses culturally appropriate hermeneutical approaches to the Bible that are indigenous to a local culture. The first component is usually done by intercultural Bible interpreters today. The second component much less so. This chapter argues that both components are necessary for holistic intercultural hermeneutics.

In a real sense, all Bible interpretation is intercultural. This is true even if the Bible interpreters, as well as the recipients of the interpretation, are from the same culture. How so? Because generational and/or socio-economic differences, and the like—even in mono-cultural contexts—may have significant impacts on the Bible interpretation task. But it is especially when Bible interpretation travels from mono-cultural encounters

1. There are many resources that speak to the interplay between hermeneutics, culture, and the Bible. Among the more significant see: Segovia and Tolbert, *Reading from this Place*; Smith-Christopher, *Text and Experience*; Sugirtharajah, *Vernacular Hermeneutics*; Dietrich and Luz, *Bible in a World Context*; de Wit et al., *Through the Eyes of Another*; Sugirtharajah, *Voices from the Margin*; Premnath, *Border Crossings*; West, *Reading Other-Wise*; Vaka'uta, *Reading Ezra 9–10 Tu'a-Wise*; Redford, *Missiological Hermeneutics*; Keener and Carroll R., *Global Voices*; Wrogemann, *Intercultural Hermeneutics*; McCaulley, *Reading While Black*; Brooks, *Interpreting Scripture* Across Cultures; Roth et al., *Reading the Bible Around the World*; and Caldwell, *Bible in Culture*. And, though not dealing with the Bible per se, cf. Xie, *Agon of Interpretations*.

to multi-cultural and cross-cultural ones such interpretation moves into the more complicated realm of intercultural hermeneutics. Here is where paying attention to the cultural dimensions of the intercultural encounters becomes even more crucial in the doing of Bible interpretation.

This chapter examines some of the complexities of intercultural hermeneutics and the interplay between cultures and Bible interpretation. Part one begins by answering three crucial questions related to the study of intercultural hermeneutics, necessary questions that shape the reality of intercultural hermeneutics as it is done today. Part two examines intercultural hermeneutics in light of the discipline of ethnohermeneutics, a discipline uniquely suited to valuing the distinct hermeneutical approaches already used by local cultures, approaches that are often neglected in the study of intercultural hermeneutics. Part three will conclude by examining the practice of ethnohermeneutics being done in one specific African cultural context as an example for the doing of intercultural hermeneutics in any cultural context.

THREE QUESTIONS RELATED TO INTERCULTURAL HERMENEUTICS

At least three questions arise in relationship to the study of the interplay between Bible interpretation and cultures known as intercultural hermeneutics. First, by referring to intercultural hermeneutics do we mean a universal, supracultural hermeneutical approach to Bible interpretation used by all cultures, whether such cultures are from the global North (Western world) or global South (non-Western world)? Or, second, do we mean the hermeneutical approach(es) that a foreign Bible interpreter (typically from the global North) brings to another culture (typically found in the global South) and, because of the dynamics of the colonization process, this receiving culture then values as their own? Or, third, do we mean Bible interpreters, primarily in global South cultures, who use indigenous hermeneutical approach(es) intrinsic to their own cultures as they do Bible interpretation in their own cultural contexts? Let's look at these three questions in more detail.

QUESTION ONE: ONE SUPRACULTURAL HERMENEUTICAL APPROACH?

First, is there one supracultural approach to hermeneutics for all cultures? Asking the question another way, is there a single universal approach to Bible interpretation which should be used by every culture of the world? If the answer to these questions is "yes," then there would be no need for intercultural hermeneutics![2] The truth, however, is that the idea of one preferred universal approach to hermeneutics grew out of the colonialization efforts of European and American missionary movements of the nineteenth and twentieth centuries. During these two centuries these global North missionaries brought their preferred grammatical-historical approach to Bible interpretation with them as they carried out their missionary activities among the cultures of the global South. Simply put, the grammatical-historical approach, using the tools of biblical criticism, stresses that a biblical passage must be understood in light of at least three factors: 1) the syntax of the words used; 2) the context in which the words are found; and 3) the underlying historical setting behind the words. While each of these factors is important, to say that the grammatical-historical approach should be the only, or even primary, approach for all cultures to use when interpreting the Bible is not only incorrect, it is contrary to the very idea of intercultural hermeneutics.

So how did the grammatical-historical approach gain privileged acceptance worldwide? While there were many reasons, one of the primary reasons was because of the founding of Bible colleges and seminaries by global North missionaries in the global South, and the wholesale implementation of global North curriculums within these schools. With such foundations the grammatical-historical approach soon became dominant and, in the minds of some, took on a universal appeal. The truth, however, is that the grammatical-historical approach *is itself a culturally influenced approach* that grew out of the post-Enlightenment context of the global North and was grounded in a rationalist worldview that permeated the hermeneutical approaches of that context. As a result, the grammatical-critical approach may be a helpful hermeneutical approach for those individuals and cultures with post-Enlightenment rationalist worldview assumption. However, for those cultures without such worldview assumptions there may be better and more appropriate hermeneutical approaches. The grammatical-historical approach is one approach to hermeneutics, and it can be a helpful one, but it is certainly not the only approach, and clearly not a supracultural approach. There is no single universal approach to Bible interpretation.

---

2. Note, however, that some scholars today still hold to at least a modified understanding of one supracultural hermeneutical approach. See, for example, Chou, *Hermeneutics of the Biblical Writers* and Brooks, *Interpreting Scripture* Across *Cultures.*

QUESTION TWO: HOW HAS COLONIZATION SHAPED INTERCULTURAL HERMENEUTICS?

The second question relates to what we've just discussed concerning a supracultural approach, but from the perspective of the receiving cultures: should the hermeneutical approach brought by global North missionaries, and subsequently taught in global North-dominated Bible colleges and seminaries, be primarily and unquestionably used by those in global South local contexts? The answer to this question is both "yes" and "no." Yes, if the foreign hermeneutical approach is appropriate for the local culture, which is indeed sometimes the case in global South contexts. For example, the use of the grammatical-historical approach may make sense in urban areas with high levels of educational attainment among the populace. At the same time, it must be said that the grammatical-historical approach does have some helpful elements for all cultures to consider. But for the majority of global South contexts the answer will be no. Why? The answer to this question is "no" because of the reality of their colonial past of many of these global South cultures and the accompanying issues of power and authoritative knowledge.

As we have already briefly touched upon above, the hermeneutical approaches of the global North were duplicated in the global South through a colonization process that was a companion to the global North's missionary enterprise of the nineteenth and twentieth centuries. This colonization often created a tendency among global South Christians to assume, without question, that the Bible interpretation approaches they were taught by their colonizers were appropriate, and necessary, to use. Even though the colonizers are now long gone, this continuing deference to colonial power structures—including the curriculums still found today in many global South Bible colleges and seminaries—has affected theological education, including hermeneutics, in many ways. This is primarily seen in regard to curriculum relevance and to dismissing local ways of teaching and learning.

Recent ethnographic research shows that this dismissing of local ways results when those who are colonized eventually take on as authoritative a certain way of thinking or knowing that was at first foreign to that particular culture. This is known among anthropologists as "authoritative knowledge." Brigitte Jordan describes how this happens: " . . . frequently one kind of knowledge gains ascendance and legitimacy. A consequence of the legitimation of one kind of knowing as authoritative is the devaluation, often the dismissal, of all other kinds of knowing."[3] Jordan's words concerning the dismissal "of all other kinds of knowing" are particularly relevant for

---

3. Jordan, "Authoritative Knowledge and Its Construction," 56.

intercultural hermeneutics. The dominance of the global North's authoritative knowledge has not allowed individuals to value "other kinds of knowing" that have mostly been categorically dismissed. Most global North individuals, as the colonizers, have not even thought of this possibility; global South individuals, as the colonized, have oftentimes forgotten the relevancy of their own culture's learning and knowing styles. Such cultural forgetfulness often results in privileging a foreign hermeneutical approach—like the grammatical-historical approach—over other possible culturally appropriate local hermeneutical approaches. As a result, it is imperative that Christians in the global South (and increasingly in the global North) reexamine the validity of other kinds of knowing to see how these other kinds might be better incorporated into how Bible interpretation is done at the local level in every cultural context. This begins to get to the heart of intercultural hermeneutics.

QUESTION THREE: ARE LOCAL HERMENEUTICAL APPROACHES LEGITIMATE?

The third question relates to the new paradigm of intercultural hermeneutics facing the theological world in the twenty-first century. It can be slightly rephrased in light of the above discussion as follows: should global South Bible interpreters, who are doing Bible interpretation in their own global South cultural contexts, use culturally appropriate hermeneutical approaches intrinsic to their own contexts even if these approaches differ from the dominate hermeneutical approaches done by those in the global North? Of course, the answer is a resounding yes! No longer under the tyranny of a supposed supracultural hermeneutical approach (Question One), nor subservient to the privileged authoritative knowledge brought about by the theological power brokers of the colonial missionary enterprise (Question Two), global South Bible interpreters today are indeed free to search for and use indigenous hermeneutical approaches that work best for themselves and their people whatever their cultural context.

Unfortunately, already oftentimes highly conversant with the globally dominate global North grammatical-historical approach to hermeneutics, most global South Bible interpreters are neither looking for nor using indigenous hermeneutical approaches that are unique to their own cultures. Instead, they are using this foreign approach to answer Bible interpretation questions from their own unique cultural situations and perspectives. As we have already seen in the introduction, however, *both* components are necessary for the doing of holistic intercultural hermeneutics: culturally appropriate understandings *and* culturally appropriate hermeneutical approaches. There are, however, a growing number of global South exceptions.

One of the first to speak to the need to look for indigenous hermeneutics, and not rely on the hermeneutics of another culture, was the late African New Testament scholar Justin Upkong. Upkong referred to this indigenous hermeneutical approach as "inculturation hermeneutics," a phrase that emphasized "using an African conceptual frame of reference in interpreting the Bible in Africa rather than using another conceptual frame for interpretation and applying the result in the African context."[4] He specifically noted the uncritical use of the grammatical-historical approach:

> In any reading practice, the conceptual frame of reference used may be that of the reader's cultural community or of another. When, for example, Africans *uncritically* use the historical-critical method, which is informed by the Western conceptual frame of reference, they are using another cultural community's conceptual grid to read. An important aspect of inculturation hermeneutics is the use, in the interpretation process, of the conceptual frame of reference of the community within which interpretation is done. Thus in inculturation hermeneutics, texts are not appropriated with a foreign conceptual frame of reference and then applied to the African context; rather, an African conceptual frame of reference is used in appropriating the text. Historical tools are used critically and made to function with the African conceptual frame of reference. In that way the African people and their contexts are made the *subject* of interpretation.[5]

In the above quote Upkong is affirming the second component of intercultural hermeneutics. Furthermore, by using the phrase, "conceptual frame of reference," Ukpong referred to, among other things, a mindset that, as he said, "comprises a particular set of worldviews, values, disvalues, and basic assumptions about reality."[6] In other words, he is referring to the first component of the intercultural hermeneutical task.

Another global South scholar, who has dived deeply into intercultural hermeneutics to arrive at his own culture's indigenous hermeneutical approaches, is Oceania Old Testament professor Nāsili Vaka'uta. His landmark work, *Reading Ezra 9–10 Tu'a-Wise: Rethinking Biblical Interpretation in Oceania*, is a study of how to do global South intercultural hermeneutics using

---

4. Ukpong, "Inculturation Hermeneutics," 23.
5. Ukpong, "Inculturation Hermeneutics," 25, his emphasis.
6. Ukpong, "Inculturation Hermeneutics," 24.

the indigenous hermeneutical approaches of the local people. Vaka'uta—drawing on the work of Ukpong,[7] Sugirtharajah,[8] and Caldwell[9]—calls his approach to the Bible "contextual biblical interpretation." He describes his use of his own Tongan culture as a valid jumping off place for an indigenous hermeneutical approach. He goes on to say: "Whatever name one uses [inculturation hermeneutics, vernacular hermeneutics, or ethnohermeneutics], they all point to the rootedness of the interpretive task in culture."[10] Vaka'uta summarizes his approach as follows:

> Reading *tu'a-wise* (Tongan *lau faka-tu'a*) is an attempt to interpret the Bible based on Tongan cultural resources and social arrangement, through the "eye-/I-s" of a Tongan commoner (*tu'a*). *Lau faka-tu'a* emphasizes contextualizing the task of biblical interpretation rather than contextualizing the Bible per se. Contextualizing interpretation uses contextual or specifically indigenous categories of analysis, while contextualizing the Bible applies the insights from one's reading to one's situation. *Lau faka-tu'a* offers "an-other," uniquely Oceanic, way of reading. . . . engag[ing] critically with existing literature on contextual biblical interpretation and existing interpretations of the chosen text, Ezra 9–10, and aims at making biblical interpretation practice-based, nonelitist, noncontinental, transparent, and accountable.[11]

As with Ukpong so, too, with Vaka'uta; both components of intercultural hermeneutics are recognized. Vaka'uta's phrase, "ontextualizing interpretation uses contextual or specifically indigenous categories of analysis," refers to the second component of intercultural hermeneutics while his phrase, "while contextualizing the Bible applies the insights from one's reading to one's situation," refers to the first component of intercultural hermeneutics.

In summary, both Ukpong and Vaka'uta seek indigenous hermeneutical approaches within their own cultural contexts. As a result, the answer to the third question—are local hermeneutical approaches legitimate?—is a resounding yes!

---

7. Ukpong, "Inculturation Hermeneutics."
8. Sugirtharajah, *Vernacular Hermeneutics*.
9. Caldwell, "Towards the New Discipline of Ethnohermeneutics."
10. Vaka'uta, *Reading Ezra 9–10 Tu'a-Wise*, 3n8.
11. Vaka'uta, *Reading Ezra 9–10 Tu'a-Wise*, from the back cover.

INTERCULTURAL HERMENEUTICS AND ETHNOHERMENEUTICS

As we have seen, both Ukpong and Vaka'uta argue for an intercultural hermeneutics done by local people using their culture's unique indigenous hermeneutical approaches (component two of intercultural hermeneutics), while at the same time being sensitive to culturally appropriate understandings, customs, and behaviors to best communicate the truths of the Bible within a culture (component one or intercultural hermeneutics). In essence, Ukpong and Vaka'uta are holistically blending the two important components of intercultural hermeneutics. Addressing *both components* of the intercultural hermeneutical task in interpreting the Bible is the heart of the discipline of ethnohermeneutics. Consequently, ethnohermeneutics warrants a closer look in any discussion of intercultural hermeneutics.

Here is a definition of ethnohermeneutics:

> Ethnohermeneutics is Bible interpretation done in cross-cultural, multi-cultural and multi-generational contexts that, whenever possible, uses culturally appropriate dynamic hermeneutical approaches already in place in the culture; the primary goal being to interpret the Bible, as well as to communicate the truths of the Bible, in ways that will be best understood from within the worldview of the receptor culture.[12]

Ethnohermeneutics encourages Bible interpreters, both within and outside a particular culture, to ask the following two questions. First, what are the cultural practices and hermeneutical approach(es), found within my own culture, or the culture of the local people among whom I am ministering? And second, how can I possibly use these cultural practices and hermeneutical approach(es) when I attempt to both interpret the Bible, as well communicate the truths of the Bible, with/to individuals found within my own culture or with/to the culture of the local people among whom I am ministering? Ethnohermeneutics embraces both components of the task of intercultural hermeneutics and, in so doing, endeavors to make the overall hermeneutical task more holistic.

Ethnohermeneutics grew out of the discipline of ethnotheology which, in turn, grew out of the contextualization movement of the 1970s and 1980s, fueled by the writings of missionary anthropologists like Charles Kraft and Paul Hiebert.[13] Phrases like "dynamic equivalence," "self-theologizing," and

---

12. Caldwell, "Cross-Cultural Bible Interpretation," 14.

13. See, for example, Kraft, *Christianity in Culture*, and Hiebert, *Anthropological Insights for Missionaries*.

the like, were inherent to the development of ethnotheologies. Today, most Bible teachers, theologians, and missiologist agree that seeing peoples and cultures develop their own culturally appropriate ways of understanding theology—in other words, developing their own ethnotheologies, is taken for granted. Ethnotheology is now seen as a legitimate discipline.

Ethnohermeneutics, as a discipline, arose in the late 1980s and early 1990s. Missiologist Larry W. Caldwell, and others, observed that, while good ethnotheologies were happening, the basic hermeneutical approaches that undergirded them were based primarily on mostly global North grammatical-historical approaches to hermeneutics.[14] It was noted that these approaches, as good as they may be, were often learned approaches that were not necessarily appropriate in a local context that used different hermeneutical approaches to their own written or oral literature. Thus, the question raised by ethnohermeneutics is this: if local theologians were learning and using "foreign" Bible interpretation techniques, then was it possible that their ethnic theologies were not completely their own? Caldwell argues that both global North missionaries and local global South theologians should look for and use interpretation approaches already present in the culture, and from this foundation local theologians can subsequently develop a more holistic ethnotheology.[15]

The basic premise underlying the entire discipline of ethnohermeneutics is this: God is at work in each culture drawing individuals from within each culture to himself. This is a simple premise, to be sure, but one that has profound implications. What ethnohermeneutics argues for is an acknowledgement that God not only works through culture, hence the need to communicate the truths of Scripture in culturally relevant forms (component one of intercultural hermeneutics), but, correspondingly, that *God also works through the hermeneutical processes inherent in each culture* (component two of intercultural hermeneutics).

Global North hermeneutical approaches—including the grammatical-historical approach—may perhaps make sense to most from the global North, or to global South cultures strongly influenced by global North ideas and media. But what must be realized is that *global North hermeneutical approaches themselves are ethnohermeneutical approaches for those from the global North*. As such, these approaches may help highly educated individuals from the global South in interpreting the Bible, but they may or may not be helpful for other global South cultures and peoples, or even for global

---

14. See Caldwell, "Cross-Cultural Bible Interpretation"; Caldwell, "Interpreting the Bible *With* the Poor"; Caldwell, "Towards the New Discipline of Ethnohermeneutics."

15. For more detailed information regarding ethnohermeneutics see Caldwell, *Bible in Culture*.

North individuals who lack the education or interest in these more technical hermeneutical approaches. In the vast majority of global South cultures around the world—and in the younger Internet and social media-savvy generations of both the global North and global South—there remains the need to look for existing hermeneutical approaches that may help to make the Bible more relevant in those cultures. In other words, a return to a more holistic intercultural hermeneutics.

SURFACE LEVEL AND DEEP LEVEL ETHNOHERMENEUTICS

The above discussion about ethnohermeneutics underscores the two levels of Bible interpretation necessary as intercultural interpretation is done in any culture: surface level and deep level. *Surface level* ethnohermeneutics involves looking for culturally appropriate practices and forms to better communicate the truths of the Bible's message to people within the culture (the first component of the intercultural hermeneutical task). *Deep level* ethnohermeneutics involves looking for culturally appropriate hermeneutical approaches that are already used within the culture to help to discover the truths of the Bible for the people of that culture (the second component of the intercultural hermeneutical task). The distinctives between the two levels are illustrated in the figure below.

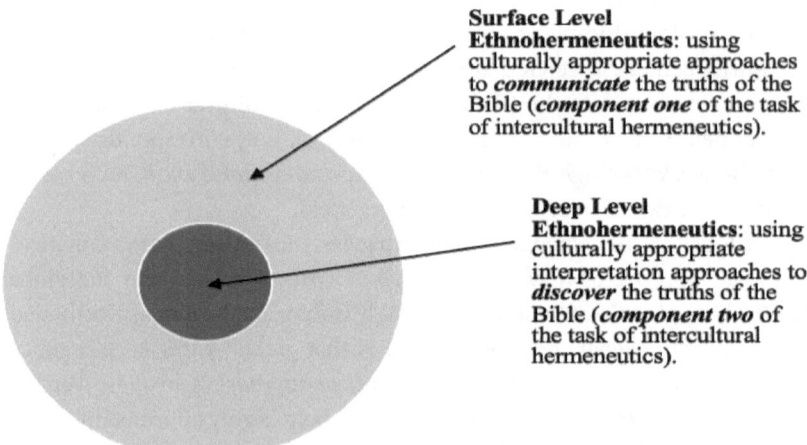

Surface Level Ethnohermeneutics: using culturally appropriate approaches to *communicate* the truths of the Bible (*component one* of the task of intercultural hermeneutics).

Deep Level Ethnohermeneutics: using culturally appropriate interpretation approaches to *discover* the truths of the Bible (*component two* of the task of intercultural hermeneutics).

It must be emphasized here that *both* levels are important for doing ethnohermeneutics. Furthermore, those individuals best able to do deep level ethnohermeneutics are the local people themselves.

Thinking about the two levels of ethnohermeneutics, and linking them to basic understandings of contextualization, can be helpful here. How so? Most Bible interpreters today would agree, in principle, that it is good to attempt to contextualize the message of the Bible in order to make it more receptor-oriented. In other words, most would agree with the need to do surface level ethnohermeneutics. In fact, good contextualizers of the Bible across cultures have been doing surface level ethnohermeneutics for two thousand years! Unfortunately, this sensitivity to the receptor's culture has not extended to exploring the best way to do hermeneutics *within* that culture. There has been a noticeable lack of concern for deep level ethnohermeneutics. Thankfully this lack is beginning to change, as we have seen with these examples from Upkong and Vaka'uta.

So how does ethnohermeneutics actually work in a specific cultural context? It is time to examine the practice of ethnohermeneutics among the Akan people of Ghana as an example for the doing of intercultural hermeneutics in any cultural context.

AN EXAMPLE OF ETHNOHERMENEUTICS: INTERCULTURAL HERMENEUTICS AMONG THE AKAN

African missiologist Akoa Kofi Amoateng, in his desire to create a truly contextualized theology for his own Akan people of Ghana, West Africa, recently completed ethnohermeneutical research using Akan Adinkra symbols in his groundbreaking book: *An Introduction to Symbolic Theology. The Case of the Adinkra Symbols of the Akan People of Ghana*. Providing an Akan theology through an Adinkra ethnohermeneutical paradigm, Amoateng attempts to provide "an illustration of what can be done if African theologians accept the challenge of helping the African [c]hurches think, understand, and express the Christian faith in terms of the traditional experience of God in our African settings."[16] For Amoateng, then, the question becomes: " . . . if African primal or folk culture is hermeneutics, then what type of hermeneutic procedure or method will be required to get to the theological messages, which are impregnated in African primal or folk cultures? . . . We cannot help but refer to these pre-Christian historical experiences of people as issues of *preparatio evangelica* for the peoples."[17]

Drawing upon Caldwell's work in ethnohermeneutics, and Barber's work in oral and written texts,[18] Amoateng proposes developing a theol-

---

16. Amoateng, *Introduction to Symbolic Theology*, 199.
17. Amoateng, *Introduction to Symbolic Theology*, 106.
18. Barber, *Anthropology of Texts*.

ogy for the Akan people based upon their commonly held Adinkra symbols which are a part of their primal past as well as their collective present:

> The Adinkra Symbols of the Akans of Ghana are art pieces that serve as metaphorical memory anchors for the Akan people. To a large extent, the Adinkra Symbols serve the same purposes of embodying and transmitting metaphors and myths from one generation of Akans to another . . . . Ghanaians have intrinsically continued to weave the Adinkra Symbols into their political, social, and religious fiber.[19]

These symbolic memory anchors are cultural texts for the Akan people. The Adinkra symbols are found in fabric designs of textile material—particularly cloth for clothing—on the walls of buildings, on pottery and wooden household items, in the logos of universities and other groups, and even on the wrappers of "Divine" chocolate bars, to name but a few. Sometimes these symbols are linked with ancient oral proverbs that communicate traditional wisdom. Adinkra symbols not only provide meaning for the Akan culture, according to Amoateng, they also "help toward identifying the theological persuasions of the Akan people" because they "have stories behind them" and "[to] get to their significant meaning, therefore, requires getting to know the stories the symbols represent."[20] In essence, such a study for Amoateng is an ethnohermeneutical one, since ethnohermeneutics, in his opinion, "presumes that cultures around the world are pregnant with issues that may constitute methods for interpreting the Bible in ways that will make the Bible understandable for the local people."[21] As a result, for Amoateng the Adinkra symbols are a form of semiotic (or "signs" or "symbolic") ethnohermeneutics.[22]

Amoateng explains his symbolic ethnohermeneutical approach:

> As an Akan African whose world is saturated with symbolism, I approach an understanding of the Bible (or hermeneutics) with a symbolic search. For African Christians, the Bible is not the word of God as independent of God. It is God's word that He watches over to perform (Jer. 1:12). The proverb "a man is as his word" explains that the truthfulness or otherwise of a person is in how that person keeps his or her word with integrity. For African Christians, the Bible itself is symbolic of God's faithfulness and ability to fulfill His promises for those who trust

---

19. Amoateng, *Introduction to Symbolic Theology*, xxxi.
20. Amoateng, *Introduction to Symbolic Theology*, 107.
21. Amoateng, *Introduction to Symbolic Theology*, 108.
22. Amoateng, *Introduction to Symbolic Theology*, 109.

Him. I have seen African Christian parents open to a verse of God's protection and place it on a newborn baby's pillow. This practice owes itself to the belief that the words of the Bible are God's words, which He will surely fulfill over the baby against the attacks of witches, demons, and evil spirits who might want to destroy the baby in Akan cosmology.[23]

Such symbolic understandings of the words of the Bible carry over to the Akan's understandings of the Adinkra symbols. As Amoateng notes, "[p]art of the reason for the popularity and usage of the Adinkra Symbols around the world is that the Adinkra Symbols are texts which communicate deep and intelligent messages."[24] Because he deeply understands his own culture, as well as hermeneutical theory, Amoateng gives hermeneutical validity to the way his ancestors developed the Adinkra symbols to better reflect their rudimentary understanding of who God is. In this way he honors his ancestors as well as honoring their early attempts to symbolize who God is. Both the Akan ancestors, and their Adinkra symbols, are crucially important to the Akan people today. As a result, any culturally appropriate hermeneutics for the Akan people must somehow incorporate both the ancestors as well as their symbols. Amoateng demonstrates how this is possible through careful analysis of both modern scholarship as well as his own Akan culture.

Specifically, by applying global North semiotic theory to the Bible, Amoateng searches for the Akan symbols lying behind the stories in the Bible that speak about God. He then identifies the stories behind the Adinkra symbols that the Akan ancestors used to communicate similar information about God, like the Adinkra symbol in the figure below: *Gye Nyame*.[25] Let us briefly examine this *Gye Nyame* symbol, and its significance for the Akan people today.

---

23. Amoateng, *Introduction to Symbolic Theology*, 109.
24. Amoateng, *Introduction to Symbolic Theology*, 119.
25. "Gye Nyame," https://www.symbols.com/symbol/gye-nyame.

Gye Nyame Symbol

THE ADINKRA SYMBOL: GYE NYAME

The words, *Gye Nyame*, mean "the final decision is with God (*Nyame*)." According to Amoateng, in pre-Christian times "the experience of the protecting power of God is part of the myth behind the *Gye Nyame* Symbol."[26] Akan tradition tells of the forerunners of the Akan people—the Gyamans—who were involved in several wars with a rival tribal group but were never defeated despite many severe trials. The Gyamans "realized that the only One who had saved them through it all was [*Nyame*] . . . the Supreme God of heaven . . . . The Ancestors realized this and started affirming the unparalleled greatness of God because they experienced the demonstrated unequaled power of *Nyame* through how He had protected them."[27]

As a result, the *Gye Nyame* symbol was created to tell future generations of Gyamans, this survival story due to the gracious and merciful safekeeping of *Nyame*. Their story forms the traditional cultural belief among the Akan people even today, a belief that includes the existence and supremacy/sovereignty of God. As Amoateng notes: "the *Gye Nyame* symbol . . . was created to evoke faith in God, even in unborn generations of the Gyamans."[28] This ancient Akan view of the Supreme Being, as exemplified through the *Gye Nyame* symbol, readily correlates with a Christian theological understanding of this Supreme Being who is omnipotent, omniscient, and omnipresent.

In a real sense, Amoateng is combining the surface level and deep level aspects of ethnohermeneutics in showing that the *Gye Nyame* symbol demonstrates how symbolic cultural texts like the Adinkra symbols, which are

26. Amoateng, *Introduction to Symbolic Theology*, 116.
27. Amoateng, *Introduction to Symbolic Theology*, 116.
28. Amoateng, *Introduction to Symbolic Theology*, 118.

neither fully oral nor fully written texts, from ancient beginnings have resonated, and continue to resonate, with Akan people even today. Furthermore, building on their past meaning the Adinkra symbols can be adapted to the present circumstances facing the Akan people and, in so doing, continue to have relevancy for today. As Amoateng says, the Adinkra symbols "were created to embody the religious significance of historical experiences for their creators in their immediate contexts, and to also transmit such broad religious understanding among the Akan people in future generations."[29]

CONCLUSION

Amoateng's use of Adinkra symbols is a good example of intercultural hermeneutics, one that incorporates both surface level and deep level ethnohermeneutics, the two components essential to a holistic understanding of the relationship between intercultural hermeneutics and the Bible. Note that Amoateng does not attempt "do away" with the global North hermeneutical approaches that he was trained in. Instead, he uses them for his own hermeneutical purposes while supplementing them with his own culturally appropriate hermeneutical approaches. All of this underscores the fact that ethnohermeneutics is not inherently opposed to the grammatical-historical approach (or any approach). To the contrary, ethnohermeneutics gives all theologians the tools they need to use the "best of both worlds" for their own hermeneutical contexts as they do intercultural hermeneutics. As Amoateng himself notes, concerning the Adinkra symbols and ethnohermeneutics:

> The difficulty in trying to get hermeneutical imports from the Adinkra Symbols is because people have not looked at the Adinkra Symbols as ethnohermeneutical texts or tools. They have only sought answers to interpretations via the historical-critical method, which contemporary exegetes require everybody to use. If we identify Africa's symbolic epistemological orientations and begin to employ symbols like art pieces, songs, dance forms, institutions, and the stories behind those institutions, we could identify that symbolisms offer an easier route toward making deeper meanings of the Christian faith for the "homo africanus."[30]

---

29. Amoateng, *Introduction to Symbolic Theology*, 96; cf. Barber, *Anthropology of Texts*, 67–68.

30. Amoateng, *Introduction to Symbolic Theology*, 50.

As a result, Amoateng's Akan people no longer need to strictly follow the dominant global North's understanding of hermeneutics in order to interpret the Bible for themselves. Instead, they can use the indigenous hermeneutical approaches found in their own Adinkra symbols as developed by their own ancestors.

As is true for the Akan culture so, too, may it one day be true for all global South cultures (as well as for global North cultures who may find the grammatical-historical approach to no longer be as culturally appropriate as it once was). At that time the hermeneutical approaches of all cultures will be equally considered and valued by the global church. No one culture's hermeneutical approach will dominate. Instead, all cultures—global North and global South alike—will contribute equally to the overall intercultural hermeneutical task of the worldwide church. The entire Christian world's understanding of the Bible, its interpretation, and its relevance to their own specific culture, will be infinitely richer as a result. This is what intercultural hermeneutics is all about.

BIBLIOGRAPHY

Amoateng, Kofi. *An Introduction to Symbolic Theology. The Case of the Adinkra Symbols of the Akan People of Ghana*. Accra: Asempa, 2022.

Barber, Karin. *The Anthropology of Texts, Persons and Publics. Oral and Written Culture in Africa and Beyond*. Cambridge: Cambridge University Press, 2007.

Brooks, Will. *Interpreting Scripture Across Cultures. An Introduction to Cross-Cultural Hermeneutics*. Eugene, OR: Wipf & Stock, 2022.

Caldwell, Larry W. *The Bible in Culture. Using Ethnohermeneutics for Reading the Bible With All the World*. Sioux Falls, SD: Lazy Oaks, forthcoming.

———. "Cross-Cultural Bible Interpretation: A View from the Field." *Phronesis* 3 (1996) 13–35.

———. "Interpreting the Bible *With* the Poor." In *Social Engagement: The Challenge of the Social in Missiological Education*, 165–90. Wilmore: First Fruits, 2013.

———. "Towards the New Discipline of Ethnohermeneutics: Questioning the Relevancy of Western Hermeneutical Methods in the Asian Context." *Journal of Asian Mission* 1/1 (1999), 21–43.

Chou, Abner. *The Hermeneutics of the Biblical Writers. Learning to Interpret Scripture from the Prophets and Apostles*. Grand Rapids: Kregel, 2018.

Dietrich, Walter, and Ulrich Luz, eds. *The Bible in a World Context. An Experiment in Contextual Hermeneutics*. Grand Rapids: Eerdmans, 2002.

Hiebert, Paul G. *Anthropological Insights for Missionaries*. Grand Rapids: Baker, 1985.

Jordan, Brigitte. "Authoritative Knowledge and Its Construction." In *Childbirth and Authoritative Knowledge*, edited by Robbie E. Davis-Floyd and Carolyn F. Sargent, 55–79. Berkeley: University of California Press, 1997.

Keener, Craig, and M. Daniel Carroll R., eds. *Global Voices: Reading the Bible in the Majority World*. Peabody, MA: Hendrickson, 2013.

Kraft, Charles H. *Christianity in Culture: A Study in Biblical Theologizing in Cross-Cultural Perspective*. 2nd rev. ed. Maryknoll, NY: Orbis, 2005.

McCaulley, Esau. *Reading While Black. African American Biblical Interpretation as an Example in Hope*. Downers Grove, IL: InterVarsity, 2020.

Premnath, D. N., ed. *Border Crossings. Cross-Cultural Hermeneutics*. Maryknoll, NY: Orbis, 2007.

Redford, Shawn B. *Missiological Hermeneutics. Biblical Interpretation for the Global Church*. American Missiological Society Monograph Series 11. Eugene, OR: Pickwick, 2012.

Roth, Federico Alfredo, et al *Reading the Bible Around the World. A Student's Guide to Global Hermeneutics*. Downers Grove, IL: InterVarsity, 2022.

Segovia, Fernando F., and Mary Ann Tolbert, eds. *Reading from this Place, Volume 2: Social Location and Biblical Interpretation in Global Perspective*. Minneapolis: Fortress, 1995.

Smith-Christopher, Daniel, ed. *Text and Experience. Towards a Cultural Exegesis of the Bible*. Sheffield: Sheffield University Press, 1995.

Sugirtharajah, R. S., ed. *Vernacular Hermeneutics*. Sheffield: Sheffield Academic, 1999.

———, ed. *Voices from the Margin. Interpreting the Bible in the Third World*. 3rd rev. ed. Maryknoll, NY: Orbis, 2006.

Ukpong, J. S. "Inculturation Hermeneutics: An African Approach to Biblical interpretation." In *The Bible in a World Context: An Experiment in Contextual Hermeneutics*, edited by Dietrich Walter and Ulrich Luz, 17–32. Grand Rapids: Eerdmans, 2002.

Vaka'uta, Nāsili. *Reading Ezra 9–10 Tu'a-Wise. Rethinking Biblical Interpretation in Oceania*. International Voices in Biblical Studies 3. Atlanta: Society of Biblical Literature, 2011.

West Gerald O., ed. *Reading Other-Wise. Socially Engaged Biblical Scholars Reading with Their Local Communities*. Atlanta: Society of Biblical Literature, 2007.

Wit, Hans de, et al., eds. *Through the Eyes of Another. Intercultural Reading of the Bible*. Elkhart: Institute of Mennonite Studies, 2004.

Wrogemann, Henning. *Intercultural Hermeneutics*. Translated by Karl E. Böhmer. Intercultural Theology 1. Downers Grove, IL: InterVarsity, 2016.

Xie, Ming, ed. *The Agon of Interpretations. Towards a Critical Intercultural Hermeneutics*. Toronto: University of Toronto Press, 2014.

Chapter 24
Racial Identity Hermeneutics
YUNG SUK KIM

DEFINITION AND NATURE OF RACIAL IDENTITY HERMENEUTICS

Racial identity hermeneutics, which is an extended version of contextual biblical interpretation, foregrounds the reader's context, concerns, interpretive lens, and methods.[1] As such, racial identity hermeneutics engages the text from the perspective factors that contribute to identity formation, asks questions about race/ethnicity matters, examines ideologies of race/ethnicity, tackles hegemonic interpretations that privilege certain voices and racial groups, and fosters diversity and solidarity for the marginalized. In doing so, racial identity hermeneutics works with other critical methods such as postcolonial, feminist, womanist, and queer criticisms. However, it should be noted that racial identity hardly remains fixed; it is permeable as it is understood from a broad spectrum of personal, communal, social, and global factors. While race or ethnicity is not changeable, one's perspective is tractable. This means even the same ethnic person may read the text differently at various times. Admittedly, any reader reads the text differently with every reading. This also implies that we should never absolutize one reading against others because meaning-making is ongoing and endless as the reader evolves over varied life experiences. Nevertheless, race or ethnicity matters not because it is absolute in our lives but because it gives a sense of belonging and meaning rooted in concrete life in one's social location. Belonging is a human need, and race/ethnicity has a greater role to play. So, race/ethnicity is a blessing and must be celebrated as a gift.

---

1. Kim, *Biblical Interpretation*, 1–57.

Considering the importance of locality and race/ethnicity, unity-driven, post-racial universal Christianity must be a phantom because, in it, there is no authentic diversity that recognizes differences in thought and culture. Indeed, early Christianity should not be understood as a movement that creates a new race of Christians. Rather, it is a movement that fosters diversity and tolerance of differences in ethnicity and culture. Christian gathering is a place of honor where members find themselves respected for who they are. They do not need to change their culture or feel ashamed because of cultural and ethnic differences. They gather in the name of Jesus Christ who cared for the marginalized. Similarly, Paul's gospel should not be construed as seeking a universal race of Christians beyond Jews. His vision is broad and lofty, and he is rooted in both apocalypticism and the new creation beginning now. He affirms the diversified community in which members receive diverse gifts of the Spirit and participate in the love of God and the grace of Jesus. In his thinking, gentiles stay as gentiles and are not to become Jews. The only thing that matters is not circumcision or uncircumcision but "faith working through love" (Gal 5:6).

Considering early Christianity's embrace of diversity, the ideology of one Christian race or a white-driven melting pot theory is an illusion and must melt away.[2] Often the ideal of oneness or unity is quixotic and hides the face of hegemonic control in which some people or groups are prioritized over against others. In the end, racial identity hermeneutics aims at dismantling the hegemonic ideology of oneness/unity and fosters a culture of care, diversity, and solidarity. What follows is in this order: "Racial/Ethnic Identity from Biblical Texts" and "Interpreting Biblical Texts through the Lens of Racial/Ethnic Identity." In the former, we will see both the importance and entanglement of race/ethnicity from biblical texts. In the latter, we will explore cases of racial identity hermeneutics with select texts from both the Hebrew Bible and New Testament.

RACIAL/ETHNIC IDENTITY FROM BIBLICAL TEXTS
RACE MATTERS FROM THE BEGINNING

The biblical story begins with a creation account in Genesis 1, which reveals the central act of God who makes things exist diverse and abundant on the earth.[3] God makes light out of chaos and darkness so that the earth may be habitable to all living beings, which need both light and darkness. So, the time of light is called Day, and the time of darkness is called Night. Both day

---

2. Kim, "Politics of Interpretation," 9–21.
3. Kim, *Monotheism, Biblical Traditions, and Race Relations*, 8–9.

and night are needed for all beings on the earth. This balanced earth with light and darkness is a sufficient condition for abundance and diversity because all living beings need the proper amount of light and darkness. After the first day of creation, God reorders the waters and makes the sky, the dry land (earth), and the seas. All these conditions are necessary for thriving beings and non-beings on the earth. On the third day, God makes the earth put forth vegetation so that plants may yield "seed of every kind and trees of every kind bearing fruit with the seed in it" (Gen 1:12 NRSVue). The earth is a place of abundance and diversity, growing all kinds of plants and seeds. The fourth-day creation is an extension of the first-day work because lights and stars come from light. On the fifth day, God makes a variety of living creatures, birds, and sea monsters. The point is every living creature is of "every kind." God says: "Be fruitful and multiply and fill the waters in the seas, and let birds multiply on the earth" (Gen 1:22 NRSVue). Then on the sixth day, God says: "Let us make humans in our image, according to our likeness, and let them have dominion over the fish of the sea and over the birds of the air, . . . and over every creeping thing that creeps upon the earth" (Gen 1:26 NRSVue). In view of his direction of creation for the first five days, God's image and likeness—although the first-person plural noun in "our image or our likeness" is a matter of debate—reflects the importance of abundance and diversity on earth. In other words, humans must fit into such a creation in abundance and diversity. Likewise, they are created as males and females, a sufficient condition for fruitful growth (Gen 1:27). God blesses them, as he did to all creatures: "Be fruitful and multiply and fill the earth and subdue it and have dominion over the fish of the sea and over the birds of the air and over every living thing that moves upon the earth" (Gen 1:28 NRSVue). All in all, humans are created to be diverse and live in abundance. From a binary perspective, *haʾadam*, though masculine singular, is biologically inclusive of both genders as verse 27b specifies the condition of *haʾadam* as specifically male and female. Gender differentiation (here) of human and animal species is conducive to procreation in order to "be fruitful and multiply." This is why Noah takes into the ark "male and female" to promote the propagation of the (general) species (Gen 6:9). While some might read God's image here as both male and female, others might object to it on ideological/cultural assumptions though feminine metaphors for God are seen elsewhere in the Bible (e.g., Isa 42:14; 66:13).

The story of the Tower of Babel (Gen 11:1–9) emphasizes the importance of diversity in human lives. That is, God wants people to thrive not in one place but throughout the whole earth. But they ignored God's will and gathered in one place and spoke the same words. They stopped migrating, settled in one place, and tried to build a big city, so that they will not be "scattered abroad upon the face of the whole earth" (Gen 11:4). Here the point is not directly about human arrogance but about their sedentary life in one place and mono language through which they try to build their own mighty fortress.[4] God wants them to live in diversity and move to all parts of the world. It is not easy to do so. Many languages may be difficult to live by because they cannot understand each other easily. It is understandable people seek safety and stability by keeping to one big city with a mighty fortress. But it is not what God intends. So, the Lord comes down to see the city and the tower, saying: "Look, they are one people, and they all have one language, and this is only the beginning of what they will do; nothing that they propose to do will now be impossible for them. Come, let us go down and *mix* their language there so that they will not understand one another's speech" (Gen 11:6–7 NRSVue, but italics is my translation). God points out the problem of "one people" and "one language." So, God "mixes" their language so that they may not understand each other. The Hebrew verb *balal* (11:7) means to mix, mingle or confound. Mixing their language is not a punishment for their arrogance but a means to prevent "one language" and to ensure diversity with multiple languages. So, the Lord scattered people, which is, again, not a punishment for arrogance but a measure that they can go back to a life of diversity. So racial diversity and multiple languages are important conditions for thriving humanity.

RACE/ETHNICITY-EMBEDDED BIBLICAL NARRATIVES

Biblical stories are entangled with racial and ethnic issues. Abraham's journey begins with motifs of migration, marginality, and hope for humanity. When God calls Abraham and blesses him, he was a poor migrant with a poor sense of who he is. There is no specific identity or tradition he could cherish and reclaim. He was just a wanderer seeking safety and security in his life. He was asked to leave his homeland for an unknown place and future, walking a long road of a faithful living through ups and downs. In Gen 12:1, he embarks on a journey of no return and seeks a God-promised future, which is a life of diversity and difficulty. In fact, God could bless him without asking him to leave his home but asked him to leave his familiar conditions of life. This injunction that he must leave is consistent with God's scattering of humans in the episode of the Tower of Babel. By leaving, he becomes a seed bearer of multitudes of people who are diverse in lifestyle and languages. God uses Abraham as a model of diverse living and culture

---

4. Croatto, "Reading of the Story of the Tower of Babel from a Perspective of Non-Identity," 203–23. See also Hiebert, "Tower of Babel and the Origin of the World's Cultures," 29–58.

through which he must move about different places constantly. Not realizing the blessings of descendants and the land in his life, he becomes a model of diverse life and culture.

Ancient Israel can be understood from the perspective of racial and ethnic conflict involving multiple factors such as political and religious ideologies. Before the Davidic kingdom, many tribes rivaled each other for hegemony. Leaders of dynasties and people were not satisfied in their places and interfered with others and invaded them to get more riches and control them. Later, rulers of Israel and Judah focused on securing their powers through expansive military campaigns at the expense of ordinary people. They also had to fend off aggressive empires.

Jesus's story in the Gospels reflects his passion and concern for the gentiles, on the one hand, and his hesitation and exclusivism, on the other.[5] The Lukan Jesus thinks his mission is for the gentiles and preaches about God's preferential option for them. In Luke 4:16–30, he is passionate about God's care for the gentiles. In his sermon, Jesus says God sent two great prophets, Elijah and Elisha, to gentiles (a widow at Zarephath in 1 Kgs 17:7–16 and Naaman, a commander of the army of Syria in 2 Kgs 5:1–19) even when there were many widows and lepers in Israel. This radical eccentric preaching disrupts his hometown people and hurts their privilege all at once. Luke embraces the good news for the gentiles because he aims at reaching them. But in doing so, he conveys a triumphant, antisemitic attitude toward Jews and others. In contrast, Jesus in Matt 15:21–28 affirms the Jewish first strategy with Jewish exclusivism, ignoring the need for the Canaanite woman who requests the healing of her daughter. In a similar version of the story in Mark 7:24–30, which is about the Syrophoenician woman's encounter with Jesus, there is no strong mood of Jewish exclusivism, as opposed to Matthew where the Canaanite woman is grilled by him and his disciples maybe because Matthew is a Jewish writer. But she gets what she needs, which is her daughter's healing, only after a tedious, tense series of conversations. In this story, we see Jesus's exclusive salvation perspective, as he says he is sent only to the house of Israel. Unlike Luke, Matthew prioritizes God's salvation for Jews. But in the end, she wins because of her persistence in blessing. In John 4:1–42, the Samaritan woman talks with Jesus at a well of Jacob, and she is transformed through a long conversation. Eventually, all people in her village come to Jesus and are transformed. How we understand race/ethnicity-entangled stories is an issue of interpretation. As seen above, early Christianity can be understood as an ongoing fight or struggle between the privileged and the marginalized; between Jews and gentiles. While race or

---

5. Kim, "Race, Ethnicity and the Gospels."

ethnicity is not the dominant factor, it is a crucial part of conflict because one can be easily noticed with certain traits of race or ethnicity. Certainly, race or ethnicity is entangled with sexism, classism, and all kinds of ideology and cultural assumptions.

Paul and his letters can also be understood from the perspective of ethnic struggles or conflict. As a diasporic Jew, he lived in marginality, dealing with many different ethnicities and people. Before his new call from God, he had a conviction that God cares for Jews only, and because of that, he thought that they must be loyal to him by keeping the law thoroughly. But he changed the course of his life completely when God revealed his Son to him and realized the good news of God differently because of this revelation (Gal 1:15–16). At the heart of this good news is the gospel of faith effective for both the gentiles and Jews (Rom 1:16). The good news is that all may become children of God regardless of who they are and that God's covenant with Abraham is intended for and extends to all people. The only condition for people of God is faithfulness and Christ. They also must be led by the Spirit (Rom 8:13–14). Otherwise, he does not promote a single race of Christians but advocates a community of diversity (with diverse ethnicities) bound by God's love and Christ's grace. He is not a champion of the gospel that rejects the law, Jews, or Judaism, or that promotes one universal Christian race or culture.

INTERPRETING BIBLICAL TEXTS THROUGH THE LENS OF RACIAL/ETHNIC IDENTITY

In this section, we will see how racial identity hermeneutics makes a difference in our interpretation, referring to the definition and work of racial identity hermeneutics, as written at the beginning of this chapter. Racial identity hermeneutics is concerned with asking race/identity-related critical questions, tackling hegemonic interpretations, and seeking alternative interpretations that foster diversity and solidarity rather than unity.

THE TOWER OF BABEL (GEN 11:1–9)

As we saw before, traditionally, the story of the Tower of Babel has been read as a story of human arrogance or pride against God, resulting in God's scattering of people and confusing their language. In this logic, multiple languages and living in diversity are the result of God's punishment. But from an alternative perspective, the issue in the story of the tower of Babel is not human pride or arrogance per se, but people getting stuck in one language and forming one empire that resists diversity.[6] In this alternative reading, multiple ethnicities and multiple languages are signs of God's blessing and conditions for thriving. The unitary Tower of Babel ends in dispersion and diversity.

FROM EXODUS TO JOSHUA'S CONQUEST NARRATIVE (EXOD 1–18; NUM 10–16; JOSH 1–12)

Exodus is a story of liberation and shows God's concern for the Israelites in Egypt who live as slaves. God called Moses and let him lead them out of Egypt. Through ups and downs on their long journey, the descendants of those who were liberated enter the promised land. God orders Joshua to conquer Canaan and annihilate all people there. At this juncture of the story, readers ask questions about the validity of such command and the justice of God. Is the ideology of the text or writer acceptable? Whose story is this? The God of Abraham was gracious, impartial, and steadfast, taking care of Abraham's descendants. But can such a good God turn into a merciless God? Is God a tribal God for Jews only? No invasion or mass killing should be justified in the name of God. Here we ask questions of ideology. Who is served by this story? Who is oppressed and relegated forever? Often the story of the biblical narrative becomes history by those who read triumphantly for themselves only, and the history of subjugation is accelerated because of the triumphant ideology/theology. A good example of that comes from European settlers who came to America with the ideology of "chosenness" and expelled American Indians from their territory. This ideology is dangerous, depriving other people of their culture, thought, and dignity.

RUTH

The book of Ruth is a short story of love, migration, economic hardships, and a family saga. It can be read diversely since such a story intersects with many factors in personal, familial, and social life. From the Jewish perspective, this story is a story of acculturation by Ruth the Moabite woman who chose Israel's God and immigrated to Israel, following Naomi, her mother-in-law. But from racial identity sensitivity, we can ask race/ethnicity questions:

- Is Ruth satisfied while living in Israel?
- Is she fully accepted as Boaz is?

---

6. Croatto, "Reading of the Story of the Tower of Babel from a Perspective of Non-Identity," 203–23.

- Is she still a Moabite or acculturated Moabite Jew?
- Did she regret immigrating to Israel?
- Did she envy Orpah at times?
- Did she feel like a surrogate mother?
- Did she exercise her agency or pretend to follow Naomi to survive?
- Is the story a happy conclusion for Ruth?
- If she goes back to Moab and faces a similar situation, will she make the same decision?
- How did she overcome when she felt alienated or scandalized because of her marriage to Boaz?

As seen above, Ruth is open-ended and defies closure of the text/story. No one can give definitive answers, and we must allow for diverse responses to the story, rejecting hegemonic voices from any side. For example, we can tackle the theory of a melting pot in which one gives up one's culture and language to belong to another culture. In other words, Ruth does not have to be Jewish to live a good life there. She is free to think and do what she wants. We do not have to agree with any ideology—from the Jewish side or from the idealized model convert theory. The truth lies somewhere on the spectrum of her emotional landscape in which she feels and faces all kinds of issues in her life—with her relationship with Naomi, other Jews, Moabites, and Boaz. So, we should not fix her feelings or issues; instead, we can engage with her story and ask critical questions about her racial identity, culture, and the meaning of life in a foreign land.

THE SYROPHOENICIAN WOMAN (MARK 7:24–30) AND THE CANAANITE WOMAN (MATTHEW 15:21–28)

According to redaction criticism, the Syrophoenician woman's story in Mark 7:24–30 has been used and redacted (edited) by Matthew, who calls the woman a Canaanite, incorporates the disciples' intervention into the story, explains Jesus's rejection of healing due to Jewish exclusivism, and elevates her faith. While the Markan version is a plain story of healing for a gentile woman's daughter, the Matthean version is a complex story of faith coupled with Jewish exclusivism along with a severe rejection of gentiles, as Jesus says he was sent only to the house of Israel. Usually, people read both texts as healing stories through the perspective of the woman's submissive faith. But from the perspective of critical racial identity, we ask the following questions:

- Is it taken for granted that Jesus rejects her request for the healing of her daughter?
- Does Jesus test her faith as often said? Can the means justify the end?
- Why does Matthew tell the story more harshly in terms of Jesus's demeanor toward her? Initially, Jesus was oblivious to her request. Then, he said he was sent only to the Israelites, ignoring her definitively.
- Why, in Matthew, do both Jesus and his disciples agree to Jewish exclusivism?
- What is the nature of her faith that Jesus elevates? Is her faith in Jesus or in God, or in both?
- Does she challenge Jesus's narrow faith?
- Why, in the end, does Jesus allow for her request to be heard? Does he change his mind? In what way? Or does he remain in his view of gentiles?

With the above questions, we must tackle hegemonic interpretations that perpetuate marginality, racism, sexism, and classism. The demeanors of Jesus and the disciples are unacceptable whatsoever. Jesus's silence, unwilling gesture, and exclusive attitude toward gentiles made a permanent scar on her soul. Why does she have to endure trauma and stigma when she expects the Jewish messiah to attend to her? Before coming to Jesus, she was already in trauma and had a stigma because of her marginality status as a woman, mother, and gentile. If she endured all these to receive blessing and healing, her faith was submissive. But we must ask further questions: What is her faith that Jesus commends? Is it submissive or challenging?[7] Did she have to show so much faith to be granted her wish and how typical is this in Matthean narratives? The alternative interpretation is to see her challenging faith, which is based on God's faithfulness and love for the gentiles as well. She believes that Jesus the Son of God, Messiah, would listen to her because he is the Messiah sent by God. So, she engages Jesus and is persistent in her faith. Her claim is that the gentiles also deserve blessings of God.[8]

THE GREAT COMMISSION (MATTHEW 28:16-20)

The Great Commission in Matt 28:16–20 is not about conquering gentiles and their countries with the gospel. Western missionaries went to Asia, Africa, and other parts of the world with this teaching so that they could

---

7. Patte, "Canaanite Woman and Jesus," 33–53.
8. Smith, *Womanist Sass and Talk Back*, 28–45.

deliver the gospel to them.[9] But the issue is whether they brought the truth of the gospel informed or taught by Jesus.[10] The gospel/good news (*euangelion*) is about God who rules people and the world with justice and love. Jesus heals the sick and talks about God's kingdom, which is "the rule of God" (*basileia tou theou*, Matt 4:23). Jesus did not preach about himself but about God's reign in which the marginalized may find their home and meaning of life. The good news is not mere knowledge or teaching. The Western gospel is based on salvific knowledge and doctrine, whose focus is on the soul's salvation, separating politics and economics from the gospel. As is often the case, missionaries thought they were given the authority to go anywhere, teach such a gospel of knowledge, and make disciples of all nations so that they may follow their Christianity. But we must ask critical questions about the Great Commission:

- Does Jesus say the gospel is about him or about the soul's salvation?
- Does he say that other countries and people must accept such knowledge?
- Is it right that they are invaded by missionaries and Western colonialists?
- Why do they not care about politics, especially social justice?
- Do they understand what Jesus taught in Matthew?
- Do they know his teaching about radical love for the least? (Matt 18:10–14; 25:31–46).
- Do they know Jesus taught the importance of God's righteousness, which is God's justice and care for the marginalized? (Matt 6:33; cf., 5:20).

With these questions, we must tackle any form of hegemonic interpretations that dishonor other cultures and people and seek an alternative interpretation that fosters a culture of impartial love of God and his justice.[11] The Great Commission is not about crossing territorial boundaries and conquering other countries with the gospel. It is simply a demand that followers of Jesus must do what he taught—the impartial love of God for all.

---

9. Lalitha and Smith, *Teaching All Nations*.
10. Soares-Prabhu, "Two Mission Commands," 264–82.
11. Patte, "Reading Matthew 28:16–20 with Others," 521–57.

THE SAMARITAN WOMAN'S ENCOUNTER WITH JESUS (JOHN 4:1–42)

Jesus passes through Samaria and meets a gentile woman called a Samaritan. He initiates a conversation with her, and she also stays interested in his talk. There is a long series of conversations in which he impresses her by telling the woman her past and underscores the worship of God in spirit and truth. In the end, her village people come out to meet him and are transformed. This story is often interpreted as legitimating Christianity's triumphant mission toward other countries. But we can raise critical questions about this story:

- Does Jesus cross the geographical boundary to subjugate Samaritans to Jewish rule and religion?
- Does he push for her conversion to Judaism?
- What does he mean when he states, "The water that I will give will become in them a spring of water gushing up to eternal life"? (John 4:15).
- Why does he say that "My food is to do the will of him who sent me and to complete his work?" (John 4:34).
- Does the Samaritan woman feel humiliated or inferior in her conversation with him?
- What motivates her to go to her village and talk about the Messiah to her village people?

With the above questions, we can reread the Samaritan woman's story and tackle hegemonic interpretations that dishonor the culture of other people and their religion.[12] First, Jesus does not push for her conversion to Judaism or to any religion. Rather, he talks about God, who is spirit. Because God is spirit, people must worship him in spirit and truth (John 4:23–24). Worship of God is not confined to Samaria or Jerusalem. Second, Jesus's offer of water is not to be understood as an exclusive message or knowledge of something, but as his work of God, which is to show the way of God (14:6), secure abundant life for people (14:6), testify to the truth of God (18:37), and deliver the word (logos) of God (17:6, 14, 17). We must note that the word of God that Jesus delivers is the same logos in 1:14: "The Word (logos) became flesh." Third, the Samaritan woman actively engages Jesus and asks questions. All is her decision and choice. She is not submissive to Jesus but finds answers to her questions about religion or ethnicity. So, the alternative interpretation seeks to explore religion and culture based on critical

---

12. Dube, "Reading for Decolonization (John 4:1–42)," 37–59.

conversation and engagement with a gradual process and a voluntary spirit. Any education or conversation under duress is detrimental to others.

"I AM THE WAY AND THE TRUTH AND THE LIFE" (JOHN 14:6)

Christian readers have long understood John 14:6 as Christ-centered, exclusive salvation. So, this understanding of 14:6 allows them to go to other countries with a spirit of triumphalism. The claim is easily made on exclusive salvation with Jesus, as he says: "No one comes to the Father except through me." Then, this claim becomes a weapon for conquering other countries and cultures. The truth of the gospel/good news is tarnished by Western colonialism. But we must ask critical questions about this text:

- How can we understand Jesus's "I am" saying in 14:6?
- Is 14:6 understood literally or metaphorically?
- If understood metaphorically, in what sense does Jesus become the way, the truth, and the life?
- How does 14:6 relate to other "I am" sayings in John?
- Can we understand 14:6 as an extension of Jesus's embodiment of the logos in 1:14?
- If Jesus embodies the word of God, can we understand 14:6b: "No one comes to the Father except through me" differently?

With the above questions, we can reexamine John 14:6 from the perspective of critical racial identity and tackle some narrow, exclusive interpretations that miss Jesus's language of the embodiment of God's love.[13] In John, the repetitive message of Jesus is he does the work of God and that he is sent by him (3:16; 4:34). He does all he can to complete that work and sends his disciples into the world so that they may do the same mission (17:18–19). So, Jesus's embodiment language will pave the way for interreligious dialogue.

"NO LONGER JEW OR GREEK; NO LONGER FREE OR SLAVE; NO LONGER MALE AND FEMALE . . . ALL OF YOU ARE ONE IN CHRIST JESUS" (GAL 3:28)

The traditional interpretation of Gal 3:28 posits the theory of a melting pot in Christ. That is, all members of the church/community are considered the same in Christ. But in fact, they are not the same! They think differently, look different, and live in different conditions. In the traditional reading of

---

13. Kim, *Truth, Testimony, and Transformation*, 47–55.

Gal 3:28, their ethnicity, social status, or gender is considered insignificant, and their differences are minimized or invisible. What is emphasized is doctrinal unity and membership in Christ. They are considered one because they are unified with the same doctrine and salvation. They think they are one because they are under the universal identity of Christ. On deeper levels, however, there is a hierarchy in this universalized community in which certain leaders, race/ethnicity, or doctrines take center stage. Indeed, Gal 3:28 is not as simple as the traditional interpretation poses. So, we must ask critical questions about this text:

- Does Paul think of the future eschatological community where all distinctions are erased, or does he think of the present community?
- How can members of the community be one in Christ Jesus?
- Is this community egalitarian or hierarchical?
- Does Paul discourage diversity or foster it, given his statement of "no longer Jew or Greek, no longer free or slave, or no longer male and female?"
- What is the meaning of "one in Christ" when Christians are still distinguished in society?

From racial identity sensitivity, we can tackle the traditional interpretation that does not allow for other readings that foster diversity and solidarity. The meaning of 3:28 is wide open, as it depends on how to interpret "in Christ Jesus" and its relationship with the status of oneness. If "in Christ" is understood as modal dative—as a way of life, members must form a beloved community, following the Christly example of life, which is to support the marginalized. In such a community, different kinds of people gather in the love of God and stay as they are, maintaining ethnic and gender differences. Seen here, though, Paul's body politics is not radical enough because there is no demand for structural change in the justice and political system or for the equality of humans. He does not ask for abolition either. He only believes that the Parousia would resolve all things in the near future. That is his limitation. We do not have to adopt his lukewarm attitude toward social justice.

"YOU ARE THE BODY OF CHRIST" (1 COR 12:12–27)

Traditionally, "the body of Christ" has been read as a metaphorical organism whose focus is unity or concord (*homonoia*). The emphasis is on members belonging to the church whose head is Christ. This understanding of the body is clearly seen in the Deutero-Pauline letters of which Pauline authorship is debated. For example, in Col 1:18, Jesus is said to be the head of the body, the church (see also Col 1:24; Eph 1:22–23; 4:12). In Paul's own letter, 1 Cor 12:12–27, however, he does not say Christ is the head of the body or associate the body with the church. Instead, whenever he refers to the community, he uses "the church (*ekklesia*) of God" (1 Cor 1:2; 10:32; 11:22; 15:9; 2 Cor 1:1; Gal 1:13).[14] As we see differences between Paul's authentic letters and later epistles, which may be written by him, we must ask critical questions about "the body of Christ":

- What is the concept of the body as Paul combines it with Christ?
- What kind of a metaphor is the body of Christ?
- Is it an organism metaphor or a site of living as in 1 Cor 6:12–20?
- Why does he not mention the head in his body talks in 1 Cor 12:12–27?
- Why does Paul say "you (the plural noun, referring to all the Corinthians) are the body of Christ"?
- In what sense do they constitute Christ? Is it in a metaphorical organism sense or in the sense of embodiment of him, as seen in 1 Cor 6:12–20?

With the above questions, we can tackle the rhetoric of unity and control that uses Christ as the head. The language of unity must be suspicious because it is often associated with a hegemonic interpretation that does not see the importance of Christ's faith and his sacrifice, which is the foundation of the church. In Paul's authentic thinking, Jesus is not the owner of the church but the foundation of it (c.f., 1 Cor 3:11). So, we can seek an alternative interpretation that affirms diversity and the importance of Christic embodiment, which is a different understanding of the body of Christ.[15] That is, we can translate and interpret it as Christ-like living and community. Here, the body is a site of living as in 1 Cor 6:20: "Glorify God in your body." The Christic body is a rendition of the attributive genitive case, as the body of sin may be translated as a "sinful body" (Rom 6:6).[16] So we can translate 1 Cor 12:27 as: "You are the Christic body individually and communally."[17] All this means members of the community embody Christ in their personal, communal lives. If they follow Christ's way and his faith, that means they

---

14. Kim, *Reimagining the Body of Christ in Paul's Letters*, 45–46.
15. Kim, *Christ's Body in Corinth*, 65–102; Kim, *How to Read Paul*, 121–33.
16. Kim, *Christ's Body in Corinth*, 65–102; Kim, *How to Read Paul*, 121–33.
17. Kim, *Christ's Body in Corinth*, 65–102; Kim, *How to Read Paul*, 121–33.

must honor one another and support each one's life and culture. In sum, for Paul, "the body of Christ" language is too important to apply to a sense of an organism. It is Christ's own body, the crucifixion body, and its implications for those who follow him.

CONCLUSION

Racial identity hermeneutics does not stand alone. Rather, it works with other critical methods such as postcolonial criticism or feminist, and womanist criticisms. Since no reading is perfect or complete, readers should attempt to read the text freshly, challenging the dominant interpretations. Therefore, it is important to *ask* critical questions about the text and the interpretations of others. With all the plausible, imaginative questions, we must *tackle* hegemonic interpretations that block diversity and solidarity. No text or interpretation can precede or prevent human dignity and equality. Then, lastly, we must *seek* alternative interpretations that foster diversity and human dignity through racial identity consciousness. Such efforts making alternative readings should be ongoing and never complete.

BIBLIOGRAPHY

Dube, Musa. "Reading for Decolonization (John 4:1–42)." *Semeia* 75 (1996) 37–59.

Croatto, Severino. "A Reading of the Story of the Tower of Babel from a Perspective of Non-Identity." In *Teaching the Bible: The Discourses and Politics of Biblical Pedagogy*, edited by Fernando F. Segovia and Mary Ann Tolbert, 203–23. Maryknoll, NY: Orbis, 1998.

Hiebert, Theodore. "The Tower of Babel and the Origin of the World's Cultures." *Journal of Biblical Literature* 126 (2007) 29–58.

Kim, Yung Suk. *Biblical Interpretation: Theory, Process, and Criteria*. Eugene, OR: Pickwick. 2013.

———. *Christ's Body in Corinth: The Politics of a Metaphor*. Minneapolis: Fortress, 2008.

———. *How to Read Paul: A Brief Introduction to His Theology, Writings, and World*. Minneapolis: Fortress, 2021.

———. *Monotheism, Biblical Traditions, and Race Relations*. New York: Cambridge University Press. 2022.

———. "The Politics of Interpretation: Paul's Gospel, Empire, and Race/Ethnicity." In *Paul's Gospel, Empire, and Race/Ethnicity: Through the Lens of Minoritized Scholarship*, edited by Yung Suk Kim, 9–21. Eugene, OR: Pickwick, 2023.

———. "Race, Ethnicity and the Gospels." In *Oxford Bibliographies*, edited by Christopher Matthews. New York: Oxford University Press, 2021.

———. *Truth, Testimony, and Transformation: A New Reading of the "I Am" Sayings of Jesus in the Fourth Gospel*. Eugene, OR: Cascade, 2014.

Lalitha, Jayachitra and Mitzi J. Smith, eds. *Teaching All Nations: Interrogating the Matthean Great Commission*. Minneapolis: Fortress, 2014.

Patte, Daniel. "The Canaanite Woman and Jesus: Surprising Models of Discipleship (Matt 15:21–28)." In *Transformative Encounters: Jesus and Women Re-viewed*, edited by Ingrid Rosa Kitzberger and Ingrid R. Kitzberger, 33–53. Leiden: Brill, 2000.

———. "Reading Matthew 28:16–20 with Others: How It Deconstructs Our Western Concept of Mission." *HTS Theological Studies* 62 (2006) 521–57.

Smith, Mitzi J. *Womanist Sass and Talk Back: Social (in)Justice, Intersectionality, and Biblical Interpretation*. Eugene, OR: Cascade, 2018.

Soares-Prabhu, George. "Two Mission Commands: An Interpretation of Matthew 28:16–20 in the Light of a Buddhist Text." *Biblical Interpretation* 2 (1994) 264–82.

Chapter 25

Race and Hermeneutics

RODOLFO GALVAN ESTRADA III

This chapter explores the role of race in Scripture, the terminology used for race, the ideologies of race that existed as part of the biblical world, and how we can reread the biblical text with attention to these dynamics. I aim to provide some interpretive insights that will help readers develop a deeper understanding of the racial language of Scripture. For the sake of brevity, our focus will primarily give attention to the world of the New Testament. This does not presume that the development of a racial conscience did not emerge in the Old Testament,[1] although it is difficult to understand the role of race and ethnicity in pre–monarchical Israel.[2] As such, the first part of the chapter provides some common definitions. The second part will cover the ideologies of race from the Greco–Roman world. Last, we conclude with thoughts on reading the Bible.

RACE AND ETHNICITY: DEFINING KEY TERMS

We may presume that the terms for "race" or "ethnicity" emerged after the colonization of the Americas or when scientists of the eighteenth and nineteenth century began to classify people into different groups. Applying the concept of "race" to the Bible is not an anachronistic move nor is it a new concept to those in the ancient world—it has been around for a long time.

---

1. The Old Testament includes many passages on "foreigners" who lived among the Israelites, although Rendtorff mentions that the identities of these people are difficult to identify; see "*Gēr* in the Priestly Laws," 77–87.
2. Edelman, "Ethnicity and Early Israel," 25–55.

When we look at how people groups were defined in ancient Greece and Rome, we see that a host of matrixes defined racial and ethnic identity, such as clothing, food, religion, language, lineage, laws, and geographical origins. For example, Herodotus records a speech by Alexander the Athenian to the Spartan envoy that explains why they did not join the Persians to enslave the Greeks. Alexander appeals to common identity markers. He refers to the "kinship of all Greeks in blood and speech, and the shrines of gods and the sacrifices that we have in common, and the likeness of our way of life."[3] Notice how aspects of Greek identity include a common descent, language, religious observance, and way of life. Isocrates provides a cultural understanding of race and its relationship to the Greek intellectual heritage. He states, "Hellenes suggests no longer a race (γένους) but an intelligence and that the title Hellenes is applied rather to those who share our culture than to those who share a common blood."[4] In Roman literature, these aspects and others were signs of racial identity. Virgil describes the diversity of the human race based upon the diversity of their clothing, weaponry, and language (*Aen.* 8.720). Likewise, Tacitus also describes the racial transformation of the Britons to a Roman identity when they started to adopt Roman customs, education, clothes, and food (*Agr.* 21.1).

Overall, the ancients used the Greek terms γένος (race), ἔθνος (ethnic), and λαός (people) to describe themselves, distinguish others, identify their descendants, or address people groups in general. Although Eric Gruen admits that the term "race" may be a misleading and erroneous category given its modern usage,[5] it is thus helpful to think about race as classification language that organizes human difference. It appears whenever the ancients attempt to define group differences and group boundaries.[6] "Us–them" language emerges specifically whenever people feel they need to emphasize group identity or indicate some sort of difference between groups. This is also why conversations about race emerge more frequently when people from different racial backgrounds come together in comparison to those who live in a homogeneous community.

In biblical literature, the term "race" is a translation of the Greek word γένος.[7] Γένος appears only twenty times in the New Testament with almost half found in Acts (nine occurrences). The term highlights distinct people

---

3. Herodotus, 8.144.
4. Isocrates, *Paneg.* 50.
5. Gruen, *Rethinking*, 197–98.
6. McCoskey, *Race*, 2; Estrada, *Race, Kinship, Empire*, 17.
7. The term refers to posterity, family, people, kind, or species. See Büchsel, "γένος," *TDNT* 1:684–85.

groups such as the Syrophoenician woman, gentiles, Jewish people, and Christians.[8] Generally, "race" is used for descendants, family, or association with land.[9] Love Sechrest notices that this term refers to people groups, language, kinship, humanity, territory, customs, government, war, and a founding figure.[10] Similarly, Denise Buell aptly suggests that the common use of the term "race" would have signaled a group classification.[11] She insists that it demarcates a group whose membership would share certain characteristics such as ancestors, rights of inheritance, knowledge, ritual practice, and ways of life.[12] This broad application should lead us to recognize that race is primary classification language, as Buell insists.

But what about the word "ethnicity?" The term "ethnicity" (ἔθνος) is also used to describe people groups within biblical literature. It appears more frequently in comparison to γένος, appearing 162 times, with most occurrences in Acts. This is a popular term used for gentiles, especially in the Pauline letters[13] and Revelation.[14] However, ἔθνος is used in reference to the Jews in the Gospel of John.[15] These diverse uses demonstrate the notion of "ethnicity" as something observable, applied to distinct groups of people, and reflective of an acknowledgment of group difference. In fact, John Balsdon finds that the Jews divided humanity into Jews and gentiles (ἔθνος) just as the Greeks divided humanity into Greeks and barbarians.[16]

The classicist Benjamin Isaac defines "ethnic group" as a people who share a long history, beliefs, traditions, distinguishable characteristics, and a cultural tradition of its own, including family, social customs, and manners.[17] Jonathan Hall notices that within ancient Greece, ethnicity was not solely a biological phenomenon but developed in opposition to other ethnic groups.[18] As Hall believes, it was the war with the Persians in 480–479 BCE that compelled the Greeks to define themselves as an ethnic group.

---

8. Mark 7:26; 2 Cor 11:26; Phil 3:5; 1 Pet 2:9.

9. Acts 4:6, 36; 7:13, 19; 13:26; 17:28–29; 18:2, 24; Rev 22:16.

10. Sechrest, *Former*, 81–90.

11. Buell, *Why This New Race*, 1.

12. Buell, *Why This New Race*, 2.

13. Rom 1:13; 1 Cor 1:23; Gal 1:16; Eph 2:11; Col 1:27; 1 Thess 2:16; 1 Pet 2:12; 4:3.

14. Rev 5:9; 7:9; 10:11; 12:5; 14:6–8; 15:4; 16:19; 17:15; 18:3, 23; 19:15; 20:3, 8; 21:24, 26; 22:2.

15. John 11:48, 50–52; 18:35.

16. Balsdon, *Romans and Aliens*, 234.

17. Isaac, *Invention of Racism*, 35.

18. Hall, *Ethnic Identity*, 33.

Although "race" and "ethnicity" are difficult to define precisely and are used synonymously throughout the biblical and contemporary era, it makes sense when people today use them interchangeably. There is a historical reason, though, why we use these terms today—partly the result of the UNESCO statements on race when the world's scientists sought to make an international declaration condemning the racial ideologies that led to World War II. These international scientists responded to the pseudoscience and myths of race that defined race in biological terms, differentiated different species of humanity, and claimed that race mixture was harmful to humanity. The UNESCO statement encouraged the use of "ethnic groups" since the term "race" contains serious errors in popular thinking.[19] Unfortunately, though, the use of the term "race" has not fallen out of use as hoped, and both terms are used interchangeably.

Given the contemporary use of the terms, their history, the potential for misunderstanding, and similar definitions, should we reject this language altogether? Certainly not. In fact, Buell argues that although "race" and "ethnicity" are modern categories, we cannot assume they were irrelevant to early Christians. She notices that early Christian strategies of self-definition resonated with both ancient interpretations of cultural difference and modern ones.[20] What is most important is recognizing how we use the terms "race" and "ethnicity" to identify boundaries between people groups. People groups share distinct identity markers such as culture, lineage, religion, territory, clothing, food, language, and myths of descent, to name a few. These boundaries, however, are not permanent but always shifting and negotiated by both members and non-members of the group.

As a result, when studying race and ethnicity in the Bible, we must be disabused of the notion that "race" or "ethnicity" are permanent, scientifically rooted in biology, and associated with skin color. This is not how the ancients thought about race. Simply because they did not associate race with skin color or biology does not mean they had no understanding of the idea. They identified differences—whether cultural, religious, territorial, or myths of descent—but these differences were not impenetrable boundaries. Instead, their view of race and ethnicity was much broader and negotiable. They could identify and classify different people groups, and knowing that racial identity was malleable, the fear of losing one's racial identity also existed if one did not remain vigilant regarding group boundaries.

---

19. UNESCO, "Scientific Basis for Human Unity," 8; Rahim et al., "UNESCO Statement on Race and Racial Prejudice," 270–72.

20. Buell, *Why This New Race*, xiii.

RACIAL IDEOLOGIES: ENVIRONMENT, GENEALOGY, AND CULTURE

One of the challenges we have in identifying race in the Bible is that we do not think about race as those in the biblical world did. Observable phenotypes such as skin color and bodily features help us make sense of the racial groups. We see blonde hair, and North American or European racial groups come to mind. We see brown skin with almond eyes, and Latin American or indigenous races are a likely guess. This way of thinking is ingrained within our society and has even found its way in children's songs. About a hundred years ago, Clarence Herbert Woolston wrote, "Jesus loves the little children, all the children of the world; red and yellow, black and white, they are precious in his sight, Jesus loves the little children of the world." Perhaps we too can recall our early childhood memories of this song. This innocent song attempts to emphasize Jesus's love for all children, but it is laced with a racial ideology that only makes sense in a modern context. Color is a racial signifier in our modern world. We use color language to distinguish people groups. Those who lived in the ancient world would have found this way of defining racial groups limiting and perhaps odd. This is not to say that skin color was not noticed or a discerning factor. They certainly did notice physical differences between people groups and linked these aspects to racial identity. But there was no such thing as a "white," "black," or "brown" identity. Instead, they turned to environmental, genealogical, and cultural factors to help explain physical and character differences among people groups.

ENVIRONMENTAL FACTORS

The Romans recognized the environment's impact among racial groups. For example, the Scythians were known to have light skin because they lived in the extreme northern region of the known world.[21] Likewise, Ethiopians, who lived in the most southern part of the Roman Empire, were known to have dark skin.[22] When we observe more closely how the Greeks and Romans explained these features, the environment did more than simply influence the physical development and appearance of racial groups. It was believed that the environment also impacted the character and intellect of its inhabitants. Balsdon finds that the Romans took this environmental racial theory to help explain their military success. The Romans believed that those who lived near the equator such as the Ethiopians were considered

---

21. Ptolemy, *Tetra.* 2.2.
22. Pliny, *Nat. hist.* 2.80.

small and to suffer from blood deficiencies that made them bad fighters.[23] Northerners, on the other hand, were tall, deep-voiced, pale-faced, and full-blooded fighters who were courageous but foolish in battle. Since the Romans lived in neither the extreme north or south, this naturally made the Rome superior to the northerners in terms of intelligence and superior to the southerners in terms of physical strength.[24] In other words, environmental determinism was a racial ideology used to explain not only differences among people groups but also why the Roman Empire was victorious.

This, however, is not simply a Roman idea. It was a deeply pervasive racial ideology that can be traced back to the early Greeks, who also made comments and observations about the various people who lived throughout the known Mediterranean world. The origins of environmental determinism can be traced to Hippocrates's *On Airs, Waters, Places*. He asserts that each region has its own weather with distinct soil and inhabitants. In comparison to both these extremes, those that live in moderate temperatures are considered healthier. He states:

> Those that lie toward the risings of the sun are likely to be healthier than those facing the north and those exposed to the hot winds . . . In the first place, the heat and the cold are more moderate . . . For the sun, shining down upon them when it rises, purifies them. The persons of the inhabitants are of better complexion and more blooming than elsewhere, unless some disease prevents this. They are clear-voiced, and with better temper and intelligence than those who are exposed to the north, just as all things growing there are better (*Aer.* 5.10–28).

Notice in the above quote how Hippocrates believes that the weather has a major impact on the aesthetic, health, moral, and intellectual aspect of human identity. One cannot avoid being sicker and aesthetically unpleasing if one resides in either a northern or southern area. Hippocrates finds a strong correlation between one's environment and character, which also includes the reason why Europeans are not ruled by kings but have a rugged individualistic, intelligent, brave, and warlike temperament.[25]

This view, also known as environmental determinism, was later developed by Greek writers such as Plato, Aristotle, and Polybius.[26] They too explained the relationship between the environment and the character and physical appearances of various racial groups. By the time the Romans

---

23. Balsdon, *Romans and Aliens*, 59.
24. Balsdon, *Romans and Aliens*, 60.
25. Hippocrates, *Aer.* 24.1–67.
26. Plato, *Leg.* 747d–e; Aristotle, *Physiogn.* 806b15; Polybius, *Hist.* 4.21.

emerged on the scene, this view was politically useful to justify the conquest and superiority of the Roman race. Vitruvius, a Roman writer, thus asserts:

> The races of Italy are the most perfectly constituted in both respects—in bodily form and in mental activity to correspond to their valor. Exactly as the planet Jupiter is itself temperate, its course lying midway between Mars, which is very hot, and so Italy, lying between the north and the south, is a combination of what is found on each side, and Saturn, which is very cold, so Italy, lying between the north and the south, is a combination of what is found on each side, and her preeminence is well regulated and indisputable.[27]

While this racial theory also contributed to Roman imperial propaganda, it is also important to note that not everyone embraced this belief. Furthermore, this view is also relative to where one considers the "center" of the world. In Jewish literature, Jerusalem is the center of the world, and all other nations are geographically spaced in relation to it.[28] This racial ideology reflected more about how one geographically arranged the environment of racial groups in relation to oneself.

While we do not find many statements that reflect the racial ideology of environmental determinism, some comments do emerge. There are hints in the New Testament that one's identity was reflective of the origin of one's region. Paul quotes a common stereotypical view of the Cretans as "liars," "evil beasts," and "lazy gluttons" (Titus 1:12). The Galatians are described as "foolish," reflective of common intellectual assessments of people who live in distant lands (Gal 3:1). Nathanael doubts whether anything good could come from Nazareth when he realizes this was Jesus's hometown (John 1:46). Some view the disciples with suspicion for speaking and coming from Galilee (Matt 26:69–73; Acts 2:7–8). And Judea is portrayed throughout Roman literature as the eastern part of the empire where corrupting influences originate.[29]

Overall, however, the boundaries of the known Roman world were not viewed with much suspicion by the earliest Christian missionaries. For example, while the Scythians and Ethiopians were viewed as those who lived in the extreme limits of the Roman world, they are also mentioned as people who should hear the gospel. Paul makes mention of his desire to preach the gospel to the Scythians (Col 3:11). Luke describes the conversion of an Ethiopian eunuch by Philip (Acts 8:30–39). Likewise, the gospel

---

27. Vitruviu, *Arch.* 6.1.11.
28. Isa 60:1–16; Jub. 8:19; Ezek 38:12; B. Sahn. 37a.
29. Lucius, *Epit. rom. hist.* 1.47.12.7–8.

given to the disciples was not for their own native region alone, it was to be proclaimed to "the remotest parts of the earth" (Acts 1:8). The universal mission of the gospel stems from Jesus's commission to the disciples and his first followers.[30]

When reading the New Testament or other ancient texts from the New Testament world, this racial ideology should help us pay more close attention to the way in which the environment and geographical regions are described. The following questions can facilitate a closer reading of the biblical text:

1. What are the environmental or geographic regions described in the text?

2. Are any judgments made about the environment and its relation to the racial group or individual who inhabits such a location?

3. Do these environmental deterministic views reflect other views commonly made about the racial group or individual?

If the text under review assesses the environment and its relationship to the moral, intellectual, or physical characteristics of the racial group or individual, then one has more than likely encountered a racial ideology.

While the environment at first helped explain phenotypes between people groups, what is most harmful is the assumption it makes between the environment and the intellectual and moral capabilities of such individuals or racial groups. Overall, this view is fundamentally contrary to the message of the gospel, which teaches in the human worth, dignity, and salvation of all people. What makes this racial belief ultimately irreconcilable with the Christian faith is that the moral, intellectual potential, and value of human beings are linked to the climate and land in which racial groups reside. Geography, in other words, is utilized to justify inhuman treatment of people.

GENEALOGICAL FACTORS

Ancients also utilized the criterion of genealogy to understand racial differences. This by far was one of the most important and fundamental aspects of defining the boundaries between racial groups. Jonathan Hall finds that the ancient Greeks used genealogies to anchor an individual to a group of ancestors of a particular racial group.[31] This does not mean that the genealogies were accurate. This really did not matter for the ancients. What mattered was that the claim for a shared descent was consensually

---

30. Matt 28:19; Mark 16:15–20; Luke 24:47; John 20:20.
31. Hall, *Ethnic Identity*, 25–28.

agreed.[32] Caroline Hodge likewise explores the importance of genealogical relations when traced through a male line and his descendants. Also known as "patrilineal ideology," Hodge explains that this ideology socially organized families through a common ancestor, included the assumption that descendants inherit the ancestor's characteristics, and understood that the corporate group was organically linked together.[33]

Genealogies were indeed utilized to invoke a particular identity that one inherited from an apical ancestor. For example, Alexander the Great was considered a descendant of Hercules which, as Diodorus remarks, gave him the "inherited the physical and moral qualities of greatness."[34] This common conviction continues within Jewish literature. Josephus, in fact, begins his life story by first pointing out his noble lineage and ancestors. He states, "My family is no ignoble one, tracing its descent far back to priestly ancestors."[35] Josephus also explains that while different races may base their claims to nobility on various options, for the Jewish people the connection to the priesthood was "the hallmark of an illustrious line."[36] There was also the recognition that King Herod, an Edomite, tried to rewrite his genealogy by commissioning Nicholas of Damascus to link his identity to a Jewish lineage descending from Babylon.[37] While this may appear humorous at first, it testifies to the need of a king to claim a more noble lineage over the Jewish people he rules.

The opening of Matthew's Gospel states the following, "This is the genealogy of Jesus the Messiah the son of David, the son of Abraham" (Matt 1:1). We may have read these verses and skipped over them. Honestly, genealogies are perhaps not the most inspiring thing to read. In the ancient world, though, one of the most popular ways of understanding racial difference and belonging was in terms of lineages. Reading the lineage of Jesus identifies not only his racial identity, but it also places him within a kingly lineage as a descendant of King David. Last, Paul himself also boasts of his lineage as well, as a "Pharisee descended from Pharisees" (Acts 23:6) and "of the people of Israel, of the tribe of Benjamin, a Hebrew of Hebrews" (Phil 3:5). He reminds people of his heritage and in a sense uses a genealogical argument to assert the honor, prestige, and status he inherited from his ancestors.

32. Hall, *Ethnic Identity*, 25.
33. Hodge, *If Sons, Then Heirs*, 22–23.
34. Diodorus, *Bib. his.* 17.1.5; 17.4.1.
35. Josephus, *Vita.* 1.1.
36. Josephus, *Vita.* 1.1–2.
37. Josephus, *Ant.* 14.9.

Tell me who your ancestors are, and I can know and understand your identity. This would have been the racial logic in the ancient world. Lineage was everything in the ancient world. It justified power and prestige, including the right to rule. Although useful in determining family relations and maintaining a cohesive group identity by appealing to shared ancestors, they also had limitations. This racial ideology certainly has the potential to justify segregationist attitudes, especially if it was believed that the quality of an entire people is determined by lineage preservation. In fact, Isaac recognizes that for some, genealogical purity signified racial superiority.[38] This racial ideology, as a result, would put immigrants and foreigners in a status of perpetual suspicion. It also could be used to rationalize the inhumane treatment of racial groups on the assumption that racial mixture among different groups would produce inferior descendants.

However, this racial ideology was important for the emergence of early Christian self-understanding. Within the New Testament we also find how the gentile mission and inclusion was explained in terms of a lineage racial logic. We see this specifically in Paul's dialogue on the role of Abraham and the role faith has in incorporating gentiles into the family of God (Gal 3:6–9). For Paul, the promise God gave to Abraham's descendants was not only to those related to him through genealogical relations, but it also includes those related to Abraham through faith in God (Rom 4:12–16). Who were those incorporated in the line of Abraham? Gentiles! In fact, Hodge remarks that Paul "constructs for them a myth of origins which is intimately tied to Jewish origins."[39] Indeed, Gal 3:27, most often quoted to explain why race does not matter, is actually a racial argument. Paul explains that since believers have faith in Jesus, they have become children of God and belong to Christ. As a result of this new linkage to Christ and God through faith, they are thus incorporated into the lineage of Abraham (Gal 3:26–29). The theology of Paul in these passages only makes sense when we understand that Paul is using a racial argument to explain how gentiles have been incorporated into the family of God and thus receive the promises God gave to Abraham and his descendants.

This is not to suggest that this racial argument was the most important factor. Sometimes, lineages were subverted. This is most specifically noticed in the Gospel of John when it asserts that the children of God are those not defined in terms of their ancestry but due to being born into the lineage of God (John 1:11–13).[40] In fact, to be "born of the Spirit" would have pri-

---

38. Isaac, *Invention of Racism*, 109–48.
39. Hodge, *If Sons, Then Heirs*, 85.
40. Estrada, *Race, Kinship, Empire*, 111–34.

marily served as a racial argument destabilizing the racial structures that defined one's identity in relation to a patriarchal ancestor. When reading the biblical text, we must stay mindful of the ways the racial logic of genealogies is used to construct or deconstruct racial identity. We can ask ourselves the following questions:

1. In what way is the genealogical argument used within the text?
2. What are the characteristics or traits within the genealogy and assumed that descendants inherit?
3. Who is mentioned in the genealogies, and what are their characteristics or traits?
4. Are genealogies used to justify or subvert racial identity?

While genealogies are mostly traced through a male figure, female figures do emerge. It is therefore important to notice how the genealogies are used and for what purpose.

Nonetheless, being a descendant of an important figure was no small matter. Identifying one's racial identity according to one's lineage also invoked the honor and privileges that come from an apical ancestor. Buell indeed notes that Christians used genealogical myths of descent to define themselves with a respected pedigree by asserting historical relation to key figures such as Abraham and Jesus.[41] This should disabuse us from the notion that race did not matter in the ancient world. It proved vital for understanding not only the identity of Jesus and Paul, but also to help explain how believers can now incorporate into the family of God.

CULTURAL FACTORS

Apart from lineage and environment, culture was an important manner for understanding oneself and others. Culture was a distinguishing mark of racial groups. Indeed, the Romans were known to value morality and culture more than lineage.[42] The Roman elite even assumed that the goal of Roman imperialism was to civilize humanity with Roman culture.[43] While culture separated various racial groups, sometimes culture also provided proof of a common racial identity. During the emergence of the Roman Empire, some writers desired to trace the beginnings of the Latin people. Virgil's *Aeneid* is one popular attempt to link the Romans as descendants of Aeneas, a Trojan

---

41. Buell, *Why This New Race?*, 75–76, 90–91.
42. Woolf, "Becoming Roman," 130.
43. Pliny, *Nat. his.* 3.6.

who escaped and migrated to Italy after the war and fall of Troy. Dionysius of Halicarnassus, a Greek historian during the reign of Augustus, also attempts to prove that the Romans are truly descendants of the Greek Trojans by appealing to their common customs,[44] insisting:

> In these cities there survived for a very long time many of the ancient customs formerly in use among the Greeks, such as the fashion of their arms of war . . . and whenever they sent out an army beyond their borders, either to begin a war or to resist an invasion, certain holy men, unarmed, went ahead of the rest bearing the terms of peace; similar, also, were the structure of their temples, the images of their gods, their purifications and sacrifices and many other things of that nature.[45]

Like Virgil, Dionysius links the Romans to the Greeks by appealing to their common lineage. But Dionysius adds further proof of this connection. He points to their similar cultural traditions which includes their weapons of war, religion, and sacrifices. More specifically, he points out that it was the "temple of Juno" that the Romans built in the same style of the one that was built in Argos, a Greek city.[46] Common cultural practices with the Trojan Greeks, in other words, served as proof of Roman racial identity.

Shared cultural traditions were not only utilized to prove the Roman identity but also to define the Greek identity. Isocrates claimed that being a Greek was not simply a lineage claim but an "intelligence," and that the name Greek could be applied to those who shared the Greek culture.[47] Alexander the Great also attempted to redefine the Greek identity as he expanded and influenced various regions with Greek culture. For Alexander, a Greek was defined in terms of virtue, and barbarians were defined in terms of their iniquity.[48] This redefinition of the Greek identity in terms of morality was not only a move away from an emphasis on lineage and environment but also opened the possibility for recently conquered subjects to become Greek. Specifically, Greekness began to be viewed as a cultural way of life; it did not simply mean having a particular association with an apical ancestor or territory. Anyone could become Greek if they decided to live like a Greek and be formed in the Greek way of life.

Cultural traditions became definitive proof of racial identity during the Roman age. It was not simply lineage or appeal to a common homeland

---

44. Dionysius, *Rom. ant.* 1.5.2; 1.89.1–2.
45. Dionysius, *Rom. ant.* 1.21.1.
46. Dionysius, *Rom. ant.* 1.21.2.
47. Isocrates, *Paneg.* 50.
48. Plutarch, *Alex fort.* 329.c–d.

that defined one's racial identity. McCoskey, in fact, points out that racial identity was both "formed and preformed."⁴⁹ This not only helps us recognize the malleability of racial identity but also the need to maintain racial identity through one's way of life.⁵⁰ Furthermore, Jonathan Hall also adds that cultural performance as a marker of racial identity seems to have been more important over time.⁵¹ That is, one can become associated, classified, or belong to a racial group based on the daily activities, habits, and lifestyle practices. Being a Greek or Roman meant living like a Greek or Roman. This also suggests that racial identity was not permanent. One could possibly be influenced by the cultures of other racial groups and thus lose or develop a racial identity.

While culture was distinguishable between people groups, what mattered most was the way in which culture structured and organized one's way of life according to the customs and habits accepted and approved by the racial group. Yet culture as a way of life also becomes an easy target to disparage, especially when compared to the "civilized" Romans or Greeks. In several instances within Greek and Roman literature, the superiority or inferiority of racial groups was judged on their closeness to Roman and Greek culture. People were considered "barbarian" simply for being non-Greek. Indeed, Edith Hall remarks that the idea of a "barbarian" was created to serve as a " . . . universal anti-Greek against whom Hellenic—especially Athenian—culture was defined."⁵² Some, however, objected to the assertion of essential differences between Greeks and barbarians. Cicero, a Roman statesman writing in 51 BCE during the Republic of Rome, narrates a debate between Scipio and Laelius on whether Romulus, the founder of Rome, was a king of barbarians. Laelius states, "If that name [barbarian] ought to be applied on the basis of men's manners rather than their language, I do not consider the Greeks less barbarous than the Romans." Scipio also responds by suggesting that "character, not race" ought to define one as a barbarian.⁵³ In this short dialogue, character and customs define the barbarian, not their association or non-association to the Greek identity.

While culture served as an important factor for understanding racial identity in the Greek and Roman world, it was also a limited marker of racial identity given that every act or material object may not have equal

---

49. McCoskey, *Race*, 81.
50. Estrada, "Racial Significance of Paul's Clothing," 1–13.
51. Hall, *Hellenicity*, 189–220.
52. Hall, *Inventing the Barbarian*, 5.
53. Cicero, *Resp.* 1.58.

significance.[54] This suggests that the cultural practices themselves must be a meaningful marker of one's identity and used to either define one's group or serve to contrast another racial group. The questions for us are the following:

1. What cultural practices are actively proclaimed, championed, defended, or highlighted as markers of racial identity?
2. Are cultural practices used to distinguish or contrast a racial group? If so, what possible motivations exist for such portrayal?
3. Is the performance or maintenance of the cultural practice being used to maintain group solidarity or cohesion?

Now, some practices of daily life were ubiquitous to all racial groups, but if one comes across a cultural practice or custom that specifically distinguishes one racial group from another and that was vitally important as a way of maintaining group cohesion, then one is more than likely to stumble across a marker of racial identity.

RACE IS EVERYWHERE

Studying race in the ancient world requires that we understand how the ancients understood this concept in their own terms, not with respect to our modern categories. Once we do so, it should help disabuse us from the notion that race did not exist in the ancient world and that they found the concept unimportant. In the Mediterranean world, the notion of race and ethnicity emerged most clearly when people groups were defined, classified, or differentiated. Race and ethnicity are terms used to understand the boundaries between people groups.

As we have observed, environmental conditions not only helped explain physical differences between racial groups, but it was also believed that the environment impacted the innate character of people groups. The Greeks and Romans used environmental determinism to justify conquest and imperial domination of foreigners. While this view ultimately was a way to stereotypically describe the intellectual and character traits of racial groups, it fundamentally stands contrary to the gospel belief in the human dignity of all people. The ancients tied racial identity to environment. "Tell me what region you are from, and I can know who you are" would have been a common way of understanding people groups.

Regarding genealogies, the ancients understood the importance of their ancestors and relation to others by means of them. Genealogies were open, negotiable, and vital for the understanding of one's identity, especially

---

54. McCoskey, *Race*, 86.

if one was related to a heroic ancestor or god. Genealogies helped people understand kinship relations, assisted in political diplomacy, were utilized to invoke moral or character traits, and in some cases, became a tool to justify the segregation between racial groups. People in the ancient world would have asked, "Tell me who your ancestors and I will know who you are." Racial identity was derived from a linkage to one's ancestors.

Culture, likewise, was an important factor in defining racial groups. It was not about how one looked, who one's ancestor was, or where one was born. One could say, "Tell me how you live, and I will know who you are." It was about how one lived that enabled one to become classified or to join a racial group. While some were open to the customs and practices of racial groups, others found cultural influences a threat. This also suggests that racial identity was fluid and liable to change. What mattered most, though, was whether the cultural marker had racial significance for the racial group.

Now that we have observed some factors that reveals how the ancients thought about race, how does this expand our hermeneutical imagination? Perhaps now, at the minimum, we are more attuned to those aspects in Scripture that we casually glanced over or did not even notice. Hopefully you can now see "race" all around you, especially as it emerges within Scripture. Racial identity was very important for the ancients, and for early Christians specifically as they emerged and defined their own identity in light of contesting ones. For them, one's homeland, genealogies, and culture were matters of race, and this too was vital for their own self-understanding.

BIBLIOGRAPHY

Balsdon, John P. V. D. *Romans and Aliens*. London: Duckworth, 1979.

Buell, Denise. *Why This New Race: Ethnic Reasoning in Early Christianity*. New York: Columbia University Press, 2007.

Edelman, Diana. "Ethnicity and Early Israel." In *Ethnicity and the Bible*, edited by Mark G. Brett, 25–55. London: Brill, 1996.

Estrada, Rodolfo. *A Latino Reading of Race, Kinship, and the Empire: John's Prologue*. Switzerland: Palgrave MacMillan, 2023.

———. "The Racial Significance of Paul's Clothing Metaphor (Romans 13:14; Galatians 3:27; Ephesians 4:24; Colossians 3:10)." *Religions* 14 (2023) 1–13.

Gruen, Eric. *Rethinking the Other in Antiquity*. Princeton, NJ: Princeton University Press, 2011.

Hall, Edith. *Inventing the Barbarian: Greek Self-Definition through Tragedy*. New York: Oxford, 2004.

Hall, Jonathan. *Ethnic Identity in Greek Antiquity.* New York: Cambridge University, 2000.

———. *Hellenicity: Between Ethnicity and Culture.* Chicago: University of Chicago, 2002.

Hodge, Caroline Johnson. *If Sons, Then Heirs: A Study of Kinship and Ethnicity in the Letters of Paul.* New York: Oxford University Press, 2007.

Isaac, Benjamin. *The Invention of Racism in Classical Antiquity.* Princeton, NJ: Princeton University, 2004.

Kittel, G., and G. Friedrich, eds. *Theological Dictionary of the New Testament.* 10 vols. Translated by G. W. Bromiley. Grand Rapids: Eerdmans, 1964–1976.

McCoskey, Denise Eileen. *Race Antiquity and Its Legacy.* New York: Oxford University Press, 2012.

Rahim, Muddathir Abdel, et al. "UNESCO Statement on Race and Racial Prejudice." *Current Anthropology* 9 (1968) 270–72.

Rendtorff, Rolf. "The Gēr in the Priestly Laws of the Pentateuch." In *Ethnicity and the Bible,* edited by Mark G. Brett, 77–87. London: Brill, 1996.

Sechrest, Love. *A Former Jew: Paul and the Dialects of Race.* New York: Bloomsbury, 2009.

UNESCO. United Nations Education, Scientific and Cultural Organization. "The Scientific Basis for Human Unity." *UNESCO Courier* 3 (1950) 8–9.

Woolf, Greg. "Becoming Roman, Staying Greek: Culture, Identity, and the Civilizing Process in the Roman East." *Proceedings of the Cambridge Philological Society* 40 (1994) 116–43.

Chapter 26
Asian Hermeneutics
K. K. YEO

To make our discussion illustrative and meaningful, the essay surveys the topic of salvation in Asia. Though the largest, most highly populated, and most iridescent continent in the world, Asia does not have one metanarrative but a myriad of lifeworlds, complex contexts, and diverse needs.[55] Asia's kaleidoscopic views of soteriology (the study of salvation) have both similar and contradictory precepts. Understanding Asia's massive and many-layered *Sitz im Leben* (life situation), as well as its relationship to the rich soteriological semantics in the Bible, is the hermeneutical task of this essay. It will demonstrate that Asian hermeneutic of soteriology is able to mirror and dialogue with its counterpoint in the robust biblical-theological world.

ASIAN LIFEWORLD AND TRADITIONAL SOTERIOLOGY

Soteriology begins with the area of need in a lifeworld, and Asian sociopolitical realities give rise to the contextual problems—of plight and terror, chaos and war, alienation and displacement, dictatorship and regional colonialism, famine and poverty, migration, and trafficking, to name a few. These contexts call for salvation at every level of Asian sentient life, and Asian soteriology inevitably addresses injustice, natural disasters, human mismanagement, and the thickness of Sin (an upper-case "S" is used to refer

---

55. Yeo, "Introduction," 1–13; Yeo, *What Has Jerusalem to Do with Beijing?*, 120–50, 208–40. All biblical translations in this chapter are mine, unless NRSV is noted and used.

to the "*power* of sin") that curses and destroys superabundant life in the cosmos and in human flourishing.

ASIAN LIFEWORLD: THREE FRAMES OF SIN AND SALVATION

There are three hermeneutical frames for Sin and salvation that will help explicate Asian soteriology, as Asian hermeneutic does not shy away from the use of the Bible. The first frame is goodness and evil in the moral sense. Almost all Asian religions or schools (Confucianism, Daoism, Hinduism, Buddhism, Islam, folk or tribal religions) understand order and chaos *morally*; thus, Sin is understood as perversion, sickness ("of the soul," Ps 32:3–5; Isa 1:4–5), and salvation is about healing (Ps 41:4), therapy, well-being (Mark 2:16–17; Jer 3:21–22), and healing (1 Pet 2:24). Despotism and bribery could be understood in terms of a fractured or sick soul that departs from the cosmic principle; poor health and famine are considered a departure from the moral law of God or gods. Salvation is about returning to God for blessings and to obey God's moral law.

In both personal and public realms, there is a strong emphasis in Asian discourse on the *ethics* of imperial worship, ancestral veneration, nationalism, tribal identity, and war in light of veterans' post-traumatic stress syndrome. Jeong-sook Kim has narrated the salvific healing that Korean shamans (*mudang*) have provided to the *minjung* (the people). In undergoing oppression, suffering, and the vicissitudes of life, the *minjung* were taught the possibility of being transformed into being fully human and becoming divine, thus attaining eternal salvation.[56] Christ's sore (*mōlōps* is a sore not arising from an illness but a blow to the body) draws "the damaged substances [of Christ's followers] so that the surrounding tissue [of Christ's followers] can become and remain healthy" (1 Pet 2:24), and this hygienic-salvific metaphor explains "Christ's sore can provide healing for all of his followers since they comprise his body."[57]

The second frame assumes a legal universe in which God is the Law-Giver establishing smooth operation of all things in the universe. Asian believers understand the biblical notion of "sin" as missing the mark (*hamartia* in 1 John 3:14 or *hattat* in Exod 20:20), to stray away (*chata'ah* in Ps 109:7), to act wrongly (*avar* in Deut 17:2) or defiantly (*awon* in Num 15:30–31); even to rebel/transgress (*pasha* in Ps 32:1) against the rules is considered law-breaking. Salvation, therefore, is forensic justification and

---

56. Kim, "Humanization and Divinization," 69–81.
57. Martin, "Christ's Healing Sore," 143–54.

atoning for guilt. But in this Internet-driven, technological, and globalized age, God's law and "sin" and "salvation" are questioned in light of the bioethics challenges to the Asian soteriological views regarding the legality of human cloning, stem-cell research, or border crossing in the global market of "need and supply." We debate the moral legitimacy of human-organ trade in colonial and postcolonial realities (e.g., a Canadian patient bought a liver from a man in Bangladesh), about the personal identity of surrogate motherhood, or exporting of maid-services.

The third frame is very relevant to the Asian lifeworld, but not well articulated in Asian churches. This frame assumes that Sin is shame (the metaphor for "nakedness" in the Gen 2–3 story), "falling short of the glory of God" (Rom 3:23), who alone creates a holy and beautiful universe by covering his creatures with his holy presence and glory. Salvation can be understood as the restoration of God's image (which is truthfully beautiful; 2 Cor 3:18; Rom 13:14; Gal 3:27) by God the wisdom (Prov 8–9; "*hokmah*" and "Sophia"; cf. Col 1:15, Heb 1:3). In the Asian lifeworld, which to a large extent is still plagued by disease, strife, pollution, and poverty, victims see Sin in terms of curse and shame. Experiences such as COVID-19, SARS, famine, wars—even massacres like the Rape of Nanjing in the Second World War—are registered as disgrace and dehumanization. With the growth of multi- or transnational corporations, resulting in an asymmetry of wealth and increasing oppression of the poor, children, women, and the environment, Asian eyes cannot simply turn to cheap forgiveness and peace but must strive for basic human dignity and ecological sustainability.

Asian Christians understand the three transcendental frames (truth, goodness, beauty), as the apostle Paul writes, "Do not be conformed to this age (*aeon*), but be transformed (a major aspect of salvation) by the renewing of your minds (*nous*), so that you all may discern what is the will of God—what is good (virtuous/morality) and acceptable (delightful/beauty) and perfect (whole/truthful)" (Rom 12:2). In other words, Asian soteriology is both a personal and a cosmic process in which honor brings truth and goodness to the authentic selves of humanity and all creation (Titus 2:11). I am suggesting in the next section that the way Asian soteriology has emerged out of its context is inevitably different from the traditional soteriology of Western Europe and North America.

TRANSCENDING TRADITIONAL HERMENEUTIC TOWARD ASIAN SOTERIOLOGY

Is Asian soteriology spiritual enlightenment, self-awakening, individual redemption, social liberation, achievement of nirvana? Yes, but it is also much more. First, the mystical Orthodox understanding of believers pursuing salvation in the divinization of human beings can be a helpful reflection of God-consciousness (F. D. E. Schleiermacher), of the Daoist soteriology of "becoming immortals" (*chengxian*), or the Buddhist soteriology of attaining Buddha-nature (*tathāgatagarbha*).[58] In the Chinese, Japanese, and Korean worlds of "mountain wizardry" and "supernaturalism of atmospheric force," in many life disciplines of Christians and non-Christians alike, this pursuit of salvation in divinization is common. Dietary discipline, herbal treatment, breathing, and meditative exercises are taught to help practitioners achieve inner peace and immortality. This Daoist and, to a certain extent the yin-yang, Buddhist, and folks' religious influence on Chinese and Korean Christianity have shaped Christian spirituality of a charismatic sort that includes questing for miracles, but now in the new semantic of "the power of the Holy Spirit." Salvation in much of Asian folk Christianity includes seeking a miraculous cure to heal sickness and to solve problems, all through the power of prayer and the supernatural.

Second, the ransom theory (Athanasius, Irenaeus, Martin Luther) can explain the soteriology of Asian Catholic and Protestant churches, whose members believe in the vicarious atonement of Jesus (Isa 53:10; Rom 3:22–25; Heb 10:12, 14; Mark 10:45) for believers. Some would see Jesus as the victor over chaos, the devil, sin and death, while others hold to the penal-substitutionary soteriology and believe Jesus's victory of self-sacrifice is expressed in his taking up, on sinners' behalf, the sin of infringing on the justice of God's law.

The Asian contexts of guilt, brokenness, shame, and honor appeal to this view readily. The ransom theory speaks volumes to Asians, but not to its victims. In the case of genocide, for example, the Stolen Generation in Australia was deprived of its culture, and do those individuals themselves need a ransom from God? To rephrase, how is God's honor wounded in their case? It is the perpetrators who need ransom. Mandy Tibbey, an Anglican barrister at Sydney, suggests correctly that a grand-scale effort such as "national Apology or constitutional change" may not necessarily be the right move to bring about change.[59]

Soteriology in an Asian context is very "messy." To Asians, settlers and colonizers who have committed atrocities need to be saved from their ethnocentrism and superiority complex; the Stolen Generation needs the salvation of honor restored to them. Similarly, the Vietnamese and their children, disabled by the Agent Orange sprayed by US forces during the

---

58. Chung, "Martin Luther and *Shinran*," 295–310.
59. Tibbey, "From Little Things Big Things Grow," 59.

war against the Vietcong and Vietnamese fighters, need not repentance but reparation and apologies. God is shamed when "justice is turned back, and righteousness stands at a distance; for truth stumbles in the *public square*, and uprightness cannot enter" (Isa 59:14 NRSV). God is honored when US citizens and Vietnamese are able to embrace one another towards mutual forgiveness and honor one another.

Third, the Asian moral lifeworld found affinity with the moral-example theory (Peter Abelard, Horace Bushnell), as believers imitate Christ's self-denial of life for the realization of a peaceful and just society. Along this view is the Confucianist impulse of self-cultivation for the sake of world's *shalom* ("inwardly a sage outwardly a king"), thus finding greater affinity with participatory soteriology—the union with Christ are those who participate in the dying and rising Christ-pattern of life, so that believers are internally transformed as they are outwardly transforming their lifeworld.

The Asian dynamic languages and holistic thinking can hardly split human actions or religious faith into "indicative and imperative," for religion and ethics are two sides of the same coin. Charles Taylor alludes to the dualistic split of Eurocentric thinking as the problem of "excarnation" living in our head "buffering" experience.[60] For just as Asian thinking is always enmeshed in life context, theology is embedded in life. As such, the distinctive feature of Asian soteriology is the way theologians or Christians weave their biographies in and out their engagement with the biblical texts in areas of need. For example, there is a common ethical aspect of salvation in both Myanmar Christianity (such as, with the Mosaic Law, the Beatitudes, and other New Testament laws) and Theravada Buddhism (the *Sila*), such as the right thought (theology), right speech (teaching), right action (living). This religious-ethical teaching could easily be a centrifugal force that brings about peaceful co-existence of different religions in Myanmar. The teachings of Gautama Buddha and Jesus are ways of life and, in that regard, are similar; they are often not regarded as abstract philosophies.

ASIAN INTERPRETATIONS THROUGH BIBLICAL SEMANTIC LENSES

While none of the Asian languages may preserve the beauty of the biblical Hebrew word, *Yeshua*, meaning "God saves" (and transliterated into Greek as "Jesus"), yet an Asian hermeneutic could embody that beauty in soteriology. The notion of "God saves" ("sotēr" in Greek) is not restrictive but expansive, seen in the biblical wealth of semantics (save, deliver, liberate,

---

60. Taylor, *Secular Age*, 771.

redeem, reconcile, set right, vindicate, expiate, propitiate, etc.) and the comprehensive repertoire (creation, redemption, consummation, personal, social, cosmic, etc.) about salvation. I wish to use these biblical semantics to guide us through Asian hermeneutic of salvation.

WORLD OF SPIRIT, HUMAN, AND COSMOS: GOD SAVES

Various Asian creation myths point to the beginning of the universe, but the notion of Creator and creation is often not differentiated in Asian languages. Asian Christians understand cognitively that God is the Creator (Isa 40:12–31) and Savior (Isa 43:14—44:6). Yet, they also wish salvation were about becoming divine, becoming one with God (*tianren heyi* [heaven and human becoming one]; becoming Buddha or at least possessing the nature of Buddha).

Asian Christians believe that if God is able to create (*bara*) by means of calling/naming (speech-act) creation into being, then human beings gifted with language could continue or participate in the creation and redemption of the world from the primordial chaos. Asian narratives and languages are an essential part of the work of Asian soteriology. R. S. Sugirtharajah (a Sri Lankan scholar living in the UK) writes of four modes of biblical interpretation (orientalist, anglicist, nativistic, postcolonial criticism),[61] each of which has different salvific functions and values. Vernacular translation becomes vernacular-soteriology, because it saves the Bible from speaking the truth imperialistically, from wiping out the "sweetness and light" (beauty and intelligence) of indigenous cultures. Vernacular translation also saves a culture, as it gives new meaning to otherwise complacent, monocultural, parochial ways of life.

The verb "save" (*sōzō* in LXX and NT [John 3:17]) or the noun "salvation" (*sōtēria*), describes the Lord or God as "my Savior" (Luke 1:47) and, expressed in the Asian context, could mean "salvation from our enemies" (Luke 1:71). The Asian world of spirits, demons, and the dead often inflicts terror, curse, and confusion upon people. Thus, salvation from demon possession or influence, fear in the spirit world, harm from the occult and witches, psychological suffering from magic and superstitions, are not entertainments of the movie world. Prayers, healing services, and sermons in churches on this topic are common, and the following biblical texts become favorites: Ps 31 (deliverance from enemies and persecutors) and Ps 35 (rescue from their ravages), Ps 91 (deliverance from the snare of the fowler, deadly pestilence); Eph 6 (standing against the wiles of the devil, the cosmic

---

61. Sugirtharajah, *Asian Biblical Hermeneutics and Postcolonialism*, 16–20.

powers of this present darkness, the spiritual forces of evil in the heavenly places).

THE WORLD OF BONDAGE: GOD DELIVERS

The Asian lifeworld of bondage and slavery is as real as any in the Bible. The Lord's Prayer uses a synonym, *ruomai* (deliver, rescue), of *sōzō* (save): "deliver us from the evil one" (Matt 6:13). This is taken in Asian contexts as referring to the harsh conditions of life, sociopolitically or otherwise. In Rom 11:26, the use of synonyms is not redundant, but a highlighted repetition: "All Israel will be saved (*sōthērsetai*), as is written, "out of Zion will come the Deliverer (*ruomenos*)." Liberation (*eleutheroō*) is a cognate of salvation, of personal, sociopolitical, and even cosmic levels, in the New Testament: "If the Son has liberated you, you will be liberated indeed" (John 8:36); "creation itself will be liberated from the bondage of decay and will enter upon the glorious liberty of the children of God" (Rom 8:21).

The Asian sociopolitical liberation theology hits a high note in *dalit* ("downtrodden") and *minjung* ("of the people") theologies, and the Asian church in India and Korea respectively have taken up solidarity soteriology in liberating the oppressed. 15 percent of the Indian population are *dalits* who make up of 60 percent of Indian Christians. Although they are perceived as the "untouchables" (*panchamas*), thought to be "polluted" by birth and thus simply not taught Sanskrit, *dalits* becoming Christians means finding hope and salvation in reading the Bible. And they find liberation in Tamil folk music and sharing meals. Siosifa Pole, working among the pasifika diaspora in New Zealand, uses a Tongan understanding of *vahevahe* (sharing) as a life of discipleship participating in the salvation of Christ.[62]

Minjung theologians spoke against dictator Park Chung Hee (1917–1979) in the 1970s. Similar to the *Minjung* theology of Korea, the Homeland theology in Taiwan claimed their right to Taiwan. Another example is the Umbrella Movement (which happened in Umbrella Square in Hong Kong) or the recent Occupy Central with Love and Peace (OCLP, which happened in the district of Central in Hong Kong). By the fall of 2014, the people of Hong Kong, including Christians, took to the streets protesting the nepotistic will of the Chinese Communist rule. This grassroots mobilization is liberation soteriology resisting the structure of what Slavoj Žižek calls the People's Republic of China's "totalitarian capitalism."[63] Using Edward Said's understanding of "occupation," Sam Tsang, a Hong Kong biblical theologian, argues that Christian responses to the Umbrella Movement have been

62. Pole, "*Vahevahe.*"
63. Ackerman and Žižek, "Slavoj Žižek."

divisive because the concept of "liberation" being contextual is rather limiting in the Hong Kong case.[64]

Biblical texts are used as a source of solace and resistance during political oppression. Both Revelation and 1 and 2 Thessalonians granted Christians prophetic hope and practical wisdom to thrive during the Cultural Revolution in China.[65] Romans was used as a hidden transcript for Christians in Malaysia to be faithful during occasional Islamic oppression.[66] Unfortunately, biblical texts often are used also to oppress the poor or spiritualized or to hold women in a place of submission. Salvation is attended to when one strives to "care for orphans and widows in their distress, and to keep oneself unstained by the world" (Jas 1:27). Liberation has to do with not only the individual level but also with empowering the poor and oppressed with a voice to bring about structural change politically, economically, and racially.

In Asia "I am the bread of life" (John 6:41–51) is not simply spiritual nourishment but also food on the table, in light of the similar context of hunger (1 Kgs 19:4–8) in Elijah and Elisha's ministry as they faced problems of natural catastrophe or government mismanagement. The Chinese saying, "[People regard] food as heaven," stressing the social meal of fellowship, thus echoes the "milk and honey" promised land (Deut 31:20). On the other hand, those, especially the powerful and the wealthy when they are autocratic and corrupt, have judgment passed on them in that their "callous heart" becomes "fatty, bloated and gorged," and the Deuteronomy diagnosis of this moral and spiritual sickness is: "He abandoned God who made him, and scoffed at the Rock of his salvation" (Deut 32:15).

Asian soteriology pays attention not just to anthropological but also to ecological poverty and repression. Global warming impinges on the Asian lifeworld; mining and water pollution also are major problems in many Asian countries.

THE WORLD OF ENMITY: GOD RECONCILES

The Asian world of enmity and hostility points to the need for reconciliation, a biblical word (*katallagē*, Rom 5:10–11, 2 Cor 5:18–20) sometimes mistranslated as "atonement" (W. Tyndale), focusing on overcoming the enmity between God and humanity. Paul here is using the Roman context of transforming conflict to friendship and love, and therefore not the OT idea

---

64. Tsang, "Exegeting the Occupation of Hong Kong," 156.

65. Yeo, *Chairman Mao Meets the Apostle Paul*, 163–228; Yeo, *What Has Jerusalem to Do with Beijing?*, 129–36, 194–241, 255–67.

66. Hii, "Contesting the Ideology of the Empire."

of atonement sacrifice (Lev 16). Kenneth R. Ross, in an essay titled, "Asia's Cry for Reconciliation," sketches a new age of conflict in Asia across ethnic, national, and religious lines such as in India and Pakistan; the Maoist insurgency in Nepal; civil war in Sri Lanka; the Christian-Muslim conflict in Indonesia; military dictatorship in Myanmar; military build-up, rebellion, and unrest in Thailand and Myanmar.[67] Reconciliation means truth-telling in speaking of corrupted power as injustice. Ross suggests that reconciliation also means following Christ so that "our wounds become a source of healing for others" and "in these deep places of faith that the resources are found which make reconciliation possible."[68]

Making Buddhism or Islam a national religion mandated by the government in any Asian country is one of the major causes of ethnic conflict and racial hatred. The Malaysian Islamic government prohibits the Arabic word "Allah" to be used by Christians referring to God. Similarly, any national churches adopting state ideology to support national self-identity and social harmony—such as Three-Self Churches in China (pressure from the government to do so)—inevitably alienates the family church; Indonesian churches under the Suharto regime in adopting *Pancasila* (literally "five principles") brought about division and hatred among local communities. In this context, a hermeneutic of reconciliation is adamant in the theological method of "interculturality" that "goes beyond binary thinking of 'us' and 'them' as well as the exoticization of diversity, in favour of an empowering in-beyond."[69] "Empowering in-beyond" is practiced in the following ways of reconciliation:

1. The people's theology of *minjung* or *dalit*, as discussed previously, in resisting the disparity structure of inequalities and exploitation towards the universal love of God in ushering God's just and egalitarian society.

2. The power of theology to save with story and memory for the Vietnamese in the atrocity of the Vietnam War, saying the liturgy re-performs the dark night of the soul, and the eucharistic "re-membering" grants new life and power.

3. The courage to forgive persons while holding them accountable for their actions. Taken in the Asian context, the Lord's prayer intends for oppressive bankers and harsh financial officials to ask God to "Forgive [their] debts, as [they] also have forgiven [their] debtors" (Matt 6:12).

67. Ross, "Asia's Cry for Reconciliation," 412–30.
68. Ross, "Asia's Cry for Reconciliation," 426.
69. Brazal and Guzman, "Intercultural Church," 71.

SECTION 3 • CONTEXTUAL INTERPRETATION
THE WORLD OF DOMINATION/UTILITY: GOD REDEEMS

The Asian world of domination and utilitarianism calls for redemption (*apolytrosis*; Rom 3:24). The redemption metaphor has a slave-market backdrop, such as: Exod 21:8's Egyptian slavery, Isa 51:11 and Isa 59:20's Babylonian captivity, or Rom 6:13–14's first-century Roman society. Other scriptural verses portray redemption from the wrath of God (Rom 5:9), from the power of Sin (Eph 1:7, 14; Rom 5) and from the power of death (Rom 6:23), from the curse of the law (Gal 3:13), and so forth. But the point is always about the *new status of freedom*, thus pointing to the soteriological goal of redeemed people as God's own possession (Exod 15:16; 1 Pet 2:9).

A culture of patriarchal domination is challenged by Asian womanist and feminist scholars. Indonesian Christian women, such as Marianne Katoppo, teach compassion despite the context of hatred and enmity.[70] Malaysian scholar Elaine Goh examines how Ecclesiastes can be used to speak to the redemption needed for Chinese who possess "the mentality of fearing death, over-confidence and workaholic tendency."[71]

Domination is found in local societies, but it also permeates countries in dynamics such as the conflict over territory. Military conquest or the exercise of soft power disrupt life across borders. Asian churches face challenges of migration, irredentism, annexation, and conquest—all of which bring about restlessness and confusion. Diaspora and migration are the "new-normal" way of life for many Asians, and much has been written on nomadic consciousness, exile and hybridity, liminality and marginality; some Asian scholars speak of the "in-betweenness" of theological method in yin-yang thought.

Because of globalization, the modern world has become once more nomadic tribes. Our modern-day caravans are Apple Pay, Amazon Prime, UPS, airplanes, and Twitter. Some Asian nations "export" maids for family and national incomes. Other international syndicates trade forced child- and sex-labors and various forms of human trafficking. Asia is a hot market for all of these enterprises.

How do Asian churches respond to the Asian need of salvation? Jonathan Y. Tan writes about the Asian theology of migration implied by the Documents of the Federation of Asian Bishops' Conferences (FABC) since 1970s. The theology of migration is based on the reign of God in its "commitment and service to life," not simply intellectually but first and foremost pastorally and missiologically "in liberating our societies from whatever

---

70. Katoppo, *Compassionate and Free*.
71. Goh, "Qohelet's Gospel in Ecclesiastes," 180.

oppresses and degrades human life and creation."[72] Becoming an intercultural church in Asia is the path of the migrant church. The migrant theology of intercultural hospitality is consistent with interpreting the Bible from the margins, the borderland, the Jebusites and Canaanites, from the outcast. Xenophilia, not xenophobia, is to be the Asian ethos of hospitality, for the God of the Bible redeems a world of domination by means of hospitality to strangers and aliens.

THE WORLD OF SHAME (DEHUMANIZATION): GOD SETS RIGHT AND HAS MERCY

The Asian world of shame and dehumanization is particularly striking, since shame and honor are intrinsic in Asian cultures. Unfortunately, the biblical phrase "being set right" (*dikiaōthēsetai*; Rom 1:23–24) is often taught by North Atlantic biblical scholarship and missionary teachers as "judicial justification and imputed righteousness." Robert Jewett's commentary on Romans attempts to provide an alternative reading: God stands with the weak and the oppressed and vindicates them by setting them right/just (Ps 82:1–3) in reversing the lowly from shame to honor (Psalm 31:1–2). Consequently, the shameful cross of Jesus in the NT *sets right* the distorted value system of glory and shame.

Being "set right" has to do with another cognate word of salvation in the Bible, *hilastērion*, which can be translated as either expiation (to be merciful) or propitiation (to placate divine justice or appease wrath of God [Rom 3:25, Heb 9:5, cf. *hilasmos* 1 John 2:2, 4:10]). As Asian Christians look to the biblical category of salvation, "expiation" is preferable, as I argue elsewhere:

> . . . as it ["expiation"] traced its theological root to the Hebrew word *kappōret*, i.e., "mercy seat" on the Ark of Covenant in the Holy of Holies, thus seeing "God loved us and sent his Son to be the expiation (*hilasmos*) of our sins" (1 John 4:10). Jesus Christ is "the expiation (*hilasmos*) not only for our sins but also for the sins of the whole world" (1 John 2:2). . . . Soteriology is not simply about atoning sacrifice but also offering of love.[73]

None in Asia is affected more deeply in the area of "set right" and "expiation" than the Oceania world. Oceania is a world of its own, though often ignored or flown over. This world has many names: Oceania, Pacific Islands, Polynesia, Micronesia, Melanesia, etc.—with many hidden gifts.

---

72. Tan, "Asian Theology of Migration," 133.
73. Yeo, "Introduction," 1–13.

Havea describes this world aptly, "Our contexts are fluid, as our cultures are oral, . . . our borders are [not] all comforting."[74]

Almost all indigenous Pacific languages were given spelling systems (orthography) by European missionaries as their way to convert the locals to Christianity. European colonizers and settlers, however, often use their mother tongues as the lingua franca, the language of the government and commerce.[75] Missionaries have brought both light and darkness to this region, so Pacific islanders need to be saved from domination of colonists, from conflicts among intra-lands. They need salvation according to the six "ecojustice" principles of intrinsic worth, interconnectedness, voice, purpose, mutual custodianship, and resistance. Havea advocates for eco-justice biblical interpretations that understand salvation for this world as belonging to the Earth's communities and mutual custodianship and resistance.[76]

Doing biblical theology without deep reflections could be dangerous. The Anti-Discrimination Act in the 1970s in Australia was meant to protect the rights of the Aboriginal people and ethnic minorities. Apology from a nation's prime minister then would mean a biblical sense of repentance if apology worked for reparation toward a better future.[77] Naden and Havea cry out, "why can't our stories be taken to be as credible as the stories of the Jewish people? . . . [And] our people are oral people, and our stories not written. And so more work needs to be done!"[78] This is a question of "outside the church is there salvation?," to which I now turn.

THE ASIAN WORLD OF THE BIBLE: "SAVED FROM" TO "SAVED TO"

The biblical narrative of soteriology moves from "saved from" to "saved to" for a complete circle. That is, the Asian soteriological *telos* is not simply being saved from death and sin, but also being saved to life and flourishing; not simply being forgiven but also becoming a blessing to all; not simply overcoming wrong and enmity but also living out mercy and love.

---

74. Havea, "Engaging Scriptures from Oceania," 7.
75. Keown, *Pacific Islands Writing*, 149.
76. Havea, "Engaging Scriptures from Oceania," 3–19.
77. Naden and Havea, "Colonization Has Many Names," 6.
78. Naden and Havea, "Colonization Has Many Names," 7.

THE CRITICAL QUESTION: OUTSIDE THE CHURCH THERE IS NO SALVATION?

The thorny issue raised by the St. Cyprian dictum still faces Asian Christians today: *extra ecclesiam nulla salus* ("outside the church there is no salvation")? How to read Acts 4:12 ("there is no salvation through any else except Jesus; for there is no other name under heaven given among human beings by which we must be saved"; NRSV)? Did missionaries bring God to Asia or did God bring missionaries to Asia?

First, some Asian scholars affirm that all religions lead to God and to the salvation of all people (universalism, pluralism). Second, other scholars affirm that salvation is universally available insofar as through Christ (inclusivism), thus Justin Martyr's "Logos among Greeks and Socrates" could be applied to *Tian* (heaven) or *Dao* (Word) among the Confucians and Daoists. Third, other scholars maintain that salvation is available only in Christ (exclusivism, or particularism). A world-renowned missiologist and missionary in India, Leslie Newbigin, holds to the position in between the second and the third views. His qualified inclusivistic view that affirms the assurance of salvation in Christ but claims agnosticism about those who have not heard the gospel of Christ.[79]

The classical paradigm of interfaith dialogue (inclusivism, exclusivism, pluralism, relativism) is restrictive and rigid. Wisdom literature often uses light and life in that cluster to overcome the chaos and destructive powers of life, so interfaith conferencing should not first ask the question of "Are we worshiping the same God?" but "Are we able to agree that we are all human beings?"—that is, all are created in the image (the light and life!) of God? If so, how do we shed light on this broken and dying world by aiming to bring about superabundant life through the combined theological and ethical resources of our faiths?[80]

BIBLE AND GOD'S WORLD

Asian soteriology raises the question of the notion of Christian canon, since the relationship of the Bible with pre- and extra-biblical Scriptures for Asians is pertinent. Is the Bible a boundary setting of norm, or is it a shared platform for making expansive connections with others in the biblical texts and with global readers, so that the central message of salvation in the Bible is effectively being realized beyond the historical biblical worlds to the ends of the earth?

---

79. Newbigin, *Gospel in a Pluralist Society*.
80. Yeo, "Light and New Creation in Genesis and the Gospel of John," 66.

We will never know the absolute logic of God, but the logic of God must give way to the God of love (who is the God of mystery and logic). The critical question must bow to the creative witness and living power of the gospel to save (Rom 1:16); that is, living out the depth and breadth of biblical salvation truly and fully, and critically of their *Sitz im Leben*. Asian believers live out their faith dynamically, holding faithful and critical tension between the Scriptures and their lifeworlds.

VERNACULAR SOTERIOLOGY: MISSIO DEI AS TRANSLATIONS

Biblical translation itself is a salvation-offering enterprise for Asian believers. Examples are many. Korean Christians use *han* (wounded love as relational consequence of sin) and *jeong* (affection) to translate the doctrines of sin and Christology. Kazoh Kitamori is a Japanese scholar who understands the pain of God in that God's self-emptying in Phil 2 is God's suffering love, not simply is his saving mercy/act but also his very divine attribute/pathos.[81] The Chinese Union Bible translates *agapē* and logos respectively into *ren* (benevolence) and *dao* (word), not only fulfilling cultural ideals, making the biblical concepts clear to the Chinese, but also perpetuating the biblical message of salvation in cultures, thus granting new life to the culture. Yin-yang, or christological metaphors of hybrid Asian theology, is one that is neither fully Chinese nor fully Asian separately, and yet it is authentically Chinese *and* authentically Asian *simultaneously*—similar to the two natures of Christ.

CONCLUSION: WORLD CHRISTIANITY AND ASIAN SOTERIOLOGY

The more complicated the contour of Asian societies and churches signified, the more powerful salvation of God will be in this land. Intercultural metabolism, global exchange, ecological metamorphosis, and multiplicity of mutation are constant, thus Asian soteriology is living and active, constantly engaging and being incorporated into the dynamic global system, consequently local actors read the same biblical text with diverse voices as a way of seeking salvation.

Asian soteriology is a self-theologizing and existential act that is well served by the deep imbrication of theology, Scripture, and readers' contexts.[82] This contrapuntal move—holding in tension the indicative and imperative mood of biblical salvation—allows Asian believers to not simply

---

81. Kitamori, *Theology of the Pain of God*.
82. Yeo, "Introduction," 11.

slip into abstract imputed righteousness but also to concretely participate in, based on merit, Christ's righteousness. This is the biblical mandate of "faith without works is dead" (Jas 2:17) and "obedience of faith" (Rom 1:5, 16:26) incarnating in Asian soil and air and light. But the theological "womb of Asia" and "Asian faces" of Jesus are constantly undergoing change, affirmed and challenged by *world* Christianity. Asian soteriology shapes, and is being formed by, ecumenical soteriology.

BIBLIOGRAPHY (*FOR FURTHER READINGS)

Ackerman, Thomas Ackerman, and Slavoj Žižek. "Slavoj Žižek: Capitalism with Asian Values." *Al Jazeera*, November 13, 2011. https://www.aljazeera.com/programmes/talktojazeera/2011/10/2011102813360731764.html

Ashcroft, Bill. "Threshold Theology." In *Colonial Contexts and Postcolonial Theologies*, edited by M. Brett and J. Havea, 3–20. New York: Palgrave Macmillan, 2014.

Brazal, A. M., and Emmanuel S. de Guzman. "Intercultural Church: A Challenge in the Asian Migrant Context." In *Christianities in Migration*, edited by E. Padilla and P. C. Phan, 71–88. New York: Palgrave Macmillan, 2016.

Chung, P. S. "Martin Luther and *Shinran*: The Presence of Christ in Justification and Salvation in a Buddhist-Christian Context." *Asia Journal of Theology* 18 (2004) 295–310.

Goh, E. W. F. "Qohelet's Gospel in Ecclesiastes: Ecclesiastes 3:1–15, 7:15–22, and 11:1–6." In *So Great a Salvation*, edited by G. L. Green et al., 159–83. Grand Rapids: Eerdmans, 2017.

*Havea, Jione. "Engaging Scriptures from Oceania." In *Bible, Borders, Belonging(s)*, edited by J. Havea et al., 3–19. Atlanta: SBL, 2014.

———, ed. *Indigenous Australia and the Unfinished Business of Theology: Cross-Cultural Engagement*, New York: Palgrave Macmillan, 2014.

Hii, Kong-hock. "Contesting the Ideology of the Empire: Paul's Theological Politics in Romans, With Preliminary Implications for Chinese Christian Communities in Malaysia." PhD diss., Garrett-Evangelical Theological Seminary, 2007.

*Katoppo, Marianne. *Compassionate and Free: An Asian Woman's Theology*. Maryknoll, NY: Orbis, 1979.

Keown, Michelle. *Pacific Islands Writing: The Postcolonial Literatures of Aotearoa/New Zealand and Oceania*. Oxford: Oxford University, 2007.

Kim, Jeong-sook. "Humanization and Divinization: The Theological Dimension of Salvation as Revealed in Korean Shamanism." *Asia Journal of Theology* 18 (2004) 69–81.

Kitamori, Kazoh. *The Theology of the Pain of God*. Eugene, OR: Wipf & Stock, 2005.

Martin, Troy W. "Christ's Healing Sore. A Medical Reading of 1 Petri 2,24." *Vetera Christianorvm* 54 (2017) 143–54.

Murniati, A. Nunuk., and I. Kuntara Wiryamartana. "An Indonesian Contribution to a Spirituality of Liberation: Two Perspectives." In *Asian Christian Spirituality: Reclaiming Traditions*, edited by V. Fabella et al., 44–68. Maryknoll, NY: Orbis, 1992.

Naden, Neville. with Havea, Jione. "Colonization Has Many Names." In *Indigenous Australia and the Unfinished Business of Theology: Cross-Cultural Engagement*, edited by J. Havea, 1–8. New York: Palgrave Macmillan, 2014.

Newbigin, Leslie. *The Gospel in a Pluralist Society*. Grand Rapids: Eerdmans, 1989.

Pole, Siosifa. "*Vahevahe*: A Tongan Concept of Receiving and Using the Bible in Relation to Matthew 4:19 and 28:19." 2015 conference presentation, Oceania Biblical Studies Association (OBSA, 2015). https://sites.google.com/site/wavesofthemoana/about-obsa.

*Rivera-Pagán, Luis. N. "Xenophilia or Xenophobia: Toward a Theology of Migration." In *Contemporary Issues of Migration and Theology*, edited by E. Padilla and P. C. Phan, 31–52. New York: Palgrave Macmillan, 2013.

Ross, Katherine R. "Asia's Cry for Reconciliation: A Challenge to the Churches." *Asia Journal of Theology* 19 (2006) 412–30.

*Sugirtharajah, Rasiah S. *Asian Biblical Hermeneutics and Postcolonialism: Contesting the Interpretations*. Maryknoll, NY: Orbis, 1998.

Tan, Joy Y. "An Asian Theology of Migration and Its Interreligious Implications: Insights from the Documents of the Federation of Asian Bishops' Conferences (FABC)." In *Contemporary Issues of Migration and Theology*, E. Padilla and P. C. Phan, 121–38. New York: Palgrave Macmillan, 2013.

Taylor, Charles. *A Secular Age*. Cambridge, MA: Harvard University, 2007.

Tibbey, M. "From Little Things Big Things Grow." In *Indigenous Australia and the Unfinished Business of Theology: Cross-Cultural Engagement*, edited by J. Havea, 47–61. New York: Palgrave Macmillan, 2014.

Tsang, S. "Exegeting the Occupation of Hong Kong: The Umbrella Movement as a Battleground for Liberation Hermeneutics." In *Theological Reflections on the Hong Kong Umbrella Movement*, edited by J. H. H. Tse and J. Y. Tan, 131–62. New York: Palgrave Macmillan, 2016.

Yeo, K. K. "Introduction: So Great a Salvation: Soteriology in the Majority World." In *So Great a Salvation: Soteriology in the Majority World*, edited by G. L. Green et al., 1–13. Grand Rapids: Eerdmans, 2017.

———. "Light and New Creation in Genesis and the Gospel of John." In *The Theological of Light and Sight: An Interfaith Perspective*, edited by K. L. Vaux and K. K. Yeo, 51–69. Eugene, OR: Wipf & Stock, 2011.

———. *Mao Meets the Apostle Paul: Christianity, Communism, and the Hope of China*. Grand Rapids: Brazos, 2002.

*———. *What Has Jerusalem to Do with Beijing? Biblical Interpretation from a Chinese Perspective*. 2nd ed. Eugene, OR: Wipf & Stock, 2018.

Chapter 27
African Hermeneutics
ELIZABETH MBURU

Interpreting the Bible is a challenging task. To be more precise, interpreting the Bible *accurately*. And yet the Bible is meant to be understood and applied in the daily lives of believers if it is to be a guide for faith and practice. One of the questions that is often asked is whether contextual readings have value. With advances in the study of hermeneutics, there is the recognition of the two-sided nature of historical conditioning. As Thiselton points out, the interpreter also stands in a given historical context and tradition and the two are in constant engagement.[1]

As an example, take the story of the tortoise and the hare that is common in many parts of the world. Tortoise challenges hare to a race and of course nobody expects him to win. What tortoise does is to recruit his relatives and place them strategically along the path of the race. Each one jumps out of the bush ahead of hare in sequence as the one behind him hides to avoid being seen. At the end of the race, tortoise is the undisputed winner. Without knowing which rules to apply, or "how to read," one might misunderstand this story to be a criticism of tortoise's deception. What this story actually teaches is that cooperation is necessary in society. It is also a story that emphasizes the importance of honour in an honour/shame culture. It "is an appeal to a higher moral ethic, and that ethic is that a family must work together in unity to see that disgrace never comes to it."[2] Our contextual situatedness leads us to different ways of reading this story.

1. Thiselton, *Two Horizons*, 11.
2. http://buchele.blogspot.com/2008/01/tortoise-and-hare-african-storytelling.html.

African readers of the Bible face the challenge that most of the approaches and methods of hermeneutics are rooted in a Global North context. This is not surprising given that missionaries came to Africa from the Global North, the churches and theological institutions that were originally founded were missionary led, and most of the theological resources are produced by writers from the Global North who inevitably brought with them cultural baggage from their contexts. Africans are still trying to imitate foreign ways when it comes to reading, interpreting and applying the Bible in our everyday lives. This chapter proposes that African hermeneutics, or Africentric re-readings, are valuable because they reveal insights that might not otherwise be seen. Like pieces of a jigsaw puzzle, different contextual readings contribute to form a more complete picture.

The purpose of this chapter is to provide an understanding of current Africentric approaches to interpretation of the Bible. It will cover reading the Bible in Africa, common assumptions of Africentric approaches, current Africentric approaches, and strengths and weaknesses of Africentric approaches. This chapter will also take a closer look at one approach—the four-legged stool approach, which is an intercultural hermeneutic.

READING THE BIBLE IN AFRICA

Hermeneutics is the theory and practice of interpretation. It involves critical reflection on the processes of interpretation and understanding. It is both an art and a science. Hermeneutics is not new to Africa. African literature demonstrates that there are rules to interpret stories, poetry, proverbs, riddles and songs that make understanding possible. Where the Bible is concerned, history records that interpretation of the Bible was being done by Africans almost two thousand years ago. Some of the most important early interpreters of the Bible include church fathers like Origen and Augustine in Northern Africa.

More recently, missionaries re-introduced biblical hermeneutics into Africa, inevitably bringing with them cultural baggage from their Global North context. Because colonization was also taking place at the same time, some Africans have objected to these approaches, preferring instead to "decolonize" hermeneutics. This has resulted in biblical hermeneutics that generally tends to be liberational and against the colonial missionary enterprise. There is the general consensus now that Africans need to move away from the approaches that have been imposed on us because they promote a "foreign" way of reading the Bible that introduces a "double hermeneutical gap." This gap is present when readers are forced to confront at least two cultures in the process of interpretation. For Africans, this is the Global North and the biblical culture.

The aim of African hermeneutics is to recover the message of the Bible and to separate it from assumptions of the Global North. The main reason for this is the recognition of the two-sided nature of contextual situatedness. While Global North assumptions and methods are by no means monolithic, either amongst communities or individuals given that there are confessional, historical, theological and ecclesiological distinctives, there are some commonalities which justify grouping them together. Some of these assumptions might include linear reasoning, a greater dependence on scientific methods and therefore more emphasis on neutrality, a more individualistic approach in understanding and representing texts, an antispirititualist approach, and a more fragmented view of reality (as opposed to African holism). African assumptions are also not monolithic. Nevertheless, there are enough commonalities (particularly south of the Sahara) that make it possible to speak generally of "African."

COMMON ASSUMPTIONS OF AFRICENTRIC APPROACHES

Africentric approaches have several common assumptions. These include faith in God, the role of the Holy Spirit as actively involved in the process of interpretation, the Bible as a significant sacred text, the Bible as powerful, the importance of the socio-cultural and religious contexts of the African reader, and interpretation viewed not just as an academic exercise, but as something that should result in transformation of believers and society as a whole.

African hermeneutics is not limited to academic study or even written forms of interpretation, but also includes oral hermeneutical reflection.[3] In fact, much biblical interpretation in Africa is done by ordinary Christians or church leaders at the grassroots level, such as in worship, prayer and preaching. It also tends to be functional. In other words, how does the text speak to concrete, contextual realities being experienced by the African people? Africentric hermeneutics are guided by several contextual concerns. These include social concerns such as poverty, oppression, gender, and ethnicity; cultural concerns such as relational issues, community, language and traditions, and globalization; religious concerns such as syncretism and false teaching; political concerns such as injustice, colonization, and war and displacement; and economic concerns such as migration. How Africans approach the discipline of biblical hermeneutics may therefore look different from that from the Global North, as these approaches include both the

---

3. Van den Toren et al., "Biblical Hermeneutics."

theories of interpretation as well as general principles and methods implicit in practices of interpretation.[4]

MOTIVATION FOR AFRICENTRIC APPROACHES

There are several motivating factors for Africentric approaches. The two that follow are adapted from Kwame Bediako's theological reflection. Although the following statement applies to theology, one of the motivating factors behind Africentric approaches is the question of "whether an African theology that is 'controlled in language and methodology by its European medium: can give adequate account of the apprehension of Christ at the "living roots of the churches' . . . 'where faith has to live.'"[5]

A corollary issue has to do with African identity. What does it mean to be Christian and African? As Bediako points out, "the African theologian's concern with the pre-Christian religious heritage becomes an endeavour to clarify the nature and meaning of African Christian identity."[6] African readers of the Bible bring their own questions to the text, a text that they believe embodies power in that it is both "a tactile object of power and a text of power."[7] These two issues affirm that Eurocentric approaches are deficient in interpreting texts in African contexts so that a consistent Christian African identity emerges.

CURRENT AFRICENTRIC APPROACHES

There are several Africentric approaches currently in use in Africa.[8] These include the following:

Ethiopian hermeneutics: This approach developed independently. *Andemta* commentary, which includes translation and commentary in Amharic on the Bible and related literature written in Ge'ez, provides highly contextual explanations that are often typological.

African Independent hermeneutics: This stems from African Initiated Churches, which evolved as a reaction to missionary churches and the colonial influence. Scripture is understood as directly related to the challenges facing African Christians, and its authority is combined with the authority accorded to African traditions. The physical Bible is itself an object of power.

---

4. Van den Toren et al., "Biblical Hermeneutics."
5. Bediako, "Roots of African Theology," 64.
6. Bediako, "Roots of African Theology," 59.
7. West, "Indigenous Biblical Hermeneutics," 87.
8. For a fuller discussion, see Van den Toren et al., "Biblical Hermeneutics."

Liberation and Black hermeneutics: These approaches address the realities of injustice, oppression and colonization. The marginalized are given epistemological privilege in that it is their reading that determines the meaning of the text for their context. The two ways of reading include a hermeneutic of trust and a hermeneutic of suspicion. Liberation hermeneutics is characterized by the sequence of see-judge-act in which the understanding of the meaning of the Scriptures begins with the realities of oppression and injustice. Black hermeneutics is similar to North American Black theology. It originated in the South African apartheid context of an oppressed majority.

Feminist/Womanist hermeneutics: This approach focuses on the struggle against the subordination of women in African contemporary societies, ecclesial, and familial roles. It has some differences with traditional Feminist approaches, given that its focus is on the religio-cultural contexts of African women. It has close affinities with liberation and intercultural hermeneutics. It is a hermeneutic of suspicion but because the Bible is esteemed as a religious symbol, it does not reject the Bible or Christianity.

Contextual Bible Study: This approach focuses on the ordinary reader who has no academic training in theology. As in liberation hermeneutics, the reading of Scripture with marginalized communities is emphasized. They have epistemological privilege in that it is their contextual situatedness and not authorial intent that determines the meaning of the text.

Pentecostal hermeneutics: This approach provides a new method of interpretation that is based on an understanding of the role of the Holy Spirit and the contemporary church in the process of interpretation. The interpretation is generally literal but some interpretive freedom is allowed.

Reconstruction hermeneutics: This approach emphasizes the interpretation of the Scriptures in the light of political, social and economic realities. Unlike liberation hermeneutics, the focus is no longer on the fight against the oppressors, but on the collaborative and inclusive task of holistic reconstruction.

Postcolonial hermeneutics: This approach analyses how literary texts themselves are shaped by power struggles and "imperialism." The texts are considered to reflect the interests of those in power. The emphasis is therefore on retrieving the subjugated voices of the oppressed.

Mother tongue hermeneutics: This approach entails using indigenous language translations of the Bible. It considers that culture and worldview are expressed through one's mother tongue and that indigenous languages are therefore resources for interpretation. It focuses on the readers' context and is a collaborative, communal task.

Inculturation and intercultural hermeneutics: These approaches emphasize a two-way dialogue between the world of the biblical text and the world of traditional and contemporary African realities. It is a hermeneutic of trust rather than suspicion, it is contextual and interdisciplinary, and the emphasis is generally on religio-cultural dimensions. Intercultural hermeneutics evolved from inculturation hermeneutics with the major development being the consolidation of a constructive dialogue.

STRENGTHS AND WEAKNESSES OF AFRICENTRIC APPROACHES

STRENGTHS

Africentric approaches have several strengths. First, the biblical text finds a home in the African heart because it speaks to the contextual realities that believers face daily. It is no longer a foreign object that has been imposed on us, but rather a relevant text that allows us to engage in constructive dialogue and find relevant application points. Second, it confronts dichotomy and syncretism by allowing for dialogue between the biblical and African contexts, thus exposing wrong doctrine and practice. Third, because it allows for fresh insights from the biblical texts, it acknowledges the multidimensional/global character of Christian faith. It provides a different way of reading that complements other readings. Fourth, rather than relegate hermeneutics to the domain of academics/intellectuals, it makes it possible for ordinary readers to participate actively in Bible interpretation. Fifth, because it promotes understanding and internalization of biblical truths within the African context, the potential for transformation of society is increased. Sixth, it promotes understanding and interrogation of African contexts and awareness of our religious spaces. This is important because Africa is very pluralistic and religious spaces are quite porous, which is why syncretism is so prevalent. Seventh, and perhaps most importantly, allows for a redefinition of Christian African identity based on biblical criteria. African identity markers are therefore not determined by ATR, culture, or even African worldviews.

WEAKNESSES

Africentric approaches also have several weaknesses. First, they may encourage syncretism. Syncretism occurs when religious and cultural forms are combined with the biblical message without any regard for whether they align with biblical truth. Although this is not just an African problem, it is one of the major challenges the church in Africa is currently facing. Second, some of the approaches above make the world in front of the text more important than the world of the text and in many instances, ignores the world behind the text. This is dangerous because the reader runs the risk of imposing meaning on the text. Third, there is the risk of collapsing the two horizons of meaning and significance. In any reading of a biblical text, there is the meaning that was intended by the biblical author and the significance that is derived by a modern reader. Fourth, there is the risk of a canon within a canon. Some Africentric approaches tend to focus on specific texts that lend themselves readily to such approaches. This means that some texts may be ignored while others may be elevated.

A CLOSER LOOK AT AN AFRICENTRIC APPROACH

The next section will provide a more in-depth description of a particular Africentric hermeneutic, namely, the four-legged stool approach.

THEORETICAL FRAMEWORK

The four-legged stool approach is an intercultural model that encourages a dialogue between the African context and the biblical context. It has five distinct steps that engage text and context in a constructive dialogue. It focuses on religio-cultural dimensions.

It is based on the concept of moving from the known to the unknown by moving directly from theories, methods and categories that are familiar in the African world into the more unfamiliar world of the Bible, without taking a detour through any foreign methods. It recognizes that parallels between biblical and African cultures and worldviews can be used as bridges to promote understanding, internalization and application of the biblical text. It is similar to what Jesus and Paul did.

It includes interrogation of assumptions. It is understood that because readers approach the text from their contextual situatedness, they come with their assumptions. While our assumptions may sometimes aid us in reading the text, we sometimes import these assumptions into the text with negative results. At the same time, the various resources that we use in Africa are also based on certain assumptions. While these resources are useful, they impose foreign assumptions on readers, which makes understanding more complicated. In addition, readers often fail to interrogate the assumptions they bring to the text from their various backgrounds. This approach addresses this deficiency.

This approach recognizes that the African cultures (material and nonmaterial) are a significant tool for the interpretive process. This includes the techniques that enable us to interpret the various genres of African literature (oral as well as post-colonial). However, it goes further by considering the worldviews represented by the reader. These are valid and form an essential interpretive bridge. The fact that there is no neutral interpretation of a text means that our worldviews will always influence our understanding of Scripture, either positively or negatively. As African readers of the biblical text, we must re-discover our cultures and worldviews and apply them in our hermeneutics. However, as we do so, we must ensure that our conclusions are in alignment with the biblical metanarrative.

This method is also similar to some approaches from the Global North in that it recognizes the value of the theological, literary and historical contexts of the text. It strives to provide a balanced reading of texts and therefore complements rather than replaces these approaches. However, while there may be some overlap with categories traditionally ascribed to Global North approaches, the conceptualization of these categories is based on African assumptions.

Effective hermeneutics requires a three-way dialogue between the "world behind the text," "the world of the text," and "the world in front of the text." Consequently, this approach does not collapse these three worlds. All three stand in a context that must be interrogated and the two horizons of meaning and significance are kept distinct. Africans generally tend to have a more holistic approach to life, which translates to the way they understand literature, the Bible included. This means that from the moment African readers begin to interact with the text, they are already deriving meaning and significance simultaneously, thus collapsing the worlds behind, of and in front of the text, and merging the two horizons of "what it meant" and "what it means." This approach therefore "makes a distinction between meaning (as intended for the original readers) and significance (as applied to the modern reader)."[9]

THE FOUR-LEGGED STOOL APPROACH

Hermeneutics requires the use of certain methods or techniques in order to produce reliable results. The approach outlined here is described using the metaphor of a four-legged stool. A stool is a familiar object in Africa. Just as a good stool is stable and supports our weight, so the hermeneutical stool will be one we can put our weight on, confident that it provides a stable or accurate interpretation of the biblical text. The process includes four legs, which in this case are 1) parallels to the African context, 2) the theological context, 3) the literary context and 4) the historical/cultural context. These

9. Mburu, *African Hermeneutics*, 85.

four legs support the seat, which represents the final stage of interpretation, the application. However, the legs are not independent of each other and one moves back and forth between them to try and find the right balance. This is because as we gain more information, our assumptions about the text change and our understanding grows.

While it is possible that this approach could be usefully adapted to any cultural context (particularly where the parallels are concerned), the hermeneutical principles that are applied to the various genres are developed specifically from East African oral and written literature.

Leg 1: Parallels to the African Context

This first leg of the hermeneutical stool aims to consciously identify and interrogate our own context and discover the points of contact (and difference) between it and the biblical context. There are two reasons why this first leg is so important. First, it enables us to begin to understand the biblical text from a familiar position. This is important because this hermeneutical approach involves moving from the known to the unknown. Second, interrogating our own worldviews and contexts puts us in a position to recognize where our assumptions fit or do not fit with the text.

The two-side nature of historical conditioning means that the context of the Bible and the context of the reader are in constant engagement with one another.[10] Some of these contexts are shared while others are not. Ukuchukwu speaks of shared contexts in terms of shared mutual interests or commonalities between the narrator and the listener.[11] These are a crucial interpretive key for the listener because they define the scope within which meaning can begin to be determined. The mutual interests guide the listener as to how to hear and interpret the story. These mutual interests also form the basis on which the narrator earns the right to be heard by their audience. Without these mutual interests, the reader is left grappling in the dark, not fully understanding either the meaning or the application of the text.

When African readers are encouraged to confront their assumptions about life, it becomes easier to hear the biblical text in its own right without imposing oneself on the text. This leg is therefore a bridge between the two contexts. For instance, in a text that has exorcisms or power encounters, or even socio-cultural issues of gender or ethnicity, an African reader can profitably use their own assumptions about external reality and anthropology to

---

10. Thiselton, *Two Horizons*, 11.
11. Ukachukwu, *Intercultural Hermeneutics*, 25.

form a bridge with the text. It therefore defines the scope or the boundaries within which meaning may be sought.

The very nature of communication demands that the speaker has something specific to say, both speaker and hearer hold some things in common that make understanding possible, and the speaker's intent is to communicate in a way that they are understood. Because of the two-sided nature of historical conditioning, this inter-dynamic process guides us in determining what is negotiable and what is non-negotiable. This will help us develop a truly biblical worldview while at the same time retain what is uniquely African.

Leg 2: Theological Context

The second leg is the theological context. Why move straight to theological concerns rather than to the historical and cultural contexts? Many scholars have noted that Africans tend to be very "religious," even in modern/postmodern Africa. By this is meant that, the spiritual dimension of life is always a factor in an African's interaction with the realities around him/her. Because of this orientation, when Africans read the Bible, they tend to look for issues that relate to God and faith and how these affect their everyday lives. This is therefore the logical next step in the way most Africans process information. Consequently, while the African approach is holistic, it is nevertheless primarily undergirded by spiritual concerns. This implies that in Africa, biblical hermeneutics is inseparable from theological reflection, as the emphasis is generally to address contextual realities within society.[12] Because of this orientation to life, an understanding of the biblical-theological emphases of the text therefore provides the foundational data for the readers, orienting their approach to the interpretation of the text. However, this emphasis has led to what is known as the fusion of the two horizons in hermeneutics. Interpretation and application are conflated. This is harmful to interpretation because it ignores the context of the Bible and prioritizes the readers' context.

It is also important to recognize that while the Bible can be regarded as literature, it is primarily a spiritual document. Key to the interpretive process, therefore, is a correct understanding of the theological emphases of a text and how these are expressed within the structural framework of the parts, as well as the whole.[13] For instance, John and Mark would have different emphases and these affect how we interpret them. Since this

---

12. West, "African Biblical Hermeneutics," 4.
13. Mburu, *African Hermeneutics*, 70.

approach recognizes a distinct separation in the two horizons of meaning and significance, application at this point can only be tentative.

Leg 3: Literary Context

The third leg is the literary context. It defines the boundaries of meaning in that "the intended meaning of any passage is the meaning that is consistent with the sense of the literary context in which it occurs."[14] Thus, the literary context establishes the flow of thought and helps us to determine the accurate meaning of the text.

There are certain aspects to cover. The first is genre. It is important to identity the genre of what one is reading so that we have some idea of how we should approach the text in order to understand what the author is communicating. Literary genre, whether in an African, Global North or biblical context, functions as a vital interpretive key in the hermeneutical process.

The second aspect is literary techniques. The techniques an author uses may vary depending on whether the material is to be presented orally or in writing. Several features of African oral literature are important here when interpreting Scripture, for much of it began life as oral literature, or as a text that was written to be read aloud in communal settings, rather than by a solitary reader. The media history of the Bible reflects this oral/written interface. Performance is therefore crucial to the engagement between narrator and hearer. Other key features of oral literature include holistic listening and interaction between the narrator and the audience. Style is also extremely important.

The third aspect is language. Issues of language such as grammar, syntax, and detailed word studies are important. Ignoring grammar and syntax means that we may fail to grasp the full meaning of the text.

The final aspect is literary flow. African storytellers are extremely skilled in ensuring that there is no breakdown in the flow of a story. There is a cyclical-linear development that allows the story to flow smoothly from beginning to end. The details that are necessary for understanding are provided when they are needed to enable the audience to interpret the story. This is also the case with other genres.

Depending on the genre, there are certain additional rules that apply from African literature. So, for instance, in analyzing a narrative text one would distinguish between 1) the world of the agents of communication, which include the narrator and the listener, and 2) the world of the story itself, which includes the plot, the spatial and temporal settings, the literary

---

14. Klein et al., *Introduction to Biblical Interpretation*, 214.

devices (such as alternation between narration and dialogue, contrastive dialogue, editorial/narratorial comments, the use of misunderstandings double entendre and irony, etc.), and characterization.

Leg 4: Historical and Cultural Context

The fourth leg is the historical and cultural context. No text arises out of a vacuum. This is just as true of biblical texts as it is of African texts. In addition to theological and literary concerns, Africans try to make sense of their lives in relation to the historical and cultural contexts in which events occur. This means that "behind the text" issues provide crucial data in the interpretive process. Thus, any interpretation must consider these crucial factors particularly because of the cultural and temporal distance between the readers and the text. If authorial intent and determinacy of meaning are to be taken seriously, we must "enter into" the world of the author and allow his world to provide the parameters that guide our understanding. In other words, we must respect the alterity or "otherness" of the text. So, for instance, in Jesus's interaction with the woman of Samaria in John 4. The original hearers/readers would have grasped the historical and cultural issues almost instinctively since they were familiar to them. These are what are known as shared mutual interests. They would also share the same understanding of the way language is used because language develops within a specific social context which those who live in that context understand. This socially conditioned nature of language must also be considered as a crucial clue in uncovering historical and cultural backgrounds.[15]

Readers must therefore make the effort to step into the world of the biblical author if they hope to understand his communication adequately. However, this is difficult to do because of the temporal and cultural barriers that are likely to hinder our full comprehension of what was written. We need to try to grasp the perspective and mindset of the author.[16] These are rarely made explicit in the writing since both the author and his audience lived at the same time and in the same cultural context. Failure to take the perspective of the author into account, means that one may miss the drama of a scene and the point the author intended to make.[17] Take the foot-washing scene in John 13. It is helpful to know that foot-washing was customarily the task of non-Jewish slaves. People who were socially inferior washed the feet of their superiors: it was never the other way around.

---

15. Mulholland, "Sociological Criticism," 302.
16. These categories are from Klein et al., *Biblical Interpretation*, 229–30.
17. Osborne, *Hermeneutical Spiral*, 127–39.

Without the cultural understanding that this task was considered too degrading for Jesus's disciples, or even Jewish slaves, we miss the significance of Jesus's action. He was demonstrating radical service to others, the kind expected of all his followers.[18]

What about mindset? In reading a text, one tries to understand not just the content but also the purpose behind the communication, as well as the intended emotional impact.[19] There are details about the text that are incomprehensible unless we know something about the period. Fee and Stuart provide an excellent example of how to relate to the mindset of the author in their retelling of the parable of the good Samaritan (this title is actually an oxymoron!) found in Luke 10:29–37.[20]

Once we understand what the writer was saying and what this would have meant to the original hearers, we can more accurately interpret the message of the text for our times.

Seat: Application

Finally, we have the seat. These four legs together reveal the probable meaning as it was intended for the original listeners. One of the basic assumptions of this approach is that a text can only have one meaning—namely the meaning that the author intended to communicate when he wrote to his original audience. This is known as authorial intent. Meaning is therefore understood to be single (as "boundaries of meaning") and determined by the author of the text. If one has done the necessary work on legs one to four of the stool, it is possible to arrive at authorial intent with a certain degree of probability.

The seat is where we derive significance. The important feature of meaning as distinct from significance is that meaning is the determinate representation of a text for an interpreter, whereas significance is fluid. This means that while a text can have only one meaning, it can have multiple applications. Once we understand what the author intended to communicate to his original audience, we can legitimately apply this message to our multiple contexts. This distinction is observed in other modern hermeneutical theories such as that of E. D. Hirsch. Even though we, the listeners, become part of the story, we do not make the story "in our image" but allow it to guide us to its true shape and form.

---

18. Köstenberger, "John," 403–5.
19. Klein et al., *Biblical Interpretation*, 230–31.
20. Fee and Stuart, *How to Read the Bible for All Its Worth*, 147.

Significance, on the other hand, is the application to the context of the listener expressed in terms that we understand in our own African society. In African oral literature, this distinction between meaning and significance is related to the authority one has earned during their career because the community has learned to trust him/her. Ukachukwu refers to this as narrative authority.[21] One implication of narrative authority is that listeners cannot impose their assumptions on a story or make it mean whatever they want it to mean.

This last step is only a confirmation of the tentative application of the text as uncovered in the legs above. Here we must de-culturize the message from the cultural form in which it is communicated. This message must then re-culturized in an African form. We must also distinguish between trans-contextual and culture-bound truths. For instance, consider the command to honour one's father and mother. This is a trans-contextual truth that cannot be applied uniformly by readers in their various contexts. At least one aspect of this for the original readers would be obedience to one's parents. One application would include entering into arranged marriages. In our own African context, obedience would still be a way to honour one's parents but unless one comes from a more traditional setup, one is not bound to an arranged marriage. Eloping would, however, be considered to be dishonouring one's parents.

CONCLUSION

The purpose of this chapter was to provide an understanding of current Africentric approaches to interpretation of the Bible. It covered reading the Bible in Africa, common assumptions of Africentric approaches, an overview of current Africentric approaches, and strengths and weaknesses of Africentric approaches. This chapter also took a closer look at one approach—the four-legged stool approach, which is an intercultural hermeneutic.

The implications for Africentric hermeneutics are tremendous. Africentric approaches recognize that the Bible speaks powerfully into the present. They reveal that the African voice is a vital contribution to the global theological conversation. Recent research shows that there is a radical shift in the growth of the church in the Global South. This has also resulted in an acceleration of reverse missions with technology contributing to even wider exposure. Going by demographics, Africa now has the sober responsibility of shaping the global church for the twenty-first century and beyond. Perhaps Africentric approaches are one way to escape the fate of

---

21. Ukachukwu, *Intercultural Hermeneutics*, 26.

Christians in the Global North, who are currently living in what is termed "Post-Christian cultures."

BIBLIOGRAPHY

Adamo, David T. *Reading and Interpreting the Bible in African Indigenous Churches*. Eugene, OR: Wipf & Stock, 2001.

An, Keon-Sang. *An Ethiopian Reading of the Bible: Biblical Interpretation of the Ethiopian Orthodox Tewahido Church*. Cambridge: James Clarke, 2016.

Anderson, Allan H. "African Initiated Church Hermeneutics." In *Initiation into Theology: The Rich Variety of Theology and Hermeneutics*, edited by Simon Maimela and Adrio Konig, 399–416. Pretoria: J. L. van Schaik, 1998

Bediako, Kwame. "Biblical Exegesis in the African Context: The Factor and Impact of the Translated Scriptures." *Journal of African Christian Thought* 6 (2003) 15–23.

Dube, Musa W., et al., eds. *Postcolonial Perspectives in African Biblical Interpretations*. Atlanta: Society of Biblical Literature, 2013

Ela, Jean-Marc. "Christianity and Liberation in Africa." In *Paths of African Theology*, edited by Rosino Gibellini, 136–53. Maryknoll, NY: Orbis, 1994.

Manus, Ukachukwu C. *Intercultural Hermeneutics in Africa: Methods and Approaches*. Nairobi, Kenya: Acton Publishers, 2003.

Mburu, Elizabeth W. *African Hermeneutics*. Carlisle: HippoBooks, 2019.

Mugambi, Jesse N. K. *Christian Theology and Social Reconstruction*. Theology of Reconstruction Series. Nairobi, Kenya: Acton Publishers, 2003.

Nel, Marius. *An African Pentecostal Hermeneutics: A Distinctive Contribution to Hermeneutics*. Eugene, OR: Wipf & Stock, 2018

Ukpong, Justin S. "Inculturation Hermeneutics: An African Approach to Biblical Interpretation." In *The Bible in a World Context: An Experiment in Contextual Hermeneutics*, edited by Walter Dietrich and Ulrich Luz, 17–32. Grand Rapids: Eerdmans, 2002.

Van den Toren, Benno, et al. "Biblical Hermeneutics." *The Bibliographical Encyclopaedia of African Theology*. https://african.theologyworldwide.com/encyclopaedia-bible-in-africa/biblical-hermeneutics.

West, Gerald O. "Biblical Hermeneutics in Africa." In *African Theology on the Way: Current Conversations*, edited by Diane B. Stinton, 21–31. London: SPCK, 2010.

———. "Locating 'Contextual Bible Study' within Biblical Liberation Hermeneutics and Intercultural Biblical Hermeneutics." *HTS Teologiese Studies / Theological Studies* 70 (2014) 1–18.

Chapter 28
Indigenous North American/ Turtle Island Hermeneutics[1]

T. CHRISTOPHER HOKLOTUBBE
& H. DANIEL ZACHARIAS

Indigenous peoples of Turtle Island, or "North America" as later called by European explorers and colonists, have had encounters with the Scriptures ever since Columbus was found lost on our shores. During and since that time, such encounters have been entangled in the colonial project. Like much missionary effort past and present, the missionary, who was socially and culturally bound to their own languages, histories, and cultural practices, mediated the Scriptures. As Indigenous followers of Jesus today seek to interpret the Bible for themselves and their communities, readers recognize that this is an act of intercultural interpretation and dialogue. Numerous patterns and emphases within Native North American interpretation can be discerned, but core to it all is the attempt to read the Bible as Creator has made us—engaging the Bible in and through our shared worldviews, lifeways, lands, experiences, histories, traditions, and struggles in order to both give due dignity to our heritage and to follow Jesus in the ways Creator has made us. Both of us, as men of mixed Indigenous and settler descent and as those trained in biblical studies, have undertaken an ongoing project that seeks to sketch out the ways in which Indigenous peoples of North America read the Scriptures, with the present essay a contribution to our evolving

---

1. Numerous thoughts from this article originate from Hoklotubbe, "Native American Interpretation the Bible"; as well as Hoklotubbe and Zacharias, "Encountering the Bible on Turtle Island."

thoughts on the issue. We do so with deep awareness and appreciation to many Indigenous theologians and practitioners that have gone on before us and shaped our thinking, as well as the robust communities of Indigenous followers of Jesus that we participate in and learn from, particularly *NAI-ITS: An Indigenous Learning Community*.

CORE ASSUMPTION

Like many ethnic groups, there is a spectrum of belief and practice within the Christian community. Many Indigenous peoples in North America do not have discernibly different approaches to the scriptural text from the wider church, and often tend towards a more conservative reading, in large part because of the theology of the missionaries. In our ongoing attempt to sketch out a "Turtle Island Hermeneutics," we seek to describe what defines the unique approach to interpreting the Christian Scriptures by Indigenous folks who have sought to practice and/or align with their cultural heritage and therefore seek to decolonize their Christian discipleship. In our readings and encounters with Indigenous authors and leaders of this persuasion, several trends are consistent, some of which will be described below. But foundational to all of them, in one form or another, is the core assumption that Creator God of Israel who revealed Godself to the Israelite Patriarchs and Matriarchs had not ignored the Indigenous Peoples of North America until the European colonizers arrived with the Bible-infused empire called Christendom.[2] Rather, Creator has always been present and made a mark upon the stories, ceremonies, lands, worldviews, and lifeways of Indigenous peoples.

In a seminal article on Indigenous interpretations of Scripture, Episcopal Bishop Steven Charleston (Choctaw) encourages Indigenous Christians to compare the Old Testament and its account of a people's history, teachings, and covenant with Creator YHWH with their own histories, traditional teachings, ancestral laws, and covenants with Creator.[3] According to Charleston, these ancestral stories, traditions, and ceremonial rites are Original Instructions given to each Indigenous nation. Indigenous Christians do not need to reject or relegate their traditions in order to accept the Old Testament as Scripture. Indigenous Christians can appreciate how the Old Testament explains Creator's unique dealings with a particular tribe and nation which culminated in the coming of the Christ, Creator with Us (Emmanuel), for all the world. The Old Testament then enters a sacred

---

2. See also, Woodley, *Living in Color*, 80–83.
3. Charleston, "Old Testament of Native America," 69–81.

circle of wisdom that shapes the Indigenous Christian—held as unique and sacred in its own particular way—alongside our own traditions. Native theologians therefore must discern how their own stories, rituals, and lifeways—the "Native Covenant"—can both *inform* and *be informed* by their interpretation of the Christian Scriptures in order to empower, inspire, and guide Indigenous lives. With the prophet Amos (9:7), Indigenous peoples recognize that Creator has had a relationship with us long before European colonization. We were not godless heathen savages in empty and unused lands.

Turtle Island Hermeneutics will forever reject the Doctrine of Discovery and *terra nullius*. The Doctrine of Discovery, which was articulated in a series of papal bulls beginning in 1455, justified European ownership and colonization of foreign and "discovered" lands occupied by disposable "pagans" and Indigenous peoples, who held no meaningful claims to the land. This is exemplified in the work of Sarah Augustine (Tewa Pueblo), who suggests that we read the story of Jacob who steals the birthright of the "foolish" Esau, "a man of open country" or "uncivilized," as a cautionary tale. "This logic of the elect," Augustine argues, "provides theological justification for the lost birthright of Native America."[4] As a cautionary tale, Augustine wonders whether we are supposed to read the story of Jacob as warning not to betray our family and kin for accumulating wealth and the broken relationships that occur as a result.

INDIGENOUS INTERPRETIVE FRAMEWORKS

Turtle Island Hermeneutics read biblical narratives according to frameworks and categories that align with and arise from their heritage and lands. Such interpretations take seriously how our "social locations" influence the questions and concerns we bring to Scripture and what broader patterns and meanings we both "discover" from and impose upon the text. We do not pretend that we can achieve a disconnected objectivity in our encounter of Scripture. Indeed, even if this could be achieved, it would not be desired, as we are individuals grounded in and formed by human communities, which themselves are grounded and reliant upon the wider community of creation. Turtle Island Hermeneutics expressly does not seek objectivity, nor is the goal a universal frame of reference. Because of the "core assumption" outlined above, Turtle Island Hermeneutics recognizes the goodness within our cultural heritage. We belong to our families, we belong to our

---

4. Augustine, *Land Is Not Empty*, 88–89.

communities, and we belong to the land. These circles of relationship form the individual and inform one's encounter with the scriptural text.

This grounded framework can often emphasize previously unnoticed elements within biblical prose and narratives or re-signify the meaning of technical terms or narrative elements and figures. For example, we can appreciate the ministries and teachings of John the Baptist and Jesus in a new light when considered in conversation with the figure of the Trickster, popular among Indigenous stories. Trickster traditions are varied within different Indigenous nations. In some traditions, tricksters often transgress cultural boundaries that encourage the people to reflect upon the meaning and function of our socially constructed conventions surrounding propriety, purity, and morality.[5] This description sounds a lot like how both John and Jesus speak and behave in the Gospels.[6] Moreover, both John and Jesus share similarities with "sacred clowns" in Indigenous traditions, which include *koshares* of the Pueblos in the Southwest and *heyokas* of the Sioux in the Plains.[7] Sacred clowns are notorious for saying and doing contrary, even offensive things, in order to shock their audiences into new insights and self-discoveries. Indigenous readers may see Jesus, in a sense, embodying the role of a sacred clown when he rebuffed a non-Jewish woman who begged him to exorcize a demon from her daughter—even going so far as to calling her a "dog" (Mark 7:24–30; Matt 15:21–28). Despite Jesus's offensive, seemingly racist portrayal of the Syrophoenician (Mark)/Canaanite (Matthew) woman as a dog, and therefore, as inferior to the children of Israel, the determined mother claims her voice and cleverly responds that even dogs receive attention and care in the form of food scraps from the table. Jesus applauds the woman's exemplary faith and announces that on account of her word the demon has left her daughter (Mark 7:29). Through his offensive response to the woman, Jesus as sacred clown provides an opportunity for audiences of the story to consider the toxic harm of socially constructed ethnic hierarchies and an opportunity in the narrative for the woman to publicly claim her dignity and her daughter's healing through her declaration of faith. Jesus's shocking response paves the way for a surprising revelation: in God's kin(g)dom, even so-called "dogs" are welcomed to the table as heirs.

Charleston reads Matthew's account of Jesus's experience in the wilderness in terms of the Native experience of vision quests.. Although the precise protocols of vision quests vary across tribes, those undertaking

---

5. Kidwell et al., *Native American Theology*, 113–25.
6. Charleston, *Four Vision Quests of Jesus*, 56–64.
7. Charleston, *Four Vision Quests of Jesus*.

such a quest often begin with a period of prayer and purification. Then their endurance and spirit are tested, which invites self-reflection, a spirit of humility, lamentation, and a recognition of their own vulnerability and need for Creator. A person may even receive a powerful vision that reveals something about their identity, character, or what role they are to serve in their community—such transformative visions are "good medicine" or divine blessings.[8] Jesus too undertakes his own vision quests. After Jesus was purified through his baptism, he set off to the wilderness to fast and focus on prayer (Matt 4:2). At the end of his forty days of prayer and fasting, Jesus encounters the tempter, who tries to persuade Jesus to misuse his spiritual power for self-serving ends.[9] Sin is understood as primarily relational rather than judicial, an imbalance in the *shalom* which God desires. *Shalom*, or the Harmony Way, is seen by scholars such as Randy Woodley (Keetoowah) as the Original Instructions to humankind.[10] For Terry LeBlanc (Mi'kmaq/Acadian), this restoration to harmony, the "restoration of right relationship and right relatedness,"[11] is also foundational for any Indigenous explorations of eschatology.

The above discussion highlights the relational framework in which the Scriptures are encountered by Indigenous readers, as relationship is a vital component to most Indigenous worldviews. One component of this relational framework is the concept of kinship. While kinship in the Christian community is basic to ecclesiology, Indigenous worldviews extend kinship to the entire community of creation. Within this community, humanity is not hierarchically over any other of our creational kin.[12] Rather, Indigenous peoples recognize they rely upon the gifts of mother earth and upon the gifts of service and sacrifice provided to us by the rest of the community of creation.[13] For Indigenous peoples, our personal and communal identi-

---

8. Charleston, *Four Vision Quests*, 10–22, 51.

9. For some Native Americans theologians, the concept of a devil who embodies pure evil as the apocalyptic enemy of Creator does not align with how they understand what evil entails. Some Indigenous readers have interpreted the devil as a literary personification of what constitutes "evil" and "sin" from an Indigenous perspective, namely, the actualization of our self-serving and destructive desires and actions that upsets the ideal balance and harmony with all of our kin—which includes humans, creatures, and creation itself. See Dellinger, "Sin—Ambiguity and Complexity and the Sin of Not Conforming," 124–25, 127.

10. See Woodley, "Harmony Way"; Woodley, *Shalom and the Community of Creation*.

11. LeBlanc, "Toward an Indigenous Eschatology," 238.

12. On this matter, Indigenous worldviews align with the biblical worldview as well. See chapters 1 and 2 of Bauckham, *Living With Other Creatures*.

13. See Zacharias, "Land Takes Care of Us," 69–97.

ties include the land, which affects how we relate to the world and read the word.[14] The land and creation are among our first teachers and vehicles for Creator's revelation—God can be encountered both in and through creation. The Indigenous understanding of the great commandment to love one's neighbor (Matt 22:39; Lev 19:18) extends out to the entire community of creation of which we are a part, an encounter with the text that is pertinent in the age of the anthropocene.

With this in mind, when we read Jesus's vision quest in the wilderness, do we consider what Jesus may have learned from creation as he observed the plants, animals, terrain, sky, and stars? Is it possible that many of Jesus's parables and teachings about the birds of the air, the flowers of the field, and the mustard seed arose from his contemplation and observation of nature? For Charleston, Jesus's visions of the stones, the sky, and the mountaintop, underscores the long-standing Indigenous conviction that we inter-exist and are interdependent with all our relations, which include non-human *persons* such as stones that Jesus was tempted to turn into bread. Rocks and stones are among our oldest relatives and according to Charleston they embody the oneness of God. In the narrative, the stones help Jesus regain his spiritual balance by recognizing his oneness and solidarity with all of creation and Creator.[15]

WRESTLING WITH SCRIPTURE: ON CANAANITES, COWBOYS, AND INDIANS

Because of the relational framework and core assumptions discussed above, Turtle Island Hermeneutics holds Scripture as a site to wrestle with the existential question of how someone can be authentically Indigenous while also identifying with an institutional religion that was complicit with the physical and cultural genocide of their ancestors and lifeways.

As an example of this, the exodus narrative, with its themes of liberation, journeying through the wilderness, and the inheritance and conquest of a promised land, is a rich, yet troubling story. Many Native readers encountering the exodus story cannot help but recall their own tribes' experiences of being displaced from their ancestral land by Christian settlers who thought the land was "promised" to them by some divine right, articulated in both the Doctrine of Discovery or Manifest Destiny. When Charleston reads Exod 13:19, which describes the Israelites as carrying the bones of their patriarch Joseph out of Egypt (Exod 13:19), he recalls the many

---

14. See Aldred, "Land, Treaty, and Spirituality," 1–17.
15. Charleston, *Four Vision Quests*, 106.

Choctaws, approximately 10 percent of whom were Christians themselves, who carried the bones of their ancestors along the Trail of Tears from Mississippi to Oklahoma.[16] Reading Exodus with a Turtle Island Hermeneutic provides an opportunity to share stories often unknown or under-appreciated by Western Euro-Americans. If we read Scripture in order to make sense of our own histories and lives, the question stands out: whose stories are we telling? To reflect on the tragic trauma of "the Long Walk" helps us to tell true stories about the past regarding how the economic growth and expansion of modern North American nations were built upon a foundation of broken treaties and the dispossession of Indigenous peoples from their lands. And yet, we hold out that Creator walked with us.

Although the exodus story has been essential to both African-American and Latino/a liberation theologians, Robert Allen Warrior (Osage) has critically asked where Native North Americans should see themselves in this narrative. Warrior argues that the story of the Canaanites, the Indigenous peoples of the promised land, whom the Israelites sought to conquer and whose land they claimed, poignantly resonates with the North American Indigenous experience. The God of Israel both liberates and conquers, Warrior warns. In a powerful response to Deut 6:10–12, in which the Lord reminds the Israelites that he has brought them to a land "with fine, large cities that you did not build, houses filled with all sorts of goods that you did not fill, hewn cisterns that you did not hew, vineyards and olive groves that you did not plant," Sarah Augustine writes:

> I am from the people who build the cities of clay on the crest of cliffs, mesas, that were seized by the Spanish; the people who originally lived in homes with good things in the river valley of what is now called the Rio Grande; the people who dug the wells in the desert that have been used and depleted by others for more than five hundred years; the people who planted the fields of corn and tobacco, the vines of squash and beans, the first people who were satisfied by these four sacred plants.[17]

While biblical scholars may continue to debate over the extent to which the book of Joshua depicts a historical or idealized story of conquest and whether the Canaanites merged with the Israelites, the story of the destruction and dispossession of Indigenous peoples of the promised land remains palpable (Exod 23:23–33). Such stories informed the imagination and sermons of Puritan ministers, including Cotton Mather, who portrayed white colonists as "the chosen people," who had a divine claim on American

---

16. Charleston, *Four Vision Quests*, 97.
17. Augustine, *Land Is Not Empty*, 119–20.

soil, and Indigenous peoples as disposable and despicable Amalekites and Canaanites.[18] "America's self-image as a 'chosen people,'" Warrior contends, "has provided the rhetoric to mystify domination."[19] In response to Warrior's take on the Canaanites, William Baldridge (Cherokee) points to the previously discussed story of the Canaanite woman (Matt 15:12–28) who begs Jesus to expel a demon from her daughter already discussed above. According to Baldridge, when Jesus hears the Canaanite woman's declaration of faith, in a miraculous moment "[t]he son of the god of Canaanite oppression repents" and the daughter is healed.[20] For James Treat (Muscogee/Cherokee), Jesus is made to recognize the Canaanite woman's story and faith—a faith that was written beyond the pages of the story of Israel.[21] And so, Baldridge concludes, if the Canaanite woman can change Jesus's mind, so too can Indigenous peoples "change the very heart of God" and "his chosen people," which results in healing, harmony, and reconciliation. Jace Weaver (Cherokee) has responded to Warrior's Canaanite Problem by directing our attention to the narrative of Zelophehad's daughters (Num 27 and Josh 17). In the biblical stories, the daughters petition Moses and Joshua for their father's inheritance, because their father had no male heirs. Since the names of the five daughters correspond to towns in northern Canaan in the land of Hepher, some suggest that these daughters were Canaanites. For Weaver, the story of Zelophehad's daughters both encourages the oppressed to speak out for themselves and validates the "maintenance of the Hepherites' cultural and territorial integrity," amid a foreign people—certainly a prophetic word for Indigenous Christians![22]

THE CROSS, CEREMONY, AND SACRED STORIES

Traditional Indigenous ceremonies and stories are also brought into conversation with Scripture and are embraced in the lives of Indigenous followers of Jesus. In this regard, one of the most important individuals in the native church was the late Richard Twiss (Lakota).[23] Twiss, along with many others that composed the NAIITS community in its earliest inception,

---

18. See for example Cotton Mather's sermon entitled "Souldiers counselled and comforted. A discourse delivered unto some part of the forces engaged in the just war of New-England against the northern & eastern Indians," September 1, 1689.

19. Warrior, "Canaanites, Cowboys, and Indians," 99.

20. Baldridge, "Native American Theology," 101.

21. Treat, "Canaanite Problem," 24.

22. Weaver, "Biblical Paradigm for Native Liberation," 104.

23. See Twiss, *One Church, Many Tribes*; Twiss, *Rescuing the Gospel from the Cowboys*.

tirelessly and patiently argued for a seat at the theological table within Christianity, particularly within evangelical spaces. The earliest battles were fought over whether Indigenous cultural ceremonies and practices could be recognized as valid forms of Christian discipleship and devotion.[24] Casey Church (Potawatomi) incorporates biblical passages into his ceremonies and justifies the practice of smudging (the burning of herbs, including sage, sweet grass, cedar, and tobacco as an incense) by pointing to the ancient Hebrew practice of burning incense over the ark of the Covenant (e.g., Exod 30:1–6, 34–6; Luke 1:8–10).[25] George E. "Tink" Tinker (Osage) has read the Passion narrative considering how Indigenous traditionalists understand what suffering on behalf of others accomplishes in the context of purification ceremonies like the Sun Dance and the Sweat Lodge.[26] The experience of discomfort or pain in such ceremonies and rituals is intended to help realign and sustain the harmony or balance of Sacred Energy within the cosmos and to reinforce prayers made to Creator. Vicarious suffering within Indigenous ceremonial contexts does not placate the anger of a wrathful god, overcome any sense of some original sin, or reconcile humanity with God. And so for some Native North Americans, Jesus's suffering at the cross is not about what God *needs* in order to forgive, but the ultimate display of Creator's love for us and the tragic culmination of humanity being out of balance and out of line with the original instructions of Creator. As Jace Weaver puts it: when Jesus was murdered, God wept, but then laughed at the folly of humanity (Ps 2), and resurrected Jesus in vindication of his life and teachings.[27] Some Lakota Christians even refer to Jesus as the ideal Sun Dancer, who suffers so that his people may live.[28]

The sacred story of the life-giving death of Christ resonates with an ancient Indigenous story, versions of which have been told across North America, namely the story of Corn Mother. George "Tink" Tinker once challenged Christians to consider the possibility that Christ, as God's eternal and pervasive *Logos* or communication of "creativity and healing or salvation to human beings," inspired our ancestral stories, like that of

---

24. In addition to the previously cited works by Twiss, numerous essays in the *Journal of NAIITS* have wrestled with this issue. See for example the inaugural essay of the journal: Twiss et al., "Culture, Christian Faith and Error," 5–35.

25. Church, *Holy Smoke*, 89–90.

26. Kidwell et al., *Native American Theology*, 62–65, 79–83. Damian Costello, a Black Elk scholar, also states that "the cottonwood tree and the Sun Dance are linked to the cross in the Black Elk tradition." See Costello, "Black Elk Speaks," 46.

27. Weaver, *That the People Might Live*, 182n172.

28. Costello, *Black Elk*, 119–22.

Corn Mother.²⁹ While Corn Mother stories may vary, each tale speaks of a divine woman who willingly accepts her death so that her people might live. In one Penobscot retelling, the First Mother, compelled by the cries of her starving children, instructs her husband to kill her and to drag her body across the fields so that her flesh, blood, and bones might mix with the soil. Months later corn begins to grow. In a word reminiscent of the Christian Eucharist, the First Man tells his people: "Remember and take good care of First Mother's flesh, because it is goodness become substance . . . she has given her life so that you might live."³⁰ Baldridge shares a Cherokee version where the mother produces corn by rubbing her body and is murdered by her own children, who mistake her for a witch upon discovering how their mom was providing food for them. In this story too, the mother's buried body produces corn forevermore, the source of life-nourishing bread for the Cherokee.³¹ The story of Corn Mother teaches us about the inter-relatedness of all creation, especially our food, and the sacred possibility that awaits us when we gather in gratitude for the meal before us each day. Similar to Jesus's sacrifice, Corn Mother's sacrifice invites people to gather around the table, recognize their shared kinship, and offer gratitude for the gifts of the Corn Mother. There are other stories of self-sacrifice within Indigenous traditions, including the Cherokee story shared by Woodley about the service and self-sacrifice of grandmother turtle, who died in her quest to retrieve mud from the bottom of the sea that would prove essential for creating the land mass we call Turtle Island (North America).³²

Patty Krawec (Anishinaabe) contrasts Noah's silence and seeming lack of concern for the deaths of countless others when warned about the flood against both the story of Abraham's willingness to argue with God on behalf of Sodom and Gomorrah (Gen 18:22–33) and the Anishinaabe story of eagle, who similarly negotiated with Creator to spare humanity for the sake of even one righteous family. Similar to the biblical story of the flood, the Anishinaabe story features a Creator that is fed up with the greed, selfishness, and violence of humans and plans to start over. However, the eagle petitions Creator to allow him to find one worthy family that is living in a good way that would merit Creator's mercy on behalf of humanity. After a lengthy, desperate search, the eagle finds one harmonious and prayerful family, thus placating Creator's wrath. Krawec juxtaposes these stories to critique humanity's tendency to mark some tribes and bodies as inferior,

29. Kidwell et al., *Native American Theology*, 76–83.
30. Erdoes and Ortiz, *American Indian Myths and Legends*, 13.
31. Baldridge, "Reclaiming Our Histories," 87.
32. Woodley, *Shalom*, 144–47.

a tendency on full historical display in how the white settler-colonialism marked native bodies. Krawec also observes that it takes faith in God, like the faith exhibited by Abraham and Eagle, to argue with God.[33] A Turtle Island Hermeneutic envisions a more comprehensive picture of how Creator has been revealed to Indigenous peoples in their ancestral ceremonies and sacred stories and finds resonance with the Scriptures.

VISIONS IN SCRIPTURE, VISIONS AND SCRIPTURE

Turtle Island Hermeneutics privileges Indigenous ways of knowing (i.e., epistemologies) and gaining knowledge and wisdom from the divine. For example, among Indigenous peoples, including "prophets" and medicine people, dreams and visions have long been esteemed as special encounters for receiving communication from and about divine and/or spiritual beings. Vine Deloria Jr. explains that for the Sioux, "dreams are critical to understanding cosmology, space and time, family structure, and relations with animals and the non-human world."[34] And so an Indigenous interpretation might appreciate the many places in Scripture where dreams and visions are essential conduits for receiving knowledge from and about the divine that are familiar to experiences in their own traditions. For example, an Indigenous eye might recognize how the dream-vision of Zechariah who sees four chariots, each led by different colored horses, which represented the four winds/directions of the earth (red/east, dappled gray/south, white/west, and black/north; Zech 6:1–8) resembles the horse dance vision of Black Elk. In this vision, Black Elk sees four groups of twelve dancing black, white, sorrel, and buckskin horses, each representing the powers of the four directions, North, East, South, and West, respectively.[35]

Hoklotubbe argues that reading Scripture in conversation with Indigenous visionaries, including Black Elk, Wovoka, and Marabel McKay can help us reframe how we interpret and imagine the apostle Paul.[36] Modern Euro-American readers have underappreciated how much Paul's understanding of the gospel, in particular how gentiles are accepted by Creator without being circumcised, seems to depend more upon his visionary experiences of the risen Christ than upon some clear method of interpreting Scripture. In Gal 1:11–12, Paul emphatically emphasizes that he received his gospel "through a revelation of Jesus Christ," and describes in a coy manner

---

33. Krawec, "Why Was Noah Silent at the End of the World."
34. Deloria, *C. G. Jung and the Sioux Traditions*, 167.
35. Costello, *Black Elk*, 99.
36. Hoklotubbe, "(En)Visioning Creator's Revelation on Turtle Island."

his visionary ascent to the third heaven in 2 Cor 12:2–7. As Richard B. Hays has acknowledged, Paul interprets and references Scripture in ways that would make modern evangelicals uneasy.[37] For Paul, Scripture's true meaning can only be "unveiled" through the Spirit (2 Cor 3) and through revelation, is sometimes allegorical, and ultimately points to Christ. Hoklotubbe suggests that "we ought to imagine the historical Paul of Tarsus as less akin to a reformed or post-Enlightenment, Euro-American reader of scripture, like Martin Luther or modern seminary trained ministers, and more akin to a visionary Indigenous medicine man."[38] Indeed, an Indigenous reader might appreciate the resonance between Paul's vision of Jesus along the Damascus Road with Black Elk's vision of Jesus, "illuminated with all colors of light," while participating in the Ghost Dance, just before the massacre of Wounded Knee.[39] Similar to Paul, Black Elk both saw the resurrected Jesus and was given a message, perhaps even a gospel to share, namely that "all earthly beings and growing things belong to [Christ]."[40] A Turtle Island Hermeneutic, then, not only appreciates and expresses curiosity and wonder about the significance of dreams and visions for advancing the story of Creator and his people in Scripture, but also toward how such phenomena remain powerful experiences for discerning the Spirit of Creator among Indigenous peoples today in conjunction with interpreting Scripture.

CONTRIBUTIONS

There is no singular Native North American reading of Scripture, but some of these interpretive trends briefly sketched above certainly represent Turtle Island Hermeneutics as we have broadly conceived it and continue to work it out. Turtle Island Hermeneutics, as its name implies, roots us not only to our social locations but to our communities and landscapes. Current Indigenous theologians approach this in different ways. A representative of a more pan-Indigenous experience is the new English paraphrase called the First Nations Version, in which Terry Wildman sought to create a translation of the New Testament that would appeal to a broad range of Indigenous peoples who only encounter the Scriptures in the English language.[41] Alternatively, Marcus Briggs-Cloud (Muscogee/Maskoke, son of the Wind Clan) advocates that we move away from pan-Indigenous theological

---

37. Hays, *Echoes of Scripture in the Letters of Paul*, 156.
38. Hoklotubbe, "(En)Visioning Creator's Revelation."
39. Neihardt, *Black Elk Speaks*, 154.
40. Neihardt, *Black Elk Speaks*.
41. Wildman, *First Nations Version*.

interpretations in favor of more localized theologies and readings of Scripture that attend to the cosmologies, ceremonies, and ideologies of a particular Indigenous community, rooted in a land.[42]

Herein lies the promise and peril of our Turtle Island Hermeneutics proposal. While Indigenous interpreters seek to reassert the dignity and wisdom of their ancestral stories and customs, Native North Americans disagree with each other on how to reconcile perceived contradictions between Indigenous and biblical conceptions of creation, divinity, sacrifice, sin, and salvation. If Creator has manifested Godself to both Native North Americans and Israelites, then which revelation "corrects" or "supersedes" the other? Should we imagine the Great Spirit/Mystery as essentially personal or as an impersonal power, as is the case with some Lakota understandings of *Wakan tanka*? Could we read Corn Mother's message of the interconnectedness of creation as inspired by Christ/Logos and even as a helpful corrective to interpretations of Gen 1:28, which has been used to endorse the domination of creation—an ideology complicit with our deforestation and scarring of the earth in order to extract its resources at unsustainable rates? There may be no simple or universally satisfying answer to these questions. And yet there are two things which are important for non-Indigenous Christians to recognize.

First, because Indigenous folks do not normally place people or things into hierarchies, the aforementioned "contradictions" are not nearly as distressing as they are for Western, Euro-American Christians. Indigenous followers of Jesus can affirm Jesus as Lord, even as we see Jesus needed to be confronted with his own people's complicated history of colonization and genocide (Matt 15:21–26)—our Christology is big enough to hold these things together.

Second, many Indigenous peoples today (including the authors of this essay) are re-asserting their personhood and proudly reclaiming their cultural heritage. This work of "healing identity" is the work to reclaim culture that was lost because of colonization.[43] This is both personal and communal work, a work of decolonization for those on the journey. The working out of these questions is ours to discern in community. Questions of "contradictions," the dialectic between the Scriptures and traditions, and the use or adaptation of traditional ceremonies, worldviews, and lifeways in one's Christian discipleship all belong with Indigenous followers of Jesus specifically. We are not seeking the approval of the wider/whiter church. In fact, we are seeking to free ourselves from the paternalism and white

---

42. Briggs-Cloud, "Creation—The New Creation," 89–118.
43. See Peterson et al., "Ways of Knowing Self," 35.

cultural hegemony that we have encountered since Columbus. We knew Creator then, and we follow Christ the Creator-made-flesh now. We invite non-Indigenous believers as fellow travelers in the journey, not as authoritative guides. Indigenous interpretations of the Bible remain fertile ground for life-affirming theology, the power of which lies in their ability to reclaim and sustain traditions threatened by cultural extinction and to energize adherents through their poetic and constructive juxtaposition of Indigenous ceremonies, experiences, and sacred stories with biblical narratives and theological concepts.

BIBLIOGRAPHY

Aldred, Ray. "The Land, Treaty, and Spirituality: Communal Identity Inclusive of Land." *Journal of NAIITS* 18 (2019) 1–17.

Augustine, Sarah. *The Land is Not Empty: Following Jesus in Dismantling the Doctrine of Discovery*. Harrisonburg, VA: Herald, 2021.

Baldridge, William. "Native American Theology: A Biblical Basis." In *Native And Christian: Indigenous Voices on Religious Identity in The United States and Canada*, edited by James Treat, 100–101. New York: Routledge, 1996.

———. "Reclaiming Our Histories." In *Native And Christian: Indigenous Voices on Religious Identity in The United States and Canada*, edited by James Treat, 83–93. New York: Routledge, 1996.

Bauckham, Richard. *Living With Other Creatures: Green Exegesis And Theology*. Waco, TX: Baylor, 2011.

Briggs-Cloud, Marcus. "Creation—The New Creation: A Maskoke Postcolonial Perspective." In *Coming Full Circle: Constructing Native Christian Theology*, edited by Steven Charleston and Elaine A. Robinson, 89–118. Minneapolis: Fortress, 2015.

Charleston, Steven. *The Four Vision Quests of Jesus*. New York: Morehouse, 2015.

———. "The Old Testament of Native America." In *Lift Every Voice: Constructing Christian Theologies from the Underside*, edited by Susan Brooks Thistlethwaite and Mary Potter Engel, 69–81. Maryknoll, NY: Orbis, 1990.

Charleston, Steven, and Elaine A. Robinson, eds. *Coming Full Circle: Constructing Native Christian Theology*. Minneapolis: Fortress, 2015.

Church, Casey. *Holy Smoke: The Contextual Use of Native American Ritual and Ceremony*. Cleveland, OH: Cherohala, 2017.

Costello, Damian. *Black Elk: Colonialism and Lakota Catholicism*. Maryknoll, NY: Orbis, 2005.

———. "Black Elk Speaks." *Journal of NAIITS* 4 (2006) 29–56.

Dellinger, Lisa A. "Sin—Ambiguity and Complexity and the Sin of Not Conforming." In *Coming Full Circle: Constructing Native Christian Theology*, edited by Steven Charleston and Elaine A. Robinson, 119–32. Minneapolis: Fortress, 2015.

Deloria, Vine, Jr. *C. G. Jung and the Sioux Traditions*. Edited by Philip J. Deloria and Jerome Bernstein. New Orleans: Spring Journal, 2009.

Erdoes, Richard, and Alfonso Ortiz. *American Indian Myths and Legends*. Pantheon Fairy Tale and Folklore Library. New York: Pantheon, 1984.

Hays, Richard B. *Echoes of Scripture in the Letters of Paul*. New Haven, CT: Yale University Press, 1993.

Hoklotubbe, T. Christopher. "(En)Visioning Creator's Revelation on Turtle Island." In *Multi-Racial Interpretations of the Bible*, edited by Esau McCaulley et al., 25–34. Atlanta: SBL, 2023.

———. "A Native American Interpretation of the Bible." *Oxford Encyclopedias of the Bible: Digital Collection*. Oxford: Oxford University Press, 2022. www.oxfordreference.com/view/10.1093/acref/9780197669402.001.0001/acref-9780197669402-e-7.

Hoklotubbe, T. Christopher, and Danny Zacharias. "Encountering the Bible on Turtle Island." In *The New Testament in Color*, edited by Esau McCaulley. Downers Grove, IL: InterVarsity, 2023.

Krawec, Patty. "Why Was Noah Silent at the End of the World: Finding the Courage to Argue with Those who Claim to Speak for God." *Sojourners*, February 2022. https://sojo.net/magazine/february-2022/why-was-noah-silent-end-world.

Kidwell, Clara Sue, et al. *A Native American Theology*. Maryknoll, NY: Orbis, 2001.

LeBlanc, Terry. "Toward an Indigenous Eschatology: Caution, Circle Ahead." In *Indigenous People and the Christian Faith: A New Way Forward*. edited by William H. U. Anderson and Charles Muskego, 229–46. Wilmington, DE: Vernon, 2020.

Peterson, Wendy, et al. "Ways Of Knowing Self: Reclamation of Real Indigenous Identity." *Journal of NAIITS* 9 (2011) 31–57.

Treat, James, ed. "The Canaanite Problem." *Daughters of Sarah: The Magazine for Christian Feminists* 20 (1994) 20–24.

———. *Native And Christian: Indigenous Voices on Religious Identity in The United States and Canada*. New York: Routledge, 1996.

Twiss, Richard. *One Church, Many Tribes: Following Jesus the Way God Made You*. Minneapolis: Chosen, 2000.

———. *Rescuing the Gospel from the Cowboys: A Native American Expression of the Jesus Way*. Downers Grove, IL: InterVarsity, 2015.

Twiss, Richard, et al. "Culture, Christian Faith and Error." *Journal of NAIITS* 1 (2003) 5–35.

Warrior, Robert Alan. "Canaanites, Cowboys, and Indians: Deliverance, Conquest, and Liberation Theology Today." In *Native And Christian: Indigenous Voices on Religious Identity in The United States and Canada*, edited by James Treat, 93–104. New York: Routledge, 1996.

Weaver, Jace. "A Biblical Paradigm for Native Liberation." In *Native And Christian: Indigenous Voices on Religious Identity in The United States and Canada*, edited by James Treat, 103–4. New York: Routledge, 1996.

———. *That The People Might Live: Native American Literatures and Native American Community*. New York: Oxford University Press, 1997.

Wildman, Terry, ed. *First Nations Version: An Indigenous Translation of the New Testament*. Downers Grove, IL: InterVarsity, 2021.

Woodley, Randy S. "The Harmony Way: Integrating Indigenous Values Within Native North American Theology And Mission." PhD Diss., Asbury Theological Seminary, 2010.

———. *Living in Color: Embracing God's Passion for Ethnic Diversity*. Downers Grove, IL: InterVarsity, 2001.

———. *Shalom and The Community of Creation: An Indigenous Vision*. Prophetic Christianity. Grand Rapids: Eerdmans, 2012.

Zacharias, H. Daniel. "The Land Takes Care of Us: Recovering Creator's Relational Design." In *The Land: Majority World and Minoritized Theologies of Land*, edited by K. K. Yeo and Gene L. Green, 69–97. Eugene, OR: Cascade, 2020.

Chapter 29
Latinx Hermeneutics
SAMMY ALFARO

As this volume demonstrates, biblical interpretation in the twenty-first century has flourished in a multiplicity of perspectives and emphases throughout the world. Among the various contextual approaches seeking to interpret Scripture through a particular set of eyes is Latinx hermeneutics. The term "Latinx" refers to Latina/o communities living in the US with the suffix "x" seeking to simply signify the gender-neutral reality of the community. Although the use of the term "Latinx" is contested and fraught with misconceptions, this chapter uses it with the purpose of indicating the broader representation of peoples from Latin American descent who reside in the US.[1] Under the umbrella descriptor of Latinx hermeneutics, then, this essay aims to survey the main perspectives and interpretative strategies of US Latinx biblical scholars and theologians.

At the outset of this study, it's important to acknowledge the difficulty of attempting to summarize biblical views and hermeneutical approaches of a large array of peoples especially on account of their continually changing demographics. In short, given the cultural, linguistic, social, and religious differences within the Latinx community, one essay cannot encapsulate various viewpoints as if distinctions could be completely erased. Nonetheless, due to the similarities of experience and faith existing in the broader Latinx culture a survey of significant themes and approaches may be attempted to

---

1. This author recognizes the difficulties that accompany terms like "Hispanic" and "Latina/o" and opts for "Latinx" for reasons of its gender inclusiveness and multicultural reach. For an excellent overview of the complexity of the use of the term "Latinx," see Agosto and Hidalgo, *Latinxs, the Bible, and Migration*, 3–6.

demonstrate its contribution to the greater field of biblical interpretation. Special attention will be given to the contextual and collaborative method signaled by the term "teología en conjunto," which forged and continues to shape interpretative approaches for reading and understanding Scripture from Latinx perspectives.

LIBERATION ROOTS OF LATINX HERMENEUTICS

In his book, *The Future of Faith,* Harvey Cox points to Latin American liberation theology as a movement which made a great impact on twentieth-century Christianity. One major influence liberation theology had around the world was to model an approach to contextualized readings of Scripture that seek to establish justice and peace. Cox celebrates the desire to establish a more humane world through the witness of Scripture with this insightful comment:

> Liberation theology is more than just a regionally specific "Latin American theology" or a passing fad. It embodies a momentous leap out of the many centuries in which Christianity has defined as a system of beliefs imposed by a hierarchy. It symbolizes the resurrection of faith-as-trust and represents the retrieval of the core of the gospel message as it was understood and lived in the earliest centuries of Christianity.[2]

Indeed, the hermeneutical strategies developed by Liberation theologians in Latin America were appropriated and applied by minoritized peoples around the world in a manner that new liberationist readings and voices surfaced. In particular, Latinx authors since the late sixties built on liberationist insights to produce their own approach to biblical interpretation and theology.

Veli-Matti Kärkkäinen summarizes the hermeneutical approach proposed by liberation theologians in the following manner.

1. Ideological suspicion: an emerging notion that perhaps something is wrong in society, especially among the underprivileged,

2. Analytical reflection on the social-value system: asking penetrating questions such as whether a situation is justified by Scripture and whether God's purposes are fulfilled in it,

3. Exegetical suspicion: an acknowledgment of the fact that theology is not relevant because of a one-sided and biased style of reading the Bible that neglects the perspective of the poor and the oppressed,

2. Cox, *Future of Faith,* 195.

4. Pastoral action: articulating an appropriate response to what is determined to be one's personal biblical responsibility.[3]

Given these foundational observations its fitting to summarize the basic appeal of Latin American liberation theology concerning Scripture. It must be recognized that the backgrounds of this theological movement lie in the social struggles within Latin America. Specifically, liberation theology arose as a response to the oppression of the marginalized poor by the more powerful ruling classes. Liberation theologians considered the plight of the poor as their need to be liberated from cultural, social, economic, and political servitude that hinder human development. Set in the context of class oppression, then, liberation theology aimed to bring the church to a more active involvement in the liberation process of the oppressed. In this struggle, the appeal to Scripture as a principal foundation for obtaining that freedom became significant.

GUSTAVO GUTIÉRREZ—OPTING FOR THE POOR

Perhaps the most prominent in delineating the basic interpretative principles of liberation theology was the Peruvian Catholic priest, Gustavo Gutiérrez. In his *A Theology of Liberation*, he suggests that the oppressed have been dehumanized and for that matter deprived of their basic human dignity as children of God. Gutiérrez explained the origins of the movement like this: "The historical womb from which liberation theology has emerged is the life of the poor and, in particular, of the Christian communities that have arisen within the bosom of the present-day Latin American church."[4] In order for the oppressed to regain their freedom a revolutionary transformation of the social structure must take place. This liberation involves political, historical, and spiritual freedom, which is inseparably joined to the all-encompassing salvific process consummated in Christ. Theology as a critical reflection, therefore, cannot stand idly as the vast majority is being oppressed, but must engage in the liberation process to bring about the freedom of the poor.

According to Gutiérrez, then, theological reflection is the second stage in the process because faith comes first and is the source of theology. This first stage is lived faith that finds its expression in both prayer and communion. Viewed from this perspective the principal task of theology can be described as "reflection on praxis in the light of faith," which means that for liberationist biblical interpreters orthopraxis and orthodoxy are profoundly

---

3. Kärkkäinen, *Christology a Global Introduction*, 225.
4. Gutiérrez, *Theology of Liberation*, xxxiii.

united in a circular relationship.[5] This key insight of praxis-oriented reflection became the model for ecclesial base communities, which gathered to read and make sense of Scripture from within their context of oppression and poverty.

JUAN LUIS SEGUNDO—THE HERMENEUTIC CIRCLE

Another early liberation theologian, Juan Luis Segundo coined this approach as the *hermeneutic circle* understanding that "the continuing change in our interpretation of the Bible which is dictated by the continuing changes in our present-day reality, both individual and societal."[6] Segundo's observation of the circular nature of this interpretative strategy is based on "the fact that each new reality obliges us to interpret the word of God afresh, to change reality accordingly, and then to go back and reinterpret the word of God again, and so on."[7] Another shorthanded way of describing this three-step dialectical process is "see-judge-act." In this hermeneutic cycle, the biblical interpreter experiences the world, reflects on the word with the weight of that experience, and goes on to live in the world again with a renewed sense of action.

In short, Latin American liberation theology's approach to Scripture is shaped considerably by the historical situations and contexts in which it developed. The Bible became the central vehicle for liberating the oppressed from the clutches of capitalism. Since the God of both the Old and New Testaments is the God of the oppressed who sides with them and seeks their freedom, their interpretation of Scripture began with the marginalized and poor, and not with the powerful and rich. In the Old Testament, God sided with the poor and the oppressed nation of Israel. In the New Testament, God's Son became incarnate within a community of the oppressed who belonged to the lower class.

By reexamining Scripture in this way, liberation theologians concluded that Western biblical interpretation was biased, ideologically controlled, and favored those in power. Interpretations coming from the "rich world," therefore, were subject to suspicion and needed to be restated in their proper context of God's siding with the poor. The exodus event, seen as "the center of Scripture," became a paradigm for liberation. The appeal for justice in the ethical teachings of the Old Testament prophets became the clarion call for the eradication of injustice toward the poor. Eschatologically, then, Christians take part in building the future kingdom of God when injustice

---

5. Gutiérrez, *Theology of Liberation*, xxxiv.
6. Segundo, *Liberation of Theology*, 8.
7. Segundo, *Liberation of Theology*, 8.

and exploitation are eliminated, and peace, justice, love, and freedom are established. As the source of these paradigms, the values and concerns of the kingdom, and the witness of the Liberator (Jesus), Scripture serves as the foundation for liberation.

In evaluating the function of Scripture in Latin American liberation theology, the efforts to make the freedom from oppression and injustice the task of theology must be applauded. Christians have the responsibility to ensure within the limits of their abilities that social and political justice is given to every individual regardless of race, sex, religion, etc. There is no doubt that the gospel is not limited to the salvation of the soul, but that it also demands our participation in social change.

MAJOR INTERPRETERS AND EMPHASES OF LATINX HERMENEUTICS

Building on the legacy of Latin American liberation hermeneutics, early Latinx scholars sought to interpret the Bible within the contexts of their own cultures and experiences. Such an approach envisioned a critical engagement with the scriptural text that takes into account the social, historical, and cultural contexts of the represented Latinx communities. Through an ongoing dialogue with liberationist premises early Latinx scholars guided their theological work focusing on the "option for the poor" of their world. This initial move led them to do theology from the perspective of the underprivileged, which served as a critique to the hermeneutical hegemony of the so-called first world countries. Key proponents of Latinx hermeneutical principles include Virgilio Elizondo, Orlando Costas, and Justo L. González.

VIRGILIO ELIZONDO—THE GALILEAN PRINCIPLE

In the early 1980s Virgilio Elizondo pioneered an essential principle for interpreting the Bible from a Latinx perspective. In his book *Galilean Journey*, Elizondo establishes parallels between the Mexican American immigrant experience and the life Jesus lived in first century Galilee. Considering the continued Latinx struggle against marginalization, oppression, and discrimination, Elizondo compares it to Jesus's lived reality like this:

> As a Galilean, Jesus grew up in contact with diverse peoples and cultures, yet far from all the "centers of belongings"—political, intellectual, or religious. Rejected and put down by all

the in-groups of their world, the Galileans had learned through their margination and suffering to relativize society's absolutes.[8]

Elizondo further relates Jesus's earthly struggles with that of the Latinx community in the US by saying:

> In the midst of this confusion, an experience of good news suddenly began among the poor and destitute of society. One of the marginated ones now became the source of solidarity and messianic hope among the masses of hopeless people. He was no well-intentioned outsider or missioner. Out of the ranks of the nobodies of the world, own of their own became the source of friendship, community and hope. This is the core of the *evangelium*.[9]

In many ways this Galilean hermeneutical principle provided early Latinx biblical interpreters with an approach to read the incarnational dimension of Jesus's life into their own lives and experience. Theological beliefs like the Son of God becoming a man become applicable insights when considering how Jesus's incarnation in the context of first-century Galilee. Jesus lived among a specific people, and in a particular time and place. He was not born in the palace of a king but began and shared his life with the despicable of his world. In other words, like Latinx peoples Jesus lived the life of a stranger in his own land. He was born in the land of his people, but it was under the control of the who oppressed them. In many ways this parallels the life of the US Latinx community; a minoritized people who continue to be marginalized by the dominant culture.

JUSTO L. GONZÁLEZ—READING THE BIBLE IN SPANISH

Other key emphases of Latinx biblical interpretation are contextual readings of Scripture. Although Latinx scholars emphasize the importance of reading the Bible in its original historical and cultural contexts, more importantly they highlight the significance of the present context of Latinx communities as an interpretative key. By approaching the biblical text in this manner, the stories of the Bible become more relevant and meaningful for the Latinx community. Drawing from their experiences as marginalized individuals or communities, Latinx scholars advocate for interpreting the Bible from the purview of those on the periphery. This approach highlights the voices and experiences of the oppressed and marginalized characters and communities in the biblical narratives.

8. Elizondo, *Galilean Journey*, 55.
9. Elizondo, *Future Is Mestizo*, 74.

Justo L. González first championed the fundamental interpretative strategy of "reading the Bible in Spanish," which has yielded a great harvest of essays and books. This is not a mere preferencing of Spanish language Bible translations over English or other translations of Scripture to modern languages. Instead, what González has in mind is a reading of Scripture that takes seriously the contexts from which one reads and, in his case, the Latinx culture and experience in particular. González puts it like this: "If it is true that we bring a particular perspective to history and to theology, then we must also bring a particular perspective to the interpretation of Scripture. And, once again, it may be that this perspective will prove useful not only to us but also to the church at large."[10]

It's not that Latinx interpreters fail to understand the Bible as an authoritative text or even that they deny the inerrancy of Scripture to put it in stronger words. Rather, the biblical text is approached with the hermeneutical suspicion that there are no innocent readings of Scripture. Everyone reads from their cultural place or location so all interpretation is in the end perspectival. González provides a helpful analogy to better appreciate this hermeneutical dilemma when he writes:

> To speak of "perspectives" is to imagine that we are all looking at a landscape. The landscape itself is the same for all of us. Yet each one sees it from a different perspective, and will thus describe it differently . . . We may certainly see it in myriad different ways; but we still are all speaking of a single landscape, of a common text. This is part of what binds us together. The primary subject of our conversation is not our varying perspectives, important as they are. Our conversation is about the landscape, and how it is illumined from each of our various wantage points.[11]

Gleaning from this valuable insight one may discern the collaborative spirit of Latinx biblical interpretation done *en conjunto*. The truth is not all Latinx people read or speak Spanish and even the Spanish or Espanglish that is understood is of a particular idiom or accent depending on the Latin American origin or corner of the US one inhabits. For this reason, even within the Latinx community itself one cannot speak of *the* definitive Latinx reading or interpretation of a biblical passage. Instead, one must speak of diverse readings of Scripture from a multiplicity of Latinx locations that enrich understandings of the text due to a variety of lived experiences and cultural belonging. In short, Latinx biblical hermeneutics envisions a rich tapestry

---

10. González, *Mañana*, 75.
11. González, *Santa Biblia*, 17–18.

or web of interpretations, which together explore interrelated dimensions of a singular text, the Bible.

LATINA BIBLICAL INTERPRETATION

One way that Latinx hermeneutics has differentiated itself from its predecessor has been by advocating for inclusivity regarding ethnicity, race, and gender. Whereas a general critique of the Liberation theology and its legacy has been the lack female voices and greater representation from diverse Latin American communities, Latinx theology and biblical studies have a much wider diversity of scholars in their ranks. Among the Latina voices who have advanced formidable biblical interpretative strategies and critiques are Ada María Isasi-Díaz, María Pilar Aquino, Elizabeth Conde-Frazier, Jacqueline M. Hidalgo, Cristina García-Alfonso, and Ahida Calderón Pilarski, to name a few.[12]

Ada María Isasi-Díaz—Mujerista Theology

Latina feminist biblical scholars have sought to underscore the roles, experiences, and agency of women in the Bible as well as explore how biblical narratives from the OT and the NT intersect with gender and race issues in Latinx communities. Ada María Isasi-Diaz "mujerista theology" places as its *locus theologicus* the daily lived experiences and insights of Latinas who are the cultural and biblical mothers of the Latinx community.

> As a theology rooted in the religious thought and practice of Latinas, *mujerista* theology has made it possible to give voice to those who so far had not been listened to in any theological elaboration, mainly because they were thought incapable of deep, systematic reflection. The experience of *mujerista* theologians has been exactly the opposite. We have always marveled at the capacity of grassroot Latinas to explain their religious beliefs and how they impact their lives. What has moved us to use the voices of Latina women as the source of *mujerista* theology is the hermeneutical privilege that theologies of liberation, among them feminist theology, claim for their communities.[13]

The hermeneutical value of this insight is that it does not privilege the typical academic spaces and scholars who at times pretend to recover the voices

---

12. Some influential essays by Latina biblical scholars include: García-Alfonso, "Latino/a Biblical Hermeneutics"; Hidalgo, "Reading from No Place"; and Calderón Pilarski, "Latina Biblical Critic and Intellectual."

13. Isasi-Díaz, *En la Lucha*, 7.

of the communities they represent. Isasi-Díaz approach is one of solidarity and empowerment; a side-by-side listening, learning, and working-with to truly capture the interpretive voice of Latinas.

Gleaning from various studies of biblical text, Elizabeth Conde-Frazier summarizes the role of the Latina lay preacher and hermeneut in this manner:

> The [Latina] interpreter interprets the biblical text in light of her present life. She uses the preaching moment to tell her story as the story of many others like her. She dares to say that which is untenable for their faith. This is a meaning-making moment of the people, who together are seeking and sharing a process of understanding God's mystery and grace (or lack thereof) in their lives.[14]

In this hermeneutical methodology, the Latinx scholar engages actively by listening and participatory in live readings and interpretations of biblical text that take place from and within the Latinx community. Instead of being *the* interpreter for the community, the Latinx hermeneut is more that of a participant narrator who attempts to carefully hear what the Spirit is saying in and through the community.

Cristina García-Alfonso—"Resolviendo" Survival Hermeneutic

The value of such a hermeneutic strategy of course lies in the capacity for agency and empowerment. In the process, the hope is for Latinas to develop their own liberating readings of texts, rather than merely hear liberating messages from others "professional" preachers, theologians, and scholars of the Bible. An example of how this takes place can be seen in the interpretative strategy of *resolviendo* developed by Cristina García-Alfonso. Dwelling on her experience as a Cuban Latina, García-Alfonso describes her approach for engaging the biblical text as that of "a feminist hermeneutics from a Cuban social location look[ing] at the realities faced by men and especially women on the island."[15] The Spanish term *resolviendo* (to find an answer or solution) refers to what García-Alfonso coins the survival hermeneutic of Cuban identity, which is deeply embedded in a people who have struggled to survive in and out of the island. Instead of seeing her cultural identity as a hindrance or baggage for understanding the biblical text, García-Alfonso considers her ethnic, social, and gendered situatedness as an asset for unpacking the meaning of Scriptures.

14. Conde-Frazier, "Evangélicas Reading Scriptures," 85.
15. García-Alfonso, "Latino/a Biblical Hermeneutics," 152.

Digging deep into her own experience as a Cuban Latina, García-Alfonso masterfully demonstrates how *resolviendo* has become a hermeneutical lens through which she reads the Scriptures.[16] In other words, the strategies of survival learned from her Cuban Latina experience provide an entry point and a source of understanding for reading biblical texts, which are similarly culturally and socially embedded in the reality of survival. Other tools García-Alfonso uses to describe and translate the experience of survival are the novels of Latin American authors like Daína Chaviano (*El Hombre, la Hembra y el Hambre*[17]) who present living parables of *resolviendo* through their stories of survival. By juxtaposing the stories of fictional prostitutes in the novels of Gebara and Chaviano with the biblical story of Rahab (Joshua 2:1–24), García-Alfonso provides a hermeneutical lens to better appreciate Rahab's struggle to survive. She explains:

> In reading the Rahab story from a lens of *resolviendo*, insights of a woman who crosses the boundaries of ideology, city walls, and gender emerge. From her unique ways of surviving and striving as a foreigner to protect her family, I appreciate a reading that allows for women's power to be born from within the same oppressive system where they find themselves. Rahab's struggle to survive pushes her to cross boundaries and to find hope for her and her people in new places, in other lands.[18]

Clearly, the hermeneutical strategy described and employed by García-Alfonso results in a powerful liberative reading through which a Latina reader may discover the value of her own experience and agency.

POSTCOLONIAL BIBLICAL INTERPRETATION—FERNANDO F. SEGOVIA

The contextual approach to Scripture from the diversity of voices and cultures of the Latinx community in turn has produced liberating readings, which not only center on eyeing the Bible as resource for communal liberation, but also aim to liberate the text itself from the hands of the biblicist hegemony that has controlled it. Whereas Latin American liberation hermeneutics in its inception focused primarily on the plight of the poor and the power of liberationist narratives in the Bible, more recent Latinx biblical hermeneutics engages directly with the impact of colonization and

---

16. García-Alfonso, "Latino/a Biblical Hermeneutics," 152.

17. The English reader perhaps misses the play on words in the Spanish title, which is translated with less rhetorical effect literally *The Male, the Female, and the Hunger*.

18. García-Alfonso, "Latino/a Biblical Hermeneutics," 163.

postcolonial realities have had on Latinx communities. Scholars like Fernando F. Segovia, Fracisco Lozada Jr., among others, continue to explore the complex interplay between the Bible, colonialism, and resistance.

The term "postcolonialism" refers to the perspective that examines the relationship between interpretation and ideology within wide-ranging fields of study; beginning with literary criticism and then turning to everything from philosophy to biblical studies.[19] In essence, "what postcolonialism did was to introduce power and politics into the world of literary criticism in such a way as to expose how some literature, art, and drama were implicitly linked to European colonialism."[20] Within this much wider field of study, Latinx postcolonial interpreters have emerged as leading voices in the movement.[21]

Fernando F. Segovia outlines some of the key elements that point to developing a postcolonial optic within biblical studies in general and Latinx hermeneutics in particular. Three primary dimensions of criticism must be distinguished as employing the postcolonial outlook. First, an analysis of the literary tradition of ancient Judaism and early Christianity should seek to set it within the greater sociocultural contexts (the ancient Near East, the Mediterranean world, the Greco-Roman period, etc.) paying attention to the sociopolitical reality (e.g., the consequences of imperialism) as directly affecting their composition.[22] To pose this parameter as a question, how did the evident imperialized setting of the biblical authors affect their perspectives and literary productions? Metaphorically, how does the shadow of the empire cast its power over and against the world of the text? Do the biblical texts highlight a "marginalized" view of the way things were in contrast to the dominant literary sources?

The second reading strategy proposed by Segovia consists in analyzing the readings and interpretations of the biblical texts "tak[ing] seriously into account their broader sociocultural context in the West, whether by way of Europe or North America."[23] Again, the sociopolitical reality from which

19. Postcolonial criticism bears witness to the unequal and uneven forces of cultural representation involved in the contest for political and social authority within the modern world order. The postcolonial critique centers directly on exposing the on-going colonial ideological dominance. Three influential prophets of postcolonialism are Edward Said, Homi Bhabha and Frantz Fanon. Their writings include: Said, *Orientalism* and *Culture and Imperialism*; Bhabha, *Location of Culture*; Fanon, *Dying Colonialism* and Fanon, *Wretched of the Earth*.

20. Sugirtharajah, *Postcolonial Criticism and Biblical Interpretation*, 21.

21. Segovia and Tolbert, *Reading from this Place*, vols. 1–2; Segovia, *Interpreting Beyond the Borders*.

22. Segovia, "Biblical Criticism and Postcolonial Studies," 125.

23. Segovia, "Biblical Criticism and Postcolonial Studies," 126–27.

the reading or interpretation is being done should be noted. What colonial perspectives can be detected in the proposed reading of a particular passage? How does the imperialistic worldview blind or color the interpreter's exegesis and resulting understanding of the text? How does the shadow of empire overlook and impose its force on the interpretation of the biblical narrative?

Third, Segovia considers that the readers or interpreters themselves need to be scrutinized from a postcolonial perspective. Is there an agenda behind an interpretation? Are texts simply being twisted in order to serve the purpose of the ideological slant of the reader? Could one detect the rhetorical function of an interpretative analysis and map the political overtones embedded in the interpretation? This postcolonial optic opened the door for biblical critiques aiming to expose colonial constructs and in turn decolonize approaches to biblical studies.

DECOLONIAL AND DIASPORIC READINGS—LUIS N. RIVERA-PAGÁN & JEAN-PIERRE RUIZ

From this decolonial standpoint but writing from the belly of the beast, Latinx biblical interpreters have taken the tools of the colonizers forging diasporic strategies for re-interpreting scriptural texts drawing parallels between themes of exile, migration, and displacement with the experiences of Latinx peoples. Indeed, influenced by the broader Latin American liberation theology movement, Latinx biblical hermeneutics continues to address issues of social justice, oppression, and liberation as depicted in the Bible, but from the experience of migration and in the vein of a diasporic consciousness the trauma of displacement produces.

Two significant monographs that serve to elucidate interpretative strategies from the Latinx experience of diaspora and migrations are *Essays from the Margins* by Luis N. Rivera-Pagan and *Readings from the Edges* by Jean-Pierre Ruiz. These works provide the significant diasporic underpinnings for reading biblical texts from the purview of the Latinx migrant experience. Writing as a diasporic Puerto Rican who has always possessed US citizenship yet is treated as an alien in his own land, Rivera-Pagán establishes the connections between Latinx diasporic existence and the diasporic realities of the Jewish and early Christian communities, which produced the Bible.

> The Bible itself, as a canonic sacred text, is a literary creature of the diaspora, for the Old Testament was born from the sufferings of the dispersed Hebrew nation and the New Testament was written in koine Greek, the lingua franca of many diasporic

peoples of the Hellenistic age. The New Testament faith is, in many ways, a devout endless wandering, by a community of "aliens and exiles" (I Peter 2:11), to the unreachable ends of the world and ends of times, in search of God and human solidarity. The concept of diaspora could thus be a significant crossroad of encounter, a dialectical hinge, between postcolonial cultural studies and theological hermeneutics.[24]

Following this bearing, Rivera-Pagán's collected essays punctuate the ways in which the diasporic experience, framework, and understandings inform the readings and interpretation of biblical texts.

In a similar vein, Ruiz follows an interpretative strategy which underscores otherness and engagement. However, for Ruiz, this is not a question of merely finding correlation and correspondence between the biblical text and Latinx contexts as a way of reading one's experience into the text (eisegesis) or proof-texting one's socially informed interpretation. Instead, Ruiz considers "a hermeneutic of otherness and engagement offers a salutary alternative, suggesting instead that mapping relationships between texts and their contexts, between readers and their contexts, and between texts and readers across contexts, is a matter of complex negotiation and not linear correspondence."[25] This meaningful observation signals a more mature and judicious hermeneutical optic, for it leads the Latinx interpreter to interrogate not only the biblical texts but even one's contextual analysis.

This hermeneutical shift is noteworthy for it recognizes the complexity of the relationship the reader has with biblical texts and fellow readers. While early Latinx theologians like Virgilio Elizondo could rightly point to the Galilean principle establishing connections between Jesus's first century migrant experience and that of modern day Latinx immigrants, a more critical understanding of the migrant experience of the first century and how it relates to the twenty-first century needs to be developed. Establishing a simplistic "this for that" correlation could be dangerous and even unbiblical without a deeper dive into the socio-cultural migrant realities in first century Galilee. Moreover, privileging the Latinx migrant experience over against the experiences of migrants from all over the world leads to myopic readings where one might only be confirming a biased reading of the biblical text. In this case, learning to read *en voz alta* (out loud) and with the other helps the Latinx exegete to acknowledge the communal migrant experience while at the same time recognize migrants from other parts of

---

24. Rivera-Pagán, *Essays from the Margins*, 50–51.
25. Ruiz, *Readings from the Edges*, 8.

the globe could read the same biblical texts differently due to the multiplicity of social locations.

DIVERSE HYBRID SPIRITUALITY

Another important feature of Latinx hermeneutics involves how biblical interpretation is informed and interacts with various spiritualities and religious practices. Woven into the interpretive strategies of Latinx scholars is the incorporation of elements from indigenous traditions, syncretic beliefs, and lived faith experience as they serve to contextualize and exegete biblical texts. Latinx peoples are religious and spiritual in ways that cannot easily be mapped. The rich religious heritage of a Latinx person could be indigenous, Catholic, Protestant, evangélico, and Pentecostal all at the same time due to the mestizaje of spiritual belongings. Rodolfo Galvan Estrada accentuates this saying: "We read the Bible with the entirety of our lives—our ethnoracial identity, culture, gendered experiences, political context, and spirituality to name a few. Diverse experiences also suggest diverse readings and approaches to the text. Indeed, no singular Latinx method can account for the totality of the Latinx experience."[26]

The diverse and hybrid spirituality of Latinx peoples leads to readings of Scripture that embrace an ecumenical ethos and a spirit of *familia*. Like a genuine Latinx family who has learned to appreciate the gift and value every member adds to the family, Latinx interpreters esteem and celebrate the religious variety of interpretations that flow from diverse spiritual wells. Although it's true that not all Latinx readers of biblical texts welcome a diversity of religious and spiritual interpretations, within the Latinx scholarly community a deep kinship has been forged by biblical, theological, and religious academicians alike due to the understanding of belonging that *familia* engenders. Thus, interpreting the Bible *latinamente* also means that biblical readers do not cut ties with their ancestral and religious spiritual inheritance, but rather incorporate the voices of their extended family into their spiritual encounters with the biblical text.

CONCLUSION

Looking back at the beginnings and development of Latinx hermeneutics, it can be said that in the last fifty years the field has progressed from being an offshoot of Latin American hermeneutics to becoming a discipline of its own. A distinct perspective and voice from the minoritized Latinx community has emerged to contribute to the larger body of biblical interpreters. The

---

26. Estrada, *Latino Reading of Race, Kinship, and the Empire*, 31.

challenge of establishing contextual hermeneutics as a valid interpretative approach was achieved in coalition with other minoritized biblical scholars. As a result, the supposed "objective" approach to biblical interpretation has been shown to be itself biased and the realization that everyone interprets from within a specific social location has become more commonplace.

Furthermore, a younger generation of Latinx interpreters is evolving without having to fight to create interpretative space in the biblical studies field. With this creative liberty to engage in contextually critical hermeneutics, a richer harvest of Latinx interpretative strategies and tools is ripening. A perfect example of the promise and future of Latinx hermeneutics can be celebrated in the recent collection of essays by upcoming and established Latinx scholars and professors who now teach in universities and seminaries all over the US, *Latinx Perspectives on the New Testament*.[27]

BIBLIOGRAPHY

Agosto, Efraín, and Jacqueline M. Hidalgo, eds. *Latinxs, the Bible, and Migration*. New York: Palgrave Macmillan, 2018.

Bhabha, Honi. *The Location of Culture*. London: Routledge, 1994.

Cox, Harvey. *The Future of Faith*. New York: Harper Collins, 2009.

De la Torre, Miguel A., and Edwin David Aponte. *Introducing Latino/a Theologies*. Maryknoll, NY: Orbis, 2001.

Elizondo, Virgilio. *The Future is Mestizo: Life Where Cultures Meet*. Oakland: Meyerstone, 1988.

———. *Galilean Journey: The Mexican-American Promise*. Maryknoll, NY: Orbis, 1983.

Estrada, Rodolfo Galvan, III. *A Latino Reading of Race, Kinship, and the Empire: John's Gospel*. New York: Palgrave MacMillan, 2023.

Fanon, Frantz. *A Dying Colonialism*. Translated by H. Chevalier. Harmondsworth: Penguin, 1970.

———. *The Wretched of the Earth*. Trans. C. Farrington. London: Penguin, 1990.

González, Justo L. *Mañana: Christian Theology from a Hispanic Perspective*. Nashville: Abingdon, 1990.

———. *Santa Biblia: the Bible through Hispanic Eyes*. Nashville: Abingdon, 1996.

Gutierrez, Gustavo. *A Theology of Liberation: History, Politics, and Salvation*. Translated and edited by Sister Caridad Inda and John Eagleson. Maryknoll, NY: Orbis, 1988.

---

27. Vena and Guardiola-Sáenz, *Latinx Perspectives on the New Testament*.

Kärkkäinen, Veli-Matti. *Christology a Global Introduction: An Ecumenical, International, and Contextual Perspective.* Grand Rapids: Baker Academic, 2003.

Lozada, Francisco, Jr., and Fernando F. Segovia, eds. *Latino/a Biblical Hermeneutics: Problematics, Objectives, Strategies.* Atlanta: Society of Biblical Literature, 2014.

———. *Latino/a Theology and the Bible: Ethnic-Racial Reflections on Interpretation.* Lanham: Lexington, 2021.

Martell-Otero, Loida I., et al., eds. *Latina Evangélicas: a Theological Survey from the Margins.* Eugene, OR: Cascade, 2013.

Rivera-Pagán, Luis M. *Essays from the Margins.* Eugene, OR: Cascade, 2014.

Ruiz, Jean-Pierre. *Readings from the Edges: the Bible and People on the Move.* Maryknoll, NY: Orbis, 2011.

Said, Edward. *Culture and Imperialism.* London: Chatto & Windus, 1993.

———. *Orientalism.* London: Penguin, 1985.

Segovia, Fernando F. *Decolonizing Biblical Studies: A View from the Margins,* Maryknoll, NY: Orbis, 2000.

Segovia, Fernando F., and Mary Ann Tolbert, eds. *Reading from this Place,* Volume 1, *Social Location and Biblical Interpretation in the United States.* Minneapolis: Fortress, 1995.

———. *Reading from This Place,* Volume 2, *Social Location and Biblical Interpretation in Global Perspective.* Minneapolis: Fortress, 1995.

Sugirtharajah, R. S. *Postcolonial Criticism and Biblical Interpretation.* Maryknoll, NY: Orbis, 2000.

Vena, Osvaldo D., and Leticia A. Guardiola-Sáenz. *Latinx Perspectives on the New Testament.* Lanham, MD: Lexington, 2022.

Chapter 30
Black Theology Hermeneutics
SANDY DWAYNE MARTIN

This chapter examines the rise, nature, and significance of Black theology, particularly during the 1966–2022 period, and places Black theology in the larger historical tradition of Black religious thought.

Let us differentiate between *Black theology* and what this chapter references as *Black religious thought*, both of which in this chapter are primarily referenced in their Christian expressions, though the latter may be inclusive of other religious traditions. Black theology is the formal, academic, sometimes philosophical-type of approach to Christian ideas, beliefs, doctrines, etc., focusing on the freedom of Blacks from social, economic, and political discrimination, oppression, and marginalization. It advocates the empowerment of Black people to escape temporal or this-worldly restrictions and confinements and to enjoy full liberty and self-determination as other groups. Black religious thought is the more general or broader category of the two, encompassing the entire range of Black religious ideas, beliefs, and doctrines, both formal or academic as well as informal or lay. Black theology has its origins in the broader category of Black religious thought, but it is most often expressed and discussed in the academic realm—seminaries, schools of theology, divinity schools, college and university departments of religion, etc. Black religious thought, as the broader rubric, covers discussion of Christian beliefs and doctrines that are both formal and informal, in the academy as well as the church, among learned experts and average laypersons. Hence, all Black theology is a part of Black religious thought, but not all Black religious thought fits the specific academic category of Black theology.

SECTION 3 • CONTEXTUAL INTERPRETATION

CONE, KING, MALCOLM X, AND THE RISE OF BLACK THEOLOGY

In terms of its *academic* debut, Black liberation theology originated in the late 1960s with James Hal Cone (1938–2018), longtime Professor of Systematic Theology at Union Theological Seminary in New York.[1] Cone argued that at the heart of the Christian faith was the call to every Christian to prioritize the liberation of Black people from economic and political oppression in the United States. He insisted that no Christian theology, regardless of how much it referenced the Bible or piety, could call itself legitimate if it did not foreground supporting freedom of Black people in North America. For the followers of Christ, the freeing the oppressed was primary because Christ himself was a liberator of the oppressed. Therefore, Black theologians held that theology without hermeneutical application was not true theology; that is, concern for the oppressed meant little without the practical application of the principle of ending oppressive social, economic, and political structures.

Cone made abundantly clear that Black liberation theology is rooted in the tradition of Black religious thought. Most immediately, Cone's theology emerged from the attempt to reconcile or bring in working relationship the thinking and activities of Martin Luther King Jr. and Malcolm X (or El-Hajj Malik El-Shabazz, the Islamic name later adopted by the former Malcolm Little).[2] King, the best known and most visible presence in the Civil Rights Movement of the 1950s and 1960s, advocated the integration of Black Americans into the mainstream of the nation's life in all arenas. He utilized (a) the progressive aspects of American history and culture, e.g., the Declaration of Independence and the US Constitution, as foundations for eradicating all acts of racial discrimination, including segregation in public facilities, disfranchisement in voting, and (b) a socially conscious approach to the Christian tradition. In addition to racial equality, King pursued the goals of peace (domestic and globally) and economic justice. In sum, King's theological, philosophical, and methodological approaches were drawn from Christian theology and the American tradition and emphasized racial reconciliation and nonviolence while concomitantly making radical critiques and challenges to the social, political, and economic system in the US.

---

1. For the life and thought of Cone, see his autobiography, Cone, *My Soul Looks Back*.

2. For a book length treatment of the two leaders, see Cone, *Martin and Malcolm and America*.

Malcolm X, on the other hand, was greatly influenced by the Islamic tradition, whether in his earlier adoption of the heterodox form of the Nation of Islam or in his later adherence to orthodox Sunni Islam. Therefore, while many of his objectives overlapped with King's, there were explicit and implicit critiques of both Americanism and Christianity in Malcolm's thought and expression. His views of Americanism were more critical than King's and at times negative; and he emphasized to a greater degree than King that the African American quest for liberation was more a matter of universal human rights than of domestic civil rights. King advocated nonviolence as a moral, rational, and practical method, but Malcolm X found King's unwavering commitment to nonviolence counterproductive and invalid, regarding King's position as abridgement of people's right of self-defense, common sense, and faithfulness to Malcolm's and Islam's understanding of religion. Rather, for Malcolm, the right to self-defense was to be safeguarded and liberation was to be achieved by any means necessary. Instead of foregrounding racial integration as the morally mandated and practically effective avenue to racial empowerment and justice as did King, Malcolm endorsed Black nationalism, an emphasis on Black pride, culture, history, property ownership, and control of those institutions in the Black community and key to the life improvement and survival of Black people.[3]

Cone, like many African Americans during the era, believed that it was possible to reconcile or bring into a productive working relationship the two apparently irreconcilable positions: (a) King's support of nonviolence, Christianity, Americanism, and integration and (b) Malcolm X's endorsement of: self-defense, Islam, priority of Blackness, and Black nationalism. Cone's theology of Black liberation, therefore, embraces King's conviction that Christianity includes the liberation of people from both spiritual and temporal oppression, something that Cone saw attested in the history of the Black experience as leaders in the Black church and Christian community had in the name of Christ sought freedom, empowerment, and equity. Similar to Malcolm X in the last couple of years of his life, Cone believed that King was correct in his position that Blacks should strive to be a part of mainstream America. From Malcolm, Cone took an emphasis on a bolder embrace of Black pride, culture, and history, and he agreed with the Muslim leader in the right of self-defense. In sum, Cone's theology combines Kingian emphasis on a liberatory interpretation of Christianity and a Malcolmian focus on Black identity and assertion.

---

3. Peter J. Paris examines King, Malcolm X, and two other leaders in his *Black Religious Leaders*. For King, see 98–143, and Malcolm X, 182–222.

Of course, Cone was not the first to seek complementarity between King's and Malcolm's approaches to Black freedom. As early as 1966 and pre-dating Cone's publications on Black theology, an impressive collection of more than 40 Black religious leaders, composed of academicians, non-academicians, pastors, and community leaders released a statement on Black power through the vehicle of the *New York Times*. It had been customary to attack Black power or Black nationalism as an ideology and approach that ran counter to the mainline Civil Rights Movement and even Christianity itself. These religious leaders, known originally as the National Committee of Negro Churchmen and self-identified as an informal grouping representing themselves and not necessarily the official stance of their respective denominations or churches. The Committee did not embrace what many considered harsh or sharp language of Malcolm X and other Black nationalists. Nonetheless, they affirmed the broad rubrics of Black nationalism—respect for culture, pride, and racial solidarity. The slogan "black power," while upsetting to many Whites and some Blacks, was not anti-Christian because power and love were not mutually exclusive. The right to seek justice through power was not something reserved only for Whites.[4]

INFLUENCE OF LIBERAL THEOLOGY

In addition to the influences of King, Malcolm, and Black religious thought in the 1960s and 1970s, Black theology in its academic formulations also reflects the influences of liberal versus conservative theology and hermeneutics. Since Cone devoted the greater part of his academic service to Union Theological Seminary in New York, a stronghold of liberal theology, one is perhaps not surprised that his understanding of theology and biblical interpretation fell on the liberal rather than conservative spectrum. Cone's theology rejects fundamentalism and its emphasis on the Bible as a literal, inerrant word of God. Rather, his writings reveal the theologically liberal position of prioritizing central values and principles of Scripture over literal interpretation or adherence to specific rules. Theologically, there is liberal emphasis on interpreting God's dealing with humanity that highlights improvement of human life on Earth rather than an emphasis on eschatology or Heavenly destination. A conservative and/or fundamentalist biblical and theological approach—that foregrounds personal over social salvation, personal piety over social responsibility, adherence to traditional Christian doctrines and traditions over freedom from this worldly political and

---

4. See the National Conference of Black Churchmen's "Black Power Statement" in Sernett, *African American Religious History*, 555–64.

economic oppression—is consistently rejected by Cone.[5] Of course, Cone's utilization of liberal theology would present problems for some in the Black tradition who would see the need for a more *Black* use of language and resources in liberation theology, which we shall note later.

INFLUENCE OF THE SOCIAL GOSPEL

The formal disciples of Black theology and liberation theology in general are not pioneers in the conviction that a full understanding of the Gospel is that Jesus Christ seeks to redeem the individual at the level of personal holiness and to bring justice and compassion to social structures. Hence, we have the appearance of Christian Socialism in England and the social gospel in the United States during the nineteenth century. The social gospel, one of whose most renowned spokespersons was Walter Rauschenbusch, insisted that God was just as concerned about eliminating social ills and bringing social redemption as freeing the individual from personal sin. In some ways the social gospel was an extension of liberal theology in that theological liberalism called for a reformulation of Christianity to fit the modern times. But conservative theology was also a parent of the social gospel, for some of the strongest advocates in the nineteenth century for remaking society so that it freed the enslaved, rescued alcoholics from the power of drink, or banished poverty were Evangelicals. At any rate, the social gospel was a significant forerunner to the advancement of liberation theology, particularly in the United States.[6]

BLACK RELIGIOUS THOUGHT AS A SOURCE OF BLACK THEOLOGY

Originators of Black theology in the 1960s and 1970s emphasized that it did not arise mainly from academic, formalized, philosophical settings, presuppositions, and theories. Rather, they claimed, the theology of liberating Black people from oppression was always present in the tradition of Black religious thought. Cone, for example, not only pointed to Martin King and Malcolm X, as has been noted. He also drew heavily on the thoughts and actions of nineteenth century religious thinkers and leaders such as David Walker and Henry McNeil Turner. David Walker, born free

---

5. A major proponent of American theological liberalism was Harry Emerson Fosdick. See a contrast between fundamentalism and liberalism and Fosdick's "Shall the Fundamentalists Win?" 417–23.

6. Walter Rauschenbusch is perhaps the most renowned advocate of the social gospel in the US. See an excerpt of his book *A Theology of the Social Gospel*, 309–21.

in North Carolina, traveled portions of the South prior to making his home in Massachusetts in the 1820s. In 1829 the first edition of his *Appeal in Four Articles . . . to the Coloured Citizens of the World . . .*, more often known as David Walker's *Appeal.* In this pamphlet or small book, Walker called on the enslaved to overthrow by violence the system of enslavement, that such was their moral and ethical duty as adults and Christians. A Presbyterian minister, Henry Highland Garnet, published a similar appeal in the early 1840s, also calling for armed rebellion against enslavement. Going beyond advocacy, some Blacks professing religious convictions actually plotted slave revolts, such as Gabriel Prosser in Virginia in 1800 and Denmark Vesey in South Carolina in 1822, and engaged in actual armed attack, such as Nat Turner of Virginia in 1831.

In the late 1800s and early 1900s, Henry McNeal Turner, a bishop in the African Methodist Episcopal Church, was a powerful spokesperson for Black freedom and pride. Cone found Turner's sermon or writing on "God Is A Negro," to be especially pertinent to the theological foundations of liberation theology, for how people envision God is often very revealing about their self-concept. Cone, hence, saw Turner's assertion emphasizing the positive relationship of Blacks with God and a move from any suggestion that Christianity is a religion for Whites or was a one less so for Blacks. Marcus Garvey, a Jamaican by birth who had lived in Central America and England, came to the United States in 1916. Headquartered in New York City, Garvey's Universal Negro Improvement Association called for Blacks outside the continent of Africa to relocate to their ancestral homeland and create a mighty Black republic, whose existence would benefit Africa and those escaping oppression in the African diaspora. Garvey's movement influenced Black nationalism and pan-Africanism among Blacks on a global scale, including in the United States. Furthermore, the Garvey Movement had a profound impact in some religious quarters in pointing to the establishment of religious approaches that centered the Black experience and the need to employ Black art, culture, and thought. One clear expression of this influence was the African Orthodox Church, founded by George Alexander McGuire, a strong supporter of the Garvey Movement. Leaders as the ones referenced above point to the reality that Black nationalism was well-represented in Black religious thought, a point relevant to the claims of Black theology.[7]

---

7. Marable and Mullings, *Let Nobody Turn Us Around*, e.g., 24–39, 51–62, 128–32.

BLACK CHURCHES, ORGANIZATIONS, AND OTHER ENTERPRISES

Black theologians cite how Black religious thought historically paved the way for formal Black theology in the founding of the Black church and organizations focused on service to the Black community. Readings of church history at the local, state, regional, and national levels reveal that Black churches had their origins in large part in the conviction that it was necessary for Blacks as a group to organize separately from Whites in pursuit of evangelism and the temporal liberation of other Black peoples, domestically and globally. Because the reality of the eighteenth, nineteenth, and even early twentieth-century America was a period of racial segregation between Whites and Blacks, one might assume that racially separated settings were the only possibilities for Black worship. Actually, many ecclesial settings permitted and even expected a biracial membership, provided that Whites occupied the power of control. Sometimes (but not always) with the encouragement, support, and active assistance of White sympathizers, Black people formed or became part of separate African American congregations, such as Silver Bluff Baptist Church in South Carolina, First African Baptist Church and First Bryan Baptist Church in Savannah, Georgia, and Abyssinian Baptist Church in New York City in the late 1700s and early 1800s. Independent Black denominations began formation in the early 1800s, as evidenced by African Methodist Episcopal Church in Pennsylvania and the African Methodist Episcopal Zion Church in New York. Regionally, there was an emergence of a number of Black Baptist organizations in Ohio, Illinois, and Michigan-Canada in the 1830s and 1840s. With the coming of the Civil War and post-Civil War periods, Black congregations, regional, state, and national organizations emerge more boldly and more prolifically. In addition to the entities such as those cited above, there was a rise of state conventions of Baptists in every state where they were not previously established, some as early as the middle and late 1860s in Virginia, South Carolina, and North Carolina. New denominational groups emerge, such as the Christian (originally Colored) Methodist Episcopal Church, the National Baptist Convention, the Church of God in Christ, and the Second (originally Colored) Cumberland Presbyterian Church during the 1870–1920 era. While Catholic Blacks do not separate from the Catholic Church prior to the 1960s, some leaders, including the first ordained Black priest in the US, Augustus Tolton, meet in their first Black Catholic lay congress called by the lay leader Daniel Rudd in 1899 to discuss matters they face in the church and society.[8]

---

8. Raboteau, *Canaan Land*, 21–39.

All of these activities, many of which are cited by Black theologians, are centrally relevant to the emergence of Black theology for a number of reasons. First, there is a sense among Blacks and some White sympathizers that Blacks can express themselves religiously speaking more fully in Black contexts. Second, these organizations and assemblies point to the need for African Americans collectively to deal with important issues facing them in church and society. Third, Black Christians affirmed that Christianity and racial freedom and empowerment were congruent—and, conversely, enslavement, racial segregation, and discrimination were inconsistent—with the true understanding of the Christian faith. Fourth, these activities convey the belief that the evangelization and service to Black community can most effectively be accomplished through the vehicle of Black groups or Black-led efforts. Fifth, closely related to the previous point, these efforts reveal the presence of some degree of pan-Africanism or pan-Blackness, the conviction that all peoples of African descent share a common origin directly or indirectly on the African continent, face a common set of racially proscribed and oppressive challenges, and must share a common struggle to participate in a common destiny of racial freedom and empowerment. These factors reflect a common marriage between the Black nationalism and Black Christianity, a fundamental element of Black theology.

In addition to the organized ecclesial groups, there surfaced early Black institutions included quasi-religious mutual aid societies, which were often interdenominational faith and community organizations, such as the Free African Society founded in the 1780s; fraternal organizations, such as Prince Hall Masons formed in the later 1700s; Black newspapers, such as the very first formed in 1827 *Freedom's Journal*; banks established especially in the Reconstruction or post-Civil War decades; and educational institutions, including Wilberforce University which became Black-controlled by the early 1860s. Of course, the few examples cited above are but forerunners to others that continued to appear for decades and generations thereafter.[9] Like the ecclesial groups, these pioneering groups and many of their successors generally (a) were heavily influenced by Christianity, (b) adhered to the conviction that Black themselves were most qualified and even "called by God" to deal with matters confronting the African American community, and (c) operated with the assumption that racial identity, pride, and solidarity were key elements to their purpose and objectives.

---

9. Franklin and Brooks Higginbotham, *From Slavery to Freedom*, 111–38, 327–68.

SPIRITUALS, PREACHING, AND THE ENSLAVED

Elements of Black nationalism also appear in the "invisible institution" of the Black religion—those beliefs, practices, secret and quasi-secret meetings, and customs of African Americans, particularly during the enslavement era, that largely went unobserved by Whites. Spirituals were songs created by the enslaved from their own experiences and incorporated hymnic and religious materials either largely derived from White Protestantism and/or shared with their White counterparts. Contemporary freed and ex-enslaved people point out how some spirituals often held double meanings for the enslaved. That is, sometimes references to Heaven and the Promised Land referred to seeking liberation from temporal enslavement in this world; singing about stealing away to Jesus might mean connecting with the Underground Railroad or the secret network of people and places assisting the enslaved to escape to freedom. Singing about having heavenly shoes were powerful assertions that the trials and tribulations of the earthly life in which racism and oppression often ruled would not last forever, thereby embracing a form of Christianity that made a strong unswerving declaration of humanity and dignity in an earthly life where ruling forces persistently sought to diminish their strength in the lives of Black people. Much of what is stated above regarding the spirituals are also applicable to much preaching by Black clergy, whether formally recognized or not by the White-controlled ecclesial bodies, and the prayers of ordinary people. Sermons and prayers, whether subtly expressed in the presence of Whites or boldly expressed in all Black contexts, clearly saw enslavement as contradictory to a true understanding of slavery and conveyed firm conviction that enslavement and oppression would sooner or later face extinction because of the power and benevolence of God.[10]

MISSIONS: DOMESTIC AND OVERSEAS

Black theology holds that Black Christianity is a more complete and faithful expression of the Christian faith than White Christianity in that the former with greater consistency has highlighted the need to preach and teach love and to work for the liberation of the oppressed. Historically, Black churches, denominations, and other organizations strongly influenced by Christianity sought to spread that faith and practice of freedom and justice among Africans and Blacks in the diaspora, a racial family that received lower attention from White Christians than did other groups. Black church, missionary, and reformed minded people held the nationalist position that Blacks were

---

10. Raboteau, *Slave Religion*, 211–88.

best suited and the ones called by God to uplift and liberate their racial kin in heavily Black populated regions in both the diaspora and on the mother continent. A Scripture passage repeatedly appearing in sermons and writings of Blacks and their White supporters from at least the 1700s into the early 1900s was Ps 68:31, which in the King James Version of the Bible reads, "Princes shall come out of Egypt; Ethiopia shall soon stretch out her hands unto God." This was understood as a prophecy announcing the return of African peoples, on the continent and elsewhere, to political and religious greatness. Hence, those spreading the Christian message were instruments of God operating in the world fulfilling God's will in that regard.

With both domestic and foreign missions, we see this operative theme that Black Christians in spreading the faith and engaging in attendant temporal uplift and philanthropic enterprises were working as God's instruments to fulfill the reclamation or affirmation of the great role in history that God had ordained for Africana peoples. All the major Black denominations—such as the African Methodist Episcopal Church, the African Methodist Episcopal Zion Church, and the various Baptist bodies at state, regional, and national levels—and African Americans in mainly White denominations—such as the Presbyterians and Methodists—during the 1800s and early 1900s either had their own mission programs or participated in those mainly sponsored by others. By engaging in one or more activities such as forming organizations specifically for African and overseas missions, raising funds to support these organizations, volunteering for active work on the mission fields, these Black Christians, such as Andrew Cartwright, Emma B. Delaney of Florida, Lula C. Fleming, and Charles and Eva Boone, were effectively operating from a pan-Africanist/Black nationalistic perspective that envisioned the necessity of Black solidarity and the conviction that Christianity promoted racial freedom, key themes in Black theology.[11]

BLACK CATHOLICS IN THE UNITED STATES

Though Black Christianity in the US has been predominantly Protestant, there has always been a significant presence of Catholics. Black Catholic numerical growth faced great challenges because of a serious lack of Black leaders, including the complete absence of self-identifying Black priests until the 1880s and then very few, as well as the often lackluster outreach to the African American population by the White-controlled American

---

11. For book-length studies on Blacks and African missions, see Jacobs, *Black Americans and the Missionary Movement in Africa*; Martin, *Black Baptists and African Missions*.

church. Yet as early as the 1820s women of Black ancestry were organizing for the specific goal of addressing the educational and spiritual needs of Black children in the Baltimore and New Orleans areas. The Oblate Sisters of Providence in Maryland were founded in the late 1820s and their received official approval in the 1830s. In Louisiana, the Holy Family Sisters emerged to serve the spiritual and temporal needs of people of color in the New Orleans area. In the 1880s Augustus Tolton became the first openly Black-identifying priest in the US. Other priests, nuns, and lay leaders will follow the same paths of creating and maintaining African American Catholic communities in the United States, finding themselves dealing with the same reality of relating their quests for racial liberation with their understanding of the Christian faith.[12]

RESPONSES TO BLACK THEOLOGY

The outline of Black religious thought has demonstrated that the emergence of academic Black liberation theology was not an aberration but an outgrowth of the longer history of Black Christians' uniting the specificity of their liberation needs with the universality of the Christian faith. These new Black theologians were insisting on liberation as a *mandate, command, insistence, and valid measure* of Christianity. The Black religious tradition had always critiqued caste or discriminatory Christianity as a deep failure to practice true Christian discipleship and, hence, offered quite severe appraisals of White Christianity in general. This new Black theology much more boldly proclaimed without any hint of apology or diplomacy that a Christianity bereft of commitment to supporting Black liberation, which Black Christians often considered an accurate description of most White Christianity, was not the true practice of the faith.

What, then, were the responses particularly from the American Christianity to this new bold proclamation of Black theology especially as expressed by Cone? As one would imagine, the responses fell (and fall) into a number of broad categories: (a) those who reject Cone's formulation as a heresy that runs counter to the essence of Christianity; (b) those who essentially embrace and celebrate the advance of Black theology; (c) those who embrace Black theology but have some major critiques regarding matters such as Cone's sources, lack of inclusion, and failure to deal with other vitally related issues and concerns. Given the limitation of space, we may quickly dispense with (a) above, that is, those who opposed Black theology as heretical, a distortion of the Christian gospel, and more ideology than

---

12. For a book length history of African American Catholics, see Davis, *History of Black Catholics in the United States*.

theology. Many in this category would emphasize the personal as opposed to the social, political, and economic application of the gospel in much the same way as the standard critiques of the social gospel or liberal theology in general.[13] It might prove more helpful to focus on those who to varying degrees supported the central liberation theology perspective that Christianity and the struggle for freedom utilizing Black pride, culture, history, and identity was compatible and perhaps even mandated by a correct understanding of Christianity.

POSITIVE RESPONSES TO BLACK THEOLOGY

Among those endorsing or concurring with Cone's explication of Black theology was the National Committee of Black Churchmen or NCBC (formerly National Committee of Negro Churchmen), James Forman, Albert Cleage, and Gayraud Wilmore. In their 1969 statement the NCBC endorsed the central premise of Black theology, that God sides with oppressed Blacks to overturn White oppression. Since their 1966 statement endorsing Black Power as consistent with Christianity preceded the publication of Cone's first book, they in effect were ratifying the professor's book as affirmation of their earlier pronouncement and broader Black religious thinking that saw Black Power as a valid expression of Christianity. The Committee was also endorsing James Forman's *The Black Manifesto*, delivered at Riverside Church in 1969. Interrupting a Sunday morning church service, Forman proclaimed racism a sin for which White America should demonstrate repentance by paying reparations to African Americans for their enslavement and suffering. The *Manifesto* certainly fit into the general rubric of Black theology and therefore was an endorsement of Cone's central thesis. Gayraud S. Wilmore's *Black Religion and Black Radicalism* provided a historical treatment of Black religious thought that concentrated on the central elements of Black theology. This work contributed immensely to authenticating formal Black theology as an integral part of the long tradition of Black religion in America, helping to secure it from being dismissed as a mere recent invention of a small group of leaders or academics.

Among those welcoming the advent of Black theology was Albert Cleage, later Jaramogi Abebe Agyeman, the founder of a Black Christian nationalist denomination more commonly known as the Shrine of the Black Madonna and whose first book, *The Black Messiah*, was published around the same time as Cone's *Black Theology and Black Power*. A former United

---

13. Joseph H. Jackson, long time President of the National Baptist Convention, USA, Incorporated, rejected Black theology as consistent with Christianity. See his appraisal in Paris, *Black Religious Leaders*, 287–93.

Church of Christ pastor in Michigan, Agyeman asserted that Christ was literally the Black Messiah sent to Black Israel to combat the oppression of imperialist White Roman Empire. Contemporary liberation efforts of Black people against the forces of contemporary racism were a literal continuation of ancient Israel's struggle. With this understanding, Black Americans should recognize the common racial heritage and challenges of all Black peoples, affirm themselves as the Chosen Nation of God, and cooperatively wage the struggle to attain their freedom. While he held a more literalist view of Black association with the Bible than Cone, Agyeman valued Cone's formulation of Black theology, believing that the latter in essence had captured the true meaning of the gospel.

CRITIQUES

There were other liberationist leaders, scholars, and thinkers who were Black theologians sharing the central premise of Cone's theology. But they offered serious and substantial critiques of some aspects of Cone's formulation or methodology. Professor J. Deotis Roberts wrote that Cone was absolutely right to state that the affirmation and liberation of Black people are at the heart of the true understanding of Christianity, but he faulted Cone for paying insufficient attention to the corresponding theme of reconciliation. God not only calls the oppressed to break free from oppression; God also calls for reconciliation between the oppressed and the oppressor so that God's universal will of love and harmony inclusive of all people may triumph. Jacquelyn Grant began while yet a graduate student of Cone's at Union Theological Seminary pointing out that both Black theology, which was dominated by Black males, and feminist theology, focused on White women, had failed Black women, who had to deal with both racism and sexism. She called for the liberation of the whole community, not just males. Grant, along with other scholars such as Delores Williams and Katie Cannon, would lay the foundation for the emergence of womanist theology, a terminology that during the 1970s and 1980s distinguished them from the White women dominated feminist theology.

Cecil Cone, a brother of James H. Cone, and a scholar and religious leader in his own right, called attention to James Cone's utilization of European and White American theologians in the formulation of Black theology. If Black theology were express fully the heart and aspirations of Black people, then it needed to incorporate with greater depth and reflect more forthrightly the rich history, experiences, culture, and thought of Black people. A Black theology speaking with the White voices of Reinhold Niebuhr, Dietrich Bonhoeffer, Rudolf Bultmann, and Karl Barth will be locked into an identity crisis. William R. Jones posed for Black theology the age old question of the problem of evil and innocent suffering and how they were to be reconciled with the belief in an omnipotent and benevolent Deity. More pointedly, Jones asked, if God is the God of liberation, then why do Black people continue to suffer oppression? Where for Black people is the exodus experience in which God has acted in history to free Blacks from oppression? According to Tom Skinner, Black theology was correct in stating that the Bible is Black and applicable to the liberation quest. But Skinner, theologically conservative and evangelical, reminded Black theology of the spiritual and orthodox dimensions of the faith, of the need to address the individual's communion with God, the reality of sin, the divinity of Christ, and eternal life.

Black theology in the United States interacted with other global cultural and liberation theology. Latin American liberation theology in its early phases said little or nothing about the reality of racial oppression in those societies or elsewhere, stressing instead the liberation of people from economic exploitation and strongly influenced by Marxist analysis. Black theology in Southern Africa was much more akin to Black theology in North America, given strength of the racism during the apartheid area. Theologies in other parts of Africa and in Asia, however, called more attention to cultural factors and the utility of non-Christian religions such as African traditional religions and Buddhism as resources for interpreting Christianity.[14]

CONCLUSION: EVOLUTION AND IMPACT OF BLACK THEOLOGY

Cone's theological evolution represents the experience of Black theology overall from its advent in the late 1960s to the 2020s. It began and still concentrates considerably on race as the central factor facing Black North Americans. But in dialogue with other theologians, religious thinkers, and theologies, Black theology has expanded to include in its orbit concerns such as gender, sexuality, the use of sources grounded in the Black experience, economic structures, and interreligious dialogue. In a decade or two, Black theology while retaining the focus on racial liberation was boldly proclaiming what is often termed intersectionality, that is, the conviction that no particular liberation quest can be completely isolated or disconnected from other liberation quests. One cannot expect racial liberation, for example, if one does not see the connections and work in concert with

---

14. Wilmore and Cone compiled an excellent documentary collection on Black theology with their *Black Theology* that included responses to Black theology from White theologians, Black women, and the Black church.

those laboring to free themselves from gender and class oppression. Concomitant with this expansion of the purview of Black theology has been its contributions in prompting "interdisciplinary-sectionality," for the call for racial liberation has challenged scholars and leaders in various disciplines to ask questions pertinent to liberation. That is, how does this discipline and my research interests—whether located in the areas of theology, philosophy, biblical studies, history, or women studies—relate to the quest of people to achieve temporal freedom in this life?[15]

BIBLIOGRAPHY

Bailey, Randall C., and Jacquelyn Grant, eds. *The Recovery of Black Presence: An Interdisciplinary Exploration.* Nashville: Abingdon 1995.

Baldwin, Lewis V. *The Voice of Conscience: The Church in the Mind of Martin Luther King, Jr.* New York: Oxford University Press, 2010.

Cone, James H. *Martin and Malcolm and America.* New York: Orbis, 1991.

———. *My Soul Looks Back: Journeys in Faith.* Nashville: Abingdon, 1982.

Corrigan, John, and Winthrop S. Hudson. *Religion in America.* 9th ed. New York: Routledge, 2018.

Franklin, John Hope, and Evelyn Brooks Higginbotham. *From Slavery to Freedom: A History of African Americans.* 10th ed. New York: McGraw-Hill, 2021.

Griffith, R. Marie, ed. *American Religions: A Documentary History.* New York: Oxford University Press, 2008.

Marable, Manning, and Leith Mullings, eds. *Let Nobody Turn Us Around: An African American Anthology.* 2nd ed. New York: Rowman and Littlefield, 2009.

Paris, Peter J. *Black Religious Leaders: Conflict in Unity.* Louisville, KY: Westminster John Knox, 1991.

Payne, Les, and Tamara Payne. *The Dead Are Arising: The Life of Malcolm X.* New York: Liveright, 2020.

Raboteau, Albert J. *Canaan Land: A Religious History of African Americans.* New York: Oxford University Press, 2001.

———. *Slave Religion: The "Invisible Institution" in the Antebellum South.* Updated Edition. New York: Oxford University Press, 2004.

Sernett, Milton C., ed. *African American Religious History: A Documentary Witness.* 2nd ed. Durham: Duke University Press, 1999.

---

15. An example of interdisciplinary analyses revolving around the theme of Black liberation is Bailey and Grant, *Recovery of Black Presence.* See, e.g., Grant's "Womanist Jesus and the Mutual Struggle for Liberation," 129–42.

West, Cornel, and Eddie S. Glaude, Jr., eds. *African American Religious Thought: An Anthology*. Louisville, KY: Westminster John Knox, 2003.

Wilmore, Gayraud S., and James H. Cone. *Black Theology: A Documentary History, 1966–1977*. Maryknoll, NY: Orbis, 1979.

Chapter 31
Womanist Hermeneutics
CHERYL A. KIRK-DUGGAN

Womanist, derived by Alice Walker, from the term "womanish," refers to women of African descent who are audacious, outrageous, in charge, and responsible—from the Black folk expression of mothers to female children, "you acting womanish," i.e., like a woman. A womanist freedom-honoring theological ethics and hermeneutics, or means of understanding, embraces hope, engenders mutuality and community, and honors the *Imago Dei,* or image of God, in everyone. Womanists welcome the experience where a woman loves other women, sexually and or nonsexually. Traditionally a universalist system, womanism appreciates and prefers women's culture and emotional flexibility and does not segregate or separate, except periodically, for health reasons. In her definition, Walker (1) defines the folk expression, (2) explores love as fluid, inclusive, emotional energy across gendered lines, (3) honors the power of love in culture, the senses, and spirituality, and (4) compares womanist to feminist as purple is to lavender. To be *womanist* invites balanced, holistic health that loves many shades of Blackness and ultimately loves all people, celebrates freedom, and confidently embraces the manifestation of woman's culture and life.[1]

Postconservative womanist hermeneutics focuses on a belief and behavioral system of love instead of doctrines and theological systems. One can have roots in evangelical, Pentecostal, liberal, denominational, non-denominational, and diverse religious beliefs—from conventional African religious traditions to Abrahamic, interreligious traditions and philosophies. Womanist thought embraces new ways of thinking about all life and

---

1. Walker, *In Search of our Mother's Gardens,* xi.

faith practices as they explore the Bible and other sacred books, including cultural artifacts. Womanists experience revelation in formal and informal settings, worship, and everyday experiences that change people's ways of thinking, doing, and being. Theology as spiritual reality is a pilgrimage, not a destination, as one grows in love for the divine, self, and neighbor. This way of thinking and being recognizes the global, historical past while not being trapped into those ways of thinking—and building on that legacy to forge a present toward a future in love, not fear. The centering factor of womanist hermeneutics is love for all people without condemnation. Using Scriptures and principles like loving the neighbor, such sacred texts provide guidelines without becoming punitive. Theology, how we think about God and our relationships with the divine, ourselves, other humans, and creation, involves community, individuals, churches, and civic institutions. Womanists respect tradition yet are not held hostage by earlier faith commitments and customs. Such interpretation emerged as practicing Black women clergy enrolled in seminary.

FORMAL WOMANIST BEGINNINGS

When pondering her scholarship, Katie Geneva Cannon recognized that Black theology problematized race and White feminist scholars historically problematized the issue of gender, but who would speak for poor Black women? Gender, race, and class were the trifecta central to Black women religious scholars' discontent at Union Theological Seminary. Cannon, joined by other first-wave scholars of womanism at Union New York—Jacquelyn Grant, Kelly Brown Douglas, Linda E. Thomas, JoAnne Marie Terrell, and Delores Williams—recognized that Black religious thought and feminism neglected and therefore discriminated against African Diasporan women through the negligence of their experience and purview in the church and academy. (While most early womanists were Christian, not all are Christian or from the United States.) Womanist hermeneutics is a radical spirituality, way of thinking, and doing scholarship formally in the lives of the founders of womanist thought that began in the 1980s. In Africa and when enslaved Black women landed on these shores, they lived womanist realities before the academic discipline emerged, in the likes of Cleopatra and the Dahomey Amazons, to Harriet Tubman, Dorothy Height, Septima Clark, Diane Nash, Ella Baker, and Myrlie Evers, among countless others. As thinkers, teachers, and practitioners, these ground-breaking movement mothers asked how and why Black people's truth often gets dismissed as anecdotal. Too often, society denies and erases Black female epistemology (way of knowing), causing a hurt that goes to the core of one's being. Some fellow Black male colleagues at Union opposed and remained vocal against women being allowed access to the seminary and pulpit. Amid the conflict of Black women being in academic and pulpit spaces, traditional feminism privileged White middle-class women in their attempts for a more egalitarian framework and praxis.

Womanist thought emerged out of the contextual liberatory praxis of two significant professors who taught at Union Theological Seminary New York: James Hal Cone (Black theology) and Beverly W. Harrison (feminist theology). They encouraged their students to engage in seminary fields from their perspectives. While the language of womanist thought, interpretation, and activism emerged within the academy, roots of womanism existed long before, minus the vocabulary and discipline. History is full of African-identified women who remain unafraid of God's clear message for them to help their community attain freedom outside of oppression. Cone affirmed and constructed a thorough critique of White/European Christianity by holding it accountable for its anti-Christian theological ethics. Still today, White Christianity (White evangelicalism, specifically) repackages White supremacy as watered-down Christianity faithful to the global oppression of minoritized people. Cone helped raise the consciousness of Black people above and beyond White America's definition of Christ and the symbols that defined Christianity. For Whites, the cross symbolizes victory at the cost of human life and continues the romanticization of suffering to be a Christian. For many African-Americans, the cross is an incredibly charged symbol in the African American community characterizing death and the promise of redemption, judgment, and the offer of blessing, misery, and the power of hope. Cone sits in tension with Christianity, which fails to address oppression.[2] This method supported some of Cone's students to question and critically analyze the state of Black theology. Black religious studies unfolded primarily from the Black male academic perspective. Cone's students also studied with feminist scholar Beverly Harrison. Accompanied by tools of such formidable scholars, a group of African American women disrupted the institution of Black theology and feminist theology with a new theo-ethical analysis and perspective called womanism. Womanist concepts include theology, ethics, Pastoral care and psychology, sociology, biblical studies, anthropology, preaching, literature and the arts, and education.

These first-wave womanists embraced Walker's writings, particularly exploring dynamics of sexism, racism, and classism. This cohort of African American women seminarians adopted Walker's definition as a framework for a unique theo-ethical analysis and praxis. Stacey Floyd-Thomas

---

2. Cone, *Cross and the Lynching Tree*, 3.

summarizes the four tenants for understanding womanist theological ethics: radical subjectivity (reclaiming one's identity from the firm grip of hegemonic normativity), traditional communalism (complete utilization of resources to benefit entire communities, unlike traditional feminists who focus solely on issues of gender), redemptive self-love (loving herself, music, struggle, the folk, roundness, and Spirit), and critical engagement. Redemptive self-love is contentious for many African American women deciding whether or not to be womanist around same-gender loving relationship possibilities. Overall, a womanist lens engages a genuine love ethic for all creation.

WOMANIST DAILY THOUGHT AND ACTIVITY

Embracing matters of society and academia, womanist theory or thought and hermeneutics always relate to daily life practice. They are defiant, complex work as it critiques class, gender, race, sexuality, age, and ability. Womanist thought includes, but is not limited to, issues in theology (identity, sacrality, subjectivity, spirituality, power); Bible and or other sacred texts (authority, characters, language, rituals, history); ethics (value, behavior, visibility, integrity, praxis); and context (power, culture, aesthetics, ecology, community). Interreligious concerns and communal solidarity toward reformation that champions immediacy, inclusivity, and justice anchors womanist thought. Womanist theory transforms women's daily oppressions towards freedom, a gift and right accorded by God. God is personal, not abstract. Since God spoke to create, many Womanists value language between God and humanity and with other human beings. The politics of language, where words and expressions can inspire or subjugate, are vital to analysis. How one communicates, uses, and interprets texts matters. Womanist theory is a critical lens for seeing and studying the seductive web of hate, exposing fear, and moving toward liberation and justice. Womanist interpretation expanded to include age, ability, and sexualities, along with the original categories of class, gender, and race.

When people think about being racist, sexist, homophobic, ageist, ablest, or elitist, the focus is often individuals. Upon self-examination, many claims: to not be racist or sexist, where one does not see color and claims to love everybody. This litany often occurs because they do not see the systemic nature of idolatrous White supremacist patriarchal capitalistic misogyny. White supremacy ritualizes, worships, codifies, and honors Whiteness as a classification superior to all else. Theologian Thandeka[3] reminds us that

---

3. See Thandeka. *Learning to be White.*

no one is born White—they are born English, German, Norwegian, etc., but they learn to be White. All immigrants to this country quickly know that they do not want to be Black. Legally concretized within dimensions of White paternal maleness, everything female is inferior, and all persons of color are unacceptable. The resulting systemic hate requires manipulation, control, domination, and even extermination of the other. The scheme resembles a broad-based, intricate seductive web of deceit. The lie is so present that it remains hidden in plain sight. Globally, from biblical times through the twenty-first century, this virulent, contagious, debilitating, self-absorbing culture of White supremacist patriarchal misogyny is death-dealing and infects everyone. No one can escape such evil. This pathology shapes faith, politics, and health. It is so present that only recently have White scholars and activists recognized that White folk must help other White folk analyze, engage, and chart courses of liberation. Biblical and Greco-Roman roots and the impact of essentialism and manifest destiny helped create fertile soil for systemic oppression that womanists address.

Race and justice have been at the forefront of many Black women scholars, even as children, when they began to wonder how and what Black people could have done if White society forbade them from participating in public activities other than church and Black schools. Some early womanist scholars grew up in all-Black neighborhoods, in Black schools, relatively privileged, and some just above poverty. Regardless of their socio-cultural location, they became aware of race. Those who grew up in the South learned the ways you had to act. Some grew up hearing the negation of Black lives and knew this was untrue. When coming to Union, they became radicalized and learned that sexism was parallel to racism. Cone shared with his students that being a woman must make a difference. Several scholars had lives where no limitations were set on them as Black girls, even in the South. When hearing a fire and brimstone sermon, Townes noted that justice could not be far behind if God loves everyone. Their lives and commitments compelled them to wrestle with hard questions. Douglas dedicated her book to her best friend, Lloyd, who died due to complications of AIDS, a terrific human being. Like many others, he loved the church, but the church did not love him back and often demonized them. To stay in the church, Douglas had to figure out how to deal with this disconnect, a painful existential dilemma. Writing the book, *Sexuality and the Black Church* was theology, faith-seeking understanding.

WOMANIST INTERPRETATION, SCRIPTURE, AND LEADERSHIP

Understanding womanist hermeneutics or interpretation and the generative moments of this work begins with Scripture to see where systemic oppression often originates. In Gen 1:26–31, the gods create humanity in the divine image, pronounce them good, and give them dominion over all creation. Problematically, throughout history, many human beings subdued and used creation for greed and self-glorification. Most have failed to understand "dominion over" as being responsible stewards for creation. Thus, we are out of balance. One of the culprits for this imbalance is White supremacist patriarchal culture, rooted in Scripture and Greco-Roman culture. In the Hebrew Bible or Old Testament, women were their fathers' or husbands' property. With the Abrahamic covenant (Gen 12:1–3), women had to marry the right man to have the right son, for YHWH promised Abram a relationship with his people in perpetuity, land, and a son. When a couple did not have a son, they assumed the woman was barren due to a sin she had committed. Any harm done to the woman was a crime against her father or husband, not her. Daughters could not inherit land, and family lineage followed a patriarchal line. The New Testament reports mixed sagas about women's capacity for authority and leadership.

Women led as priests, bishops, and prophets in early church history but experienced subordination with the rise of Christianity. Augustine and Aquinas, following Socrates, Aristotle, and Plato, believed women are inferior by nature and thus incapable of leadership. Conversely, Jesus challenged social convention and saw women and men as equal. Paul's letters indicate that women were apostles, evangelists, congregational leaders, and prophets. Women were leaders and patrons in house churches during the first two centuries. Women had power in the household but not in public.

By the third century, with the church's institutionalization, a male ethos dominated. Greco-Roman social order of public/private dichotomy connected men with honor and women with shame. Christianity connected women and female characters with sexuality, sin, and church history. Women were significant players in the social, informal Jesus movement. Women and men were patrons and householders, prophets, and priests. Christian women were professional prophets and diviners employed by government officials as consultants. With Constantine's elevation, Christianity became a public religion, the religion of the Roman State, reversing the radical change, particularly around gender equity Jesus created. By the fourth century, Christians could worship in public temples. Then tension between social norms about women and women's long-standing roles in the church caused heated controversy. Men demanded the oppression of women and relegated women to the private sphere.

Female sexual promiscuity was the greatest threat to women's character. Christian writers and others used sex to intimidate and shame women, calling female leaders disreputable and promiscuous. So-called good women were married or chaste and private. So-called evil women were unchaste, single, and public. Tertullian and Origen, early church leaders whom a woman had sponsored, insisted on women's subordination. From these beginnings in Scripture and the church, patriarchal rule became rule of law, then and now. Such concepts undergird everything that limits women's leadership in church and society, from unequal pay and domestic violence to double standards around sexuality. The intensity of sexism, sexual violence, and the need to control women's bodies parallels some of the racist bigotry that allowed enslavement in the fifteenth century and brutal murders by police for driving while Black or eating ice cream in one's apartment in the twenty-first century.[4]

BLACKNESS AND IDOLATROUS WHITE SUPREMACY

The Eurocentric and American curiosity about Black culture and Black people influences White supremacist patriarchal misogyny in three ways: (1) violence as a tool of contempt and conflict; (2) fascination about and fear of the stereotypical sexual prowess of Blacks, and (3) intrigue about the color Black. Simultaneously, desire and disdain around Blackness have existed deep within Western culture and psyche since the Greco-Roman era, notes Robert Hood. From then, Whiteness signals excellent and superior, and Blackness signals negative and inferior. Originally Blackness was ambiguous, not negated. The Greek philosopher Homer introduced the notion of dark-skinned people eighth century BCE. In Christianity, early theologians like Origen began to interpret Blackness as mysterious and a witness to divine salvation. Blackness became a metaphor for evil with the third-century Manichean heresy, a dualistic worldview: dividing things into good or evil, light or dark, Black or White. While there was a connection between Africa—the peoples of Egypt, Ethiopia, and North Africa during the development of early Christianity, Blackness implied chaos during the rise of the Roman Empire within Christian mythology. Ethiopia referred to gentiles, indicating malevolence, eros, and sin until one knew salvific cleansing. Blackness now signified the devil and the demonic. Hood contends three medieval historical events sealed the negation of Blackness and Black skin:

4. Torjesen, *When Women Were Priests*, 1–154.

the twelfth-century fall of Edessa, causing Islam to rise; the impact of the fourteenth-century Bubonic plague; and the fifteenth-century inception of African slave trade. Just as oppression occurs in creation with dominion over, and Blacks and Blackness become demonized, that same ethos supports exceptionalism and manifest destiny.

Kelly Brown Douglas[5] posits that Tacitus created the Anglo-Saxon myth in his volume *Germania* (98 CE), which supported the Nazi's heinous final solution celebrating racial purity and the ideological, social creed of the United States that fuels "stand your ground." Thus 60 years after Jesus's death, 200 years before the institution of Christianity, and 1,914 years before George Zimmerman murdered Trayvon Benjamin Martin, this myth supported Anglo-Saxon superiority and subjugation and elimination of non-Anglo-Saxon peoples. Transported to the United States, seventeenth-century Puritans and Pilgrims imported their understandings of common law, jury trial, and the relationship between Crown and parliament. Their beliefs helped frame American exceptional identity, blending their ideas of freedom, virtue, and being the divine New Israel. Their political identity mirrored Anglo-Saxon essence, including chauvinism and ethnocentrism, around individual rights and liberty. The religious American grand story or narrative connecting Christianity and race produced American civil religion. American civil religion, a term coined by Robert Bellah, is a sociological theory that claims a nonsectarian pseudo-religious faith exists within the United States with certain sacred symbols of national history, a cohesive spirit, and a standard set of socio-cultural values. The term American civil religion, as opposed to United States civil religion, seems pretentious given that other countries and continents include America in their name: Central America, South America, and North America, which includes Mexico, Canada, and the United States. This tapestry of civil religion with Protestant evangelicalism framed Anglo-Saxon exceptionalism, which became American exceptionalism. Exceptionalism is the belief that a species, country, society, institution, movement, or individual and the quest for human origins, indicated by one's bloodline, heightened Anglo-superiority and diminished others. This belief morphed into snobbery and arrogance, defining the collective American psyche. As history became liturgy, Christian and civil tapestries created a language of exclusion for immigrants to ensure that English was the United States' language, protecting Anglo-Saxon exceptionalism. As many immigrants acclimated and became White, over against Blacks, Whiteness became the landmark of privilege and cherished property rooted in religiosity. "God bless America" meant God blessed Anglo-Saxon

---

5. Douglas, *Stand Your Ground*, 3–108.

exceptionalism, which believed Black bodies have no value. The Declaration of Independence, which stated "all men are created equal," designated all White male protestant landowners.

Thus, Black bodies, especially Black males, cannot have the privilege of Whiteness in "stand your ground culture" forged in the United States' collective consciousness. This ethos constructs and reinforces the guilty Black body. Stand your ground culture promoted by Anglo-Saxon exceptionalism connects and subconsciously convicts unarmed Black corpses for the White, guilty perpetrator turned killer. In short, Anglo-Saxon exceptionalism theology and ideologies project a "truth" that privileging Whiteness is a lived fact. This natural law amid enslavement made the Black body chattel and the free Black body hypersexualized and sinful. This idea legitimated White supremacy. Brown Douglas notes that such negation of Black bodies, rooted in multiple biblical creations, legitimated differentiation between Whites and Blacks. Such negation creates random sexual exploitation of Black bodies, permits White men to rape the alleged Black female temptress, and supports the belief that Black men were allegedly predatory and obsessed with White women. Ask Emmett Till and Walter McMillan of *Just Mercy* about the cost to Black males being around a White woman. Too often, because the body's experience of sexual excitement and violent impulses are similar, the hypersexualized, beastly Black body is also the hyper-violent body—dangerous, forever threatening. Enslaved, chattel Black bodies become criminalized Black bodies, which require an aggressive "stand your ground" culture that developed during Reconstruction and thus becomes institutionalized in the prison industrial complex. Psychologist Resma Menachem frames it as the docile White body, the threatening Black body, and the militarized police body. Society perceives the innocent Black body as dangerous targets of "stand your ground culture." Founded in violence, the United States has used *violence* to become the globally so-called "greatest, wealthiest, most powerful country." The mantra of "make America great again" is a conquering, subduing mentality fashioned as Manifest Destiny. Few recognize it as violence. Manifest destiny uses political, economic, or religious reasons and clout to claim the right to manipulate and have power over something or someone. Rarely do those who exact such violence see themselves as doing something wrong. The negation of Blackness, supported by "stand your ground" ideology, exceptionalism, and manifest destiny, affects how we do theology and life—opposite of freedom. As fear-based hate grows, Sweet Honey in the Rock, an all-female a capella, reminds us, "We who believe in freedom cannot rest until it comes/Until the killing of Black men, Black mothers' sons/ Is as important as the killing of white men, white mothers' sons."

Womanist hermeneutics remind us that White supremacist patriarchy has a sophisticated, seductive web of deceit that established a strong foundation during enslavement with long oppressive fibers rooted from those times. Emancipation supposedly freed the formerly enslaved without having had previous access to literacy, property, marriage, or their bodies. Following a failed Reconstruction, enslavement morphed into other forms of legalized oppressive confinement. Bells of freedom tolled briefly and then shifted to the muffled drums of chain gangs, convict leasing, lynching, Black Codes, and Jim and Jane Crow laws. Urban renewal ran interstate highways through thriving Black townships, decimating communities, properties, and businesses, where integration never happened. More disillusion occurred, including losing Black teachers who demanded excellence in their Black students. School boards moved many excellent Black teachers to elite White schools; more so-called Christian schools developed so little Black boys would not be seated next to little White girls. The emergence of these private and new charter schools gutted budgets for public schools. Where teachers of excellence remain, they have too many students and insufficient resources. Besides decisions to cancel the arts and physical education, with more attention deficit disorders and obesity on the rise, the so-called war on crime and drugs erupted when there was no drug problem. Militarized weapons were dumped in impoverished communities, followed by mass incarceration and unfair sentencing laws. Today, death while being Black—where innocent Black people have been executed by police, mostly with impunity—is almost normative.

Womanist hermeneutics sees that it is impossible to understand all oppressive issues without assuming that all suppression is unjust, abusive, and dehumanizing. Society must transcend, dismantle, and dissolve all oppression for any actual change toward justice and healing. There are many areas of study where womanists study and engage in thought, research, and activist life, including spirituality, theology, ethics, biblical studies, culture, and practical theology.

WOMANIST SPIRITUALITY, ECOWOMANISM, AND BIBLICAL HERMENEUTICS

Womanist spirituality[6] is a vibrant, significant, life-changing personal and communal resistance-based way of life and academic study, building from African diaspora women in relationship with God, celebrating life, and exposing injustice and oppression. The tremendous capacity for love involves

---

6. Kirk-Duggan, "Womanist Spirituality," 644–46.

the spectrum of culture, creation, Spirit, people, and self. *Womanist* spirituality embraces hope and transformation towards creating mutuality and community, builds on the essential goodness of humanity, and focuses on liberation amid personal and societal fragmentation in general and faith-based discourse in particular.

Womanist spirituality is a creative life experience not exclusive to religion, worship, or denominational commitments. Such power denotes an influence and way of thinking where one embraces change responsibly and believes in possibility when all is lost and efforts to make a difference are futile. Rosita deAnn Mathews states that womanist spirituality is energy with prophetic awareness and power from the margins or periphery that gains strength to exist. In creative faith, such spirituality works within its ethical framework to nurture personal and communal spirituality and responsibility with integrity, dignity, and truth, disrupting oppression. Womanist spirituality honors love as respect for courage, compassion, and completeness, as a paradox from bell hooks's idea of "killing rage."

Killing rage disrupts cultural creations and pedagogical guidelines that celebrate White privilege, capitalistic bullying, and male supremacy: all hegemonic oppression that denies and destroys ideas, possibilities, spirits, communities, individuals, and bodies. Without an outlet, such rage destroys and causes intense misery. Killing rage helps us name, unmask, and engage God, ourselves, and others towards audacious action and antagonism that helps one change and develop: a potent peripheral tool for human transformation.

Emilie Townes explains that womanist spirituality emerges amid goal orientation and catastrophic dimensions in redemption and salvation. Such energetic commitment presses one toward the social witness, social analysis, ethical examination, biblical and theological reflection, and collective wisdom or mother wit to challenge all oppressive, violent systems. The lived experience of justice and love, central to the womanist experience, involves respect and dignity, viewing all persons as innocent children of God. This prophetic spirituality embraces awareness of what is, moves to challenge and confront wrongs, and commits to working for righteousness. Karen Baker-Fletcher positions God, the Creator, and Source, amid embodied spirituality. As human beings connect with the source of life within, amid intimate relationships, they connect with God's voice and word metaphorically, as in Anna Julia Cooper's "A Singing Something," which celebrates communal freedom, wholeness, and flourishing. The dynamic energy-matter in creation holds and interconnects all humanity towards healing and provides knowledge, insight, fortitude, new meaning, living harmoniously with God, and ecologically, promoting respect and dignity for all life. This life-affirming, embodied spirituality supports deliverance and salvation towards balance as justice and provides a powerful wholeness and healing with many gifts from voice and imagination to flourishing and liberation. These gifts signal humanity's interconnection with God/Spirit.

Womanist spirituality knows and shares the community's past and present stories, where everyone's health and well-being are significant, notably given toxic oppression. Hope, love, and intergenerational, communal wisdom provide a healthy context for womanist spirituality and desires and work for wholeness and wellness. Self-awareness shapes womanist spirituality and allows individuals and communities to be assertive, curious, persistent, astute, and oppose the hegemonic status quo with integrity for gathering knowledge about self and the community. Kelly Brown Douglas views womanist spirituality as an intimate connection with God/Spirit, thus celebrating one's sensuality and sexuality as sacred. Human beings, created divinely, are sensual, personal, emotional, affective, sexual, and relational. Spirituality involves everything about human life, the power to be relational, empowered, and fully engaged in freedom. In womanist spirituality, one lives in the presence of Mystery, the Beautiful, where human beings have ultimate intimacy with a power that is both within and more splendid than themselves. Such a spirituality allows for human beings, as co-creators, the manifestation of beauty in culture and embraces justice that teaches one to celebrate differences and see new possibilities of engagement. Interconnections with God and all creation produce ecological empowerment and embodied spirituality.

Womanist spirituality personifies an attitude and commitment to love via compassion, justice, worship, and dedication as a social witness. Rosetta Ross posits that activity as a witness connects faith with protest, where God within shapes how people see, understand, and connect with the world, and allows one to meet external challenges with authority, trusting God will provide amid unspeakable joy.

Just as womanism responds to feminism, ecowomanism emerges as a consciousness that humanity has an obligation beyond other humans. So often, we mistreat the land, where pollution and landfills exact environmental injustice. We fail to care for creation. Ecowomanists carefully identify the inattention of both ecofeminists (race) and womanists (intentional environmentalism). Ecowomanism juxtaposes the reclamation of ancestral heritage with earth care and incorporates race and economics to dismantle and transcend White-male driven institutional ecology authenticated for and by White males.

Karen Baker Fletcher, bell hooks, and Alice Walker explored ecowomanism before the label's popularity. Baker-Fletcher develops an earthy potential of womanist thought rooted in reclaiming ancestral history while honoring the land. She juxtaposes her theory of earth care against an autobiographical experience of earth throughout life. Seeking to recover and reclaim connections of African diasporan persons with land, Baker-Fletcher reflects on the embodiment of God, Spirit, Christ, creation, and humanity amid the survival, liberation, and wholeness of all communities with ecological justice. hooks explores the import of connecting systemic injustice experienced by people of color and see a disconnect between African Americans and the land, which parallels migration to the urban North. Through centuries of enslavement and the restraints around owning property, literacy, marriage, and voting, the impact of sharecropping, convict leasing, the imagery of White supremacy via lynching from a tree, tenant farming/sharecropping, and the policies robbing Black farmers from any government subsidies, African Americans experience a significant interference amid their ancestral cosmological worldview as people of African descent. Peter Paris investigates the African cosmological worldview regarding the interconnectedness of humanity, nature, and spirit. The calculated and systemic influence of Whiteness maintains power at the expense of African Americans' unfamiliarity and unawareness of the importance of land connection and stewardship. Ecowomanism disrupts this narrative and removes the scarph of self-hate, leading to communal spiritual and physical unhealthiness. The destruction of creation is no longer limited to the purview of White academic scholars and preachers. The emergence of ecowomanism counters the message of silence among African Americans and shatters the destructive perspective of earth care rooted in a history of enslavement and migration north.

The advent of ecowomanism emerges from a quest to expand social justice analysis from a womanist perspective to include all of creation—regardless of race, sex, class, gender, age, sexual orientation, and ability. This expansion supports womanist writings as a disruptive voice to heteronormativity in the public sphere, classroom, and pulpit. Expanding womanism provides foundations for justice work that are entirely communal and embrace the environment among womanist scholarship. In sum, ecowomanists maintain that connecting issues of race, gender, class, age, ability, and sexual orientation with the oppression of land and animals gives a powerful and bold consideration of making this connection to womanist activism without disparaging humanity and honoring all creation. Given the state of global warming, climate change, and ongoing patriarchal misogyny, not only do Black women continue to be Zora Neale Huston's construct of "mules of the world," the earth for many, has become an "other," to be used, enslaved, and dominated without any responsible stewardship. Ecowomanists stand firmly in requiring our conversation about freedom and social justice work to include all creation. Freedom is a gift and a right endowed by a personal God.

We take seriously the politics of language, where words and expressions can inspire or subjugate and inspire freedom. This strategy is vital to the analysis of biblical texts. A womanist reading of biblical texts involves a hermeneutics of (1) tempered cynicism, (2) creativity, (3) courage, (4) commitment, (5) candor, (6) curiosity, and (7) the comedic. (1) Tempered cynicism, sometimes equated with reasonable suspicion, invites us to question with a sensitivity that knows the joy of impossibility, the hope of rooted faith, with study that helps us celebrate and honor the complexities of such work. (2) Creativity affords an environment where conventional interpretations and traditions do not hinder exploring oral or canonical texts in new ways. (3) Courage offers the cushion for doing analysis that leads to similarity or Mystery, daring to ask questions and engage comparative analysis of unique and seemingly antithetical texts and themes. (4) Commitment to the hearing and justice-inspired, honest living of these texts undergird relevant discovery. (5) Candor provides the impetus to reveal the oppression within texts and communities that have helped produce an oppressive, mainline faith. (6) Curiosity presses one to keep searching the realm of the sacred to push toward an atmosphere of inclusivity, mercy, justice, and love. And (7) the comedic reminds us not to take ourselves so seriously that we fail to grow and respect other ways of seeing, despite disagreement.[7]

Womanist biblical scholars wrestle with Scriptures as they deal with the absurdity of oppression: calling for new kinds of interpretation, accountability, and change. Womanist theology emerges from the rich yet oppressive experience of women of African descent. Such theology or God-talk analyzes human individual and social behavior in concert with the Divine. Womanist hermeneutics embody a God/Spirit who cares and looks with disgust at anyone who dismisses, disregards, or denigrates a person made in the Divine image. Every person is essential and relational. Womanist biblical theology merges the study of theology, exegesis, and African American oral and cultural traditions to examine and learn from biblical texts toward the empowerment of all people. Womanist biblical interpretation wrestles with Scripture to study questions of sexuality and gender, advocacy and agency, marginalized women, and biblical children. Womanist thought, across various disciplines and social activism, provides a robust, rich, expansive, illuminating framework for critical, creative analysis. We

---

7. Kirk-Duggan, "Hot Buttered Soul and Cold Icy Truths," 783.

must name, expose, and do all we can to encourage love—freedom, appreciation, compassionate communication, trust, and sincerity.

From protests to political campaigns, womanist hermeneutics, and embodiment occur on the streets. Womanist engagement happens in diverse contexts, from school board meetings around reproductive justice, food deserts, and mass incarceration, to social organizations, on social media, and supportive of entrepreneurial businesses. In all engagements, womanist hermeneutics expose the oppression and offer liberation, ways to reflect critically, and center Black women's religious and moral perspectives in analysis and activity. In sum, womanist hermeneutics involves many aspects of religious engagement, including theory, thought, beliefs, practice, and activism. This discussion focused on the spiritual attention of womanist rituals and practices, while some women work outside of religious thought and ideas, especially literature.

Womanist hermeneutics take all people, institutions, and systems seriously. Womanist thinkers agree that a womanist is confessional and names herself. To embody womanism is to be a woman of African descent. Some indicate that anyone can do womanist analysis by asking questions about oppression; others disagree. From the 1980s through the twenty-first century, many women of African descent found womanist hermeneutics an ideal context for their thought and work. In exploring life and faith, womanist hermeneutics focuses on liberation for all people, for oppressed and oppressor. This spiritual hermeneutic is vital, expressive, revolutionary, embodied, personal, communal resistance-based way of life and theoretical discourse, based upon the rich lived yet violated experiences of women from the African diaspora. A wide-sweeping panorama confronting all forms of oppression and misuse of power, this hermeneutic celebrates women's lives and cultures, including wholeness and healing. The analysis involves viewing people as sacred, made in God's image, and listening to past and present stories amid social witness as justice work. This analysis and activism embrace the beauty of the Sacred and creation. Womanist hermeneutics expose fear-based rhetoric and bullying attitudes by persons who lust for power, who often have church memberships and ascribe to civil and denominational religions, where they honor mom, the flag, and apple pie. Such belief systems include daily mass shootings, food desserts, climate change, lynchings, mass incarceration, book burnings, and assaults against trans and non-binary persons; stand your ground brutality, from elected and appointed politicians' intent on demonizing "wokeness" to neighbors claiming to stand their ground and shoot people who mistakenly come to the wrong address. Womanist hermeneutics continues to expand and heightens the awareness in town and gowns, the academy, and the world where theological engagement happens in celebration of freedom.

BIBLIOGRAPHY

Baker-Fletcher, Karen. *Sisters of Dust, Sisters of Spirit: Womanist Wordings on God and Creation*. Minneapolis: Fortress, 1998.

Baker-Fletcher, Karen, and Garth Kasimu Baker-Fletcher. *My Sister, My Brother:* Womanist and Xodus God-talk. Maryknoll, NY: Orbis, 1997.

Byron, Gay, and Vanessa Lovelace. *Womanist Interpretations of the Bible: Expanding the Discourse*. Atlanta: Semeia, 2016.

Douglas, Kelly Brown. *Sexuality and the Black Church: A Womanist Perspective*. Maryknoll, NY: Orbis, 1999.

———. *Stand Your Ground: Black Bodies and the Justice of God*. Maryknoll, NY: Orbis, 2015.

Floyd-Thomas, Stacey. *Mining the Motherlode: Methods in Womanist Ethics*. Cleveland: Pilgrim, 2006.

Gafney, Wilda. *Womanist Midrash: Reintroduction to The Women of the Torah and the Throne*. Louisville, KY: Westminster John Knox, 2017.

Hood, Robert E. *Begrimed and Black: Christian Traditions on Blacks and Blackness*. Minneapolis: Fortress, 1994.

hooks, bell. *Killing Rage: Ending Racism*. New York: Henry Holt, 1995.

———. *Sisters of the Yam: Black Women and Self-Recovery*. New York: Routledge, 2014.

Kirk-Duggan, Cheryl. "Hot Buttered Soul and Cold Icy Truths: The Hermeneutics of Biblical Interpolation in R&B (Rhythm & Blues)." In *African Americans and the Bible: Sacred Texts and Social Textures*, edited by Vincent Wimbush, 782–803. New York: Continuum, 2000.

———. "Womanist Spirituality." In *The New Westminster Book of Christian Spirituality*, edited by Philip Sheldrake. Louisville, KY: Westminster/John Knox, 2005.

Laughinghouse, Candace. "Nobody's Free Until Everybody's Free: Expanding Coalition Politics Through Antispeciesist Ecowomanism." PhD diss., Chicago Theological Seminary. 2023.

Mathews, Rosita deAnn. "Using Power from the Periphery: an Alternative Theological Model for Survival in Systems." In *A Troubling in My Soul: Womanist Perspectives on Evil and Suffering*, edited by Emilie Townes. New York: Orbis, 1993.

Menaken, Resmaa. *My Grandmother's Hands: Racialized Trauma and the Pathway to Mending Our Hearts and Bodies*. Las Vegas: Central Recovery, 2017.

Paris, Peter. *The Spirituality of African Peoples: The Search for a Common Moral Discourse*. Minneapolis: Fortress, 1995.

Phillips, Layli. *A Womanist Reader*. New York: Routledge, 2006.

Ross, Rosetta E. *Witnessing and Testifying: Black Women, Religion, and Civil Rights*. Minneapolis: Augsburg/Fortress, 2003.

Sanders, Cheryl J., et al. "Roundtable Discussion: Christian Ethics and Theology in Womanist Perspective." *Journal of Feminist Studies in Religion* 5 (1989) 83–112. http://www.jstor.org/stable/25002114.

Thandeka. *Learning to Be White: Money, Race and God in America*. Sacramento, CA: Continuum, 2000.

Torjesen, Karen Jo. *When Women Were Priests: Women's Leadership in the Early Church and the Scandal of Their Subordination in the Rise of Christianity*. Repr. San Francisco: HarperSanFrancisco, 1995.

Townes, Emilie. *In a Blaze of Glory: Womanist Spirituality as Social Witness*. Nashville: Abingdon, 1995.

Walker, Alice. *In Search of our Mother's Gardens: Womanist Prose*. New York: Harcourt Brace Jovanovich, 1983.

———. *Living By the Word*. Orlando: Houghton Mifflin Harcourt, 1989.

White, Monica A. *Freedom Farmers: Agricultural Resistance and the Black Freedom Movement*. Chapel Hill: UNC Press, 2018.

Williams, Delores. *Sisters in the Wilderness: Womanist God-Talk*. Maryknoll, NY: Orbis, 2013.

Chapter 32

Gender and Hermeneutics

Spacious Ambiguities

KAREN STRAND WINSLOW

Gender and hermeneutics, as well as the concepts and practices they represent, are diverse and defined by theorists and practitioners in various ways. I will necessarily attend to the complexities of both terms. Nonetheless, in keeping with the purposes of this project, I will narrow my discussion to the effects of using gender as a lens for interpreting the ancient texts of Jewish and Christian Scripture in a postconservative context. The architects of this paradigm have sought to create space for faithful interpreters who adapt to culture, revise theology, nurture the imagination, and produce fresh insights, while recognizing the motley history of the Christian church and its biblical interpreters.[1]

Before we discuss how gender is deployed as a hermeneutical lens, I will land upon a serviceable definition of the concept. I will then describe how "gender" is used by theorists across the fields of philosophy, rhetoric, literary studies, social sciences, and understood by most people. This will lead to tracing gender criticism's roots in feminist theory and how gendered approaches to the Bible are exemplified by secular, Jewish, and Christian feminist biblical interpreters. I shall proceed with examples from my own research on women characters in the Bible, showing that its producers intentionally included women and outsiders as vital contributors to Israel's story of redemption. Their stories occur at crucial junctures, ensuring Israel's survival and showing the subversive spaciousness of God.

---

1. See the Preface and Introduction to this volume.

DEFINING HERMENEUTICS/BIBLICAL INTERPRETATION

We will not be discussing hermeneutics in general, but rather biblical hermeneutics. "Hermeneutics" refers to shifting theories of interpretation and a variety of approaches to texts, whose emphases depend on multiple influences and agendas, such as changing concepts of language and history. These include "rules of interpretation" created by authorities within religious communities and academic guilds, and by the positions, biases, and assumptions of the interpreters.[2] Social and physical location as well as platforms and power are determinative. Who has authority? Who has a voice? For whom are they speaking? Are they in developed or developing worlds, urban or rural, the academy, the church, or the workplace?[3]

With the complexities in mind, a basic definition is in order. In my view, as a professor of biblical studies for decades, teaching most of biblical library, as well as exegesis, Bible formation, and women in religion, biblical interpretation involves hearing or reading biblical texts by receivers of scriptural textual traditions to understand and explain them. Translating, retelling/writing, preaching, teaching, reflecting upon, analyzing, and applying biblical passages by anyone who regards and uses the text as authoritative and/or sacred continues the process of authorizing—scripturalizing—these texts. The intertextuality found within the library of the Bible indicates such procedures were happening among its many producers before the canon was fixed.[4] Clearly, the New Testament overtly interprets and imaginatively reapplies the Old Testament, the Deuterocanon, and Pseudepigrapha, just as passages within books of the Jewish Scriptures/Old Testament were responding to earlier oral and literary texts. The translations of the Hebrew Bible and the many ancient extra-canonical examples of rewritten Bible and midrash also exemplify the practice of interpretation as giving new life to and honoring old traditions. Living interpreters within faith communities are thus part of the process of preserving its status as living Scripture. On the other hand, the effect may be the opposite. The traditional authority of the text may be defused, decried, and denied. This is the case with some feminist interpreters and gender critics; some reject the entire Bible and others seek to retrieve and redeem the liberating, life-giving themes.

---

2. See the survey in Soulen, *Handbook of Biblical Criticism*, 73–76.

3. See Demers, *Women as Interpreters of the Bible*, 5–24, a review of feminist interpretation up to 1992.

4. I use "producer" to include all oral and written tradents of the material that became Scripture: speakers, performers, writers, redactors, editors, copyists, preservers, translators, and those who read and explained the sense to hearers.

In my view, biblical interpretation is a literary, historical, and theological[5] enterprise that benefits from the critical methods that have been developed over time by confessional and non-confessional scholars.[6] Most interpreters emphasize a few methods to practice and promote. I maintain that interpretation unfolds in steps, beginning with careful observations of a biblical passage within its closest literary context, noticing genre, stylistic techniques and what this requires for interpretation. Close readers observe seams and other criteria indicating potential sources and the hands of reactors. Certain genres, such as song and dialogue within narratives indicate the possibilities for oral and performance-based transmission. Without ignoring the descriptions of settings provided within the text itself, interpreters should also discover and/or speculate on the historical contexts of *the time of writing*, noting the possible agendas of people groups behind the texts. For example, the writer gives the narrative setting for the book of Ruth as "the time when the judges ruled," and yet it was probably composed by and for Jews of the Second Temple period who needed to be reminded of the Moabite great grandmother of David and other good foreign women during a time of conflict over the marriages of Jewish men who had returned from exile to women of the land (non-exiled wives, called "foreign" by Shecaniah and Ezra).[7] Indications of intertextuality across the library of the Bible should also be explored for what they add to understanding.[8] Good interpreters find that Bible is truly a "radically layered, plurally authored, multiply motivated garden of delight to the exegete." We embrace its fascinating mysteries, gaps and inconsistencies.[9] Trying to avoid the sin of certainty, we fumble, flounder, and wrestle with it, resting in the partially known.

DEFINING GENDER

Gender theorists, and most others understand "gender" to describe a pervasive, but variable, *social construct*. Although firmly established within

---

5. Although the Bible is interpreted by scholars who may not be people of faith, its theological meanings continue to be discussed in all sorts of contexts.

6. I was trained in the inductive method of close reading, as well as in multiple modern and postmodern critical methods. Traditional critical approaches developed by male scholars are problematic for some interpreters for they belong to the domain of male oppression (Fuchs, "Neoliberal Feminist Scholarship," 160–79).

7. Winslow, *Moses' Wives*, 68–72, 88–92, 108–11; Winslow, "Ethnicity, Exogamy, and Zipporah"; and Winslow, "Mixed Marriage."

8. Application is a final step urged upon preachers, but it should not be strained and usually left for the Holy Spirit to do.

9. Ostriker, "Word Made Flesh," 11–13.

cultures, it is diverse and fluid *across* cultures. Gender is an ideological product of social conditioning and expectations, and its various manifestations of masculinity and femininity can be rejected and/or reconfigured. Thus, it can be deconstructed—observed, analyzed, broken apart—and reconstructed. Gender provides a series of seemingly determinative, albeit resistible, assumptions about what it means to be feminine or masculine, woman or man, female or male.[10] Gender is about difference, not universality of experience or expression.[11] The philosopher and gender theorist, Judith Butler, argued that gender is a reiterated social *performance* rather than the expression of a prior reality, saying that the constant repetition of stylized acts, "gender performativity," creates the illusion that there are substantive genders, gender is real only to the extent that it's continually performed.[12] Subsequent theorists have continued this use of the term, so that "gender" is widely understood and deployed this way. Butler applied the same ideas to "sex." She argues that a phenomenon "the body," is reiterated, formed, and performed, produced and reproduced through language. This process is considered "constructivism."[13] Nonetheless, many prefer to retain a distinction between "sex" and "gender," in order to acknowledge "natal sex" based on physical characteristics, while describing gender formation as the result of the social conditioning and/or how a person identifies.[14]

The concepts of constructivism, discourse, and deconstruction are buzzwords of the academy and are useful for understanding gender criticism, which has its roots in feminist theory, as well as in post-structuralist and postmodernist philosophy. All of these have influenced feminist biblical hermeneutics, from which gender as an approach to biblical hermeneutics

---

10. Brenner acknowledges that "most humans are socialized into their gender roles according to the norms of their communities," and that texts and traditions, because they are authored and read by gendered people cannot be strictly neutral (*Intercourse of Knowledge*, 1). Texts—both oral and written, ancient and modern also serve to gender; they are part of the processes of social, political, religious, power processes that include gendering.

11. Showalter, "Feminist Criticism in the Wilderness," 179–205.

12. Butler, *Gender Trouble*, esp. xv–xvi, 35, 189–92.

13. Butler, *Bodies that Matter*, 1–5. Butler questions the category "woman," claiming that traditional feminism is wrong to assume and use a natural, essential notion of the female. See Low, *Bible, Gender, and Reception History*, 18–21.

14. In her introduction to *The Intercourse of Knowledge*, Brenner shows the complexity of the issues regarding "sex" and "gender" and provides reasons for distinguishing the two, especially regarding reading biblical texts. "[I]t is convenient shorthand for differentiating sex identities from social identities—and for assessing when and how the two 'identities' are conceived of as indistinguishable or interchangeable," 2–3. See "Sex and Gender: Meanings, Definition, Identity, and Expression," https://www.medicalnewstoday.com/articles/232363. See Peter Enns's chapter in this volume.

also stems. Constructivism is the theory that discourses are invented as powerful, but malleable systems of language and thought. Discourse is a post structuralist "constructivist" term representing linguistic and non-literary systems that have the power to produce realities. Discourses generate and limit knowledge, the shape it will take, and what people can do, their identities and roles within communities and societies. Even while theorists recognize that a particular discourse may seem determinative and unyielding, their argument is that all discourses are malleable—questionable and resistible. "Gender" is a discourse. This is true for race, ethnicity, people groups, and cultures as well. For example, cultural/ethnic identity formation, like gender, is based on words and practices/rituals and language, which implement inclusion and exclusion. Deconstruction involves questioning assumptions and procedures of prevailing discourses, including religious texts and practices, theories and methods of biblical interpretation, as well as past and present discourses about feminism and gender.[15] Before discussing relate to the Bible, I will briefly describe how gender criticism, feminist theory, and feminism relate to each other.

Feminist theory has multiple definitions and permutations, but a brief definition is: "feminist theorists examine the oppression of women and the power structures working against them," seeking to understand the nature of gender inequality in social roles throughout cultures globally, as well as within academic disciplines and politics.[16] Feminist theories first emerged in 1792 with *A Vindication of the Rights of Woman* by Mary Wollstonecraft, which was followed by publications and activism on behalf of women, including voting rights. Later analysts identify this movement as the first wave of feminism.[17] Feminist theory is a type of ideological criticism that investigates the power differentials in social relationships and in the production of the texts (who wrote it, when, why, which is also of concern to biblical exegetes).[18] Feminist theory is the theoretical and academic arm of feminism, which is political and activist, but they are mutually informing and overlap in purpose.

In my book, *Imagining Equity: The Gifts of Christian Feminist Theology*, I wrote:

> Feminism is the practice of supporting equality for all people in the face of centuries of gender (and other) inequality. Feminists believe in equal opportunities, wages, and justice for everyone

---

15. Elam, *Feminism and Deconstruction*, 12.
16. Ruane, "When Women Aren't Enough," 244.
17. Showalter, "Feminist Criticism in the Wilderness," 179–205.
18. Ruane, "When Women," 244–48.

and that women should have access to the same rights, resources, and opportunities as men. They affirm in word and action that gender equality is to be valued and pursued in all aspects of society, including the church. Feminists advocate not only for women, but also for other marginalized sets of society because they desire equality for all. Anyone is a feminist who believes in equality for women, men, and all people groups; feminism is for men and women alike.[19]

When Butler and other gender theorists challenged feminists to avoid the gender binary of feminine and masculine/woman and man and to discard the practice of making women the subject of feminism, they created a dilemma for feminists advocating for equal rights and opportunities for women around the world. Butler says that feminists should instead reveal the ways the gender binary of male/female is produced, regulated, and naturalized and then attempt to *revolutionize* the categories of gender. The response among feminists was to ask, how then will this view of "gender" as constructed and performance-based affect feminist politics and the lives of living women? What is the danger for women and those at the intersections of race/gender/class/sexuality? of claiming that gender is so fluid and malleable, so indeterminate, that women are not seen as women?[20] Could the social gains made by feminists be nullified when theorists reject the category of woman? Some feminists responded that this could unravel social equality and affirmative action for those who identify as women.

A further obvious question is this: Can we operate without reference to a gender binary? Even those who seek to dissolve it, affirming a continuum of gender expressions, still use gendered terms while making claims about gender within and across cultures. This includes interpretations of biblical narratives, law codes, assumptions, and biblical figures. Further questions are pertinent to this essay. Is "gender" considered more neutral, safe, and acceptable; less controversial and political than "feminist"? Is it more inclusive of masculinity, going beyond feminist theory to stress the fluidity of gender and include transgender and queer? What is the relationship of gender criticism to feminist criticism of the Bible? How have they contributed to biblical interpretation? These questions will be explored throughout the remainder of this essay.

---

19. Winslow, *Imagining Equity*, 3–4.
20. Ruane, "When Women," 248–49.

FEMINIST AND GENDER CRITICS APPROACH THE BIBLE: WHAT HAPPENED TO ZIPPORAH?

Gender criticism explores the role of gender in society and cultural products, such as sacred texts and their interpretations, while simultaneously revealing the instability of categories and norms associated with gender, such as "man" and "woman," masculine and feminine.[21] Gender criticism includes the insights from feminist theory, as well as masculinity studies, intersectional analyses, and queer theory. Gender criticism of the Bible is based on the work of feminist theologians and biblical scholars, just as the work of gender theorists is based on feminist theory.[22] Like feminist critique, it is a revisionist project and leads to questioning accepted conceptual structures, expanding the analytical, deconstructionist project to apply to masculinity, male figures, and how the writer genders them as masculine and male. Thus, gender criticism is *not* more neutral or safe than "feminist" interpretation, but more expansive and inclusive to focus on male figures, God, and processes of gendering throughout the Bible.

Gender critical and feminist projects, like that of other poststructuralist theories and methods are concerned with exposing the position of the interpreter. Positionality determines results, whether the interpreter is from academic guilds, the synagogue, or the church. The first step to deconstructing and reconfiguring powerful discourses and structures is recognizing the position—the backgrounds and agendas—of those who control the discourses, i.e., the dialogue, communication, and information produced, whether it be academic, theological, or ecclesial discourse. Philosophers, literary critics, and other theorists consistently observed the perspectival bias of scientific and philosophical theory and traditional biblical interpretation. Since exposing the position of the interpreter is a foundational aspect of their critiques, these late twentieth century feminist interpreters eventually began to openly claim their own positions and agendas to avoid asserting false, universal objectivity. They thus affirmed that they cannot speak for other marginalized groups, including women further subjugated by race, class, and economics. Given their stance that everyone has a stance, these feminist interpreters confessed their limitations at speaking for other women. They learned to listen to and support liberationist, womanist, and post-colonial interpretive approaches, as well as the perspectives of non-academics.[23]

---

21. Yee, *Hebrew Bible*, 25; Ruane, "When Women," 243–60.

22. Yee, *Hebrew Bible*, 5; Ruane, "When Women," 248.

23. This was a prolonged process that involved resistance to essentialism, associated with French feminists, that promotes "naturalized" options about gender, and also was in response to the protests of other women (Yee, 7–14; Ruane, "When Women," 243–47).

Biblical scholars and feminist theologians were influenced by the development of feminist theory, postmodern discourses, and women's studies. Feminist interpreters, who use "women's experience" as their primary hermeneutical lens, deploy a "hermeneutics of suspicion" as they approach the Bible. This means that, since the Bible serves the interests of those who 1 it—males, it must be questioned, its androcentrism and what we now call "patriarchy" identified, and its power to oppress resisted.[24] Feminist and gender critics of the Bible claim that conventional, ingrained, and powerful paradigms of knowledge, including Scripture itself and methods of biblical interpretation, must be investigated, reflected upon, and sometimes dismantled in the interest of new approaches that reflect the values of a wide variety of interpreters from across the gender spectrum and from around the world.[25]

Some secular feminist interpreters, and others with religious ties, have concluded the Bible *only* promotes male dominance, androcentrism, and gender injustice. Arguing that the diverse work of most other feminist biblical interpreters falls into a "neo-liberal" camp *because* they use the critical methods of biblical scholarship, they call for a complete transformation of interpretive tools, a radical revolution of the male-centered interpretive paradigm.[26] They thus reject the Bible and critical methods, seeing them as tools used to oppress women and others by the elite who have access to the production and interpretation of authoritative texts.[27] Nonetheless, they still actively place the Bible at the center of their investigations to expose its pervasive influence.

Christians who were not part of the academy also began publishing critiques of traditional biblical interpretations, beginning also in the second half of the twentieth century, recognizing their antecedents from earlier

---

24. See "Patriarchy is Not Destiny" by Angela Saini, whose studies emphasize the complicated societies of the past, including matriarchal cultures, in which power was shared. Carol Meyers points out that the term patriarchy is a social-science theory, not a biblical construct, and is problematic for understanding the biblical past ("Gender and Heterarchy," 443). Compare Day and Pressler, *Engaging the Bible*, xvii; and Fuchs, *Feminist Hermeneutics of Resistance*, 153–56.

25. Scholz, *Oxford*, xxvi–xxxi provides a history of feminist scholarship of the Hebrew Bible to 2020.

26. Scholz demonstrates that feminist interpreters use critical methods to a variety of effects in "Gendering the Hebrew Bible," 67–84; summary, 83–34. But Fuchs refers to Lourde's phrase, "the master's tools" to describe critical methods in "Neoliberal Feminist Scholarship," (160) and throughout "Sexual Biblical Politics." Fuchs also criticizes feminists who find portions of the Bible as freeing, enlightening, and/or useful in any sense.

27. Fuch's "Sexual Biblical Politics," 35–51; Fiorenza on post-biblical feminists (*Bread Not Stone*, 9–10); and Milne ("Milne and Scholz," 28–31).

centuries.[28] They also began to deconstruct traditional interpretations in their publications and presentations. They exposed biblical content regarding biblical women characters and women as a social group that had been ignored, minimized, and/or misinterpreted by centuries of male interpreters. This included demonstrating how male clergy, exegetes, interpreters, and theologians not only minimize(d) the significance of women characters and other Others in the Bible; they also establish(ed) cultural and ecclesial practices to promote hierarchy and "complementarianism" among Christians. Noting that theologians and churchmen often ignored the liberating messages of the Bible taken as a whole, "evangelical egalitarians" and "Christian feminists" exegeted biblical narratives and law codes by closely reading the texts with redemptive agendas for women.[29]

Christian feminism and egalitarianism overlap but are not always synonymous. Evangelical women in the late 1960s and 70s preferred "egalitarian" to distinguish themselves from secular feminists. Nonetheless, both focus on equality for women in the church, appealing to Scripture, Christian history, and women's experience.[30] Feminist interpreters have focused on women characters, how women as a group are gendered as women, included or marginalized, and the reversals or subversions of patriarchy.[31] At present, the Bible has been interpreted less by explicitly self-identified gender critics; fewer scholars have examined how the narrator genders/masculinizes male characters. Several studies exist, but this is an area ripe for research for Christian biblical interpreters.[32]

As a biblical scholar and woman of faith, I count myself among the feminist biblical interpreters who focus on the biblical characters who are textually gendered/identified as women. I examine what they do, how they are acted upon, legislated, controlled, used and/or abused within the world of the story, but also by the narrators, redactors, and eventually by interpreters. We see both negative and positive use and treatment of women. We recognize that the Bible includes "pornoprophetic" metaphors and allegories from which contemporary readers recoil.[33] And yet, within this large

28. Winslow, "Recovering Redemption," 279–89; Winslow, "Egalitarian," 525–42.

29. Winslow, "Recovering Redemption," 274–83; Winslow, "Egalitarian," 526–31.

30. I describe the distinction between Christian "feminists" and egalitarians in "Recovering Redemption," 269–89, where I also trace their origins and debates with "complementarians, who interpret the Bible to enforce their stance against women in church leadership (also "Egalitarian," 525–42).

31. Brenner, "Intercourse of Knowledge," 1–8.

32. Ruane's study cites several gender critical approaches that include attention to masculinity in the Bible. Ruane, "When Women," 249–52, esp. citations 10–12.

33. Brenner, "Intercourse of Knowledge," 153–174, esp. 154–55, n4–11.

library of books, we also see that many books, narratives, pericopes, and oracles serve to subvert, deconstruct—in both overt and subtle ways—other biblical assumptions and perspectives that women and outsiders are inferior or less valued than males or Israel. We argue that the biblical meta-narrative and many biblical texts can be interpreted as liberating for women and all people.[34] The songs of both Hannah and Mary are more about leveling the ground between the lowly and the exalted than they are about motherhood, and in my view, explicitly express one of the most important themes of the entire Bible.[35]

Religious feminists and egalitarians continue to oppose interpretations of Scriptures that restrict women from leadership in synagogues and churches and seek to enforce gender roles in families. We offer positive, constructive interpretations to preserve the Bible for women and others who have been blocked from roles of authority and influence. Therefore, we consider the Bible to be salvageable, that is redeemable, especially because it is itself redemptive of oppressed people. Both testaments regularly and actively disparage hierarchy and ethnocentrism; the Bible, overall, is a picture of God's impartiality. Its attention to particular, ancient situations are not rules for all time, all contexts. Thus, its meaning and messages are retrievable from their historical and literary contexts, even as they necessarily rely upon roots in history.

In sum, unlike the feminist interpreters who claim that the Bible is primarily a tool to promote patriarchy and gender injustice, who thus reject it, we find that the Bible provides a basis for overcoming sexism, racism, colonialism, and classism. It supplies grounds for revising or rejecting traditional interpretations. While understanding that Israel was a patriarchal culture and is the context for the Bible's producers, we claim that they—the shapers of Scripture—intentionally produced and preserved the stories of women, and/or as non-Israelites so that these Others will be seen as exemplars for the people of God. These foreigners demonstrate ideal faith confessions (Jethro, Exod 18; Rahab, Josh 2) and model practices for receivers of these texts (Tamar, Gen 38; Zipporah, Exod 4).[36] Those constructed as women and/or outsiders to Israel, such as Tamar, Rahab, Jethro, Ruth, Uriah, Naaman, are represented in the Bible as aligned with God's purposes,

---

34. Winslow, "Recovering Redemption," 269–89; Winslow, *Imagining Equity,* 26–49; "Egalitarian," 525–542.

35. 1 Sam 2:1–10; Luke 1:46–55.

36. Winslow, *Moses' Wives,* 68–72, 88–92, 108–11; Winslow, "Ethnicity, Exogamy, and Zipporah"; and Winslow, "Mixed Marriage in Torah Narratives."

even though leaders (such as Ezra and Nehemiah) threatened "outsiders" with expulsion or worse.[37]

Tamar, a helpless Canaanite widow, at the mercy of the whims and paranoia of her father-in-law, Judah, took the future of Israel into her own hands and pretended to be a prostitute in order to produce progeny and (eventually) the royal tribe of Judah and kings of Israel and Judah. Throughout the ages of redacting traditions and texts that became Scripture, those who handled the ancient traditions had plenty of opportunities for this story about a Canaanite woman who played a prostitute in order to have sex with her father-in-law to be suppressed and excised from the traditions that became the Bible. This did not happen. Tamar's story remains a witness to the erstwhile wife, innovative outsider, a pretend prostitute, who was crucial to the preservation of Israel. The shapers of Scripture purposely included this story to describe Israel's origins, just as they included the stories of Abraham's call, acts of obedience, and trials of faith. Furthermore, Zipporah, the Midianite shepherd wife of Moses, acted swiftly to save him from death by performing the priestly act of covenant cutting and male-bonding, circumcision. Rahab, a Canaanite prostitute, confessed her faith and shrewdly manipulated the spies and in order to preserve her family's life and assimilate into Israel. The conscious choices of these women led to the enhancement, not the destruction, of Israel; they created and preserved the people of God.

I recognize that women characters disappear from the larger story after their contributions are stressed. Nonetheless, they remain models of faithfulness to God's ways for every receiver of the text. It is more important to remember that these stories did not have to be told; they did not have to be included in the Jewish-Christian Scriptures. They are here to show how conventional perspectives and practices can be overturned by the most surprising people.[38] These stories show that community of God is for everyone who looks at the evidence and chooses to join. Israel and the church was formed from all sorts of people from all sorts of backgrounds with all sorts of motives. They are here for our instruction and to build faith and hope (1 Tim 3:16) for they show that what people say and do, not who they are or from whence they come, brings them into the people of God. You cannot be excluded if your motives are self-preservation, personal salvation, fear, desire to be on the winning side, or a new identity. Any of these are good reasons to join the people of God. The fact that these stories are Scripture

---

37. Ezra 10–11; Neh 13, especially 13:23–31.
38. Spina, *Faith of the Outsider*.

says something very powerful about and to people constructed as marginal, strange, and dangerous.[39]

CONCLUSION

To use gender as a hermeneutical lens is to take a step back from assumptions based on operating in a binary gendered world and watch how the text informs us about a character in the text. This includes, but goes beyond, names and adjectives like woman/man, wife/husband. It notices how the narrator makes something of the actions, words, descriptions, and roles reported or presumed. Recognizing gendering is to observe how a textually gendered person is treated within the world of the story that seems to be connected to their gender and/or is different than other characters, gendered differently.

Maleness has been considered the "norm," and male biblical characters are far more numerous, and judged, if not presented, as more important than female characters. Females are the Other. When they have not been ignored and minimized, they have been objectified by traditional interpreters. Thus, women in the Bible became the subjects and objects of feminist criticism when women began to interpret the Bible. Masculinity construction has been analyzed far less; how males are gendered in the Bible has only recently been examined by a few interpreters. Nonetheless, gender critics focus on the descriptions, terms, actions, contexts, and other means by which characters are identified as male, asking what is the effect of this process of observation showing how these characters are shown to be male?

The same is true for God. For most interpreters, God's 'maleness' was assumed, or, if not, male pronouns were considered a *natural* way of referring to a God that cannot be confined to a sex or gender.[40] But a gendered lens would help interpreters take issue with this, and, while observing that God is gendered by masculine, singular pronouns and metaphors of king, warrior, commander, and father, female metaphors for God also appear, as feminist interpreters have consistently shown.[41] This brings us back to the

39. Ezra 9–10 represents the fear of mixing and impurity on the part of some of the post-exilic leaders, who called the returned Israel "holy seed." Many of the other biblical stories oppose that perspective, showing tension among Second Temple Jews over Jewish identity and intermarriage. I have treated this topic at length elsewhere (*Moses' Wives*; "Ethnicity, Exogamy, Zipporah"; "Mixed Marriage"; "Moses' Cushite Marriage"; and "Moses Married a Cushite Woman").

40. McFague *Metaphorical Theology*, and *Models of God*; Peeler, *Women and the Gender of God*.

41. Num 11:12; Deut 32:11–12, 18; Isa 42:14, 44:2,24, 46:3–4, 49:15, 66:13; Jer 1:5; Hos 23:8; Matt 23:27; Luke 1:34, 15:8–10 (Winslow, *Imagining Equity*, 3, 62–63, 77–79).

significance of gender as difference. To attempt to abolish a gender binary is to refuse to honor and celebrate difference whether it is developed through social conditioning and is flexible or based in biology or both. This would preclude the compelling contributions of many feminist interpreters, including *Mourner, Mother, Midwife: Reimagining God's Delivering Presence in the Old Testament* and *The Female Face of God in Auschwitz: A Jewish Feminist Theology of the Holocaust*.[42]

Although a gendered lens of interpretation shows up problems in the Bible that emerge from the cultures of its producers, it also highlights the countercultural confessions and actions of outsiders and women to belie a view that they are less important than males. Should women reject Scripture when they recognize its problems? Should we leave the church founded originally by our compassionate Savior to continue its history of male dominance and documented practices of ignoring the abuse of children, women, the oppressed, and the poor?[43] Should we leave the church in the hands of men only?

Post-biblical feminist interpreters claim that to retrieve the Bible for women, to claim that it is still a foundation for delivering the oppressed, maligned, and marginalized, is to support the androcentric, patriarchal, and unjust agendas of the male writers and interpreters of the Bible. On the other hand, confessional Jewish and Christian feminist biblical interpreters seek to re-present, magnify, the voices of women in the Bible, women interpreters, and other Others in order to spread justice for all. Whereas traditional interpretation ignored has aligned itself with the patriarchy, hierarchy, and exclusivism scattered throughout the Bible, feminist interpreters recognize the word of God in Scripture on behalf of the non-aligned and the powerless. The Bible more consistently carries a message of inclusivism and leveling of ethnic, social, economic, and gender categories. We emphasize Scriptural affirmations of women and biblical metaphors about God taken from nature and women's experience or the prophetic critiques of social injustice and oppressive religion. These interpretative approaches supply biblical foundations for what ecclesial practice, i.e., practical theology. Recognizing and deploying these biblical grounds for ordination without regard to gender,

---

42. Claassens and Raphael, respectively.

43. We know the church has been a cooperative covenant partner with God throughout its history in countless venues and ways. However, its abusive practices in some segments continue to come to light. This is demonstrated by the ongoing sexual abuse by leaders not only in Catholic churches and the Southern Baptist Convention. Investigative reporters from *The Houston Chronicle* and *San Antonio Express-News* collected 380 allegations spanning twenty states. The SBC is complementarian; they do not allow female teachers or preachers. But member churches have hired convicted sex offenders (Robert Downen, et al, "Abuse of Faith," *Houston Chronicle*, 10).

ordaining called and trained women to pastor, teach, and lead is a primary way the church can help God to raise up the oppressed, the least of these, and to preserve life.

BIBLIOGRAPHY

Brenner, Athalya. *The Intercourse of Knowledge: On Gendering Desire and 'Sexuality' in the Hebrew Bible*. Biblical Interpretation Series 26. Atlanta: Society of Biblical Literature, 1997.

Butler, Judith. *Bodies that Matter: On the Discursive Limits of Sex*. London: Routledge, 1993.

———. *Gender Trouble: Feminism and the Subversion of Identity*. New York: Routledge, 1990.

Claassens, L. Juliana. *Mourner, Mother, Midwife: Reimagining God's Delivering Presence in the Old Testament*. Louisville, KY: Westminster, 2012.

Day, Linda and Carolyn Pressler, eds. *Engaging the Bible in a Gendered World: An Introduction to Feminist Biblical Interpretation in Honor of Katharine Doob Sakenfeld*. Louisville, KY: Westminster John Knox, 2006.

Demers, Patricia. *Women as Interpreters of the Bible*. New York: Paulist, 1992.

Downen, Robert, et al. "Abuse of Faith: 20 years, 700 Victims." *Houston Chronicle*, February 2019. https://www.houstonchronicle.com/news/investigations/article/Southern-Baptist-sexual-abuse-spreads-as-leaders-13588038.php.

Elam, Diane. *Feminism and Deconstruction*. London: Routledge/Taylor & Francis, 1994.

Fuchs, Esther. "A Feminist Hermeneutics of Resistance." In *Feminist Interpretation of the Hebrew Bible in Retrospect*, edited by Susanne Scholz, 2:151–87. Sheffield: Sheffield Phoenix, 2014.

———. "Neoliberal Feminist Scholarship in Biblical Studies." In *The Oxford Handbook of Feminist Approaches to the Hebrew Bible*, edited by Susanne Scholz, 160–79. Oxford: Oxford University Press, 2020.

———. "Sexual Biblical Politics as Interventionist Interrogation." In *Feminist Interpretation of the Hebrew Bible in Retrospect*, edited by Susanne Scholz, 3:35–51. Sheffield: Sheffield Phoenix, 2017.

Low, Katherine. *The Bible, Gender, and Reception History: The Case of Job's Wife*. Edited by Claudia Camp et al. Scriptural Traces: Critical Perspectives on the Reception and Influence of the Bible, Library of HB/OT Studies 586. London: T. & T. Clark/Bloomsbury, 2013.

McFague, Sallie. *Metaphorical Theology: Models of God in Religious Language*. Philadelphia: Fortress, 1982.

———. *Models of God: Theology for an Ecological, Nuclear Age*. Minneapolis: Fortress, 1987.

Meyers, Carol. "Gender and the Heterarchy Alternative for Re-Modeling Ancient Israel." In *The Oxford Handbook of Feminist Approaches to the Hebrew Bible*, edited by Susanne Scholz, 443–59. Oxford: Oxford University Press, 2020.

Milne, Pamela. "Milne and Scholz: A Conversation." In *Feminist Interpretation of the Hebrew Bible in Retrospect*, edited by Susanne Scholz, 3:28–31. Sheffield: Sheffield Phoenix, 2017.

Ostriker, Alice. "A Word Made Flesh: The Bible and Revisionist Women's Poetry." *Religion and Literature* 23 (1991) 11–13.

Peeler, Amy. *Women and the Gender of God*. Grand Rapids: Eerdmans, 2022.

Raphael, Melissa. *The Female Face of God in Auschwitz: A Jewish Feminist Theology of the Holocaust*. Abingdon: Routledge, 2003.

Ruane, Nicole. "When Women Aren't Enough." In *Feminist Interpretation of the Hebrew Bible in Retrospect*, edited by Susanne Scholz, 3:243–60. Sheffield: Sheffield Phoenix, 2017.

Saini, Angela. "Patriarchy is Not Destiny." *National Geographic* 243 (2023) 15–18.

Scholz, Suzanne, ed. *Feminist Interpretation of the Hebrew Bible in Retrospect: Social Locations*. Recent Research in Biblical Studies 8. Sheffield: Sheffield Phoenix, 2014.

———. ed. *Feminist Interpretation of the Hebrew Bible in Retrospect: Methods*. Recent Research in Biblical Studies 9. Sheffield: Sheffield Phoenix, 2017.

———. *Introducing the Women's Hebrew Bible: Feminism, Gender Justice, and the Study of the Old Testament*. London: T. & T. Clark/Bloomsbury, 2017.

———. ed. *The Oxford Handbook of Feminist Approaches to the Hebrew Bible*. Oxford: Oxford University Press, 2020.

Schussler Fiorenza, Elizabeth. *Bread Not Stone: The Challenge of Feminist Biblical Interpretation*. Boston: Beacon, 1984.

Showalter, Elaine. "Feminist Criticism in the Wilderness." *Critical Inquiry* 8 (1981) 179–205. https://www.journals.uchicago.edu/doi/epdf/10.1086/448150.

Soskice, Janet Martin. *The Kindness of God: Metaphor, Gender, and Religious Language*. Oxford: Oxford University Press, 2007.

Soulen, Richard N., and R. Kendall. *Handbook of Biblical Criticism*. Louisville, KY: Westminster John Knox, 2001.

Spina, Frank Anthony. *The Faith of the Outsider: Exclusion and Inclusion in the Biblical Story*. Grand Rapids: Eerdmans, 2005.

Winslow, Karen Strand. *Early Jewish and Christian Memories of Moses' Wives: Exogamist Marriage and Ethnic Identity*. Lewiston, NY: Edwin Mellen, 2005.

———. "Ethnicity, Exogamy, and Zipporah." *Women in Judaism: Multidisciplinary Journal* 4 (2006) 1–13.

———. "'For Moses Had Indeed Married a Cushite Woman': The LORD's Prophet Married Well." *Lectio Difficilor* 1 (2011) 1–18.

———. *Imagining Equity: The Gifts of Christian Feminist Biblical Theology.* Nashville: The General Board of Higher Education and Ministry, the United Methodist Church, 2021.

———. "Mixed Marriage in Torah Narratives." In *Mixed Marriages, Intermarriage, and Group Identity in the Second Temple Period,* edited by Christian Frevel, 132–49. London: T. & T. Clark International, 2011.

———. "Moses' Cushite Marriage: Torah, Artapanus, and Josephus." In *Mixed Marriages, Intermarriage, and Group Identity in the Second Temple Period,* edited by Christian Frevel, 280–302. Library of Hebrew Bible/Old Testament Studies 547. London: T. & T. Clark, 2011.

———. "The Purpose, Principles, and Goals of Egalitarian Biblical Interpretation." In *The Oxford Handbook of Feminist Approaches to the Hebrew Bible,* edited by Susanne Scholz, 525–42. Oxford: Oxford University Press, 2020.

———. "Recovering Redemption for Women: Feminist Exegesis in North American Evangelicalism." In *Feminist Interpretation of the Hebrew Bible in Retrospect,* edited by Susanne Scholz, 2:269–89. Sheffield: Sheffield Phoenix, 2014.

Wollstonecraft, Mary. *A Vindication of the Rights of Woman,* 1792. https://revolution.chnm.org/d/579.

Yee, Gail, ed. *The Hebrew Bible: Feminist and Intersectional Perspectives.* Minneapolis: Fortress, 2018.

Chapter 33
Intersex Hermeneutics[1]
MEGAN K. DEFRANZA

I grew up in a fundamentalist Christian family and learned at a very young age that God only created male and female. I was raised to be a good Christian woman, but I wasn't ever fully comfortable in that role... I was 22 when I learned about my intersex variation, and I was horrified. I knew it was true and that I was born both male and female. I was terribly ashamed of my body, tried hard to fit in, and to appear more female.

I didn't have the courage to be authentically intersex in my culture—to recognize myself as someone who was fearfully and wonderfully made. Because there isn't yet an honest place for intersex people in the world of my upbringing, I questioned the whole establishment. The teachings felt irrelevant because I knew that my existence rocked the whole system. To remain in that culture as fully female began to feel dishonest. I didn't want to have uncomfortable conversations, so I gradually pulled away.

I am still untangling my own conditioning around gender roles and giving myself permission to exist in this body. As that relates to my faith, I am developing a more expansive view of God. I no longer see God as having a gender—or even an agenda—but as a massive force of love and divine grace. God is the love and the fabric that connects everyone and everything.[2]

—SARAH BECK

---

1. Author note: Special thanks to Sarah Beck and Rev. Laura Bethany Buchleiter who provided feedback and editorial assistance on this chapter.

2. Sarah Beck, personal email (May 26, 2023).

After I came out, the first spiritual community that I landed with was this recovery community. I thought, 'I relate to these people. I belong here but I don't know why. I don't have 'an addiction.' . . . but the more I thought about it, my faith, doctrine, everything I'd grown up with and preached, I realized I was strongly addicted to being able to explain things. Being able to explain things means that there had to be some absolutes . . . certainties . . . . beyond a shadow of a doubt.

Embracing my intersex variations pushed me outside of a need for binary explanation, has pushed me outside of the need for 'true' or 'false'. . . . It changed how I came to Scripture because I wasn't looking for Scripture to give me answers about God. I was looking to Scripture to inform a journey, to understanding God in a more experiential and personal way.

I lean into the mystery of understanding God. I think one of the challenges of modern Christianity is we tend to make certain what should be mystery and hold ambiguous what should be certain. We claim to know God and yet get confused about loving our neighbor.[3]

—Rev. Laura Beth Buchleiter

INTERSEX THEOLOGY IN CONTEXT

Intersex people have biological sex traits that vary from medical definitions of male or female—variations in chromosome patterns, gonadal development and function, hormone levels, internal reproductive structures, external genital shape, or secondary sex traits. Between 0.05 percent and 1.7 percent of the population are born with an intersex variation—the upper estimate is similar to the number of red-haired people. Most health professionals are not trained to care for intersex people, and those who are typically attempt to hide or medically alter intersex bodies.

Children whose intersex traits are visible at birth are routinely subjected to medically unnecessary, non-consensual plastic surgeries in the first months and years of life to make them appear more male or female. Others have had gonads removed without their consent and under false pretenses. Many have had medical records hidden from them by parents and doctors. Because of frequent follow-up care, many have experienced medical and sexual trauma from doctor after doctor peeking under the sheets or taking

---

3. Laura Beth Buchleiter, Zoom Webinar, "Language for Understanding: Engaging the Transgender and Intersex Community With Empathy And Compassion" (May 22, 2023, 7:00 p.m. EST).

photographs of their genitalia. Many are put on hormone blockers or given synthetic hormones to force naturally non-binary bodies closer to the medical definitions of male or female. These interventions have been identified as human rights violations and likened to torture by the United Nations. Intersex activists have been raising their voices for decades to end unnecessary medical procedures on healthy children and adults without their consent (most often before the age of consent).

Attempts to hide intersex traits have contributed to a lack of education in the general public; however, even most medical professionals are not educated about intersex healthcare. On the positive side, more intersex people have come out in recent decades to protest their treatment and educate the public at large. On the negative side, there are concerted political efforts, often endorsed by right-wing Christians, to deny the facts of human biological sex diversity and demonize those brave enough to share details about their bodies and their trauma. Intersex people have been erased and injured by a society influenced by an interpretation of Genesis which reads Adam and Eve, male and female, as the only two kinds of humans God created, or intended, or calls "good."

DIFFERENCE OR DISORDER?

There is no doubt that Genesis describes the creation of male and female but what of those who do not fit this pattern? Many Christians, upon first learning about intersex, quickly assume this must be a consequence of original sin. Similarly, in the 1950s, our Western medical community labeled intersex traits as "disorders of sex development" (DSDs), likening them to diseases, birth defects, or disabilities, and began surgically and hormonally altering intersex children and adolescents.

In recent decades, intersex people have advocated terms like "differences of sex development," "variations in sex traits," "intersex traits," or their precise diagnoses such as "androgen insensitivity," "ovo-testes," "adrenal hyperplasia," etc. Some intersex people view their traits as primarily medical in nature while others argue that their bodies should not be seen as problematic. A child born without an urethra certainly has a medical need for surgery on their genitals; however, a child born with a larger than average clitoris does not need it to be surgically amputated because it is deemed "too large for a girl." Separating which aspects of sex traits are health concerns and which are cultural or theological concerns is imperative.

MALE, FEMALE, AND BODIES IN BETWEEN

Interestingly, the most important biblical passage for understanding intersex is not found in Genesis but in Matthew chapter 19. It is not merely the *fact* that Jesus speaks of people with variations in sex traits but *how* he talks about them. In a passage where Jesus is asked to weigh in on a first century Jewish debate about divorce, he quotes Genesis one and Genesis two then pivots to speak about eunuchs.

> Not everyone can accept this teaching, but only those to whom it is given. For there are
> *eunuchs who have been so from birth*, and there are
> *eunuchs who have been made eunuchs by others*, and there are
> *eunuchs who have made themselves eunuchs for the sake of the kingdom of heaven.*
> Let anyone accept this who can. (Matt 19:11–12)

Jesus names eunuchs as those who do not fit the categories of male and female found in the first chapters of Genesis. He identifies two kinds of eunuchs familiar to his ancient audience before introducing a third. More significantly, the Messiah does not speak of eunuchs as proof of the fall or as people in need of healing. On the contrary, Jesus recommends his disciples learn from eunuchs, indicating that some people even "make themselves eunuchs for the sake of the kingdom of heaven." Christians debated for many centuries how to interpret this puzzling passage.[4]

First-century Christians were very familiar with the second type of eunuch. Some took Jesus literally, castrating themselves to show that their devotion was equal to priests of the Great Mother who practiced self-castration as part of their worship. Other men took a more metaphorical approach, flouting masculine dress, hairstyle, and comportment; giving up male privilege in a patriarchal society. Others chose to become like angels who were usually depicted as beardless men—the identifying mark of a eunuch. These men subordinated their masculinity in order to inaugurate the kingdom of God. "Thy will be done on earth as it is in heaven" (Matt 6:10) where people "no longer marry or are given in marriage but will be like the angels" (Matt 22:30). Angels were understood as mediators between the divine and human.

Like angels, eunuchs were servants and mediators. Their in-between bodies were seen as well suited to go between upper and lower classes, sacred and secular spaces, and between men and women. In first-century

---

4. For a detailed history of the interpretation of this passage see DeFranza, *Sex Difference in Christian Theology*, chapter 2.

Rome, they were mostly enslaved people: boys kidnapped, castrated, and sold into slavery as living sex toys and as servants in aristocratic households. The latter were trusted with financial responsibilities and as guardians of the harem because they couldn't impregnate royal women to threaten a dynasty. Thus, historian Kathryn Ringrose calls them "perfect servants."[5]

The church too found uses for eunuchs. Eastern and Western Christian leaders believed women must be silent in church but still wanted soprano voices in their choirs; so, they castrated boys to sing the high notes. Alessandro Moreschi, "The Last Angel of Rome," was the last castrato to sing at the Sistine Chapel. He died in 1922 a mere 101 years ago. In the later Byzantine empire, some Christian parents would castrate a son to give him a career opportunity serving as a eunuch of the imperial court or the church. Castrating an adult was considered an offense but castrating a child was seen as a method for retaining the values natural to children: beauty, lack of sexuality, lack of aggressive behavior, and willingness to serve.

Before Jesus speaks of castrated eunuchs in Matthew 19, he first mentions those who have been eunuchs from birth. Here the Messiah employs language developed by Rabbis for the identification of those born with bodies different from male and female. In Judaism, it is of utmost importance to know who should or should not be circumcised. When questions arose as to sex of a newborn, a rabbi would be called in to make a determination. Over the years, they noticed a sufficient number of variations in sex traits that they created the following additional categories, providing language and religious places for everyone in their community:

> *Saris Chamah*—born masculine of center (eunuch from birth)
> *Aylonith*—born feminine of center
> *Androgynos*—equally male and female, *hermaphrodite*[6]
> *Tumtum*—sex is unclear but believed to become clear in time
> *Saris Adam*—eunuch made my humans (castrated male)

In Matthew 19, Jesus uses the first term and the last term in this list above. *Saris chamah* translates literally as "eunuch of the sun" (i.e., from the first day the sun shone on the child). The practice of differentiating between castrated eunuchs and eunuchs from birth has roots in the Torah. Deuteronomy 23:1 reads "No one who has been emasculated by crushing or

---

5. Ringrose, *Perfect Servant*.

6. "Hermaphrodite" and "androgynos" are terms used in the ancient world to describe people with certain kinds of intersex traits. These terms are considered offensive to some intersex people today while others self-identify as hermaphrodites. It is best to avoid the language of hermaphrodite unless encouraged to do so by an intersex individual in reference to themself.

cutting may enter the assembly of the Lord." The verses that follow prohibit Israelites from marrying foreigners of various tribes. Ritual castration was practiced in the religions of some of Israel's neighbors. Prohibitions of mixing with foreigners may have motivated the exclusion of cut eunuchs from the assembly. Eunuchs whose surgically altered bodies blurred the lines between male and female were considered foreign, and separation from foreigners is an important theme throughout the Old Testament.

Castrated eunuchs were excluded from religious assemblies, but eunuchs from birth were not. To integrate naturally born eunuchs into society, Rabbis pulled from laws for men and laws for women to clarify religious obligations for naturally born eunuchs as well as those who fell into the other sex/gender categories. Contemporary Jewish scholars continue this practice often employing stricter rules so that nothing is left undone.

Many Christian leaders today interpret Jesus's teaching in Matthew 19 as a commendation of celibacy for single-minded service to God (as Paul does in 1 Cor 7:32–35) but this does not explain why the Messiah would employ the gender diverse figure of the eunuch, one legally excluded from worship by Deuteronomy 23, in order to make his point. On the other hand, it is very much like Jesus to pay attention to those on the margins of society, despised by the majority; honoring them with his attention and including them in his message of good news.

WELCOMING THOSE FORMERLY EXCLUDED

Jesus was not the first to call into question Deuteronomy's exclusion of eunuchs and foreigners from worshiping in the assembly. In the book of Isaiah, this change is already underway. Through the prophet, God speaks words of comfort to the very people outlawed by Deuteronomy 23.

> Do not let the foreigner joined to the Lord say,
>   "The Lord will surely separate me from his people";
> and do not let the eunuch say,
>   "I am just a dry tree."
> For thus says the Lord:
> To the eunuchs who keep my sabbaths,
>   who choose the things that please me
>   and hold fast my covenant,
> I will give, in my house and within my walls,
>   a monument and a name
>   better than sons and daughters;
> I will give them an everlasting name
>   that shall not be cut off.

> And the foreigners who join themselves to the Lord,
>> to minister to him, to love the name of the Lord,
>> and to be his servants,
> all who keep the sabbath, and do not profane it,
>> and hold fast my covenant—
> these I will bring to my holy mountain,
>> and make them joyful in my house of prayer;
> their burnt-offerings and their sacrifices
>> will be accepted on my altar;
> for my house shall be called a house of prayer
>> for all peoples. (Isa 56:3–7)

Despite all the marks against eunuchs and the suspicion of foreigners, God assures these outsiders of their place in the community; but this good news is more than mere inclusion. The Lord does not promise to heal eunuchs or restore them to one of the two categories established in the book of Genesis. Yahweh does not declare these "dry trees" fertile so that they can perpetuate their name as Jewish men did, by begetting sons who begat sons. The Lord does not seem concerned to restore these ambiguous bodies to some creational pattern or ideal. They are promised, *not* the same blessing as those given to Jewish men, but something "*better* than sons and daughters . . . an everlasting name that shall not be cut off" (v. 5). Rather, they are blessed *as eunuchs*. The passage goes on to assure the foreigner that they too have a place in the community. Instead of doing everything to separate God's people from outsiders, Yahweh declares, "my house shall be called a house of prayer for all peoples" (v. 7). God was doing something new.

In light of the good news preached to eunuchs and foreigners by the prophet Isaiah, Jesus's positive inclusion of those whose bodies fall between male and female in Matthew 19 should not come as such a surprise. But the true fulfillment of Isaiah's prophecy is found in Acts chapter 8 in which an angel tells the apostle Philip to share the good news with a eunuch and a foreigner who is traveling home to Ethiopia after a religious pilgrimage to Jerusalem. Philip overhears the Ethiopian eunuch reading from the book of Isaiah and shares with him the good news about Jesus. "As they traveled along the road, they came to some water and the eunuch said, 'Look, here is water. What can stand in the way of my being baptized?'"

Here was an individual who fit the profile of eunuchs in the first century—a high-ranking slave to the queen of the Ethiopians. High status allowed him the freedom and funds not only to make the pilgrimage from Ethiopia to Jerusalem but to have his own copy of the scroll of Isaiah. His devotion to the Scriptures indicates that he would certainly have been familiar with the exclusion of eunuchs from the assembly in Deut 23:1. As a gentile, he would also have recently experienced the limitation that his foreigner status placed upon his proximity to the holy of holies—surrounded as it was by the court of men, then the court of women, and finally the court of gentiles.

Is it any wonder that, when he heard the good news about Jesus, he would ask, "What can stand in the way of my being baptized?" He may very well have been wondering what his status would be in this new community. Would he remain a second- or third-class citizen among God's people? Would his body continue to prevent him from coming as close to God as Jewish men or Jewish women could come? Could he also be conformed to the image of Jesus, or would the form of his body perpetuate his place as an outsider?

Acts does not record Philip's answer but he might have responded similarly to the apostle Paul, whose letter to the Galatians was also attempting to clarify the relationship of Christians to the old law. "All of you who were baptized into Christ have clothed yourselves with Christ. There is neither Jew nor Gentile, neither slave nor free, nor is there male and female, for you are all one in Christ Jesus. If you belong to Christ, then you are Abraham's seed, and heirs according to the promise" (Gal 3:27–29). Whatever Philip said in response must have satisfied him because someone "gave orders to stop the chariot. Then both Philip and the eunuch went down into the water and Philip baptized him. When they came up out of the water, the Spirit of the Lord suddenly took Philip away, and the eunuch did not see him again, but went on his way rejoicing" (Acts 8:38–39).

REREADING ADAM AND EVE

How do we reconcile the inclusion of those whose bodies fall in between male and female with the opening chapters of Genesis and exclusionary laws in Deuteronomy? As noted above, the deuteronomic prohibition is found in the context of commands to maintain separation from foreigners. While often confusing to contemporary readers of the Bible, many of the laws found in Leviticus and Deuteronomy—naming certain foods and animals as abominations, prohibiting mixing of plants in the garden, mixing textiles at the loom, and animals at the plough—make sense as everyday reminders that God's people were to remain separate from their neighbors. Israel had been set apart, not to remain separate forever but so that eventually "the blessing given to Abraham might come to the Gentiles through Christ Jesus" (Gal 3:14).

The theme of separation begins in Genesis. "God separated the light from the darkness" (1:4), then "the waters from the waters" (v. 6), climaxing in the creation of "humankind" (v. 26) separated into "male and female"

(v. 27). Even the animals are named in separate categories: "the fish of the sea," "the birds of the air," and "every living thing that moves upon the earth" (v. 28).

While some Christians have argued that people whose bodies fall in between the "creation categories of male and female" are a result of the fall, they do not draw the same conclusion about frogs or penguins or lobsters–creatures that mix the categories outlined in Gen 1:28. Even if one argues that some of these hybrid creatures are identified as "unclean" early in Hebrew history, the remainder of the canon shifts the focus from ritual symbols of separation, such as food and circumcision, to faith and virtue, "circumcision of the heart" (Rom 2:12–29). Pointedly, the Jerusalem council would declare that people should not be judged by whether they had an operation on their genitals but by their relationship with God—a relationship based on grace through faith.

How then should Christians read the theological significance of Adam and Eve? Are they the *pattern* that God established for all people or the first *parents*? Are they God's *best* or the *beginning* of the story? Are they the exclusive *model* for all humans or the statistical *majority*?

Most humans fit into the categories of male or female fairly adequately, just as many animals fit into one of the three categories named in Genesis 1:28. Could the author of Genesis simply have been painting the story of creation in broad brushstrokes rather than listing an exhaustive inventory of all God's good creatures? The text does not indicate whether Adam and Eve represent the ideal *form* of masculinity and femininity to which all people must conform or the *fountainheads* of the beautiful variety of human beings who come after.

Theological anthropology begins in Genesis but the apostle John reminds us that true humanity is not to be found in some Edenic past but in God's eschatological future, a future breaking into the present but not yet fully realized. "Beloved, we are God's children now; what we will be has not yet been revealed. What we do know is this: when he is revealed, we will be like him, for we will see him as he is." (1 John 3:2–3). At the end of the story, Revelation 7 describes "a great multitude . . . , from every nation, tribe, people, and language" (v. 9). There was no diversity of nations, tribes, peoples, and languages in the garden of Eden, yet these differences are preserved at the End.

As God's revelation unfolds, more and more "outsiders" are brought in. Eunuchs and foreigners are promised a place in God's house *as they are*, not after restoration to an Edenic pattern (Isa 56:5). While this was a surprise to many followers of Jesus, it shouldn't have been. God had said long before, "My house shall be called a house of prayer for all peoples" (Isa 56:7).

NOT (YET) A HOUSE OF PRAYER FOR ALL PEOPLE: INTERSEX EXPERIENCES IN CHRISTIAN CHURCHES

> *It's more the church that I have trouble with, not necessarily God. When people go through cancer or their kids go through cancer, people are supportive; but with an intersex kid there is no support from the church. These kids are shamed. Families are asked to leave their churches. [Christians] treat us like lepers. The intersex community needs fellowship. I'm still a born-again believer but I struggle. I know God still loves me. It's just the church.*[7]

Intersex people should not be forced to alter their bodies or hide the truth about their sex traits in order to be welcomed into communities of faith. Sadly, there are churches where fellowship is revoked when the truth about intersex bodies comes into the light.

Anunnaki Ray Marquez was born with the intersex variation Congenital Adrenal Hyperplasia or CAH (i.e., XX chromosomes, ovaries and higher levels of testosterone than a typical woman) and assigned female at birth. From a young age, Anunnaki understood himself as a boy but he was given hormone suppressors to prevent natural masculinization, and prescribed estrogen to force an unnatural feminizing puberty. Anunnaki tried to live as a woman and married a man, but when years of feminizing medical protocols resulted in a wheelchair-bound body, he decided to stop all artificial medical intervention. As he progressed from wheelchair to a cane, to full health, the clergy at his Roman Catholic Church celebrated this miracle. When Anunnaki explained to the priest that feminizing medications were the cause of his ill health, that he was allowing his body to naturally masculinize, and choosing to live as a man, the priest excluded him and his husband from receiving communion. He and his family were devastated.[8]

Intersex activist and educator in Ireland and the UK, Sarah Haveron, explains "Sex characteristics can become apparent at any age. Sex at birth is not written in stone." Rather, it is "an imprecise approximation based on what sex genitalia was visible initially . . . Such choices are not infallible and later elucidation means the choice was incorrect."[9]

> *I was told that since my mother chose male for me and I married a woman, the sacrament of marriage dictated I shouldn't live as a woman. By stopping male sex affirming hormones, my body went into a natural female puberty, and my physical feminisation no*

---

7. Konrad Blair, personal email and phone interview (May 26, 2023).
8. Marquez in DeFranza et al., *Stories of Intersex and Faith*.
9. Sarah Haveron, personal email (May 28, 2023).

longer allowed me to live as a man or perform the responsibilities of a husband.

[I was told] same sex marriage was both not legal and against God's intentions. Due to my natural gender evolution they removed me from any further involvement, withheld the sacrament of communion, and insisted I could not receive Holy burial unless I continued as the sex assigned by my mother. I was told since I accepted my physical variations that I was already lost, in the grip of Satan. By refusing anointing by Elders and their prayers for my repentance, I was told that I was bound for Hell. Excommunication by my then denomination, left me feeling that God had created me as a failed person, incapable of living in faith.

Some of my first memories are as a tiny child having to be lifted onto a chair to sing 'Jesus Loves Me.' I went from being a lifelong Christian, a church committee member, and teacher of Youth Church to persona non grata; *from an involved church member, friend, and communicant to an unwelcome sinner, even though I was still a practicing Christian.*

Fortunately, before I lost all faith, I found a truly welcoming, loving church who accepted me as I am and allow[s] me the sacrament of communion. When a sex variation becomes apparent later in life, one that contradicts the sex assigned at birth, it isn't a sin to begin living in a more accurate sex.[10]

Anunnaki and his family also had to find a new church home. They found welcome with the Unitarian Universalists.[11] While their UU church was not familiar with intersex variations, they were committed to embracing all people, regardless of sex, gender, or sexuality. Anunnaki has since become an activist and educator in an effort to help the world make space for intersex people, as demonstrated in his TEDx talk, "Born Intersex: We Are Human."[12] Anunnaki is now a Master of Divinity student at a Unitarian seminary serving intersex people and their families as a chaplain as well as continuing his work as educator and activist. He wants all religions to embrace intersex people as they are.[13]

---

10. Sarah Haveron, personal email (May 28, 2023).
11. Marquez in DeFranza et al., *Stories of Intersex and Faith*.
12. Marquez, "Born Intersex."
13. https://anunnakiray.com.

WHAT DO INTERSEX CHRISTIANS WANT?

I want all surgeries on intersex babies and children stopped, right away. I want people to know that we know that we exist, that we are a part of this world.[14]

I am not a mistake.[15]

I am fearfully and wonderfully made.[16]

It's society that needs to be healed, not us.[17]

I want people to judge me by the good deeds I leave behind, not by my chromosomes, I'm much more than that![18]

Activists identify two main priorities 1) education that variations in sex characteristics are natural human physical phenomena, and 2) the cessation of medically unnecessary surgeries, forced hormone suppression and/or supplementation on infants and children. Intersex Christians want their faith communities to know about natural variations in sex traits so that intersex people are not treated as evil or sinful, or asked to pray away their physical differences; and so that parents do not agree to medical interventions out of religious obligation. They want to be judged by their character, by the fruits of the Spirit, by a life of virtue. Parents of intersex children want to feel safe leaving their children in the nursery, in Sunday School classes, in youth groups, knowing they will be loved and cared for like any other child. Jen and David Brukiewa are conservative Christian parents of several intersex children. Jen says, "I want the church to talk about these things so that [for] people like my Megan it won't be so scary." They want Christians to become more comfortable not knowing all the answers, "God wants to wrestle with us in areas that are hard."[19]

THE RAINBOW-COLORED ELEPHANT IN THE ROOM

The hardest issue for Christians is the connection between intersex and LGBTQ. For many, the concept of homosexuality begins to fray in the face

---

14. Adams in DeFranza et al., *Stories of Intersex and Faith*.
15. Bruikiewa in DeFranza et al., *Stories of Intersex and Faith*.
16. Sarah Beck, personal email (May 26, 2023).
17. Simon in DeFranza et al., *Stories of Intersex and Faith*.
18. "Jorge," in DeFranza et al., *Stories of Intersex and Faith*.
19. "Beginning with Bodies and Better Dialogue" in DeFranza, *Fearfully and Wonderfully Made*.

of the complexity of intersex bodies. Advocates for LGBTQ people often use the facts of intersex traits to prove that sex and gender are a spectrum. (Unfortunately, this has often been done without attention to the unique concerns of intersex people for human rights protections.) For many Christians the conversation is more complicated.

Slightly more than half (52 percent) of intersex people identify as non-heterosexual.[20] This percentage is higher than the general population (7.2 percent) and points to significant biological influence on sexual orientation and gender identity.[21] Most intersex people identify as men or women. At the same time, approximately half of all intersex people do not want to be associated with LGBTQ people. Some intersex Christians are very conservative about sexual ethics, marriage between one man and one woman, and disapprove of transgender people.

A growing number are identifying as non-binary because that language is more accurate than male or female. A minority of intersex people transition from the sex they appeared to be at birth. Some of these identify as intersex as well as transgender; while others only identify as intersex.

Some conservative Christian leaders have said that they make exceptions for intersex people who transition from the sex they were assigned at birth; but in practice, when intersex people who cannot pass as clearly male or female show up at church, they are usually treated with suspicion. No one should have to present a doctor's note to be allowed fellowship, communion, or church membership; yet, this is exactly what some intersex people have been asked to provide.

Dawn-Mark Bacon Johnson was born intersex, also with CAH. His birth certificate originally indicated a male named Mark but was "corrected" to "Dawn" and "female" at 8 months when he experienced his first of many surgeries to "reshape" his genitals to make them appear more feminine. Raised as a girl, Dawn-Mark recalls a life of gender dysphoria, shame, silence, multiple painful surgeries, and sexual pain. Dawn-Mark recalls always being sexually attracted to women but knew the Missouri-Synod Lutheran Church did not approve of same-sex relationships. When he was finally able to access his original birth certificate at age 50, he decided to begin the process of transitioning to living as a man, eventually electing medical procedures to alter his sex traits to better align with his sense of self. Dawn-Mark has found a spiritual home in the Evangelical Lutheran Church of America (ELCA), particularly in ELCA churches which have implemented their LGBTQ inclusive curriculum "Reconciling in Christ" (RIC). He continues to

20. Jones et al., *Intersex*, 177.
21. Jones, "U.S. LGBT Identification Steady at 7.2%."

serve his church and educate Christians, doctors, and the general public about the urgent need to stop genital surgeries on children. "If there was no God, I would not be here. I would not have survived without the strength my faith has given me. I feel compelled to believe. I also know that while I'm here, I have purpose. I'm glad that I've been given gifts."[22]

INTERSEX THEOLOGICAL INTERPRETATION

Understanding the presence of non-binary bodies in the Bible and Christian history shows that there is nothing in Scripture or Tradition that justifies medically unnecessary procedures to force naturally non-binary bodies into male or female forms without the consent of the individual. Given the challenges facing intersex people to secure their human rights, to find informed medical care and safe Christian communities, it should come as no surprise that there is not a vast body of intersex theological interpretation. In truth, this chapter is a prelude to intersex interpretation—an introduction into the realities of intersex life, Scriptural justification of the rights of intersex people to exist as they are without forced medicalization, and a call to create safer, more welcoming churches.

As an endosex theologian (someone without intersex traits), I work to raise up the voices of intersex people and the theological reflections of intersex Christians. My own theological conclusions can be found in various publications, especially in *Sex Difference in Christian Theology: Male, Female and Intersex in the Image of God*. Those in search of postconservative theology, biblical commentary, and preaching from an intersex person's perspective would do well to begin with the work of Donovan Ackley III, who taught theology for fifteen years at a conservative Christian university until forced to resign in 2013 after coming out as transgender. As a child and teenager, Donovan had been prescribed hormone blockers and estrogen to force his body into an unnatural female form. Over time, these medical interventions caused his physical and mental health to deteriorate. A few years after losing his faculty position, a medical exam confirmed he is intersex. Reflecting on the parable of the Lost Sheep, Dr. Ackley observes how the Good Shepherd does not keep the lost sheep separate from the flock in order to comfort it or keep it safe; rather, He returns the one to the ninety-nine. "This one percent of us is a game changer for the church. It is really important that we get carried back by our Shepherd to the rest of the flock, more for them than for us."[23]

---

22. Dawn-Mark Bacon Johnson, phone interview (May 16, 2023).
23. "Light for Our Feet," in DeFranza, *Fearfully and Wonderfully Made*.

BIBLIOGRAPHY

Ackley, Donovan, III. *Queer Preaching and Exegesis for Revolution and Resistance: Collected Sermons, Bible Commentaries, and Liturgies of Donovan Ackley, III, PhD.* Self-published, 2021.

———. *Sex and Sacrament: A Queer Liberation Theology of Prayer and Worship.* Queer Liberation Theology & Praxis. Self-published, 2021.

Budwey, Stephanie. *Religion and Intersex: Perspectives from Science, Law, Culture, and Theology.* New York: Routledge, 2022.

Cornwall, Susannah, ed. *Intersex, Theology, and the Bible: Troubling Bodies in Church Text and Society.* New York: Palgrave MacMillan, 2015.

Cornwall, Susannah. *Sex and Uncertainty in the Body of Christ: Intersex Conditions and Christian Theology.* London: Equinox, 2010.

DeFranza, Megan K., dir. *Fearfully and Wonderfully Made: Scripture and the New Science of Gender.* Video curriculum. Beverly, MA: Van Ness Creative, 2021.

DeFranza, Megan K. *Sex Difference in Christian Theology: Male, Female and Intersex in the Image of God.* Grand Rapids: Eerdmans, 2015.

DeFranza, Megan K., et al., dirs. *Stories of Intersex and Faith.* Documentary. Beverly, MA: Van Ness Creative, 2018.

Jones, Jeffrey M. "U.S. LGBT Identification Steady at 7.2%." February 22, 2023. https://news.gallup.com/poll/470708/lgbt-identification-steady.aspx.

Jones, Tiffany, et al. *Intersex: Stories and Statistics from Australia.* Cambridge: Open Book, 2016.

Marquez, Anunnaki Ray. "Born Intersex: We Are Human!" https://www.youtube.com/watch?v=WpPTf-oo0b0.

Ringrose, Kathryn M. *The Perfect Servant: Eunuchs and the Social Construction of Gender in Byzantium.* Chicago: University of Chicago, 2007.

Simon, Lianne. *Confessions of a Teenage Hermaphrodite.* Faie Miss, 2012.

United Nations, Office of the High Commissioner. "Fact Sheet: Intersex." 2017. https://unfe.org/system/unfe-65-Intersex_Factsheet_ENGLISH.pdf

SECTION 4

Scripture and Interpretation

Chapter 34
Deconstruction Hermeneutics and the Old Testament
PETER ENNS

WHAT IS DECONSTRUCTION AND WHY DOES IT HAPPEN?

Few people live out their lives never changing what they think. Mercifully, our understanding of the world around us will morph and adjust over time. Who at sixty years of age thinks as they did at forty, let alone twenty? Who would want to? I think this innocent observation is true and requires little defense. But why is this the case? Why don't we just stay as we are? Because, as our knowledge of our world and our place in it grows, we eventually see the inadequacies of the thinking patterns that emerged before such knowledge. This process happens, I would surmise, in any area of our lives, not the least of which are the life of faith and our beliefs about God, and (for Christians) of Christ, the Christian Bible, and other theological matters. As life becomes less tidy and scripted with age and experience, we eventually see where our inherited beliefs are not up to the task of dealing with our growing consciousness of the world around us. Does God, for example, really answer prayers if we keep at it long enough? Does God truly reward the righteous? Children are often taught this very lesson, but when their cognitive development and experiences mature, they see that such a simple, transactional model of faith, though certainly present in Scripture, spits and sputters.

This pattern of being confronted in due time by the inadequacies of our belief systems is often called "deconstruction," a term that has proven itself to be useful, even if I want to quibble a bit with how that word tends to be used. Often when I hear someone say they are deconstructing their faith, they mean that they are in a process of *examining closely* what they believe and voting thumbs up or thumbs down. This conventional understanding of the term is fine as far as it goes, but it misses the deeper meaning and significance of the term. Deconstruction, in its more philosophical usage, describes the step prior to the conscious act of analysis, namely *becoming aware* that one's thinking patterns are becoming inadequate. It is that initial moment of insight where one begins to sense, often reluctantly, that nagging feeling that something isn't right—what I like to call "uh oh moments."[1]

To give a brief example, one such moment for me was when I truly began thinking about the nature of the cosmos as we understand it today—an essentially limitless expanse, that we are told may only be one universe among an infinite number. When I was first confronted by this scientific model of the universe, I began to sense that my conventional, inherited view of God—as a "being" who is "up there," "looking down" on us, and who occasionally makes cameo appearances—could not be squared with the reality of the multiverse. What sense does it make to think of God as "up" when there *is* no "up?" Is the eternal Creator "located" somewhere in the cosmos? If so, where? Such questions were driven by a model of the universe that is no longer workable.

Getting to my main point, I did not ask for the universe to lay waste to my views of God; it just did. I did nothing to instigate this process. I simply *became aware* of the disconnection between my understanding of God and the world around me, and as a result my system of thinking proved to be inadequate. Such information led to an internal upheaval, which led not to a quickly constructed alternative answer, but to that nagging sense that something is wrong with how I see God and bigger change is needed. *That*, I would argue, is where the term deconstruction is rightly at home. Deconstruction is a sudden awareness. The process of beginning to think through to do with that awareness—what to believe and not believe—is a conscious act that follows upon deconstruction and is called "reconstruction." Deconstruction is the earthquake that comes unexpectedly and topples the home. Reconstruction is what one does to rebuild once the shock has worn off and it is time to continue forward.

To put this another way, and with respect to postconservative theological interpretation, deconstruction is about the exposing of inadequacies of our conceptions of God. And all our conceptions of God are *necessarily open to being exposed,* since all of our conceptions of God are by definition incomplete, limited by our limited humanity. Acknowledging as much has

---

1. I ran a blog series in 2014 on "uh oh" moments some scholars have experienced. The first post in that series can be accessed here: https://thebiblefornormalpeople.com/aha-moments-biblical-scholars-tell-their-stories-1-me/.

a huge implication: already baked into our mental structures are the very seeds of the deconstruction of those structures. John Caputo sums it up succinctly: "Deconstruction is organized around the idea that things contain a kind of uncontainable truth, that they contain what they cannot contain. Nobody has to come along and 'deconstruct' things. Things are auto-deconstructed by the tendencies of their own inner truth."[2]

I believe that all conceptions of God are primed to be "auto-deconstructed." What Caputo describes holds, I believe, for any thoughts of God—including those articulated by the biblical writers. They all spoke to their sense of truth, but their very words "contain what they cannot contain." Baked into Scripture are the very ingredients that invite its own deconstruction, especially given the subject nature of Scripture: the infinite Creator, whose ways are not our ways, and whose thoughts are not our thoughts.

THE HEBREW BIBLE BEARS WITNESS TO A PROCESS OF DECONSTRUCTION

On one level, for many, simply reading the Hebrew Bible (Old Testament) is an entry point to deconstruction, because it seems particularly adept at creating cognitive dissonance. How many faithful Bible readers have begun questioning the very foundation of their faith when first confronting, for example, the violent manner in which Israel's God is depicted at regular intervals in the Hebrew Bible? Who has not wondered what relevance the Hebrew Bible's ancient legal codes, pro-kingship propaganda, and anti-Assyrian rhetoric has for people of faith today? Who has not squirmed at the prospect of trying to square Genesis 1–3 with cosmology or evolution?

I believe that Scripture itself—including the New Testament[3]—creates challenges to faith, because it seems reluctant to make peace with the rather sanitized and scripted formulations of God our theological systems give quarter to. The disconnection between the contexts of ancient Scripture and contemporary life is felt, I dare say, by anyone who has taken seriously the study of Scripture while also remaining awake to the world around them.[4]

As important as this phenomenon has been for understanding contemporary journeys of faith, this essay will not focus on the Hebrew Bible

---

2. Caputo, *What Would Jesus Deconstruct?*, 29.

3. I am thinking here primarily or the varied, and often irreconcilable, depictions of Jesus in the four Gospels, and the rather clear disagreement concerning the role of works in James vis-à-vis Paul (especially in Galatians).

4. A foundational discussion of this hermeneutical challenge of merging the present and ancient contexts is Gadamer, *Truth and Method*.

and deconstruction in that sense. Rather, I will focus on a more fundamental matter, namely: *the manner in which the Hebrew Bible itself bears witness to the deconstructive process*. To put it that way simply amounts to addressing the *diversity* of viewpoints one finds in the Hebrew Bible on many topics, not the least of which is how God is portrayed.[5]

Having said that, and before we move on to considering some examples, I would like to clarify my intention. I am not claiming to have cracked the code of the Hebrew Bible by pointing out its inner-deconstructive properties. I believe the Hebrew Bible in particular, and the Christian Bible as a whole, are open to various models by which we can draw together it's disparate parts. But this essay nevertheless takes as its point of departure *the notion that the passage of time and the changing circumstances of the various writers of the Hebrew Bible do indeed bear witness to the inner-deconstructive dynamic of the Hebrew Bible in two senses*: (1) It is certainly the case that later writers engage earlier ones and lay out competing visions for God; (2) Theological diversity can also be a product not of consciously competing points of view over time, but simply differing traditions that may have no connection with each other whatsoever.

I have generally found it very difficult to tease out the differences between these two perspectives. Whether one writer is consciously engaging another is not often self-evident, but for our purposes we do not need to settle the matter. As much as I hold the historical study of Scripture in high regard, I also recognize its canonical structure—whether one is considering the Jewish or (various) Christian canons. Theologically, I regard the diverse voices of Scripture, which the ancient Jewish scribes took great care to include in the canonical process, as an irrevocable and constructive property of Scripture, one that has great theological value for contemporary readers of the Bible. To put it another way, both the Bible's historical roots and its very canonical structure model for contemporary readers the normalcy of the deconstructive process. At least, that is my point of view, due in no small part to my watching Scripture's behavior, some examples of which are the following.

WHAT DOES GOD THINK ABOUT HEBREWS HAVING HEBREW SLAVES?

In Exod 21:2–11, God reveals to Moses on Mt. Sinai that a Hebrew male who is enslaved to a fellow Hebrew has the right to be granted his freedom after six years of service, should he want it. The fate of the female Hebrew

---

5. I look at this in more detail in *The Bible Tells Me So* and *How the Bible* Actually *Works*.

slave, however, depends on her marital status at the time her servitude began. If she is married she will accompany her freed husband. If she came in single, she remains the owner's property. Verse 7 adds that a daughter who is sold into slavery by her father "shall not go out as the male slaves do."

Though presented to the reader as a reiteration of the law given forty years earlier to Moses from Yahweh, the Hebrew slave law in Deut 15:12–18 sounds a very different note. "If a member of your community, *whether a Hebrew man or a Hebrew woman*, is sold to you and works for you six years, in the seventh year you shall set that person free" (Deut 15:12). Then, after laying out the details of the process for the release of male slaves, the writer adds, "You shall do the same with regard to your female slaves" (v. 17). Females slaves are allowed to elect freedom just as men are, without their fate being tied to theirs.

Leviticus 25:39–43 claims yet another divine revelation from Sinai. This author mentions specifically Hebrews who sell themselves to a fellow Hebrew out of financial need, and makes clear that they are not to be considered slaves at all but "hired or bound laborers" bound to the owner until the year of jubilee, at which time they will be set free from their obligation (v. 40). It seems that women are included along with men as well as their children. The rationale given for not enslaving fellow Hebrews (that is, not buying a Hebrew slave from someone) is that they too were delivered from Egyptian servitude.

I am not suggesting that these three laws about Hebrew slaves can be easily laid out chronologically from most restrictive to least restrictive. I do, however, find it reasonable to say that Deuteronomy and Leviticus are reacting to the law in Exodus, even if indirectly, though I do not think Leviticus is necessarily a later revision of Deuteronomy. The two could just as easily be seen as see as two distinct yet coterminous legal traditions.[6] The point, however, remains the same. Within the legal sections of the Torah, all of which are purported to be the product of the same divine revelatory act, we see different ways of conceiving of the divine will. The conventional explanation, which I find compelling, is that these laws differ because they arose at different times and under different circumstances. Further, the wording of Deuteronomy in particular suggests strongly that this writer disagreed with the law in the Exodus tradition. I do not hesitate to say that Deuteronomy is more socially enlightened than Exodus, and perhaps Leviticus more so than either.

To put it another way, Deuteronomy's understanding of the revealed divine will differ from that of the writer of Exodus because he found that

---

6. See Kugel, *How to Read the Bible*, 296–300.

earlier law to provide an inadequate understanding of God for his time.[7] Within his own religious tradition, a view of God had been espoused that did not sit well with him in his time and place. The actual version of the law we find in Deuteronomy is the act of reconstruction motivated by the writer's deconstructive insight.

WAS JEHU'S COUP DIVINELY APPROVED?

During the period of the divided monarchy, Jehu, the commander of the Israelite (northern) army, usurped the throne by ridding the nation of the corrupt house of Omri, a dynasty that lasted thirty-three years and included the infamous King Ahab. Jehu's coup began by assassinating Joram, the last of the Omride kings. He then killed Ahaziah, a southern (Judahite) king who posed a threat to Jehu, because he was a close relative of Joram. Jehu next authorized the slaughter of the seventy sons of Ahab and ordered that their heads be brought to him in Jezreel. To seal the deal, Jehu killed all who remained from the house of Ahab, including "all his leaders, close friends, and priests until he left him no survivors" (2 Kgs 10:11), as well as all the priests of Baal (vv. 18–27). For his efforts, the Deuteronomistic historian praises Jehu for being aligned with the divine will: "The LORD said to Jehu, 'Because you have done well in carrying out what I consider right, and in accordance with all that was in my heart have dealt with the house of Ahab, your sons of the fourth generation shall sit on the throne of Israel'" (2 Kgs 10:30). It seems clear enough that the LORD approved greatly of Jehu's bloody coup.

Moving to the book of Hosea, we find quite a different evaluation of Jehu's act. After taking for himself a "wife of whoredom" with whom he is to have "children of whoredom," by God's command, Homer's wife Gomer bears him a son: "And the LORD said to him, 'Name him Jezreel; for in a little while I will punish the house of Jehu for the blood of Jezreel, and I will put an end to the kingdom of the house of Israel. On that day I will break the bow of Israel in the valley of Jezreel'" (Hos 1:4–5).

Hosea lived roughly 100 years after the time of Jehu, and was an active prophet long enough to see the end of Jehu's dynasty. And not a minute too soon, as far as Hosea was concerned. Rather than be praised for his faithfulness to God for exterminating the previous dynasty, Hosea predicts

---

7. Benjamin D. Sommer explains these variations in the biblical law codes as reflecting the notion of "participatory revelation," meaning, the divine revelation at Mt. Sinai was not in and of itself clear but needed to be interpreted by the Israelite community (*Revelation and Authority*). The three communities that gave us these three takes on Hebrew slave laws were each interpreting the divine revelation for their time and place, and in that sense were participating in the revelation of God.

the end of Jehu's dynasty *for that very same act*. The Deuteronomistic Historian is evaluating Jehu's coup against the backdrop of the main tenets of Deuteronomistic theology, in this case the disastrous religious influence of Jezebel, who massacred the LORD's prophets (1 Kgs 18:4). The will of God in this regard is clear:

> Thus says the LORD the God of Israel: I anoint you [Jehu] king over the people of the LORD, over Israel. You shall strike down the house of your master Ahab, so that I may avenge on Jezebel the blood of my servants the prophets, and the blood of all the servants of the LORD. For the whole house of Ahab shall perish; I will cut off from Ahab every male, bond or free, in Israel. I will make the house of Ahab like the house of Jeroboam son of Nebat, and like the house of Baasha son of Ahijah. The dogs shall eat Jezebel in the territory of Jezreel, and no one shall bury her. (2 Kgs 9:7–10)

Hosea, however, understands Jehu's coup not as a fulfillment of the divine will but as an egregious act of bloodshed that is deserving of divine retribution. Hosea's condemnation of Jehu's coup may also have had something to do with his disapproval of the alliances the house of Jehu formed with Assyria and Egypt (see Hos 12:1 and 14:1–4). The eighth-century BCE prophets in general were strongly disapproving of Judahite kings making political alliances, especially with the Assyrian war machine, rather than maintaining fidelity to the covenant with God.[8]

The treatment of Jehu's coup in 2 Kings and Hosea is a particularly clear example of different theological perspectives in the Hebrew Bible. It may be that one is responding to the other, though I am not confident that one can arrive at a clear conclusion. On the one hand, the events surrounding Jehu's coup in 2 Kings predate Hosea's evaluation by 100 years, so one might be tempted to conclude that Hosea is reacting to the Deuteronomistic historian. On the other hand, the Deuteronomistic history was written probably no earlier than the seventh century BCE and then edited well into the sixth and perhaps fifth centuries—in other words, after Hosea's time. To add to the ambiguity, few would argue that Hosea was written wholly in real time in the late eighth century BCE but has itself a subsequent history of redaction. Indeed, historically speaking, there may be no direct relationship

---

8. The book of Deuteronomy, which forms the theological basis for the Deuteronomistic History, is itself a lengthy admonition to its seventh-century BCE readers to trust their alliance with Yahweh rather than making an alliance with Assyria. The book's structure strongly resembles seventh-century Assyrian Suzerain-Vassal treaties, that is, treaties between the conquering Assyrians and those conquered by them.

between these two texts at all. They may simply be two independent traditions of Jehu's coup.

My point, however, is that the canonical placing of these stories in a "literary chronology" (rather than an actual historical chronology) invites readers to see Hosea as a reaction to 2 Kings. Whether that is historically true is irrelevant. The positive evaluation of Jehu in 2 Kings is nevertheless unacceptable to the writer of Hosea. Why, exactly, is a matter of debate, but Hosea could not go where Jehu led.

WHAT KIND OF KING WAS MANASSEH?

Manasseh was king of Judah for forty-five years (687–642), beginning at the tender age of twelve. According to the Deuteronomistic historian, Manasseh was the most abysmally religiously corrupt of any king, north or south (2 Kgs 21:1–18). The list of Manasseh's offenses in verses 2–7 reads like a checklist of standard Deuteronomistic false worship practices; Manasseh rebuilt high places and instituted other Canaanite religious practices, not the least of which was child sacrifice. In fact, Manasseh's reign was so problematic that it is cited as the cause for the exile of Judah to Babylon in 586 BCE nearly 100 years after his death (see vv. 12–15). Even the sweeping, godly, and praiseworthy reforms of his grandson Josiah (reigned 640–609; see 2 Kgs 22–23), which righteously and systematically dismantled all of Manasseh's corruptions, were not enough to deter God from punishing Judah for Manasseh's acts. What Manasseh did could only be redeemed by punishing the nation as a whole.

The depiction of Manasseh's reign in 2 Chr 33:1–20 shares with 2 Kings 21 the condemnation of Manasseh's acts, but it also differs in one vital aspect. Rather than a wholesale repudiation of the evil Manasseh committed, the Chronicler adds a scene of Manasseh's personal redemption, which, at least in my opinion, has little historical value; it shows us more of the author's theology than it does of history.

The scene added by the Chronicler is of Manasseh's prayerful repentance for his sins, which was prompted when the Assyrians took him captive and brought him to Babylon. Alone with his thoughts, Manasseh repented of his many sins and God responded by bringing him back to Jerusalem and restoring him as king. As I mentioned, Manasseh's repentance and restoration to his throne are of highly questionable historical value. An Assyrian invasion of Judah in the seventh century would certainly be known to us by other sources, but it is not. Further, it is worth pondering why the King of Assyria (unnamed) would exile anyone to Babylon in the first place.

These historical incongruities are indications that something other than historical accuracy is the writer's intention. The repentance and restoration of Manasseh illustrates a central theological motif in Chronicles of "immediate retribution": God treats all as they deserve. The one who sins is punished. The one who repents is rewarded. We do not suffer from the sins of others nor benefit from their obedience. And the fact that Manasseh is "exiled" to Babylon is central to the Chronicler's rewriting of Manasseh's reign. Such a historical faux pas is a clue: Manasseh is a stand-in for what had happened to Judah as a whole: they were taken captive to Babylon but returned when God's term of punishment had been completed. The Chronicler's account of Manasseh isn't so much about Manasseh-in-history as it is about using Judah's worst king as a model of repentance for readers in his own day. After all, if even Manasseh can gain God's favor by repenting, there is no reason to think that God will not act accordingly with anyone else.

Working this out is a major concern of 1 and 2 Chronicles. The Deuteronomistic historian ruthlessly condemns Manasseh because the question he is addressing is the cause of the exile. The Chronicler, living centuries later, is not interested in explaining the exile, but of giving encouragement to his readers that they are not going to continue bearing the burden of their ancestors' sins, and thus give up altogether. The time and circumstances of the Chronicler require a rewriting of the story of Manasseh in order to make their sacred stories speak to their circumstances. The older story of Manasseh will not do. A god who punishes sixth-century Judahites for something a seventh-century king did is denounced by the Chronicler, and he adapts the story of Manasseh to that end.

This example clearly concerns a later author specifically engaging an earlier tradition and adapting it for a circumstance that the Deuteronomistic historian did not anticipate, nor should he be expected to. The recognition on the part of the writer (and his community) that the inherited portrait of God will not do is the moment of deconstruction. His re-presentation of God is his act of reconstruction.

WHAT DOES GOD THINK OF ASSYRIANS?

The Neo-Assyrian empire[9] was a persistently malevolent force in Israel's history by the middle of the ninth century BCE until their downfall at the hands of the Babylonians in the late seventh century: the capital Nineveh

---

9. The Assyrian empire that reigned during the period of Israel's monarchy is actually the fourth phase of Assyrian civilization, the first phase having begun around 2600 BCE. This neo-Assyrian empire was the most expansive and powerful of them all, and dominated the Fertile Crescent.

was sacked in 612, the last Assyrian king was ousted in 609, and the remaining vestige of an army was finally crushed in 605 at the Battle of Carchemish.

We see the Assyrian presence in Israel's affairs already during the reign of Jehu, who paid homage to the Assyrian kind Shalmaneser the III in 841 BCE, a scene depicted on the Black Obelisk monument. The height of Assyrian dominance in Israel began with the aggressive expansions of Tiglath-Pileser III in 745 BCE and continued through to the fall of the Samaria, the capital of the northern kingdom of Israel, in 722 BCE under Sargon II. Later followed the unsuccessful attempt by Sennacherib to raze Jerusalem during the reign of Hezekiah in 701 BCE. For the remainder of the seventh century, the Assyrians remained a lurking, if also somewhat less aggressive, presence until their aforementioned defeat at the hands of the Babylonians.

We should not pass over the fact that the Assyrians, by sacking the northern capital of Samaria, were responsible for seizing most of the land the Israelites believed was theirs by divine right since the days of Abraham (Gen 12:1–3). And after the tragedy of 722 BCE, the southern kingdom of Judah was understandable nervous about an Assyrian attack. One persistent temptation recorded in the prophetic literature was for Judahite kings to make alliances with Assyria in order to secure their own well-being, despite prophetic warnings that their God alone is their sovereign.

With the fall of Nineveh in 612 BCE, the nation of Judah and of the surrounding nations, who had also felt the brunt of Assyrian aggression, were understandably relieved. The book of Nahum minces no words that the fall of Nineveh was an act of divine wrath, payback for Assyria's largely unchecked history of wickedness, bloodshed, and plundering.

> I am against you,
>   says the LORD of hosts,
>   and will lift up your skirts over your face;
> and I will let nations look on your nakedness
>   and kingdoms on your shame.
> I will throw filth at you
>   and treat you with contempt,
>   and make you a spectacle.
> Then all who see you will shrink from you and say,
> "Nineveh is devastated; who will bemoan her?"
>   Where shall I seek comforters for you? (Nah 3:5–7)

The relentless negative assessment of Assyria on the part of the biblical writers is well-justified and unanimous—with one exception. The book of Jonah is much more than a tale of the great fish that swallows a reluctant prophet. It is actually a story that undermines Israel's longstanding—dare I say, justified—hatred of the Assyrians. The same God who has always been against the Assyrians is now telling Jonah to offer the Ninevites a chance to repent. Jonah famously wants none of this, since he knows God is merciful and compassionate, which is the last thing any true child of Abraham would want to see accorded to their archenemy. Hence, Jonah scurries away, finds himself on a boat heading in the opposite direction, and is tossed overboard (at his own suggestion), lest the ship be lost to a raging storm caused by God to get Jonah's attention. After the fish vomits Jonah up onto the shore, Jonah reluctantly delivers half-heartedly an uninspiring message of repentance: "Forty more days, and Nineveh shall be overthrown" (Jonah 3:4). Despite his attempts to sabotage God's desire that Nineveh be saved, the Ninevites do indeed repent—from the king on down to the animals—and so God relented from bringing destruction upon them. This is all too much for Jonah to bear. He goes off sulking, wishing he were dead (4:3).

The story of the reluctant prophet Jonah is about God's unexpected—even obscene—compassion on Israel's ancient enemies. It is not a historical account, since the Assyrian war machine certainly never turned to the worship of Israel's God, not do fish swallow humans who survive for three days under water. The story of Jonah, rather, is an object lesson about Israel's need to adjust its understanding of God. God now is believed to have compassion on a nation that was responsible for relocating, assimilating, and making disappear a majority segment of the nation of Israel (not to mention harassing the southern nation for a few decades thereafter). Our author poses not a God of uncompromising harsh judgment for Israel's enemy. Rather, in his fictional story, he is posing a question: What if God is not our private deity who aims to wipe out our enemies? What if God's heart has room for everyone, even the people we hate most?

This adjustment didn't come out of the blue. It grew out of an experience, namely the sixth-century Babylonian exile. Most scholars suggest that the author of Jonah wrote in the wake of this national tragedy. One might easily imagine our author living in exile, side-by-side with the enemy, and coming to see the Babylonians as people, rather than simply objects of God's wrath. However despised the impersonal Babylonian war machine might have been, the every-day Babylonians, whom the captives got to know as neighbors, were another matter. They were people, too, who were Babylonians by birth, not choice, and where just trying to farm, tend their livestock, raise their families, and survive. We can well imagine ancient Judahites asking, "Are these Babylonians really any different from us? Maybe—dare we hope—God cares about them just as God cares about us?" The author of Jonah used Israel's long-gone Assyrian enemies to make his rhetorical point about their present enemies.

A common story I have heard in my life, and one that I have experienced myself, is that familiarity with the "other" humanizes them and makes demonizing them much more difficult, even absurd. To rephrase the message of Jonah, it is much more than, "We must love our enemies," but "*God loves our enemies* and therefore so should we" (a thought clearly echoed in Matt 5:43–48). Jonah is a dramatic reframing of the very nature of God, and that reframing was born out of the experience of exile. For Jonah, the God portrayed in Nahum and elsewhere in the Hebrew Bible will no longer do.

HOW DOES GOD FEEL ABOUT INTERGENERATIONAL PUNISHMENT AND REWARD?

The prophet Ezekiel lived at the time of the Babylonian Exile. A prophet's job was to interpret the events of the day from God's point of view—in Ezekiel's case, to proclaim (among other things) that the sack of Jerusalem and the exile were no accident of history, but God's punishment for generations of corruption, namely worshiping false gods.

Having said that, Ezekiel chapter 18 raises a legitimate complaint. Apparently, a saying was making the rounds at the time: *The parents have eaten sour grapes, and the children's teeth are set on edge* (verse 2). As the following verses make clear, this saying is a complaint: "Why are children exiled in Babylonian for what their parents did? If the parents were the ones who ate the sour grapes, why should the children's teeth be "on edge"? One can easily imagine that some of the deported Judahites, who were perhaps too young to have actually done anything all that wrong, or who were born in captivity, might have an issue for being punished for something they didn't do.

Ezekiel's answer—better, God's answer spoken through Ezekiel—is: "As I live, says the LORD God, this proverb shall no more be used by you in Israel. Know that all lives are mine; the life of the parent as well as the life of the child is mine; it is only the person who sins that shall die" (Ezek 18:3–4). Ezekiel then proceeds to lay out various scenarios to make it absolutely clear what God means. God will bless a righteous and lawful man, but if his son is wicked, that son will be treated as he deserves: he can't appeal to his father's reputation. Likewise, if the son is righteous and does not follow in his father's wicked footsteps, he will not bear his father's punishment. Everyone is treated by God as they deserve, on the basis of their actions.

Of course, all this makes perfect sense, but Ezekiel's prophecy, his word from the LORD, collides with an earlier word from the same LORD—the Second Commandment against false worship (the making of idols). In Exod 20:4–6 (and the later version in Deut 5:8–10), false worship merited a punishment extending *three or four generations.* The blessings for obedience will linger for *a thousand generations*. This bit of numerical hyperbole is common in Scripture, but the point remains: according to Torah, when it comes to worshiping God, *obedience and disobedience have multigenerational effects*.

We should keep in mind that the sin that resulted in Judah's exile was not some general offense, but the very same topic that occupies the Second Commandment: false worship. I find it hard to miss the implication of Ezekiel's words: God clearly said one thing to Moses in the Second Commandment at the beginning of Israel's journey, and then God clearly says something different through Ezekiel centuries later.

That *both* Exodus and Ezekiel claim to be relaying God's speech indicates either that God is being portrayed here as having a change of heart, which certainly has precedent in the Hebrew Bible (see for example Gen 6:5–8), or that these texts reflect different views of God at two different moments in Israel's story. I am not convinced these are necessarily mutually exclusive options, though laying out the reasoning would take us far afield. I would simply suggest that Ezekiel is at the very least distancing himself from a commonly known, older tradition that happens to be in Exodus. The circumstances of Ezekiel's day required a different "word from the LORD" than what had been in effect earlier.

God is never fully captured by our perceptions. As people continue to live and breathe and experience life, how they see God changes, too. In Ezekiel's day, the God presented in the older tradition cannot bear the weight of the needs of the exilic community.

CONCLUSION

Deconstruction, as I have defined it, is an inevitable process when it comes to any human articulation of God, including the biblical writers. The Creator will always be beyond human limitations to comprehend and articulate. This inevitable process is evinced in the Hebrew Bible itself, a collection of writings that span—in common estimation—roughly a millennium.[10] As Israel's journey march on over that time, her understanding of God deconstructed and reconstructed to account for Israel's lived experience.

---

10. The earliest writings in the Hebrew Bible are estimated on linguistic grounds to arise from roughly the twelfth century BCE and include the poems Genesis 49, Exodus 15, and Judges 5. Even though it contains older material, the youngest book of the Hebrew Bible, Daniel, was written no earlier than the end of the reign of the Seleucid emperor Antiochus IV Epiphanies in 164 BCE.

BIBLIOGRAPHY

Brueggemann, Walter. *Texts Under Negotiation: The Bible and Postmodern Imagination*. Minneapolis: Fortress, 1993.

Caputo, John D. *What Would Jesus Deconstruct: The Good News of Postmodernism for the Church*. Grand Rapids: Baker, 2007.

Enns, Peter. *The Bible Tells Me So: Why Defending the Bible Has Made Us Unable to Read It*. San Francisco: HarperOne, 2014.

———. *How the Bible Actually Works: In Which I Explain How an Ancient, Ambiguous, and Diverse Book Leads Us to Wisdom Rather Than Answers—and Why That's Great News*. San Francisco: HarperOne, 2019.

Gadamer, Hans-Georg. *Truth and Method*. 2nd rev. ed. Pearl River, NY: Crossroad, 1991.

Hanson, Paul. *Dynamic Transcendence: The Correlation of Confessional Heritage and Contemporary Experience in a Biblical Model of Divine Activity*. Minneapolis: Fortress, 1978.

Kugel, James L. *How to Read the Bible: A Guide to Scripture Then and Now*. New York: Simon and Schuster, 2008.

Sommer, Benjamin D. *Revelation and Authority: Sinai in Jewish Scripture and Tradition*. New Haven, CT: Yale University Press, 2015.

Williams, Rowan. "The Bible." In *Being Christian: Baptism, Bible, Eucharist, Prayer*, 21–40. Grand Rapids: Eerdmans, 2014.

Chapter 35

Deconstruction Hermeneutics and the New Testament

CHRIS TILLING

This chapter title, "deconstruction and the New Testament," is rather broad and suggestive of several different possible trajectories. As A. K. M. Adam astutely pointed out many years ago, deconstruction "is not one thing,"[1] which makes talking about it in relation to another subject more challenging. As we shall see, however, this offers a chance for creative rethinking of broader New Testament related interpretative concerns that speak directly into the postconservative spirit of this volume. In what follows, I will outline the ways in which "deconstruction" has been understood and related to New Testament scholarship. But I will capitalize on the fact that "deconstruction" has come to mean something different in contemporary Christian discourse. In light of this, in the second part of this chapter, I will turn to defend the importance of "deconstruction," understood in a particular way, then point to areas of weakness. In so doing I will champion, in the final section, what I take to be a postconservative response to "deconstruction" and New Testament studies.

DECONSTRUCTING NEW TESTAMENT TEXTS: FROM DERRIDA TO SOCIAL MEDIA[2]

This is not a volume, nor a chapter, to delve into the theory in depth, so I will not canvas what sets deconstruction apart from structuralism, what

---

1. Adam, "Deconstruction and Exegesis," 100.
2. We could reach behind Derrida, of course, to enlightenment responses to Christendom and, behind that, to apophatic theology, see, Jersak, *Out of the Embers*.

Derrida's *differance* is all about, "slippage," "play" and more besides. But some comment must be made when the word "deconstruction" is used as it has come to mean many different and nebulous things. Theological scholarship in the 1980s and 1990s was primarily preoccupied with reflecting on the implications of specifically *Derridian* deconstruction, as an opportunity, on the one hand,[3] or as a problem to be defeated, on the other.[4] Naturally, this specifically theological engagement evolved, with scholars inevitably finding more creative positions.[5]

In New Testament scholarship, however, Derridian deconstruction was more limited and rather less theoretically sophisticated. Although aspects of generally overlapping and broad "postmodern" thought were skillfully appropriated by certain New Testament scholars, Derrida was not often directly engaged for the purposes of exegesis. And this is not without reason for deconstruction is not a discrete method or set of tools that one could apply to reading texts.[6]

Hence, in only a few earlier works do we find engagement with Derrida directly. David Seeley's work is a major, if imperfect, attempt to allow specifically Derridian deconstruction to sharpen New Testament exegetical endeavors.[7] Although he presents a rather limited account of Derrida, by means of an analysis of just *Of Grammatology* and Derrida's essay, "Structure, Sign, and Play," he rightly presented deconstruction as something that emerges from the text itself—it is not something imposed upon it. However, Seeley tended to imagine deconstruction as merely a destabilizing and cynical event, which has been rightly critiqued. This is a trend that will continue even more imprudently into current discourse, as we shall see. But as Adam noted over two decades ago: "deconstructive criticism honours the text's important role in the world's complex systems of signification. Deconstruction may thus be orientated towards the preservation of a tradition as much as to its demise."[8]

A more radical appropriation of Derrida is undertaken in the work of Stephen Moore, who is arguably the most important name in any consideration of deconstruction and the New Testament.[9] Here we encounter a

---

3. See, e.g., Taylor, *Erring*, and a number of his other works.
4. E.g., Ellis, *Against Deconstruction*.
5. See, e.g., Smith, *Jacques Derrida*.
6. Adam, "Deconstruction and Exegesis," 103.
7. Seeley, *Deconstructing the New Testament*.
8. Adam, "Deconstruction and Exegesis," 104.
9. His contributions are vast and continue to the present day, but see Moore, *Bible in Theory*.

far less methodologically restrained approach (as found in Seeley). A much more playful engagement with the New Testament texts emerges, that pushes beyond the bounds of usual exegetical practices and sensibilities. Certainly, it tends towards something Marcus Gabriel might dismiss as "'postmodernist' constructivist hyperbole."[10] Adam more generously describes Moore's work as "adventuresome interpretationeering,"[11] while a still friendlier voice admits that despite Moore's "penchant for 'strategic anachronism,'" he still offers "culturally specific insights"![12] Either way, aspects of Derridian deconstruction are woven into his colorful analysis of New Testament texts. He destabilizes metaphysical concepts, with their concomitant hierarchical oppositions, and extends this beyond Derrida into postcolonial approaches, third-wave feminism and queer theory. He emphasizes the "exclusions, omissions, and systemic blind spots that enable texts, and entire societies, to function."[13] In other words, deconstruction, for Moore, is one thread of a wider poststructuralist panoply of impulses, ranging from Michel Foucault's emphasis on power, Jean-François Lyotard's questioning of metanarratives, Judith Butler's "queer theory," postcolonialism and much more besides.

This kind of approach to deconstruction and the New Testament remains alive and well, diffused through a multitude of poststructuralist strategies. Scholarship now is deeply sensitive to the need to diversify the interpretative task in ways that challenge a myopic western perspective. But let us note one example representative of others, namely Arminta M. Fox, *Paul Decentred*.[14] In what could be broadly understood as a deconstruction inspired move, à la Moore, she questions the often unexpressed but controlling assumption of the veracity of Paul's perspective when reading 2 Corinthians. By deploying identity reasoning, feminist and postcolonial (or better, *decolonizing*) tools, Fox traces numerous "kyriarchal" tendencies in Paul's rhetoric, which she understands to perpetuate colonialism. By taking seriously the diverse Corinthian community, she thereby decenters Paul.

What to make of all this? To the extent that deconstruction draws attention to the margins, to the location of the reader in their particularity, to the unstable nature of all discourse and the tensions within texts, it is a welcome ally in postconservative New Testament exegesis. There remain questions, of course. As one would expect, deconstruction, so diffused and

10. Gabriel, *Fields of Sense*, 22.
11. Adam, "Deconstruction and Exegesis," 106.
12. This is from Amy-Jill Levine's foreword to Moore, *Bible in Theory*, xiii.
13. Moore, *Bible in Theory*, 2, but see his entire introductory chapter for a useful overview of the scope of his work.
14. Fox, *Paul Decentred*.

applied, has been co-opted into rather specific contemporary political accounts that, by and large, find most energetic expression in North America, and they—whether acknowledged or not—remain bound to that specificity. What I mean is that such work tends to project labels and narratives it finds compelling in that context on to all other readers, in a rather lazy generalizing and, dare I say, colonizing manner. But matters are arguably less transferable than one might expect, as an emerging tide of monographs are now urging.[15] Terms such as "whiteness" and specific accounts of identity arguably lack sufficient nuance beyond North America, with the result that matters of greater local importance, such as the massive import of *class* in the UK, are neglected. These applications of "deconstruction" strategies are not as welcome.

Deconstruction, therefore, has a colorful and varied history in New Testament interpretative work. From fairly limited and methodologically temperate approaches (Seeley) it has travelled through Moore's "adventuresome interpretationeering," through to more recent applications, and sometimes blunt extensions, of myopic and zero-sum north American identity politics.

But all of this is rather distant from popular and contemporary usage of the word "deconstruction." A scan of the use of the word "deconstruction" on social media, for example, will judge it, in the opinion of some, to be synonymous with *apostasy*. But, and because you can always trust social media to polarize and foster groupthink, others will described "deconstruction" not negatively but as the life of faith *simpliciter*! There remains some link with the more theoretically heavy accounts of Derridian deconstruction, as we shall see, but it has taken on an almost wholly destructive hue, such that accepting "deconstruction" aligns one with "progressive Christianity" and the rejection of traditional faith. Meanwhile, refusing the destructive forces of "deconstruction" is an important way of "keeping the faith pure."

Take, for example, Alisa Childers' claim that "something progressive Christians call deconstruction" is the "dismantling of doctrinal tenants—where all the beliefs someone was raised with and had never questioned are systematically pulled apart."[16] A result of such "deconstruction," she asserts, is that "[t]raditional understandings of the Cross, the Bible, and the gospel get taken out with the trash."[17] Chad Bahl, on the contrary, argues in his edited volume, *Deconstructing Hell*, that his book has emerged "out of the larger process of Christian deconstruction happening within the church

---

15. See, e.g., Owolade, *This Is Not America*; Malik, *Not So Black and White*.
16. Childers, *Another Gospel?*, 7.
17. Childers, *Another Gospel?*, 24.

today," and that however uncomfortable it might be, we should "encourage, not judge, such deconstructing."[18]

In both cases it is clear that deconstruction is seen as the dismantling of traditional beliefs, which does not necessarily align it with Derridian deconstruction as noted above. It does correspond to more philosophical accounts of deconstruction in its attempt to relentlessly question and point out tensions and alternative interpretive options, but "deconstruction" has evolved as a concept. Indeed, some authors are alert to these developments, and I cite Bradley Jersak as an example, who admits that in popular usage the word deconstruction has become a "trendy catchword for the dismantling . . . of the beliefs and values of a person or culture,"[19] something he calls elsewhere "ex-vangelical pop-deconstruction."[20] Instead, his own account of deconstruction aligns it with numerous streams, from ancient apophatic theology, through Enlightenment critiques of Christendom, to technical and philosophical deconstruction.[21]

So what do we mean by deconstruction in this essay? Deconstruction in its more philosophical variety has always been broad and difficult to define. It effectively encompasses any analysis of the relationship between text and meaning, as "negotiating . . . the radical difficulty in all the interpretive transactions of academic (and everyday) life."[22] But it seems clear that it will be better understood in our contemporary climate to be specifically "deconstruction" if there is also a measure of *subversion* involved. Hence, deconstruction and the New Testament can be understood—for the purposes of this chapter at least—as the process whereby problems and textual difficulties for more conservative cohorts are emphasized when interpreting the New Testament. By foregrounding interpretative turbulence it subverts and questions assumptions.

My claim, to which we now turn, is that this account of deconstruction will facilitate a more interesting way forward when tackling the question of deconstruction and New Testament studies, especially, as we shall see, in relation to this Handbook. In what follows I will argue that a postconservative approach to New Testament scholarship, and this account of deconstruction, is a fruitful juxtaposition. I will focus on Paul's letters in what follows as this textual corpus is, theologically speaking, a load-bearer—what we make of Paul is wrapped up in accounts of what "the gospel" is and means. This

18. Bahl, *Deconstructing Hell*, 3–4, 5.
19. Jersak, *Out of the Embers*, 18.
20. Jersak, *Out of the Embers*, 21.
21. Jersak, *Out of the Embers*, 19.
22. Adam, "Deconstruction and Exegesis," 100.

matters massively of course for ecclesial communities. But beyond church life, Paul is also implicated in political accounts of what justice means, both how it is to be understood and enacted. Hence, debating interpretations of Paul is far from an intellectual curiosity, merely on the academic fringes. So much is at stake here. So, and first, I shall justify the importance and centrality of deconstruction, understood more widely, for New Testament scholarship when reading Paul. As we shall see, it serves a vital task. But it is inadequate as a complete project, as we shall explore in the final section, which returns us back to the burden of particularly postconservative concerns.

PAUL AND "DECONSTRUCTION" DECONSTRUCTION AT THE HEART OF HISTORICAL-CRITICAL EXEGETICAL WORK

Deconstruction, understood as suggested, goes hand in hand with the task of spotting, elucidating and resisting anachronisms and ethnocentrisms in the interpretative task, for precisely at this point the relationship between text and meaning are juxtaposed. As such it is at the heart of exegetical work. I will focus on anachronisms in what follows to give the reader a feel for how extensive and important these are to acknowledge. An anachronism is a chronological inconsistency (the Leviathan, in Job, must be a dinosaur because the fossil record; the locusts of Revelation 9 are attack helicopters, etc.) But a gift of New Testament scholarship is to alert the general reader to the more subtle and insidious ways anachronisms invade our interpretation. This is the key point: to certain cohorts this will be received as deconstruction (again, understood in the sense urged above). Nevertheless, these deconstructive elements are not imposed from without but emerge from close readings of the New Testament in its historical particularity. As New Testament scholars will argue: these subversive and disruptive annotations and interpretations are crucial to the interpretive process. To do without them is simply to project our own voice and expectations onto the text of the New Testament uncritically, and therefore run the risk of misunderstanding Scripture.

Let us dip our toes into just one verse as an example of these concerns, namely 2 Cor 1:1. I cite the recent NRSVue, which is representative of many others:

> Paul, an apostle of Christ Jesus by the will of God, and Timothy our brother, To the church of God that is in Corinth, together with all the saints throughout Achaia.

Scholars usually point to two anachronisms here, namely the meaning of "Christ" and "church." In both cases, these rank anachronisms are countered will alternative translations, namely "Messiah" (or perhaps "King") and "Assembly." The purpose of these alternative glosses is to subvert expectations, to disrupt the expected relationship between text and meaning, and to reorientate the reader to different semantic possibilities. Now all of this is well trodden ground, so I will not comment on it further.[23]

Yet there are at least two more anachronistic glosses in just this verse! "Paul, an *apostle* of Messiah Jesus"? "Apostle" is surely to our ears an exclusively religious term. Not so for Paul, at least the word does not connote such by itself. An *apostolos* was an envoy or emissary, whose work overlapped with systems of ancient patronage and benefaction. They went to represent the sender and were, likewise, to be received with the honor that would have been accorded the sender. This is why Paul is, for the Corinthians, *apostolos Christou*, an emissary of Messiah. A deconstruction of expectations is vital at this point, hence I argue that "emissary" hits a less anachronistic tone than "apostle."

Finally, a rather exciting line of reasoning is now being explored by New Testament scholars about "holy ones." Paul writes, so says the NRSVue, to recipients including "all the *saints* throughout Achaia." But "saints" mobilises a set of connotations today, such as the "prayers" of or to the saints, canonized individuals, and more besides. And they are anachronisms all of them, which breezily take us past a matrix of scriptural themes that would have been familiar to Paul. The "holy ones" (*hoi hagioi*) is a phrase in Paul's Bible that rarely denoted humans. Rather, the *hagioi* were primarily understood as angels or celestial beings. Some scholars now understand Paul, when speaking of "holy ones," to denote the Spirit infused new celestial substance of these pagan Messiah-followers; their very nature is changed into something celestial or angelic. This aligns with some very strange readings of Paul, odd, that is, to most conservative ears anyway, that build on the "ethnic essentialism" of Paul's day.[24] The Spirit enables pagans to enjoy eschatological life, but contrary to their "nature" (cf. Rom 11:23), whereas Jewish ethnicity involves an activity of the Spirit in eschatological life that is "according to" their "nature" (Rom 11:21, 24). As the lens of modern genetics is an overt anachronism, care is needed here and Paul's "ethnic essentialism," whereby Jews were Jews by nature, and gentiles are sinners, again because of their nature, will be received as a deconstruction of a set of theological

---

23. But see Novenson, *Christ Among the Messiahs*; Korner, *Origin and Meaning of Ekklēsia in the Early Jesus Movement*.

24. On this, see the useful introductory essay, Thiessen and Fredriksen, "Paul and Israel."

and traditional anthropological motifs. The point is this: "saints" is not only unhelpful but completely misses all of these themes. Misunderstandings follow anachronisms. Paul is made *too familiar* by the NRSVue at this point.

New Testament scholarship on Paul is particularly "cutting edge" when it makes Paul *odd* again. Ecclesial and reception history lenses can obscure. Deconstruction, understood as suggested above, is therefore a necessary part of the task of New Testament scholarship. And our examples are just the tip of the iceberg; we noted four examples in just one verse!

New Testament post conservative interpretation, therefore, has nothing to fear from the task of deconstruction. It is necessary to create conceptual space between, in this example, Paul's Greek words in their particularity, and our own expectations and distortive lenses. Without deconstruction, we will only ever project our own voices onto Paul, creating interpretative mischief as a result.

DECONSTRUCTION IN EXEGESIS AS AN ETHICAL OBLIGATION

But the closer we press into the heartbeat (real or imagined) of Pauline theology the more is at stake and the more prescient deconstruction becomes. The case to be made now is that deconstruction is also vital in interpreting Paul for ethical reasons.

To focus on a particularly load-bearing text, we turn to concerns around Romans 1–4, in order to explicate how "the Jew" can be understood, first, then how conceptions of justice are illegitimately mobilized. This second issue leads to problems associated with construals of "justification" and the saving significance of Jesus.

David Seeley's work, *Deconstructing the New Testament* makes much of fissures in traditional readings of Romans, though he illegitimately assumes that the traditional reading is the only option. He drills into what he calls "a broken theological landscape."[25] As Seeley argues, Rom 1:18–32 "shows that an understanding of God's will is universally accessible."[26] The point, therefore, is that all are culpable and, therefore, guilty.[27] This entails, as Seeley explains, a theology of desert, which seems to stand in "stark contrast to Paul's claim that no one is justified by the law . . . and to his conception of sin as a cosmic power that controls people."[28] All of this is "a bit odd"[29] and ends up creating not only contradiction in Paul but also "a

25. Seeley, *Deconstructing the New Testament*, 129.
26. Seeley, *Deconstructing the New Testament*, 132.
27. Seeley, *Deconstructing the New Testament*.
28. Seeley, *Deconstructing the New Testament*.
29. Seeley, *Deconstructing the New Testament*, 134.

startling statement, to say the least" about Jewishness.³⁰ Worse, Paul then does an "about-face" in his argument about Judaism in the earlier chapters of Romans,³¹ "taking back" what he earlier asserted.³² So Seeley rightly asks: if "'no human being will be justified . . . by the works of law' . . . where does this leave the Jew who receives 'glory and honor and peace' on the Day of Judgment for doing good (2:10, cf. 2:5)?."³³ A very good question! Indeed, we would also add that the account of Judaism in the first few chapters is profoundly antisemitic, because it misrepresents Judaism by presenting "the Jew" as the paradigmatic works-based legalist. This impulse, which labelled the Jew as the way *not* to do religion, contributed to the evil treatment of Jews in Europe in the twentieth century.

Seeley points to many more fissures and difficulties in Romans 1–8, but this gives a flavor. While his proposed solution to these textual seems and contradictions is less helpful, oh that more exegetes had read his, or similar, arguments more closely! Yet rather than seizing upon these reasonable observations as an opportunity to reflect on received theological traditions, many took a posture that assumed the traditional reading must be defended at all costs, despite numerous internal contradictions. Meanwhile, others stayed satisfied with textual fissures, with a Paul who leaves behind a shattered theological landscape, with a Paul who constructed theology "on the go" without any central theological axioms to provide coherence. It was "job done" in simply pointing out these problems. We shall see that a post-conservative approach wants to navigate between these options.

Second, Romans 1–4 also raises questions about justice. Justice is a complicated concept and can be understood in a variety of different ways.³⁴ But traditions, especially those of a more conservative variety, tend to impose certain negative retributive notions of justice on the interpretive task of reading Paul,³⁵ and these concepts are then mobilized to understand Paul's use of the *dik-* words ("justice," "righteousness," "righteous," "just," "to justify," are all common glosses of the *dik-* word group found in many Bible translations). Why scholars do this relates more, arguably, to their cultural, church historical, socio-ideological and philosophical situatedness than

30. Seeley, *Deconstructing the New Testament,*, 143.
31. Seeley, *Deconstructing the New Testament,*, 134.
32. Seeley, *Deconstructing the New Testament*, 135.
33. Seeley, *Deconstructing the New Testament*.
34. See, e.g., Sandel, *Justice*, which proffers numerous accounts of justice and not one of them articulates it as negative retribution.
35. Negative retribution presents justice as done when punishment is exacted. This is not about positive retribution involving compensation, which is an entirely different matter.

because it has anything to do with textual analysis of Paul's letters. Either way, this impulse impacts how "justification" is understood, how the death of Jesus is conceived as salvific, and what is understood by hell.

To take just the first two (justification and the meaning of the death of Jesus), we can trace what happens when negative retributive notions of justice are imported into our reading of Paul. The immediate result is that we lose sight of the liberative dimension of Paul's *dik-* language and end up forcing Paul into "justification" providing a solution to individual guilt (as we saw in Seeley's deconstruction). The result is that justification equals "forgiveness with bells on." But as Paul hardly ever speaks about forgiveness (or guilt) in his letters, we should already be alert to problems here. Either way, Paul's justification discourse is put out of shape, distracting from central christological and liberative aspects.[36] As if this were not disturbing enough, by importing these notions of justice into Paul, readers create an account of justice that can be weaponized politically (a point to which we will return in a moment). To deconstruct these notions, to untangle the interpretative mess, is thus an important part of Christian discipleship.

The interpretive baggage from imported notions of "justice" overflows into how the death of Jesus is understood. "Penal" is a word deployed in atonement theology to bring particular forensic notions into play, namely those that associate justice *with the exactment of a penalty*, understood in terms of punishment and desert. It is related to the Latin *punire* to mean the infliction of a penalty, "to cause pain for some offense."[37] As Douglas Moo, representative of many others, recently opines: "Christ's death atones because he suffers and dies in the sinner's place. This 'place taking' is then often elaborated in terms of punishment."[38] Moo elaborates the logic involved, thereby helping us coordinate his account of what is "just" in this scheme: those "in Christ can be certain of escaping God's wrath on that day because . . . it has been fully absorbed by Christ on the cross."[39]

It follows that "penal" as an adjective names an attribute of the noun "substitution" to present a particular account of justice, namely a retributive one understood negatively. It is one in which justice is served by means of the exactment of a penalty understood in terms of deserved punishment. In US court justice this reappears, as the death penalty's logic is arguably sustained by this theology of Christ's death; it gives it "divine" validation.[40]

---

36. On this, see, e.g., Tilling, "Evil."
37. Campbell, *Pauline Dogmatics*, 343.
38. Moo, *Theology of Paul*, 393.
39. Moo, *Theology of Paul*, 398–99.
40. See, e.g., Campbell, "Mass Incarceration."

Once penal notions of justice are inscribed into the gospel, into the heart of core theological truths, we necessarily have a God who can endorse the death penalty. In parts of the world, like Texas or Belarus, this costs lives.

Deconstructionist readings are thus urgent and will question why this account of justice is imputed into Paul. As already noted, it's not the only one to hand, so why prioritize this one? Paul indeed announces, in Romans 1:16–17 (cf. also 3:21–22), that God's *dikaiosunē* (typical glosses being "righteousness" or "justice") is revealed *in the gospel*. Justice for Paul is, in other words, to be parsed according to gospel-driven grammar and cannot be projected into Paul's theology willy-nilly. The relationship between text and meaning, here, needs to be urgently assessed. And noticing these dissonances requires a mindset that will be familiar to almost all varieties of deconstruction. It involves noticing the gap between signifier and asserted meaning with particular ethical urgency.

So deconstruction has played an important part in New Testament scholarship. It is part of the vital task of creating hermeneutical space between us, on the one hand, and Paul, on the other. It displays fissures in traditional readings and alerts the readers to toxic readings. It follows, therefore, that deconstruction *should* play an important part in interpreting the New Testament. But all is not as clear-cut as this account might suggest. The problems of deconstruction need now to be addressed, simultaneously foregrounding a postconservative response to deconstruction in New Testament interpretation.

DECONSTRUCTION AS INCOMPLETE: A POSTCONSERVATIVE RESPONSE

Deconstruction is vital, but dangers are afoot! Too many historical-critical scholars tend to think "job done" when the deconstructive task is undertaken when, in truth, it has only begun. Moreover, those who revel in Paul's alterity can sometimes remain hermeneutically unreflective. It is often expressed as follows: "we are doing the proper historical-critical work, not naive theology dressed up as historical exegesis. Everybody except me is an apologist!" The theological reception of the New Testament in the theological work of the Fathers is then often handled as a suspicious force, indeed sometimes not entirely without reason! Witness, for example, Paula Fredriksen's sideswipe at using the language of "monotheism" in relation to New Testament God-talk. Monotheism isn't merely anachronistic for her (though we agree that its philosophical variety is). It is also associated with what she calls "tortured Chalcedonianism" which she describes as "austere and exclusive."[41] Surely this evidences hermeneutical agendas beyond the properly historical-critical. But resistance to such tendencies are inchoate and disorganised. For this reason, a postconservative interpretative posture has an important contribution to make. It suggests that the deconstructive approach is not critical enough. We also need to interrogate the ideological axioms by means of which the deconstructive agenda is propelled. As Barth famously put it: "The critical historian needs to be more critical."[42]

Another way to frame this is to suggest that the siren call of endless equivocation sometimes blots out the work of constructive exegetical and conceptual labor. Take, as our first example, the correct instinct to reject anachronistic readings. When scholars examine Paul's theology in terms of its seeming trinitarian dynamics, the same scholars will breezily, and anachronistically, presuppose the Nicene-Constantinopolitan settlement of 381 as the interpretative gauge. This is often done because, in so doing, they can easily undermine the claim that Paul was a such a Trinitarian. But is also means they can ignore the hard labor of figuring out Paul's own complex theological coherence. It short-circuits the constructive task and distracts from appreciation of Paul's own trinitarian grammar.[43]

Take, as our second example, the Seeley trajectory, which settles on an account that assumes the incoherence of Paul's theology in Romans. But why not assume that the incoherence lies with a certain (traditional) reading of Paul, not Paul himself? A postconservative response will be *more* critical, not less, because it also works hard to evaluate alternative constructive accounts. It will not insist on absolute inerrancy in Paul's letters but assume a preference for general coherence. This is therefore to be distinguished from a conservative response to the challenges people like Seeley and others raise. When the deconstructive challenge is accepted and not ignored, however, alternative and liberating solutions indeed become evident. Here I think of the work of Douglas Campbell and his apocalyptic rereading of Romans, which follows the text of Romans 1–3 as closely as traditional readings, but resolves problems conservative readers have usually pretended are not there.[44] A postconservative exegetical posture, in other words, goes beyond the elucidation of fissures and seems to a constructive solution that helps deepen our understanding of the coherence of the text. Despite the reception of Campbell's work in certain circles, his reading is presently the only one that both solves real problems and does so by sticking closely to the

---

41. Fredriksen, "Retirement," 35, 37.
42. Barth, *Romans*, 8.
43. On this, see Tilling, "Paul the Trinitarian."
44. Campbell, *Deliverance*.

text in historical-critical mode. It is therefore currently the best reading of Romans and, gladly, also the one that presents the most beautiful vision of Paul's theology.[45]

Finally, take the matter of justice and justification, with the corresponding account of the nature of the saving significance of Jesus noted above. The constructive work that is being done on these questions places us at the cutting edge of Pauline exegetical work. It recognizes that constructive work must also attend to necessary theological axioms in presenting theological coherence: the knowledge of God begins with God. As such, it seeks to integrate, synthesize, and speak theologically in light of the *reality* of the risen Messiah.[46] At the very least, it will mean that, to understand the *dikaiosunē* of God in Rom 1:17, a broader account of the event of God in Christ, for Paul, is necessarily involved. It will discover that God's act in Jesus Christ is the content of God's justice. As such it is an act of *unconditional* love and benevolence precisely "while we were still sinners" (Rom 5:8). This is to say that it does not operate according to the dictates of negative retribution and desert (contra Moo). God's "righteousness" revealed in the gospel will be seen as an event of loving *solidarity*, to the point of death—even death on a cross—for one died, therefore all died (2 Cor 5:14; Phil 2:6–11). It will be seen as *incorporative*, for Paul insists that we shall also be raised with him (2 Cor 4:14). It is an act which, in resurrection and by the Holy Spirit, *liberates* us from the powers of Sin and Death (Rom 6; Gal 5). This is further evidenced in the way Paul predominantly talks about freedom from enslavement rather than forgiveness of guilt. It is, thus, an event that *delivers*, pressing us toward forensic liberative notions of justice. At least this would all be a good start in unpacking a Pauline account of justice.[47]

These constructive labors also present us with an account of the meaning of the death of Jesus that is likewise about solidarity all the way down. As Andrew Rillera explores in his book, *Lamb of the Free*, a historical-critical subverts conservative accounts of the saving significance of Jesus. But he likewise creatively rethinks New Testament language with emphasis on the historical-critical method to present a far more compelling and very different account of the significance of the death of Jesus that has *nothing at all* to do with penal substitutionary accounts.[48] Postconservative exegesis

---

45. Campbell elucidates this positive vision more completely in Campbell, *Pauline Dogmatics*.
46. See Wolter, "Which Jesus Is the Real Jesus?"
47. On these issues, see now Campbell and DePue, *Beyond Justification*.
48. Rillera, *Lamb of the Free*.

deconstructs but also works harder. It is simultaneously constructive and is so with theological alertness.

CONCLUSION

I have argued that an account of the meaning of deconstruction, inflected with modern connotations, provides a suggestive way forward for examining the relationship between New Testament studies and deconstruction. In this light, I argued that deconstructing readings of the New Testament is an important task, indeed a key part of historical-critical work and, beyond even that, a moral imperative. However, by itself it falls short of the constructive work that postconservative postures would encourage. The latter allows for the moment of deconstruction, indeed welcomes it, but as a tool in the process of creative reengagement with the text. In my lectures I insist that all first-year undergraduates grasp two principles when engaging the New Testament texts on the journey to become wiser readers and interpreters. First, they need to take seriously the historical particularity of these texts, to recapture their oddness, to notice the fissures, to be *troubled* by the alterity, *to allow deconstruction*. If this is not done, the danger is that we only ever project our own voice onto the New Testament, which ultimately means we learn very little. Worse, we may end up projecting rotten theological presuppositions onto central New Testament theological dynamics, thereby baptizing our sinful and even idolatrous images and perspectives, granting them—oh the shame—divine confirmation. Deconstruction alerts us to the idols and urges we refigure assumptions. However, there is a second principle I adjure students consider. It is a vital postconservative moment that says we cannot be satisfied with the destabilizing effect alone, revelling merely in the alterity of these texts. It insists that, in addition to appreciating historical particularity, a good reading of the New Testament will also lead us to a greater appreciation of the unconditional love of God revealed in Jesus Christ and by the Holy Spirit. It will insist that historical criticism needs to go further, to be more critical, and to prayerfully receive and respect the *scopus* of Scripture. But as it does this, if it is to be a truly constructive and Christian theological account, it must orientate its reading of the Bible as a whole to *the* Word of God, namely Jesus Christ (see, e.g., John 5:39–40; Heb 1:1), which is effectively what Paul insist in Rom 1:17. God's "justice" is revealed *in the gospel*. This must be our primary and most important orientation otherwise *unevangelized* concepts will determine our core theological axioms. And that won't end well. Taken to its worst ends, we will end up inscribing idolatrous conceptions into the heart of the God-human relation.

BIBLIOGRAPHY

Adam, A. K. M. "Deconstruction and Exegesis." In *Exegese und Methoden Diskussion*, eds. Stefan Alkier and Ralph Brucker, 99–110. Tübingen-Basel: Francke Verlag, 2000.

Bahl, Chad, ed. *Deconstructing Hell: Open and Relational Responses to the Doctrine of Eternal Conscious Torment*. Grasmere, ID: SacraSage, 2023.

Barth, Karl. *The Epistle to the Romans*. Translated by Edwyn C. Hoskyns. 1968. Oxford: Oxford University Press, 1933.

Campbell, Douglas A. *The Deliverance of God: An Apocalyptic Rereading of Justification in Paul*. Grand Rapids: Eerdmans, 2009.

———. "Mass Incarceration: Pauline Problems and Pauline Solutions." *Interpretation* 72 (2018) 282–302.

———. *Pauline Dogmatics: The Triumph of God's Love*. Grand Rapids: Eerdmans, 2019.

Campbell, Douglas A., and Jon DePue. *Beyond Justification: Liberating Paul's Gospel*. Eugene, OR: Wipf & Stock, forthcoming.

Childers, Alisa. *Another Gospel? A Lifelong Christian Seeks Truth in Response to Progressive Christianity*. Carol Stream, IL: Tyndale Elevate, 2020.

Ellis, John M. *Against Deconstruction*. Princeton: Princeton University Press, 1989.

Fox, Arminta M. *Paul Decentred: Reading 2 Corinthians with the Corinthian Women*. London: Lexington, 2020.

Fredriksen, Paula. "Mandatory Retirement: Ideas in the Study of Christian Origins Whose Time Has Come to Go." In *Israel's God and Rebecca's Children: Essays in Honor of Larry W. Hurtado and Alan F. Segal*, edited by David B. Capes et al., 25–38. Waco, TX: Baylor University Press, 2007.

Gabriel, Markus. *Fields of Sense: A New Realist Ontology*. Speculative Realism. Edinburgh: Edinburgh University Press, 2015.

Jersak, Bradley. *Out of the Embers: Faith After the Great Deconstruction*. New Kensington, PA: Whitaker, 2022.

Korner, Ralph J. *The Origin and Meaning of Ekklēsia in the Early Jesus Movement*. Leiden: Brill, 2017.

Malik, Kenan. *Not So Black and White: A History of Race from White Supremacy to Identity Politics*. London: Hurst & Company, 2023.

Moo, Douglas J. *A Theology of Paul and His Letters: The Gift of the New Realm in Christ*. Grand Rapids: Zondervan, 2021.

Moore, Stephen D. *The Bible in Theory: Critical and Postcritical Essays*. Atlanta: Society of Biblical Literature, 2010.

Novenson, Matthew V. *Christ Among the Messiahs: Christ Language in Paul and Messiah Language in Ancient Judaism*. Oxford: Oxford University Press, 2012.

Owolade, Tomiwa. *This Is Not America: Why Black Lives in Britain Matter*. London: Atlantic, 2023.

Rillera, Andrew. *Lamb of the Free*. Eugene, OR: Wipf & Stock, forthcoming.

Sandel, Michael J., ed. *Justice: A Reader*. Oxford: Oxford University Press, 2007.

Seeley, David. *Deconstructing the New Testament*. Leiden: Brill, 1994.

Smith, James K. A. *Jacques Derrida: Live Theory*. London: Continuum, 2005.

Taylor, Mark C. *Erring: A Postmodern a/Theology*. Chicago: University of Chicago Press, 1984.

Thiessen, Matthew, and Paula Fredriksen. "Paul and Israel." In *The Oxford Handbook of Pauline Studies*, edited by Matthew V. Novenson and R. Barry Matlock, 371–88. Oxford: Oxford University Press, 2022.

Tilling, Chris. "Paul, Evil and Justification Debates." In *Evil in Second Temple Judaism and Early Christianity*, edited by Chris Keith and Loren T. Stuckenbruck, 190–223. Tübingen: Mohr, 2016.

———. "Paul the Trinitarian." In *Essays on the Trinity*, edited by Lincoln Harvey, 36–62. Eugene, OR: Cascade, 2018.

Wolter, Michael. "Which Jesus Is the Real Jesus?" In *The Quest for the Real Jesus*, edited by Jan Van Der Watt, 1–18. Leiden: Brill, 2013.

Chapter 36
Ancient Near East Hermeneutics
JOHN H. WALTON

ASSUMPTIONS IN COMMUNICATION

It is the nature of communication between insiders that much "goes without being said."[1] Communication would be inefficient and cumbersome if it did not allow for a basic set of commonly understood ideas, even regarding the meanings of words being used. Such communication is permeated with cultural presuppositions. Penetrating such communication is daunting for outsiders who do not share the inherent perspectives and assumptions of the insiders. Examples abound and include the mundane (listening to traffic reports in a city we might be visiting), the technical (wading through an advanced textbook in a discipline with which we have little acquaintance), the esoteric (such as the philosophy of the Kabbalah), and the exotic (trying to read the poetry of another culture).

It rarely occurs to Bible readers, however, that they are in such an outsider position. They are used to feeling ownership of the Bible as the foundation of their theological beliefs as they also seek guidance for their lives. Such readers often consider the Bible to be authoritative, even when that concept remains largely undefined in their minds. It is often not obvious to them that they are outsiders trying to penetrate an insider-to-insider communication. Such unawareness can be addressed by the reminder that as much as the Bible can be considered to have been written *for* us, it was not written *to* us—most prominently attested by the fact that it is not in our language. We consequently need the help of translators, but our need does not stop there. The fact that the texts are written in an ancient language inevitably means that they are written in the context of an ancient culture with

---

1. Richards and O'Brien, *Misreading Scripture with Western Eyes*, 9–19.

all of the expected assumptions that characterize insider-to-insider communication. We therefore not only need language translators, but we also need cultural brokers who can decipher the cultural subtleties and unlock those insights that will make the text more communicative to us.

For those who subscribe to the concept of biblical authority, this recognition that the Bible is the product of a different cultural context must be an essential component of doctrine and faithful interpretation. If the authority of this literature is to be respected, readers must hold themselves accountable to something outside themselves, but inherent in the text. This accountability requires an understanding of cultural elements that "went without saying" in the biblical text. This can be provided in part by the study of the literature of the ancient Near East, and only in that way, since such understanding is not intuitive to modern readers. Biblical authority is always premised on some level of understanding the literary intentions of the writers, which comprise the language, culture, and genres that are features of their works.

Most who believe that the Bible has authority (however defined) would insist that the literature of the ANE does not. They might therefore question whether using the literature of the ANE as a tool for interpretation might admit a corrupting influence into interpretation. Nevertheless, though examples could be garnered where the literature from the ANE has been used to undermine the theological significance of the Bible, the tool itself is not inherently corrupting.

The operative premise to this hermeneutical approach is that the implied audience of the Hebrew Bible consisted of an ancient Israelite people embedded in the culture of the ancient Near East. In order to most fully understand their culturally embedded, insider to insider communication ("high context"), knowledge of the ancient world must be discerned to the extent that our access to ancient sources allows. Such knowledge will inevitably enrich our understanding of the Hebrew Bible with regard to the world behind the text and will enable more informed interpretation of the text. This approach represents a commitment to first reading the Old Testament in isolation from the New Testament—"seeking to listen to it as Ancient Israel would have heard it."[2] As evidenced by Bartholomew's insistence, this hermeneutical desideratum is even being recognized by those inclined to theological interpretation of Scripture.

---

2. Bartholomew, *Old Testament and God*, 80.

APPROACHES

Two distinct, though not mutually exclusive, approaches have characterized comparative studies. One is most interested in *literary indebtedness*, the other in *cultural embeddedness*. The first approach, and arguably the one most frequently manifested in comparative analysis, interrogates biblical texts for their possible dependence on texts known from the ANE. A range of potential relationships and influences could be recognized, from outright adaptation and light revision to vague literary echoes.[3] Such a comparative exercise is oriented toward literary content. Any proposed literary dependence must be demonstrated in light of internal investigation (e.g., overlapping of content) as well as external investigation (Israelite access to ANE literature that purportedly contributed to the development of the HB text under consideration). This sort of comparative analysis may be motivated by purely literary interests, but can also take place in discussions concerning the assessment of HB as Scripture. The latter interests are at times apologetic in nature as those working in a confessional context seek to undergird the validity of the HB as Scripture, or alternatively at times seeking to neutralize its Scriptural status by revealing its derivative nature. Confirmation of indebtedness is not easily achieved. Potential literary trails are difficult to establish in the absence of transitional or contemporary manuscript evidence. Content can be compared, but observation of overlapping content does not demonstrate dependence. Two pieces may both draw from a common stream of tradition that is widely disseminated. Alternatively, other parties may be involved in transmission though their texts are not extant. When comparing pieces like the flood stories in the Gilgamesh Epic and the Epic of Atrahasis, the large amount of overlapping content, the many phrases shared between them, and the similarity in the narrative arc makes dependence between them clear. In contrast, the flood account in Genesis evidences a narrative arc that is comparable, but with many differences, and shared phrases are not as easily identified. Though it is entirely likely that the flood account in the HB is interacting with traditions that circulated in the ancient world, it remains arguable whether this relationship is best described as literary indebtedness or cultural embeddedness.

The second approach can be referred to as cognitive environment criticism due to its interests in the conceptual world.[4] This approach also has interest in the literature of the ANE, but more because of its ability to provide windows to the conceptual world. Understanding that conceptual world has more significant an exegetical payoff than demonstrating literary

---

3. Frahm, *Babylonian and Assyrian Text Commentaries*, 364–68.
4. Walton, *Ancient Near Eastern Thought and the Old Testament*, 11.

dependence does. Beyond the insight such knowledge can provide to specific passages in the HB, information gained about the conceptual world can be applied to abstract knowledge (from how they thought about topics such as history or law, to understanding their epistemological and ontological preconceptions). This approach will be interested in human inter-relationships (sociology) as well as relationships between the divine and humanity. This approach does not need to be as concerned about Israelite access to ANE literature and is ambivalent to the question of scriptural status.

It is far too easy for modern readers to impose a grid of modern perspectives on an ancient text unwittingly. For example, we might assume that they interrogated the world of experience in moral terms, as we often do today, or that they were attuned to a divide in causation between natural or supernatural that characterizes current philosophical thinking. Such assumptions would be unwarranted and would skew our interpretations in subtle ways. In contrast, we need to be reminded continually of the foreignness of the Israelite culture. Israelites thought more like Babylonians than they do like us. That should motivate us to understand the Babylonians.

The hermeneutical mandate in both approaches is to attend to both similarities and differences, a truism in comparative hermeneutics. This dictum generally pertains to the similarities and differences between the world and literature of the Israelites over against that of the surrounding ancient Near Eastern world. At the same time, it equally applies to the similarities and differences between the modern world and the ancient one.

BASIS FOR COMPARISON

For informed comparison to take place, it would be helpful for us to have a sense of how much of the literature of the ancient world would have been familiar to the Israelites (whether the common folks or, perhaps more importantly, the scribal elites). Just how cosmopolitan were the scribal schools that presumably operated in Iron Age Israel? It is not difficult to imagine that, even before the exile, there was awareness of the great literature, such as the Gilgamesh epic, or that such literary traditions circulated orally among the general population. But what about the Ugaritic Baal epic or the mythology found in Sumerian literature? We might consider it inevitable that during the time of living in Egypt the Israelites encountered Egyptian mythology, at least as traditions, even if not in written forms. But how much of it would have been sufficiently encountered that it could serve as conversation partner to the Israelite scribes in later periods? Evidence to answer such questions is in short supply, so interpreters are left to infer such knowledge based on vague hints combined with general assumptions about cultural diffusion.

Yet even if the Israelites encountered very few pieces of ancient literature, traditions would have circulated and the perspectives they held regarding the world, humanity, society, and the gods would reflect defaults native to the ANE rather than those with which we are familiar. To be sure, the ancient world was not monolithic, yet a perspective that can be documented even in one of the dominant cultures of the ancient world may serve to provide a backdrop for a biblical text more readily than our modern impulses. Moreover, many of the most significant insights can be demonstrated to find support in numerous ancient cultures over a long period of time. Here we may include topics such as community identity, shame/honor, ritual provision for the gods, and the role of the gods in causation, as only a few among many.

Even if the book of Genesis, for example, is not in conversation with specific pieces of ancient literature, though many have proposed evidence that they were, it is in constant conversation with the cultural ideas and the cognitive environment of the ancient world. We need not assume such interaction to be intertextual, nor does it necessarily admit to being employed for (re)constructing biblical traditions. Alternatively, the interrelationships could be understood in a cultural diffusion model that can be discussed using the metaphor of a cultural river.

METAPHOR OF THE CULTURAL RIVER

A cultural river includes the default perspectives that are commonly held (regionally) in areas as diverse as politics, economics, social values, science, religion, law, psychology, metaphysics, and more. Our own Western cultural river therefore values concepts such as freedom, democracy, tolerance, diversity, individualism, personal rights, etc. It includes capitalism, big bang cosmology, and consumerism, as well as, more recently, social networks and rapidly changing ideas about gender. These provide the backdrop for cultural perspectives and conversation, whether individuals or groups like these ways of thinking or not. Nothing in this modern cultural river profile, however, would be recognizable or assumed by people in the ancient world. For that reason, a hermeneutic attending to cognitive environment would not assume that any of these impulses would be present, and would therefore would not interpret in light of them.

Instead, we need to perceive the shape of the ancient cultural river, largely discernible from the literature produced by the various cultures of that world, now made available to us from the massive number of texts excavated by archaeologists and published by linguists. The features of that cultural river are very different from ours. Its ideas of law, kingship, marriage and community, as basic examples, would all be very different from what is familiar to us today. Even if the Israelites were largely unaware of the literature from which we gain knowledge of the ancient cultural river, they were unquestionably characterized in similar ways. We would not describe this relationship as "influence" but as an inherent commonality. If these common, ancient ways of thinking characterized the insider communication by Israelites to Israelites, then it is essential that they be understood when we engage in the act of interpretation. If, instead, we interpret intuitively, without engaging the ancient cultural river, we will inevitably be reflecting various aspects of our own cultural river, which means that we will be imposing something foreign on the HB.

REFERENCE AND AFFIRMATION

All readers recognize that hallmarks of ancient culture inevitably pervade the Bible, but they often figure in what could be called "reference" rather than in the "affirmations" of the biblical message.[5] Even in the most conservative of views of the Bible, i.e., that which argues for the inerrancy of the Bible, the qualification is made that it is inerrant in all that it affirms.[6] Such a caveat implies that there are statements found in the Bible that it does not affirm. Most obviously, this would be applied to statements made by Satan or by Job's friends. Nevertheless, once the qualification is admitted, sound interpretation demands identifying what parts should be classified as present in the text, but not affirmed.

The alternative description given to statements that are not affirmed is "reference"—that is, that the text neutrally refers to that which was said or even to something that stands behind the text. New Testament examples have long been recognized and discussed: Jesus's reference to the mustard seed as the smallest of seeds; Paul's insistence that women be veiled. At the same time, these are often the subject of vigorous debate. In the HB, ready examples of reference without affirmation could be identified in cosmic geography. Most are convinced that the Israelites, would have shared the same view as those around them that would have included a solid sky with some way to suspend it, and something on which the earth was anchored. These would be assessed as offering reference to how Israelites thought without

---

5. Walton and Walton, *Demons and Spirit in Biblical Theology*, 16–18.

6. "Chicago Statement on Biblical Inerrancy," 289–96. Qualifications to inerrancy throughout the document use words such as "teachings," "assertions," and the like to limit the application of the term. See particularly the exposition on p. 295.

suggesting that serious Bible readers must adopt such views as biblical and therefore accepted as indisputable truth.

Once we acknowledge the ANE backdrop to the HB, we can advance to the recognition that *everything* that we read is reference (since it is all rooted in the ancient world), but that *some* of it is also affirmation (supported teaching of the Bible). In this we encounter one of the most fundamental of all hermeneutical questions: How do we tell when something is being affirmed?

Perhaps one of the most practical guidelines that can be applied to such a question concerns whether or not what is found in the HB is also identifiable thinking in the ANE. That is, if what we find in the HB is something that can be attested in the ANE (even if only in one culture), the default would be to categorize that idea as reference rather than affirmation. It is of course possible that in some cases the biblical writer desires to reiterate something that is well-known in the ancient world and give it an emphasis as something that is also considered important. For example, long before the time of Sinai, cultures would have commonly prohibited murder. Consequently, stating that the Israelites should not commit murder would not offer any new information—everyone in the ancient world would have embraced such a value. It would therefore be difficult to label this as "revelation" because revelation would not be an appropriate descriptor for common, well-recognized ideas.

Nevertheless, such observations do not mean that the sixth commandment should not be considered affirmation. It only means that that which is being affirmed may be more subtle than we might have originally imagined. For example, though the prohibition of murder may not be new information, one possibility is that its incorporation into covenant stipulations constitutes a new perspective.[7] Consequently, we must be asking a literary question: "Why is this here?" Whatever solution the interpreter might suggest, it is clear that the distinction between reference and affirmation requires familiarity with the ancient Near Eastern world.

RELEVANCE THEORY

Another important perspective that factors into this approach to interpretation is what has been called "Relevance Theory."[8] Relevance theory proposes that hearers or readers will process information in order to achieve optimal results based on the path of least effort with regard to the context

---

7. Walton and Walton, *Lost World of the Torah*, 255.
8. Hilber, "Contextual Method through the Lens of Relevance Theory."

in which the communication takes place (including language, literature, culture, and circumstances). "Speakers and listeners share implicit assumptions, and listeners employ a loose logic to infer meaning from an utterance."[9] Furthermore, this inference-based model of communication is "facilitated by principles of cooperation that people tacitly employ: listeners expect a relative economy of words, truthfulness, relevance in relation to their needs, and a clear manner of expression."[10] That means that people from differing cultural contexts speaking different languages might draw different interpretive conclusions. This is important for the ancient Near East hermeneutic presented in this essay because it demonstrates that if we want to arrive at legitimate interpretations of an ancient text like the HB, we should make an attempt to grasp the factors to which relevance theory would suggest the ancient hearer or reader would have been responsive.

If pieces of literature are known to both speaker and hearer, relevance may be perceived on the basis of that common knowledge. Inversely, if either the speaker or hearer are unaware of a given piece of literature, that literature cannot figure prominently on the relevance spectrum. If, in a class lecture, I make a passing reference to a phrase from a movie that none of my students have seen, they will have no relevance path by which to make the intended connection.

SUBVERSION

We will now consider what might be the best way to characterize the posture of the HB toward the literature and cognitive environment of the ANE. I have already suggested above that "borrowing," though perhaps defensible in isolated cases, would not provide a broad enough paradigm. Another common paradigm is "polemic," suggesting that the Israelite elites who produced the literature of the HB were arguing against ANE religious ideas. Several examples of polemic are identifiable in the HB (e.g., Isa 44; Jer 10), but such a paradigm fails to account for many other types of texts and does not provide an adequate basis for making full use of the background that the ANE can provide.[11] Frahm offers other categories of interplay such as counter-texts and echoes. Admittedly, diffusion of literary ideas across cultures can take many forms and such ideas may be reflected in either subtle or obvious ways.

---

9. Hilber, "Contextual Method through the Lens of Relevance Theory," 184.
10. Hilber, "Contextual Method through the Lens of Relevance Theory," 184.
11. Walton, "Interactions in the Ancient Cognitive Environment," 334–35.

Crouch has proposed that the concept of "subversion" is more descriptive of the posture of Israelite tradents and writers. When one literature subverts another, it is both dependent on that literature and distinct from it. Subversion in the context of literary criticism means "to challenge and undermine (a conventional idea) [. . .] the description of an act as subversive establishes the action as reactive, responding to an entity—personal, social, political, textual, *et cetera*—that already exists."[12] As reactionary, such literature interacts with other literature which it is subverting. As Crouch points out, subversion assumes a knowledge of those ideas that are being challenged, and it seeks to change the mind of the audience.[13] J. Harvey Walton summarizes: "These three ideas combined—that the text is written to tell the implied audience something in a context of pre-existing belief; that some of the existing beliefs of the audience are expected to change; and that some (many) of the existing beliefs of the audience are expected to remain the same—provides a justification for reading the biblical text as an argument with an illocution of subversion."[14] He continues by making a distinction between the HB using the comparative literature as sources (rare) and using texts as exemplars of particular way of thinking. "Individual ancient Near Eastern texts operate within a worldview and reflect a particular way of thinking. It is elements of this worldview, rather than any given individual text, that the argument of Genesis intends to subvert. References to themes and images which also appear in ancient Near Eastern texts serve to orient the implied audience towards the conceptual arena in which the argument is intended to operate."[15] When subversion is in play, the intended objective to change the opinions of the audience requires that the subversive literature "operates within the context of the opinion it intends to change."[16] Consequently, the subversive text (HB) will not be able to be well-understood absent the relevant material from the ancient world.

I would readily agree with the conclusion that a subversive posture is often represented in the HB, but still, we cannot stop there. Many contributions that the ANE cognitive environment can make to interpretation could be described simply as evident in the way that the HB reflects that cognitive environment. When we read about the customs practiced by the Israelites, we will understand them more deeply as we explore the shape of similar

12. Crouch, *Israel and the Assyrians*, 16. In this and much of what follows in this section, I have been influenced by the unpublished St. Andrews dissertation Walton, "Knowing Good and Evil."
13. Crouch, *Israel and the Assyrians*, 21.
14. Walton, "Knowing Good and Evil."6.
15. Walton, "Knowing Good and Evil."7.
16. Walton, "Knowing Good and Evil."8.

customs in the ancient world. For example, Israelite marriage reflects many of the same aspects as that practiced in the world around them. The HB does not subvert the practices of others; it reflects some of the same values and traditions. Recognizing these reflections should also be the result of applying ANE hermeneutics to our reading of the HB.

Two brief contrasting examples will illustrate the point. The first pertains to the community of the gods. Israelites, like everyone else in the ancient world, thought of themselves in terms of community identity, and therefore it is no surprise that they understood the divine realm as a functional community. Polytheism is not just about numbers, it is about community identity and operations in the divine realm. Israel reflects this sort of understanding in its perception of the divine council (1 Kgs 22; Job 1–2; Isa 6; Ps 82). Yet, this idea was problematized as they increasingly understood the singular claims of Yahweh, and it was subverted in the instruction that they should have no other gods before him (presumably, in his presence in the temple). As interpreters we need to understand the acceptance of the ANE idea of divine community by Israel to understand the way they thought about the divine realm. We furthermore need to understand that way of thinking in order to discern how they are subverting it and to what degree they are doing so. Incorporating both the similarities and differences requires knowledge of the ancient world. A final piece of the puzzle falls into place when we realize that Yahweh's community is not populated by other gods, but by the people he has made in his image and by the nation with which he has made a covenant. This example illustrates partial acceptance (community in the divine realm) and partial subversion (revised ideas of what constitutes the community).

A second example can be seen in the objectives served by ritual. Throughout the ANE, sacrifices were viewed as providing food for the gods. The gods had need for food (as well as housing, clothing, etc.) and, in their view, people had been created to meet those needs. The contrast with the previous example is found in that on this count the HB is entirely subversive. Yahweh has no needs, and sacrifices (despite the continued use of vestigial terminology) are not his food. In a case such as this one, when interpreters are unaware of the mentality in the ANE, they will not see that the HB is being subversive. In contrast to the first example, this one illustrates a more pervasive subversion. In either case, however, interpreters need to understand the ANE in order to interpret well.

COGNITIVE LINGUISTICS

A more specific discipline that describes the role of ANE material in biblical interpretation is called cognitive linguistics. In this discipline we recognize that categories of general interest to most cultures, despite common generalities, nevertheless feature very different ways of thinking. For example, all cultures show an interest in life and death, but they may differ radically on how they understand life and its source or how they understand the point of death. They may all talk about afterlife, but their conceptions of it will differ widely. As another example, ANE cultures show an interest in the past and write about it. Yet they do not all share a common view of the significance of the past. Do Israelites reflect the same sort of thinking found among their neighbors in these cases, or are they subversive on some counts? Given some thought, we would at least admit that we could not expect them to think and write about the past in the same way that we do. They would not prioritize empiricism or naturalism the way that modern culture does. Similar cognitive linguistic awareness would equally extend to issues like "creation" or "law." We would even have to investigate what is meant by "existence." They will not necessarily share our views of ontology or epistemology. More practically, we could not imagine that we intuitively understand how they think about the temple or about ritual, and we could not assume that they all think the same way.

One area where cognitive linguistics takes on great import for interpretation concerns the components of a human. In modern conversations we debate the adequacy of Platonic or Aristotelian concepts as we talk about body, soul, and spirit. Yet we dare not imagine that Egyptians, Babylonians, or Israelites would have thought in those terms. Here translations undermine our ability to understand as they adopt the familiar modern terms to represent Hebrew ideas. We cannot begin with modern (or classical Greek) categories, but neither can we assume that all those in the ANE thought in the same ways. Egyptian anthropology differs markedly from Babylonian anthropology.

COMPARATIVE SEMITICS

Another aspect of ANE hermeneutics is represented in Comparative Semitics. In this category, we recognize that many Hebrew words share cognate roots with other Semitic languages, Aramaic, Ugaritic, and Akkadian being the most important among them. Comparative Semitics is especially helpful when trying to understand a Hebrew word that occurs infrequently and is not clarified by context. In such cases, a cognate in a related language may help to clarify the semantic range, particularly when the semantic range evident in the cognate language appears to fit the Hebrew context. At the same time, we remain aware that semantic range of the same root word can develop in very different directions in different languages.

Further use for comparative Semitics can be found when we compare what are obviously differing semantic ranges. For example, the Hebrew root *qdš* ("holy") has cognates in both Ugaritic and Akkadian, but its meaning in Hebrew only overlaps slightly with that in the cognate languages. It would be a mistake to impose the meanings in Ugaritic or Akkadian on the HB. Yet nuanced understanding can be gained by investigating how they are different.

UNDERSTANDING GENRES

One of the most notable ways that ANE literature can help us interpret the HB better is by helping us to be more informed about ancient literary forms and intentions, which we call genres. Without this information, interpreters would have little option but to think of the biblical genres in modern ways. For example, should we consider ancient genealogies to represent the same kind of thinking that is present in our modern genealogical interests and records? Are the genealogical data preserved in the HB and in the ANE of similar rigidity as in our modern perspective? Do genealogical records represent the same sort of data and make the same sorts of affirmations? We ought not presume that to be true. We must, instead, explore the dynamics of the ancient use of genealogies.

As another example, in the ANE we encounter much literature that we designate as mythological in nature. Much ink has been spilt over attempting to define the ancient genre as well as in discussion of whether the HB has anything comparable. These are important conversations. We cannot decide whether any biblical exemplars should be deemed mythological until we can understand how this category of literature was defined and functioned in the ancient world. Our modern definitions will not suffice.

As a final example, when we read the conquest accounts in the book of Joshua, we are unsurprisingly inclined to read them from our own intuitive ideas about what characterizes a historical report of a conquest. Reading that way, we can become somewhat unsettled when the comprehensiveness of the conquest in Joshua seems contradicted by territorial disputes indicated in Judges 1. The solution is not found by concluding that the HB contains contradictory material, but by understanding the many ways in which Joshua reflects the genre of conquest accounts in the ancient world, where universality is rhetorical rather than actual.[17]

Many other aspects of comparison beyond interpreting individual texts could be explored. For example, cultural knowledge can help us understand how texts are composed and compiled. We can delve into the purpose of writing and the power that it had in ancient culture. Ultimately, we want to understand how people think about themselves, the world, the gods and the interrelationships between all of those.

In some cases, a single point of comparison can be significant even lacking any possibility of literary tracking. For example, the claim that David is a man after God's own heart (1 Sam 13:14) is familiar to many Bible readers. It often serves as the basis for inspirational challenges for readers to nurture a deeper piety, purportedly as David evidenced. Comparative study, however, offers a revised picture. When reading royal inscriptions from as early as the Sumerian texts of the mid-third millennium, all the way through the Babylonian inscriptions of the mid first millennium, we find that this sort of claim is commonplace: that an idealized ruler was appointed "after the god's own heart."[18] It becomes evident that this refers to the exercise of the determinative will of the god, not to a personal, spiritual quality of the king. No literary trail leads from the royal inscriptions to the book of Samuel. This is not a case of borrowing, but a case of dissemination of a particular royal rhetoric. Even if we had only one example (say, a Sumerian inscription fifteen hundred years before David), that would be enough to indicate that the statement in Samuel should not be used as an inspirational call to piety. Only one example is necessary to conclude that this statement in Samuel is an example of ancient royal rhetoric—it is not unique to biblical theology or expression.

In the end, interpreting the HB in light of its ANE setting has ramifications for whatever eventual theological ideas are derived from the text. For those who believe that the HB has a significant role to play in shaping theology (as I do), it is important to realize that any theological conclusions that are drawn must be based on an accurate understanding of the text-in-context.

BIBLIOGRAPHY

Chavalas, Mark W., and K. Lawson Younger, eds. *Mesopotamia and the Bible: Comparative Explorations*. Grand Rapids: Baker Academic, 2002.

---

17. Younger, *Ancient Conquest Accounts*.
18. Walton, *Ancient Near Eastern Thought*, 262–65.

"Chicago Statement on Biblical Inerrancy." *Journal of the Evangelical Theological Society* 21 (1978) 289–96.

Crouch, C. L. *Israel and the Assyrians*. Atlanta: SBL, 2014.

Frahm, Eckart. *Babylonian and Assyrian Text Commentaries*. Münster: Ugarit-Verlag, 2011.

Greer, Jonathan S., et al., eds. *Behind the Scenes of the Old Testament*. Grand Rapids: Baker, 2018.

Hilber, John W. "The Contextual Method through the Lens of Relevance Theory." In *"Now These Records are Ancient": Studies in Ancient Near Eastern and Biblical History, Language and Culture in Honor of K. Lawson Younger, Jr.*, edited by James K. Hoffmeier et al., 183–99. Münster: Zaphon, 2022.

Hundley, Michael B. *Gods in Dwellings*. Atlanta: Society of Biblical Literature, 2013.

———. "Here a God, There a God: An Examination of the Divine in Ancient Mesopotamia." *Altorientalische Forschungen* 40 (2013) 68–107.

———. *Keeping Heaven on Earth: Safeguarding the Divine Presence in the Priestly Tabernacle*. Forschungen zum Alten Testament 50. Tübingen: Mohr Siebeck, 2011.

———. *Yahweh Among the Gods*. Cambridge: Cambridge University Press, 2022.

Keel, Othmar. *The Symbolism of the Biblical World*. New York: Seabury, 1978.

Launderville, Dale. *Piety and Politics: The Dynamics of Royal Authority in Homeric Greece, Biblical Israel, and Old Babylonian Mesopotamia*. Grand Rapids: Eerdmans, 2003.

LeFebvre, Michael. *Collections, Codes and Torah: The Re-characterization of Israel's Written Law*. New York: T. & T. Clark, 2006.

Lewis, Theodore J. *The Origins and Character of God*. Oxford: Oxford University Press, 2021.

Malul, M. *The Comparative Method in Ancient Near Eastern and Biblical Legal Studies*. AOAT 227. Kevelaer: Verlag Butzon & Bercker; Neukirchen-Vluyn: Neukirchener Verlag, 1990.

Pongratz-Leisten, Beate, ed. *Reconsidering the Concept of Revolutionary Monotheism*. Winona Lake, IN: Eisenbrauns, 2011.

Porter, Barbara Nevling, ed. *One God or Many? Concepts of Divinity in the Ancient World*. Bethesda, MD: CDL, 2000.

———. *What Is a God?* Winona Lake, IN: Eisenbrauns, 2009.

Radner, Karen, and Eleanor Robson. *The Oxford Handbook of Cuneiform Culture*. Oxford: Oxford University Press, 2011.

Richards, E. Randolph, and Brandon J. O'Brien. *Misreading Scripture with Western Eyes*. Downers Grove, IL: InterVarsity, 2012.

Rochberg, Francesca. *Before Nature: Cuneiform Knowledge and the History of Science.* Chicago: University of Chicago, 2016.

Van de Mieroop, M. *Philosophy before the Greeks: The Pursuit of Truth in Ancient Babylonia.* Princeton: Princeton University Press, 2016.

van der Toorn, K. *Family Religion in Babylonia, Syria and Israel: Continuity and Change in the Forms of Religious Life.* Leiden: Brill, 1996.

Walton, John H., ed. *Ancient Near Eastern Thought and the Old Testament.* Second edition, Grand Rapids: Baker, 2018.

———. "Genesis and the Conceptual World of the Ancient Near East." In *The Cambridge Companion to Genesis*, edited by Bill T. Arnold, 148–67. Cambridge: Cambridge University Press, 2022.

———. "Interactions in the Ancient Cognitive Environment." In *Behind the Scenes of the Old Testament,* edited by Jonathan S. Greer et al., eds. 333–39. Grand Rapids: Baker, 2018.

———. "Knowing Good and Evil: Values and Presentation in Genesis 2–4." Unpublished diss., St. Andrews, 2023.

———. *The Zondervan Illustrated Bible Backgrounds Commentary: Old Testament.* Grand Rapids: Zondervan, 2009.

Walton, John H., and J. Harvey Walton. *Demons and Spirit in Biblical Theology.* Eugene, OR: Cascade, 2019.

———. *Lost World of the Torah.* Downers Grove, IL: InterVarsity, 2019.

Westbrook, Raymond, and Gary M. Beckman. *A History of Ancient Near Eastern Law.* Leiden: Brill, 2003.

Younger, K. Lawson. *Ancient Conquest Accounts.* Sheffield: JSOT Press, 1990.

Zevit, Ziony. *Religions of Ancient Israel.* New York: Continuum, 2001.

Chapter 37
Biblical Cosmology Hermeneutics
ROBIN PARRY

SCRIPTURE AS ANCIENT TEXT

The biblical cosmos is a strange place. There are two dangers to avoid when trying to make sense of it. One is the temptation of thinking that if the Bible is inspired by God, then it must teach a scientifically accurate cosmology, otherwise it would be "untrue." This approach is motivated by a respect for the text, but ironically ends up disrespecting it by forcing it into conformity with modern science. For instance, witness the discomfort of some creationists with the biblical descriptions of waters above the firmament (Gen 1:6–8). This, some have proposed, must be a water canopy that used to surround the earth, facilitating paradisical conditions. In Noah's time, they suggest, it came crashing down, flooding the earth (an explanation seeking to account for the current absence of "the waters above" and how there was enough water for the Flood). This interpretation of Genesis 1 fails to make sense of the details of that text nor of others passages in which the ocean above the sky is still in place (e.g., Ps 148:4). If we are to respect the biblical text, we need to listen to it and allow it to be the kind of text it is, rather than making it submit to our requirements. And what kind of text is it? Amongst the many things it is, the Bible is a set of ancient writings penned by ancient people for their contemporaries. In countless ways it demonstrably reflects the worlds in which it was written. Honoring the Bible means, in part, that we should not prematurely collapse the distinction between the horizon of the text and that of the modern reader.

Seeking to interpret biblical books against the background of their ancient contexts is not a simple task and it needs to be done cautiously and carefully. In the case of cosmology, this involves seeking to piece together the diverse cosmologies—as far as we are able from the extant evidence—of other ANE cultures that Israel was in contact with: Egyptian, Canaanite, Assyrian, Babylonian, and such like. These cosmological ideas were, to varying degrees, part of the cognitive environment of the authors and original audiences of biblical texts. It is not that the Bible has to say the same things as we find elsewhere, but awareness of such concepts helps us to see where biblical texts are engaging them—whether to affirm them, reject them, modify them, subvert them, or simply use them as a springboard of shared background understanding of the world to make a point about something else entirely.

We also need to be aware that interpreting some of the imagery about cosmology can be tricky. It is not always easy to tell when cosmological language is simply poetic and metaphorical and when it is to be taken more literally. For instance, are references to "the pillars of the earth" simply a metaphorical way of speaking about the stability of the world or were they taken as physical descriptions? Care should be taken not to jump straight to literal interpretations, but equally we should not assume that everything was poetic. It is impossible to believe that the ancients did not have physical models of the cosmos to help them make sense of their observations of the world. Decisions on such matters are not always straightforward and cannot always be made with certainty. We can be increasingly confident that a more-then-metaphorical conception is in play in Scripture if (a) the conceptuality appears in multiple genres: poetry, law, narrative, prophetic oracles, etc., if (b) it is a sensible way of integrating the available observational data into a mental model of the world, and if (c) the same conceptuality seems to be at play within cosmologies from other ANE cultures.

We also need to be aware that ancient Israelites were not interested in crafting an entirely coherent cosmography. Some of their concepts may raise all sorts of questions for us that ancients may simply not have had answers to, in part because they were not interested in them. For instance, suppose you asked some ancient Mesopotamian people what it was like at the edges of the flat disk of the earth where the sky-dome meets it. They may never have even entertained such a question nor tried to integrate it into a tidy picture of the cosmos. We must allow the ancients fuzzy and fluid edges to their physical models of the world.

What follows is a very quick sketch that offers no more than a heuristic snapshot to give an initial orientation. It obviously would need a lot of fine tuning and qualifications.

ANCIENT BIBLICAL COSMOGRAPHY

Across the ANE, the cosmos was seen as essentially tripartite, comprising heaven, earth, and the underworld.[1] Israel shared that view (Amos 9:2–3), though often the OT divides the world into heaven, earth, and sea (Exod 20:11).[2]

EARTH

Flat Earth

Ancient Israelites, along with everyone in the ancient world, believed that the earth was flat, not sphere-like. (The notion of a spherical earth was first argued for by a Greek astronomer in the third century BCE, with the idea gradually taking hold over the following centuries.) The Bible's flat earth is perhaps hinted at in some of the language about its "corners" (Isa 11:12), "ends" (Isa 41:9), "edges" (Ps 19:4), and its foundations and pillars (Ps 75:3), though some care must be taken with what may be poetic language. More telling are scenarios that only make sense if the speakers envisage a flat earth. Thus, Nebuchadnezzar dreams of a tree so tall it could be seen from all over the earth (Dan 4:10–11); the devil showed Jesus all the kingdoms of the world from a high mountain (Matt 4:8); Jesus's return in the clouds is visible to all the inhabitants of the earth (Rev 1:7). None of this imagery works against the background of belief in a spherical earth.[3]

Geo-centrism

Not only was the earth flat, but it lay at the center of the cosmos. It wasn't until Copernicus (1473–1543) that anyone thought otherwise. Remember, at the time people had no reason at all to think that reality was other than how it appeared. And it certainly appears that the sun moves around us. Thus, for biblical writers, the earth was fixed in place (Ps 93:1) and the sun circuits the earth (Ps 19:4c–6), not vice versa. And on special occasions God can reverse the direction of the sun (2 Kgs 20:8–11) or, on one interpretation of the text, stop it still (Josh 10:12–14).

---

1. On ANE cosmology in general, see Horrowitz, *Mesopotamian Cosmic Geography*, and in Israel, see Keel, *Symbolism of the Biblical World*.

2. We should note that in the OT the "sea" has a link to the concept of the underworld, because the earth was not simply surrounded by the sea but was also *founded upon* the waters beneath. This link is possibly present in the concept of the "abyss" (Ps 135:6), which may include the underworld.

3. On whether the "circle" on the face of the deep (Prov 8:27) or "the circle of the earth" (Isa 40:22) teach a spherical earth, see Parry, *Biblical Cosmos*, 19–21.

The Sea

In various ANE cultures, everything began with a vast, "chaotic," uninhabited sea. From this, the world we know arose. A notable ANE motif is that of creation of the world through conflict with, and defeat of, a sea deity. Most famously, in the Babylonian *Enuma Elish*, Tiamat, goddess of saltwater ocean, is slain by the god Marduk. He divided her watery corpse to form the heaven and the earth and sculpted the habitable world from her remains.

Genesis 1 also begins with water: a dark, churning sea, shapeless and empty (1:2). Life cannot thrive here. The Genesis 1 creation story concerns God bringing form to that which is formless and putting the sea in its place, creating a vertical habitable zone between the waters above, held at bay by a solid sky-dome, and the waters below, the seas and oceans we are familiar with (Day Two). God also pulls the sea back on the horizontal plane so that dry land is exposed (Day Three). This activity creates the zones of the heavens, the sea, and the land, which are subsequently populated (Days Four to Six).

Israel shares with other ANE cultures a use of the sea as a symbol of, for want of a better word, "chaos." It needs taming for life to thrive. But in Genesis 1, unusually, there is no conflict. God creates effortlessly, simply by speaking his commanding word. And the watery "chaos" is not banished from creation but kept within limits (cf. Prov 8:27–29; Jer 5:22); furthermore, within those limits it makes a *vital* contribution to the flourishing of creation, full of life and facilitating life (Gen 1:20–23; Ps 104:25). But if those limits are breached, as in the Flood (Gen 6–8), creation in thrown into reverse and undone.

One surprise about the biblical cosmos is the presence of *an ocean beneath the land*. The earth is often spoken of as being "upon" the waters (Pss 24:1–2; 136:6), not simply alongside them. Hence the need for stabilizing "pillars." Another surprise is the presence of *an ocean above the sky*, held back from us by the firmament (*raqia'*) (Gen 1:6–8; Ps 148:4), a solid sky-dome like an upside-down bowl.[4] We find the idea that the sky was solid to be odd, but it was a universal belief in the ANE. In Genesis 1, the sun, moon, and stars are set into that solid sky, like jewels. And on the other side if it—beyond the astral bodies—lies a vast ocean, held back so we have a habitable zone in which to live. This sky-ocean was not to be confused with the clouds, for the clouds lie on *this side* of the firmament.[5]

---

4. On these, see the two-part article by Seeley, "Firmament and the Waters Above."

5. Rain normally comes from clouds (1 Kgs 18:43–45), not from the sky-ocean beyond the firmament. In the Great Flood, however, God open windows in the heavens and let the water back (Gen 7:11), an act of de-creation, partly undoing Genesis 1.

So, water *in its place* is a great good, but it remains a dangerous force within creation, and various biblical texts echo the ANE conflict-with-chaos motif in describing God's relation with it. Sometimes it is pictured as a dragon, rebuked and defeated by God (Ps 18:10–16; Rahab in Job 26:12–13 and Ps 89:9–10; or the many-headed Leviathan in Ps 74:12–15, the latter text drawing on Canaanite mythology). In other texts, the sea or the sea monster is God's powerful and dangerous pet, which only he can tame (Job 41; Ps 104:25–26).

This water symbolism helps us to understand features of biblical stories, such as the exodus, in which crossing the Reed Sea is presented poetically as God's defeat of the sea monster Rahab (Isa 51:9–10; cf. Ps 74:12–15); or the "great fish" that swallowed Jonah, which has overtones of the sea dragons (not cuddly whales from children's books); or Jesus "rebuking" the wind and commanding the sea to "be still" (Mark 4:36–41) in the same way he does with demons (Mark 1:25); or Jesus walking not simply on water but "on the *sea*" (Mark 6:47–53), just as YWHW walks "on the sea" (Job 9:8), demonstrating his power over it. It also helps us understand why the symbolic chaos beasts of Daniel 7 and Revelation 13 (representing political powers) arise out of the sea and why the new creation in Revelation has no sea (Rev 21:1). We miss these layers of meaning if we do not grasp the place of the sea in Israelite cosmology.

Land

The land was much more familiar to Israelites than the water, for they were not a seafaring people. It was a place of towns and villages, surrounded by cultivated fields, and of wilderness and desert inhospitable to humans. (But, as God reminded Job, very fitting habitats for certain wild animals that he cares for; Job 38–39.) Although Israelite understandings of dry land are less peculiar to modern minds, there are many layers of interest that we might miss if we do not pay attention. For the land was a *meaning-full* space.

Consider mountains. In the ANE, mountains were not just rocky landscape features but had cosmic significance, for they linked heaven and earth, with roots going down underground and tops reaching towards the sky.[6] ANE gods were often pictured as inhabiting mountains and could be encountered on mountains. The Bible plays with precisely this symbolic idea. This is why shrines were on "high places" (1 Kgs 3:4–15). Indeed, in one tradition, the paradise of Eden was on God's holy mountain (Ezek 28:13–16). And consider some of those significant mountains of divine

---

6. On mountains, see Clifford, *Cosmic Mountain*.

encounter in the Bible: Abraham's offering of Isaac on Mount Moriah (Gen 22) and Elijah's battle of the deities on Mount Carmel (1 Kgs 18:20–40). And we cannot forget the two monumental mountains of divine encounter in the OT: Mount Sinai, where Moses met God at a burning bush (Exod 3–4), and where God met with the representatives of the children of Israel after the exodus, making covenant and giving them the law (Exod 19:1—Num 10:13), and where Elijah met God in the stillness (1 Kgs 19). This was a place of dramatic theophany. Then there is Mount Zion, the most holy location on earth, from an Israelite perspective. Here lay the place that YHWH had chosen and caused his Name to dwell—the Jerusalem temple. All Judahite religious life came to be orientated around the divine presence on this "holy hill." And although it was not a large hill, in prophetic rhetoric it was destined to become established as "the highest of mountains," the focus of international religious life, with all nations streaming to it to learn from YHWH (Isa 2:1–4). All this helps us see the importance of mountains in the NT as well. In Matthew's Gospel Jesus is tempted on a mountain (4:8), preaches a pivotal sermon on a mountain (5–7), prays alone on a mountain (14:23), heals on a mountain (15:29–31), is transfigured on a mountain (17:1), and gives his great commission to the disciples on a mountain (28:16). Mountains are places of divine encounter.

It is also worth making mention of wilderness in Israelite perspective. Here food and water were scarce, making them difficult places for humans to thrive (Job 38:26). And the animals that inhabited those dry places were, in Israelite perceptions, unclean creatures, not suitable for consumption. These were liminal spaces between the order of civilization and the disorder of "chaos"—places associated more with death than life, bandits and outlaws (cast out from civilization), unclean beasts, and even demons. The children of Israel (and later Elijah, 1 Kgs 17:2–6) could only survive there because of miraculous divine provision (Exod 16:1—17:7). It is no coincidence that Jesus was tested by the devil in the desert (Matt 4:1) and that the Gadarene demoniac had been driven by the demon into the wilderness (Luke 8:29). And it makes good sense in this context that the book of Isaiah envisages the restoration of Israel in terms of the wilderness becoming fertile land (41:17–20).

Israelites also viewed land in terms of their covenant relationship with God. Canaan was the land promised to Abraham and his descendants by YHWH (Gen 12:7, etc.). This theme looms large in the OT. In the religious imagination, the promised land is a kind of Edenic paradise (Deut 8:7–9; 11:11–15), or at least will be one day (Isa 51:3; Ezek 36:35). And this promised land was perceived to lie at the center of the world, certainly in terms of significance and perhaps too in literal terms (Ezek 5:5; 38:10–12). Later

Christians believed that Jerusalem, where Christ was crucified, was the literal and symbolic "mid-point of the earth" (Cyril of Jerusalem's phrase), an idea beautifully presented cartographically in the medieval Mappa Mundi, in which Jerusalem lies at the crux of the world (pun intended).

Indeed, horizontal space was perceived in terms of a graded holiness in the Bible. At the center, most holy of all, was the temple in Jerusalem. As one moves away from this center, from the divine dwelling place on earth, the holiness of the space declines, we move from divine "order" towards "chaos": from Jerusalem to the promised land to the wilderness, out towards the churning and dangerous sea. There was a spirituality to the geography in the Israelite world.

Sheol/Hades

In the Hebrew Bible, sheol (Greek, hades) is the realm of the dead.[7] It is a dark (Job 10:21), prison-like (Job 16:22) zone whose inhabitants exist in a pale echo of life on earth (Ps 88:2–12). And it was always spoken of as "below" (Deut 32:22), "the pit" (Jonah 2:6), "the depths of the earth" (Ps 71:20). One goes "down" to it and "ascends" from it. We tend to see such language as metaphor, but narrative texts suggest that it was understood more literally by biblical writers. In Num 16:23–34, the ground opens up and swallows Korah and his fellow rebels alive, taking them down into sheol—literally under the ground. Similarly, the witch of En-Dor brings Samuel "up" from sheol, and sees him "coming up out of the earth." In the NT, Jesus is pictured as defeating death, breaking open the gates of hades/sheol, and leading its prisoners free.

THE HEAVENS

In Scripture, "the heavens" is paired with "the earth," and refers to everything that is "up" in the sky: whether visible things on this side of the sky-dome (clouds, sun, moon, stars) or invisible things on the other side of the sky-dome (God, angels, the divine council, seraphim, etc.). And, just like earth and sea, it had inhabitants: sun, moon, stars; and heavenly beings in the highest heaven.

To get a quick glimpse of differences between ancient and modern ways of classifying celestial entitles, compare the following two tables. First, modern:

---

7. On sheol, see Johnson, *Shades of Sheol*.

Types of celestial entity	Modern typology of astral entities
Stars	*(including the sun)*
Planets	*(including Mercury, Venus, Mars, Jupiter, Saturn, and the earth itself)*
Moons	*(including our moon)*
Comets, asteroids, etc.	

And here is how biblical authors did it:

Type of celestial entity	Ancient typology of astral entities	
Sun		
Moon		
Stars	Falling stars	*Comets, etc.*
	Fixed stars	*Stars (grouped in constellations)*
	Wandering stars	*Mercury*
		Venus
		Mars
		Jupiter
		Saturn

We immediately notice that in this geocentric cosmos the earth is not an astral entity at all. It wasn't spinning in space; and the sun is not a star; and what we differentiate as stars, planets, and comets, etc., are all considered different kinds of star. This is all perfectly sensible, given the available evidence. It is not that the ancients did not study the sky carefully—they knew its visible inhabitants and its movements intimately. Indeed, they could predict the movements of the sky with considerable accuracy. The sky was their clock and their calendar, and was often seen as a place in which messages from the gods were revealed in astral signs.

Celestial Bodies

Even more weird to modern minds is the way in which astral entitles were considered by ANE cultures to be closely associated with divine beings—gods.[8] They were possibly understood as the heavenly equivalents of the idols that populated the temples across the ancient world. These idols

---

8. On stars and gods, see Rochberg, "Stars Their Likeness."

represented the gods and were believed to be animated by the gods—such that to worship the idol was to worship the god. However, a god could not be reduced to its images, but transcended them all. So too sun, moon, and stars were understood as the astral images of gods, but the gods transcended those counterparts. This is why the movements of stars were understood to be messages from the gods. Deities communicated their will to humans through their astral bodies. And this too is why the sun, moon, and stars were worshiped across the ANE . . . except in Israel.

Israel was unique in developing a religion in which the worship of stars was forbidden; *YHWH alone* was to be the object of Israel's worship and service (Deut 4:19). And when Israel fell into worshiping stars (2 Kgs 23:5) it was strongly rebuked by the prophets (Amos 5:25–27; Jer 8:1–2). So too, while heavenly signs were seen as significant (portending judgment, e.g., Isa 13:10, or most famously announcing the birth of Christ), biblical religion was unusual in not developing any significant interest in astrology, even exhibiting certain hostility to it (Isa 47:13).

Nonetheless, there are reasons to think that at least some of the biblical authors shared the common ANE belief that the stars were manifestations of heavenly beings, indeed, of gods. We need to be clear: in biblical texts, these astral gods were not the Creator, they were creatures; so they were not on a par with YHWH and they were certainly *not* to be worshiped. But they could still be spoken of gods, heavenly beings with great dignity. And YHWH, the Creator, was "the God of gods" (Ps 136:2).

Here we could compare the Ugaritic conception of the divine council with Israel's. In Ugarit we have:

1. El, the chief god, and his wife, Athirat.
2. The sons of El—the gods. There appear to have been seventy of them.
3. The craftsmen gods.
4. Minor deities, including the messenger gods (*ml'km*)—servants.

In Ugarit the council of El is called "the assembly of the gods," "the circle of El," "the assembly of the sons of El." The divine council was a large divine family, with servants, who convened on El's sacred mountain. Now it appears that the sons of El were *astral* deities. They are called "star gods" and "the assembly of stars" and individual members have astral associations.

This is not at all dissimilar to what we find in some biblical texts:

1. El, the *chief* god (i.e., "*the* god" or, what we would call, "God with a capital G") and ruler of the council.
2. The "sons of El" or "gods."

3. The messengers (*ml'km*, i.e., angels)

Our interest here is in the members of the divine council. In the OT they are called, amongst other things, "gods" (Ps 82:1), "sons of the Most High" (Ps 82:6), and "holy ones" (Ps 89:6–7). They are assigned governance, by YHWH, over the seventy nations of the world.[9] Their responsibility is to do justice—although they do not always achieve this (Ps 82). Now, just as Ugaritic literature refers to the divine council as "the assembly of stars," so too parts of the OT seem to associate the members of the divine council with stars.

> Where were you [Job] when I [YHWH] laid the foundation of
> the earth? . . .
> when the *morning stars* sang together
> and all the *sons of God* shouted for joy? (Job 38:4, 7)

Here the "sons of God" (i.e., the members of the divine council, see Job 1:6; 2:1) seem to be identified with "the morning stars." The two lines in verse 7 are parallel and the subjects of each line would appear to be the same or, at very least, linked. We may also note that the stars/sons of God were not involved in creating—YHWH did that—but they were around when God made the earth and they responded to God's creative activity with joy.

- Job 4:18 and 15:15 seem to contain the same idea and need to be interpreted in the light of each other:
- "Even in his servants he puts no trust, // and his angels he charges with error" (4:18).
- "Behold, God puts no trust in his holy ones, // and the heavens are not pure in his sight" (15:15).

By "heavens" the poet most likely has the heavenly bodies in mind. This would also make the stars parallel to "his servants," "his angels," and "his holy ones." The point of 15:14–16 is that God is *so* pure that *even* his heavenly servants seem impure by comparison.

Various other texts suggest this same star-deity link (Ezek 1:4–28; Isa 14:12–15; 24:21–23; Pss 89:5–7; 148:1–6).[10]

The stars were sometimes seen as God's heavenly hosts/armies (Deut 4:19; 17:3). As such, they could be actively involved in warfare:

> The kings came, they [i.e., the tribes of Israel] fought;
> then fought the kings of Canaan, . . .

---

9. On which, see Heiser, *Unseen Realm*.
10. On all these texts, see Parry, *Biblical Cosmos*, ch. 5.

> *From heaven the stars fought,*
> from their courses they fought against Sisera.
> (Judg 5:19–20)

Here the stars in heaven are pictured as joining the armies of Israel in fighting against Sisera. The earthly battle had a heavenly counterpart.

Nevertheless, because they were not objects of worship, though the stars were gods they were a matter of relative disinterest in biblical religion. YHWH was the focus. He created the sun, moon, and stars (Ps 136:5, 7–9; Isa 40:22, 25–26); they are called to worship him (Ps 148:3) and they declare his glory (Ps 19:1). He is sovereign over them (Dan 4:35; Job 9:7–10) and they are to obey his commands. Their predictable behavior is a testimony to God's fidelity to creation (Ps 148:6; Jer 33:20–22), and they serve to mark times and seasons for the worship of God (Gen 1:14–19). These created gods are servants of YHWH.

God's Heaven

Beyond the firmament is God's heaven, hidden from human sight and inaccessible to earthly creatures, unless admitted by God (like Elijah ascending on chariots of fire). This heaven is literally "up." Thus, Jesus ascends into heaven (Acts 1:9–11)—an act that is, of course, symbolic of his enthronement but was also taken literally. And at the parousia he will descend from heaven (1 Thess 4:15–17).

The imagery of heaven draws in large part on earthly royal courts. Heaven is God's palace, where his throne room is, from which he governs the world (Rev 4). There are numerous heavenly beings that are also pictured as inhabiting heaven—the sons of God (i.e., the divine council; 1 Kgs 22:19–23), cherubim (Isa 37:16), seraphim (Isa 6:3), angels (who serve as messengers), archangels, multi-faced living creatures (Rev 4:6–9), and so forth. Similar heavenly creatures (i.e., messengers of the gods and unearthly, hybrid beings) can be found in the heaven imagery of Egypt, Assyria, Babylon, and elsewhere. In Scripture, all these are servants of the King, YHWH. The focus is always directed towards the one who sits on the throne.

This imagery is a human attempt to speak of that which was understood to be beyond speech. Notice Ezekiel's very guarded language describing his vision of the heavenly creatures (who possibly represented divine constellations): what he saw staggered his mind; he could not say what it was, only that it had the *appearance* of this or that (Ezek 1). And God transcends heaven itself. Heaven, remember, is a dimension of creation, and creation cannot hold God: "Behold, heaven and the highest heaven cannot contain you" (1 Kgs 8:27).

THE COSMOS AS A TEMPLE

Another aspect of the biblical cosmos was that it was closely associated with the sanctuary. Many scholars have argued that temples in the ancient world were seen as microcosms, symbolic models of the cosmos. And the reverse was true too: the cosmos was perceived to be a temple.[11]

> He built his sanctuary like the high heavens,
> like the earth, which he has founded forever.
> (Ps 78:69)

The basic pattern of the tabernacle shown by God to Moses on Mount Sinai was simple enough. It was composed of three sections: (a) an outer courtyard, containing a large altar for sacrifices and a laver full of water, (b) a chamber called the holy place, containing a seven-branched lamp stand, a table for bread, and an altar for burning incense, and (c) a central chamber, the holy of holies, containing the ark of the covenant. There is reason to think that these represented different zones of creation.

The outer court arguably represented the land and sea. Some clues include: a large bronze basin containing water called "the sea" (1 Kgs 7:23–26), with representations of plants (gourds) and animals (oxen) on the basin, the latter facing to the four points of the compass; and an alter originally composed of earth and uncut stones (Exod 20:24–25). This area was accessible to any ritually clean Israelite.

The holy place represents the sky (this side of the firmament). Some clues here include the seven-branched candlestick, arguably representing the seven fixed lights that could be seen with the naked eye in the sky: the sun, the moon, Mercury, Venus, Mars, Jupiter, and Saturn. (Incidentally, the word Gen 1:14–18 uses for the sun, moon, and stars is "lights," *māʾôr*, a word only used elsewhere for the sanctuary lights.) We should also note that the curtain separating the holy place from the outer court was blue, purple, and scarlet and was held up by blue loops—all sky colors.

One might think that the garden symbolism in the holy place (the floral decorations; the bread, made from grain; the candlestick, which can be interpreted as a stylized tree of life) undermines such sky claims, but this is to forget the close association of temples with mountains[12] and the idea

---

11. On the temple-cosmos, see Beale, *Temple and the Church's Mission*.
12. Parry, *Biblical Cosmos*, 141, 49–56.

that Eden was located on a mountain (Ezek 28:13–16). It would make sense in the symbolic world of ancient Israel for the garden paradise to be located skyward, up a mountain, allowing the holy place to contain both sky and paradise imagery.

The most holy place represents God's heaven, beyond the firmament. The curtain separating the holy place from the holy of holies was decorated with cherubim, symbolic of those heavenly creatures that guard the divine throne. Its colors of blue, purple, and scarlet were those of the sky (indeed, it may have represented the sky-dome) (Exod 26:1). Within the chamber itself was God's cherubic throne (1 Kgs 6:23–28) and his royal footstool, the ark of the covenant (1 Chr 28:2). Appropriately, humans cannot see into this heavenly throne room and are not permitted to enter it. The only exception is the high priest on one day a year, and even then, only when surrounded by a thick cloud of incense, obscuring his sight (Lev 16).

So the temple is the cosmos writ small. When the priests and the high priest move around the temple performing their sacred duties, they are symbolically moving around the biblical cosmos. And when humans move around in the world, they move around in the outer court of God's holy house.

THE BIBLICAL COSMOS TODAY

How can we inhabit the biblical cosmos? The first thing to say is that it is not possible for those with modern scientific understandings of the world to inhabit the biblical cosmos in the way ancient Israelites did. Belief in a flat earth, for instance, or that heaven is literally upwards, is simply not a live option (the Flat Earth Society notwithstanding).

Second, Christians have long recognized that in revealing himself God accommodates to the capacities and conceptualities of his audience to facilitate communication. God in love stoops down to communicate in ways his audience would understand. (Reminding me of how my chemistry teacher first explained to me that a molecule is atoms holding hands.) The idea of revelatory accommodation can be found in the work of Christian theologians since the time of the church fathers. And such accommodation would include working within the parameters of ancient understandings of the cosmos.[13] That biblical cosmology is not scientifically accurate does not

---

13. For a survey of the concept of accommodation throughout church history, see Hilber, *Old Testament Cosmology*, ch. 3. Hilber's book seeks to develop the notion in more nuanced and sophisticated ways through use of the use of linguistic concepts from relevance theory.

mean that the biblical texts are not divinely inspired, nor that God was not revealing truth through them.

Third, we should refuse to reduce the notion of "truth" to that of "scientific truth." And here is where the weird and wonderful world of the Bible has so much to offer us today. Not *despite* its weirdness but precisely *because of* it. The strangeness of the biblical cosmos grabs our attention and wakes us up to the *meaning* biblical writers saw in the world. God can speak afresh through their words today.

Some biblical cosmology transfers into the modern world without much effort, even if we no longer take it literally. Most obviously, we still speak of the sun rising and setting, because that describes how it appears from where we stand. Nobody takes such speech scientifically, but neither is it considered problematic. The same could be said of talk about "the ends of the earth" and such like.

Now consider the image of heaven being above us. That is not literally true, and we do not expect space missions to discover God's throne room. Heaven is not, in our conceptuality, a physical space within the cosmos. (And arguably ancient Judaism developed a much more sophisticated understanding of it than that too.) Nevertheless, talk of heaven being "above" is still very useful because it metaphorically conveys something importantly true of heaven: its eminence and its transcendence. Today we still use height and depth language to speak of value and rank and such like. John was brought down; Sarah went up in public opinion. It functioned exactly the same in Scripture. Heaven was the most exalted dimension of creation—through which God presences himself within creation—and so it was pictured as *above* everything else. That was *always* the idea embedded in the ancient cosmography. And it's true. Heaven is invisible and inaccessible to us—another truth integral to biblical imagery—and it is still "up above" in every way that matters. Talk of a royal throne room in heaven is not to be taken literally—and presumably most biblical writers realized this: God doesn't have a body, for starters, so a throne isn't much use—but it is a true symbol of divine rule. Jesus "ascending" into the sky remains an image that captures the meaning of Jesus's cosmic enthronement—ascending to the heights of God's heaven. The ascent image was *always* about that.

Now of course, modern Christian theologians need to ponder afresh how we think about heaven and the ascension and such like, reflecting on how such talk integrates with our current scientific and philosophical ways of thinking, but that is no different from what Christians have always done. Theology is a never-finished task. And the biblical imagery remains at the very heart of that project. (Similar things could be said about the underworld, which, while not literally below the earth, is an image that can still resonate with us.)

Talk of the cosmos as a temple is also inspirational, even in a modern secular world which has only the vaguest memory of what temples are about. For a temple is a royal house, for a monarch to live in and reign from. And that is not a difficult idea. To picture the whole universe as a stunning palace built by God for divine habitation serves simultaneously to bestow great value on the cosmos (it is sacred and holy) and to see it as infused with divine presence. This is a fecund metaphor with many implications for how we see the world, how we find God in it, and how humans should behave in it.

What about star deities? Stars are, in the words of Pumba, "balls of gas burning billions of miles away." They ain't gods. Even so, they can still serve as powerful symbols of the divine realm, pointing us beyond themselves to transcendent spiritual realities. And they are not arbitrary symbols, for their light speaks to us of the divine Light. As such, they still declare the glory of God (Ps 19:1).

And chaotic oceans surrounding us—above us, below us, and encircling us? Obviously, we cannot believe in this as a physical reality, but it can still function as a picture that speaks to us of the presence in creation of powerful forces beyond our control that are a great good when contained and channeled appropriately but that can endanger and undo us. Creation is good but also potentially dangerous. Those forces can by physical or sociopolitical or spiritual. Indeed, Scripture itself employs water-dragon imagery to speak of unruly political powers, which God opposes. So the process of "deliteralizing" cosmic imagery is going on within the Bible itself. Scripture invites us to consider how we might do likewise.

In sum, while some aspects of biblical models of the cosmos cannot be taken as truths about the physical structure of the world, they can still serve to speak truth—symbolic, metaphorical, theological, spiritual, and metaphysical truth about God, the world, and how we should inhabit it.

BIBLIOGRAPHY

Beale, G. K. *The Temple and the Church's Mission: A Biblical Theology of the Dwelling Place of God*. New Studies in Biblical Theology. Leicester, UK: Apollos, 2004.

Clifford, Richard J. *The Cosmic Mountain in Canaan and the Old Testament*. 1972. Repr. Eugene, OR: Wipf & Stock, 2010.

Heiser, Michael S. *The Unseen Realm: Recovering the Supernatural Worldview of the Bible*. Bellingham, WA: Lexham, 2015.

Hilber, John W. *Old Testament Cosmology and Divine Accommodation: A Relevance Theory Approach.* Eugene, OR: Cascade, 2020.

Horrowitz, Wayne. *Mesopotamian Cosmic Geography.* 2nd ed. Winona Lake, IN: Eisenbrauns, 2011.

Johnson, Philip. *Shades of Sheol: Death and Afterlife in the Old Testament.* Leicester, UK: Apollos, 2002.

Keel, Othmar. *The Symbolism of the Biblical World: Ancient Near Eastern Iconography in the Book of Psalms.* Translated by Timothy J. Hallett. Winona Lake, IN: Eisenbrauns, 1997.

Parry, Robin A. *The Biblical Cosmos: A Pilgrim's Guide to the Weird and Wonderful World of the Bible.* Eugene, OR: Cascade, 2014.

Rochberg, Francesca. "'The Stars Their Likeness': Perspectives on the Relation between Celestial Bodies and Gods in Ancient Mesopotamia." In *What Is a God? Anthropomorphic and Non-Anthropomorphic Aspects of Deity in Ancient Mesopotamia,* edited by Barbara Nevling Porter, 41–91. Winona Lake, IN: Eisenbrauns, 2009.

Seely, Paul H. "The Firmament and the Waters Above. Part I: The Meaning of raqiaʿ in Gen 1:6–8." *Westminster Theological Journal* 53 (1991) 227–40.

———. "The Firmament and the Waters Above. Part II: The Meaning of 'The Water above the Firmament' in Gen 1:6–8." *Westminster Theological Journal* 54 (1992) 31–46.

Chapter 38
Penultimate Hermeneutics
DAVID STUART

Selecting the appropriate hermeneutical lens to interpret the biblical text has been endlessly debated, leaving the interpreter often feeling at a crossroads with no sense of direction. The number of chapters in this book is clear enough indication that there is no obvious or simple solution to the problem of selection. And yet the Christian cannot avoid selecting one (or more) of the available options because the Bible cannot be read without also engaging in hermeneutics. Even those who seek to avoid a precise method of interpretation cannot help but implicitly interpret the text through a particular lens and according to a set of presuppositions which invariably determine the meaning they draw from the text. Whether it is intentional or nascent, selecting and using a hermeneutic is a necessary part of reading Scripture.

But the problem runs far deeper. Even if we could determine the most reliable hermeneutic, the interpreter would not necessarily be able to rely on their conclusions due to the more fundamental problem of limitation. Our human situation is inescapably conditioned by finitude and fallibility. As finite beings, we can never see things from God's infinite perspective because finitude restricts our viewpoint and creates the possibility of being wrong. As we are unable to guarantee the faithful use of any chosen interpretative method, the importance of the selection of method seems negligible. The reliability of the interpreter is more fundamentally at stake. We are not only lost at a crossroads, then, but we cannot rely on our ability to navigate to find the right path.

We could consider simply accepting our situation of being lost in uncertainty and dismiss the desire to be correct. If the quest for truth is ultimately futile, there seems little need to continue pursuing it. But such a move undermines a typical Christian reason for interpreting the Bible, that of Christian formation. This was classically the meaning behind the reformational principle *sola scriptura*. Scripture was viewed as the primary authority for Christian belief and praxis, and as such was the main source of greater conformity to Christ.[1] Connected to the principle of *solus Christus*, as the Christian encounters the text, they, too, expect to encounter Christ who will renew them and conform them to his image. But by connecting hermeneutics directly with ethics, the problem of limitation takes on much higher stakes. A misinterpretation here impacts the interpreter's beliefs *and* actions. And if *sola scriptura* comes to function as a self-authenticating principle as it did in its late-modern renderings, abhorrent ethical actions may be justified with little to no room for criticism. This has led many to renounce the text itself as the primary principle of interpretation but, as Willem Dekker notices, another principle will inevitably fill its place and which may be something even more contestable.[2] The problem in either case is that whatever principles are used to determine hermeneutics seem to be thoroughly human and ultimately arbitrary, leaving us with haphazard justifications for derived interpretations or ethical actions. Christian formation demands the search for reliability within our limited context but depending how it is resolved can lead to significant rational, ethical, or pastoral consequences.

A penultimate hermeneutic seeks to respond to the problem of limitation, but not by providing a principle which we can simply rely on to do the interpretative work for us. Originating from Dietrich Bonhoeffer's ultimate/penultimate distinction, it rather seeks to approach things from a theological perspective, contextualizing the hermeneutical process and the problem of limitation within the interrelated and ongoing activity between God and humanity.[3] Within this theological landscape, "penultimacy" will be shown to be a more theological and fruitful term than "limitation" in describing the human situation. The difference in terminology helps relocate our limited ways of knowing and the possibilities of erring within the larger

---

1. Dekker, "Hermeneutical Theology as Contemporary Rendition of the *Sola Scriptura*," 106.
2. Dekker, "Hermeneutical Theology," 106.
3. The circularity of this approach is not lost on me. I am starting as an insider by reading Scripture *as Scripture* rather than as an outsider. However, given that faith depends on perceiving the meaning of reality differently, it seems one of many appropriate starting points for considering hermeneutics.

narrative of God's relating to humanity through these limitations. That is to say that our human, penultimate activity, relates to God through Christ and in the Spirit as the ultimate "origin, essence and goal" of all life.[4] When considered according to this theological framework our limitations become reconceived as possibilities for encounter with the self-communicating God who seeks to reconcile and conform us to his image.

This will be shown to have significant effect on how the interpreter interprets. Instead of seeking a reliable method that might lead to the most verifiable propositional truth-claims, reflection on penultimacy will lead us to ask, how does the interpreter encounter God through interpretation and what might enable or hinder their conformity to Christ in the interpretative process? Penultimacy will be shown to contain an internal imperative to seek to encounter and to conform to God whilst also retaining the ever-present possibility of mistaking God's voice and putting one's faith in something other than God (i.e., engaging in idolatry). By identifying the ways which are conducive or which inhibit encounter with God, a penultimate posture will be identified as conditioning how the interpreter interprets. This will have wide-ranging implications for interpretation as we contextualize the interpreter, the text, the interpretations and the interpretative community within an ultimate/penultimate framework. The problem of selection will dull in significance due to the possibility of utilizing many different forms of interpretative method. Moreover, a penultimate posture will help us navigate on the road as we learn to rely on God as our travelling companion and ultimate destination. It will do so by centralizing focus on God and remaining open to challenge and reinterpretation through regular encounter with God. Two practices will be identified as particularly prudent to enable this task: acts of witnessing to God and acts of repentance for ways that attentiveness has morphed into some form of idolatry or self-justification.

All of this analysis relies on identifying a penultimate interpretative posture which requires understanding the theological context from which it emerges. We turn, then, to the place from which "penultimate" language is borrowed: Bonhoeffer's ultimate/penultimate distinction.

THE ULTIMATE/PENULTIMATE CONTEXT

The language of penultimacy as used here originates in Bonhoeffer's ultimate/penultimate distinction which seeks to make sense of all reality in its united duality. It claims that Jesus Christ is located at the center of all created reality and is reconciling all things to himself (cf. John 1:1–3; Col 1:15–20).

---

4. Bonhoeffer, *Ethics* (henceforth DBWE 6), 251.

Christ is the mediator of everything, becoming in himself the fundamental meeting point of Creator and creation.[5] Bonhoeffer goes on to understand all things and events through what sort of relation they have to Christ. To do so, he uses the language of ultimate and penultimate, referring to whether an activity is directly attributable to Christ or is indirectly attributable to Christ as an effect of his direct action. He illustrates this by unpacking the logic of the doctrine of justification by faith.

For Bonhoeffer, justification by faith connotes a believer being restored to a relation with Christ not through their own action but through Christ's action in them, which elicits their response of faith.[6] Christ can thus be attributed as the primary or *ultimate* agent who actualizes a relationship of dependence, situating the human agent in a responsive position in relation to Christ. The giving of grace and the illumination of faith within the believer is thus directly attributable to Christ and is considered an ultimate event. The receiving of grace and responding in faith is the consequence of Christ's action which elicits this response in the believer. These receptive, dependent and responsive types of actions are considered penultimate. The ultimate thus remains transcendent from the penultimate as the penultimate's "origin, essence and goal," and so can never be contained by it. As such, ultimate events are never fully comprehendible as they remain ungraspable by the penultimate, Moreover, penultimate events are only discernible as such only after an ultimate event has occurred, which has related those events to itself.

This dependent relation is cached out by Bonhoeffer in two ways. First, there is a qualitative difference where the penultimate's dependence on the ultimate is not reciprocal as the ultimate is the one who initiates the relation. The penultimate's identity is inextricably linked to the initiating (and sustaining) action of the ultimate but the ultimate does not gain its identity from the penultimate. In classical terms, the Creator's relation to creation is characterized by his aseity as he remains free from creation's influence, but creation is in a dependent relationship with the Creator.[7] Only because of God's ultimate actions are the creature's existence, response and identity possible.

Along with this qualitative sense, Bonhoeffer draws out a temporal and telic sense of the distinction and its logic is worth reflecting on in greater detail. This relies on the more typical use of ultimate/penultimate language

5. DBWE 6, 58.
6. DBWE 6, 148.
7. It should be noted that Bonhoeffer preferred using terminology of "promeity" as he resisted notions of freedom as being abstracted from things but rather being free for another. Nonetheless, the meaning is not significantly changed in this context. Cf. Bonhoeffer, "Lectures on Christology" (henceforth DBWE 12), 310–15.

as referring to the last thing and the thing which immediately precedes the last thing, respectively. Here, Bonhoeffer stresses how Christ culminates the life prior to faith rather than on how he initiates faith. More than just a temporal fact, the significance of the ultimate coming last is that, from this final position, it reorders all that comes before it. The point here seems twofold.

First, that which previously did not consider itself penultimate (or inherently related and ordered towards God) can now, after the fact, be considered as such. This speaks to how our conceptual framework is altered by encounter with the ultimate where we begin to perceive the ultimate in ways we previously would not have. Augustine's autobiography *Confessions* is exemplary on this point given how he reconceives his childhood and early adulthood in light of the faith he acquires later on.[8] This speaks to the way in which Christ reconciles our past lives that may previously have opposed him but, through his ultimate action, have been reconciled and ordered to him. When perceived as penultimate, events can no longer be considered in and of themselves as if they could be described apart from their relation to the ultimate.

Bonhoeffer reflects on forgiveness to illustrate the logic here. Whilst we may be inclined to look on our past with regret, guilt and shame regarding various sinful actions, when we encounter Christ's forgiveness, no longer can we perceive them according to our actions alone. Looking back through the lens of Christ's forgiveness, Bonhoeffer argues that we are invited to see not only the destructive intentions and effects of our actions but also the way God is at work in reconciling our past to himself, justifying us despite our sinfulness and moving us to perceive and participate in that reconciliation.[9] The relation of our penultimate past and present are all to be understood through our relation to Christ and no longer in or of themselves. An ultimate encounter of Christ thus leads us to reconsider our past and present identities primarily through the lens of how Christ has related us to himself.

The second temporal sense is more eschatological in nature, which expands the aforementioned logic to a cosmic scale.[10] This is the idea that we have encountered the ultimate *as the ultimate* but only through a *penultimate* frame. We see now "through a glass, darkly" (1 Cor 13.12) and so our perception of the ultimate never itself amounts to being an ultimate event. Rather, we always perceive the ultimate in a penultimate and provisional way. This does not preclude ultimate events from happening but

---

8. Cf. Augustine, *Confessions*, 3–70.
9. Bonhoeffer, *Act and Being*, 156–57.
10. Cf. Harvey, *Taking Hold of the Real*, 22.

rather emphasizes our epistemological location in relation to them, that an ultimate event must be affirmed and attested to rather than possessed and objectively understood. The penultimate thus defers to the ultimate and relies on the ultimate as the end goal or telos of its existence. Moreover, an ultimate event points away from itself to the end of time where the ultimate will fulfil and finally reorder the penultimate which can only now be accessed in a conditional way. The eschatological action of God thus is discerned in the present through ultimate events and orders the penultimate to God's final action in restoring all things.

To claim an ultimate event has occurred can be nothing other than a statement of faith which cannot be rationally deduced from an impartial standpoint. This is because the penultimate always responds to the ultimate and points towards it but never encompasses it so that the penultimate transforms into the ultimate. The person who recognizes their own penultimacy thus points away from themselves to the ultimate who is the source, sustenance and goal of their existence.

This complicates the task of distinguishing between the penultimate and the ultimate for the ultimate could either be conflated with the penultimate or go unnoticed. Bonhoeffer thinks this keeps us in a position of openness to the penultimate where the penultimate acts as a "cover of the ultimate."[11] Our task is to be attentive to where the ultimate has occurred, is currently occurring or may occur in the future and, in the case of the latter, we can "prepare the way" to enable us to recognize the ultimate better.[12] We might do so by embodying a penultimate posture which, crucially, does not dismiss the penultimate for not being the ultimate but seeks to listen to the penultimate and discern the ultimate through it.

Conversely, the penultimate should not be blanketly affirmed as if it were itself the ultimate or always the site of God's revelatory activity. The ultimate must always remain distinguishable from the penultimate so as not to divinize creation or unduly promote or justify our own points of view. To claim something is penultimate is not to guarantee validity or appeal to an inscrutable authority; it is rather to account for its radical provisionality and need to rely on another (the ultimate) for verification. The claim here is that Christ, through his ultimate action, relates to the penultimate; it is not that the penultimate is inherently good on its own terms. By emphasizing God's activity to the penultimate, the penultimate has the lexical range to encompass both good and bad things. That is, it encompasses actions which respond to Christ in faith or oppose Christ in sin. Whilst God may be at

---

11. DBWE 6, 158.
12. DBWE 6, 161–62.

work reconciling them to himself, the sinful actions remain in opposition to God and are attempts to exclude or overcome the ultimate. There are thus two ways of enacting penultimate identity, either consistent ways of acting in faith or ways which contradict the relation to God by trying to oppose that relation.[13] The penultimate person who seeks to take their penultimacy seriously thus seeks to live by faith in God which entails attesting to Christ's ultimate centrality and turning from ways which have hindered that focus. We can condense this into two primary actions: acts of witness and of repentance.

To witness in this context involves attesting to Christ as the ultimate source of a revelatory event which led to the believer perceiving Christ's activity. Such an event can be rationally investigated but cannot be comprehended in such a way that the person no longer has to attest to Christ as the source of the event or as ultimate. For this reason, Bonhoeffer talks of Christ not as the conclusion of rational investigation but the premise of our theological reflection.[14] Christ is not to be categorized according to our preconceived notions of reality but rather is deferred to as the one who establishes himself as the center of reality and enables us to reconceive reality in this way. Such a move dislocates the position of the human subject in relation to Christ, putting Christ rather than the self in the center. Rather than attempting to master what Christ is, the theologian can only defer to who Christ has revealed himself to be through repeated acts of witness. The focus of witness will thus naturally be on Christ's incarnation who remains outwith the immediate vicinity of the penultimate enquirer today and thus to Scripture which itself attests to the reality of Christ's centrality. The witness will also attest to the encounter of Christ in the life of the believer which inspired faith and the (ongoing) reorientation of their worldview. Such a position also resists the ways in which humans might seek to overcome Christ by instrumentalizing an idea of him for their own purposes. Whilst no Christian is immune from this possibility, witnessing to Christ reduces their actuality as there remains a constant deferral to Christ. The Christian seeking to witness to Christ thus prays with him, "Not my will, but yours, be done" (Luke 22:42). The act of witness can thus be summarized as deferring to an encounter which remains outwith the subject's control and defers to the source of that encounter (that is, Christ) to repeatedly authenticate himself to the believer and through the life of the believer.

---

13. Bonhoeffer describes these respectively as "natural" and "unnatural." DBWE 6, 173–85.

14. DBWE 12, 350.

Repentance refers to a two-step process which is facilitated by dependence on Christ's ultimate activity. Repentance requires first an awareness of ways the self has become disoriented from God and requires reorientation to God. This is where the Christian realizes their life of faith has been once again infiltrated by sinful desires, actions and/or effects. Whilst this presumably can arise simply through self-reflection, Bonhoeffer stresses that this typically arises through encounter, primarily with God but also with others. Through encounter, we may be challenged and emotionally convicted of ways in which our ethical existences have not conformed to our dependency on God in the way we either had previously intended or now seek to reorder them. It seems particularly pressing that this leads Christians to be unable to ignore those who are different to them (be that sociologically or ideologically) simply because they are challenging or are presupposed to be wrong in their perspective. By encountering others—even when radically different to us—we may be led by God into discerning ways in which we need to repent.

After recognizing the reality of the situation, the second step is to reorient one's beliefs and actions to Christ. Rather than being a one-off act performed at conversion, Bonhoeffer shows his Lutheran roots by arguing for the ongoing need for repentance.[15] As Luther stated, "humanity lives in sins and daily is either justified or more polluted."[16] The Christian thus should seek out regular encounter with God to be continually reoriented by God's reconciling activity in the life of the believer. The act of repentance seeks to realign the self to the ultimate in ways it has, accidentally or intentionally, sought to reduce the ultimate's significance.

Acts of witness and of repentance are both conditioned by being dependent on encounters with God. Neither seeks to rely on their own abilities in a way that could amount to self-justification, but each consistently seeks to defer away from the self to God. Each presupposes the contemporaneity of God's action, not simply deferring to prior historical revelation but also to God's relational activity within the life of the penultimate individual. The person who realizes their penultimate identity is thus invited to actively seek out ways in which God may have already encountered the individual which they had not realized at the time and to be attentive to ways in which God may encounter them in the future. Both also seek to remain or become aware of ways in which they have intentionally or inadvertently contradicted God in sin through ignoring, forgetting or opposing him, perhaps even in their attempts to appeal to him through witness or repentance. The

---

15. DBWE 2, 156–57.
16. *Die Disputatio de homine*, 177, my translation.

penultimate individual is thus invited to adopt a posture of deference, attentiveness, anticipation and self-criticism or, in sum, a penultimate posture. This enables the Bonhoefferian scholar Ross Halbach to summarize that "Theology . . . is repentance. Its goal is not to speak for God but to prepare the way for the surprise of God's speaking."[17]

PENULTIMATE INTERPRETATION

With the theological context expounded, we can now turn to applying penultimacy to the task of biblical interpretation. Because Christ and his direct actions are perceived as ultimate, all things to do with interpretation can be viewed as nothing other than penultimate, including the text, the interpretations deduced, the method of interpretation, the interpretative community and the interpreter themselves. We will consider the relevance of penultimacy in relation to each feature.

Beginning with the biblical text, penultimacy invites us to distinguish the biblical text from both the historical revelatory events which it attests to and from a contemporary encounter with God which the reading of the text facilitates but neither necessitates nor becomes. The biblical text is itself conditioned by historical acts of witness given how it seeks to attest to revelatory encounters of individuals and communities with God occurring in antiquity.[18] It is thus penultimate in a historical sense insofar as it attests to God's prior ultimate activity. As seen through Christian usage today, the text functions not only as a historical witness but also a contemporary witness to God's activity. That is to say that the bible has become a site for God's ultimate encounter with Christians. To make this claim does not entail a corollary affirmation of either the text's infallibility or inerrancy; it is to say that as a penultimate witness to God, the text can be utilized by God to cause an ultimate event for the interpreter. The text, as a penultimate thing, can be used providentially by God in the life of its reader to cause an ultimate event in which their existence becomes reordered and reanimated by God through Christ in the Spirit.

This is similar to the claims of hermeneutical theologians like Gerhard Ebeling or Eberhard Jüngel who focus on the way language affects the reader. In short, they claim that rather than being a descriptive imposition on reality, language is the basic structure of reality which enables reality to affect us. Applied to reading the biblical text, an event occurs where the language

---

17. Halbach, *Bonhoeffer and the Racialized Church*, 10.

18. This is not to claim every event in the bible happened in the way it is written about; it is rather to claim that the authors of the biblical texts attest to direct encounters with God they or their communities experienced.

of the text affects the interpreter in such a way that it changes their beliefs and/or actions by addressing them and eliciting a response from them.[19] In our terms, when this occurs during interpretation, an ultimate event can be said to have taken place where God has encountered the reader by addressing them through the text and the interpreter responds by interpreting and acting. The interpreter should always then be ready for God to use the biblical text to cause an ultimate event where they are challenged or changed by God to become more fully conformed to his image, without presuming an ultimate event will occur. The interpreter relates to the text with an openness to God speaking through it but without the ability to create or force an ultimate event. Encountering God remains God's prerogative. In sum, the biblical text is penultimate in its origins and in its contemporary effects on the interpreter and can be the location of ultimate events of encounter with God.

This position moves away from any notion that might divinize the biblical text, suggesting that either the text itself or the interpretation derived from it are inscrutable. As Maarten Wisse reminds us, "Scripture witnesses to the incarnation, but it is not in itself incarnational."[20] This can only be done by continuing to distinguish between the possibility and the necessity of God using the text to create an ultimate event. There must remain a chance for God not to act through the text or for his activity to be misconstrued as something other than it is. Such a possibility is what enables the text to be utilized to justify sinful actions or beliefs and considering the text as in some way ultimate perpetuates these eventualities. The text must instead be affirmed as penultimate, something which points towards the ultimate and may, at times, be the location of the ultimate, but is never itself ultimate. In more classical terminology, God's word operates through the written word of the text but cannot be reduced to the text and cannot be presumed to be operant.[21] The interpreter's relation to the text is thus one of being a witness to a witness where God's ultimate activity is constantly attested to as giving order and meaning to the text which the text itself refers to. And as the text is presently engaged with, encounter with God is sought after but never presumed.

The interpretations derived from the text follow this logic. Despite the purported relation to the ultimate, the interpretation can never itself become ultimate; it remains penultimate. This is because the interpretation

---

19. For a critical appraisal of Hermeneutical Theology, see Dalferth, "God and the Mystery of Words."

20. Wisse, "*Contra et Pro Sola Scriptura*," 32.

21. Ziegler, "On the Present Possibility of Sola Scriptura," 577–80.

is an abstraction from an ultimate event, attesting to that event but unable to replicate or contain it. Because interpretations inherently reduce the ultimate to something penultimate and inadequately express the ultimate even in their attesting to it, they must undergo persistent scrutiny. A hermeneutic of suspicion thus seems a fruitful lens through which to read the text as well as reflect on one's own interpretations.[22] In this way, the interpretation is provisionally located in the overarching economy of God's action and ongoing encounter with God is sought to affirm or criticise the ongoing relevance of a particular interpretation. Interpretations derive their authority not from the method used or the apparent rationality of the claim, but from their ongoing connection and affirmation from God who continually reorders our penultimate activity towards him.

Practically this means interpretations taken from the text can have authoritative weight to act upon them in response to what is thought to be God's address, but they must also be subjected to suspicion given how they could have originally been misinformed or become unsuitable for a new context in which they are now being applied. Whatever interpretation is derived from the text must constantly be referred to God as the foundation of its authority and as its greatest critic, who is hoped in to illumine ways in which the interpretation requires reordering. Helping to resist confirmation bias, the central place given to criticism resists the ultimacy that interpretations might otherwise claim. Moreover, encounters with God should not be expected to simply affirm prior interpretations or perceptions about reality, but to *change* the interpreter to be further conformed to Christ by faith.

The interpreter is left being able to use a range of interpretative methods insofar as they remain viewed through the lens of penultimacy. No interpretative method can claim for itself ultimacy and so cannot be used as the exclusive hermeneutical method. There may be good reasons for preferring one method over others, perhaps because it is presumed to grant the most favorable conclusions, but no principle or method can be definitive in leading to theological truth. The theological subject matter of God cannot be compelled through method to disclose himself, but rather will only disclose himself on his own terms, which will be irreducible to our terms. Our interpretative methods can thus be ways in which we approach ultimate encounters with God through the text but can never amount to a way of conjuring those encounters nor a definitive way of analyzing them. Conversely, the penultimacy of interpretative methods leads us to be

---

22. Cf. Garrett Green comments that "There is indeed a valid, even necessary, Christian suspicion; it will be discovered, though, not by the application of secular hermeneutics but rather theologically—that is, by attending to the sources and norms implicit in Christian faith itself." In *Theology, Hermeneutics and Imagination*, 190.

suspicious of methods which would affirm the overall competency and ability of the interpreter to arrive at truth through rational investigation. Any method which claims ultimacy must either be reconceived or avoided by the penultimate interpreter.[23] A variety of interpretative methods can then be utilized by the penultimate interpreter conditioned on their penultimate use and interpretation which resists claims of ultimacy, deferring to God in his ultimacy.

The interpretative community also plays a significant role in penultimate hermeneutics. As seen earlier and in relation to the text, the penultimate can cover over the ultimate so that an encounter with the penultimate can also be an ultimate event. This can be seen in how persons' communal engagement with the text (perhaps through study, prayer or liturgy) do not only offer resources for reflection but also may constitute God's ultimate address to the individual. In this way, another's witness to God may become the source of furthering our own witness or function as a critical lens towards our misinterpretations of the ultimate. Feminist hermeneuts have tended to emphasise the critical function of the community in perceiving God, where the community uses their contemporary situation and perceptions to guide their interpretations of Scripture rather than blanketly deferring to what Scripture says without any further thought. Whilst this can inadvertently reposition the individual to an ultimate position, it more often aids in the re-centering of God where previous interpretations may have attempted to displace him.[24] The Christian community can thus aid in the interpreter's tasks of witness and repentance in both penultimate and ultimate ways.

There are other communities within which the Bible can be read, too, and penultimate hermeneutics makes them seem beneficial to the task of interpretation. Reading the Bible in the context of an interreligious community is useful where the aim is not to synthesise the truth-claims between discussion partners but to use differing truth-claims and interpretations to refine one's own position. Peter Ochs's practice of Scriptural Reasoning (SR) is an excellent case in point.[25] The main reason a penultimate interpreter might seek out encounters like this is to reconsider assumptions which are taken for granted within the Christian community, enabling the exposure of these as nascent views and bringing them before the ultimate for judgment

---

23. I largely have some historical-critical accounts of the gospels in view here, which for a helpful history of these approaches see Wright, *Jesus and the Victory of God*, 3–124.

24. Cf. Lisa Isherwood's insightful "Wanderings in the Cosmic Garden" is a good illustration of reconceiving anthropology, protology and cosmology according to feminist concerns.

25. Ochs, *Religion Without Violence*.

and new life. It thus gives the Christian greater opportunity to both witness and repent to God.[26]

We finally come to reflecting on the significance of penultimacy applied to the interpreter. All other hermeneutic features hinge upon the interpreter's posture towards them, for the orientation of the text, the method, the interpretation and even the community depend on how they are used by the interpreter. The interpreter could consider the text as a penultimate thing but if it is used to justify the interpreter's presuppositions it fails to be used in a penultimate way. It, instead, centralizes the interpreter rather than attesting to God's centrality. Due to the prevalence of sin, the interpreter is constantly vying for who will be central, seeking either to conform in their penultimacy to God's centrality or to oppose God by claiming ultimacy for the self. The interpreter can never fully escape this situation which is why they must rely on ongoing encounters with God to sustain and reorient the interpreter's focus. The point of claiming the interpreter's penultimacy is thus to dislocate the interpreter from the center and relocate them at the peripheries, pointing towards God in Christ who is rightfully at the center not only of their interpretation but also of reality itself. The interpreter who seeks to be penultimate should then adopt the ongoing practices of witness and repentance, seeking to reaffirm God's centrality and their dependence on God. These can be enacted in the ways in which the aforementioned hermeneutic features have been considered in penultimate ways.

The interpreter thus perceives themselves and the things which they use or rely on for interpretation as penultimate and seeks to become more coherently penultimate through the hermeneutic process. As they continually seek to attest and repent to God as the ultimate, they embody their penultimacy and are able to arrive at provisional conclusions which are sufficient for faith in God but insufficient to make timeless truth claims. The quest for truth remains ever-present for the penultimate interpreter as they seek to attest to the One who is true in their changing circumstances. The grounds for certainty and the truth of their convictions rely on the veracity of Christ which, due to Christ's ultimacy, remains out of reach but not out of view. Christians can witness to Christ even if they cannot possess him or verify him through independent criteria. The interpreter is thus relieved from the burden of being right in their interpretations as long as they point to Christ through their interpretations. Moreover, there is confidence that where their statements misrepresent Christ that he will reorder them to become truly *pen*ultimate.

---

26. Cf. Mike Higton's use of SR in "Christian Doctrine and the Discipline of Reading Scripture," 103.

CONCLUSION

We can now return to where we started, at the problem of limitation. Penultimate hermeneutics does not solve our limitations by somehow giving us unlimited access to eternal truth or by providing a trustworthy principle by which we can flawlessly interpret. To claim otherwise would make this an account of *ultimate* hermeneutics.

Penultimate hermeneutics, however, reinterprets our limitations through a theological lens, which itself must remain provisional and subject to further scrutiny and adaptation. When considered in isolation, the problem of limitation remains pronounced due to the manifold ways in which we continually obscure objective reality and the way we use these misinterpretations to justify our ethical practices. Reconceiving this according to penultimacy does not reduce the poignancy of the problem but provides Christians with a means of understanding and responding to it. They come to understand their situation and their own identities as being inherently related to God who sustains and repeatedly reorders them through ultimate encounters. Their failures and their misinterpretations continue to have significant, penultimate consequences but, as penultimate things, they are also reconciled and reordered by God's ultimate actions. These problems derive, in part, from the penultimate's dependency on God but they need not be seen as inherently problematic. Rather, penultimacy invites us to reconceive human limitations as means to become more attentive to God's ultimate action by acknowledging our contingency and dependency on him.

Regarding interpretation, the penultimate interpreter seeks to recognize God's ultimate acts within and through penultimate things. Their posture is deferential to God who is relied on to authenticate his revelation through ongoing ultimate events in the life of the interpreter. The interpreter is left in a position from where they can attest to the fact that they have perceived an ultimate event and point towards God who is affirmed to have revealed himself through that event. There is thus reason for hope in the process of interpretation as the interpreter turns to God as a witness of who he has revealed himself to be as well as the judge of their oppositional views and actions which are to be reordered by his reconciling activity. There is also scope to adopt many different hermeneutical methods to analyze or to prepare the way for God's ultimate action, aiding the interpreter's acts of witness or repentance. When separated from God's ultimate action and not perceived through a penultimate frame, the various features of hermeneutics can seem arbitrary, meaningless and/or erroneous; but when God is perceived as the ultimate, these things become penultimately ordered towards God, being reconciled and utilized by his ultimate actions.

Penultimate hermeneutics does not answer all of our problems, but it tries to point us in the right direction. Or, better, it tries to allow God to reorder us towards himself. The interpreter may find themselves at many different crossroads in their lifetime, but they are never completely lost. Just like the disciples on the road to Emmaus, they may discover that Christ is and has always been travelling with them. And if they begin to perceive him more clearly through recurrent ultimate encounters, they may discover how Scripture and all of reality point to him. The route the interpreter takes falls into insignificance as they realize their travelling companion and their destination are one and the same. As a fellow traveller, the penultimate interpreter needs not know which route to take but, through witness and repentance, seeks to travel with and towards Jesus Christ.

BIBLIOGRAPHY

Augustine, *Confessions*, Oxford: Oxford University Press, 2008.

Bonhoeffer, Dietrich. *Act and Being*. Dietrich Bonhoeffer Works 2. Minneapolis: Fortress, 2009.

———. *Ethics*. Dietrich Bonhoeffer Works 6. Minneapolis: Fortress, 2009.

———. "Lectures on Christology." In Dietrich Bonhoeffer Works 12, 299–360. Minneapolis: Fortress, 2009.

Dalferth, Ingolf. "God and the Mystery of Words." *Journal of the American Academy of Religion* 60 (1992) 79–104.

Dekker, Willem. "Hermeneutical Theology as Contemporary Rendition of the *Sola Scriptura*." In *Sola Scriptura: Biblical and Theological Perspectives on Scripture, Authority, and Hermeneutics*, edited by Hans Burger et al., 105–20. Boston: Brill, 2018.

Green, Garret. *Theology, Hermeneutics and Imagination: The Crisis of Interpretation at the End of Modernity*. Cambridge: Cambridge University Press, 1999.

Halbach, Ross. *Bonhoeffer and the Racialized Church*. Waco, TX: Baylor University Press, 2020, 10.

Harvey, Barry. *Taking Hold of the Real: Dietrich Bonhoeffer and the Profound Worldliness of Christianity*. Cambridge: James Clarke & Co, 2016.

Isherwood, Lisa. "Wanderings in the Cosmic Garden." In *Through Us, With Us, In Us: Relational Theologians in the Twenty-First Century*, edited by Lisa Isherwood and Elaine Bellchambers, 121–36. London: SCM, 2010.

Luther, Martin. "Die Disputation de homine." In *D. Martin Luthers Werke: Kritische Gesamtausgabe*, 39:174–80. Weimar: Hermann Böhlaus Nachfolger, 1926.

Ochs, Peter. *Religion Without Violence: The Practice and Philosophy of Scriptural Reasoning*. Eugene, OR: Cascade, 2019.

Wisse, Maarten. "*Contra et Pro Sola Scriptura.*" In *Sola Scriptura: Biblical and Theological Perspectives on Scripture, Authority, and Hermeneutics*, edited by Hans Burger et al., 19–37. Boston: Brill, 2018.

Wright, N. T. *Jesus and the Victory of God: Christian Origins and the Question of God*. London: SPCK, 1996.

Ziegler, Philip. "On the Present Possibility of Sola Scriptura." *International Journal of Systematic Theology* 24 (2022) 565–83.

Chapter 39
Figural Hermeneutics
DAVID NEY

In his essay, "From creation to New Creation: The Mission of God in the Biblical Story," Anglican bishop of the Horn of Africa, Grant LeMarquand, described the experience of receiving a report from Mennonite missionaries who had surveyed an area of South Sudan around the town of Rumbek. The report, which came into his hands just before Christmas, detailed "atrocities beyond description." For LeMarquand the most striking detail in the report was that in a vast area of hundreds of square miles the missionaries had found no living children. They had been killed, succumbed to disease and starvation, fled as refugees, or been carried off as slaves or child soldiers.[1] Shortly after receiving the report, on December 28, LeMarquand opened his Bible to read the gospel lesson for the daily office, which concludes with the following words:

> Then Herod, when he saw that he had been tricked by the wise men, was in a furious rage, and he sent and killed all the male children in Bethlehem and in all that region who were two years old or under, according to the time which he had ascertained from the wise men. Then was fulfilled what was spoken by the prophet Jeremiah: "A voice was heard in Ramah, wailing and loud lamentation, Rachel weeping for her children; she refused to be consoled, because they were no more." (Matt 2:15–18)

December 28, of course, is the Feast of the Holy Innocents, and this haunting festal reading united forever in LeMarquand's mind the plight of the

---

1. LeMarquand, "From Creation," 10.

Sudanese and the coming of our Lord. This association is thoroughly linguistic; but the figural reader insists that it is not merely so. For the figural reader asks, "Where is Rachel weeping for her children?" and answers "in Bethlehem and Rumbek both" as he searches after the identity they share as creatures of the One Word.

LEXICAL SPECIMENS AND LIVING WORDS

Modern biblical exegesis is based on the presupposition, which Benjamin Jowett famously voiced in *Essays and Reviews* (1860), that the goal is always to "read Scripture like any other book."[2] Jowett's progressivist assumption was that he stood at the dawn of a new horizon as one who, with enlightened sensibilities and sharpened historical-grammatical tools, could precisely demarcate textual meaning by stripping away the obfuscating layers of historical testimony.[3] He believed his forbears had failed to fully appreciate that Bible words are human words whose meanings, as historically embedded, are determined by the definitions of these words and the psychologies of those who used them. Whatever the virtues of Jowett's approach, he failed to note that he did not, as a modern interpreter, stand outside of history. Every interpretation he mustered was equally a product of his context and person. As an interpreter all that Jowett was as a Christian, as an Anglican, as a man, as an English citizen, as a Victorian, and as a scholar was brought to bear on the words he penned, as human words.

This is just to say, as Gadamer noted in the introduction to *Truth and Method*, that each representation of a text (whether privately or publicly enacted) is itself equally the product of history.[4] Augustine had already observed as much when he noted that the past, like the future, can only be thought of but present. "My childhood," he observes, "which no longer is, is in time past, which now is not; but when I call to mind its image and speak of it, I behold it in the present, because it is yet in my memory."[5] And just as the one who remembers the past does so in the present, Augustine holds, so too the one who reenacts it. Were we able to inhabit past, present, and future we would be creators and not creatures, for the punctiliar moments of the disappearing present do not merely mark our lives but constitute them. As creatures the present moment is all we have been given to take hold of,

---

2. Jowett, "On the Interpretation," 339.

3. The reader, Jowett insists, must, "clear away the remains of dogmas, systems, controversies." Jowett, "On the Interpretation," 338–39.

4. Gadamer, *Truth and Method*, xi–xv.

5. Augustine, *City of God*, 11.18.23.

whether we choose to look to the past or to the future. And it is all we have been given to take hold of our Creator.

While many conservative biblical scholars have refused to acknowledge this presentist orientation, concealing themselves within Jowett's constructed bastion of objectivity, to acknowledge the delimited temporal location of the interpreter is not to embrace relativism. It is simply to say that meaning stands at the intersection of text and reader. And we might point out further, to return to Jowett, that his understanding of textual meaning was itself the product of a particular context which was, as Gadamer insisted, infatuated with the scientific method. As Jowett waxes eloquent about the need to strip the text of historical accretions he is merely echoing the rhetoric of the leading lights of the so-called scientific revolution. This scholarly movement, which received its mandate from Bacon's *Novum organum*, was a great taxonomic enterprise, confident that it had the tools to overcome Adam's impotence and accurately name all God's creatures (Gen 2:19). It comes as no surprise, therefore, that its flowering was accompanied by the rise of modern lexicography. Indeed, Dr. Johnson's epoch-making English dictionary was a self-conscious response to the Baconian mandate, which insisted that ambiguity in communication (Idols of the Marketplace) stood as the most glaring hindrance to the advancement of learning. In his *Plan for an English Dictionary* Johnson proposed that:

> The value of a work must be estimated by its use: it is not enough that a dictionary delights the critic, unless at the same time it instructs the learner; as it is to little purpose, that an engine amuses the philosopher by the subtilty of its mechanism, if it requires so much knowledge in its application, to as be of no advantage to the common workman.[6]

Despite this democratic impulse, Johnson is equally concerned to protect the English language from the common workman, for he states that his object is to "preserve the purity and ascertain the meaning of our English idiom."[7] The invention of the modern dictionary is the basis of the modern valuative distinction between connotation and denotation, which presupposes that proper use is governed by the strictures of lexicography. This creates the impression that meanings are found in dictionaries. And yet, there can be no denying that the meanings of lexical terms, as Johnson still perceived, depend upon their place within the wider world.

On one hand, the scientist is justified in colonizing humane learning with lexicography's taxonomic approach: since words are things they can be

---

6. Johnson, *Plan*, 5.
7. Johnson, *Plan*, 4.

placed in petri dishes as specimens to be examined, dissected, atomized. But taxonomy, like taxidermy, presents dead specimens as dead specimens in order to give the impression that they are alive. In *The Death of Scripture and the Rise of Biblical Studies*, Legaspi observes, following Northrop Frye, that while the Bible had been "the great code" of Western civilization, serving as the foundation of not just its academic theology but its moral universe, the divided churches of the Reformation struggled to maintain an integral account of the Bible as Scripture.[8] "Because both Roman Catholics and Protestants claimed the Bible, in different ways, as their own," Legaspi observes:

> What had functioned centrally in the life of the Church became, in the early modern period, a kind of textual proving ground of the legitimacy of extrascriptural theoretical understandings: at first theological and polemical and then, over time, literary, philosophical, and cultural. As a text, an object of critical analysis, the Bible came into clearer focus; however, as Scripture the Bible became increasingly opaque.[9]

For Legaspi, the German critics that perfected the method successfully wrested the Bible from the hands of the Catholic, Lutheran and Reformed confessionalists that had weaponized it, planting it in the greener pastures of the ancient Near East to represent scriptural texts as "ancient cultural products capable of reinforcing the values and aims of a new sociopolitical order."[10] It is important to note the contradiction that underlies this approach, namely that dead specimens alone can birth new life.

But perhaps the words of the Bible aren't dead. To begin, there are at least two ways in which all words are alive. The first, which words have in common with all created objects, is that they are alive as in flux, as Heisenberg's uncertainty principle illustrates: even that which has been painstakingly observed and measured as a specimen is no longer what it once was. And as the object is evolving so too the perceptions of the subjects that observe and measure it. Words may or may not be justifiably regarded as a special class of object, philosophically or physiologically, but they are unique among objects in their central mediatorial location within society. It is this location which makes them alive in a second sense. To carefully observe two humans in conversation is to witness subtle shifts in meaning which accompany the use of words and phrases. And these shifts, while problematic from the standpoint of lexicographic science, are concomitant in the explosive formative power of speech. The wonder of human language

8. Legaspi, *Death*, 3.
9. Legaspi, *Death*, 4.
10. Legaspi, *Death*, 5.

is not just that it manages to describe the world truthfully, but that it is constantly evolving as it attempts to speak more accurately about a world which is itself given over to change.

Rigorous philological study has been the province of biblical interpretation since at least the third century—a bit of research confirms there is nothing remarkable about the work of Luther or Calvin in this regard. And when Jowett proposed that the Bible, like any other book, could be fruitfully studied in dialogue with other period texts and artifacts, he failed to note that this had been readily acknowledged since at least the work of Scaliger and Grotius. But the question is not whether the Bible can be appropriately given over to critical industry or set alongside other texts, but whether prevalent assumptions about the conditions underlying such work are justified, and, urgently, whether they should be deployed to generate a positivist worldview which, in turn, returns to govern exegesis.

The scientist stands over the presumably dead specimen and operates upon it, subject over object. Though biblical interpreters in the modern west learn, as Legaspi observes, to "operate on the Bible as an inert and separated body," the curated conditions of this encounter are peculiar.[11] Whatever else can be said of this curated encounter, it evidently trains students to read the Bible in a very different way than they would read "any other book." Reading is a fluid, dialogical, temporal encounter between reader and text. When any other book is read the reader does not merely work upon the text, subject upon object: the text, as subject, works upon the reader, as object. This had been obvious enough in premodern aural contexts: as language was received as that which was spoken and heard in homes and in the marketplace, it was received as a powerful and often sacral divine causal force. Thus the downside of the modern scientific approach is twofold; not only has it proved to be unable to offer immutable certainty, it has, in pursuing this impossible outcome, fashioned lexical specimens out of living words.

LITERAL AND FIGURAL INTERACTIONS WITH THE WORLD

The way that the human subject reads any other book is the way he or she reads any other thing. The world and the things that comprise it confront the human subject as subjects, and act upon human senses that, in this encounter, must equally be understood as objects. As the first encounter with the world, infancy is, Radner observes, "a pure encounter," in which "[e]verything is close by and immediate." To be born into the world is to be

---

11. Legaspi, *Death*, 5.

"given things over which we have little control" and thus to be given over to "touching, seeing, listening, receiving, the intimacy of literal physical presence with parents and family and with surroundings."[12] This first encounter is emblematic of human experience from the cradle to the grave. The human mind is forced to respond to a world that is actively bombarding it with a remarkable variety of sensory data. Neuroscience offers key insights in this regard which dismantle the Lockean conceit that the human mind is a blank slate. The world itself is the backdrop that is devoured by the human mind from birth through innate mechanisms of learning and socialization which are constituted neurologically as new pathways are absorbed into existing ones, growing, shrinking, shifting.

To say that figurative or figural language is, as many literary scholars insist, the most fundamental aspect of language is simply to acknowledge that language takes its place in this larger theater of unruly and evolving appositional interaction. If we take a toddler's first word as our starting point, we might describe it, in its referentiality, as a literal statement. This is obvious enough if it happens to be a noun like "mom." But soon enough the child will have to reckon with the fact that other people use the word too–and not only siblings but parents and playmates–in ways that confront the confusing variety of the world. The point here is not just that there are now multiple "moms" but that these utterances open up, to the child, a whole host of new relations, possibilities, and boundaries: this is that and that and that, and that is this and this and this. As it turns out, even that precious first association of the word "mom" with the person is a figural association, since it compares two things within a larger appositional context.

The interplay of words and the world they describe is masterfully captured by Gadamer in a section of *Truth and Method* on play. Gadamer begins by reflecting upon the lexical definition of play, as a word used to describe a "to-and-fro motion" which is "without goal or purpose" and which also takes place "without effort." Gadamer's interest in this state of being, which he describes as a subjective experience of relaxation, is that it is "so close to the mobile form of nature." We might say that the structure of the world demands the creation of the word "play." "It is obviously not correct," Gadamer concludes, "to say that animals *too* play, nor is it correct to say that, metaphorically speaking, water and light play *as well*. Rather, on the contrary, we can say that man too plays." This observation might be taken to imply, in a metaphysical or perhaps even specifically Platonic sense, the existence of an abstract form which goes by the name "play" in which various fleshly realities participate more or less. But this line of inquiry is

---

12. Radner, *Time to Keep*, 139.

not of particular moment for Gadamer. He is interested in what play communicates about human language, and he concludes that "it becomes finally meaningless to distinguish between literal and metaphorical usage."[13]

The answer to the question, "which appellation is the literal one?" is not only difficult to find. It is proved in Gadamer's example to be a somewhat uninteresting question in the first place. As Aquinas observes, the world we receive as humans is a world in which words, as things, do not merely denote things but denote them *as* things. And they do so in a way which populates the world of things with the properties presumed to belong exclusively to words. In the west, the provenance of this insight can be traced to Augustine of Hippo, who grasped that a world comprised of words and things is a symbolic world in which the figural and literal are intractably intertwined.[14] As Gadamer observes, it is not merely the case that we have to say, in the end, that "this one plays, and that one plays, and that one plays," but also, "this one plays as that one plays as that one plays, as does the first."[15] Those that play, in this instance, are figures of one another, juxtaposed in commonality and difference both.

As a case in point Augustine begins his monumental *Literal Meaning of Genesis* by promising to forsake unnecessary allegorical speculations. As Radner observes, literal meaning for Augustine, "seems to indicate that Scripture, taken in the specificity and order of its distinct words, remains something concrete."[16] When it comes to interpreting the first chapter of Genesis, interpreting referents concretely means acknowledging them as words which refer to objects of the natural world, and in this there is something inherently empirical, if not "scientific," about the enterprise. But since these words and objects are all creatures of the one Word they are all words which communicate the mind of the divine artificer. The scientific study of specimens in this respect is to be affirmed–but also affirmed as incomplete. While it can answer a delimited set of physiological questions, it easily slips into the conceit that having answered these questions it has answered them all. For Augustine, on the other hand, to study an artifact is to open a window through which new vistas of inquiry are beheld, and it is thus that his literal commentary embraces the patristic practice of extended and often circuitous figural exploration of the world. One way of describing Augustine's semiotics is to say that the literal contains within itself the figural, as his medieval descendant Thomas Aquinas implied when he spoke of

---

13. Gadamer, *Truth and Method*, 109.
14. See Markus, *Signs and Meanings*, 1–44.
15. Gadamer, *Truth and Method*, 109.
16. Radner, *Time and the Word*, 53.

the *sensus literalis*. But it is perhaps even more accurate to say that readings can only be said to be literal within a larger figural framework which just is the universe itself as created by God and given, moment by moment, to creatures as a language they are innately disposed to understand. It is only because the world, as a creature of the one Word, is already playing that humans can speak of this one and that one at play.[17]

THE SLAUGHTER OF THE INNOCENTS IN FIGURAL PERSPECTIVE

I can vividly recall a presentation done by a leading proponent of figural reading in which the first question in the question and answer period was raised by an international student from Africa. "Are you saying," the student humbly asked, "that I am allowed to read the Bible in the way I did back home?" It was obvious from this question that his seminary professors had, hopefully unwittingly, been systematically pulling him away from his roots, his culture, and his piety—taking the Africa out of him, we might say. And it was equally evident that they had been doing so by insisting upon the use of their western historical-grammatical tools. I quietly hoped that he—and the hundreds of international students at seminaries across the continent—would throw his graduation certificate into the ocean on the trip back home and resume his native figural practice as Watchman Nee, arguably the greatest Chinese expositor of Scripture of all time, had once done. After all, figural reading has been the lifeblood of not only the most vital churches of history, but the ones that are transforming the global south today. But what the presentation opened up for this international student wasn't, in the first place, a justification to pursue a particular figural method which he had once embraced and presumably loved. Rather, it was the blessing he needed to stand before the face of the text as he once did, as a creature who stands before his Maker.

With this in mind we can return to the African bishop's reading of Matthew 2, which was at once an encounter with Bethlehem and Rumbek. The good bishop observes that this encounter revolutionized the way he reads the text. But while Jowett might ask him to put aside this experience to approach the text objectively as a scientist he might with reason counter that it is impossible to do so. And what is more, he might ask why this should be demanded of him in the first place. The text, given his experience, becomes a kind of memorial, and the bishop's future encounters with it a fitting liturgical commemoration of the people of South Sudan. In this case

---

17. On the ontological priority of divine speech see Chrétien, *Ark of Speech*, 48–58.

reading Matthew 2 becomes an offering unto God of the lives of the countless murdered children in that land. The person who has come face to face with such madness has a special access to the interior of Matthew's text. We would of course not wish this experience upon even our worst enemies, but we must also see that the fruit of this horror is a newfound appreciation of the explosive power of the text which, as George Lindbeck famously said, "absorbs the world."[18]

The claim that Matthew 2 is about both Bethlehem and Rumbek might be taken in a strictly psychological and therefore individualized way–nothing more than a connection forged in the mind of the interpreter. But the person exposed to the carnage in South Sudan is doing more than sharing personal feelings. For the figural reader the apposition of Bethlehem and Rumbek is itself a figure. The brute fact that Bethlehem and Rumbek stand side by side is revelatory of the nature of the world, the Scriptures, and the God who made them both. It confirms, in this case, that the world is not merely an assortment of random happenings but is rather a language. The Scriptures, likewise, as the syntax of this language, are seen to reveal the true form of the world. And the God who made them both is likewise revealed as the God whose creative work in giving the world and the Scriptures is always also, as the word's work, the work of divine self-revelation. Regarding figural reading as an exegetical method may in fact mislead: it is, in the first place, the reading practice that accompanies the conviction that the world, as depicted in the Scriptures, is revelatory of God in Christ.

The figural reader comes to the text of Matthew 2 bearing the knowledge that the world which God has made is a world in which Rachel weeps for her murdered children. This can be seen as a straightforward affirmation of the historicity of the text; that Rachel weeps for her children is, for this reader, an incontrovertible historical fact. But the figural reader is not intent on pinning down the historical referents here described (something that is probably impossible to do). The figural reader is ever conscious of Paul's exhortation to embrace the limits of creaturely knowledge: "Now we know in part and we see in part, then we shall see fully even as we are fully known" (1 Cor 13:12). This fullness of knowledge is perhaps best captured by the future perfect tense: at that time there will be no doubt that the history the Scriptures describe *will have* taken place. Then and only then will the people of God behold the true form of the Rachel who weeps for her children.

To bicker with the good bishop about whether or not Rumbek can in fact be compared with Bethlehem is somewhat beside the point, just as arguing with the Matthean author about his deployment of Ramah as a figure of

---

18. Lindbeck, *Nature*, 118.

Bethlehem is to misunderstand New Testament hermeneutics. What counts in this case is that the world of which Ramah is a part and Bethlehem was a part is also the world in which Rumbek belongs. They are confirmed to be part of the same world by the fact that the Isaian, Matthean, and Mennonite texts can be placed next to one another on a table. But they could be set side by side in this way and still have nothing substantial to do with one another in terms of the meaning they convey. The great marvel, in this case, is that the words they contain are proved to be a part of the same world by the fact that the meaning each text conveys in one context can be fruitfully received, understood, and thus applied to another.

SCRIPTURE'S TRUTH

When the reader of Scripture reads figuratively, the reader is in fact reading Scripture as one would intuitively read any other book. Reading is only possible because the words deployed by the author to describe their world can be received by readers as truthfully descriptive of their own. This process of meaning-making presupposes the temporal priority of both world and word.[19] Wherever the interpreter is, the words were there first. The rich and variegated figural application of the words, which precedes the reader, is always only partially known to her. But it is equally a history upon which her meaningful reception and use of words depends. As Chrétien puts it, the act of speech demands more than just a simple duality of you and me:

> As soon as you speak to me, we are already all there, even the dead, and those who will one day come also. The interlocutors do not address one another in the vacuum of a telepathic communication, they speak to each other in the world within which they exist along with everyone and in the language of a community. There are never only two people: even a face-to-face conversation is heavy with a distant rumour, and even intimacy has its own wide-open spaces.[20]

The expansive temporal framework of reading, which Chrétien here describes, pressures many contemporary moral readings of scriptural texts. The preacher of the Matthean text under consideration who does nothing but use the text as an imperative to liberate the oppressed may, as is well known, succeed in this task and yet fail as a scriptural expositor. We might even appeal to Augustine and say that such a reading is not to be rejected inasmuch as it has managed to promote love of God and love of neighbor.

19. Chrétien, *Ark of Speech*, 1–2; Radner, *Time and the Word*, 44–110.
20. Chrétien, *Ark of Speech*, 10.

We could also add that it has only been able to do so inasmuch as it has managed to find the words of the text in the world. After all, the homiletical force of the text is not found in the existence of an abstract and ubiquitous principle of social justice but rather the fact that there exists, in the text and in the world, children that have been slaughtered and mothers that weep. The power of the Scriptures is that they name just this world before the face of the Lord. This is demonstrated by a simple observation: the sermon preached to a grieving mother in the face of such loss is nothing like the sermon that does not have to or chooses not to reckon with this tragedy.

Language is the object humans use to create integrative conceptions of the world they inhabit; language also works as subject quite apart from the intentions of those who hear and use it. But while language effectively helps individuals, it also actively distorts their view of the world and sets them at odds with one another. The story of the Tower of Babel, in this instance, isn't just a primitive euhemeristic account of the origin of linguistic obfuscation and diversity. It is, rather, a figure of human linguistic use which some theorists have gone so far as to call "death." Blanchot calls the first name given in the Garden of Eden, "woman," a "deferred assassination:" "For me to be able to say 'This woman,' I must somehow take her flesh-and-blood reality away from her, cause her to be absent, annihilate her."[21] Other theorists, such as Chrétien, are more optimistic, rightly pointing out that what is given to the man is not just an object to define but rather "bone of my bones and flesh of my flesh" (Gen 2:23)! Thus while the Genesis account begins with "the imposing of names on mute beings" it thus quickly becomes "a dialogue that takes place within a liberty that is at once intimate and open."[22]

However well dialogue partners feel the joy of being properly named and understood, the words they use will inevitably, like the subjects they name, remain only partially understood as *other*. While the deconstructionist is correct to despair the ability of a singularly human language to achieve unmuted communication, it is a despair which has already precluded the possibility of a human word which is at once divine. While humans can never fully grasp communicated truth, divine speech contains a fullness which extends beyond what humans are able to receive. In the Hebrew Scriptures this insight is embedded in the very first words of the text: God creates by and with and in his word. Every artifact which is made is thus an embodied word or *logoi*, to borrow a term from Maximus the Confessor, which contains within itself a particular blueprint of its divine original, the *Logos* in whom all things were made (Col 1:16). Maximus's way of articulating

---

21. As quoted in Chrétien, *Ark of Speech*, 6.
22. Chrétien, *Ark of Speech*, 6.

the relationship between created artifacts and their divine artificer is merely one way of capturing the seminal Christian insight that created artifacts, as parts which contain the imprint of the whole, are microcosms. The Latin West took hold of the microcosm-macrocosm participatory framework, but it was more likely than the Byzantine East to describe the relationship between the part and the whole in horizontal or empirical terms. Augustine's notion of God's two books—the book of Nature and the book of Scripture-enabled Latin scholars to do so in a compelling way. Scripture, in this case, stood in for the whole so that artifacts named scripturally became parts within it.

The great sixteenth-century Hebraist Reuchlin described the enrapturing mystical experience of reading Hebrew characters as follows: "when reading Hebrew I seem to see God himself speaking."[23] But while few Christians today embrace Reuchlin's kabbalistic framework, many continue to take for granted that Scripture words address them. Scripture words are able to speak in this way because "The grass withers and the flowers fall, but the word of our God endures forever" (Isa 40:8). Human words are as grass, going in and out of existence even more quickly than the flowers they name. Even words that endure as legibly transcribed are subject, in their meaning, to the mutable minds that perceive them. Describing how words expressed in space and time can be described as eternally true may well escape human cognitive capacity, no less than the hypostatic union. But it is possible to at least describe the eternality of the divine word in act. The eternal Word of God is "living and active, sharper than any two-edged sword, piercing until it divides soul from spirit, joints from marrow; it is able to judge the thoughts and intentions of the heart" (Heb 4:12). This is to state little more than Paul when he says, "These things happened to them as examples and were written down as warnings for us, on whom the culmination of the ages has come" (1 Cor 10:11).

The figural reader affirms that the divinity of Scripture words is enfleshed in their enduring power. Scripture words are true for all time, and not just as words from which abstract doctrinal or philosophical principles can be fashioned and reapplied. They are true for all time because at *every* time they describe the world as it stands before the Lord. Thus to say, as Paul does, that the death and resurrection of Jesus happened "according to the Scriptures" (1 Cor 15:3) is not merely to say, as modern evangelicals often have, that a few select details of Christ's life can be matched with Old Testament texts as prophetic fulfillments. It is, rather, to say that the death and resurrection of Christ are revelatory of the whole of history as proceeding

---

23. Reuchlin, *Breifwechsel*, 105.

according to the divine plan. History, in this case is, as Augustine saw, a carpet which is wrapped up in the divine counsel and unrolls moment by moment as the present is given to the people of God as their means of encountering the Christ in whom they "live and move and have our being" (Acts 17:28). To say that Scripture is a divine word—whether the red letters or the canon as a whole—is to say that this word bombards creation from the outside and addresses the whole because it addresses each and every part.

To emphasize the ability of Scripture words to speak across time is not to deny this to non-scriptural words. But for non-scriptural words this ability depends upon the scriptural claim that "the earth is the Lord's and the fulness thereof" (Ps 24:1; 1 Cor 10:26). It is by searching the Scriptures, rather than reading other books, that all things can be seen as revelatory of God in Christ; and as revealed in the Scriptures, each creature is beheld, as it truly is, in relation to the God who is all in all. It is easy to scoff at the many ancient Christian interpreters that sought to prove that Plato had read the books of Moses. However incredible their historiographical reconstructions, they must be appreciated as those who, having been inundated by Scripture words, couldn't help but find these words at work in the world, proclaiming the glory of God everywhere they looked.

CONCLUSION

While the goal of modern scientific exegesis is, to borrow Chrétien's turn of phrase, to create a "vacuum of a telepathic communication," which attempts to atomize textual meaning by approximating the conditions of the petri dish, the goal of figural reading is to allow text and reader to "speak to each other in the world within which they exist along with everyone and in the language of a community." Thus, to return to our initial example, a figural reading of the slaughter of the innocents presses beyond the bounds of a reconstructed communication from the Matthean author to his original readers. To begin, the figural reader notes that his narrative is saturated with the language of the Old Testament. The Matthean author locates Herod's rage within the larger context of the exile of God's people and thus salvation history through an explicit quotation of Jer 31:15. And as this text is already something of a midrashic "play" upon Genesis 31, where Rachel dies as she comes to Ramah while her child Benjamin and his brothers live on and eventually take possession of the land, so too the story of the slaughter of the innocents. In Jeremiah 31 Rachel weeps because she has given her life so that her offspring might live and inherit the land though it is now spewing them out. In Matthew 2 Rachel weeps again, though now the christological significance of these murders is heard explicitly in her wailing. Since Christ was, in the fullness of time, "born of a woman" (Gal 4:4), the devil's appointed means of making war on Christ is to destroy her children (Rev 12:17). The figural reader who beholds the women of Rumbek weeping in Ramah is thus compelled to see the murder of the young Sudanese within this cosmic battle as an assault on the gospel itself. For human flourishing is bound to the gospel in the speech that issues forth from God's children, even "the least of these" (Matt 25:40): "Through the praise of children and infants you have established a stronghold against your enemies, to silence the foe and the avenger" (Ps 8:2). And when the children and infants are gone so too is their efficacious praise (Ps 6:5).

Modern theorists often paint the distinction between modern and premodern exegesis as a methodological conflict, but the difference has more to do with the location of biblical interpretation itself. Pre-modern exegesis was flagrantly figural because it was pursued within the church and not the laboratory. As the people of God in the world, the church finds that the Scripture words it speaks and receives attach themselves to the people, places, and things that comprise its world. In this the Church affirms scriptural authority as the authority to unveil the true identity of every created thing as particular acts of divine praise, and figural reading is the means by which it accomplishes this end. The importance of figural reading, however, isn't just that it gives account of the unique kerygmatic place of each created thing. It is in every case, but especially in cases of unspeakable horror, an act of Christian hope. The bereaved woman who in searching the Scriptures finds that she is weeping in Ramah finds a place for herself and for her children within the enduring promises of God.

BIBLIOGRAPHY

Chrétien, Jean-Louis. *The Ark of Speech*. Translated by Andrew Brown. New York: Routledge, 2004.

Augustine. *City of God*, Volume 2, *Books 11–22*. Translated by William Babcock. New York: New City, 2013.

Gadamer, Hans-Georg. *Truth and Method*. Translated by William Glen-Doepel. London: Sheed and Ward, 1979.

Johnson, Samuel. *The Plan of a Dictionary of the English Language*. Repr. Farmington Hills, MI: Gale ECCO, 2010.

Jowett, Benjamin. "On the Interpretation of Scripture." In *Essays and Reviews*, 330–433. London: John W. Parker and Son, 1860.

Lemarquand, Grant. "From Creation to New Creation: The Mission of God in the Biblical Story." In *Waging Reconciliation: God's Mission in a Time of Globalization and Crisis*, edited by Ian T. Douglas, 9–34. New York: Church, 2002.

Lindbeck, George. *The Nature of Doctrine: Religion and Theology in Postliberal Age*. Philadelphia: Westminster, 1984.

Markus, R. A. *Signs and Meanings: World and Text in Ancient Christianity*. Eugene, OR: Wipf & Stock, 2011.

Radner, Ephraim. *A Time to Keep: Mortality and the Shape of a Human Life*. Waco, TX: Baylor University Press, 2017.

———. *Time and the Word: Figural Reading of the Christian Scriptures*. Grand Rapids: Eerdmans, 2016.

Reuchlin, Johann. *Breifwechsel*. Edited by by Ludwig Geiger. Tübingen: Ulan, 1875.

Chapter 40
Scapegoat Hermeneutics
JENNIFER GARCIA BASHAW

WHAT ARE SCAPEGOAT HERMENEUTICS?

In this chapter, I use the term "Scapegoat hermeneutics" to describe a range of hermeneutical approaches that use the thought of René Girard to interpret biblical literature. Although scholars from fields as diverse as sociology, anthropology, and political philosophy have built upon Girard's theory for their work, this essay focuses on the ways that scapegoat hermeneutics can be used as a theological lens for interpreting the Bible. Girard's theory has been called an "anthropological apologia for Christianity" because he proposes that biblical literature helps us understanding the nature of human violence and provides the solution for ending that violence.[1] Applying Girard's insights to Scripture—as an array of biblical scholars has done in the last several decades—produces fresh and faithful interpretations that refocus readers on the context of the literature and on the transformative power of the Bible in human history. Scapegoat hermeneutics aligns with postconservative principles in several ways—it values the revelatory work of the Bible, it provides new perspectives on Scripture's context and function, and it can be catalytic and transformative for believers and their communities.

Before learning how to use and apply scapegoat hermeneutics, one must first understand the interlocking pieces of Girard's complex and comprehensive theory. Girard's thought cannot be contained in one discipline; his work does not provide a solution to a single problem but to many. Girardian theory proposes an answer to sociological questions: what is at the heart of human interaction, rivalry, and violence? It also explores anthropological

1. Alison and Palaver, *Palgrave Handbook of Mimetic Theory*, 1.

questions: How did humans form culture and what prompted their development of religion? In the field of religious studies and theology, the theory addresses a host of questions—what is the function of sacrifice in ancient religions? What purpose do myths serve? What do the Christian Scriptures teach us about the nature of humanity and God? Why did Jesus die and what difference does that make in the world? Because these last questions are at the heart of the Christian faith, theologians and bible scholars who have engaged Girard's ideas have produced much interpretive fruit from them. We will get to that fruit soon; but first, the theory.

A SKETCH OF RENÉ GIRARD'S THEORY

MIMETIC VIOLENCE

Girard's ideas, though descriptive of religion and society, owe their formation to his critical analysis of literature. Girard was a literary critic before he began to study ancient cultures and anthropology and he believed that great literature provides us with a window into the true nature of humanity and social conflict. The first part of Girard's theory, concerning the mimetic nature of desire, arose from his discovery of imitation in the antiheros of great modern novels.[2] Each of the characters he studied acts out of an intense desire for something another person has or is. Girard's conclusion in his book, *Deceit, Desire, and the Novel,* is that these literary characters represent an authentic problem with which all of humanity struggles, a problem Girard names *mimetic desire.* Girard explores the mechanism of mimetic desire through other literary genres such as Shakespeare's plays, the tragedies of ancient Greece, and mythical texts throughout history, and each of his examples demonstrate poetically how imitation is the most basic and destructive force of human civilization.

Plunging from literary study into the adjacent spheres of sociology and anthropology, Girard then began to investigate ancient cultures and their myths to support his view that the problem of mimetic desire is a human reality present even from the earliest accounts of civilization. What Girard found in his study of ethnology confirmed his hypothesis: Imitation has always been at the center of human interactions. The very process by which humans grow from infancy to adulthood and develop into functioning members of society involves constant imitation, learning to desire what those around us desire and modeling our lives and actions after others.

---

2. For example, Emma in *Madame Bovary*, *Don Quixote*, Dostoevsky's protagonist in *Crime and Punishment*, and Stendahl's protagonist in *The Red and the Black*.

In his book *Violence and the Sacred*, Girard theorizes that mimetic desire not only fuels human learning and interaction, it also drives communities to widespread violence. Humans imitate the possessions, desires, and qualities of others, often their social relations. When two people desire the same objects, there is conflict and violence inevitably arises. The desire for an object or quality of another becomes the desire actually to be the other; consequently, the one imitated becomes both a model and a rival. Girard labels this desire *conflictual mimesis* and concludes that the violence resulting from mimetic rivalry produces reciprocal violence in response and soon causes a cycle of violence, infecting everyone in a group.

THE SCAPEGOAT MECHANISM

If endemic conflict among the members of a community persisted, that community would destroy itself. What prevents the destruction is an unconscious process Girard uncovered in the literature of many ancient groups, something he calls the scapegoat mechanism, or single victim mechanism. When imitation leads to conflict, cooperation between members of a group ceases and they cannot agree on anything. What finally unites these members is focusing their rising violence on one surrogate victim. Their mimetic conflict, the violence of *all against all*, becomes the violence of *all against one*. This is a key finding in Girard's study of ancient societies. With the violent expelling or killing of innocent victim by what amounts to a lynching mob, a temporary peace covers the community and brings the mimetic crisis to a conclusion. For Girard this mob violence against a scapegoat produces a society—the unification of people toward a goal of peace and order.[3]

In addition to a unified society, the sudden resolution of conflict appears to be a miraculous deliverance and the scapegoat, who was at first blamed for sins they did not commit, also takes on the role of savior. Girard finds the roots of religion and culture in this transformation of victim into the sacred. The new society realizes it needs prohibition against imitation and violence and so they start enforcing law. Prohibition (law), then, is the first pillar in the construction of religion. When conflict and violence inevitably rise again, the society enacts sacrificial rituals in order to reproduce the miraculous event that ended the crisis in the first place. Whereas prohibition wards violence off by *avoiding* mimetic crises, ritual sacrifice avoids mass violence by *performing* mimetic violence. Ritual is the reenactment of an original act of violence, which serves to ward off mass violence with its

---

3. See Girard, *Scapegoat*.

"little doses of violence, like vaccination."[4] The third pillar of religion that works together with prohibition and ritual to control violence in society is the device of myth. Girard maintains that myth is necessary for the scapegoat mechanism to continue its peaceful regeneration in society. Without the illusion that myth brings to ritual sacrifice, communities would uncover the terrifying violence they both practice and elude and such knowledge would create a sacrificial crisis resulting in chaotic violence and destruction. The statement Girard makes about religion and myth shocks and rivets with its simple accusation, "Religion dupes; this is its only way to conquer violence."

Girard's explanation for the origin of religion and culture is fascinating and has produced a vast quantity of commentary from scholars; however, the figure of the scapegoat is the central and most illuminating aspect of Girard's system for social theory and biblical interpretation. The scapegoat serves as a substitute victim for the community's violence; it unifies the community by focusing it on one salvific task and establishes peace by taking away the violence that would divide the community. Though scapegoats are selected arbitrarily by communities, Girard discovers several characteristics common to scapegoats that emerge from history. First, a scapegoat is similar enough to the members of a society that it can bear its pollution but dissimilar enough to be singled out for blame. Scapegoats are accused of crimes that a society abhors, often extreme taboos, but are themselves usually innocent of these crimes. The scapegoat must be seen as removed from society by some characteristic or circumstance. Scapegoats, then, tend to be chosen from those who are outsiders, marginalized, or have physical differences that causes them to stand apart from the majority. They also tend to be people without family or allies, in order to preclude retaliation from someone on their behalf. Girard's description of those who have served as innocent victims throughout human history strikes a chord of familiarity for those of us who have seen immigrants, members of the LGBTQ community, and other "outsiders" suffer as the scapegoats of our contemporary society.

BIBLICAL LITERATURE EXPOSES THE SCAPEGOAT MECHANISM

To recap, the reality of mimetic violence is the human problem Girard recognizes in his examination of great literature. Then, in his research on ancient civilizations, Girard uncovers the scapegoat mechanism, a temporary solution to mimetic violence enacted by a society that builds a religious system of rituals and hides the workings of the mechanism in myth. In the

---

4. Girard, *Violence and the Sacred*, 290.

last part of his theory, Girard reveals the solution to mimesis and scapegoating, and he finds it in biblical literature. As Girard was studying ancient myths, he mined the Hebrew Bible and the New Testament for evidence of the typical veiling of violence and victimization. What he finds in the Scriptures of the Jewish and Christian religions becomes the revelatory cipher to his theory. In the Bible, as in other cultures' myths, violence becomes sacred as humans project their own mimetic violence onto God and fail to grasp that it originated with them. However, Girard sees the Bible as a text in "travail between myth and gospel," one that reveals the system of sacred violence through many of its stories and teachings.[5] Whereas myths usually hide the scapegoat mechanism by telling stories from the perspective of the persecutors, the biblical stories regularly speak from the perspective of the victim. In the stories of Hebrew Bible, we hear Abel's innocent blood cry out from the ground, we see Joseph prevail and forgive despite the unjust blame forced upon him, and we experience Hagar's abuse and expulsion along with her naming of God.

Hebrew prophetic literature also takes the side of the victim when it rebukes Israel for their abuse of the poor and exhorts them toward justice for the oppressed (as exemplified in Amos and Micah). The prophets set forth a vision of God's forgiveness that is not tied to law or the sacrificial system but is part of God's love for God's people: "I will put my law within them, and I will write it on their hearts, and I will be their God, and they shall be my people . . . they shall all know me, from the least of them to the greatest . . . I will forgive their iniquity and remember their sin no more." (Jer 31:33–34).

Girard also locates a key disclosure of the victimization mechanism in Isaiah 40–55, when the author describes the servant of YHWH as a suffering scapegoat, despised and forsaken by others. The plight of this suffering servant, so poetically narrated by the prophet, puts on display the workings of scapegoating violence so that one day it may be fully revealed and reversed.[6] Through the stories and the prophetic literature of the Hebrew Bible, we are introduced to a God who cares for the neglected and marginalized in society, not a god who requires the sacrifice of the innocent.

According to Girard, this storytelling from the underside crescendos in the New Testament when the Gospel writers narrate the story of the messiah who identifies with society's victims and calls out the power structures that perpetuate violence. Jesus dies at the hands of those powers and the Gospels reveal him not as a victim of God but as an innocent victim of a

---

5. Girard, *Violent Origins*, 145.
6. Girard, *Things Hidden Since the Foundation of the World*, 155–57.

mimetically violent humanity. Through this victimhood, Jesus becomes the *scapegoat to end all scapegoats.*

Girard's practice as a literary critic surely influenced his study of the Bible because his exegesis proves both bold and profound as he gleans universal insights from Gospel stories. For example, one of Girard's central insights involves the passages in which Jesus denounces the Pharisees for their role in killing the prophets and others: "Therefore I send you prophets and wise men and scribes, some of whom you will kill and crucify . . . that upon you may come all the righteous blood shed on earth, from the blood of innocent Abel to the blood of Zechariah the son of Barachiah, whom you murdered between the sanctuary and the alter" (Matt 23:34–36).

Girard sees beyond Jesus's chastisement of a group of religious Jews and asserts that Jesus here unveils the sacred violence at work in all religions. It will be helpful to repeat Girard's analysis of the above passage because it exemplifies how Girard reads and interprets the Gospels throughout his works:

> The text gives us to believe that there have been many murders. It only mentions two of them, however: that of Abel, the first to occur in the Bible, and that of a certain Zechariah, the last person to be killed in the Second Book of the Chronicles, in other words, the last in the whole Bible as Jesus knew it. Evidently, mention of the first and last murders takes the place of a more complete list. The victims who belong between Abel and Zechariah are implicitly included. The text has the character of a recapitulation, and it cannot be restricted to the Jewish religion alone, since the murder of Abel goes back to the origins of humanity and the foundation of the first cultural order. Cainite culture is not a Jewish culture. The text also makes explicit mention of 'all the righteous blood shed on earth'. It therefore looks as though the kind of murder for which Abel here forms the prototype is not limited to a single region of the world or to a single period of history. We are dealing with a universal phenomenon whose consequences are going to fall not only upon the Pharisees but upon this generation, that is, upon all those who are contemporary with the Gospels and the time of their diffusion, who remain deaf and blind to the news that is being proclaimed.[7]

Girard's interpretation here universalizes the words of Jesus and explains the violence that plagues not only those who killed the prophets but all humans whose mimetic rivalry results in the murder of innocent

---

7. Girard, *Things Hidden*, 159.

scapegoats. If Jesus's contemporaries would have listened to Jesus's teaching and heeded the truth that his coming kingdom demonstrated, then they would have understood the hidden predicament of sacred violence that had continually poisoned humanity.

The work of revelation does not peak in Jesus's teaching but in his innocent death, which comes at the hands of all the human forces that turned against him in Jerusalem. The Gospels' presentation of victim and persecutor is revolutionary because it portrays elements of the violent sacred that religious mythology had been masking for all of history. The unconscious nature of violence is a truth revealed in Jesus's words on the cross: "Father, forgive them for they do not know what they are doing" (Luke 23:34).

In the end, Girard's analysis of the gospel message is fascinating and provocative, especially considering that he is neither a theologian nor an official apologist for Christianity. Girard finds that Jesus's teaching, especially his exchanges with the scribes and Pharisees, uncovers the violence inherent in their religion and all religions, and reveals what societies have always kept hidden. Girard's commentary on Jesus's passion and death helps us see that Jesus is a typical scapegoat like the scapegoats present in all religious rituals; however, unlike myths and other literature, the Gospels are transparent about this fact. The Gospels expose the scapegoat mechanism because they proclaim Jesus's innocence. A scapegoat that is knowingly innocent completely reverses the effect of scapegoat sacrifice. Salvation from the violence in religion, then, comes with the truth that the Gospels reveal about Jesus's death and the workings of the scapegoat mechanism. Jesus's teaching and the unveiling of his innocent death make him more than just the scapegoat; they establish him as the cure to the need for scapegoats and the possible conclusion to sacred violence in humanity.

SCAPEGOAT HERMENEUTICS: IMPLICATIONS OF GIRARD'S THEORY

René Girard wove together the pieces of his ambitious theory over the course of four decades and during that time he remained in conversation with other scholars about his work, clarifying and reformulating when it was needed. Although scholars from an impressive range of fields have taken Girard's thought in new directions (philosophers, anthropologists, political theorists, and sociologists) it has been the theologians, religious scholars, and biblical interpreters who have most enthusiastically adopted and adapted Girard's ideas. The implications of Girard's theory for their fields are far-reaching. Below, I address some of the major subjects that have benefitted from reassessment through a Girardian lens and demonstrate how using scapegoat hermeneutics can transform our perspective on the Bible and its theology.

GOD'S CHARACTER AND HUMANITY'S PLIGHT

Christians have long struggled with the portions of Scripture that seem to portray God as a vengeful, violent, or angry deity. Such passages contrast sharply with ones that demonstrate God's lovingkindness and mercy, as we see in Hosea 11 and the parable of the prodigal son (which should be named the parable of the forgiving father). Contradictory portrayals of God have caused some strands of Christian tradition to split the character of God in two, separating "the angry God of the Old Testament" from "the merciful God of the New Testament." This misinterpretation of the Hebrew Bible finds a constructive reversal in light of Girard's theory. Applying scapegoat hermeneutics to the portraits of God in the Hebrew Scriptures causes readers to consider that the violence attributed to God by the authors does not originate from God. As Girard argues, we often hide our own mimetic violence in myth, projecting attitudes and practices that originate with humans onto the divine.

This has been a productive area of study for interpreters of Girard. Raymond Schwager, one of the first biblical scholars to apply Girard's theory, does an in-depth analysis of Hebrew literature with a scapegoat lens and discovers how the authors cloak human violence in God language. Although a vengeful or angry YHWH shows up in about 1,000 OT passages, Schwager finds that this violence is usually a consequence of evil human deeds carried out by human powers. Prophetic books especially tend to communicate that YHWH, in anger, intends to destroy humans but the action of the stories show nations invading nations or people inciting violence against their neighbors. God does not actually participate in the violence; it is committed by humans against humans. The writings attribute this sacred violence to God instead of to its true source, humanity. The only violence God commits involves hiding God's own presence from people or withdrawing, as we read about in the first murder, when Cain kills his brother Abel.[8]

This brings us to the real source of violence, humanity. Popular Christian explanations about the character of humanity include the doctrine of original sin or the Calvinist emphasis on the hopeless sinfulness of individuals. Girard locates the source of humanity's greatest sin in the formation of societies that use victimization to evade mimetic crises. This perspective acknowledges individual participation in mimetic conflict, but the emphasis is on the collective. The formation and perpetuation of the

---

8. See Schwager, *Must There Be Scapegoats*, 53–70.

scapegoat mechanism is a communal affair. A Girardian reading of Genesis acknowledges the mythological character of stories like the Fall and the first murder but points to their revelatory nature as well. James G. Williams, in *The Bible, Violence, and the Sacred*, builds upon Girard's thought and highlights that it is the story of Cain and Abel more than the story of Adam and Eve in the garden that reveals the nature of humanity and the function of mimetic violence.[9] After Cain murders Abel out of mimetic rivalry, God protects him from becoming a victim of vengeance by putting a prohibitive sign on him. Out of this generative murder (or "founding murder"), cities and civilizations arise. Eventually, one of Cain's descendants, Lamech, boasts of his violent vengeance and the story reveals the destructive force of cyclical violence in civilizations.[10] If Christians who exalt an individualistic idea of sinful human nature and salvation were to view the larger picture humanity through Girard's theory, they would be able to appreciate better the collectivist nature of human sin and the communal conception of redemption, perspectives that fit much closer with the socio-historical context of the biblical authors and their message.

THE NATURE OF SCRIPTURE: A CANON IN CONFLICT WITH ITSELF

One outworking of Girard's thought on sacred violence is his conviction that the diversity of texts in the Bible cause parts of the canon to conflict with one another. The Jewish and Christian Scriptures, he insists, contain both mythological texts, which hide the scapegoat mechanism, and truth-telling texts, which counter or reveal the scapegoating process. For the Hebrew Bible, when laws and narratives enforce the sacrificial system, they fall prey to the mythological instinct, ascribing the victimization and violence practiced in rituals to God rather than to its true source, human mimetic conflict. These texts stand in contrast to the stories mentioned above that highlight the innocence of the victim and the ganging up of all against one, for example, the narrative of Joseph and his brothers and the prophetic voices in Micah and Isaiah.

Like the Hebrew Bible, the New Testament also seems to contain stories that unmask the scapegoating nature of humanity *and* texts that put the comfortable mask of hidden victimization back on. The Gospels, Girard's canon-within-the-canon, are truth-telling literature par excellence. They are transparent about the innocence of Jesus, meticulously characterizing him as the scapegoat of the religious and political powers of his day. The Gospel

---

9. Hamerton-Kelly, however, focuses on the story in the Garden as revelatory, casting the serpent as a metaphor of mimetic desire. See *Sacred Violence*.

10. Williams, *Bible, Violence, and the Sacred*, 33–38.

writers describe how the whole city of Jerusalem turned against Jesus during Passover—first the religious leaders, then the crowds, then the soldiers, and finally his own disciples (save for the women disciples at the cross). The Gospel of John, in Caiaphas's ironic speech preceding the passion, explicitly clarifies Jesus's role as a scapegoat: "It is better for you to have one man die for the people than to have the whole nation destroyed" (John 11:50).

On the other hand, some New Testament writers use the sacrificial language of the Hebrew Bible to describe Jesus's salvific work, something that Girard sees as a return to sacred violence. For example, the author of Hebrews implies continuity with previous sacrifices in his or her imagery of Jesus as a priest and a sacrifice. This interpretive move would lead later Christian thinkers like Anselm to a misreading of the atonement and God's character (represented in the satisfaction theory of Anselm).[11] When Paul utilizes sacrificial metaphors in his letters to first-century Christians (e.g., Rom 3:24–26), he retains vestiges of the sacrificial system as well, but he uses a variety of other images alongside these, signaling that even within Paul's own writing, there is a diversity of expression about sacrifice and salvation.

Any serious reader of texts, from Bible scholars to literary critics like Girard, should not be bothered by the fact that the Christian Scriptures represent differing and even contradictory perspectives on sacrifice. A Girardian reading prioritizes certain texts over others—the ones that free people from the cycle of violence are favored and the ones that conceal human scapegoating in myth are devalued. However, Girard's assertion that the Bible is in conflict with itself and needs an interpretive lens (like a Gospels-centered or anti-sacrificial hermeneutic) could help bring to light what we usually deny—that we all have a canon within a canon. Like Girard, perhaps all Christians should acknowledge our lenses and start interpreting from that transparent foundation. Such honest interaction with biblical literature could start some important conversations about inspiration, canon, and the tension that Bible readers must hold when they study the diverse Christian teaching found in Scripture.

NEW PERSPECTIVES ON CONTROVERSIAL TOPICS

An anti-sacrificial reading of the Bible like Girard's has the potential to turn traditional doctrines of the church on their heads. Girard's literary analysis

---

11. Girard, *Things Hidden*, 228. Some New Testament scholars disagree with Girard's analysis of the sacrificial language in Hebrews, arguing that he and theologians like Anselm have misinterpreted the Hebrews on sacrifice. See Webb, "René Girard and the Symbolism of Religious Sacrifice," 165–84.

alongside the insights of his later theological interpreters has produced new perspectives on several of Christianity's most debated topics: the figure of Satan, the theme of sacrifice in the Bible, and the inner workings of salvation.

Satan

There is not agreement among scholars about how the figure regularly known as Satan functions in biblical literature. Interpreters are often frustrated by the superstition surrounding the character, so they ignore its presence or focus solely on the literary purpose it serves in the literature. Many would agree, though, that the satan (the accuser) of Job's introduction and the character who shows up to tempt Jesus in the wilderness (called *satanas* or "satan" in Mark and *diabolos* or "devil" in Matthew and Luke) then makes appearances in other places in the New Testament have some connection. Christian tradition often interprets these figures to be the same person throughout the biblical witness, a literal entity known by a host of names: the devil (e.g., Matt 4:1), Satan (used over fifty times), the evil one (Matt 13:19), Beelzebul (Matt 12:24), the deceiver (Rev 12:9), the father of lies (John 8:44), and the ruler of this world (John 14:30).

On this subject, Girard forms a bridge between scholarship and Christian folk tradition, affirming that the satan figure is the same one throughout the biblical witness, but insisting that it must be demythologized. Satan, in Girardian analysis, is the personification of the scapegoat mechanism, the force that drives humans to mimesis, conflict, and then the violent victimization of all against one. Satan's work is finally made transparent in the Gospels' passion accounts, when we see the function the crucifixion performs, a temporary quelling of unrest achieved by an innocent man's torture. Although Jesus's suffering is a *product* of the satanic mechanism of victimage, the Gospels' narration of the process makes it also the *unveiling* of Satan's work. This is how Jesus's passion becomes the act that (potentially) defeats Satan. If humans heed the gospel's revelation and recognize the satan working among us, then Jesus will truly be the scapegoat to end all scapegoats.[12]

Sacrifice

The atonement theory that has stubbornly dominated Protestant history and become the cornerstone of evangelical Christian ideology (penal substitutionary atonement) takes very seriously the necessity of sacrifice for salvation. Defenders of the theory will pluck a verse fragment out of

---

12. Girard, *I See Satan Fall Like Lightning*, 32–38.

Hebrews—"without the shedding of blood there is no forgiveness of sins" (Heb 9:22)—and use it as a trump card to insist that the Father sacrificed Jesus in order to satisfy God's wrath against sinners (or substituted him to pay the price for our sins). Girard's anti-sacrificial reading of the Bible cuts the legs out from under penal substitutionary atonement. If "all religious rituals spring from the surrogate victim," then the sacrifices described in the Hebrew Bible, and repurposed in Hebrews, are a part of humanity's enslavement to the scapegoating system, not the desire of a merciful God.[13] Girard's argument that humans project their own violence onto the divine and trap themselves in systems of sacrifice is one that has the potential to deconstruct traditional views of Scripture, God, and salvation. Therein lies the great power of scapegoat hermeneutics. Reading texts that have been foundational to the evangelical faith through the lens of scapegoat theory disrupts what lay at the heart of our inherited beliefs. Scapegoat hermeneutics may also impact humanity's relationship to God and interactions with one another for the better. For many, the risk of losing a treasured (but destructive) belief is well worth the reward and revelation it brings.

Salvation

What is one left with after burning up the dregs of a sacrificial view of atonement? What are we saved from if not the wrath of God or the punishment for sins? Girard's view of salvation is not an *objective* atonement theory, one that purports to affect something in God, as if God needed to be appeased or paid back. His is a *subjective* atonement theory, one that produces changes in humanity. Through a Girardian lens, our salvation comes from the revelation of our own human nature. When we learn about the mimetic rivalry that ravages the hearts of individuals, the violence that ensues, and the innocent victims that we unknowingly sacrifice, then we can interrupt the cycle of violence. We can stop blaming others to hide our own culpability, and we can save victims from their unjust fates by calling out the powers and systems that oppress them. We can, effectively, end the scapegoat mechanism. Scapegoat hermeneutics show us that we do not need to be saved from a wronged or disappointed God—we need to be saved from ourselves and our violent processes. This is the truth that we require, according to Girard, and it is this truth that will set us free from the disease that plagues all human societies, our inclination to allow injustice to reign and victims to suffer.

When we are finally released from our hidden prison, then we will be free to practice the good kind of mimesis; imitation is, after all, at the center

---

13. Girard, *Violence and the Sacred*, 306.

of the human experience. The destructive kind of mimetic desire produces envy for what our neighbor has or who our neighbor is; the good kind of mimesis imitates the life of Jesus. Jesus's teaching reveals the patterns of violence and victimization in our society and his death uncovers the workings of the scapegoat mechanism. It is Jesus's *life and ministry*, however, that model for us how we might protect future victims and end scapegoating before it has a chance to run its course. Jesus enacted his upside-down kingdom ministry among the most vulnerable people in his context. He loved and empowered the people on the margins of his world—the women who bore the brunt of oppression and scorn, those people who moved unseen through life with illness and disability, the poor who suffered under the high taxes of empire, and societal outsiders who were one calamity away from being scapegoats for the insiders. When Jesus raised the voices of these potential scapegoats and opposed the people complicit in systems of violence and hierarchy, he was showing us the priorities of God, the characteristics of God's reign on earth.[14] Salvation, according to the Gospels, does not come to individuals who believe in their hearts that God sacrificed Jesus for us. Salvation is a systematic affair—a society that has been flipped on its head with God's preference for the poor, a community transformed by the inclusion of enemies and outcasts, a people who turn from ritual and sacrifice to finally recognize the extravagantly merciful character of their God.

APPLICATION OF SCAPEGOAT HERMENEUTICS

As productive as Girard's work has been for theologians and biblical scholars, it has even more potential to revitalize the faith and lives of laypeople who are dissatisfied with the narrow interpretations of Scripture handed down to them. Christians who have begun to deconstruct or have concluded that their inherited view of God, the Bible, and salvation are insufficient will find much to ponder when they read with a Girardian lens. Applying scapegoat hermeneutics to biblical literature offers new ways of understanding Scripture and prompts fresh questions of the text, such as: "How does the idea of God sacrificing Jesus fit with the portrayal of God and humanity throughout the Bible?"; "How does Scripture's perspective on victims change the way we read the stories in it?"; "What do the Gospels tell us about why Jesus died and how does that implicate human systems of power?"

The way I have used scapegoat hermeneutics in my classroom is first by introducing students to the idea that we all have lenses through which we interpret the Bible. Then, I outline the basics of Girard's theory and ask how

---

14. See Bashaw, *Scapegoats*.

it might give us a different perspective on key themes in the biblical text. Students end up fascinated and/or discomfited by Girard's anti-sacrificial interpretation because it challenges the way the church has traditionally understood the cross. In addition, I turn my students' attention to how scapegoat hermeneutics can help us see Jesus's ministry as a model of love and inclusion. Although Girard's interpreters have tended to emphasize the atonement in their application of scapegoat hermeneutics, I maintain that Jesus's whole life provides a paradigm for ending the victimizing mechanism. Jesus's ministry among the poor, sick, and rejected in society offers us an alternative way to be human. A Girardian lens can help students and laypeople alike recognize this liberative message that has been in the text all along. With the revelation that the Gospel writers offer, those of us who follow Jesus can live into the reign of God that he announced and continue his work to end scapegoating and violence in our world.

BIBLIOGRAPHY

Alison, James, and Wolfgang Palaver, eds. *The Palgrave Handbook of Mimetic Theory and Religion*. London: Palgrave Macmillan, 2017.

Burkert, Walter Burkert, et al., eds. *Violent Origins: Walter Burkert, René Girard, and Jonathan Z. Smith on Ritual Killing and Cultural Formation*. Stanford: Stanford University Press, 1987.

Bashaw, Jennifer Garcia. *Scapegoats: The Gospel through the Eyes of Victims*. Minneapolis: Fortress, 2022.

Girard, René. *I See Satan Fall Like Lightning*. Maryknoll, NY: Orbis, 2001.

———. *The Scapegoat*. Baltimore: The Johns Hopkins University Press, 1986.

———. *Things Hidden Since the Foundation of the World*. Stanford: Stanford University Press, 1987.

———. *Violence and the Sacred*. Baltimore: The Johns Hopkins University Press, 1977.

Hamerton-Kelly, Robert. *Sacred Violence: Paul's Hermeneutic of the Cross*. Minneapolis: Fortress, 1992.

Schwager, Raymund. *Must There Be Scapegoats: Violence and Redemption in the Bible*. San Francisco: Harper & Row, 1987.

Webb, Eugene. "René Girard and the Symbolism of Religious Sacrifice." In *René Girard and Creative Reconciliation*, edited by Vern Neufeld Redekop and Thomas Ryba, 165–84. Lanham, MD: Lexington, 2014.

Williams, James G. *The Bible, Violence, and the Sacred*. New York: HarperCollins, 1991.

Chapter 41
Christ-Shaped Hermeneutics
JASON BYASSEE

Intellectual movements should be careful with their self-definitions. The so-called New Critics are a century old now. Ask any postmodernist whether they have actually been able to leave behind their modernism. What we claim to be done with—"post"—can go on defining us indefinitely.

"Conservative" and "liberal" are fine words in a sense. The one suggests we treasure what we have received; the other means we are generous with others. Yet in our frayed cultural fabric in North Atlantic cultures, they usually obfuscate rather than clarify. In biblical hermeneutics the one treats the bible as a source of diktats, timeless truth to be obeyed, not investigated. Some conservatives treat the bible as if we were Muslims reading the Koran. For Islam, Mohammad falls into a trance and transcribes the Koran, without human participation. This is no Christian view of Scripture. For us, human beings write Scripture, lend it their personality, and their views matter in how we interpret Scripture. They are under the guidance of the Holy Spirit, of course. But Scripture is a living word, in reflection of an incarnate Word. We wrestle with it like Jacob at the Jabbok. It leaves us changed, holy, for having been in its presence. And the best way to tell that we've read it correctly is that our community has grown in faith, hope, and love. No hermeneutic can be judged in a vacuum. It has to be evaluated for the sorts of people it produces.

A postconservative hermeneutic must avoid over-correcting, lurching too far from its moorings. It is good to step past a positive and simplistic hermeneutic in which truth is deposited in the text and we extract and apply it today. It is also good not to pretend anything goes, that the text can be abandoned for individual preference, or worse still, dropped in acid. Better to restore a chastened historical hermeneutic in which the Holy Spirit forges the body of Christ through our worship of God mediated through Scripture and sacrament. This will yield no single, stable "meaning," since with God there is always more depth. It will, rather, gather and sanctify a people who long to see God's face in Jesus Christ. Such a trinitarian hermeneutic will treasure what we have received, while being flexible in how we learn from it—drawing strength from "conservative" and "liberal" approaches alike, avoiding the pitfalls of each. But its primary goal will be to meet the living God, who is determined, despite our foibles, to use the church to bless the world.

I propose to use the prophet Isaiah to show a Christ-shaped communal hermeneutic. There are few places in Scripture more perfect to show the gaping difference between ancient Christian approaches to the bible and modern, historical-critical ones. Of course the author(s) of Isaiah are not thinking of Jesus of Nazareth or the church he will gather. Yet they are coining language without which Jesus's church could not have arisen. Conservatives are often in the awkward place of having to act like Isaiah knew exactly what was coming. Liberals in the even more awkward place of insisting Isaiah was describing anything other than Jesus. But the church's tradition of worship and preaching is wiser. It knows we cannot gather in Advent without reading these texts: "He shall be called 'Wonderful Counselor, mighty God, everlasting Father, Prince of Peace.'" Those words were not written with Jesus in mind. Yet we cannot now describe Jesus without them. To root them out of Christian speech, to disqualify them from the church's lexicon, is to do immeasurable violence to the church's worship. These are poets' words, and they have shaped the church's imagination for millennia. We need more such words of wonder, not fewer. Modern interpretation had good reason to object: the author did not intend these meanings; the church has often used them to berate Israel. All true. Yet remove them from the church's speech and imagination and you are left with no church at all. The right response to abuse is, of course, right use, not suspension altogether.

WHERE OX AND ASS ARE FEEDING

A short one to start, Isa 1:3, "The ox knows its owner, and the donkey its master's crib; but Israel does not know, my people do not understand." The prophet begins diagnosing the people's unfaithfulness by saying even these two dumb animals know their owner. The church has often included an ox and an ass in its iconography of Christmas, drawing on St. Luke's imagery of a manger it has included this image from Israel's Scripture. These two dumb animals are not so dumb. What's dumb, in the sense of silent, is the Word in the crib. These two pay homage. St. Ambrose says "Let us then know the Lord's crib where we are nourished, fed, and refreshed."[1] The fathers often point out that one creature, the ox, is ritually clean in Israel, the other, the ass, is not. All people, Jew and gentile alike, are drawn to the one in the manger. Gregory Nazianzus contrasts us gentiles as those loaded down with sins and idolatries to Jews who are blessed by the yoke of God's law.[2] Positive references to Judaism are few in the fathers, so we should treasure those we find. St. Augustine suggests we "not be ashamed of being the Lord's donkey . . . you walk along the way, and the Way is sitting on you. Let the Lord sit on us and take us wherever he wants."[3] This is homiletical playfulness, following an animal image throughout he canon and the church's imagination into our lives now. It proves nothing—but it preaches. It can of course do harm. Everything can. The church has tried to dodge Isaiah's condemnation of God's people by saying that's about the Jews, not us. Wrong on our part—if we claim to be God's people, the prophet aims at us. But of course suspending the figural interpretation doesn't free you from anti-Judaism. A reading technique cannot keep you from sin. Only God's mercy can do that.

Now notice what these readings do and don't do. They don't prove anything. Offer Isa 1:3 to a Jew or a pagan as a prooftext and they will rightly laugh at you. It is a tenuous reading—attentive to the letter, but only intelligible in light of Christ. But for those who worship Christ as God, who see his incarnation as the salvation of all that God has made, who sing these hymns and surround themselves with this art and chase their children around horns in live nativity scenes, a reading like this is beautiful. The animals are there as a model for us. We're to recognize our Lord, gaze on him, adore him, eat him up, let him ride on us and direct us in where we are to go. The reading shapes imagination and faithful living and joy. That is why it's a reading that lives in church and dies in the university. In a place committed to praising the God who has mixed himself up in the stories of Israel and church, the reading soars. For a place committed to critique and puncturing certitudes and setting itself up as the guardian of truth, it falls flat. If those preparing to lead the former sort of community by the latter aren't shown these readings, their perils and their glories, they'll be left to their own devices to preach.

---

1. McKinion, *Isaiah 1–39*, 5. Quoting from Ambrose's letter 36 (13.6).
2. Sawyer, *Fifth Gospel*, 119.
3. Wilken, *Isaiah*, 22, quoting from Augustine's "Sermon on the Birthday of the Lord."

There is in this chapter also a note of grace, one that cannot be found by a community that will close its ears to Isaiah's condemnation: "Come now, let us argue it out, says the Lord" (1:18). A biblically attentive reader will think of Abraham sticking his neck out on behalf of Sodom and Gomorrah, or Moses pleading with God not to destroy the Israelites (Gen 18, Exod 32). Israel's God not only notices every ill, the Lord also listens when faithful people advocate on behalf of others. This verse is also often used in ecclesial traditions that place a high premium on philosophy: even God asks for rational argument. The Lord continues with a word of grace, like dew-born grass in the middle of a thicket of thorns: "Though your sins are like scarlet, they shall be like snow; though they are red like crimson, they shall become like wool" (1:18). This is a hinge verse for this chapter, perhaps for the entire book of the prophet. Isaiah lays out human sin in graphic detail, and then features a divine promise to wash it cleaner than wool, whiter than snow. Prophetic denunciation is not denunciation alone. It is the grace of sin confessed so it can be forgiven; a wound uncovered for the physician so she can offer healing, a moral fault so gruesome none would show it to another unless showing it would mean repair. This repair will not be easy: "I will smelt away your dross as with lye and remove all your alloy" (1:25). Forgiveness in Christian vocabulary is free but not cheap, it comes with a purging, a penance, a mandate for reconciliation. For example, Zoe Ministry in southern Africa is an empowerment program that offers training in micro enterprise to AIDS orphans. They tell a story in which some formerly abused children found themselves with extra goats in their newly successful business. What should they do with them? They decided to offer a goat to the adults in their village who had abused them.[4] One cannot imagine the anguish of a powerless child mistreated by a powerful adult. And one cannot imagine the reconciliation made possible when forgiveness is offered, with material signs, instead of violence. Well, almost no one can imagine. Isaiah can. And he can help us to also: "Afterwards you shall be called the city of righteousness, the faithful city" (1:26).

IN THE DAYS TO COME...

"In the days to come," Isaiah 2 opens, before closing with a famous image, "they shall beat their swords into plowshares" (Isa 2:2 and 5). There are not many more important passages in Israel's Scripture for the church's self-understanding than this one. John Sawyer's book *The Fifth Gospel* says no verse has been more "in the headlines" than the swords to plowshares over

---

4. I heard this story on a "Come and See" pilgrimage in Rwanda in 2014 to learn about Zoe's ministry there.

the last 50 years—witness the Soviet artist's rendering of it in front of the UN building in New York.⁵ An expression of confidence that diplomacy could bring about the end of wars, or perhaps Soviet propaganda claiming that only the people's revolution can do what the UN hopes for.

Of more interest to us is the church's ecclesiocentric way of reading this text. "In the days to come" is an eschatological signal. In those days, mountains shall rise and fall. Rock will be flimsy and nations fluid. Peoples will stream to Zion. The gentiles, even the gentiles, can you believe it? Will find their way to Zion to worship Israel's God. God's promises in Genesis will be fulfilled. Israel was first chosen by God not for itself, but for everyone else: "in you all the nations of the earth will be blessed" (Gen 12:4). Since St. Paul the gentile church has seen ourselves as the fulfillment of these promises in Genesis and Isaiah (Rom 15:8–12). We are ascending to Zion in Christ, learning God's Torah and being changed into people of peace (Rom 12:25–32).

One common charge against theological readings like allegory is that they elide specifics, hover above materiality, platonize away the specific. Allegory can do that. But not always. St. Athanasius suggests that barbarians, gentiles, us, are warlike by nature due to idolatry. But when we hear of Christ we turn from war to farming, and stretch out our arms in prayer.⁶ Far from allegorizing this passage away, Athanasius insists it means Christians have to be people of peace, like it or not. A century earlier, St. Irenaeus boasted that we have forgotten how to wage war, "when struck, we turn the other cheek," because of the "one who brought these things about." These church fathers write before Constantine's settlement between church and empire, and before Augustine's limited blessing of violence. For them the fulfillment of the prophet's promise requires Christian non-violence. Irenaeus goes farther.

> It was our Lord himself who made the plough, and introduced the scythe, that is, the first sowing of the seed that led to the creatin of Adam, and the gathering in of the produce "in the last times" by the Word. For this reason he joined the beginning to the end, and is Lord of both. He has finally displayed the plough in which the wood is joined to the iron and has cleared his land. For the Word, being firmly united to the flesh, and nailed to the cross, has reclaimed the savage earth.⁷

---

5. Sawyer, *Fifth Gospel*, 233.
6. Cited in Wilken, *Isaiah*, 41–42, quoting from *On the Incarnation* paragraph 52.
7. Wilken, *Isaiah*, 40–41, citing Irenaeus's *Against Heresies*, 4.34.4.

Jesus is the one who taught farming to Adam, giving him Eden's tools, like plough and scythe. He is also the last Adam, and like a plow, he's the one in whom metal is joined to wood, in the soft saving flesh of his hands. Modern imagination suggests diplomacy can bring peace. That's good. Not uncontentious, but good. Irenaeus's suggests the beating of weapons into farm equipment is of a piece with humanity destroying the son of God. He, in that very action, joins the first and second Adam in making humanity new. This is what I sometimes call "christological maximalism": seeking Christ in all places and in depth.[8] But notice it requires something of us: repenting out of violence into peace.

And note: this is the way the New Testament reads the Old. It is New Testament convention to say the church is in the last days (Heb 1:2, Acts 2:17). Paul's eschatological promises in Rom 11:26–27 include the words *ex Sion* from Isa 2:3, as instruction comes forth from Zion. Reading this way is reading Israel's Bible with the earliest church. Irenaeus has learned it from Paul. He makes a move beyond Paul, but defensible, playful, wise, and demanding upon its readers.[9]

HOLY, HOLY, HOLY LORD

It is hard to think of a more important OT passage for us Christians than Isaiah 6, with its glimpse of the Lord with the two seraphim, the "holy holy holy" oft repeated in eucharistic liturgy. Liturgy doesn't just reflect meaning. It carries it. Bears it. And, of course, changes it.

Origen suggested the two seraphim as a glimpse of the Son and the Spirit. Their wings cover the Father's face, since no one can see God. Later Trinitarians would attack this reading for its subordinationist overtones. As Jerome thunders, "the eyes of the flesh are unable to see the divinity of the Father, nor that of the Son, nor that of the Holy Spirit, because in the Trinity there is one nature."[10] Jerome is right of course: the divinity the persons share is equally invisible to all flesh. Yet Origen's glimpse of the Trinity has a recent defender in Robert Jenson.[11] What do the Son and the Spirit do but praise the Father and submit to his will? This is no diminution of the other persons, for their submission is no loss, it is, if anything, perfectly appropriate for God to defer in the inner triune life. Note this multi-millennia

---

8. Byassee, *Psalms*.

9. Hays has shown the biblical fidelity and pastoral fruitfulness of entering into the New Testament's interpretation of the Old in such places as *Echoes of Scripture in the Letters of Paul* and *Echoes of Scripture in the Gospels*.

10. Wilken, *Isaiah*, 69.

11. See the essays on Origen in Jenson and East, *Triune Story*.

debate undoes one of the common criticisms of allegory: that it is absurd, that anyone can find anything that way. No, Origen and Jerome and Jenson all agree there are rules, it is worth arguing over. It might be wrong, but it's not unruled or unboundaried.

You won't be surprised that the ancient church sees a glimpse of the threefold nature of God in the three-time repetition of the sanctus. St. Ambrose says "the seraphim spoke the name not once, lest the Son be excluded, not twice, lest the Spirit be overlooked, not four times lest something created be included."[12] Ambrose is aware this proves nothing to the unconvinced. For those already convinced by arguments from elsewhere in Scripture and tradition that God is triune, this reading is appropriate, fitting, even delightful. Allegory proves nothing. It's not allowed to. It demonstrates what we already know in a surprising new place. It's a preacher's practice. It allows what Robert Wilken calls "homiletical playfulness." Hearers go from perplexed. Hm. To enlightened. Oh, right. To delighted. There God is again. And wouldn't a glimpse of the divine nature in the throne room calling the prophet give us some granular insight into the divine nature?

In textbooks, Theodore of Mopsuestia is taken to be a non-allegorizing Antiochene, a sane but lonely voice in the wilderness. Yet he sees the coal that touches Isaiah's lips as a sign of the Eucharist. Ordinary bread on its own, "but when it is brought to the fire it becomes luminous and hot . . . by the coming of the Holy Spirit it is transformed into body and blood, and thus it is changed into the power of a spiritual and immortal nourishment."[13] St. Ephrem the Syrian, also often described as non-allegorizing, takes Theodore one step farther, suggesting the seraphim and the prophet in Isaiah 6 don't get to do what every Christian does in the Eucharist. "The seraph could not hold it, Isaiah did not consume it, but our Lord has allowed us to do both."[14] Liturgy shapes Scripture, and then in turn, Scripture shapes liturgy, both shape us, to see what we couldn't have on our own. The Eucharist is a live coal we swallow. The closer you are to Christian liturgy, this way of reading makes more sense. The farther, it seems more fanciful.

PREGNANT VIRGINS

There is no more contentious text for us as we adjudicate critical scholarship and ancient Christian exegesis. Yet this need not be so. Ancient interpreters can allow multiple conflicting interpretations. It is usually a modernist

12. Wilken, *Isaiah*, 77.
13. Wilken, *Isaiah*, 82.
14. Sawyer, *Fifth Gospel*, 64.

assumption of a single author's intent that cannot. So Sts. Cyril of Alexandria and John Chrysostom are happy to admit that Isaiah is referring directly to the birth of a new Israelite King, probably Hezekiah. St. John says "There is much to learn from Isaiah bout the wisdom of God and his care for the Jewish people."[15] God allows a trial, and also makes provision for Israel's deliverance. No historical critic could have said it better.

Yet for ancient Christians, as for ancient Jews, texts take on new meanings as a community's life progresses. Again, despite modern disdain, the fathers were well aware that an *almah* is not a virgin in Hebrew, just a young girl. It is *parthenos,* the Septuagint's translation of *almah,* that means a woman who knows not a man. St. Jerome pushes back a little, suggesting an *almah* is a *concealed* virgin, which would make conception a bit difficult. These issues are not usually resolved with better translation. The fathers ask, nearly as one, why the blaring trumpets, promise of a sign, the bestowal of the name Emmanuel, if this were an ordinary human birth? It's not all that surprising that a young girl falls pregnant, that's in fact how these things usually work. Yet Isaiah itself ratchets the rhetoric up to the level of the miraculous.

For the church fathers, the virgin birth is an affirmation of human embodiment. God graces a womb. It is gnostics who shudder at this. Christianity delights in it. Moderns have asked whether a virgin birth means a disparagement of sex. I'll let the fathers speak for themselves in response. Tertullian: "It is to be expected that the one who was going to inaugurate a new birth had to be born in a new way."[16] That's a conclusion from faith for faith. He goes further. If the first Adam was taken from virgin earth, unplowed or seeded or tended, "All the more reason that the second Adam would come forth from a virgin earth."[17] If Eve was beguiled by the serpent's words, Mary is enchanted by Gabriel's, and conceives by believing. St. Gregory of Nyssa analogizes here with the burning bush. A natural phenomenon working differently than nature normally works. As the bush is filled with the fiery presence of God and not destroyed, so Mary is filled with the fiery presence of God and not destroyed. Instead she gives life where we didn't expect it.[18] The virgin birth brings out our forebears' lyrical and aesthetic best. And we try to trip it up, interrupt it, with "excuse me, the Hebrew doesn't mean that." No wonder our church is so bereft of wonder.

---

15. Wilken, *Isaiah,* 92–93, referring to Daniel 3 and 6.
16. Wilken, *Isaiah,* 98.
17. Wilken, *Isaiah,* 98
18. Wilken, *Isaiah,* 101.

The fathers' best argument is their simplest. If you're willing to believe that God can enter human life and divinize it, why would a virgin birth be heard to believe? Chrysostom again, God "was conceived as a human being and went through the nine-month term, was born and kept in diapers and nursed by his mother."[19] All the might there is dependent on a young girl's assent, then her child care. There is no more distinctive Christian word than that.

UNTO US

One of the most important questions for any hermeneutic is how it determines what is and is not a problem. Isaiah 9:6 puts St. Ambrose in a defensive crouch.[20] If the Son is sent, he must be less than the sender, some say. The Son is a counselor, but God the father *needs* no counselor, Isaiah elsewhere insists (Isa 40:13). The Septuagint version is even more problematic: how can the Son be called an "angel of mighty counsel"?

Ambrose responds by noting the passive construction: a son *is* given, *is* sent, with no subject denoted. The sender is, of course, the whole Trinity. The Son is sent by the Father, but also by the Spirit, and even, in his divine nature, by himself. There is no subordination in the Trinity, except with regard to the incarnation, in which the Son is even less than himself. The scrambling around of expected subjects and objects shows the heart of this passage, and the heart of the gospel: God becomes one with us. This is no loss to God. It shows who God eternally is: with us and for us. John Chrysostom responds more directly to the counselor worry: "When scripture wishes to show that God needs no one, it says he has no counselor. When it wishes to show the equal honour of the Only Begotten, it calls the Son of God his counselor."[21] The Son is counselor to the One who needs no counsel.

The problem in this passage is also its great possibility. These seeming contradictions actually show the mystery of the incarnation. Passages in which the Son seems lesser show his kenosis among us to save. Those that show his equality show his shared divinity. This is the key to fourth-century biblical interpretation and all Christianity that stands on the shoulders of the Council of Nicaea (325): those defending Nicaea have a way to explain passages that speak to the Son's divinity and also that speak to his lesser status. Anti-Nicene opponents have no way to explain the equality verses.

---

19. Wilken, *Isaiah*, 94 quoting from Chrysostom's commentary on Isa 7:1.
20. McKinion, *Isaiah 1–39*, 71.
21. McKinion, *Isaiah 1–39*, 72.

The key to reading Scripture well is to be able to embrace the widest swath of differing Scriptures. Nicaea can do that. Its opponents cannot.

For our purposes, how would we describe Jesus Christ without Isaiah's language as "wonderful counselor, mighty God, everlasting Father, prince of peace"? The depth of language for our Christology is much reduced without Isaiah's words. It is hard to imagine a worse fate than loss of language with which to praise God. The language is not unproblematic. The fathers don't get around to addressing the Son's being called "everlasting Father" (Aquinas does later—it's a reference to the Spirit as Father of the Poor). Accepting that Isaiah's language is christological puts the fathers to work. We don't worry about the application and so don't sweat it. And so our language, our praise, our interpretive skills, atrophy, and our Christology loses the tang of Israel's speech. Disaster.

SPIRIT REST

To risk pointing out the obvious, much of the power of these chapters comes from the future tense verbs and the lack of specific referent. Isaiah looks forward to a shoot from Jesse on whom the Spirit pours seven-fold gifts who will usher in peace in creation, but it does not say who that will be. Once Christians think we have a specific referent, the meanings lock in place for us, and the church's worship is shaped accordingly, giving birth to later and equally imaginative and faithful readings.

St. Paul started it. He quotes this passage in Romans 15: "The root of Jesse shall come, the one who rises to rule the Gentiles." Revelation describes Jesus as a "rod" in several places, though of David rather than his father Jesse, same tree. Most patristic figures deepen these New Testament hints by speaking of the order of salvation. St. Augustine preaches, "If you seek the fruit in its root, you will not find it. But neither would you find the fruit in the branch, unless it had first come from the root."[22] The organic metaphor of the tree gets at both continuity and change. Ambrose is more specific still: "The root is the family of the Jews, the rod is Mary, and the flower is her Christ."[23] St. Cyril of Alexandria knows this Marian interpretation and, surprisingly, doesn't like it. For him, the rod refers to Christ's royal authority, his vocation as shepherd of the sheep. The blossom at the end of the staff is the blooming of human nature into immortality, and God's people as a fragrance to others. Cyril is the great bard of one nature Christology, but he surprises by cutting Mary out here. Chrysostom does stop to

---

22. McKinion, *Isaiah 1–39*, 96.
23. McKinion, *Isaiah 1–39*, 96.

poor some disdain on those who say this is "just" a rod.[24] Always look out for that word "just," it's a tell that some highly unimaginative interpretation is coming. Nothing is just anything. "No one would be so senseless as to say that the grace of the Spirit came down on a piece of wood." Isaiah himself speaks in poetry, please, pay attention. The fact that it's a shoot blossoming is miraculous, suggesting an unlikely conception, without a father, or staying in the metaphor, without tending or cultivation. And the beauty of the image of a branch blossoming has made this one stick in the church's liturgy, hymnody, and art—witness hymns like "Lo How a Rose E'er Blooming" and "O Come O Come Emmanuel." Once you long to see Christ everywhere, you see him especially in the Scriptures that bear witness to him, the same ones he learned bouncing on Mary's knee.

CHILD LEADERSHIP

It would be hard to overstate the degree to which the sevenfold gifts of the Spirit in Isa 11:2 for the church's thinking about the Holy Spirit. As is natural with the Spirit, sources tend to turn to liquid metaphors: the Spirit is poured out so lavishly on Christ that it overflows on the rest of us in the form of the Spirit's gifts.[25] For Ambrose, the Spirit is like an eternal river that is constantly overflowing its banks, in a "copious stream" of "overflowing greatness."[26] St. Cyril of Alexandria deepens this hermeneutical tradition by suggesting the Son's reception of the Spirit is a sign of his self-emptying. For why does the Son need a deluge of the Spirit whom he breathes forth eternally within the life of the Trinity? Isaiah 11:2 suggests then the Son's kenosis, since "he who is the giver of the Spirit received the Spirit."[27] Several patristic sources, beginning with Origen, argue that Isaiah's description that the Spirit "rests" on him echoes St. John's language of the Spirit "abiding" with Jesus: with all the rest of us sinners the Spirit is occasionally present, in our share of the gifts here described (wisdom, understanding, knowledge etc). Only on Jesus does the Spirit descend, remain, and abide.[28] Irenaeus, writing early on in the second century, uses daring language when he describes the Spirit growing "accustomed to dwell in the human race" by dwelling in Jesus. Having

---

24. Wilken *Isaiah*, 145.

25. So Novation in McKinion, *Isaiah 1–39*, 98.

26. McKinion, *Isaiah 1–39*, 99.

27. Wilken, *Isaiah*, 136. Cyril offers this partly as a rebuff of a possible adoptionist reading of Isaiah 11.

28. So Origen: "The spirit of wisdom did not rest on Moses, the spirit of wisdom did not rest on Joshua . . . not on Isaiah nor on Jeremiah . . . John saw only one on whom it remained," Wilken, *Isaiah*, 146.

become so accustomed the Spirit can now alight on us. Irenaeus goes on to describe the Spirit as the water that, mixed with flour, can become bread, or even more gracefully, as the "dew of God," defused throughout the earth after beginning with Jesus.[29]

It is not insignificant that the gifts of the Spirit are sevenfold. Yet precisely what is that significance? Patristic writers like to treat such passages as so many stair steps for spiritual ascent. Yet this one presents some difficulties. Tertullian lays the gifts of 1 Corinthians 12 atop those of Isaiah 11 to insist they are the same gifts, given by the same Spirit. He may be right, but his argument feels strained (are prophecy, discernment of spirits, tongues and interpretation of tongues, really the same thing as the Spirit of knowledge?).[30] St. Augustine suggests the gifts described in Isaiah 11 are the same as those laid out in the Sermon on the Mount, yet they appear in reverse order. Here Isaiah begins with the most elevated gift, wisdom, but Scripture elsewhere insists the fear of the Lord is the beginning of wisdom (Ps 111:10), and Isaiah includes that last. Elsewhere Augustine plays with Jesus's warning that unless a demoniac replaces her evil spirits with the Spirit of God, seven more devils may enter inn (Matt 12:45). He suggests those demons are the opposite of the spiritual gifts in Isaiah: they are folly and error, rashness and cowardice, ignorance and impiety, and pride.[31] Gregory the Great, ever the imaginative one, connects these seven gifts with Job's question of who "joined together the stars of the Pleiades" (Job 38:31). Those are, of course, seven stars. Gregory ties Job with Zechariah: "It belongs to this stone to have seven eyes in the sense that at the same time it retains in operation every virtue of the Spirit's sevenfold grace."[32]

Isaiah then famously turns to the effects of the righteous branch's coming on the natural order. Or, rather, not so famously. It was not until the paintings of Edward Hicks, the American Quaker, that Isaiah 11 took such a ferocious hold on the church's popular imagination about this passage.[33] Hicks' own trajectory on this passage is instructive: John Sawyer describes the way he began by painting the image in a way that accentuated the child who leads all the surprisingly tame animals. Yet over time his images came to accentuate the animals more than the child, the branch in the child's hand became an olive branch rather than the more obviously eucharistic vine, until the peace in the natural order became the image's focus rather than

---

29. Wilken, *Isaiah*, 144.
30. Wilken, *Isaiah*, 139.
31. Wilken, *Isaiah*, 148–49.
32. Wilken, *Isaiah*, 150.
33. Sawyer, *Fifth Gospel*, 236.

the One whose coming inaugurates and consummates that peace. Being a Quaker, Hicks also linked the image to the signing of a peace deal between William Penn's Pennsylvania colony and indigenous peoples in 1681.

How does Isaiah 11 look now, bathed in the waters of baptism, refracted through the prism of history? Such a reading may, surprisingly, emphasize Jesus's Jewishness more, since the chapter is at such pains to emphasize Jesse's status as the origin of the righteous branch. It will describe the nature of the Holy Spirit with fulsome detail, as wisdom and knowledge and counsel and fear of the Lord and might are poured out on Jesus and overflow onto us, like dew miraculously present every morning. And such a reading will note that salvation is not limited to our souls, but includes the entire natural order. Christian faith looks forward to the day when all believers can put their hands over asps as well, and all nature sings praise to God together in tones that will remind us of the church's praise as it has long been inspired by Isaiah 11. As St. Leo the Great said, we Christians are those who "adore aided by the instruction of the prophets."[34]

WHAT READING IS FOR

Christians have long been impressed by the degree of detail with which our Lord's incarnation, passion, resurrection, and calling of the church are described in the book of Isaiah. It is the fifth gospel precisely because nothing in the gospel is left out here. We might go further and say that excising Isaiah from theological imagination tragically limits the range of praise we might lift to God, the depth and richness of speech with which we understand salvation and most else in Christian theology. In the end it leaves us without an Old Testament at all. For a desire to learn and adore more of Christ and the Spirit can send us into the pages of the Old Testament with fresh and eager eyes. To have such readings forcibly excised from the pages of the Scriptures will leave us with a book but little read. This is not to say patristic sources are always right, far from it. They not only disagree with each other, they undercut the very gospel at times, not least when they cut the Jewish trunk onto which the church has been grafted. Yet we cannot ignore their readings as we serve the church now. Christian faith is a matter of coming to see all the world slowly being transfigured into what God intended and intends for it, as Isaiah 11 imagines most fulsomely.

I hope I have shown here that postconservative hermeneutics will look surprisingly Jewish in form. Jews know one cannot access the riches of the Scriptures without the multi-generational debate about the Scriptures of the

---

34. Wilken, *Isaiah*, 141.

rabbis. There are jokes in Israel about Moses turning up to correct his interpreters. He gets a strange look, and is sternly asked, "but have you read this rabbi, and that rabbi, and the other rabbi?" I hope I've shown the activity of reading with our ancient forebears to have a sort of playfulness about it. The most delightful reading wins in most cases. Most importantly, I hope I've shown such readings are community-forging. They only make sense to those who know enough of the story to be committed to it. Who care enough about it to want to contribute to it. The very activity of learning the tradition leaves learners with something to say—something that contributes to further tradition, and blesses the church God is bringing.

BIBLIOGRAPHY

Byassee, Jason. *Psalms 101–150*. Grand Rapids: Brazos, 2018.

Hays, Richard, *Echoes of Scripture in the Letters of Paul*. New Haven, CT: Yale University Press, 1993.

———, *Echoes of Scripture in the Gospels*. Waco, TX: Baylor University Press, 2017.

Jenson, Robert, and Brad East. *The Triune Story: Collected Essays on Scripture*. New York: Oxford University Press, 2019.

McKinion, Steven A. *Isaiah 1–39*. Ancient Christian Commentary on Scripture 10. Downers Grove, IL: InterVarsity, 2004.

Sawyer, John. *The Fifth Gospel: Isaiah in the History of Christianity*. Cambridge: Cambridge University Press, 1996.

Wilken, Robert W,. *Isaiah. The Church's Bible*. Grand Rapids: Eerdmans, 2007.

Chapter 42
Memory Studies Hermeneutics
MEGAN C. ROBERTS

THE UBIQUITY OF MEMORY

The phenomenon of human memory takes many forms, serves many functions, and has been both the source and object of much human contemplation and activity. The ubiquitous presence and influence of memory on every aspect of life is a reality that leads sociologist Jeffrey Olick to argue for conceiving of memory as a phenomenon so important that it is "a medium of our existence in time."[1] Memory is a process of both remembering and forgetting, which provides meaning and orientation for individual and corporate identity, enables learning, and affords interpretative templates for understanding experiences so that we can relate our past to our present to make decisions for the future. As an interpretive template that provides meaning, memory is inherently selective. Only those things that are experienced and assessed, consciously or subconsciously, as meaningful and significant are retained; everything else is allowed to fade or is intentionally suppressed. Given memory's ubiquity and significance, making it a topic of focus concerning hermeneutics and theological interpretation is not only reasonable but deeply valuable. After all, Christianity claims that the Bible presents a metanarrative that provides the true identity of God and humans and the true meaning of our existence. Memory, in all its complexity, is the faculty through which we know ourselves and others and understand the meaning of our existence. Thus, understanding memory and its relationship to biblical interpretation is, arguably, essential.

Memory studies is an inter-discipline that draws on the diverse fields of neurology, psychology, history, anthropology, sociology, literature, and

1. Olick, "Willy Brandt in Warsaw," 28.

philosophy. These various streams within memory studies emphasize aspects of memory ranging from individual to group dynamics, from present time to the recent and distant past, from public commemorations and civic holidays to religious rituals, from oral traditions to written texts, and from individual brains to patterns of social and collective thought. Memory studies intersects with biblical studies at the nexus of written text, but biblical scholars can use all of the streams and aspects of memory for interpreting the biblical text. The world of memory studies is complex because of its interdisciplinary nature, and those who use memory studies as a hermeneutical lens should be careful to identify the stream of memory studies that is best suited to their specific interpretative question.

Amidst the complexity, however, memory studies has proven useful as a hermeneutical lens to explore what the biblical text is and what is behind, within, and in front of it. The following survey of memory studies as a hermeneutical lens for theological interpretation provides an orientation to the characteristics, concepts, people, and terminology of memory and memory studies. Representative examples from Old and New Testament studies will then demonstrate how the various streams function in textual interpretation. I must stress that this introduction is the smallest tip of the iceberg! As an entry point into the world of memory studies, those wanting to know more can follow the trail of breadcrumbs laid out below to discover for themselves the wealth of perspective offered by memory studies that can expand and benefit our hermeneutical endeavors within biblical studies.

CHARACTERISTICS AND FUNCTIONS OF NEURO-PSYCHOLOGICAL MEMORY

In his *Theaetetus*, Plato described memory by using the analogy of impressions made on a wax tablet, and this analogy has been the basis for a common conception among westerners that memories are fixed images and pieces of information that we file away in our brains so that we can retrieve them when required. In English, we often equate the word "memory" with our capacity for factual recall, or lack thereof. However, memory studies provides abundant data that this is a simplistic and faulty conception of memory. Rather than simple recall of impressions in our brains, memory is an ongoing process of the human "effort after meaning" that is rational, embodied, emotional, neural, psychological, social, and cultural.[2]

---

2. Baddeley et al., *Memory*, 165.

Memory can be broadly divided into two categories: semantic and episodic.[3] Semantic memory is our "store of general knowledge" about the world.[4] It is general and conceptual, rather than being tied to a specific context or experience. Episodic memory, on the other hand, is tied to specific and contextual experiences that are sensory and emotion-laden. Semantic and episodic memory are mutually informative, and they work together to inform our effort after meaning.

As an ongoing process, memory includes active remembering and active forgetting, even when this activity is not conscious. Though we may experience frustration over things we forget, researchers agree that memory is remarkably good and that the selectivity processes that retain some things and not others "are in fact the necessary consequences of the virtues that make our memories so rich and flexible."[5] We should note that memory research seeks to understand how memory works in general by studying what happens when memory is disrupted by disease, injury, disorders, social factors, the passage of time, various kinds of trauma, etc. Given that the literature focuses so much on memory problems, we may get the impression that memory is quite faulty, fallible, and unreliable. This impression, however, would be incorrect, a fact that will be important for our discussion on the use of memory studies as a hermeneutical lens.[6] We must not equate memory's selectivity with an inherent bent towards unreliability or fabrication. Rather, this characteristic of memory should provoke questions concerning what and how a biblical text remembers and forgets and why.

Many factors contribute to what we remember and forget. Our intrinsic desire to understand the meaning of our experiences and knowledge is inherent to our memory processes. Memory research has demonstrated that we retain more information and encode experiences more deeply and accurately when they are meaningful. This meaningfulness that leads to deeper encoding occurs in several ways: when we can integrate new information and experiences with existing knowledge; when meaningful remembering happens repeatedly; when an experience is multi-sensory and emotional; and when experiences or knowledge contain something unexpected.[7] We tend to forget that which is not deeply encoded because the content simply fades away. We are, however, also capable of intentional, or motivated,

---

3. Semantic and episodic memory are, more technically, two kinds of *explicit* memory. Implicit memory includes skills like riding a bike and other such habitual knowledge (Baddeley et al., *Memory*, 114–40).

4. Baddeley et al., *Memory*, 208.

5. Baddeley et al., *Memory*, 3.

6. Bauckham, "Psychology of Memory."

7. Baddeley et al., *Memory*, 174–98 and 223–30.

forgetting, and pain is the key factor that motivates active forgetting. We actively forget negative feedback about ourselves and experiences that are painful or traumatic. Painful or traumatic experiences are almost always deeply encoded, but we can activate neural processes that suppress conscious recall of these memories so that we do not continue to encounter the pain, especially when the pain disrupts our effort after meaning.[8]

Since memory is an ongoing process of remembering and forgetting, any given memory is not a static thing that can be retrieved from a single location in our brains. Advances in neurology have enabled researchers to connect psychological and social findings about memory to the biological processes that are the basis of memory. With these advances, we know that multiple areas of the brain are involved with memory processes and that every act of remembering and forgetting is a construction of a given memory initiated by and dependent on retrieval cues and other contextual factors.[9] The research on memory storage, retention, and retrieval has also demonstrated the extent to which memory is a whole-self and whole-context process. While the remembering and forgetting processes are a biological fact of our neural networks, the encoding and content of our memory involves our bodies, physical surroundings, social and cultural contexts, and emotional-relational contexts. Additionally, the content of what we encode in our memory is guided and shaped by the whole context of complex interactions between our individual selves and our context.

Our socio-cultural location plays a significant role in our individual memory for a number of reasons, one of the most important of which is that it provides us with patterned structures and frameworks through which we understand, store, and recall in order to create meaning. The term *schema* is often used to refer to this concept of memory structures.[10] A schema is an interpretive grid that organizes and creates meaning out of our experiences and knowledge about ourselves, others, and the world around us. Because of memory's selectivity, schemas are composed of experiences and information that have been socially- and culturally-determined to be meaningful, useful, and pertinent to our present questions and concerns, especially those related to identity and meaning. Schemas are very helpful for organizing our experiences and creating meaning out of them, though their perspectival and predictive nature also entails that they can organize and create meaning incorrectly.[11] Schemas are generally stable and fixed but are capable of

8. Baddeley et al., *Memory*, 318–39.
9. Baddeley et al., *Memory*, 237–54.
10. Baddeley et al., *Memory*, 163–65.
11. Baddeley et al., *Memory*, 258–60.

adaptation in response to changing contexts.[12] This concept of schemas is significant as we consider the genre, content, and perspective of a biblical text and ask questions about what schema the text contains and intends to pass on to a given audience. That many biblical texts are concerned with forming correct memory in the face of incorrect memory is explicit in texts like Deut 8–9 and Isa 43–46; the schema concept explains these memory dynamics within the biblical text in ways that other interpretive methods cannot.

The characteristics of memory discussed thus far are based on the research findings of individual memory and neural/biological processes. I have made a few notes concerning this information's pertinence to biblical interpretation, and it is pertinent for two additional reasons. First, some biblical texts are written from the perspective of an individual or are directed toward an individual. Thus, characteristics of individual memory processes may illuminate these texts in new ways. Second, the characteristics of individual memory map onto analogous processes at the social, corporate level of memory. I have already noted that individual memory is inextricably tied to socio-cultural context, and we will see in what follows that social and collective memory process are, in turn, a reflection of individual memory processes.

CHARACTERISTICS AND FUNCTIONS OF SOCIOLOGICAL MEMORY

While human memory has been the object of philosophical, theological, and literary contemplation going back to the ancient Greek philosophers, French philosopher and sociologist Maurice Halbwachs (1877–1945) is credited with pioneering the modern field of sociological memory studies and the concept of collective memory.[13] Two of Halbwachs's key contributions were to demonstrate the extent to which individual memory is dependent on its social context and the reality that our present needs and questions shape and determine our past recollections. This emphasis on the power of the present to determine how the past is remembered is called presentism. In this view, "memory is not primarily a past-oriented function of the individual; it is a present-oriented function of the individual-in-society."[14] Halbwachs argued that an individual's memory is shaped by the multiple social frameworks within which an individual is embedded, such

---

12. Baddeley et al., *Memory*, 223–30.
13. Halbwachs, *On Collective Memory*.
14. Keith, "Social Memory Theory, (Part 1)," 359.

as family, religion, and nationality. Collective memory, then, in Halbwachs's view refers to each group's shared construction of the past that creates and sustains collective identity.

Subsequent cultural, sociological, and neuro-psychological memory research has given credence to Halbwachs's argument that individual memory is inextricably bound to socio-cultural contexts, but the same research does not support Halbwachs's view that the present so thoroughly determines the construction of the remembered past. Halbwachs's presentist perspective was based on his distinction between collective memory as being particular and ideological and history as being universal and neutral. However, this distinction is a key weakness of Halbwachs's theory because it does not account for how collective memory and identity are sustained across many generations and changing times.[15] The nature of collective memory and its relationship to history continues to be an important area of discussion within memory studies theory and one that is also hermeneutically significant for biblical studies, which will be further discussed below.

Three scholars have developed Halbwachs's ideas in ways that are particularly pertinent for biblical studies: Jan and Aleida Assmann in Germany and Barry Schwartz in the United States. In this development, they have added new terminology, nuanced concepts, and incorporated insights from their fields of expertise. Jan and Aleida Assmann come to Halbwachs's work from Egyptology, primarily Jan, and English literature, primarily Aleida. They study how ancient peoples passed on their cultural identity from one generation to the next beyond the limits of the living community of three or four generations. In particular, they have studied the role of written texts as a uniquely-suited medium for preserving and passing on cultural identity.

The Assmanns took Halbwachs's concept of collective memory and divided it into two distinct kinds of memory: communicative memory and cultural memory. Communicative memory is the memory of the living community that is verbalized and participated in across the living community of three or four generations. Cultural memory, on the other hand, is formalized memory contained in written texts and commemorative artefacts and practices that reaches into the present from the distant past, beyond the living memory of the community.[16] J. Assmann thus argues that "what communication is for communicative memory, tradition is for cultural memory."[17] The Assmanns retain Halbwachs's theory that social frameworks influence

---

15. Buster, *Remembering the Story*, 18–19.
16. Keith, "Social Memory Theory, (Part One)," 364–65.
17. Assmann, *Religion and Cultural Memory*, 8.

individual memory,[18] but they nuance Halbwachs's presentist perspective by recognizing that the present is shaped by cultural memory even if the present also shapes cultural memory for its own purposes.[19]

Barry Schwartz (1938–2021) was a sociologist who developed Halbwachs's ideas along a somewhat different trajectory than the Assmanns. Schwartz retains Halbwachs's term "collective memory" but defines it as "the *distribution* throughout society of what individuals know, believe, and feel about the past, how they judge the past morally, how closely they identify with it, and how much they are inspired by it as a model for their conduct and identity."[20] This broad yet nuanced definition captures the complex interplay between the past and the present and strongly affirms that the past shapes the present just as much as the present shapes the presentation of the past. This affirmation is a nuanced disagreement with Halbwachian presentism, which can argue so strongly that the present constructs the past that the past almost entirely disappears. Schwartz represents the continuity perspective, which affirms the reality of the past as that which has produced the present; therefore, the past lives in the present even as present questions and concerns shape the presentation of the past. Importantly, this perspective aligns with the neuro-psychological memory characteristics already discussed.

Because memory is concerned with our effort after meaning, we interpret our present in light of our past in order to move towards a particular future. Schwartz describes the mechanism through which this interpretive effort after meaning occurs as "keying" and "framing." He explains that, "[b]ecause effective preservation maintains the past as a living thing, it requires a cognitive bridge connecting past and present. . . . *Keying* makes this connection by aligning current events with happenings in the past and by activating *frames* that shape the meaning of these current events."[21] Keying and framing thus function as a bridge between the past and present in two ways: "as 1) a model *of* society—reflecting its needs, interests, fears, and aspirations; and 2) a model *for* society—a template for thought, sentiment, morality, and conduct."[22] The mechanism of keys and frames functions in this way because of memory schemas, and Schwartz's explanation of the mechanism aligns with the function of schemas.

18. Hübenthal, "Social and Cultural Memory," 184–87.
19. Keith, "Social Memory Theory, (Part One)," 365–66.
20. Schwartz, "Rethinking the Concept," 10. Italics original.
21. Schwartz, "Rethinking the Concept," 15. Italics original.
22. Schwartz, "Rethinking the Concept," 15. As a model for society, a key can be both positive and negative. A positive key suggests that the present *should* imitate the past, whereas a negative key suggests that the present should *not* imitate the past.

Another important mechanism at work in connecting the past to the present is memory media. Memory research studies the significance of the diversity of memory media that record, enact, depict, commemorate, cue, and shape remembering and forgetting for individuals and communities. *How* we remember and forget is as important as *what* we remember and forget. Together, the *what* and the *how* of memory help determine the *why*. In our effort after meaning, memory is purposeful and goal-oriented. We cannot understand memory by only identifying *what* is being remembered and forgotten; the media of memory—the embodied and tangible *how* of memory—are also essential for understanding how memory creates identity and meaning.[23] Biblical studies also recognizes the significance of literary form and genre for correct interpretation. That narratives communicate differently than poetry and that epistles communicate differently than prophecy is basic to biblical interpretation. However, though this recognition in biblical studies closely aligns with research on memory media, the two are not hermeneutically the same for one key reason: a hermeneutic shaped by memory studies is able to ask and answer what a given form or genre is capable of *doing* to shape memory.[24]

If a text's shaping of memory can be analyzed, then we can also better understand how the text participates in the embodied and tangible realities of identity and meaning formation. In this way, biblical studies can move beyond identifying *what* memory a text records to elucidating the *how* and *why* of the text's remembering and forgetting, which is hermeneutically significant for perceiving the multidimensionality of a text's communicative weight. This multidimensionality un-flattens the text, helping us to better perceive and imagine the world of the text as well as to better connect the dots from that ancient world to our world today. For confessional scholars and communities who affirm that the biblical metanarrative is the true narrative for identity and meaning, a memory studies hermeneutic has the potential to incorporate Christians more deeply into the biblical metanarrative by engaging us in the memory-formation process enacted by the text so that our identity is shaped by the biblical memory schemas.

MEMORY'S HERMENEUTICAL AND EPISTEMOLOGICAL CLAIMS

The theological affirmation that the biblical metanarrative provides true identity and meaning is to claim, in memory studies terminology, that the

---

23. Olick, "Willy Brandt in Warsaw"; Buster, *Remembering the Story*, 6–35.
24. Buster, *Remembering the Story*, 6–35; Culp, *Memoir of Moses*, 7–32.

memory recorded in the Bible provides the correct memory schema for interpreting reality. Furthermore, to claim that a correct and true memory schema exists is to claim conversely that incorrect and false memory schemas also exist. Texts like Isaiah 40–55 make this argument explicitly, claiming that God's covenant people are remembering and forgetting incorrectly and have thus falsely interpreted the exile event, their identity, and God's identity.[25] This begs the question, then, about memory's epistemological and hermeneutical claims and what memory studies research can tell us about these claims.

I have been describing the complex ways in which memory processes function to create and sustain identity and meaning through the ongoing activity of selectivity that is guided by our need to interpret our present in light of our past in order to move towards an envisioned future. In this way, memory is inherently epistemological and hermeneutical in its claims to know, interpret, and understand. These claims are not the same as those of modernism, which pursues objective historical facts and what "actually happened," because memory is concerned with a meaningful past that is subjective in its selectivity. On the other hand, these claims are neither those of postmodernism that eschews the possibility of objective truth and relegates knowing and understanding to the relativity of the self and personal experience. Memory's epistemological and hermeneutical claims, it would appear, fit somewhere in between modernism and postmodernism.

As noted above, memory is remarkably reliable and accurate. Thus, memory's selectivity does not make it inherently unreliable, as modernism might argue. Memory research also disagrees with modernism's pursuit of the "actual past" because it recognizes that the past always comes to the present by way of mediated forms, genres, schemas, socio-cultural patterns, etc. In agreement with postmodernism, memory research affirms that we do not have access to the objective, actual past. In disagreement with postmodernism, however, memory's subjectivity does not mean that it has no connection to external truth and reality. While memory is fallible, our ability to document fallibility means that we have access to a standard by which that fallibility can be determined. A precise, philosophical understanding of the relationship between memory and modernism and postmodernism is outside the scope of this chapter, but we can illustrate how a memory studies hermeneutic functions from its place between the two.

One way to illustrate a memory studies hermeneutic in biblical interpretation is to observe how biblical scholars use the terminology and concepts from memory studies to discuss the biblical text. Memory studies

---

25. Roberts, "Remembering and Forgetting."

terminology is challenging to grasp because of its inter-disciplinary nature; terminology from one stream may not mean the same thing in another stream, and biblical scholars may not use the terminology correctly. For example, the idea of memories being constructed or created is the neuro-psychological way of describing the fact that memories are not stored in a single place in our brains. Within social, collective, or cultural memory, however, the term "(re)constructing/creating memory" does not refer to a neurological process within an individual brain. Rather the term is used to describe the group dynamics involved with selecting what is remembered and forgotten for the community, which is motivated by the need to sustain collective identity and meaning. The concept of (re)constructing memory is also used in the memory studies stream called social constructivism, which is a maximalist view of Halbwachs's presentist perspective. As a theoretical commitment, the concept of memory construction within social constructivism no longer describes an observable process in a brain or social group but rather states a presupposition that the needs and concerns of the present are so dominant that all constructions of the past can be explained as refractions of the present.[26]

An important note regarding this terminology of (re)constructing and creating memory is that, within neuro-psychological and sociological memory studies, this terminology in and of itself makes no claims about the reliability, authenticity, or factuality of memory. The terminology is descriptive of observed and repeated processes and does not make ontological or epistemological claims concerning the content of what is remembered and forgotten. This neuro-psychological and social fact that is described as the (re)construction or creation of memory is, however, taken out of context by some biblical scholars so that the term "construction" or "creation" is used to "prove" that at least some narratives in the Bible were fabricated out of thin air such that the recorded "memory" is entirely fictional. This is, however, a misuse of terminology.[27]

Memory research *is* interested in studying the reliability and factuality of remembering and forgetting, which is one reason why some biblical scholars use aspects of memory studies to augment their research concerning the Bible's historical reliability. However, we must take great care to discern the different presuppositional and epistemological foundations of the disciplines we combine. On the question of reliability, scholars who discuss the historicity of biblical events often assume that the question of reliability in memory studies is precisely the same kind of question in

---

26. Hübenthal, "Social and Cultural Memory."
27. Pioske, "Retracing a Remembered Past," 292–95.

historical-critical studies. This is not the case, however, precisely because the epistemological commitments of historical criticism are different than the epistemological commitments of memory studies.

For some biblical scholars, historical criticism is a hermeneutical framework that categorically denies the historicity of miraculous events and thus seeks to recover the facts of the "actual past" before the stories were embellished by tradition with mythological and theological significance. To substantiate their interpretation, these scholars use research that demonstrates how memory can be unreliable, fabricated, embellished, and otherwise faulty and inaccurate. Therefore, they conclude that the Bible is cultural memory that is historically unreliable. Alternatively, other biblical scholars who employ historical criticism as their hermeneutical framework accept the legitimacy of miracles as historical events. These scholars choose to highlight memory research that demonstrates how and why various kinds of memory are generally reliable and how difficult it is to alter or fabricate memory. They therefore conclude that memory studies "proves" the historical reliability of the Bible.

However, memory studies does not resolve questions regarding the historical reliability of the Bible by either confirming or denying our ability to recover the "actual past" behind the text. Recovery of the "actual past" is a pursuit of higher criticism, but it is not a pursuit of memory. The necessary point to make here is that memory research does not adhere to one set of presuppositions or a single epistemology, and the presuppositions and epistemologies within memory studies may or may not align with those within biblical studies. In my assessment, scholars who use insights from memory studies within a different hermeneutical framework, usually historical criticism, often fail to account for these differences with the result that their work misuses memory studies and is methodologically disjointed.[28]

MEMORY STUDIES AND THE OLD TESTAMENT

In Old Testament studies, scholars have used the Assmanns's concept of cultural memory to develop tradition criticism and to shift conversations away from historicity debates towards an understanding of how cultural memory accomplishes identity-formation.[29] The difference between analyzing a text through the lens of historical-critical methods and analyzing a text through the lens of cultural memory is the difference between asking whether or not the text is factually accurate and asking in what way the content of the text is

---

28. Pioske, "Retracing a Remembered Past."
29. Pioske, "Retracing a Remembered Past," 291–94.

emotionally meaningful for making sense of collective identity in the present. This affective aspect of memory is a key way in which cultural memory analysis has deepened and expanded tradition criticism.[30]

Jan Assmann and those who follow him represent the kind of scholarship noted above that denies the possibility of the miraculous and thus rejects the historicity of any such biblical narratives. These scholars perceive a clear divide between the "actual past" of history and the identity-formation function of cultural memory. In Assmann's assessment, the exodus events are not factually, historically true. In their function as cultural memory, however, they are symbolically true and explain why the Jews, of all ancient peoples, have survived as a distinct cultural group to this day without geographical stability.[31] In this view, the actual past of history and the creation of a symbolically-meaningful past of cultural memory are two separate things. However, the relationship between history and memory is more complex than such interpretations allow, and the denial of miraculous events is a presupposition of Enlightenment thought, not of memory studies. Daniel Pioske rightly argues that this kind of scholarship does not have a robust understanding of memory since "what memory is for these authors and why it should replace the notion of history for considerations of the biblical narrative is never addressed, leaving the meaning of memory and the reasons behind its appeal for the reader to determine."[32]

Ehud Ben Zvi has pioneered a different use of sociological memory studies for Old Testament research. Ben Zvi focuses on the phenomenon of social memory, a term he uses to describe to the formal processes and memory content within a specific group at a specific time and location.[33] For Ben Zvi, the small group of literate Judeans in Persian Yehud, who were responsible for copying, editing, and preserving the authoritative texts that became the Old Testament, provide the specific group, time, and location for reconstructing social memory based on these polyvalent texts. By reading across the texts, social memory analysis answers questions about what was being remembered, why one memory site was more prominent than another, how polyvalent memories formed complex memory spaces that held multiple options for imagining the future, and how the negotiation of social memory shaped social cohesion and identity.[34] As a historian, Ben Zvi wants to understand how the Judeans of Persian Yehud constructed their

---

30. Wilson, *Kingship and Memory*, 31–33.
31. Roberts, "Remembering and Forgetting," 37–38.
32. Pioske, "Retracing a Remembered Past," 294.
33. Roberts, "Remembering and Forgetting," 39–40.
34. Ben Zvi, "Remembering the Prophets."

social memory in the aftermath of exilic upheaval that had threatened their annihilation as a people. His work avoids the methodological disjointedness noted above because he does not subsume his social memory hermeneutic under the epistemological commitments of historical criticism.

Though Ben Zvi's questions are historical in nature—namely, how the Judean *literati* of Persian Yehud constructed their social memory from their authoritative texts, he does not first scrutinize the text according to the modernist pursuit of a demythologized "actual past." Rather, he allows the texts to stand as they are and then seeks to understand the memory processes that shaped social identity and meaning. Another strength of Ben Zvi's social memory work is that it demonstrates how multiple memory schemas interact in memory formation processes. In contrast to historical-critical analysis that seeks to prove one narrative as historically accurate and a different one as false or fabricated, Ben Zvi's analysis explains the function of telling a story in multiple ways, all of which were accepted by the Judean *literati* as authoritative representations. For example, much scholarly debate swirls around the differences between Kings and Chronicles. Historical criticism assesses one narrative as a (more) reliable representation of the past and the other as unreliable and thus as fabricated cultural memory. Ben Zvi, in contrast, asks how the two different representations could have worked in dialogue for the Judean *literati* in their pursuit of social cohesion, identity, and ways to imagine possible futures.

These cultural memory and social memory analyses approach the biblical text as an artefact of memory, a text containing memory that was produced to preserve memory. A. J. Culp's work helpfully distinguishes between this kind of analysis that views the text as a "memory product" and memory analysis that views the text as a "memory producer."[35] The former is interested in the world behind the text, while the latter is interested in the world within the text and the world that the text influences as it is received by each subsequent generation. The two approaches are hermeneutically different since viewing the text as a memory product does not invite or require the modern interpreter to consider how the text's memory has any bearing on our memory formation today. The text is viewed as a stabilized artefact that was significant for the collective identity of the ancient context alone. In contrast, viewing the text as a memory producer takes seriously that texts can do things and that memory formation processes can be discerned within the biblical text. It takes seriously that the memory formation processes in the text both invite and require the modern interpreter to consider how that memory formation process might involves us today.

---

35. Culp, *Memoir of Moses*, 7–26.

Culp's memory analysis of Deuteronomy reveals not only *what* memory Deuteronomy contains but also *how* and *why* Deuteronomy pursues memory formation for each subsequent generation of God's covenant people. Deuteronomy argues that there is correct and incorrect memory and that the two produce the opposite outcomes of life or death for the covenant people. The text intends to produce the kind of memory that leads to life.

Aubrey Buster is similarly interested in what memory forms can *do* to not only carry cultural memory from one generation to the next but also to form social memory for collective identity in any given generation that participates in a text's memory formation process. Buster focuses on how the historical summary form, which can be textualized in multiple genres, accomplishes memory formation in Second Temple Judaism through the participatory commemoration that a given text envisions. Taking seriously that memory media are essential for understanding memory formation, Buster demonstrates how "literary *form* motivates and facilitates common memory."[36]

MEMORY STUDIES AND THE NEW TESTAMENT

In New Testament scholarship, most memory studies work is done in the Gospels. Gospels scholars use memory studies to augment or reframe discussions concerning the Jesus tradition, historical Jesus research, and the formation of the Gospels. Scholars who use memory studies within an overarching framework of historical-critical presuppositions and goals present rather different textual analyses and conclusions than those scholars who employ memory studies as their primary hermeneutical framework. Jens Schröter and Sandra Hübenthal are representative of presentism/social-constructivism Gospels research,[37] and they are skeptical of the miraculous and the idea that memory preserves access to "actual events from the past,"[38] because memory cannot meet historical-critical criteria for reliability and authenticity.

Richard Bauckham, on the other hand, employs memory studies as hermeneutical framework on its own.[39] While he is still interested in the Gospels' formation and their reliability, Bauckham argues for the appropriateness of "personal event memory" as a useful lens for considering Gospels

---

36. Buster, *Remembering the Story of Israel*, 24.
37. Hübenthal, "Social and Cultural Memory."
38. Schröter, "Memory, Reception of Jesus," 87.
39. So also Kirk, "Memory Theory and Jesus Research."

narratives as stemming from eye-witness accounts.[40] Bauckham argues that many Gospels narratives bear the marks of "personal event memory" and thus argues that the Gospels have a greater likelihood of being grounded in eye-witness accounts than previously thought. The key hermeneutical difference between Bauckham's and Schröter's analyses is that Bauckham allows the epistemological claims of memory theory to govern his textual analysis while Schröter maintains the epistemological commitments of historical criticism. The former produces a much more positive assessment of our access to the historical Jesus than the latter.[41]

Memory studies in the NT outside of Gospels research is less developed but holds potential for deeper and more nuanced interpretation.[42] For example, Stephen Barton discusses the apostle Paul's recounting of his meeting with the Jerusalem church leaders in Galatians 2 and notes Paul's inclusion of the leaders' injunction that he should "remember the poor" (Gal 2:10). Barton notes that, "under the influence of Cartesian epistemology, moderns tend to think of remembrance primarily in subjective, psychological terms," which reduces remembrance to "bringing [the poor] to mind in individual reflection for detached consideration."[43] However, the kind of remembrance enjoined here "involves . . . social engagement and practical action arising out of a moral recognition, theologically grounded, of ties of mutual obligation."[44] In other words, the kind of remembering commanded in Gal 2 flows from a schema that properly orients Paul's perspective on reality and consequent behavior. In this way, memory shapes ethics, and memory theory moves our interpretation of "remember the poor" beyond simple factual recall to the complex reality that memory shapes behavior choices and why this is so.

CONCLUSION

Far more could be said about memory studies as a hermeneutical framework for biblical interpretation. This survey merely gestures towards the significance of memory for biblical interpretation and the potential it has for opening the biblical text in new ways as modern western interpreters regain awareness of memory's complexities. A memory studies hermeneutic can transcend and reframe historical criticism's pursuit of the "actual

---

40. Bauckham, "Psychology of Memory."
41. Keith, "Social Memory Theory (Part One)"; Keener, *Christobiography*, 365–496.
42. Keith, "Social Memory Theory (Part Two)," 517–18.
43. Barton, "Memory, in Paul," 331.
44. Barton, "Memory, in Paul," 331.

past," explain memory formation processes within texts, and incorporate faith communities today into the biblical metanarrative that provides true identity and meaning.

BIBLIOGRAPHY

Assmann, Jan. *Religion and Cultural Memory: Ten Studies*. Translated by Rodney Livingstone. Stanford: Stanford University Press, 2005.

Baddeley, Alan, et al., eds. *Memory*. New York: Taylor and Francis, 2020.

Barton, Stephen C. "Memory and Remembrance in Paul." In *Memory in the Bible and Antiquity*, edited by Loren T. Stuckenbruck et al., 321–40. WUNT 212. Tübingen: Mohr Siebeck, 2007.

Bauckham, Richard. "The Psychology of Memory and the Study of the Gospels." *Journal for the Study of the Historical Jesus* 16 (2018) 136–55.

Ben Zvi, Ehud. "Remembering the Prophets through the Reading and Rereading of a Collection of Prophetic Books in Yehud: Methodological Considerations and Explorations." In *Remembering and Forgetting in Early Second Temple Judah*, edited by E. Ben Zvi and Christoph Levin, 17–44. Forschungen zum Alten Testament 85. Tübingen: Mohr Siebeck, 2012.

Buster, Aubrey E. *Remembering the Story of Israel: Historical Summaries and Memory Formation in Second Temple Judaism*. Cambridge: Cambridge University Press, 2022.

Culp, A. J. *Memoir of Moses: The Literary Creation of Covenantal Memory in Deuteronomy*. Lanham, MD: Lexington/Fortress Academic, 2020.

Halbwachs, Maurice. *On Collective Memory*. Edited and translated by Lewis A. Coser. Chicago: University of Chicago, 1992.

Hübenthal, Sandra. "Social and Cultural Memory in Biblical Exegesis: The Quest for an Adequate Application." In *Perspectives on Hebrew Scriptures and its Contexts* 17, edited by Pernille Carstens et al., 175–99. Piscataway, NJ: Georgias, 2012.

Keener, Craig S. *Christobiography: Memory, History, and the Reliability of the Gospels*. Grand Rapids: Eerdmans, 2019.

Keith, Chris. "Social Memory Theory and Gospels Research: The First Decade (Part One)." *Early Christianity* 6 (2015) 354–76.

———. "Social Memory Theory and Gospels Research (Part Two)." *Early Christianity* 6 (2015) 517–42.

Kirk, Alan. "Memory Theory and Jesus Research." In *Handbook for the Study of the Historical Jesus*, edited by Tom Holmén and Stanley E. Porter, 1:809–42. Leiden: Brill, 2011.

Olick, Jeffrey. "Willy Brandt in Warsaw: Event or Image? History or Memory?" In *Double Exposure: Memory and Photography, Memory and Narrative*, edited by Olga Shevchenko, 21–40. New Brunswick: Transaction, 2014.

Pioske, Daniel. "Retracing a Remembered Past: Methodological Remarks on Memory, History, and the Hebrew Bible." *Biblical Interpretation* 23 (2015) 291–315.

Roberts, Megan C. "Remembering and Forgetting in Isaiah 40–55: Memory and the Problem of Comfort." PhD diss., McMaster Divinity College. 2020.

Schröter, Jens. "Memory, Theories of History, and the Reception of Jesus." *Journal for the Study of the Historical Jesus* 16 (2018) 85–107.

Schwartz, Barry. "Rethinking the Concept of Collective Memory." In *Routledge International Handbook of Memory Studies*, edited by Anna Lisa Tota and Trever Hagen, 9–21. New York: Routledge, 2016.

Wilson, Ian D. *Kingship and Memory in Ancient Judah*. Oxford: Oxford University Press, 2017.

SECTION 5

Pastoral-Applicational Interpretation

Chapter 43
Apprenticeship Hermeneutics
DAVID STARLING

THE INTERPRETER'S TASK

Faithful interpretation of Scripture is not an easy or effortless endeavor. Even Martin Luther, in the context of mounting a vigorous argument for a bold set of claims about the clarity of Scripture, still insisted, graphically and memorably, that there is "sweat" and "assiduous endeavor" involved in the task of interpreting it.[1]

Interpreting Scripture is hard work for a number of reasons. It is hard work, at times, because of the demanding and difficult ideas that Scripture contains. It is hard work, too, because of the rich diversity that Scripture embraces, as a collection of sixty-six books, produced across more than a millennium by a vastly varied cast of authors, editors, and compilers. It is hard work because of the complexity of the world in which we seek to understand the Scriptures and live out the life to which they call us. It is hard work because of the cultural and historical distance between our own context and the contexts in which the biblical texts were written and originally received. It is hard work because of our own finitude and fallenness, including the various and particular vices, biases, and limitations of vision that impede the clarity of our understanding. And it is hard work because of the spiritual battle we are engaged in against the principalities and powers that exert their authority over the social order that we inhabit, surrounding us with their threats, distractions, and enticements.

For all of those reasons, the approach we take to the discipline of hermeneutics should not be premised on the assumption that what we are

---

1. Luther, *Assertio Omnium Articulorum*, Weimarer Ausgabe 7, 97.3–9 (my translation).

learning (and what we are teaching to others) is a simple set of understandings and skills that can be summed up neatly in a three-step method, or a system that can be diagrammed and hung on the wall. Biblical interpretation, like numerous other important disciplines and practices, is learnt best through a process that involves much more than just the apprehension of a set of abstract principles or the mastery of a set of technical skills. As a species of wisdom, biblical interpretation involves character as well as competency, practices as well as principles, and intuitions as well as ideas. It is therefore learned best through a process that is slow, recursive, and relational.[2] In short, the best method for learning and teaching the wisdom that is required of us to read and apply the Scriptures wisely and well within our context is a kind of apprenticeship.

A THREEFOLD APPRENTICESHIP

The apprenticeship through which we become more wise and well-formed readers of Scripture takes place on at least three levels.

APPRENTICESHIP IN THE CLASSROOM AND THE CHURCH

First, and most obviously, our apprenticeship as readers and interpreters of Scripture takes place within the face-to-face learning community of a classroom or a local congregation of believers and fellow-readers.[3] Within a context of this sort there is opportunity for the student to observe the teacher at work as an interpreter of Scripture, to participate with the teacher and fellow-students in the group process of co-interpretation, and to attempt and obtain feedback on the student's own interpretive tasks. And there is opportunity, too, within such a context, for the learner to acquire more than just skills and ideas; a face-to-face community of learning creates a context for learners to observe and imitate (and, where necessary, critique and challenge) the way in which the reading of a text shapes and is shaped by dispositions of the heart, habits of practice, and structures of community life.

A delightful cameo of the local church as a learning community of this sort can be found in Col 3:16–17, where Paul depicts the church as a metaphorical dwelling-place inhabited by the word of Christ and believers as a community of mutual instruction, forming one another in wisdom,

---

2. Cf. Starling, *Hermeneutics as Apprenticeship*, 72–74, 205–6.

3. For those who grow up within believing households, the learning community of the church contains within it the micro-community of the family as the first and (in many cases) most formative context in which this apprenticeship takes place. Cf. Deut 6:4–9, 20–25; Prov 1:8–9; 2 Tim 1:5; 3:14–15.

singing together in psalms, hymns, and songs of the Spirit, and serving one another in ministries of word and deed. Similar pictures can be found in other places within Paul's letters (e.g., 1 Cor 4:17; Phil 3:17; Titus 1:7) and elsewhere in the New Testament (e.g., Matt 13:51–52; Heb 13:7), where the formation of Christian disciples is depicted as a process in which wisdom is passed on through word and example within the communal context of the household of faith.[4]

APPRENTICESHIP TO THE INTERPRETIVE TRADITION OF THE GLOBAL CHURCH

But face-to-face apprenticeship between teacher and students within the local church or the hermeneutics classroom is not the only kind of apprenticeship that is required for the getting of hermeneutical wisdom. The metaphorical "classroom" within which we learn to read Scripture is far older, larger, and more diversely populated than the literal classroom in which teachers and their students meet to do the work of learning and teaching. The local church, likewise, possesses its identity in solidarity with "all those everywhere who call on the name of our Lord Jesus Christ" (1 Cor 1:2);[5] the wisdom its members pass on to one another ought to be a humble, receptive wisdom, shaped by a grateful recognition that the word of God did not originate within it and its members are not the only people whom the word of God has reached (cf. 1 Cor 14:36).

Accordingly, as learners of the art of interpreting Scripture, we would do well to acquaint ourselves with the interpretive work done by our forebears within the traditions that have shaped us and to engage with readings from outside those traditions and from socio-cultural locations that are remote from our own. In some cases, the aim of such engagement will be to challenge and unsettle the unreflective, taken-for-granted assumptions that we bring with us to the text of Scripture from the local traditions in which we have been formed as readers. In other cases it will be to provide ourselves with the reinforcement and reassurance that come from knowing we are participants in the consensus of a grand tradition that is far older and broader that we might otherwise have realized. In all cases, it will be to remind us that the Scriptures were not given to us alone, and that we have much to learn from other readers, past and present, who have grappled with the same texts.

---

4. Cf. Starling, "Scribe, the Steward, and the Inhabiting Word," 17–28, for a discussion of three of these verses (Matt 13:52; Col 3:16; Titus 1:7) and their implications for a theology of Christian formation.

5. Biblical quotations within this chapter are from the NIV, unless otherwise stated.

APPRENTICESHIP TO THE CANON

Thirdly, and most importantly of all, an apprenticeship hermeneutic responds to the unique character and authority-claims of Scripture by requiring us all, teachers and students alike, to be apprentices to the interpretive practices of the canonical authors themselves.

The biblical writings should never be thought of merely as objects for our analysis or our use. Nor should we think about the work of interpretation as if it were, at its heart, a matter of bringing to bear on the text a set of resources (traditional, theoretical, and/or technical) derived from some other source. If Scripture is to have the kind of authority that we say it has within the communities of faith in which we read it, then the way in which we read, interpret, and apply it needs to be pervasively shaped by the interpretive wisdom that we find within the canon itself. Our task, therefore, as learners and teachers of the art of biblical interpretation, includes the work of observing and, where appropriate, emulating the practices of the biblical writers as they receive and use the texts and traditions that functioned as Scripture (or its closest equivalent) for them.[6]

The shape taken by this kind of interpretive apprenticeship to the canon will vary from case to case depending on the various biblical corpora and genres that we are learning to read, and the various ways in which they are read and interpreted elsewhere in the canon. In some instances, where the texts that belong to a particular biblical corpus or genre have an obvious and accessible inner-biblical reception history, an apprenticeship to the canon includes taking that inner-biblical usage into account as we discuss the way in which they should be received and used by Christian readers today.

In other instances, in the absence of any inner-biblical reception history for a particular text or corpus of texts, there is still a wealth of interpretive wisdom to be gained by attending carefully to the invitations and directions, explicit and implicit, that the biblical writers extend to their intended readers. A wise reader of the book of Revelation, for example, will take note of the various ways in which the author encourages his readers to receive and make use of the vision reports contained within the book, beginning with the intimations of genre that are conveyed within the opening verses (cf. Rev 1:1–5) and extending through the book to the blessings, warnings, and invitations of the closing paragraphs (cf. Rev 22:8–21).

---

6. See especially Vanhoozer, *Drama of Doctrine*, 331; Starling, *Hermeneutics as Apprenticeship*, 1–21; Graves, *How Scripture Interprets Scripture*, 1–24; Hays, *Echoes of Scripture*, 154–92; Childs, *Introduction*, 73; Fishbane, *Biblical Interpretation*, 525–44; Blocher, "Analogy of Faith," 37–38; Barker, Chan, Davis and Starling, *Hermeneutics*, ch. 2.

The canonical contribution to our interpretive wisdom should not be thought of merely as a process in which later writings provide a frame or starting point for the interpretation of earlier ones. In numerous cases the intertextual connections that a later biblical text establishes with an earlier one imply a relationship between the two that is *mutually* interpretive; the hermeneutic that is taught and modelled within the Gospel of Matthew, for example, involves not only the interpretation of Scripture in light of the Christ event (cf. Matt 5:17) but also the interpretation of the Christ event, with all its attendant mystery and scandal, in light of Scripture (cf. Matt 11:2–6; 12:1–8; 21:33–42).[7] The art of biblical interpretation, in other words, requires the ability to read both forwards and backwards. We read Scripture both as a path of promise, foreshadowing, and testimony that leads us toward (and ever back toward) Christ, and as a path of discipleship, formation, and reformation onto which we are sent (and endlessly re-sent) by Christ in our journey of discipleship. The combined effect, where the Spirit of God is at work and we are keeping in step with the Spirit, is a kind of virtuous circle—or, to borrow language from Matthew's Gospel, a discipling process through which, in the midst of life's trials and the challenges of mission, we learn the wisdom of the kingdom of heaven (cf. Matt 13:52).

TWO LESSONS FOR APPRENTICES

In the remainder of this chapter we will zero in on two case studies in canonical apprenticeship, sampling from the myriad of ways in which the interpretive practices of the biblical authors offer us wisdom for our own task of interpreting and applying the Scriptures within the context in which God has placed us.[8]

RUTH AND THE HERMENEUTICS OF HESED

In recent decades a growing number of writers have made the point that good interpretation requires not just skill but character—that, all else being equal, virtuous people, whose interactions with the world are characterized by habits of attentiveness, charity, honesty, courage, and humility, are most likely to understand the texts they read and do justice to them in the way in which they respond. Stephen Fowl makes the claim succinctly: "Given that

---

7. Cf. the more detailed discussions in Starling, *Hermeneutics as Apprenticeship*, 93–104, and Hays, *Reading Backwards*, 35–54.

8. The case studies in the paragraphs that follow are adapted and abridged from Starling, *Hermeneutics as Apprenticeship*, chs. 3, 5, and used with permission from Baker Academic, a division of Baker Publishing Group.

Christians are called to interpret Scripture as part of their ongoing journey into ever-deepening communion with God, it is not surprising that those who have grown and advanced in virtue will tend to be masterful interpreters of Scripture."[9]

Whilst there is much in the claims made by proponents of virtue hermeneutics that seems both obvious and important, the approach has not been without its critics. To begin with, there are the questions that might be asked about the notion of "virtue" itself, and its origins within ancient pagan cultures in which wealthy, freeborn men competed with one another to demonstrate their prowess, display their magnanimity, and accumulate titles of honor.[10]

In addition to these general questions about the concept of virtue itself are the particular questions we might ask about its applicability to our interaction with the text of Scripture. Fowl's picture of the "masterful" interpreter who brings to the text a full complement of virtuous dispositions raises some obvious theological questions. Is faithful reading of Scripture really a matter of "mastery"? And if there is a place for "virtue" in the way we describe the interaction between Scripture and its readers, is it in the description we offer of the character which the reader brings to the Scriptures, or of the character which the Scriptures form in the reader?

One corner of the canon to which we might turn in contemplating questions of this sort is the book of Ruth. In form, the book of Ruth presents as a heart-warming, gently comic short story or novella, but in function it serves at least in part as a kind of case study in hermeneutics. Lurking just beneath the surface of the story are a string of interpretive questions about how the commandments of the law of Moses are to be understood and applied—in particular, the law on redemption of land in Leviticus 25, the levirate marriage provisions in Deuteronomy 25, the stipulations regarding gleaning in Leviticus 19 and 23, and the ban on Moabites in Deuteronomy 23. Behind these, in turn, stand questions about the character of YHWH, as it is described in the core confessions of the nation of Israel, and how it is to shape the conduct of his people.

Within the story that is told by the book of Ruth, there is much that can be read as offering support to an approach that emphasizes the importance of virtue in interpretation. Viewed from one angle, Boaz could be seen as the paradigm of the virtuous interpreter, the "blessed . . . one" celebrated in texts like Psalms 1; 41; 112 as the ideal reader of Torah. As an *'îš gibbôr*

---

9. Fowl, "Virtue," 838.

10. Cf. the criticisms and cautions stated in Hauerwas and Pinches, *Christians among the Virtues*, 57.

ḥayil—a "man of standing" (2:1)—he reads the law of Moses from a position of wealth and social prestige, and uses these resources liberally for the good of others. He has a proper sense of honor and shame, prudently averting the potential scandal that could have arisen from Ruth's nocturnal visit to the threshing floor (3:14) and expertly navigating the public transactions at the city gate the following day (4:1–12).

But Boaz is not the only reader of God and his purposes presented to us within the book of Ruth. Among the other characters of the story the most prominent are Naomi and Ruth, whose interpretations of the words and actions of God are arrived at from a very different angle, and provide a challenge to the sufficiency of "virtue" as a category for theological hermeneutics. In contrast with Boaz's virtuous fullness as an *'îš gibbôr ḥayil*, Ruth and Naomi arrive in Bethlehem "empty" (1:21). Unlike Boaz, whose place in the world of the story is a settled one, as a blessed and prosperous occupant of the land, they enter from stage left, returning (in Naomi's case) or arriving (in Ruth's) after a tersely-narrated episode of marriages and bereavements in Moab.

From the standpoint of Ruth and Naomi, the action of God in ending the famine, the Mosaic provisions for gleaners to find grain at the margins of the field, and the generous hospitality of Boaz are interpreted, taken together, as expressions of the "kindness" (*ḥesed*) of YHWH (2:20). The actions that they take in returning to Judah and gleaning in Boaz's field are recognized by Boaz as a decision on their part to "come to take refuge" under the wings of YHWH (2:12). As "empty" readers, their primary recourse to the word of God is not to clarify the extent of its demands on them but to take refuge in its promises and in the God whom it makes known.

Boaz's virtuous reading of the requirements of the Mosaic law and Naomi and Ruth's bold ventures of trust, in which they cast themselves upon YHWH's kindness, do not take place as disconnected, independent events. The honor and generosity with which Boaz treats Ruth is motivated, at least in part, by what he has heard of her kindness and fidelity to Naomi, and of her decision to throw in her lot with the people of Israel and take refuge under the wings of their God (2:11–12). And the rising hopes of Naomi, culminating in the potentially scandalous scheme of chapter 3, are encouraged in turn by what Ruth reports back to her about the extravagant generosity of Boaz (2:18–23).

Underlying both developments—the swelling tide of Boaz's generosity and the rising boldness of Naomi and Ruth—are intuitive, imaginative connections that each of them draws between the actions of the other and the kindness of YHWH. In the two widows' situation of need, and in Ruth's status as a foreigner in the land (highlighted in her first words to him, in

2:10), Boaz is provided—if he has eyes to see it—with a mirror of his whole nation's story, and a reminder of the identity of "the LORD, the God of Israel" (2:12) as a refuge for the widow and the foreigner (cf. Deut. 10:18–19) and the original giver of all the abundance he enjoys (1:6; cf. Deut. 8:6–18). Within that context, Ruth's fidelity to Naomi is interpreted by Boaz (as it was by Naomi before him, in 1:8) as an act of *ḥesed* analogous to the kindness of YHWH with which he hopes she will be rewarded (2:11–12; 3:10). Naomi and Ruth, in turn, are emboldened by the words of his blessing in 2:12 ("May you be richly rewarded by the LORD, the God of Israel, under whose wings you have come to take refuge") to risk everything on a nocturnal appeal to Boaz to "spread the corner of your garment [literally "your wing"] over me" (3:9), daring him to act in line with his words.

Connected with all of these convergent assessments of character and circumstance is a bold and striking reading of the law of Moses, which informs both Ruth's proposal in 3:9 and its acceptance by Boaz. In linking her appeal to Boaz to extend his garment over her in marriage with his status as *gōʾēl* to Naomi and her family, Ruth is implying a connection between the rationale of the law of levirate marriage and that of the provisions for redemption of property, and appealing for an action on Boaz's part that goes far beyond the letter of the law of Moses. What she is asking for from Boaz is deeply and explicitly informed by the laws and customs of Israel, but it reads those laws and customs not merely as prescriptions of duty but also as expressions of the *ḥesed* of YHWH, which is to be imitated and manifested in the actions of his people.

What the book of Ruth suggests, one might conclude, is that the proper interpretation of Torah is not simply a matter of the skilful application of objective principles of scientific jurisprudence. Rightly reading the law and knowing how to interpret its implications for the shaping of one's conduct requires the exercise of love, courage, generosity, and humility. But the moral universe within those readerly virtues flourish—and in which they can be understood as the equal possession of a destitute, widowed, Moabite *ēšet ḥayil* and a wealthy, landowning, Israelite *ʾîš gibbôr ḥayil*—is a far more expansive one than the universe presupposed by the virtue ethics of the Graeco-Roman philosophers.[11] The generous reader is not merely a person who understands the public honor accorded to the virtue of generosity, but a person who understands himself or herself as a recipient of the generosity of God; the courageous reader does not simply navigate the channel between rashness and timidity, but interprets and acts with a boldness that is invited and sustained by God's favor and faithfulness.

---

11. See especially the classic discussion in Aristotle's *Nicomachean Ethics*.

And the social matrix within which the story of God's kindness is remembered and re-echoed is one that requires something much more complicated and beautiful than the small circle of wealthy, free-born, virtuous men among whom Aristotle imagines as necessary to safeguard the flourishing of good character.[12] The bold and risky ventures of kindness that are enacted within the book of Ruth come about as the commandments of YHWH and the story of his ways are read together by rich and poor, men and women, outsiders and insiders, full and empty, as their lives intersect within the community of God's people and under his sovereign hand.

JOB AND THE HERMENEUTICS OF WISDOM

Scripture furnishes us not only with exemplars of interpretive wisdom for us to imitate but also with an abundance of examples of interpretive folly and vice for us to learn from and avoid. Perhaps the most famous (and the most pious-sounding) example of hermeneutical malpractice to be found within the Scriptures is the speeches of Eliphaz, Bildad, Zophar, and Elihu, recorded in the lengthy cycle of debate and mutual acrimony that makes up the majority of the book of Job.

Taken as a whole, the contributions of Job's friends provide us with a powerful reinforcement of the warnings repeatedly given in the book of Proverbs that the sayings of the wise are not, in and of themselves, a shortcut to wise living. It is true that wisdom may be learned from the proverbs (cf. Prov 1:2), but it is also true that wisdom is a requirement for those who wish to understand and use them in a way that is right and just (cf. Prov 1:6; 8:8–9). The journey toward wisdom is, it seems, a long, slow spiral, in which the same wisdom that offers "prudence to those who are simple, knowledge and discretion to the young" also invites the wise to "listen, and add to their learning," and the discerning to "get guidance" (Prov 1:4–5).

The hermeneutical circle involved in the appropriation and use of proverbial wisdom derives, in part, from the nature of proverbs as generalizations from experience—an aspect of the nature of proverbs that is frankly admitted within the collection (e.g., Prov 26:4–5). The ability to decide, or instinctively to recognize, whether a given situation is one in which a fool must be answered according to his folly (so that he does not become wise in his own eyes) or one in which a fool must *not* be answered according to his folly (so that one does not become a fool like him) requires something more than just verbal recall and comprehension of the relevant proverbs: wise use of the proverbs requires not only an accurate understanding of the text but

---

12. Cf. the discussion in Hauerwas and Pinches, *Christians among the Virtues*, 31–51.

also an insightful assessment of the people and circumstances to which it is to be applied.

We cannot for certain say whether the book of Job is an interpretation of the final form of the canonical book of Proverbs, but the debate which it contains is certainly constructed as one in which his friends present themselves as mouthpieces of proverbial wisdom. The lacerations they inflict as they circle around him in their wearying iterations of debate and accusation provide a vivid demonstration of the warning in Prov 26:9 that "a proverb in the mouth of a fool" can be as dangerous and damaging as "a thornbush in a drunkard's hand."

The function of Job's friends as self-appointed wisdom teachers is most obviously evident in the case of Eliphaz, the first of the friends to offer a reply to Job's complaint. From the start, his speech is permeated with allusions to the language of the proverbs. He begins politely: Job's piety (more literally, his "fear") should be his confidence (Job 4:6; cf. Prov 3:26; 14:26), and he should take comfort from the fact that—as Eliphaz's own observations have confirmed—"those who plow evil and those who sow trouble reap it" (Job 4:8; cf. Prov 22:8). As his tone toward Job darkens and becomes more hostile, Eliphaz's ideas and language continue to draw upon proverbial sources: Job is implictly depicted as included among the common herd of fools who "die without wisdom" (Job 4:21; cf. Prov 5:23; 10:21), and is urged not to "despise the discipline of the Almighty" (Job 5:17; cf. Prov 3:11–12); only if he submits to the discipline of his sufferings will he "come to the grave in full vigor, like sheaves gathered in season" (Job 5:26; cf. Prov 10:27). When Job continues to repudiate his unsolicited advice, Eliphaz vents his frustration. "Are you the first man ever born?" he asks Job, exasperatedly. "Were you brought forth before the hills? Do you listen in on God's council? Do you have a monopoly on wisdom?" (Job 15:7; cf. Prov 8:25). Job must "submit to God" by submitting to Eliphaz, since the torrent of proverbial wisdom proceeding from Eliphaz's mouth is really coming from the mouth of God (Job 22:21–22; cf. Prov 2:6).

Whilst Eliphaz is the one who takes the lead in appropriating the wisdom tradition and applying it to Job's predicament, Job's other friends are not far behind in following his example. Thus, Bildad commences by appealing to "the former generation" and "their ancestors" (Job 8:8) in support of his warning to Job about the perishing hopes of the godless (Job 8:13; cf. Prov 10:28; 11:7) and his assurances that "if you are pure and upright, even now he will ... restore you to your prosperous state" (Job 8:6). Zophar, similarly, draws on the language of proverbs to express his frustration at Job's recalcitrance: the very first line of his opening speech is a rhetorical question about whether "all these words" can be allowed to go unanswered

(Job 11:2; cf. Prov 10:19). When Elihu's turn finally comes around, he is quick to point out that "it is not only the old who are wise, not only the aged who understand what is right" (Job 32:8–9), but the content of his speeches draws as heavily as the other friends' did on the language and ideas of the proverbs (e.g., Job 34:11; cf. Prov 24:12; similarly Job 35:6–8, cf. Prov 8:36; 9:12).

Job's speeches in reply to his friends make it clear that they are not the only ones who are familiar with the language and ideas of the proverbs. Throughout his speeches, Job rails against the assumption of his friends that his situation is a sign of divine displeasure and evidence of a secret sin, and he sharply questions the way in which his friends have taken the generalizations of Proverbs as if they were easily-verified universal laws. If Bildad is happy to echo the sentiments of the proverbs about the snuffing out of the lamp of the wicked, wielding them against Job as menacing warnings (Job 18:5–6; cf. Prov 13:9; 20:20; 24:20), Job insists in return that he take an honest look at all the situations around him in which the wicked are *not* snuffed out, but "spend their years in prosperity and go down to the grave in peace" (Job 21:13).

Goaded by the intensity of his sufferings and the smug assumptions of his friends, Job asks sharply-worded questions about the frequency with which the generalizations of Proverbs come true and their adequacy as an answer to the phenomena of (unpunished) evil and (undeserved) suffering. But this does not mean that he rejects the message of the proverbs outright. If his friends wield proverbs as weapons against him, Job himself is capable of wielding proverbs as weapons against his friends (e.g., Job 13:5; cf. Prov 17:28), and in the defense that he mounts against his friends' accusations, he frequently appeals to the ethical and theological axioms that the proverbs teach: he is as happy as they are to affirm that God sees all (Job 31:4; cf. Prov 5:21; 15:3), that God is the one who drew the boundaries of the universe (Prov 8:29 in Job 26:10), that rich and poor are formed in the womb by the same hands (Job 31:15; cf. Prov 22:2), that the concealment of sin is pernicious and futile (Job 31:33; cf. Prov 28:13), and that sin itself is a culpable crime and a destructive fire (Job 31:9–12; cf. Prov 6:27–29). His screams of protest against the contradictions that he sees between the phenomena he has witnessed and experienced and the ordered world depicted in the proverbs are, in their own way, an affirmation of the rightness of that order in his eyes.

Whilst the proverbial sayings echoed by Job and his friends are a prominent and important focus of the interpretive tug-of-war between them, they are not the only biblical traditions that are echoed and interpreted within the book. Job's anguished wrestling with the proverbs and the way in which his friends have interpreted and applied them is accompanied by a string of additional intertextual references to the Torah, the psalms, and the prophets. The echoes of the proverbs in Job's speeches (and in those of his friends) are generally in the context of speech *about* God, but Job's echoes of the psalms and prophets are frequently in the context of speech directed *to* God, or of complaints and imprecations that seem to be intended for God to hear. The pattern is set in the searing complaint with which he breaks the silence in chapter 3, which opens with an extended echo of Jeremiah's laments (cf. Jer 10:18; 15:10; 20:14–18) and closes with a string of echoes from the psalms (e.g., Pss 6:6; 22:1, 14; 38:8; 42:3–4; 80:5).

Job's anguished parodies and echoes of the psalms and prophets underline the high expectations of God that deepen and intensify his interaction with biblical wisdom and its interpreters. He expects of God not merely the distant supervision of a neat system of retributive equilibrium, but a personal concern that finds expression in visiting, redeeming, and comforting his people. The God he believes in (and against whom he protests so vehemently) is an interventionist God, however much the logic and timing of his interventions may remain shrouded in mystery.

In the end Job gets his wish. YHWH himself speaks to Job from out of the storm and (after Job's reply in 42:1–9) acts to restore his fortunes. Whilst YHWH's words to Job include an element of stern rebuke (e.g., 38:2; 40:2) they are certainly not an endorsement of the approach taken by Job's friends (cf. 42:7). Neither should Job's "repentance" in 42:6 be taken as a concession to their accusations; read against the background of YHWH's speeches in chapters 38–41 and Job's responses in 40:4–5; 42:1–5, Job's words of repentance in 42:6 function not as a vindication of the wisdom of his friends but as an admission of the limits of his own—a concession that "I spoke of things I did not understand" (42:3; cf. 38:2).

The divine verdict on the "wisdom" of Job's friends is searingly negative (42:7). However accurately Job's friends may have reiterated the content of proverbial wisdom, the way in which they have related it to Job's circumstances makes it clear that they have understood neither it nor him. Their failure results in part from their unwillingness to listen to Job (6:27), to weigh his sufferings (cf. 6:1–3), and to deal honestly with the evidence before their eyes (13:7–8); it is compounded by their inability to see the gap between the total knowledge and perfect wisdom possessed by God and the true but partial insights granted to humans.

It is this gap that is the principal theme of YHWH's speeches in chapters 38–41, with their vertigo-inducing tour of the majestic, mysterious, uncontrollable and inexplicable corners of the creation. This perspective, implied so powerfully by the vivid imagery and the barrage of rhetorical questions in chapters 38–41, is anticipated explicitly in the wisdom poem of chapter 28. True human wisdom, as that poem reminds us, is not a God's-eye view of the universe but an engagement with the mysteries of the world from a stance of humility and integrity: "The fear of the Lord—that is wisdom, and to shun evil is understanding" (28:28).

The crucial formulation at the end of Job 28 must not be read in isolation from the concentric circles of debate and narrative that surround it. "The fear of the Lord" is, after all, a traditional motif within the language of Israelite wisdom, and even within the book of Job it can hardly be said to emerge at the end of chapter 28 as a brand-new idea. From the very first paragraphs of the opening speech of Eliphaz, Job's friends have had no trouble in speaking of "piety" (4:6) and "fear" (15:4; 22:4) as the basic stance which they are commending to Job. But it is Job, not his friends, who perceives how much more "the fear of the Lord" involves than the sententious recitation of biblical texts (cf. 6:14–15), and it is Job who is described from the start as living a life that *practices* that kind of fear (1:1; 1:8–9).

The fear of the Lord that is at the heart of the interpretive wisdom taught by the book of Job is not a magic key that unlocks the meaning of difficult texts or resolves the tensions between Scripture and experience. It does not transform the task of Bible reading into an easy or painless exercise; nor does it amount to an unquestioning willingness to swallow all the traditional nostrums of conventional piety. What it amounts to, this side of the general resurrection, is a way of living with unanswered questions that still bears true witness, keeps faith with friends, maintains integrity, and hopes in God. If we wish to interpret the Scriptures with integrity and authenticity, relating its message to the complicated and at times bewildering circumstances of our lives, we would do well to apprentice ourselves to Job, following his path through the whirlwind and seeking to emulate the fierce and faithful wisdom that he models for us.

SCRIPTURE, CHRIST, AND HERMENEUTICAL APPRENTICESHIP

The two case studies briefly sketched out above are, of course, just a tiny sample of the vast treasures of hermeneutical wisdom contained within the Scriptures. Every part of Scripture is, for the church, not only a text requiring interpretation but a living and active word that forms its interpreters and a rich supply of the wisdom that is required for its interpretation. And at the center and climax of the story Scripture tells stands the figure of the risen Jesus, opening the minds of the disciples to understand the Scriptures and commissioning them to play their part in the unfolding story of salvation (cf. Luke 24:25–27, 44–47).[13] To apprentice ourselves to Scripture is, in the end, to apprentice ourselves to Christ, following all of the multitudinous paths of Scripture as they lead us in faith toward him, sitting at his feet and learning from him how to read the Scriptures and recognize their fulfilment, and being sent out by Christ to labor together in his mission, helping one another to understand and do the will of God. May the God who gave us the Scriptures work through them within us, so that we might rightly receive and rightly respond to his voice, for the glory of his Son's name.

BIBLIOGRAPHY

Barker, Kit, et al. *Hermeneutics: A Guide for Apprentices*. Grand Rapids: Zondervan, 2024.

Blocher, Henri. "The 'Analogy of Faith' in the Study of Scripture: In Search of Justification and Guidelines." *SBET* 5 (1987) 17–38.

Childs, Brevard S. *Introduction to the Old Testament as Scripture*. Philadelphia: Fortress, 1979.

Fishbane, M. *Biblical Interpretation in Ancient Israel*. Oxford: Oxford University Press, 1985.

Fowl, Stephen E. "Virtue." In *Dictionary for Theological Interpretation of the Bible*, edited by K. J. Vanhoozer, 837–39. Grand Rapids: Baker, 2005.

Graves, Michael. *How Scripture Interprets Scripture: What Biblical Writers Can Teach Us About Reading the Bible*. Grand Rapids: Baker, 2021.

Hauerwas, Stanley, and Charles Robert Pinches. *Christians among the Virtues: Theological Conversations with Ancient and Modern Ethics*. Notre Dame: University of Notre Dame Press, 1997.

Hays, Richard B. *Echoes of Scripture in the Letters of Paul*. New Haven, CT: Yale University Press, 1989.

———. *Reading Backwards: Figural Christology and the Fourfold Gospel Witness*. Waco, TX: Baylor University Press, 2014.

Starling, David. "The Scribe, the Steward, and the Inhabiting Word." In *Theological Education: Foundations, Practices, and Future Directions*, edited by A. M. Bain and I. Hussey, 17–28. Eugene, OR: Wipf & Stock, 2018.

Starling, David I. *Hermeneutics as Apprenticeship: How the Bible Shapes Our Interpretive Habits and Practices*. Grand Rapids: Baker, 2016.

Vanhoozer, Kevin J. *The Drama of Doctrine: A Canonical-Linguistic Approach to Christian Theology*. Louisville, KY: Westminster, 2005.

---

13. Cf. Starling, *Hermeneutics as Apprenticeship*, 116.

Chapter 44

Trauma Hermeneutics

RICHARD RICE

THE MEANING OF TRAUMA

In a horrific traffic accident college professor Jerry Sittser lost three members of his family—his mother, his wife, and one of their three children. A drunk driver crashed into the van he was driving. When he climbed out of the wreck and saw the effects of the collision a powerful sensation settled over him. By the time the ambulance reached the hospital, two hours later, he knew he could never go back to the life he had before the trauma. In his words, he "stepped out into a whole new world."[1]

Sittser's account of this tragic accident gives us a useful description of trauma. A traumatic event or experience is one which results in a life-changing loss. Trauma is a special kind of loss. There are many life-changing experiences that do not involve significant "loss." Some are just transitions; some are life-changing gains. When a student starts college she leaves high school behind, perhaps along with some of the friends she had in previous years and organizations she belonged to, as well as classes that were less demanding than what lay ahead. When two people get married, they leave behind their lives as single persons. From then on, they arguably lose a measure of independence. Losses of this sort, however, are not traumatic in the sense we have in mind.

Neither are experiences that are painful when they occur, but actually lead the way to something that turns out to be better than what was lost. In other words, the net effect of some losses is actually a gain. Years ago I was promised a job that I eagerly looked forward to, only to have it given to someone else. I was devastated until I realized that it came with problems

---

1. Sittser, *Grace Disguised*, 21.

that I had not been aware of, and the person who got it was much better prepared for it than I was. In addition, the position I was given instead proved to be an important step toward a career that I was more suited for. So, not all losses are traumatic. Neither are losses that may be painful when they occur, but lead to benefits we only come to know later.

A traumatic loss, in contrast, is one that arguably outweighs whatever gains may follow it. Both the title and subtitle of Sittser's book may seem to contradict this—*A Grace Disguised: How the Soul Grows Through Loss*. For, in spite of the life-changing and irreversible loss of three of his close family members, Sittser found that he experienced grace and growth after the tragedy. What Sittser never says, however, is that whatever gains or benefits may have followed the sudden loss of his loved ones somehow made up for the loss, or turned it into something beneficial in the long run. The net effect of trauma is essentially negative.

What then is trauma? One source defines *trauma* as "anything that results from experiences that overwhelm an individual's capacity to cope," and goes on to list a dozen examples, ranging from abuse and neglect, sexualized violence, and family conflict, to life-threatening illness, war, grief and loss.[2] Another section of the same website defines no fewer than seven trauma types, ranging from "acute," "repetitive," "complex," and "developmental," to "vicarious," "historical," and "intergenerational." So, trauma may be caused by any number of factors and may take a variety of forms.

The expression "trauma hermeneutics" raises the possibility of two ways of approaching the Bible. We may think of trauma as the kind of experience that often drives people to "search the Scriptures" in hopes of finding encouragement and reassurance. What does the Bible provide that can help people face the serious challenges, or crises, that life sometimes brings?

We may also think of the experience/category of trauma as an interpretive lens through which to view various passages of the Bible. The Bible contains numerous accounts of life-changing losses that people experienced. And they sometimes describe the ways that people responded to these losses. Then there are passages which provide reassurance and encouragement without identifying specific types of suffering or mentioning particular causes. In spite of the various challenges we encounter, no matter how formidable, they encourage us to continue to believe that our lives have meaning and purpose.

As described in the Bible, people often suffered the consequences of their personal mistakes. A well-known example is David, who arranged for the death of Uriah the Hittite, in order to cover up his affair with Bathsheba,

---

2. "BC Mental Health and Substance Use Services," http://www.bcmhsus.ca/

Uriah's wife. When the prophet Nathan denounced David for his horrible deed, David was filled with self-reproach and remorse, and begged God for forgiveness, as we see in the great penitential Psalm attributed to him.[3] Though David received divine forgiveness, what he had done still had important consequences. By many accounts, this abuse of his status as king was a turning point in David's reign. To mention just one of the negative events that followed, David's favored son Absalom sought to replace his father as king and was killed as a result of his treachery.

Besides the sort of trauma that one may bring on oneself, there are traumatic experiences caused by various other factors, including the actions of other people, sometimes deliberate, as in the case of child abuse, sometimes accidental, as in the case, say, of many traffic collisions. And there is trauma that results from life-threatening illness, or the death of someone we love, like a family member or a close friend. Trauma also results from natural catastrophe, such as the massive earthquakes that cost thousands of lives in Turkey and Syria in early 2023. Then there is the widespread trauma caused by war. The extensive conflicts that occurred during the twentieth century, along with the terrors of the Holocaust, have led some to identify it as "the century of death."

If we identify trauma as life-changing loss, we can think of other losses that threaten the very meaning of life. Some people find it traumatic to lose their position in society, to no longer enjoy the status or respect they once had. Sometimes this results from the mistakes one has made. Sometimes it is more or less due to the passage of time. Discovering that one is no longer regarded with the esteem he or she enjoyed during an influential career can be a painful, even traumatic.

TRAUMA IN THE BIBLE

The Bible is filled with examples of people undergoing suffering for various reasons—some physical, some social, some spiritual, and some all three. Many of them may qualify as forms of trauma. But there are two biblical figures in particular—one in the Old Testament, one in the New—whose experience was unquestionably traumatic. These experiences are clear demonstrations that people sometimes find themselves in circumstances where they seem to have lost everything that gave their lives meaning—friends, social respect, their very sense of identity, and most significantly their relation to God.

---

3. Psalm 51.

Job is the classic case of massive and undeserved suffering. He lost everything that seems to give life value—his possessions, his children, eventually his health, and arguably the respect of other people, including several friends who came to "comfort" him, but wound up saying things that only added to his misery. Then he listened to God give an account of divine glory and majesty, and he concluded that it was presumptuous of him to question the character of God. His response to God's revelations ends with these words: "I had heard of you by the hearing of the ear, but now my eye sees you, therefore I despise myself, and repent in dust and ashes."[4]

Jesus, the central figure of the New Testament, suffered more profoundly than any other person in history. He was subjected to crucifixion, a painful form of execution and one which involved disgrace and social condemnation. And judging from his agonizing exclamation, "My God, my God, why have you forsaken me?"[5] he felt condemned and rejected by God as well. Some people might say that Jesus on the cross experienced the full measure of God's judgment against sin—complete exclusion from the presence of God.

As suggested by several New Testament passages, the suffering of crucifixion, painful as it was, was central to the purpose of the incarnation and to the fulfillment of Jesus's mission.[6] A famous passage in Paul's letter to the church in Philippi states that Christ Jesus, who, "though he was in the form of God," "emptied himself," and "became obedient to the point of death—even death on a cross." As a result, God gave him "the name that is above every name, so that at the name of Jesus every knee should bend, in heaven and on earth and under the earth, and every tongue soul confess that Jesus Christ is Lord, to the glory of God the Father."[7]

From Paul's perspective, then, Jesus's crucifixion, excruciatingly painful and socially humiliating—vividly traumatic—was central to Jesus's mission, indeed the climax of the incarnation. His execution and the trauma it brought him revealed the extent of his submission to God and the depths of his love for those he came to save.

The summary description of Jesus's person and work we just cited from Paul's letter to the church in Philippi appears in a passage that begins by urging believers in that city to follow Jesus's example in the way they

---

4. Job 42:5–6.

5. Matt 27:46; cf. Ps 22:1.

6. Although he was a Son, he learned obedience through what he suffered; and having been made perfect, he became the source of eternal salvation for all who obey him (Heb 5:8–9).

7. Phil 2:5–11.

treat one another. "Let the same mind be in you that was in Christ Jesus."[8] Actually, this letter is filled with advice to church members to remain strong in their faith in the face of trying circumstances. Here's another example: "For [God] has graciously granted you the privilege not only of believing in Christ," he wrote, "but of suffering for him as well."[9]

As the apostle describes it, then, one of the things that believers have in common with their Lord is the prevalence of trials and difficulties in their lives, while these challenge their faith, they also provide opportunities for them to receive God's help and learn from the traumatic difficulties that Jesus endured, especially during his final hours on earth. It appears, then, that even traumatic experiences and dramatic losses can be occasions for believers to grow in their confidence in God's care.

The biblical book of Psalms, the longest book of the Bible, gives full expression to the depths of human woe. In fact, fully one-third of these ancient songs concern what one writer calls "the wintry landscape of the heart." There is great comfort in these poems, because suffering people need to know their sufferings are acknowledged.

Martin Luther was particularly attracted to the Psalms of lament. "What is the greatest thing in the Psalter but this earnest speaking amid the storm winds of every kind? . . . Where do you find deeper, more sorrowful, more pitiful words of sadness than in the psalms of lamentation? There again you look into the hearts of the saints, as into death, yes, as into hell itself. . . . And that they speak these words to God and with God . . . is the best thing of all. This gives the words double earnestness and life."[10]

We have already referred to one of these Psalms in describing the suffering of Jesus, viz., Psalm 22. It begins with the plaintive cry, "My God, my God, why have you forsaken me?" These words express the pervasive reason for lament in this category of Psalms—the sense that God is not with us, that we are exposed to the trials and losses that life often brings. Yet these Psalms typically conclude with assurance that our troubles do not have the last word and God purposes will eventually find fulfillment.[11] Psalm 22 ends with these reassuring words: "Posterity will serve him; future generations will be told about the Lord, and proclaim his deliverance to a people yet unborn, saying that he has done it."

Pervasive and painful as it is, the Psalms affirm, suffering does not have the last word. God's purposes will eventually be fulfilled. Traumatic

---

8. Phil 2:5.
9. Phil 1:29.
10. Luther, *Word and Sacrament*, 1:255–56.
11. Psalm 88 is an exception.

experiences may be unavoidable and costly. But in light of God's love, they need not empty our lives of all meaning. The very fact that they could be the central concern of so many of the biblical Psalms underscores the value of faith in God's care as a resourceful way of responding to trauma. They assure us that we are not alone when trauma invades our lives. God is aware of what we are going through, and we have reason to hope.

Throughout history, the Psalms of lament have provided believers with the means of expressing both their misery and their hope, indeed their confidence that God's purposes will eventually find fulfillment. And both elements are essential to honest communication. God's care for us is strong enough to permit us to express the anguish we sometimes feel. After all, God shares our sorrows as well as our joys. One of the most moving scenes in the Gospels is the description of Jesus weeping at the tomb of Lazarus.[12] If we are forthright with God, our prayers will express, not just praise and thanksgiving, but our disappointments and despair as well.

TRAUMATIC EXPERIENCES

If we think of trauma as the sort of experience that threatens the very meaning of life, then trauma hermeneutics could be understood as a study of the Bible with the hope that we can find in it a basis for confidence that our lives do have meaning, in spite of the sort of events that threaten it.

There are times when events that disappoint us turn out to be beneficial, and what appeared to be a loss was actually a benefit. Years ago the president of a company I was working for promised me a position that was beyond my wildest dreams. But when his official letter arrived several weeks later, it said that things had changed and I would be given a different assignment instead. I was bitterly disappointed. I wondered why God had let me down. But in a few months I realized that I was better off in my new situation than the one I was expecting. What looked like a setback turned out to be a blessing, and I was grateful for God's leading in my life. Experiences like this support the conviction that there is a purpose behind the apparent tragedies that come to us. God sends them, or allows them, or at least uses them to benefit us. As the famous text in Romans says, "all things work together for good."[13]

In contrast, there are instances of suffering that refuse to fit this reassuring pattern. Years ago, for example, a college friend of mine lost his son when an airliner crashed into the ocean, the daughter of another friend was

---

12. John 11:35.
13. Rom 8:28.

brutally murdered, a teaching colleague died of cancer leaving her husband with two small children, and a teenager I knew became a quadriplegic when a car crash broke his neck. We can see God's hand in life's minor disappointments, but what do we do when faced with traumatic loss, or "horrendous evils," as one writer calls them? But in cases like this the loss apparently outweighs any possible good that could come from it. So, where is God when it really hurts? Why doesn't God protect us from harm or deliver us from evil?

The question is inescapable because nothing is more pervasive than suffering. And with it come inevitable questions. In his best-selling book on the subject, Rabbi Harold Kushner asserts, "There is only one question that really matters—why do bad things happen to good people. All other theological conversation is intellectually diverting."

Many people turn to religion for help in the face of suffering, but religion does not offer a uniform answer to the problem, and people often respond to religion in unexpected ways. If religion is a genuine resource to victims of trauma, and to those who assist them, we need to clarify its role and acknowledge its limitations. Although we often speak of "the meaning of pain and suffering," that's not exactly something religion provides. The real concern of religion is not suffering, it is the sufferer.[14]

On two occasions, according to the Gospels, Jesus had the opportunity to explain why tragedy strikes—one was the case of the man born blind; the other was the collapse of a tower that killed several people.[15] When the disciples asked Jesus why the man was born blind, he turned the discussion in another direction. The important thing, he said in effect, is not the reason for suffering, but our response to suffering, not why we suffer, but what we do when suffering comes.

TRAUMATIC QUESTIONS

Traumatic experiences present us with a number of perplexing paradoxes. One is the fact that traumatic suffering always seems to take us by surprise. Nothing is more obvious than the fact that everybody suffers to some degree, yet nothing seems more incomprehensible to us than our own suffering. As Elizabeth Kubler-Ross said of our attitude toward death, "it comes to thee and to thee, but not to me." Similarly, author William Saroyan wrote, "I knew that everybody died. But in my case I thought there would be an exception." And the fact is, there are no exceptions. Suffering enters every life sooner or later in one form or another.

14. As Sittser's experience illustrates, traumatic losses have no meaning in themselves, but it is possible for our lives to have meaning *in spite of* such suffering.

15. John 9:1–3; Luke 13:1–5.

The greatest paradox trauma presents us with is the apparent discrepancy between the power of God and the downsides of life. If God is all good and all-powerful, why does anyone suffer?[16] An omnipotent being has power to create any kind of world he wants to, and change anything in the world he wants to. If such a being existed, wouldn't he eliminate suffering, or prevent it, or at least limit it?

Historically, people have responded to this problem in various ways. One is to place suffering *outside* God's will, to maintain that God is not responsible for suffering. The most popular version of this approach appeals to free will. God endowed the creatures with the capacity to obey or disobey. They disobeyed, and the world now suffers the consequences. So, it was human rebellion that ultimately accounts for the sorrows of the world. God did not cause it or will it. It was never God's plan that we suffer.

The contrasting response to the problem of evil is to place suffering *inside* God's will. Things may *appear* to be out of control, goes this line of thought, but God is nevertheless completely in charge of the world. And everything that happens, including traumatic events, has its place in the divine plan. We may not understand why God lets things go the way they do. But we can be sure that it is all for the best. Everything we go through, even the traumatic events in our lives, is just what we need. God uses this painful process to develop our characters. In time, we will see that God's will is perfect.

Each of these responses generates a long list of questions. Some people can't understand how creatures who were perfect at the moment of creation could ever rebel against their maker. Others wonder why an all-powerful creator couldn't create beings who are free, but always use their freedom to do the right thing.

As for the idea that everything happens for the best, it seems contradicted by our experience. The soul-making, or character development, God is bringing about doesn't seem very cost effective. Is it really necessary for the world to contain this much suffering in order for our characters to develop? History's massive traumas hardly seem to be justified by whatever lessons we learn from them.

There are responses to these questions and further questions about these responses, and so on, in an endless cycle of philosophical point-counterpoint. They may show how perplexing suffering can be, but their success in demonstrating that traumatic experiences have meaning is limited. Even if they take us part way down the road to understanding or a measure of

---

16. Bart D. Ehrman identifies "why we suffer" as our most important question and argues that the Bible fails to answer it.

comprehension, none of them provides a fully satisfying solution to the problem of evil. And the obstacle that brings even the best of them to a halt is horrendous, traumatic, human suffering. All the theories in the world seem to pale in light of the intense misery that some people experience.

One of the most powerful expressions of this insight comes from Fyodor Dostoyevsky. In a memorable exchange in *The Brothers Karamazov*, the skeptical Ivan is challenging his brother Aloysha, a tender soul who has become a novice monk. "Imagine that you are building the edifice of human destiny with the object of making people happy in the finale, of giving them peace and rest at last, but for that you must inevitably and unavoidably torture just one tiny creature, . . . raise [the universe] on the foundation of her unrequited tears—would you agree to be the architect on such conditions? Tell me the truth." "No, I would not agree," Aloysha said. And neither would we. Theories founder on the shoals of traumatic suffering. No explanation makes it intelligible. Something is obviously wrong when solutions turn out to be problems, and our attempts to make things better wind up making them worse. When we're not getting good answers to our questions, the problem isn't always the answers. Sometimes it's the questions we are asking.

THE CHRISTIAN STORY

The cross and the resurrection of Jesus are central to the Christian story, and they are indispensable to a Christian perspective on suffering. According to the Gospels, Jesus approached the cross with fear and apprehension. During the last night of his life, he asked his closest friends to watch with him, and he fervently prayed that God would spare him the bitter cup that lay ahead. His hopes notwithstanding, he endured the agony of the cross. And his cry of desolation, "My God, why hast thou forsaken me!" reveals the depths of anguish to which he sank. With his resurrection, of course, Jesus broke the power of death, reversed the condemnation of the cross, and reunited with the Father.

The cross points to the inevitability of trauma in this world. Jesus did not avoid suffering, and neither can we. At the same time, Jesus's anguish confirms our basic intuition that suffering is wrong. There is a tragic abnormality to our existence. We know that we are susceptible to suffering and death; we also sense that we were not meant for them.

The cross also affirms Jesus's solidarity with us in our sufferings. It reminds us that we are never alone, no matter how dark and oppressive our situation may be. Because Jesus endured the cross, nothing can happen to us that he has not been through himself—physical pain and hardship, the distress of family and friends, the loss of worldly goods and whatever social status we had, the animosity of those we try to help, even spiritual isolation—he knew it all.

If the cross reminds us that suffering is unavoidable, the resurrection assures us that suffering does not have the last word. Jesus could not avoid the cross, but he was not imprisoned by it. The empty tomb assures us that suffering is temporary. From the perspective of Christian hope, the time will come when traumatic experiences will be a thing of the past.

For Christian faith, cross and resurrection are inseparable, and we must always see them together. Without the resurrection, the cross would be the last sad chapter in the story of a noble life. Jesus's death would simply illustrate the grim fact that the good often die young, with their dreams unfulfilled and their hopes dashed. In light of the resurrection, however, the cross is a great victory, the central act in God's response to the problem of suffering. So, the resurrection transforms the cross. It turns tragedy into triumph.

At the same time, the cross illuminates the resurrection. Standing alone, the resurrection might seem to offer an easy escape from the rigors of this world. It might lead to us to look for a detour around life's difficulties. If God has the power to raise the dead, then surely he can insulate us from pain and sorrow; he can prevent us from suffering. But before the resurrection comes the cross. And this leads us to recognize that God often takes us *through* traumatic experiences, rather than around them. He does not promise to lift us dramatically and miraculously out of harm's way. Just as Jesus had his cross to bear, his followers have theirs as well (cf. Matt 16:24). Jesus's promise to be with us in *our* sufferings also calls us to be with him in *his* sufferings.[17]

RESPONDING TO TRAUMA

This general view of things has several applications to our attempts to help people who are enduring traumatic experiences. People undergoing trauma need to know, first of all, that suffering is real and suffering is wrong. Suffering involves the loss of good things, especially traumatic suffering. Our instinctive response to such an experience is "Oh, no! This can't be right.

---

17. A short distance from Rome there is a small chapel on the Appian Way whose front wall bears the inscription, "Quo Vadis, Domine?" According to legend, Peter was fleeing Rome during a time of persecution when he encountered Christ heading toward the city. "Where are you going, Lord?" he asked. And Jesus answered, "I'm going to Rome, to be crucified again." With that, Peter realized he was traveling in the wrong direction, so he turned around to be with Jesus.

This is not supposed to happen to me." We were not meant to suffer. It was not God's plan for us. Trauma detracts from the value of life.

This insight rules out some of the familiar things people say to sufferers. "Compared to other people's problems, yours aren't so bad." "Your troubles are all for the best. Someday you will understand." "This happened for a reason. Either you deserve this, or you need it. Or perhaps God let it happen to teach you a lesson." When we tell people their problems are not so bad, compared to those of others, or their difficulties are all for the best, or that this was supposed to happen for some inscrutable reason—because they need it, or will somehow benefit from it, or perhaps worst of all, that they are being punished—we may actually increase their suffering rather than relieve it.

Several years ago a friend of ours learned she had ovarian cancer the day her second child was born. As she struggled with the disease, well-wishers assured her that God was testing her, or that God had chosen her for this special mission, or that God was getting ready to work a miracle on her behalf. All these approaches denied the traumatic reality of what she was facing. Not surprisingly, rather than ease her suffering, they compounded it. If there are any benefits that accompany suffering, they come not because suffering is good, but in spite of the fact that suffering is bad.

Church historian Martin Marty describes losing his wife to cancer after nearly thirty years of marriage. During the months of her final hospitalization they took turns reading a Psalm at the time of each midnight medication. He read the even numbered psalms, she read the odd numbered psalms. But after she had a particularly difficult day, I did not feel up to reading Psalm 88. I didn't think she could take it tonight, and I knew I couldn't. "Please read it for me," she said. All right: *I cry out in the night before thee. For my soul is full of trouble. Thou hast put me in the depths of the Pit, in the regions dark and deep.* "Thank you," she said, "I need that kind the most."

"After that conversation we continued to speak," Marty recalls, "slowly and quietly, in the bleakness of the midnight but in the warmth of each other's presence. We agreed that often the starkest scriptures were the most credible signals of God's presence and came in the worst time. When life gets down to basics, of course one wants the consoling words, the comforting sayings, the voices of hope preserved on printed pages. But they make sense only against the background . . . of the dark words."[18] Marty's experience affirms the right of people to face their suffering openly. It can help people to know that their trials and trauma are appreciated.

---

18. Marty, *Cry of Absence*, xi–xii.

In a book responding to the loss of his son, philosopher Nicholas Wolterstorff describes the struggle to "own his grief," as he put it. "The modern Western practice is to disown one's grief: to get over it, to put it behind one, to get on with life, to put it out of mind, to insure that it not become part of one's identity." To see his point we have only to think of the facile way newscasters talk of "healing" and "closure" just hours after some terrible tragedy has occurred. "My struggle," Wolterstorff said, "was to own [my grief], to make it part of my identity: if you want to know who I am, you must know that I am one whose son died."[19] In a similar vein Jerry Sittser speaks of embracing the sorrow that engulfed him when he lost three members of his family. To deal with the tragedy effectively, he found he could not go around his grief, he had to go through it. He had to penetrate its depths.[20]

Although it is important to acknowledge that suffering is real and suffering is wrong, it is equally important to insist that suffering does not have the last word. Suffering may be an inescapable part of our story, but it is not the whole story. Our story is larger than our sufferings.

People transcend traumatic suffering in several ways. One is courageously refusing to let suffering dominate them. This is the central point in Viktor Frankl's well-known book *Man's Search for Meaning*. When every freedom is taken away, one freedom always remains—the freedom to choose our response. When we cannot change our situation, we are challenged to change ourselves. And of course, the greater the challenge, the greater our courage must be. Frankl quotes Dostoyevsky: "There is only one thing that I dread, not to be worthy of my sufferings!"[21] No matter how desperate our situation, we can surmount it by refusing to let it define our significance. We can be greater than our sufferings.

It helps us transcend our sufferings to realize that we do not suffer alone. God is with us in our sufferings. According to Christian faith, the story of Jesus is God's own story, and its great climax is the crucifixion—a moment of indescribable anguish. Some people believe that Christ suffered so we won't have to. But the cross represents solidarity as well as substitution. Christ not only suffers *for* us, Christ suffers *with* us.

From the Christian perspective, this is a testimony to the fact that God is with us in our suffering, that everything that happens to us makes a difference to him. Paul's letter to the Romans contains the ringing assurance that nothing can separate us from the love of God in Christ Jesus—not

---

19. Wolterstorff, *Philosophers Who Believe*, 273–75.

20. Significantly, the subtitle of Sittser's book is "how the soul grows through loss." It does not read "the soul grows *because of* loss" or "the soul grows *in spite of* loss."

21. Frankl, *Man's Search for Meaning*, 87.

trouble, or hardship, or persecution, or famine, or nakedness, or danger, or sword. Neither death, nor life, nor angels, nor rulers, nor things present, nor things to come, nor powers, nor height, nor depth, nor anything else in all creation"—nothing can separate us from him (Rom 8:35–39). None of these things can separate us from God, not because he is waiting for us after they are over, but because he is with us when they happen. In the words of the most famous passage in the Bible, "I will fear no evil, for thou art with me."[22]

Traumatic suffering does not have the last word for those who have confidence for the future, so a final element in the Christian perspective on trauma is hope. One form of hope is the conviction that suffering counts for something, that it contributes to the achievement of some worthy goal. We have an instinctive desire to respond to tragedy by using it for some good purpose. We want our suffering and the suffering of those we love to count for something. It must not lie there, like a gaping hole in the fabric of life. We must somehow mend it, learn from it, grow beyond it. And religious faith sustains this hope with the assurance that in everything God works for good.[23]

My uncle died of Parkinson's disease and was bed-ridden for the last four years of his life. My aunt cared for him day and night during that entire time, with the exception of a one-hour visit each day from county caregivers. The other night I asked her the questions that form the title of our conference—What hurts? What works? One of the things she mentioned was the fact that his caregivers allowed him to contribute to them. In spite of his situation, his good nature, his faith, his sense of humor, came through, and they made an impact. In fact, not long after he died, one of the caregivers made a life-changing decision in part because of his influence.

What is the meaning of pain and suffering? Suffering has no meaning. But we can find meaning *in spite of* suffering. And religious faith is our greatest resource for doing so.

BIBLIOGRAPHY

Adams, Marilyn McCord. *Horrendous Evils and the Goodness of God*. Ithaca, NY: Cornell University Press, 1999.

Boyd, Gregory A. *Is God to Blame? Beyond Pat Answers to the Problem of Suffering*. Downers Grove, IL: InterVarsity, 2003.

Clark, Kelly James, ed. *Philosophers Who Believe: The Spiritual Journeys of Eleven Leading Thinkers*. Downers Grove, IL: InterVarsity, 1993.

---

22. Ps 23:4.
23. Rom 8:28.

Davis, Stephen T., ed. *Encountering Evil: Live Options in Theodicy*. Atlanta: John Knox, 1981.

Ehrman, Bart D. *God's Problem*. HarperOne, 2008.

Frankl, Victor E. *Man's Search for Meaning*. Washington Square, 1985.

Fretheim, Terence. *Creation Untamed: The Bible, God, and Natural Disasters*. Grand Rapids: Baker Academic, 2010.

Hasker, William. *The Triumph of God over Evil: Theodicy for a World of Suffering*. Downers Grove, IL: InterVarsity, 2008.

Hick, John. *Evil and the God of Love*. Rev. ed. New York: Harper & Row, 1978.

Kushner, Harold. *When Bad Things Happen to Good People*. New York: Schocken, 1981.

Luther, Martin. *Luther's Works*, Volume 1, *Word and Sacrament*. Edited by E. T. Bachmann. Philadelphia: Fortress, 1960.

Marty, Martin E. *A Cry of Absence: Reflections for the Winter of the Heart*. HarperSanFrancisco, 1993.

Rowe, William L., ed. *God and the Problem of Evil*. Malden, MA: Blackwell, 2001.

Sittser, Jerry. *A Grace Disguised: How the Soul Grows Through Loss*. Grand Rapids: Zondervan, 1996.

Chapter 45

Disability Hermeneutics

THOMAS E. REYNOLDS

Recent developments in theology have taken seriously the experiences of disability, moving beyond seeing disability as a personal diminishment, tragedy, or moral flaw that requires cure or management, or that provides opportunity for non-disabled Christians to show benevolence and goodwill. With such developments, calls for accessibility, justice, inclusion, and belonging have become prevalent, challenging church communities to honor the perspectives people with disabilities and reimagine what genuine togetherness means as the Body of Christ. Resisting both exclusionary practices and paternalistic charity approaches, theologies of disability resource new ways to understand Christian faith in light of disability, seeking to dismantle barriers—environmental and attitudinal—that stigmatize or prevent participation. More constructively, they affirm diverse embodiments in a way that fosters communion among all and a richer sense of God's loving presence.

Essential to this work is the task of hermeneutics. Disability is always an interpretation laden with cultural and religious meanings, understood in various ways. Hermeneutics not attuned to the experience of disability risk reinforcing ableism and normalcy, perhaps interpreting disability as an abnormal and demeaning flaw contrary to God's creative and loving purpose. Identifying three ways of approaching disability portrayed in Scripture, Hector Avelos notes that scholars may take a *rejectionist, historicist,* or *redemptionist* position.[1] First, some writers highlight the irresolvably problematic nature of religious interpretations from Scripture and theology,

---

1. Avelos, "Redemptionism, Rejectionism, Historicism," 91–92.

suggesting they perpetuate negative attitudes toward disability as divine punishment or curse, a sign of lack of faith, or alternatively, a chance for displaying faith that isolates and demeans disabled people as spectacles. On this basis, there is cause to reject or repudiate scriptural accounts of disability as irredeemably oppressive. An alternative approach might provincialize such accounts through historicizing methods that locate their meaning as mainly relevant to an ancient context, taking little interest in the consequences for a contemporary situation. Redemptionist interpretations, while still privileging a disability perspective, seek to redeem biblical texts that might seem to promulgate a negative view of disability, recontextualizing for contemporary applications and "rescuing" the Bible from itself. Each of these approaches has value and can even work simultaneously in tension, though one or another tends to predominate.

Instead of adopting mainly rejectionist or historicist approaches, theologies of disability work largely in the redemptionist mode to critically appraise yet retrieve generative resources from Scripture and tradition through a *disability hermeneutic*. Amos Yong describes this hermeneutic as an approach to the Bible that is informed by the experience of disability and by the understanding that people with disabilities are created in God's image, are agents in their own right and not defined by disability, and that "disabilities are not necessarily evil or blemishes to be eliminated."[2] Such a hermeneutic, even if unstated, is operative throughout the literature since its beginning in Nancy Eiesland's ground-breaking book *The Disabled God*, appealing to Scripture as an authority while interpreting it anew in light of disability experience and interdisciplinary insights from disability studies.[3] Disability hermeneutics, as Bethany McKinney Fox further notes, is a way of "honoring the perspectives of people with disabilities both in the present day and those in the biblical text," in the latter case, remembering that "people with disabilities in the healing narratives are more than mere object lessons."[4]

Building on Yong, Eiesland, and McKinney Fox, I take a disability hermeneutic to describe an approach that takes seriously the formative power of the Bible as testifying to God's creative and saving work in the world even while acknowledging its complexities and ambivalences relative to disability. In some cases, this requires reading intratextually: that is, reading passages with negative views of disability in light of others with

---

2. Yong, *Bible, Disability, and the Church*, 13.

3. Eiesland, *Disabled God*. Eiesland's work employs all of Avelos's three approaches and holds them in tension, though tilting toward a liberative redemptionist approach.

4. McKinney Fox, *Disability and the Way of Jesus*, 76.

more positive views and in light of larger canonical themes with theological relevance (to be enumerated in section three below). Central to this task is reading against interpretive traditions held captive by ableism and normalcy—that is, by principalities and powers that normalize certain "abilities" as prototypically human. This chapter, rather than catalogue the variety of approaches represented in the literature, aims modestly to sketch broad issues particularly relevant to developing a theologically-oriented disability hermeneutic, aware that more extensive analysis is required.

Essential to a disability hermeneutic are both a hermeneutics of suspicion and a hermeneutics of retrieval which engender a multidisciplinary approach that honors experiences of disability and the voices of disabled people. In light of this, disability interpretations engage in a reflective way with the gospel, God, and humanity in order to reimagine the life of the church as a people of God joined in vulnerable communion. The chapter begins by learning from disability studies, exploring several models that frame attention to disability, identifying and critiquing ableism and normalcy as fundamental problems. Then, refining a disability hermeneutic with regard to biblical representations of disability, especially the healing narratives in the Gospels, will be a key testing site encouraging re-reading the Bible against ableist framings. Third, the discussion will culminate in a brief examination of five theological themes that should inform the theological character of a disability hermeneutic. The overall aim is to highlight the importance of foregrounding disability as an integral part of embodied human life within the arc of God's creative power and loving embrace, prophetically resisting the distortions of normalcy and constructively empowering new forms of radical belonging together as the Body of Christ.

DISABILITY AS A CATEGORY AND MODELS OF DISABILITY: ENGAGING DISABILITY STUDIES

The World Health Organization (WHO) recently noted that disability "results from the interaction between health conditions such as dementia, blindness or spinal cord injury, and a range of environmental and personal factors." It estimates about 1.3 billion people—or 16 percent of the global population—experience a significant disability today, the number growing due to an increase in noncommunicable diseases and people living longer.[5] The term "disability," however, is a modern European construction, the origins of which date to the sixteenth century. It is an *interpretation* of embodied difference in human life, conveying complexity, interdependence,

---

5. See World Health Organization, "Disability and Health."

and vulnerability in ways that problematically come to be understood as a diminishment, blemish, or disordering problem to be remedied or managed. Stigma and discrimination accompany such interpretations. Yet the category of disability is unstable and complex, and can include many things related to motor, sensory or cognitive impairments that restrict participation in social environments—from intellectual disabilities to mental health challenges, dyslexia to cerebral palsy, chronic illness, blindness, and physical mobility issues. These represent a diverse range of experiences that resist a simple definition. They do, however, often find common cause in a struggle to access social spaces. Barriers to participation in community are a common reference point in the experience of disability. And this carries over into church participation, where disabled people are often excluded, perceived as objects of pity, in need of healing, or designates for "special" programs.

What thinking hermeneutically can do is unsettle and complicate dominant or taken-for-granted images of disability as a universal, natural condition appearing in the same way across cultures and historical periods. Disability may be an integral part of human experience (e.g., as humans age and eventually die), but how this is understood is not a given. Recent work in disability studies challenge ableist depictions of a standard or "normal" physiology, ability, agency, and social identity. Indeed, ability and disability are discursive constructs developed in particular contexts; their meanings are historically and culturally contingent interpretations of the human, and often intersect with other experiences of marginalization. The WHO underscores that "persons with disabilities are a diverse group, and factors such as sex, age, gender identity, sexual orientation, religion, race, ethnicity and their economic situation affect their experiences in life and their health needs. Persons with disabilities die earlier, have poorer health, and experience more limitations in everyday functioning than others."[6]

The emergence of disability studies thus represents a shift away from focusing on certain kinds of bodies designated as problems to be remedied by medical treatment or managed by caregiving assistance to examining the means by which disability itself is produced, interpreted, and attributed to such bodies. This contrast is characterized as between "medical" and "social" models of disability. The former understands disability to be an individual's impairment resulting in personal and social consequences; the latter takes disability to be a factor of the relationship between an impairment and social environment. As a social construct, the pathology is in *the disabling social system*, not the individual body. This insight builds on developments

---

6. World Health Organization, "Disability and Health."

in the 1970s and 1980s, as people with disabilities and their allies joined to resist discrimination and advocate for human rights, widening conceptions of accessibility beyond "pity" and "charity" models towards full inclusion.

Exploring how representations of disability are produced and embedded in cultural systems opens a line of inquiry that characterizes a "cultural model" of disability. The cultural model exposes the cracks in society's pathological pretenses to normalcy, its preoccupation with shoring up resources against deviation by enforcing processes of normalization that regulate and "expect" certain kinds of "able" bodies.[7] Furthermore, it assesses the ways that normalcy produces and privileges the "normate" figure—that is, the prototypical able/normalized ideal through which people identify as "definitive" human beings.[8] The addition of the cultural model to the medical and social models of disability provides added nuance, assessing the complex manner by which representations of disability are produced as part of normalcy. Disability serves to represent a kind of counter example marking disruption, the effect of which generates normalizing mechanisms, producing and maintaining normalcy.

RETHINKING DISABILITY REPRESENTATIONS IN SCRIPTURE: INTERPRETING HEALING NARRATIVES

In light of the insights of disability studies, briefly sketched above, we now examine how Christian attitudes toward disability often operate under the sway of normalcy, particularly in biblical interpretation.

Perceptions of disability as "flaw" associate it with the presence or absence of God, a deprivation that signals problematic inner character traits and deeper spiritual or moral realities. At one extreme is Martin Luther's remark encouraging drowning a child with disabilities, understood as a subhuman threat to others and the work of the Devil. It was common in Luther's day to believe that the Devil took on forms—sometimes attributed to misshapen human figures and diseases—that were a danger to be resisted.[9] In many ways, disability continues to be interpreted in Christian terms as a physiognomic sign of God's absence, a sign of reprobation, or the effect of evil and sin. For example, drawing from personal experience as a parent with a child who identifies on the autism spectrum, well-meaning Christians have inquired about potential evil or demonic forces at work in some behaviors representative of autism. Interpretations of certain mental

---

7. On the production of normalcy, see my *Vulnerable Communion*, ch. 2.
8. See Garland-Thomson, *Extraordinary Bodies*, 8.
9. See Hueser, "Human Condition as Seen from the Cross."

illnesses and epilepsy have also drawn similar conclusions, influenced by stories from the Bible about demon possession. Fear of disability's disruption, interpreted via systems of normalcy, often fosters a desire to account for disability by pointing to underlying causes such as destructive spiritual forces.

Moral and spiritual meaning is given to disability by assigning blame to the individual in a kind of physiognomic chain of causation. If God is thought to be humanity's moral and provident ruler, and if disability is assumed to be a bodily defect accompanied by suffering and from which nothing good can come, it is a short path to interpreting disability as an index of God's intentions or framing it as the result of wrongdoing on the part of a person or family. The Bible carries examples of this logic, linking righteousness with blessing and sinfulness with suffering as a punishment or curse, whether collective (as in the case of guilt and suffering on part of the Israelites for failing as a people to honor the covenant with God) or individual (as in Job's friends who falsely surmise that he has brought suffering upon himself (e.g., Job 4:7-9, 8:4-7, 11:14-20) or in passages like those in Proverbs which state, "Misfortune pursues sinners, but prosperity rewards the righteous" (Prov 13:21). Jesus himself seems to illustrate this when speaking a man he has just healed: "See, you have been made well! Sin no more, that nothing worse befall you" (John 5:14). The stigmatization of disability as a desecration or harmful flaw is thus given religious rationale.

Interpretations like these were common not only in Jesus's time but persist today in many Christian communities. Part of the reason for the persistence is that they, as in the examples above, rely on a hermeneutic that assumes the biases of normalcy. When interpreted simplistically, selectively, or without a depth of contextual and historical understanding, biblical passages can be appropriated in ways detrimental to people with disabilities, unwittingly reproducing normalcy as a hermeneutical vantage point. Recent studies by biblical scholars and theologians alike have noted this problem.[10] Simplistic hermeneutics can grant unqualified authority to select biblical references that depict disability as a curse. This not only overlooks the ambivalence of the Bible on disability; more, it conceals while reaffirming ableist biases in readers that operate in advance and hermeneutically govern the selection of particular texts as definitive over others. Ironically, such interpretations submit Scripture to the power of normalcy even while claiming "authority" as the privileged property of the word. Hence, approaches to the Bible can serve circularly to justify pretensions to normalcy

---

10. For example, see McKinney Fox, Yong, as well as Avelos et al., *This Abled Body* and also Black, *Healing Homiletic*.

rather than attend to the complexity, polyphony, and ambiguity of the Bible itself as a normative canon of texts.

The case of healing as divine intervention deserves special consideration here. Analogous to modern medical approaches that view disability as an affliction, yet with a focus on supernatural mediation and a corresponding stress on the spiritual or moral transformation of the person, healing employs divine power as a resource for restoration. Key to this approach are stories that portray Jesus's healing powers as a demonstration that God was doing something special through him.[11] And, as Colleen Grant notes, they generally serve a twofold function in the Gospels. First, they often illustrate the messianic status of Jesus, focusing not on the people being healed but instead on the identity of Christ: emphasizing his authority, for example, to forgive sin (which only God can do) or heal on the Sabbath (which supposedly went against Jewish law). Second, if they do focus on those being healed, they do so to commend their discipleship and faith in Jesus. In the first sense, Jesus's power to forgive sins is often coupled with healing, confirming the link between sin and disability.[12] In the second sense, these stories often attribute successful healing to the faith of the person, a sign of spiritual transformation among those who were healed.[13] Under the sway of normalcy, both depictions can provide a basis for identifying disability as a means to demonstrate God's healing power, signalling grace in its removal but attributing blame to the person when attempts to heal fail. Failure to be healed often is deemed a personal flaw.

The logic here of expectation and resultant blame serves to objectify and demean people with disabilities. Not only does this individualize disability as a defect, it also introduces further social burden by making people with disabilities responsible for their own condition and cure. Further, it presents people with disabilities as agents only insofar as they desire restoration, willfully seeking to become able-bodied, symbols of brokenness in need of and pursuing wholeness on normalcy's terms. The Bible can be read in a way that fuels such dynamics, usually rendering invisible people with illnesses and disabilities in the healing narratives except as they appear as object lessons. Disabled people thus bear the burden of a socially inscribed pathology, compelled to internalize normalcy's stigmatizing gaze and take responsibility for their own cure. This is reinforced by the Bible's metaphorical use of impairments (blindness, deafness, paralysis, etc.) to

---

11. For examples see Mark 1:23-28, 2:1-12, 7:31-37; and John 5:1-47.
12. Grant, "Reinterpreting the Healing Narratives," 75. For example, Mark 2:1-12.
13. For examples, see Matt 9:22; Mark 5:34, 10:52; and Luke 8:48, 17:19, 18:42.

describe deficient moral and spiritual states. Individual bodies thus become indexes of transcendent meanings that embed normalcy.

Such analyses show the important hermeneutical insights gained by drawing from social and cultural models of disability as a way of re-reading biblical texts. A disability hermeneutic thus adopts a hermeneutics of suspicion: a critical interpretive standpoint that does not take things at face value without questioning, interrogating common beliefs and practices from the position of disability as a marginalized human experience.[14] This can disrupt pretensions to normalcy in faith communities that authorize portrayals of disability as an embodied deficiency with transcendent physiognomic meanings, inviting constructive alternative readings. The challenge is to articulate anew the gospel's power to disrupt normalcy and make possible new ways of living together in embodied differences, where disability is recognized as an integral part of embodied human life and people with disabilities are welcome participants in community.

There are subtle currents in scriptural texts themselves that may, when read with a disability hermeneutic, open up such possibilities. John 9:1–41 provides one case. John depicts Jesus's disciples encountering a blind man, about whom they ask Jesus, "who sinned, this man or his parents, that he was born blind" (John 9:2). In a striking reply, Jesus subverts a common assumption that disability is a consequence of sin, claiming that neither the man's parents nor he had sinned to cause the disability. The man was born blind that "the works of God may be made manifest in him" (9:3). The narrative subverts the causal link between healing and faith; the man is healed without any stated expectation and only gradually develops an articulation of faith as he confronts challengers (9:24–34). Furthermore, the blind man is not represented as one who seeks out his own healing.[15] Even so, however, he still is portrayed as an object lesson highlighting the "works of God" through Jesus and the man's own growing discipleship. So this text is ambiguous and contains contrasting elements to the stereotypical interpretations of disability mentioned above, even as it also contains some of these residual components. The main point is that this story complicates overly glib interpretations that would simply reassert normalcy.[16] Addressing these and other subtleties and ambivalences in the Bible is an important and fruitful way for Christians who assert the authority of Scripture for Christian life to harness a disability hermeneutic in critically engaging and retrieving

---

14. See Yong, *Bible, Disability, and the Church*, 63.

15. See Grant, "Reinterpreting the Healing Narratives," 75–85.

16. Yong, *Bible, Disability, and the Church*, 50–57 and McKinney Fox, *Disability and the Way of Jesus*, 96–98, 136–39.

biblical texts from interpretive barriers erected in the clutches of normalcy, and in so doing expand awareness that Jesus engages people in his context to create greater liberations for people, including those he healed.

Working to avoid readings of the healing narratives where disabled people are depicted solely as object lessons or passive victims, McKinney Fox helpfully identify seven marks of Jesus's healings.[17] First, there is a positive reception by the healed person, a mutual participation that acknowledges agency and regards the outcome as beneficial, even if it was not explicitly sought after. Second, there is an attention to the body and its healing/transformation in ways that count against a focus on physical cure as the main marker of healing. Bodily healing is not the end of transformation; it also involves transformed social relations and community. Third, Jesus was present to others with compassion and respect, not dismissive or condescending. He listens receptively and responds with care. Fourth, healing impacts and transforms the broader community, eliciting responses from witnesses that range from confusion to anger to worship and praise. Factoring this point widens the aperture for considering healing beyond something happening to an individual. Healing can unmask injustice and exclusion, a prophetic part of remaking the world and building a new kind of community. Fifth, healing clarifies the identities of the person healed and of Jesus. People see themselves as beloved children of God, forgiven and reconstituted spiritually, and the identity of Jesus is affirmed as Lord and Savior, Messiah. Sixth, the healing narratives display spiritual and communal dimensions at work, as well, which contribute to a more holistic sense of healing—that is, a sense of wholeness and belonging beyond stigma and exclusion. Finally, healings expand categories and enlarge the imagination of all, provoking new and boundary-expansive ways of thinking, a window into hope beyond the conventions of normalcy.

These takeaways from re-reading healings narratively through a disability hermeneutic lead to deeper insights on healing and the Bible that motivate a more expansive relational imagination regarding disability. Seemingly obvious, it is worth noting that not every person with a disability who met Jesus was healed. The Gospel narratives give accounts with broader significance than merely a curative paradigm where Jesus heals everyone; that is, rather, something new is happening and the kingdom of God is at hand, with the inbreaking love of God in Jesus. Moreover, healing and curing do not necessarily mean the same thing. Scholars are shifting interpretive focus away from a narrow sense of healing as curing bodies or a restoration to normalcy, to a wider sense of healing as shalom: a graced

---

17. McKinney Fox, *Disability and the Way of Jesus*, 145–53.

wholeness and well-being that includes restoration to communal belonging and renewed dignity in relationships of mutual regard. This is not to say simplistically that the elimination of disability made restoration to community possible. Instead, Jesus deliberately crossed social boundaries which were established to control and contain dangerous and impure bodies, to offer radical acceptance and reconcile people to God, each other, and themselves in a way that brought well-being, and which exposed and subverted structures perpetuating exclusion and marginalization.

A key ramification is that healing can happen without cure, which takes the focus off people with disabilities as seeking a "fix" so as to conform to standards of normalcy and be included. Yong shows how Luke-Acts undercuts ways the dominant culture diminishes particular bodies as of lesser status through physiognomy. Here, God's work of salvation included people otherwise belittled—for example, an Ethiopian eunuch (ethnically and anatomically devalued) and Zacchaeus (undesirable shortness of size or stature)—yet whose demeaned condition was not reversed but rather accepted as it was. God's liberative work exposes and undoes restrictive social barriers by actively embracing different kinds of bodies, showing no partiality (Acts 10:34), and so challenging discriminatory attitudes and policies based upon dominant society's standards of desirability.[18] Healing then can be rethought in ways that emphasize broader personal and social transformation that takes place through Jesus, recognizing disabled people as already part of God's beloved community prior to any physical transformation.

This focus correlates with the larger narrative plot of Jesus's ministry as depicted in the Gospel accounts. Jesus's ministry—including healing—calls attention to exclusion by constantly challenging the status quo and overturning assumptions about what normal is, refocusing community away from the center toward the margins, welcoming the uninvited outcast as the honored guest, pointing toward those shunned by society as, in fact, treasured vessels of the new community of God.[19] God-in-Christ ushers in communal transformation and establishes right relations between people. Healing stories can be understood within the larger arc of the gospel message of liberation, the release of those held captive by debilitating systems of normalcy and their power to discriminate and exclude, aspiring to a new kind of community founded upon kinship and interdependence in God's love.

---

18. Yong, *Bible, Disability, and the Church*, 63–69.
19. See Reynolds, *Vulnerable Communion*, 219–28.

THEOLOGICAL THEMES INFORMING A DISABILITY HERMENEUTIC

We already see theological themes at work above in reframing attention to disability in the Bible. I propose five themes as essential to a disability hermeneutic. These are not an exhaustive account, but a way of briefly sketching how a disability hermeneutic can offer substantive vision and more fruitfully nourish and guide faithful practices for the Church's life.

First, the priority of God's creative and loving will. This affirmation relativizes human abilities and mechanisms that would control God's presence by parsing it out according to finite standards managed by normalcy. God's love is not a reward for human achievement, something bestowed according to abilities or capacities framed within normalcy and measured by criteria that favor only a select few. God is sovereign and free, and from a prodigal abundance offers the gift of grace and love for all. The worth of human life ultimately resides in God's inestimable and gratuitous welcome, which transcends every system of normalcy.[20] This cuts to the core of the gospel message: the good news of Jesus Christ is that God reaches out lovingly to embrace people where they are, as they are, neither because of virtues and abilities nor because of vices or disabilities. This subverts physiognomic interpretations of disability. All people fall short of the glory of God, being sinful (Rom 3:23); and yet all are loved into being by God and accepted into the love of God, and so should accept one another (Rom 15:7). Divine grace thus undercuts the ability/disability distinction as of any merit for estimating human worth and importing moral and spiritual meanings onto disabled bodies. It also undercuts the illusion of self-sufficiency and control before God, for divine grace searches out and grasps human beings prior to any effort on their part, making it a gift, not an achievement. As such, normalcy is itself an idol that warrants deconstructing; it feigns to be an ultimate matrix of value and worth, when indeed only God is ultimate. And God's love extravagantly transgresses human-made boundaries and barriers; even more, it relativizes and levels them, liberating all held captive by their power, those who are marginalized as well as those who marginalize, and opening all to consider each other as neighbor.

Second, the embodied diversity of creation is good. God loves creation into being and affirms it as good. Creation itself is diverse and multiplies, finite and subject to change. Creatures have integrity as beings with bounded identities, with limits, *and* are good because of it. Such goodness affirms embodied limits and its accompanying vulnerability as part of being

---

20. See Reynolds, *Vulnerable Communion*, chs. 5–6.

creaturely.[21] A deficit model of anthropology begins from positing a normative condition and from this vantage point focuses on what is lacking, disability framed as an unusual and abnormal defect. A "limits model," for Deborah Creamer, begins with disability as one of the intrinsic features of "normal" embodied existence, theologically understood as part of a good creation.[22] Rather than being an exception to the rule, disability is one aspect of limits and how they are manifest differently in human life, some being more profound than others. Creamer helpfully foregrounds how this challenges "binary categories of 'us' and 'them,'" and invites the recognition "that it is not only those who are labeled 'disabled' that experience limits; limits are something inherent in the experience of humanity. Rather than identifying this as an inherently negative or evil characteristic, limits are understood to be part of creation."[23]

Furthermore, third, affirming the vulnerable limits of embodied life implies a relational theological anthropology, wherein human interdependence is primary over autonomous independence. Each creaturely life has its own integrity and is woven into life with others within shared relational fabric of reciprocity and connection. However, anthropologies built upon modern notions of the person as an autonomous and self-reliant subject have nourished ableist ideals and fueled normalcy, rendering dependency a disabling flaw to be remedied. But we are born, grow, live, and die in multiple matrices of interdependent relations. A relational anthropology understands, then, that *imago Dei* is not a substantive property encased in individuals who in their ideal state are independent authors of their own being, but as something reflected differently among all in relations that mediate value and cultivate life, ultimately reliant upon God. The image of God founds a relational ontology, an image pointing toward wholeness found in being together and with God.[24] Solidarity among people finds roots in the image of God, not as sameness among all people, but in a deep respect for and obligation to the infinite value and particular difference of every person, whether non-disabled or disabled. And in this, the image of God opens to the holiness of life together and to God. Yet human life is degraded by the distortion of sin, one aspect of which is embedded in disabling systems of normalcy that obscure the more basic reality of the image of God in

---

21. On limits, see Creamer, *Disability and Christian Theology*, 31–34, 93–96. On vulnerability, see Reynolds, *Vulnerable Communion*, 104–32.
22. Creamer, *Disability and Christian Theology*, 93–96.
23. Creamer, *Disability and Christian Theology*, 109.
24. See Reynolds, *Vulnerable Communion*, 177–88.

all persons. A disability hermeneutic thus requires deep engagement with redemption in Christ.

A fourth component, then, building from the above, is the affirmation of God whose creative love is attuned to and draws near to the world. The gospel testifies to such power, a sympathetic attunement that affirms the vulnerable limits of finite creatureliness by becoming creaturely, the Word made flesh. It is *within* such limits that God encounters humanity in solidarity through Jesus Christ. As Eiesland notes, this entails a basic re-symbolizing of God in ways that subvert dominant symbols that create barriers to participation in the church for people with disabilities. For Eiesland, the understanding of God incarnate in Jesus as the Christ means that God identifies with human bodies in a way that makes the limits and vulnerabilities of bodies "partially constitutive of God."[25] If Jesus is Emmanuel, God with us (Matt 1:22–23), embodied interdependence is a central ingredient, not absolute power and control. God reaches to share the divine self with humanity, participating in humanity in all its elements, including a tragic death on the cross. In this, God reveals the divine nature as compassion not only by "undergoing" or "suffering with" human limits and vulnerability, but also by raising them up into God's own being. This is what makes the resurrection crucial for the disciples' understanding of who Jesus was in connection to God. Eiesland puts it eloquently:

> In the resurrected Jesus Christ, they saw not the suffering servant for whom the last and more important word was tragedy and sin, but the disabled God who embodied both impaired hands and feet and pierced side and the imago Dei. Paradoxically, in the very act commonly understood as the transcendence of physical life, God is revealed as tangible, bearing the representations of the body reshaped by injustice and sin into the fullness of the Godhead.[26]

The fact that Jesus's body remains scarred in the resurrection signals that God is "with us" in the fullness of embodied limits and contingencies, as disabled.

Importantly, this does not negate limits by representing the ideal invulnerable and perfectly whole human body. Rather, it reveals God in solidarity with humanity, who knows injustice, experiences vulnerability, and discloses a new humanity, one "underscoring the reality that full personhood is fully compatible with the experience of disability."[27] Here, the image of

---

25. Eiesland, *Disabled God*, 99.
26. Eiesland, *Disabled God*, 99–100.
27. Eiesland, *Disabled God*, 100.

God in humanity is inclusive of disability, not despite it but through it. This delegitimizes theological rationales for marginalization disability through stigmatization. God's grace has priority over mechanisms of human valuation, conditioned as they are by normalcy, and underscores the vulnerability and limits of embodied human life in a disability affirming way. Eiesland links the two themes brilliantly in a Christology that resymbolizes God as disabled. God identifies with the experience of finitude and disability such that it becomes part of God's own being, so that to exclude one is to exclude the other. This challenges Christian communities on many levels toward living into the fullness of faithful life together as the Body of Christ.

Fifth, then, is a reimagined conception of living into the fulsomeness of being the Body of Christ, that place where members are joined equally, where welcome, access, and accommodation are central features of life together, through which all members "have the same care for one another" (1 Cor 12:25). Church is a household/family of God (Eph 2:19) in which "dividing walls" based upon human ordinances are abolished (Eph 2:14–15) and gifts are received from all members of the body (Rom 12:4–5; 1 Cor 12), some of whom may be seen (interpreted) to be weaker but who are in fact indispensable (1 Cor 12:22). This last point highlights the subversive power of what Paul calls "weakness." This is not to romanticize or valorize disability as a weakness. Yong articulates that the language of what "seems" to be weaker and what "we think" is less honorable is actually an indictment of normalcy, a provocative rebuke of elitist and hierarchical attitudes that demean certain members of the community as worthless and deficient.[28] For Paul, church is a body with many parts, none of which can denounce the other as inconsequential (1 Cor 12:21). It is worth quoting: "God has so composed the body, giving greater honor to the (alleged) inferior part, that there may be no discord in the body, but that the members may have the same care for one another. If one member suffers, all suffer together; if one member is honored, all rejoice together" (1 Cor 12:24–26). The so-called weakest members are the key to community, for the church is a place where all people are members of one another (Rom 12:5), so that discrimination against one part "disables" the whole community.

A disability hermeneutic thus provides tools to re-examine "weakness" as a site of provocative disruption, calling for reform and transformation, and more, to reconceive what "being together" means, for the Spirit of God freely distributes gifts to all members for the common good (1 Cor 12:7), each having a vocation that is distinct and valuable. The language is important: disability as such does not mean giftedness, but because the Spirit

---

28. Yong, *Bible, Disability, and the Church*, 93.

chooses to work where it may, not according to hierarchical arrangement or calculable human standards of worth framed within normalcy. The Spirit makes many gifts and abilities possible, making everyone both recipient and provider of care. This is perhaps the meaning of Paul's encouragement that all members "have the same care for one another." The church is a place of interdependency, of giving and receiving by and for all, people with disabilities being contributors instead of only recipients of care.

Love of neighbor, as a principal ethic of compassion and justice in the Bible, in this way can be conceived as a process of mutual respect and hospitality, working outside paternalistic mechanisms of care that "do to" others. In this, way the biblical ethic of love of neighbor and hospitality are connected as central ingredient in the work of God's Spirit: all people are loved by God and, in turn, called to hold one another in loving regard, such that receiving one another in care is a way of receiving God's gifts.[29] The church, ideally, is then that place where the Spirit comes to hearth: a vulnerable communion of mutual gift exchange. And since God's image includes disability, and this image dwells among all human beings, the church is summoned into a radical kind of belonging, opened up to different embodiments—including disability—as if welcoming each other is to host the divine in our midst.

CONCLUSION

All five of the theological components named above work together in an organic way to present a vision that not only resists and seeks to transform normalcy, but that also may nourish a more robustly accessible, inclusive and welcoming life together in Christian community. Such a community is one where people with disabilities are not merely welcomed and included as an afterthought, but rather are active participants and co-creators in the making of community, leaders. In this sense, a theologically informed disability hermeneutic moves beyond interpreting disability as something subject to exclusion, demeaning and thinned out versions of healing and curative practices, or as an object of charity that serves to showcase the benevolence of non-disabled people. Disability is an integral part of embodied human life within the arc of God's love.

A disability hermeneutic requires interdisciplinary theological sensitivity in honoring the experience of disability and re-reading biblical texts accordingly. This chapter has only scratched the surface, highlighting a select sample of issues that address the need to take seriously the experiences

---

29. See Reynolds, *Vulnerable Communion*, 239–47.

and voices of people with disabilities. More can be found in the robust and growing literature in theology and biblical studies relevant to disability. Lay people and leaders alike would do well to think through the implications of how a disability hermeneutic might invite transformation in their own faith communities. Such would be an act of faithful witness to God's love in the midst of vulnerable life together.

BIBLIOGRAPHY

Avelos, Hector. "Redemptionism, Rejectionism, Historicism as Emerging Approaches to Disability Studies." *Perspectives in Religious Studies* 34 (2007) 91–100.

Black, Kathy. *A Healing Homiletic: Preaching and Disability*. Nashville: Abingdon, 1996.

Creamer, Deborah Beth. *Disability and Christian Theology: Embodied Limits and Constructive Possibilities*. Oxford: Oxford University Press, 2009.

Eiesland, Nancy L. *The Disabled God: Toward a Liberatory Theology of Disability*. Nashville: Abingdon, 1994.

Goodley, Dan. *Disability Studies: An Interdisciplinary Introduction*. 2nd ed. London: Sage, 2017.

Grant, Colleen C. "Reinterpreting the Healing Narratives." In *Human Disability and the Service of God, Reassessing Religious Practice*, edited by Nancy Eiesland and Don E. Saliers, 72–87. Nashville: Abingdon, 1998.

Hueser, Stefan. "The Human Condition as Seen from the Cross: Luther and Disability." In *Disability in the Christian Tradition: A Reader*, edited by Brian Brock and John Swinton, 184–215. Grand Rapids: Eerdmans, 2012.

Melcher, Sarah J., et al., eds. *The Bible and Disability: A Commentary*. Waco, TX: Baylor University Press, 2017.

McKinney Fox, Bethany. *Disability and the Way of Jesus: Holistic Healing in the Gospels and the Church*. Downers Grove, IL: Inter Varsity, 2019.

Moss, Candida and Jeremy Schipper, eds. *Disability Studies and Biblical Literature*. New York: Palgrave Macmillan, 2011.

Reynolds, Thomas E. *Vulnerable Communion: A Theology of Disability and Hospitality*. Grand Rapids: Brazos, 2008.

World Health Organization. "Disability and Health." https://www.who.int/news-room/fact-sheets/detail/disability-and-health.

Yong, Amos. *The Bible, Disability, and the Church: A New Vision of the People of God*. Grand Rapids: Eerdmans, 2011.

Afterword

The Emergence and Trajectory of Postconservative Thought

JOHN R. FRANKE

In the prologue to this volume, Roger Olson tells the story of the emergence of what he described as postconservative evangelicalism in his May 1995 article "Postconservative Evangelicals Greet the Postmodern Age" in the *Christian Century*. While he was not, as he later discovered, the first to coin the term, he was perhaps the most influential in making part of the mainstream conversation in the mid-1990s. This brand of evangelical theology as also been called, among other things, liberal evangelical theology, postmodern evangelical theology, progressive evangelical theology, or the theology of the evangelical left.

I still remember reading Roger's article in my office at Biblical Theological Seminary where I had been teaching since joining the faculty in the fall of 1993 after returning from three years of doctoral research in England. The school at that time had moved away from its fundamentalist roots and was establishing its identity as a conservative evangelical, but not fundamentalist school, in the mold of Trinity Evangelical Divinity School and Gordon-Conwell Theological Seminary. I had been a student at Biblical and was excited to join a seminary "on the move" theologically.

The palpable sense of theological openness within an evangelical framework encouraged me to engage with postmodern thought in the development of an evangelical theology for the fast-approaching twenty-first century. Indeed, the first book I read in preparation for teaching my theology courses in the fall of 1993 was the volume of Stanley Grenz on reimagining evangelical theology for the fast approaching twenty-first century, published in the spring of that same year.[1] I was captivated. Over the next two years, I started working his postmodern evangelical perspective into successive theology classes. When Roger's article appeared at the end of my second year of teaching in 1995, I was hooked and started to more vigorously pursue the postconservative evangelical agenda he and Stan Grenz were describing and constructing.

In looking back, I realize that the combination of the shifting perspective at Biblical away from its fundamentalist roots toward a more broadly evangelical perspective, coupled with its relatively small size and therefore limited influence, gave me space to develop my thinking in ways that would likely not have been possible at other more established institutions. I became friends with the small cadre of evangelical scholars who were developing the postconservative perspective, particularly Stan Grenz who made a memorable visit to Biblical Seminary in the spring of 1997 in support this work. He was brilliant, engaging, and inspiring. Many attended his lectures left with a fresh sense of the exciting possibilities of a postconservative evangelical theology. A theology that attempted moved beyond the liberal-conservative divide that had dominated the discipline throughout the twentieth century with negative consequences for the church and Christian witness.

My friendship and collaboration with Stan resulted in a co-authored book on theological method from a postmodern and nonfoundational perspective.[2] I followed this up with a postconservative evangelical introduction to theology.[3] However, with the publication of these volumes, the criticism from evangelical critics and gatekeepers intensified. Shortly after the publication of my book devoted to the expression of what Merold Westphal calls in his foreword to this volume "perspectival pluralism,"[4] it became clear to both the leaders of the seminary and me that our relationship was no longer one that enabled us to flourish together and I resigned from the faculty. This development made me acutely aware of the difficulties associated with doing postconservative and postmodern theology in churches and contexts typically associated with a more conservative outlook. More on this in a bit.

As Roger Olson points out in the prologue, the beginnings of postconservative evangelicalism were inspired to some extent by the emergence of postliberal theology. Postliberal theology is marked by two distinctive tendencies. The first is the rejection of philosophical foundationalism in its classic iteration and its attempt to find a neutral and ultimate vantage point

1. Grenz, *Revisioning Evangelical Theology*.
2. Grenz and Franke, *Beyond Foundationalism*.
3. Franke, *Character of Theology*.
4. Franke, *Manifold Witness*.

from which to assess the truth and coherence of theological statements. Nonfoundational approaches resist this effort, arguing the all theological ideas and formulations are situated and shaped by the contexts from which they emerge. They suggest that the notion of secure "foundations" from which to launch theological projects is a chimera, particularly espoused by those with social privilege and power as a means of justifying their epistemic and theological claims. This nonfoundational approach to theology leads to a second tendency, that of understanding Christian theology primarily as an act of communal self-description. Theology in this model is not so much the attempt to explain the "way things are" for everyone as it is the description of particular communal convictions.

One of the two most significant figures in the development of the postliberal perspective in theology is Hans Frei. His book on the relationship between the Bible and theology established him as one of the leading thinkers in the development of this conception of theology.[5] In another significant work, based on lectures and published after his untimely death, we are able to glimpse Frei's conception of the developments in theology during the twentieth-century and many of the ideas inculcated in his students that gave rise to the Yale School of Theology also known as postliberal theology.[6]

In this work Frei attempts to sort out the approaches of various modern theological alternatives to the perennial question of the relationship of theology to philosophy. He achieves this by posing a spectrum of opinion ranging from strong foundationalism, the belief that Christian theology is subordinate to the discipline of philosophy which sets forth the rules of correct discourse for all fields of knowledge, to strong non-foundationalism, the belief that Christian theology is an internal, contextual exercise in self-description that rejects in principle the notion of general, universally valid theories of knowledge that apply to all intellectual disciplines.

The question that Frei seeks to address concerns the very nature of the discipline: Is Christian theology primarily a philosophical discipline that is open to *external* description (that is, explication from outside the believing community) or is it primarily an *internal* act of Christian self-description (i.e., faith seeking understanding)? In the former, theology is subject to the current canons of reason in philosophy and is therefore best done in the context of the academy while the latter account suggests that theology is subject only to explicitly Christian discourse and is thus best pursued in the context of the church.

---

5. Frei, *Eclipse of Biblical Narrative*.
6. Frei, *Types of Christian Theology*.

In addition to Frei, the other formative influence on the shape and development of postliberal theology is fellow Yale theologian George Lindbeck. His work on nature, formation, and significance of doctrine and theology became one of the seminal texts for postliberal thought and made Lindbeck the other standard bearer of the movement.[7] He offers a program for theology that reverses the direction of conformity he thinks characterizes the revisionist paradigm of liberal theology.

Instead of seeking to contextualize the biblical message in such a way as to conform it to the conceptualities of the modern world, as in the revisionist program, Lindbeck calls for an approach to theology that seeks to redescribe and contextualize the modern world using the stories, symbols and categories of the Bible. From his perspective this allows Christian Scripture to play the lead role in the process of Christian culture formation, rather than the secular world whose thought forms are alien to those of the Bible. He calls this program "intratextual theology" and defines its task as follows: "Intratextual theology redescribes reality within the scriptural framework rather than translating Scripture into extrascriptural categories. It is the text, so to speak, which absorbs the world, rather than the world the text."[8]

Postconservative thinkers drew inspiration from the postliberal program and sought to reimagine evangelical theology, leading to divisions similar to those that divided postliberals from liberals. In attempting to describe these division, commentators identified a variety of taxonomies. Conservative theologian Millard Erickson identified postconservative thinkers as the "evangelical left."[9] He maintained that postconservative thought was in fact, merely a nuanced shift to the older liberal agenda. Wheaton College theologians, Timothy Phillips and Dennis Okholm suggested that the emergence of postliberalism accounted for the emerging tension within evangelical theology and identified three distinct groups. On the right are those who followed Carl Henry's established forms of evangelical theology and its rejection of all forms of liberalism. On the left are the postconservatives who linked their proposals with the postliberals. And in between are a group of moderates who shared common concerns with the postliberals while sharply questioning the postliberal agenda.[10]

Roger Olson identified the emergence of two loose coalitions among evangelical theologians. On one side are the "traditionalists," who uphold

7. Lindbeck, *Nature of Doctrine*.
8. Lindbeck, *Nature of Doctrine*, 118.
9. Erickson, *Evangelical Left*.
10. Phillips and Okholm, "Nature of Confession," 14–15.

"traditional interpretations and formulations as binding and normative" and tend "to look with suspicion upon any doctrinal revisions and new proposals arising out of theological reflection." On the other side are the "reformists," who value "the continuing process of constructive theology seeking new light breaking forth from God's word."[11] Olson provides a perceptive description of the attitudes of these two constituencies toward three significant issues: theological boundaries, the nature and progress of doctrine, and interaction with other theologies and culture in general.

Olson describes traditionalists as responding to the question of theological boundaries by viewing Christianity as a "bounded set" category and seeking to determine those who are "inside" the community and those who are on the "outside." They believe that the only way to avoid the slide into debilitating relativism and pluralism is to develop firm boundaries. Reformists, on the other hand, understand Christianity as a "centered-set" category. They insist that the boundaries remain open and relatively undefined and look to broad, central Christian commitments has providing coherence for their approach to theology.

As to the nature and progress of doctrine, Olson suggests that traditionalists emphasize the close identification of central doctrinal affirmations with what is directly taught in Scripture. Therefore, they tend to see doctrine as lying at the heart of the enduring essence of Christianity. For reformists, the enduring essence of Christianity is not to be found in the fallible doctrines of the church but rather in the work of God in the lives of human beings. Doctrinal and theological progress for the reformist involves the discovery of "new light" and better comprehension of the Christian faith through the careful study of the biblical narratives and their witness to the gospel in the context of various social and historical contexts and circumstances.

Because traditionalists understand established doctrines as communicating the essence of Christianity and therefore normative for Christian faith, they tend to view the theology produced those who do not share their particular convictions has being of little positive value in the development and formulation of theology. These theologies must be exposed as false and dangerous in order to properly safeguard the theological boundaries of the church. Hence, traditionalists tend to be resistant to the incorporation of culture as an integral part of the theological enterprise believing that doing so will lead to the sort of cultural accommodation they tend see in various forms of liberal theology. For reformists, the provisional and ongoing nature of theology means that we can learn from new theological perspectives

---

11. Olson, "Future of Evangelical Theology," 41.

that raise new and appropriate questions that may have been overlooked by traditional conservative formulations. These can stimulate fresh perspectives for theological reflection.

In the same way, reformists believe that they can learn from the study and examination of the thought forms and insights of contemporary culture. Since all truth is God's truth, theology must remain open to the contributions of any and all serious thinkers who honestly seek truth. Reformists emphasize dialogue as the proper approach to the ideas of the broader theological community and contemporary culture. This open stance is to culture and other theological voices and traditions is particularly important in addressing the failure of the church to listen to the voices of the marginalized and oppressed who have long been excluded from theological discourse.

From this perspective, the diverse voices represented in this volume can be seen as part of the broadly reformist paradigm with each attempting to reform and reframe theological interpretation so that it more appropriately reflects the good news of God's love for all people. This, at least to me, represents the flowering of postconservative thought beyond the evangelical world that spawned it.

Ironically, one of the general critiques of postliberals by liberals has been that they have become conservative, while conservatives have accused postconservatives of becoming liberal. However, it seems to me that some of the most fruitful conversation in contemporary theology has been and will continue to be between postliberals and postconservatives who share aspects of postmodern thought, particularly the linguistic and nonfoundational turns. George Hunsinger's words with respect to postliberals apply equally as well to postconservatives: "They can be recognized by a common set of goals, interests and commitments, especially their ecumenical interests and their desire to move beyond modernity's liberal/evangelical impasse. As made newly possible in our culture by the rise of nonfoundationalism they have begun to think through old questions like the truth of theological language, interdisciplinary relations, and religious pluralism."[12]

One final thought, as I read through the essays in this volume, I'm struck by the sense that postconservative theology is also progressive theology. While the label postconservative describes the context from which these various perspectives emerge in their various way, the label progressive helpfully describes, at least for me, what they are in search of. To the extent that this is true, it creates a challenge for postconservatives of all types who are regularly accused of simply adopting the liberal paradigm of the past

---

12. Hunsinger, "Postliberal Theology," 57.

and attempting to dress it up in new and fashionable ways while holding fast to its main contours.

In response to this, I believe the outlook of Gary Dorrien is especially helpful. In the final volume of his magisterial survey and interpretation of American liberal theology, he makes this important observation:

> Regarding the relation liberal and progressive, many religious thinkers discussed in this book employ these terms interchangeably. This usage has historical weight, because for many years liberalism *was the* progressive tradition in theology. The idea of a progressive Christianity was first imagined and developed by theological liberals. However, I believe that "progressive" should be treated as a wider category than "liberal" and that the fundamental divide in Christian theology is between various forms of conservative orthodoxy and progressivism. The latter includes liberal theology, so-called neo-orthodoxy (including its Catholic forms), liberation theology, and post-modern theology. The former includes fundamentalism, conservative evangelicalism, and conservative confessionalism. The conflict between these approaches to Christianity runs deep within and between denominations.[13]

In keeping with this perspective, I understand postconservative theology as a form of progressive theology that is committed to open-ended theological discourse and principled theological pluralism for the sake of bearing witness to, and living out God's love for the world. I believe this volume admirably displays the diversity of postconservative thought as it has developed over the past thirty years and hope that it will stimulate further thought along these lines in the years to come.

BIBLIOGRAPHY

Dorrien, Gary. *The Making of American Liberal Theology: Crisis, Irony, and Postmodernity 1950–2005*. Louisville, KY: Westminster John Knox, 2006.

Erickson, Millard J. *The Evangelical Left: Encountering Postconservative Evangelical Theology*. Grand Rapids: Baker, 1997.

Franke, John R. *The Character of Theology: An Introduction to Its Mature, Task, and Purpose*. Grand Rapids: Baker Academic, 2005.

Franke, John R. *Manifold Witness: The Plurality of Truth*. Nashville: Abingdon Press, 2009.

---

13. Dorrien, *Making of Modern Liberal Theology*, 6.

Frei, Hans W. *The Eclipse of Biblical Narrative: A Study in Eighteenth and Nineteenth Century Hermeneutics*. New Haven, CT: Yale University Press, 1974.

———. *Types of Christian Theology*. New Haven, CT: Yale University Press, 1992.

Grenz, Stanley J. *Revisioning Evangelical Theology: A Fresh Agenda for the twenty-first Century*. Downers Grove, IL: IVP Academic, 1993.

Grenz, Stanley J., and John R. Franke. *Beyond Foundationalism: Shaping Theology for a Postmodern in a Postmodern Context*. Louisville, KY: Westminster John Knox, 2001.

Hunsinger, George. "Postliberal Theology." In *The Cambridge Companion to Postmodern Theology*, edited by Kevin J. Vanhoozer, 42–57. Cambridge: Cambridge University Press, 2003.

Lindbeck, George. *The Nature of Doctrine: Religion and Theology in a Postliberal Age*. Philadelphia: Westminster, 1984.

Olson, Roger E. "The Future of Evangelical Theology." *Christianity Today* (February 9, 1998).

Phillips, Timothy R., and Dennis L. Okholm. "The Nature of Confession: Evangelicals and Postliberals." In *The Nature of Confession: Evangelicals and Postliberals in Conversation*, edited by Timothy R. Phillips and Dennis L. Okholm, 7–20. Downers Grove, IL: IVP Academic, 1996.

Afterword

Do Evangelical Biblical Practices Make Sense?

TELFORD WORK

"Postconservative" denotes a shared past more than a present. Our authors in this book seem to have little else in common. Some sound like *former* conservatives who are now progressives. (Whereas "postliberals" have turned out to be more *liberal* than *post*, "postconservatives" seem more *post* than *conservative*. Both camps may be adjuncts of dominant elite modern liberalism more than they realize.) Some are traditionalists who have found refreshment in premodern *resourcement*. Some have become disciples of a particular contemporary school or specialty, often from outside evangelicalism. Some, like me, are basically conservatives who for various reasons just don't completely fit one or another definition. Can some conclusion be drawn from our jumble of voices?

At a nondenominational church, I overheard a new parent talking to his pastor about infant versus believers' baptism. "What should we do?" he asked in complete innocence. "Just show me the Bible passages." On another occasion my evangelical college held a faculty exchange about homosexuality. When we saw how differently we appealed to the Bible, we held another faculty exchange on biblical hermeneutics. Evangelical Christians constantly go back to Scripture to answer our questions.

Back to Scripture?! Ha! In graduate school I could always count on my non-evangelical colleagues to cluck at such fundamentalist naïveté. It's not that simple! All observation is theory laden![1] Meaning is not transparent! The Bible must be read through tradition! My colleagues had a point. Our simple talk covers a range of evangelical biblical practices that is complex to

---

1. Simmons, chapter 1, "Phenomenological Hermeneutics," herein.

the point of contradiction. Evangelicalism's many camps, forms of life, biblical practices, and entangling alliances take our common respect for Scripture in different directions and produce a rich variety of evangelical "Bibles."

This volume's dizzying array of hermeneutical visions may leave readers bewildered and skeptical of a hermeneutical solution. But a pattern emerges from the apparent chaos as we survey the Bible's life and activity in our actual communities. This yields a set of metaphors: ways we treat the Bible as a certain kind of thing.[2] Each characteristic use involves distinctive hermeneutics and visions of Scripture's character and purpose. We generally use the Bible in multiple ways even if we have favorites.

Since at least Irenaeus the Bible has been an *ultimate narrator* locating everything in its story of creation, judgment, and redemption. Evangelicals often draw from this ancient vision, from Restorationist Alexander Campbell to creedalists who consider the ecumenical *credos* the Bible's most profound narrative summaries.[3] Both see us in the Bible's world more than vice versa. Figuration traces the deep continuities across the centuries of God's economy across biblical eras to the present and the end of the age.[4]

A distinct type sees the Bible as a *treasury of truth* about God and the world. Apologists insist that its histories really happened, moralists mine its lessons for universal ethical principles, and fundamentalists read its creation stories as literal accounts in accommodative premodern language. Grammatical-historical background helps readers distinguish cultural and cosmological assumptions about these ancient texts from the truths they properly convey.[5] Historical critics belong here too; they just treat the Bible as yielding its truth more stubbornly and partially. Thomas Jefferson is Charles Hodge with scissors.

A related variant understands the Bible as a *past and future timeline*. Ellen G. White and John Nelson Darby followed in Joachim of Fiore's footsteps. Adventists and Dispensationalists synthesize Scripture's genealogies, chronologies, and apocalyptic passages to decode the past and especially the future, often drawing figural connections as in the first two types.[6]

---

2. Thus, Ney's treatment of biblical language in "Figural Hermeneutics" (chapter 40) applies to the Bible itself.

3. Moore, chapter 14, "Creedal Hermeneutics."

4. For continuities across the Testaments see Byassee, chapter 42, "Christ-Shaped Hermeneutics." Literary and narrative approaches to Scripture are often congenial: for example, Peel's chapter 5, "Literary Theory and Hermeneutics."

5. Parry, chapter 38, "Biblical Cosmology Hermeneutics," especially its conclusion.

6. So Byassee's "Christ-Shaped Hermeneutics" might help a present-day Joachim of Fiore as much as an Augustinian amillennialist.

"Evangelical" once meant "Protestant." Protestants hear the Bible as a *judge*—God's designated canonical authority, to be heard and trusted. Scripture proclaims our relationship with God, particularly our forensic condemnation and justification. Its covenantal and kerygmatic passages are Lutheran and Reformed highlights.

Evangelicalism owes its name not just to the gospel but to practices that share it with new audiences, or old audiences in more persuasive ways.[7] Like William Tyndale, translators render the Bible in the languages of the nations, and like William Carey, missionaries convey its good news. Indigenous churches receive Scripture with the Holy Spirit's power and enculturate it. For all these the Bible is *a means of mission*.

Witness evokes opposition. Those who bear Jesus's good news meet the world's defensiveness and enmity towards its Savior. For these the Bible is also *a means of power*. Guided by its conflict narratives and armed with its ever-sharp Word, armies of spiritual warriors—Pentecostals, charismatics, therapists, liberationists—wield the Bible to advance Christ's victory and pray it to wage spiritual warfare, overcome adversaries, defeat addictions, and heal relationships. Charles Fox Parham and Martin Luther King Jr. are two famous commanding officers.[8]

To receive Scripture's judgments with faith is to become God's new creation. Those whom the Bible convicts and changes learn it's *a means of conversion*. Wesleyans, revivalists, and sanctificationists encourage us to follow the Bible's saints in taking on lives of grace, forgiveness, and holiness.

Especially in the patristic, Catholic, and "Anabaptist" traditions, the Bible is *God's word to the church*. Biblical rituals structure these communities, their liturgical calendars, and their life events. Benedict developed a biblical ethic for his rule; Thomas Cranmer left the Bible at the heart of England's reformed Sunday liturgy; Menno Simons centered ethics in the Sermon on the Mount and other passages most directly relevant to the life of disciples. Key to Baptist missionary David Watson's phenomenally successful disciple-making strategy is God teaching through biblical passages that are heeded and shared.[9]

Many find our own story there, making the Bible *a mirror of personal life experience*. Augustine pioneered the reading of Scripture for self-understanding. Ignatius of Loyola took that in one direction, while the Reformation's Spiritualists, Pietists, later modern individualists, and socially

---

7. Caldwell, chapter 24, "Intercultural Hermeneutics."

8. Section 3's liberationist chapters present one cluster of varieties of this metaphor, Mather's chapter 13 "Spirit Hermeneutics" another.

9. Watson and Watson, *Contagious Disciple Making*.

marginal as well as dominant groups took others.[10] Evangelicals practice identifying with biblical figures and voices, especially its psalmists.[11]

We evangelicals, then, are "a factory of Bibles." We produce different visions of Scripture in the overlapping communities in which the Bible governs Christian life. Our distinctive metaphors for Scripture generate correlated images for everything.[12] For a case study, consider how *Islam* means different things to different evangelicals in ways that reflect our biblical practices.

Where the Bible is *a treasury of truth*, apologetics establish its veracity and document its detractors' errors, and Islam becomes *a false ideology*. R. C. Sproul and Abdul Saleeb contrast Muslim and Christian teachings on Scripture, God the Father, Trinity, sin, salvation, Christ's crucifixion, and his deity.[13] Saleeb and Norman Geisler offer a Christian response to orthodox Islamic doctrines, then defend the orthodox Christian perspective.[14]

Focus and rhetoric shift profoundly where the Bible is *a means of mission*. Here Islam is *a fallow mission field*.[15] Ron Rhodes resists the urge to convince Muslims about Trinity or Christ's divinity. Instead he offers conversation seasoned with leading questions that engage Islamic imagination in order to lead Muslims beyond it—and into Scripture and its world. "Do not hesitate to quote from the Bible," Rhodes advises. "Remember, 'Faith comes from hearing, and hearing from the Word of Christ.'"[16] An Indonesian disciple-maker I know mentions the Quran's allusions to God's six-day creation, then invites curious Muslims to learn what happened over those days. The Quran becomes a bridge to Genesis 1–2's very different picture of humanity made to represent God in creation.

These two approaches apparently contradict. Geisler demands that we acknowledge the problems in Muslim faith, while Rhodes treats it as persuasive and powerful. Apologists tend to defend the Bible defensively whereas intercultural and insider missionaries promote it. We disagree and talk past one another in part because we treat Scripture differently.

Where the Bible is *a means of conversion*, Islam—with whose categories Muslims must first interpret it—becomes *a basis for conversion*.

---

10. E.g., Kirk-Duggan, chapter 32, "Womanist Hermeneutics."

11. Rice's chapter 47, "Trauma Hermeneutics" shows that those experiences may not offer transcendent meaning.

12. Figuration is a natural disposition of evangelical interpreters worldwide: Ney, "Figural Hermeneutics."

13. Sproul and Saleeb, *Dark Side of Islam*.

14. Geisler and Saleeb, *Answering Islam*, 8.

15. McKinzie, "Missional Hermeneutics."

16. Rhodes, *Reasoning from the Scriptures with Muslims*, 280.

Evangelical missionaries love giving Muslims the Bible. Scripture's voices are often closer to Muslim worlds than western ones. They proclaim the faith apart from later distortions of Constantinianism, crusades, imperialism, and globalization. Reading the Bible is how my Indonesian friend came to faith in Isa al-Masih. It convinced an Indian Shi'i who knew Christ as the highest prophet that he was Savior and Lord.[17] The undeterred Jesus of Scripture bypasses readers' objections and engages interlocutors on his own terms. Through the Bible's patient, suffering witness the Jesus of Christian faith gets a hearing. Scripture's lines of silent text "plant the Word of God in [Muslim] hearts."[18] They absorb readers' counterarguments without retaliating, allowing roots to grow and shoots to spring up.

No one metaphor seems to encompass or govern all the others. How can Geisler's false ideology be a tutor for the gospel? Yet it is.[19] How can biblical texts addressed to churches speak to untutored Muslims? Yet they do. The Bible's translatability into languages and categories even of rivals reveals Islam to be *a language for faith*, a platform for evangelism. Speaking into every culture, Scripture manifests the universality of Christ's reign and the catholicity of his body.[20] So the Bible is also a versatile *hermeneutical bridge between communities*.

The academy is one such community. In my circles the Bible is *an object of fascination*—an ambiguous image. Scholars today increasingly commit themselves to "making readings" of Scripture as *a means of social action*.[21] Yet even as the Bible funds our theological entertainments and projects, its wilder side obstructs our pursuits, whispers answers to other concerns, and shifts thinking and scholarship into uncomfortable territory. Scripture in its rawness holds the authority to bypass centuries of discourse and advance its own agendas.

What happens then? Apologists expect Scripture to overcome critique, whereas missionaries and new disciples expect it to nurture Christian faith dialogically. The reality is less predictable and more dramatic. In the

---

17. Hanna, *True Path*, 21.

18. Safa, *Inside Islam*, 122.

19. So apologetics, not always wedded to modernist assumptions, is vital to many evangelicals' testimonies, including mine. Contrast Penner, chapter 9, "Hermeneutics and the End of Apologetics."

20. Caldwell, "Intercultural Hermeneutics."

21. Neusch's chapter 18, "Nonviolent Hermeneutics" critiques using the Bible to license violence for some goal, then advocates harnessing biblical strands to pursue nonviolence. Macallan's chapter 21, "Embodied Hermeneutics" associates biblical themes with contemporary political *desiderata*. Hunt's chapter 22 "Ecological Hermeneutics" "makes a reading" shaped by ecological concerns.

wilderness Deuteronomy was Jesus's means of power against the devil. Charismatics today subdue spiritual forces and deliver the oppressed with Bible passages in power encounters and intercessory prayer. Where the Bible is *a means of power and presence*, Islam becomes *a domain of principalities and powers* that dominate Muslims and harass Christians.

Is Islam itself one of those spiritual forces? Franklin Graham provoked widespread ire and embarrassment for his 2001 comments that Islam is "a very evil and wicked religion," but his judgment is echoed by nearly every popular evangelical book on Islam. Hal Lindsey sees Islam as an eschatological enemy of God's people.[22] "Islam denies the deity, death and resurrection of Jesus; therefore, it is an antichrist religion," says Reza Safa, who calls Islam "Satan's weapon to oppose God, His plan and His people."[23] A speaker in the 2019 documentary "Sheep among Wolves" says Islam manifests the spirit of Haman (Esth 3:6). What does all this say about evangelicalism? Is the Bible *hate speech*, and Islam *one of its targets*? The "fundamentalist" Bible is often so characterized.[24]

Before jumping to conclusions, consider the spirit of the 2002 Veggie Tales film *Jonah*. God points Jonah, a comfortable moralist, to a map of the Middle East with Nineveh off in a forbidding corner that astute viewers would recognize as the northern no-fly-zone of Saddam Hussein's Iraq. The film's wisest character is a prophetic caterpillar named Khalil (as in Gibran). While Muslims were killing and enslaving Christians in the Sudan and south Asia and as George W. Bush's America was preparing for war in Iraq, these evangelical Christians *inserted an Arab prophet* to stress the irony of grace that pervades Jonah, and young families came in droves to see it. Bicoastal elitists may scoff at fundamentalist Midwesterners, but one of 2002's most introspective and culturally subversive films came from the heart of American conservative evangelicalism.

After all, where the Bible is *a judge* it renders God's dialectical verdict of *apocalyptic judgment and loving affirmation*, and Islam is *an object of both*. Graham's organization poured relief supplies into Bosnia, Kosovo, Sudan, Afghanistan, Turkey, and Iraq. Graham later said that "if we obey the teachings of Jesus we will love all Muslims."[25] Safa, a former Shi'i Muslim, introduces his book by forbidding readers to reach spiteful or resentful conclusions about Muslims, who "in general are very loving and hospitable."[26]

---

22. Lindsey, *Everlasting Hatred*.
23. Safa, *Inside Islam*, 17–18.
24. Section 3's "Contextual Hermeneutics" voices such complaints.
25. Graham, "My View of Islam."
26. Safa, *Inside Islam*, 9–10.

Missionary outsiders and Muslim background believers discover that Jesus has preceded them in dreams and signs with his mercy, and love and forgive their persecutors. Uncompromising negativity and unconditional love exist side by side in most evangelical analyses of Islam.[27]

These complexities are natural, not formidable hermeneutical challenges. The Bible narrates the cosmos, the nations, Israel, and human lives from their beginnings through Christ's cross to their final ends. In that story we discover not only God but also ourselves[28]—and everyone else, for where the Bible is *the ultimate narrator* of all histories, Islam is *a narrative figure*.

Which one though? I am persuaded that Muslims are not best understood as Genesis's Ishmaelites, the prophets' enemy empires, Acts' God-fearing *goyim*, Jerusalem's Sanhedrin or its church's cultural conservatives, Haman, Revelation's false prophet, nor even the Gospels' Pharisees or Samaritans. They are closer to us, right in the middle of the story. In my humble opinion, Islam is *Simon bar-Jonah*. The oft-perplexed fisherman is a walking contradiction: an adversary, a beneficiary, and a trustee of God's grace all in one. Simon's difficulty is not that he has the wrong God or wrong Messiah, but that he construes the right God and Messiah in the wrong way (Matt 16:13–28). Islam is not the blasphemous idolatry of a Herod or Caesar but the opposition of a follower who rebukes Jesus for promising suffering. All our partial accounts of Islam fit Peter's character. And if Islam *is* satanic, it's no less satanic than the rest of us who trail our Lord without picking up our crosses. "*Every spirit* that does not confess Jesus . . . is the spirit of antichrist . . . the spirit of error" (1 John 4:3–4, 6). Happily, more Muslims are finally beginning truly to recognize their Masih.[29]

Islam-as-Simon-Peter is not a metaphor I found elsewhere; I arrived at it myself. Disagree if you like. How is such a conclusion made, or evaluated? David Yeago argues that understanding the Bible involves judgments that cannot be made through "Scripture alone," hermeneutical technique, or formal method. True understanding must appreciate "the *force and implications* of what the text says." This requires resources "embedded in the form of ecclesial life."[30] Using Scripture well *both requires and cultivates* healthy community, obedience, exposure, training, skill, and virtue. Imitating

---

27. By contrast, approaches such as Wandinger's chapter 10 "Dramatic Hermeneutics," Bahl and Oord's chapter 16 "Open and Relational Hermeneutics," Neusch's "Nonviolent Hermeneutics," and Bashaw's chapter 41, "Scapegoat Hermeneutics" all reflect a contemporary trend in which one dramatic theme seems to eclipse another.

28. Kallenberg, *Live to Tell*, 104–19.

29. Garrison, *Wind in the House of Islam*.

30. Yeago, "Bible," 52, 56.

Peter's expanding fellowship in Acts 2:40–47, Muslim background believers study the Bible together in discovery groups that become networked house churches. These communities express Scripture's messages from within cultures in which the word takes root in discipling communities that multiply under pressure. They learn that where Scripture is *God's word to the church*, Islam is *a social order both oppressive and supportive of Christ's body*.

We don't really fabricate or choose these metaphors for Scripture; evangelical images of Scripture emerge as our biblical practices shape us. Our varieties of interpretation manifest our facets and varieties of evangelicalism.

Then is the Bible whatever we make it? Does all this variety allow one coherent account of Islam or anything else, or just a hodgepodge of readers' perspectives?[31] Do evangelical biblical practices make *sense*?

Not always. R. R. Reno blames the weaknesses of mainline Protestant churches not on techniques such as historical criticism but a deeper pattern of modern and postmodern distancing that coopts them. "The very core of Christian life and practice is alienated from the Bible," he says, in churches where the plain sense of Scripture is "ruled out" as a norm for church discipline, family life, worship, or evangelism.[32]

This is increasingly true among evangelicals—as this volume demonstrates. Our debates shift from the content of Scripture to hermeneutics, history, philosophy, and politics as we seek other ground on which to justify our interpretations. Among us too the Bible is "the site of contest and conflict rather than our instrument of adjudication."[33] Not because of hermeneutical complexity; that's been with us all along. Rather, Scripture can become our adversary.[34] We oppose God's word when we use it as reactionaries or revolutionaries rather than apostles, as an instrument of our own wills rather than as Holy Scripture (Matt 22:29, 1 Cor 3:1–3, Gal 4:21; cf. 2 Pet 1:4).

We're in good company. Where the Bible is *a mirror of life experience*,[35] Islam is also *Saul of Tarsus*. Many Muslim- as well as Hindu-background believers told missionary Lesslie Newbigin that they identified with Paul. "At the point of crisis Jesus appeared to them as one who threatened all that was most sacred to them. In the light of their experience of life in Christ

---

31. So Merold Westphal's foreword might suggest.
32. Reno, *In the Ruins*, 90, 136–37.
33. Reno, *In the Ruins*, 136.
34. And if we respond poorly to its obstinate challenges, possibly an ironic Girardian scapegoat, cf. Bashaw's "Scapegoat Hermeneutics."
35. Gschwandtner, chapter 2, "Postmodern Hermeneutics" and Raschke, chapter 3, "Deconstructive Hermeneutics."

they now look back and see that he has safeguarded and fulfilled it."[36] Our adversarial Bible voices the familiar contradiction of grace. To respond to it as Saul did invites what Richard Hays calls "conversion of the imagination" with which Paul read Scripture in the new light of Jesus Christ.[37]

When we evangelicals are in trouble and prone to looking outside the tradition for quick fixes to our problems, Yeago's advice is good for us too. Greater technical expertise, inventive hermeneutics, and even just knowing the texts better will not solve our problems. "Renewal of the church requires . . . renewed practices of being the church, and chief among these are practices of understanding and applying the scriptures."[38] Back to Scripture, we might say!

Yet Reno's advice is just as important. He describes three kinds of distance between readers and Scripture. Biblical scholars have acknowledged *historical* distances between themselves and their ancient texts at least since Origen. And philosophers and theologians constantly wrestle with the *metaphysical* limits of human language. Reno diagnoses our most serious problem as *spiritual* distance: "we are unwilling to enter into the spiritual discipline necessary to travel the distance between what we hear and what is said."[39] It is not enough to be more skillful scribes; we must become scribes *trained for the kingdom of heaven* (Matt 13:52), by obeying Scripture as *our spiritual disciplinarian.*[40]

Many would use traditional liturgies[41] and figural exegesis[42] for that. I prefer the ways of disciple-making movements (DMM) that are the little-told missionary story of our century.[43] DMM's "naïve realism," biblicism, and practical inerrancy may not attract many postconservatives, but its commitment to obey God's biblical teachings and commands is proving orders of magnitude more fruitful globally than legacy traditions in terms of kingdom transformation.[44] DMM practices unsettle some conservative and

---

36. Newbigin, *Open Secret*, 177.
37. Hays, *Conversion of the Imagination*.
38. Yeago, "Bible," 93.
39. Reno, *In the Ruins*, 180.
40. The canon apprentices readers in Starling's chapter 44, "Apprenticeship Hermeneutics."
41. Edie's chapter 8, "Convictional Hermeneutics" describes James K. A. Smith on liturgy.
42. Along lines found in MacGregor's chapter 12, "Sacramental Hermeneutics."
43. Coles and Parks, *24:14—A Testimony to All Peoples* and Farah, *Motus Dei*.
44. Here the "nurturant" and "authoritative" from Sanders's introduction do not pull apart, because sociological dualisms do not describe our Triune Authority who gives and sustains our life. Besides, DMM's power structures are flatter than traditional

evangelical assumptions, but they spring from evangelicalism's devotional and missional heart rather than being grafted in. They even harmonize forces that often strain traditional evangelicalism: service and evangelism, spiritual devotion and action, social margins and centers, canon and charismata, spirits and materiality, and persecution and establishment. They're an emerging form *of* conservative evangelicalism rather than a successor.

Our different Bibles don't just artefacts of modern deficiencies, indiscipline, division, sin, or hypocrisy. They *do* manifest such confusions, of course; we fall short. Yet the multiplicity of evangelical metaphors and correlative images also springs from our movement's healthy heart. It reflects our mixed Calvinist, Wesleyan, Pietist, Baptist, and Pentecostal heritages. It enlivens our different reading communities: When we read with strangers, Scripture is a means of mission. With brethren, God addresses his people through it. In solitude, it mirrors our souls. Against opponents, it witnesses and defends. Its timeline and geography place our own generations and peoples. In our Lord's presence, it judges and releases. Among scholars, it fascinates. With allies, it reassures.[45] Our Bibles are what they are—the Bible is what it is—in the many roles Scripture plays in God's mysterious economy of salvation whose mission seeks the lost, addresses us, displays us in its mirror, judges and forgives us, converts us, conquers our sin, renarrates us, acquaints us with one another, and equips us for its future.[46] Rather than contradiction I prefer another term: reconciliation, through the word's power and grace.

BIBLIOGRAPHY

Coles, Dave, and Stan Parks, eds. *24:14—A Testimony to All Peoples*. Spring, TX: Independently published, 2019.

Farah, Warrick, ed. *Motus Dei: The Movement of God to Disciple the Nations*. Pasadena: Carey, 2021.

Garrison, David. *A Wind in the House of Islam*. Monument: WIGTake, 2014.

Geisler, Norman, and Abdul Saleeb. *Answering Islam: The Crescent in Light of the Cross*. Grand Rapids: Baker, 2012.

Graham, Franklin. "My View of Islam." *The Wall Street Journal* (December 9, 2001).

---

church hierarchies.

45. Not all these audiences are primary. Some aren't even necessary nor particularly helpful. So not all this variety need be honored or accommodated.

46. Along the lines of Mather's Spirit hermeneutics, as well as David Stuart's chapter 39, "Penultimate Hermeneutics."

Hanna, Mark. *The True Path: Seven Muslims Make Their Greatest Discovery*. Colorado Springs: International Doorways, 1975.

Hays, Richard. *The Conversion of the Imagination*. Grand Rapids: Eerdmans, 2005.

Kallenberg, Brad J. *Live to Tell: Evangelism in a Postmodern World*. Grand Rapids: Brazos, 2002.

Lindsey, Hal. *The Everlasting Hatred: The Roots of Jihad*. Murrieta: Oracle House, 2002.

Newbigin, Lesslie. *The Open Secret*. Grand Rapids: Eerdmans, 1995.

Reno, R. R. *In the Ruins of the Church*. Grand Rapids: Brazos, 2002.

Rhodes, Ron. *Reasoning from the Scriptures with Muslims*. Eugene, OR: Harvest, 2002.

Safa, Reza F. *Inside Islam: Exposing and Reaching the World of Islam*. Lake Mary: FrontLine, 1996.

Sproul, R. C., and Abdul Saleeb. *The Dark Side of Islam*. Wheaton: Crossway, 2003.

Watson, David, and Paul Watson. *Contagious Disciple Making*. Nashville: Nelson, 2014.

Yeago, David. "The Bible." In *Knowing the Triune God*, edited by James J. Buckley and David S. Yeago, 49–93. Grand Rapids: Eerdmans, 2001.

About the Contributors

Sammy Alfaro is Professor of Theology at Grand Canyon University. He received a PhD in Theology (2008) from Fuller Theological Seminary (Pasadena, California). Books include *Divino Compañero: toward a Hispanic Pentecostal Christology* and the co-edited *Pentecostal and Charismatic Movements in Latin America and among Latinas/os*.

Chad Bahl is a DThM candidate at Northwind Theological Seminary, where he studies Open and Relational Theology. Bahl is the author of *God Unbound: An Evangelical Reconsiders Tradition in Search of Truth* and the editor of *Deconstructing Hell: Open and Relational Responses to the Doctrine of Eternal Conscious Torment*.

Gregory A. Boyd (PhD, Princeton Theological Seminary) is founder and Senior Pastor of Woodland Hills Church (Maplewood, Minnesota) and adjunct Professor of Theology at Northern Seminary. He has worked in the areas of theology, apologetics, the problem of evil, Christian spirituality, church and culture, and most recently, in developing a cross-centered hermeneutics.

Jason Byassee (PhD, Duke University) is the senior minister of Timothy Eaton Memorial Church in Toronto. He previously held the Butler Chair in Homiletics and Biblical Hermeneutics at the Vancouver School of Theology. His work in Christ-shaped hermeneutics began with his book *Praise Seeking Understanding: Reading the Psalms with Augustine* (2007), continued with his commentary *Psalms 101–150* (2018) and came to fruition with his *Surprised by Jesus Again: Reading the Bible with the Communion of Saints* (2019).

ABOUT THE CONTRIBUTORS

Larry W. Caldwell (PhD, Fuller Theological Seminary) is Professor of Intercultural Studies and Bible Interpretation at Sioux Falls Seminary/Kairos University. He has taught worldwide, including over twenty years at Asian Theological Seminary, Manila. His research interests include ethnohermeneutics, hermeneutics of the New Testament, and cultural exegesis. His publications include *Doing Bible Interpretation*.

Megan K. DeFranza (PhD, Marquette University) is an author and filmmaker. Her works include *Sex Difference in Christian Theology: Male, Female, and Intersex in the Image of God*; *Two Views on Homosexuality, the Bible, and the Church*; *Understanding Transgender Identities*; "Stories of Intersex and Faith."

Fred P. Edie is Associate Professor for the Practice of Christian Education at Duke Divinity School/Duke University. He earned a PhD at Emory University, and partnered with Mark Lamport to write *Nurturing Faith: A Practical Theology for Educating Christians* (2021).

Rodolfo Galvan Estrada III (PhD, Regent University) is the Assistant Professor of the New Testament at Vanguard University. His research focuses on race and ethnicity in the Greco-Roman world, the Gospel of John, and Latino/a readings of the New Testament.

Brian Felushko (ThD cand, Northwind Theological Seminary) has served as a teaching pastor for more than 35 years in churches in the US and Canada. His current research is in open and relational theology for a doctoral treatise titled, *An Open and Relational Reading of Genesis 1–11*.

Jacqueline N. Grey (PhD, Charles Sturt University) is professor of Biblical Studies at Alphacrucis University College in Australia, and research fellow at the University of South Africa. She recently co-edited *Key Approaches to Biblical Ethics* (2021).

Christina M. Gschwandtner (PhD, University of Durham; PhD, DePaul University) teaches Continental Philosophy of Religion at Fordham University. She is author of *Degrees of Givenness: On Saturation in Jean-Luc Marion*, *Marion and Theology*, *Welcoming Finitude: Toward a Phenomenology of Orthodox Liturgy*, and *Reading Religious Ritual with Ricœur: Between Fragility and Hope*, besides many articles at the intersection of phenomenology and religion.

T. Christopher Hoklotubbe (ThD, New Testament and Early Christianity, Harvard; Choctaw & Settler) serves as an Assistant Professor of Religion at Cornell College (Iowa) as well as an adjunct professor with NAIITS: An Indigenous Learning Community.

Cherryl Hunt (PhD, Biological Sciences; PhD, Theology, University of Exeter, UK) trains ministers and others at South West Ministry Training Course, Exeter. Her theological publications cover the use of the Bible in environmental ethics and congregational engagement with Christian Scriptures.

Wemimo Jaiyesimi (PhD candidate, theology and ethics, Baylor University) recently published "The Recovery of Human Dignity in Protestant Christianity and Its Ethical Implication" (with Paul Martens) *Religions* 14 (2023) 425.

Yung Suk Kim (PhD, Vanderbilt University) is Professor of New Testament and Early Christianity at Virginia Union University. He is the author of 20 books, including *Monotheism, Biblical Traditions, and Race Relations* (2022), *How to Read Paul* (2021), and has edited *Paul's Gospel, Empire, Race, and Ethnicity* (2023). Kim serves as a member of the Bible Translation and Utilization Committee that oversees the NRSV, RSV, and NRSVue.

Cheryl A. Kirk-Duggan (PhD, Baylor University), retired from Shaw University Divinity School (North Carolina), and an Ordained Elder in the Christian Methodist Episcopal Church, is author of over 25 books and CEO for Dr. Cheryl Enterprises, where she focuses on grief journeys and writing excellence. Her related volumes include *Baptized Rage, Transformed Grief*, and *Breaking Free to Write: From Fear to Finish*.

Kirk R. MacGregor (PhD, University of Iowa) is Associate Professor of Philosophy and Religion and Department Chair at McPherson College in McPherson, Kansas. He is the author of *Contemporary Theology: An Introduction* and *A Molinist-Anabaptist Systematic Theology*.

Hannah Mather (PhD, London School of Theology) is Honorary Fellow of the Edward Cadbury Centre for the Public Understanding of Religion, University of Birmingham, and a Certified Professional Coach. She is author of *The Interpreting Spirit: Spirit, Scripture, and Interpretation in the Renewal Tradition* (2020).

Elizabeth Mburu (PhD, Southeastern Baptist Theological Seminary) is Associate Professor of New Testament and Greek at Africa International University, Kenya and regional coordinator of Langham Literature, Anglophone Africa. Her latest book is *African Hermeneutics* (2019).

ABOUT THE CONTRIBUTORS

Greg McKinzie (PhD, Fuller Theological Seminary) is an adjunct faculty member of Lipscomb University (Nashville, Tennessee) and the executive editor of *Missio Dei: A Journal of Missional Theology and Praxis*. His publications focus on missiology, missional theology, philosophical hermeneutics, and theological interpretation of Scripture.

Mark Moore (PhD, Liberty University) is Professor of Theology at William Jessup University in California. His research interests include creedal theology, racial justice, mercy, and theological contextualization. His publications include *The Rhythm of Prayer* and *Early Creedal Formulations*, and *Theological Discourse: Toward a Systematic Understanding of Theology Via the Creedal Process*.

Jared Neusch (PhD, King's College London, UK) lectures at St. Mellitus College in London, teaching Greek and a variety of other topics in New Testament. His research interests include Paul (with special interest in Galatians), nonviolence, soteriology, and Christocentric hermeneutics.

David Ney (ThD, Wycliffe College, University of Toronto) is Associate Professor of Church History at Trinity School for Ministry (Pennsylvania). His primary research areas are the history of biblical interpretation and the Church of England of the eighteenth century. He is co-editor of *All Thy Lights Combine: Figural Reading in the Anglican Tradition* and author of *The Quest to Save the Old Testament: Mathematics, Hieroglyphics, and Providence in Enlightenment England*.

Thomas Jay Oord (PhD, Claremont Graduate University) directs the doctoral program in Open and Relational Theology at Northwind Theological Seminary and the Center for Open and Relational Theology. An award-winning author, professor, and speaker, Oord has published 30+ books, including *Open and Relational Theology* and *The Uncontrolling Love of God*.

Robin Parry (PhD, University of Glouchestershire) is an academic book editor for Wipf & Stock Publishers and a priest in the Church of England, whose ministry is directed towards fostering a more creation-attuned spirituality. He has published on various biblical and theological issues, including *The Biblical Cosmos: A Pilgrim's Guide to the Weird and Wonderful World of the Bible* (2014).

Oliver Peel is a PhD candidate at King's College London, focusing on the theology of George Herbert's poetry. With a background in both literature and theology, he seeks to bring these disciplines into dialogue, with a firm belief that they are mutually informative and enriching.

ABOUT THE CONTRIBUTORS

Myron Bradley Penner (PhD, University of Edinburgh) is Rector of St. Paul's Anglican Church in Edmonton, Alberta. Most recently his publications include: "Christian Witness in a World Full of Fascists," in *Theological Reflections: Eastern European Journal of Theology* 20 (2022); "Postmodern Christianity," in *Handbook of Contemporary Christianity in the United States*, edited by Mark A. Lamport. His book is *The End of Apologetics: Christian Witness in a Postmodern World* (2011).

B. Keith Putt (PhD, Rice University) is Professor of Philosophy at Samford University in Birmingham, Alabama. Among his recent publications are "Debating the Art of an Anatheistic Wager" in *Research in Phenomenology*, "Structuralism" in *The Encyclopedia of Philosophy of Religion*, and "The Symbol Gives Rise to Faith (Perhaps)" in *A Companion to Ricœur's* The Symbolism of Evil.

Carl Raschke (PhD, Harvard University) is Professor of Philosophy of Religion at the University of Denver and University Lecturer for 2020–2021. He is the author of over 20 books on philosophy, religion, theology, and culture who is internationally recognized for having originally introduced the concept of "deconstruction" to theology and the study of religion.

Thomas E. Reynolds (PhD, Vanderbilt University) is Associate Professor of Theology at Emmanuel College, of Victoria University in the University of Toronto and the Toronto School of Theology. His teaching and research interests include disability theologies, hermeneutics and theological method, and interreligious dialogue. His publications include *Vulnerable Communion: A Theology a Disability and Hospitality*.

Richard Rice (PhD, University of Chicago Divinity School) is Emeritus Professor of Religion, Loma Linda University. He has taught a range of courses in Christian theology and philosophy of religion. His publications include various books and articles on the openness of God, the relation of faith and reason, and the problem of suffering.

Megan C. Roberts (PhD, McMaster Divinity College) is Assistant Professor of Old Testament at Prairie College, Three Hills, Alberta. Her research focuses on memory negotiation and formation in Isaiah and the intersection of memory studies and the Old Testament.

J. Aaron Simmons (PhD, Vanderbilt University) is Professor of Philosophy at Furman University. His authored and edited books include *God and the Other*, *Kierkegaard's God and the Good Life*, *The New Phenomenology*, *Christian Philosophy*, and *Reexamining Deconstruction and Determinate Religion*.

ABOUT THE CONTRIBUTORS

David Starling (PhD, University of Sydney) is Professor of New Testament and Chief Academic Officer at Morling College in Sydney, Australia. His publications on New Testament exegesis and hermeneutical method include *Hermeneutics as Apprenticeship* and *Not My People: Gentiles as Exiles in Pauline Hermeneutics*, as well as commentaries on Ephesians, Colossians, and 1 Corinthians.

David Stuart (PhD candidate, University of St. Andrews) researches theological hermeneutics and epistemologies, particularly regarding their relation to Christology and ontology. He has wider research interests in modern theology, fundamentalist theologies, and interreligious dialogue.

Chris Tilling is Head of Research and Senior Lecturer in New Testament Studies at St. Mellitus College and is particularly interested in historical-critical New Testament scholarship and its interface with systematic theology Chris co-authored How *God Became Jesus* (2014). He is presently co-editing the *T&T Clark Handbook of Christology* (2022), and writing the NICNT commentary on the Second Epistle to the Corinthians (2023). Forthcoming, also, is his *Reading Romans* for the Cascade Companions series.

Jonathan Tran (PhD, Duke University) is Associate Professor of Great Texts (Theology) at Baylor University where he is also Associate Dean of Honors College. He is author of *Asian Americans and the Spirit of Racial Capitalism* (2022) and other books and articles focused on language and theology.

John H. Walton (PhD, Hebrew Union College) is Professor of Old Testament at Wheaton College. His nearly 30 books, include commentaries, reference works, textbooks, monographs, and popular academic works ("Lost World" books). He was the Old Testament general editor for the *Cultural Backgrounds Study Bible* and the author of *Ancient Near Eastern Thought and the Old Testament*.

Nikolaus Wandinger (Dr. theol, Universität Innsbruck, Austria), is associated professor of dogmatic theology. His research interests are the application and further development of the approach of Dramatic Theology, as initiated by Raymund Schwager SJ. Special areas of application so far have been Christian anthropology, soteriology and eschatology, as well as the theological interpretation of some works of popular fiction.

Karen Strand Winslow (PhD, University of Washington) is a professor of Biblical Studies at Azusa Pacific Seminary. Her publications focus on the Hebrew Bible, Judaism, Scripture formation, women in religion, the science and theology dialogue, and ethnicity and identity formation and include *Imagining Equity: The Gifts of Christian Feminist Theology* (2021).

K. K. Yeo (PhD, Northwestern University) is Harry R. Kendall Professor of New Testament at Garrett-Evangelical Seminary and affiliate professor at the Department of Asian Languages and Cultures at Northwestern University, Evanston. His publications on critical studies of Bible and cultures include *What Has Jerusalem to Do with Beijing?* (2018), and the editor of *The Oxford Handbook of the Bible in China* (2021).

H. Daniel Zacharias (PhD, Highland Theological College/Aberdeen; Cree-Anishinaabe) serves as the Professor of New Testament Studies at Acadia Divinity College in Mi'kma'ki (Nova Scotia) as well as an adjunct professor with NAIITS: An Indigenous Learning Community.

Jens Zimmermann (PhD, University of British Columbia; PhD, Johannes Gutenberg University, Germany) holds the J. I. Packer Chair for Theology at Regent College, Canada. His publications cover the fields of continental philosophy (philosophical hermeneutics), theology, and literary theory. His works include *Hermeneutics: A Very Short Introduction*, *Humanism and Religion: A Call for the Renewal of Western Culture*, and *Dietrich Bonhoeffer's Christian Humanism*.

Index of Names and Subjects

1 and 2 Thessalonians (books of), 404
1 John (book of), 398, 407
1 Kings (book of), 404
1 Peter (book of), 398, 406
2 Corinthians (book of), 399, 404, 440

Abel, 623, 624, 626, 627
Abelard, Peter, 401
Abraham, 368, 370, 371, 389, 391, 439, 517, 536, 537, 577, 636
Absalom, 683
Abyssinian Baptist Church, 467
Achaia, 547
Achley, Donovan, III, 523
Acts, book of, 382–83, 387–89, 409
  narrative of, 281, 289, 616
Adam and Eve, 512, 517, 518, 606, 627, 638, 640, 644,
Adam, A. K. M., 541
Adinkra's ethnohermeneutical paradigm, 357, 358
  symbols in, 357, 358, 359, 360, 361, 362
Adventists, 720
Aeneas, 391
Aeneid, 391
Africa, 415–17, 419–21, 423, 427, 636
  Africans, 415–16, 421, 423, 425
  African Christians, 417
  African Initiated Churches, 417
  African Methodist Episcopal Church, 467, 470
  African Methodist Episcopal Zion Church, 467, 470
  African Orthodox Church, 466

"Against Theory" (Knapp and Micahels), 71
Agent Orange, 400
Agyeman, Jaramogi Abebe, 472–73
Ahab, King, 532–33
Ahijah, 533
Akan, 357–62
Alexander the Athenian, 382
Alexander the Great, 389, 392
Allah, 405
Aloysha, 689
Altizer, Thomas J. J., 30
Amalekites, 436
Amazon Prime, 406
Ambrose, 208, 635, 639, 641, 642, 643
American civil religion, 484
Americas, 381
Amharic, 417
Amoateng, Akoa Kofi, 357–62
Amos (book of), 431, 580, 623
anatheism, 103
Anatolios, Khaled, 205
  hermeneutics precedes theology, 205–6
Anaziah, 532
ancient biblical cosmography, 574
Ancient Near East cultures, 573–76, 579–80, 607
angels, 578
  archangels, 582
Anglican, 605
Anishinaabe, 438
Anselm, 628
  satisfaction theory of, 628

anthropological apologia for
    Christianity, 619
anthropology
    relational, 706
    theological, 705
antichrist religion, 724
Anti-Discrimination Act, The, 408
apologists, 400, 720
Apology (Plato), 5
apostle, 131–33
Apostles' Creed, 206–7
    and Melchior Hittorp, the canon of
    Cologne, 206
Apostolic Tradition (Hippolytus), 208
*Appeal in Four Articles . . . to the
    Coloured Citizens of the World*
    (Walker), 466
Apple Pay, 406
Aquinas, Thomas, 85, 167, 482, 610,
    643
Aquino, María Pilar, 452
Archer, Kenneth, 281, 283
Archer, Melissa, 284
Argos, 392
Aristotle, 386, 675
Arius, 210–14
Ark of Covenant, 407, 437
aseity, 591
Asia, 397, 404–7, 409, 411
    Asians, 400, 406, 409–410
    Asian Christians, 399, 402, 407, 409
    "Asia's Cry for Reconciliation"
    (Ross), 405
Assmann, Jan and Aleida, 652–53,
    657–58
    cultural memory, 657
    identity formation, 657
Assyria, 533, 536, 537, 582
astral entities, ancient typology of,
    579
    modern typology of, 579
    Moon, 579
Athanasius, 158, 179, 211, 214, 400,
    637
Athenian, 382
Athirat (El's wife), 580
atrocities beyond description, 604
Attridge, Derek, 71

Auerbach, Eric, 82
Augustine, 39, 65–66, 119, 160, 167,
    174, 178–79, 182, 415, 482, 592,
    605, 610, 615–21, 635, 642, 644
    amillennialist view of, 720
    Confessions, 39
    semiotics of, 610
Augustine, Sarah (Tewa Pueblo), 431,
    435
Augustus, 392
Australia, 400, 408
Australian Pentecostal Community,
    287
Autero, Esa, 289, 291, 292
authorial intention, 282, 290
authority, 131
Autism spectrum, 699
Avelos, Hector, 695
AWARE study, 316

Baal, 532
Baasha, 533
Babel, Tower of, 367–68, 370, 371, 614
Babylon, 389, 534, 535, 537, 582
    Enuma Elish, 575
    exile, 538
Bacon Johnson, Dawn-Mark, 522
Bacon, Francis, 606
    mandate of, 606
Bahl, Chad, 544
Baker, Ella, 478
Baker-Fletcher, Karen, 487, 488–89
Baldridge, William (Cherokee), 436,
    438
Balsdon, John, 383, 385
Balthasar, Hans Urs von, 139, 165
Bangladesh, 399
baptism, infant versus believers, 719
Barr, James, 322
barriers to participation in
    community, 698
Barth, Karl, 86, 164, 165, 206, 220,
    271, 473, 552
Barton, Stephen, 661
Basileia, 142
Bathsheba (Uriah's wife), 682, 683
Bauckham, Richard, 333, 660, 661
    personal event memory, 660, 661

INDEX OF NAMES AND SUBJECTS

Bayer, Oswald, 164
Beatitudes, 401
Beck, Sarah, 510
Becoming the Gospel (Gorman), 230
Bediako, Kwame, 417
Being and Time (Heidegger), 11
Ben Michaels, Walter, 71
Ben Zvi, Ehud, 658, 659
    phenomenon of social memory, 658
Benedict, 721
Benjamin, 389, 616
Berger, Peter L., 85
Bernard of Clairvaux, 180–81
Bernstein, Ellen, 331
Bethlehem, 604, 605, 611–13
Bible, 281, 282, 288, 289, 290, 300, 572, 588, 604, 607, 608
    authority and reliability of, 282, 340
    authorial intention, 282
    biblicism, 727
    interpretation, 347, 348
    Spanish, 451
biblical personalist anthropology, 156
Biblical Theological Seminary, 711
bicoastal elitists, 724
Bio-Psycho-Social model, 317
Bird, Michael, 204
Black
    clergy, 469
    missionaries, 469–70
    power, 472
    religious thought, 461
    spirituals, 469
    theology, 461–76
Black Elk, 439–40
Black Manifesto, The (Forman), 472
Black Messiah, The (Cleage/Agyeman), 472
Black Obelisk monument, 536
Black Religion and Black Radicalism (Wilmore), 472
Black Religious Leaders (Jackson), 472
Black Theology and Black Power (Cone), 472
Blanchot, Maurice, 614
Boaz, 672–75
Bodies That Matter (Butler), 497

body of Christ, 377–79, 695, 697, 701
Boersma, Hans, 171, 173, 176–77, 178–80, 182
Bonhoeffer, Dietrich, 124, 129–30, 157–59, 164–65, 473, 589–95
Bookless, Dave, 331–32
Boone, Charles, 470
Boone, Eva, 470
Bosch, David, 221
Brenner, Athalya, 497
Bretherton, Luke, 52–53, 56
Brooks, Peter, 67
Brothers Karamazov, The (Dostoyevsky), 689
Brown, Shaun, 80
Brukiewa, David, 521
Brukiewa, Jen, 521
Brukiewa, Megan, 521
Buber, Martin, 162
Buchleiter, Rev. Laura Beth, 511
Buddha, Gautama, 400–402
Buddhism, 398, 405
Buell, Denise, 383–84, 391
Bultmann, Rudolf, 473
Bush, President George W., 265–56, 724
Bushnell, Horace, 401
Buster, Aubrey, 660
Butler, Judith, 497, 499, 543
Byzantine East, 615
    Byzantine empire, 514

Caesar, 725
Caiaphas, 628
Cain, 626, 627
Caldwell, Larry W., 355
Calvin, John, 608
Campbell, Alexander, 720
Campbell, Douglas A., 45–49, 272, 552
Canaan, 371, 436, 577, 581
    Canaanites, 407, 435–36
    culture, 624
    mythology, 576
    problem, 436
    woman, 369
Cannon, Katie Geneva, 473, 478
canon within the canon, 627

canonical authority, 721
Cappadocian fathers, 163
Caputo John D., 18, 30, 32, 96–104, 529
Carchemish, Battle of, 536
Carey, William, 721
Cargal, Timothy, 283
Cartesian epistemology, 661
Cartledge, Mark, 287, 288
Cartwright, Andrew, 470
Cassian, John, 252
Cassin, Barbara, 18
Catechism of the Catholic Church, 173
Catholic, 519, 607
  Black and, 467
celestial bodies, 579
  entities, Ancient and modern ways of classifying, 578
Chan, Simon, 280
Charleston, Bishop Steven (Choctaw), 430, 432, 434
Chaviano, Daína, 454
Chenoweth, Mark, 177
Cherokee, 436, 438
cherubim, 582, 584
child soldiers, 604
Childers, Alisa, 544
Chimera, 713
China, 403–5
  Chinese, 400, 404, 406, 410, 611
  Chinese and Korean Christianity, 400
  Chinese Union Bible, 410
Choctaws, 430, 435
Chrétien, Jean-Louis, 613, 614
Christ Jesus 517, 527, 550, 554, 590–96, 617, 634, 635, 708
  conformity to, 589
  forgiveness, 592
  mediator of everything, 591
Christian Century, The, 711
Christian, 588, 589, 596, 605, 623, 627, 628
  community, 292, 304, 306, 312, 342
scripture in, 714
  Christendom, 430
  culture formation, 714
  early, 455

enduring essence of, 715
eucharist, 438
formation, 588
scripture alone, 725
socialism, 465
tradition, 314, 315, 316, 318, 320, 323, 329, 339, 340, 626
Christian Imagination, The (Jennings), 71
Christian Methodist Episcopal Church, 467
Christology, 410, 441
  Christification (Christformation), 167
  christological criterion, 147–48, 150–51
  christological maximalism, 638
Chrysostom, John, 175–76
Church Dogmatics (Barth), 164
Church of God in Christ, 467
church tradition, 306
  Calvinist, Wesleyan, Pietist, Baptist, and Pentecostal heritages, 728
Church, Casey (Potawatomi), 437
Cicero, 393
circle of El, the, 580
Clark, Septima, 478
Classical Pentecostalism, 291
Cleage, Albert, 472
Clement of Alexandra, 177
Cleveland School, 283
climate change, 321, 322, 324
"Cogito and the History of Madness" (Derrida), 34, 36
cognitive impairments, 698
colonialization, 348, 350
Colossians (book of), 387, 399
Columbus, 429, 442
comets, asteroids, 579
communal self-description, 713
Conde-Frazier, Elizabeth, 452, 453
Cone, Cecil, 473
Cone, James Hal, 462, 463–64, 474, 479
confessions, 592
confessionalists, 607
Confucians, 409
  Confucianism, 398

Congenital Adrenal Hyperplasia
    (CAH), 519
evangelicalism, conservative, 633, 728
    orthodoxy and progressivism, 717
    outlook, 712
Constantine, 637
Constantinopolitan Creed, 212
contemporary theology, 716
    and contemporary culture, 716
contextual exercise, 713
    contextualization movement, 354
conversion
    basis for, 722
    of the imagination, 727
    means of, 721
Cooper, Anna Julia, 487
Copernicus, 574
Corinthians (book of), 612
Corn Mother, 437, 438, 441
Costas, Orlando, 449
Council
    of Chalcedon, 212
    of Jerusalem (Acts 15), 283, 292
    of Milan
    of Nicaea, 204, 210–14, 641
Course in General Linguistics
    (Saussure), 64
Cox, Harvey, 446
Cranmer, Thomas, 721
Creamer, Deborah, 706
creation, 302, 306, 318, 320, 326, 329,
    331, 333, 336–39, 366, 367
creatio ex nihilo, 161
creation care, 331
creationist realist cosmology, 156
creator, 402, 429–31, 433, 435,
    437–42, 528
    stewardship of, 333–34
creedalists, 720
    ecumenical credos, 720
Cretans, 387
Critical Race Theory, 8
critical realism, 156
*Crucifixion of the Warrior God:
    Interpreting the Old Testament's
    Violent Portraits of God in Light
    of the Cross, The* (Boyd), 276
Culp, A. J., 659–60

memory product, 659
memory producer, 659
cultural accommodation, 715
Cultural Revolution in China, 404
Cummings, Brian, 62
cyclical violence in civilizations, 627
Cyril of Alexandra, 182, 640, 642, 643
Cyril of Jerusalem, 578

Damascus Road, 440
Daniélou, Jean, 173
Dao, 409
Daoism, 398, 409
Darby, John Nelson, 720
David (biblical), 389, 682
Davies, Jamie, 46
Dayton, Donald W., 284
de Beistegui, Miguel, 7–9
de Lubac, Henry, 258
De Man, Paul, 29, 31
de Saussure, Ferdinand, 64–66
De Witt, Calvin, 331
Declaration of Independence, 485
Deconstructing Hell (Bahl), 544
Deconstructing the New Testament
    (Seeley), 39, 548
DeFranza, Megan K., 510
Dekker, Willem, 589
Delaney, Emma B., 470
Delay, Tad, 69
Deloria, Vine, Jr., 439
Dempster, Murray W., 283
demythologized, 629
Derrida, Jacques, 6–7, 30, 29,
    33–42, 65–66, 95–96, 98, 99, 112,
    115–17, 543, 544, 545
Descartes, 36, 122
Deuteronomy (book of), 398, 404,
    578
Dilthey, Wilhelm, 33, 63
Diodorus, 389
Dionysius of Rome, 210, 392
disability, 702, 706
    and Christian theology, 706
    complexities and ambivalences
        relative to, 696
    consequence of sin, 702
    cultural model of, 699

effect of evil and sin, 699
hermeneutics of, 695–97, 702, 705, 707, 709
modern European construction, 697
marginalized human experience, 702
physiognomic sign of God's absence, 699, 700
sign of reprobation, 699
stigmatization of, 700
Disabled God, The (Eiesland), 696
disciple-making movements (DMM), 727
practices, 727
disciples, 602
Dispensationalists, 720
Dissemination (Derrida), 37
divine council, 578
divinize the biblical text, 597
doctrinal affirmations, central 715
Doctrine of Discovery, 431, 434
Dombrowski, Dan, 325
Dorrien, Gary, 717
Dostoyevsky, Fyodor, 689, 692
Douglas, Kelly Brown, 478, 484, 485, 488
Drama of Jesus, The, 141–44
Dramatic Theology/Theologians, 139

Eagle, 439
Eagleton, Terry, 72
Earth Bible, 338, 342
Project, 336–37
earth, 578
ends of, 585
Ebeling, Gerhard, 596
ecclesial life, 725
Ecclesiastes (book of), 406
Eclipse of Biblical Narrative, The (Frei), 77
Eco, Umberto (model reader), 231
Ecowomanism, 488
Eden, Garden of, 576, 584, 614, 638
Edenic pattern, 518
Edmund Pettus bridge, 317, 319
Edomite, 389
Egypt, 316, 371, 434, 533, 582

Eiesland, Nancy, 696, 707
El (the chief god), 580
Elijah, 369, 404, 577, 582
Elisha, 404
Elizondo, Virgilio, 449, 457
Ellington, Scott, 191, 285
Elliott, Jane, 71
embodied human life, 702
Emmanuel, 430
Emmaus, 602
empirical science, 128
end of apologetics, 127, 129, 132
Enlightenment, 127–29
Enns, Peter, 527
Ephesians (book of), 402, 406
Epilepsy, 700
epistemic and theological claims, 713
epistemological location, 593
Erickson, Millard, 714
Esau, 431
eschatology, 321–23, 326, 330, 335, 337, 341
escapist, 321–23, 326
eschatological action of God, 593
eschatological liberation and reconciliation, 341
Essays from the Margins (Rivera-Pagán), 456
Estrada, Rodolfo Galvan, 291, 458
ethics, embodied, 317, 319–21, 323, 325–26
embodied theological ethic, 318, 319
Ethiopia, 516
Ethiopians, 385, 387
eunuch (ethnically and anatomically devalued), 704
ethnohermeneutics, 348, 353–58, 360–61
deep level, 356
ethnotheology, 354–55
surface level, 356
Eucharist, 639
Europeans, 386
evangelical left, 714
progressive, 711
theology of the, 711

INDEX OF NAMES AND SUBJECTS

Evangelical Lutheran Church of American (ELCA), 522
evangelical theology and agenda, postmodern, 711–12
  reimagining, 711
evangelicalism, 282, 301, 322
  devotional and missional heart of, 728
  postconservative, 711–12
  thought, flowering of, 716
  scholars, 712
  various streams of, 301, 305
Eve, 627, 640, 644
Evers, Myrlie, 478
evil, problem of, 307–8
Exégèse médiévale (de Lubac), 171
Exeter Project, 339, 340
Exodus (book of), 371, 398, 406, 434–35, 437
  exodus from Egypt, 448
extrascriptural categories, 714
Ezekiel, 538, 539, 582
Ezra, 505

Face of the Deep, The (Keller), 70
faith
  responding in, 591
  ways of acting in, 594
Falque, Emmanuel, 18
Feast of the Holy Innocents, 604
Fecund metaphor, 586
Federation of Asian Bishops' Conferences (FABC), Documents of the, 406
Fee, Gordon D., 281, 282, 426
Felski, Rita, 72
Female Face of God in Auschwitz, The (Raphael), 506
feminist hermeneutists, 599
  feminist theory, 498–507
Ferretter, Luke, 66
figural perspective, slaughter of the innocents in, 611
finitude and fallibility, 588
First African Baptist Church, 467
First Bryan Baptist Church, 467
First Man, 438
  First Mother, 438

Flat Earth, 574
  Society, 584
Fleming, Lula C., 470
Flood and Fury (Lynch), 276–78
flood, 572, 575
Floyd-Thomas, Stacey, 479–80
Fodor, James, 78–79
Forman, James, 472
Forum on Missional Hermeneutics (annual meeting of the Society of Biblical Literature), 222
Fosdick, Harry Emerson, 465
Foucault, Michel, 8, 112–13, 543
Fowl, Stephen, 671–72
Fox, Arminta M., 543
Franke, John, 229, 711
  recontextualization language, 229
Frankl, Viktor, 692
Fredriksen, Paula, 551
Free African Society, 468
free will, 688
Freedom's Journal, 468
Frege, Gottlieb, 40
Frei, Hans, 77, 82, 713
Freud, Sigmund, 67
Freud and Philosophy (Ricoeur), 36
Fry, Stephen, 92
Frye, Northrop, 607
Fuch, Esther, 501
fundamentalism, 20–22, 322, 720
  conservative evangelicalism, and conservative confessionalism, 717
Future of Faith, The (Cox), 446

Gabriel, Marcus, 543
Gadamer, Hans-Georg, 19, 31, 63, 93, 155, 161, 283, 286, 605–6, 609
Gadarene demoniac, 577
Galatians (book of), 387, 390, 399, 406, 439, 617
Galilean Journey (Elizondo), 449–50
Galilee, 387
García-Alfonso, Cristina, 452–53
Garnet, Henry Highland, 466
Garvey, Marcus, 466
Gaventa, Beverly Roberts, 45, 47, 54
Gebara, Ivone, 454

Geertz, Clifford, 84–85
  and worldview, 227
Geisler, Norman, 722
gender theory, 496–97
Genesis (book of), 330, 332–33, 366, 399, 438, 441, 606, 614
  chapter 1, 572, 575, 583
  Ishmaelites in, 725
  literal meaning of, 610
genius/apostolic distinction, 132
genocidal portrait of God, 251–54
  and killing, 261,
  and violent acts, 253
Gentiles, 390, 517
Geocentric cosmos, 574, 579
German, 607
Ghost Dance, 440
Girard, René 619
  theory of, 620
Global North hermeneutics, 348–51, 355–56, 359, 361–62, 415–16, 421, 424
Global South hermeneutics, 314, 348–52, 355–56, 362, 427
God Is Unconscious (Delay), 69
God, 512, 518, 527–29, 530, 532–33, 535–39, 551, 553, 554, 596–600, 612, 616, 623, 626, 628, 630, 634–35, 697, 700
  angry God of the Old Testament, 626
  and judgment against sin, 684
  cherubic throne, 584
  fidelity to creation, 582
  Godself, 430, 441
  heaven, 582
  Holy Mountain, 576
  merciful god of the New Testament, 626
  will, place of suffering inside, 688
  outside God's will, 688
Goh, Elaine, 406
Goh, Jeffrey, 86–87
Gomer, 532
Gomorrah, 438
González, Justo L., 449, 450–51
Gordon, Gabriel, 241

Gordon-Conwell Theological Seminary, 711
gospels, 432
Goyim, 725
grace, 591
Grace Disguised, A (Sittser), 681, 682
Graham, Franklin, 724
grammatical-historical approach, 349–52, 362
  background of, 720
Grant, Colleen, 701
Grant, George, 161
Grant, Jacquelyn, 473, 478
Great Commission, 373, 374
"Great Disembedding, the" (Taylor), 127, 129–30–31
Great Spirit/Mystery, 441
Greece, 382–83
Greek, 383, 385–86, 388, 392–93, 401, 409
Greekness, 392
Greek Trojans, 392
Green, Joel, 231
Gregory of Nyssa, 179–80, 182, 252, 640
Green Bible, The, 330, 331, 334
Gregory the Great, 644
Grenz, Stanley, 711
Grey, Jacqueline, 287, 290, 291
Grotius, Hugo 608
Gruen, Eric, 382
Guardini, Romano, 166
Gutiérrez, Gustavo, 447
Gye Nyame symbol, 359, 360

Habel, Norman C., 336, 337, 338
Hagar, 623
Halbach, Ross, 596
Halbwachs, Maurice, 651–53, 656
  presentist perspective, 656
Halicarnassus, 392
Hall, Christopher, 204
Hall, Edith, 393
Hall, Jonathan, 383, 388, 393
Haman, 724–25
Hannah, 503
Harmony Way, 433
Harrison, Beverly W., 479

hate speech, 724
Hauerwas, Stanley, 204
Havea, 408
Haveron, Sarah, 519
Hays, Richard B., 440, 727
healings
  attention to the body, 703
  healing clarifies the identities of the person healed, 703
  healing impacts and transforms the broader community, 703
  healing narratives display spiritual and communal dimensions at work, 703
  healings expand categories and enlarge the imagination, 703
  marks of Jesus's, 703
  others with compassion and respect, 703
  positive reception by the healed person, 703
health, 319, 323–26
heaven, 582
heavens, the, 578, 581
Hebrew Bible, 578, 623, 626–28
  prophetic literature, 623;
  scriptures, 614
Hebrew, 407, 615
Hebrews (book of), 399–400, 407
Hee, Park Chung, 403
Heidegger, Martin, 11–14, 19, 33, 63–64, 119, 155, 161
Height, Dorothy, 478
Heisenberg, Werner, 607
Hellenes, 382
Henry, Carl 714
Hepher, 436
heralding, 296, 312
Hercules, 389
hermeneutic(s), Pentecostal, 280–85, 287–93
  contextual-Pentecostal approach, 283
hermeneutical circle, 63, 300, 308
  foot-stomping, 8–9
  framework/paradigm, 133–35
  lens, appropriate, 588
  theologians, 596
hermeneuticist, 108

hermeneutics
  challenges, 725
  definition, 495–96
  epistemology of, 156
  feminist, 498–507
  in Black theology, 461–75
  interconnections between the Spirit, Scripture, and humans, 190
  Latinx, 445–59
  models, 302, 304
  Womanist, 477–92
  spiral, 232
  of suspicion, 336, 598, 702
hermeneutics, biblical 720
  inventive, 727
  and phenomenological, 720
hermeneutics, biblical cosmology, 572
  biblical cosmos today, 584
hermeneutic, conventionalist, 311
hermeneutics, creedal, 203–17
  assessment of cultural influence, 216
  ecumenical unity, 216
  marks of, 213–17
  objectivity with freedom, 215
hermeneutics, cruciform, 249–64
  beautiful nature of God, 259
  conflict of commitments, 250
  cross as summation and culmination, 250
  and discipleship, 256–57
  divine accommodations, 260
  literary crucifixes, 261
  ugliness of the cross, 259
hermeneutics, diacritical, 97, 98
hermeneutics, ecological, 329, 336
  ecotheological, 342
hermeneutics, embodied, 314, 317, 319, 320, 321, 323, 326
hermeneutics, evangelical, 296, 297, 302, 303, 304, 306, 307, 308, 309, 310, 311, 312
hermeneutics, figural, 604
  figuration, 720
  figural exegesis, 727
hermeneutics, holistic evangelical, 296–97, 302–4, 309, 311–12,
hermeneutics, inculturation, 352, 361

hermeneutics, intercultural, 228, 347,
   348, 354, 356, 361
hermeneutics, missional, 218–33
   contextualization of, 226
   ecumenical and evangelical
      approaches, 218–33
   four streams, 224–26
   narrative theology of, 225
   reading scripture missionally, 230
hermeneutics, New Testament, 613
hermeneutics, nonviolent, 265–78
   in the character of God, 270–72
   definitions of, 266–67
   and love, 267
   and peace, 268
   and road to Emmaus, 272
   and suffering, 274–75
hermeneutics, open and relational,
   235–47
   biblical violence, 2238
   centrality of the cross, 254–59
   and divine providence, 238
   and freedom, 239
   and inerrancy, 241–43
   interpretative case study, 244.
   primacy of love, 236
   open and relational theology
      (ORT), 235–47
   scripture as dynamic, 242
   uncontrolling God, 239–40
hermeneutics, penultimate 588, 589
   interpretation, 596
   interpretative posture, 590
hermeneutics, radical, 97–102, 104
hermeneutics, Spirit, 186–201
   through affective, ethical, and
      cognitive, 190
   application, 190
   and communal discernment, 198
   communicates to us, in us, and
      through us, 192
   interpretation, 190, 195
   spirit interprets scripture, 187, 188
hermeneutics, ultimate, 601
   ultimate/penultimate distinction,
      589
   ultimate/penultimate framework,
      590

hermeneutics
Hermes, 92–94
Herod, 604, 616, 725
Herodotus, 382
heterogeneity, 296, 312
Hezekiah, 536
Hicks, Edward: 644–45
Hidalgo, Jacqueline M., 452
Hiebert, Paul, 354
higher criticism, 289
Hillel, 35
Hinduism, 398
   Hindu-background believers, 726
Hippocrates, 386
Hirsch, E. D., 426
historical-grammatical method, 281
Hodge, Caroline, 389–390
Hodge, Charles 720
Hoklotubbe, 439, 440
Holocaust, 68
Holy Family Sisters, 471
Holy of Holies, 407
Holy Spirit, 280, 281, 283, 285, 286,
   288, 289, 292, 293, 301, 302, 400,
   416, 418, 554
   gifts of the Spirit, 302, 306
Homer, 532
homosexuality, 719
Hong Kong, 403–404
   central district in, 403
Hood, Robert, 483–484
Horrell, David, 340, 341, 342
Hosea, 532, 533, 626
hospitality, 296, 297, 312
house churches, 726
Hübenthal, Sandra, 660
Hubmaier, Balthasar, 175, 183–84
human reason, 132
Humanism and Religion, 64
Hunsinger, George, 716
Huston, Zora Neale, 489

Ignatius of Loyola, 152, 721
illumination of Faith, 591
image of God, 318, 330, 332–33
   imago Dei, 318, 322
Imagining Equity (Winslow), 498–99

INDEX OF NAMES AND SUBJECTS

In Search of our Mother's Gardens
(Walker), 477
incarnation, purpose of, 684
  incarnational worship, 118
India, 403, 405, 409
  Indian Christians, 403
  Indian Shi'I, 723
indigenous Christians, 430–31, 436
  indigenous peoples of North
    America, 430
Indonesia, 405
  Indonesian disciple-maker, 722
Intercourse of Knowledge, The
  (Brenner), 497
Interpretation of Dreams, The (Freud),
  67
interiori luce veritatis, 160
International Missionary Council
  (Willingen, Germany, 1952), 219
  church's participation in God's
    mission, 219
  critique of ecclesiocentrism, 219
  and the kingdom of God, 220
  theology of, 223
intratextual theology, 714
  reading, 696
Ireland, 519
Irenaeus of Lyons, 160, 163–64, 209,
  400, 637–38, 643–44, 720
Isa al-Masih, 723
Isaac, 390, 577
Isaac, Benjamin, 383
Isaiah, 634
Isaiah (book of), 398–400, 402, 406,
  577, 615, 627
Isasi-Díaz, Ada María, 452–53
Islam, 398, 405, 463, 722
  Muslim, 722, 725
  Orthodox Islamic doctrines, 722
Islam, 633
Islam-as-Simon-Peter, 725
Isocrates, 392
Israel, 381, 389, 403, 430, 432,
  435–36, 536–37, 539, 623
Israelites, 434–35, 441, 573–74, 576,
  577, 580, 583–84, 634, 635, 636
  patriarchs and matriarchs, 430
Italy, 387, 392

Jackson, Joseph H., 472
Jacob, 431, 633
Jakobson, Roman, 67
James, Aaron, 6
James (book of), 411
Jasper, David, 73
Jebusites, 407
Jefferson, Thomas 720
Jehu, 532, 533, 536
Jennings, Willie James, 71
Jenson, Robert, 638–39
Jeremiah, 39, 604, 616, 623
Jeroboam, 533
Jerome, 167
Jerome, 638, 640,
Jersak, Bradley, 31, 545
Jerusalem, 387, 516, 534, 536
  council, 518
  temple, 577
Jesus Christ, 513, 518, 520, 554,
  576–78, 582, 585, 628, 684, 725,
  727
  Latinx perspective, 449–50
Jewett, Robert, 407
Jews, 383
  Jewish, 623, 627
  culture of, 624
Jezebel, 533
Jezreel, 532
Joachim of Fiore, 720
Job, 576, 577, 578, 581, 644, 675–79,
  684
  friends, 675–79
John Chrysostom, 640–43
John Paul II, Pope, 331
John the Baptist, 432
John, 423, 432, 518, 532, 585
John, gospel of, 383, 387, 390, 402–4,
  425
Johns, Cheryl Bridges, 282, 285–86,
  287, 288
Johnson, Samuel, 606
Jonah, 536, 537, 538, 578
Jonah (2002 Veggie Tales film), 724
Jones, William R., 474
Joram, 532
Jordan, Brigitte, 350

Joseph, 434, 623, 627
Josephus, 389
Joshua, 435–36, 454
Josiah, 534
Jowett, Benjamin, 605, 606, 608, 611
Judah, 535, 536, 539
　Judea, 387
Judahite(s), 538, 577
Judaism, 585, 635
　ancient, 455
　Second Temple, 660
Jüngel, Eberhard 596
Juno, 392
Jupiter, 387
Just Gaming (Lyotard), 18
justification by faith, 591
Justin Martyr, 175

Kant, Immanuel, 8
Kärkkäinen, Veli-Matti, 446–47
Katoppo, Marianne, 406
Kearney, Richard, 18, 27
Keats, John, 98
Keener, Craig, 190, 286, 289
Keetoowah, 433
Keller, Catherine, 70–71, 322
Kelly, J. N. D., 207
kenosis, 641, 643
Kearney, Richard, 96–104
kerygmatic passages, 721
Khalil (as in Gibran), 724
Kierkegaard, Søren, 97–98, 131, 132
Kim, Jeong-sook, 398
King, Martin Luther, Jr., 317, 462, 721
kingdom of God, 300, 302, 310, 318, 338, 369, 374, 448–49
Kitamori, Kazoh, 410
Knapp, Steven, 71
Korah, 578
Koran, 633
Korea, 403
Korean Christians, 410
Kraft, Charles, 354
Krawec, Patty (Anishinaabe), 438–39
Kubler-Ross, Elizabeth, 687
Kuhn, Thomas, 84
Kumar, Johnny, 285, 288
Kushner, Rabbi Harold, 687

Laelius, 393
Lakota Christians, 437
Lakota, 436, 441
Lamb of the Free (Rillera), 553
Lamech, 627
land, 576
Land, Steven J., 284
language, metaphysical limits of, 727
Latin American theology, 446–449
Latin West, 615
Latinx Perspectives on the New Testament (Vena and Guardiola-Sáenz), 459
leap of faith, 98–99
Learning to be White (Thandeka), 480
LeBlanc, Terry (Mi'kmaq/ Acadian), 433
Leclercq, Jean, 180
lectio divina, 168, 184
lectura creyente, 289
Legaspi, Michael 607, 608
LeMarquand, Grant 604
Leo the Great, 182, 645
Levering, Matthew, 171, 173–74
Leviathan, 576
Leviticus, book of, 405, 434
Lewis, C. S., 161
liberal theology, 464–65, 717
　evangelical theology and, 711
　paradigm, 716
　liberal-conservative divide, 712
　liberalism, adjuncts of dominant elite modern, 719
liberal, 633–34
liberation theology, 446–49, 717
Limits of Critique, The (Felski), 72
Lindbeck, George, 77, 79, 88, 612, 714
Lindsey, Hal, 724
Lippman, Walter, 5
liturgical animals, 119
Locke, John, 609
logic of incarnation, 108, 113
Logos, 437
　Christology, 174
　Logoi, 614
Lord, 515, 533, 605, 613, 616, 635
Lord's Prayer, 403, 405

Lozada, Francisco, Jr., 455
Lubac, Henri du, 171
Luckmann, Thomas, 85
Lukács, György, 69–70
Luke, 387, 634
Luke (Gospel of), 42, 402, 426, 437, 594, 625, 629
Luther, Martin, 181–82, 258, 400, 440, 595, 608, 685
    Lutheran, 595, 607, 667
Lyotard, Jean-François, 17–18, 112, 543

MacIntyre, Alisdair, 84
Malaysia, 404
Malcolm X, 462, 463
Manasseh, 534, 535
Manifest Destiny, 434
Mappa Mundi, 578
Marcellus (336–341), 207
Marduk, 575
marginalization, 698
    marginalized and oppressed, 716
Maritain, Jacques, 161
Mark (Gospel of), 400, 423, 432
Marquez, Anunnaki Ray, 519, 520
Mars, 387
Martin, Trayvon Benjamin, 484
Martyn, J. Louis, 45
Martyr, Justin, 409
Mary (mother of Jesus), 503
Mary, 640, 642–44
Masih, 725
Mather, Cotton, 435
Mathews, Rosita deAnn, 487
Matthew (Gospel of), 387, 389, 403, 432, 434, 436, 441, 577, 612, 617
Maximus the Confessor, 163, 614
McCoskey, Denise Eileen, 393
McGuire, George Alexander, 466
McKay, Marabel, 439
McKinney Fox, Bethany, 696, 703
McLean, Mark, 283
McMillan, Walter, 485
media via, 176
medical and social models of disability, 698–99
Meditations (Descartes), 36

Melanesia, 407
Memory Studies, 647
    framing, 653
    keying, 653
    schema, 650
Menachem, Resma, 485
Mennonite, 604, 613
Menzies, Robert, 282
Merleau-Ponty, Maurice, 120
messengers (ml'km, i.e., angels), 581
Messiah, 513, 514, 547, 623, 725
Mi'kmaq/ Acadian, 433
Micah, 623, 627
Micronesia, 407
middle knowledge, 172–73
Midrashic "play" upon Genesis 31, 616
Miller, J. Hillis, 31
Mimesis (Auerbach), 82
mimetic conflict, 627
    human reality present even from the earliest accounts of civilization, 620; conflictual mimesis, 621
    rivalry, 627
    violence, 620, 627
missio Dei, 221
    in the biblical story, 604
    mission, means of, 721
    missionaries, 604
Missional Church in Perspective, The (Van Gelder and Zscheile), 223
missionary movements, European and American, 349
Mississippi, 435
Missouri Synod Lutheran Church, 522
Moabite(s), 672, 674
modernism, 65
    actual past, 655, 657, 658, 659, 661–62
    modernity, 109–11, 127–29, 131–32–33–35
Mohammed, 633
Moltmann, Jürgen, 54
Monta, Susana, 73
Moo, Douglas, 550
Moore, Rickie D., 283

Moore, Stephen, 542, 543, 544
moralists, 720
Moreschi, Alessandro ("The Last Angel of Rome"), 514
Moses, 436, 531, 539, 583, 646, 672
　book of, 616
　Mosaic Law, 401
Mount Carmel, 577
Mount Sinai, 530, 577, 583
Mourner, Mother, Midwife (Claassens), 506
Mujerista Theology, 452
Murphey, Nancey, 315, 316
Muscogee/Cherokee, 436, 440
Must We Mean What We Say? (Cavell), 31
Myanmar, 401, 405
　Myanmar Christianity, 401

Naaman, 369
Naden, 408
Nahum, 538
NAIITS: An Indigenous Learning Community, 430, 436
Naomi, 371–72
Naomi, 673–74
Nash, Diane, 478
Nathan, Prophet, 683
Nathanael, 387
National Baptist Convention, 467
National Committee of Black Churchmen, 472
National Committee of Negro Churchmen, 464
Native America, 431
　Native North Americans, 435, 437, 441
Native Covenant, 431
Nature of Doctrine, The (Lindbeck), 80, 88
nature of God, creational (Father), redemptive (Son), and reconciliational (Spirit), 193
Nazareth, 387
Nazianzus, Gregory, 635
NDEs (near-death experiences), 316
Nebat, 533

neo-orthodoxy (including its Catholic forms), 717
Nepal, 405
New Critics, 633
New Testament, 381–82, 387–88, 390, 401, 403, 440, 623, 627, 618
New York, 637
New Zealand, 403
Newbigin, Lesslie, 220, 409, 726
Next Reformation: Why Evangelicals Need to Embrace Postmodernity, The (Raschke), 30
Ney, David, 604
Nicene Constantinopolitan settlement of 381, 552
Nicene Creed, 205, 211
　and ecumenical unity, 212
Nicholas of Damascus, 389
Niebuhr, H. Richard, 41, 42
Niebuhr, Reinhold, 473
Nietzsche, Friedrich, 6, 7
Nigeria, 56
Nineveh, 536, 537, 724
Noah, 438, 572
nonfoundational perspective, 712–13
non-Indigenous Christians, 441
non-reductive physicalism, 316
North America, 399, 429, 437–38, 544
North Atlantic, 407
Northern Africa, 415
Northerners, 386
nouvelle théologie, 173
Novum organum, sive Indicia Vera de Interpretatione Naturae, 606
Numbers, book of, 398, 578

O'Donahue, John, 323
Obadare, Ebenezer, 56–57
Oblate Sisters, the, 471
Occupy Central with Love and Peace (OCLP), 403
Oceania, 407
Ochs, Peter, 599
Of Grammatology, 542
Okholm, Dennis, 714
Oklahoma, 435
Old Testament, 381, 430 615, 616
　prophets, 448

Olick, Jeffrey, 647
Oliver, Simon, 160–61
Oliverio, L.William Jr., 282, 283
Olson, Roger, 76, 711
Omri, 532
Omride kings, 532
On Airs, Waters, Places, 386
One Word, 605
Oord, Thomas Jay, 240
ordo salutis, 179–80
Origen, 175, 176–79, 181, 252, 415, 483, 638, 639, 643
Original Instructions, 430, 433
original sin, 626
Orthodox, 400
Osage, 435, 437

Pacific Islands, 407
Pakistan, 405
Palmer, Richard, 93
Pancasila, 405
panentheism, 319, 320, 322
pantheism, 306–8
parable
 of the forgiving father, 626
 of the prodigal son, 626
Parham, Charles Fox, 721
Paris, Peter J., 465, 472, 489
parousia, 582
Parry, Robin, 572
Pascalian dictum, 120
passover, 628
"Patriarchy is Not Destiny" (Saini), 501
Paul Decentred (Fox), 543
Paul, 162, 387, 389–91, 399, 404, 420, 439, 440, 545–53, 612, 615, 637–38, 642, 661, 668–69, 684, 692, 726–27
 Saul of Tarsus, 726
Penn, William, 645
Pentecostal Republic, 56–57
Pentecostalism, 280–81, 283–93, 301, 322
 scholastics, 282
 theology, 284
 tradition, 280, 283
penultimacy, 589, 596
 activity, 590

 of interpretative methods
People's Republic of Rome, 393
Persians, 383
Peter, 725
Phaedrus, 34
Pharisee, 389, 725
Philip, 387, 516–17
Philippi, 684
Philippians (book of), 389, 410
Phillips, Timothy, 714
Philo, 177
philosophical foundationalism, 712
 point-counterpoint, 688
philoxenia, 176
phronesis, 303
physiognomic meanings, 702, 704
Pilarski, Ahida Calderón, 452
Pillars of the Earth, 573
 Planets, 579
Pinnock, Clark, 240
Pioske, Daniel, 658
pity and charity models, 699
Plan for an English Dictionary
 (Johnson), 606
Plato, 34, 386, 616, 648
pluralism, 304, 310
 perspectival, 712
 principled theological, 717
 truth of theological and religious language, 76
pneumatic, hermeneutics. *See* hermeneutics, Spirit, 197
Pole, Siosifa, 403
Polybius, 386
Polynesia, 407
postcolonialism, 455
post-Enlightenment context, 349
postliberal theology, 712, 714
postmodern, 128–29–30, 283
 theology, 717
 thought, 711
Potawatomi, 437
Potsdam Day (1933), 265
power, means of, 721
practical inerrancy, 727
pragmatism, 284
premillennial, 281
Presentist orientation, 606
Prickett, Stephen, 61

Priminius, Saint, missionary manual, *de Singulis Libris Canonicis Scarapsus*, 207
primitivism, 284
Prince Hall Masons, 468
Principle of Interconnectedness, 336
  of Intrinsic Worth, 336
  of Mutual Custodianship, 337
  of Purpose, 336
  of Resistance, 337
  of Voice, 336
progress, 128, 130
progressive theology, 716
prophets, 580
prosopological exegesis, 179
Prosser, Gabriel, 466
Protestants, 607, 629
  mainline, 282
Proverbs, book of, 399
Psalm, book of, 398, 402, 407, 578, 617, 685, 686
  Penitential Psalm, 683
  psalmists, 722
psychoanalysis, 67, 69
Pueblos, 432
Pumba, 586
quadriplegic, 687
Quran, 722

race/ethnicity, 365, 366, 368, 371–72, 376–77
  racial identity hermeneutics, 365, 366, 370, 379
Rachel, 604, 605, 612, 616–17
Radner, David, 608
Rahab, 454, 504, 576
Rahner, K., 146, 152
Ramah, 604, 612, 616–17
Randall, James Mark, 89
Rape of Nanjing, 399
Rauschenbusch, Walter, 30, 465
Reading for the Plot (Brooks), 67
Readings from the Edges (Ruiz), 456
reason, current canons of, 713
Reconciling in Christ (RIC), 522
"Recovering Redemption" (Winslow), 502–3

Recovery of Black Presence (Bailey and Grant), 475
redemptionist interpretations, 696
Reed Sea, 576
Reformation, 607
  spiritualists and pietists, 721
Reformed, 607
  Reformists, 715
  Reformed and Always Reforming, 76
  reformist paradigm, 716
relativism and pluralism, debilitating nature of, 715
Religion and Literature (journal), 73
Religious Right, 10
Reno, R. R., 726
repentance
  acts of, 590, 594–95
  ongoing need for, 595
Republican party, 322
rescuing the Bible, 696
responding to trauma, 690
Reuchlin (Hebraist), 615
  kabbalistic framework of, 615
revelation, 725
  revelation *sub contrario*, 148
Revelation (book of), 383, 404
revisionist paradigm, 714
revivalists, 721
Reynolds, Thomas E., 695
Rhodes, Ron, 722
Rice, Richard, 681
Ricœur, Paul, 19, 31, 36, 94–95, 98, 103, 155, 283
Rillera, Andrew, 553
Ringrose, Kathryn, 514
Rio Grande, 435
Rivera-Pagán, Luis N., 456–57
Roberts, J. Deotis, 473
Rock, 404
Romans (book of), 390, 399–400, 403–4, 406–7, 410
Rome, 382, 386, 393, 514
  Romans, 385–86, 391–94, 692
  Roman Empire, 385–386, 391
Romulus, 393
Rorty, Richard, 38
Ross, Kenneth R., 405

Ross, Rosetta, 488
Rudd, Daniel, 467
Rufinus (c. 390), 207, 208
Ruiz, Jean-Pierre, 456, 457
Rumbek, 604, 605, 611–13, 617
Ruth (book of), 371–72, 671–75
Ryle, Gilbert, 83–84

Sacramentum futuri: études sur les origines de la typologie biblique (Daniélou), 173
Sacred Energy, 437
Saddam Hussein's Iraq, 724
Safa, Reza, 724
Sahara, 416
Said, Edward, 403
Saini, Angela, 501
Saleeb, Abdul, 722
Samaria, 375, 425, 536
    Samaritans, 426, 725
    Samaritan woman, 375
Samuel, 578
sanctificationists, 721
Sanhedrin, 725
Sanskrit, 403
Sarah, 585
Sargon II, 536
Saroyan, William
Satan, 520, 629
    Beelzebul, 629
Saturn, 387
Sawyer, John, 636, 644
scapegoat hermeneutics, 619
    aligns with postconservative principles, 619
Schleiermacher, Friedrich, 19, 33, 63, 400
Schmitt, Carl, 52, 53
Schröter, Jens, 660, 661
Schwager, Raymond, 139, 626
Schwartz, Barry, 652, 653
scientific truth, 585
Scipio, 393
Scott, Nathan, 29
Scriptural Reasoning (SR), 599
Scripture(s), 280–93, 300–306, 312, 314–15, 330, 334, 338, 342, 355, 578, 588, 607, 611–13, 616, 695

as ancient text, 572
inerrancy of, 282
as infallible, inerrant, 301
and intention of author, 281–83
Scythians, 385, 387
Sechrest, Love, 383
Second Cumberland Presbyterian Church, 467
second naivete, 103
Second World War, 399
secularity, 128
Seeley, David, 38–40, 542–44, 548, 549, 552
Segovia, Fernando F., 455–56
Segundo, Juan Luis, 448
semiotics, 93–94
Sennacherib, 536
sensus literalis, 611
Septuagint, 640, 641
seraphim, 578, 582
Sermon on the Mount, 338
Sex Difference in Christian Theology: Male, Female and Intersex in the Image of God (DeFranza), 523
sexual abuse, 506
Sexuality and the Black Church, 481
Shaimaneser the III, 536
Shalom, 433
SHE (sustainability, health, ethics), 319, 323, 324, 325, 326
Sheldon, Charles, 30
Sheol/Hades, 578
Shi'i Muslim, 724
Shrine of the Black Madonna, 472
Sila, 401
siloing of opinions, 21–22
Silver Bluff Baptist Church, 467
Simon bar-Jonah, 725
Simon, 725
Simon, Menno, 721
sin, 397–399, 406
Sinai, 531
Singer, Peter, 325
Sioux in the Plains, 432
Sioux, 432, 439
Siricius, Pope, 208
Sisera, 582
Sittser, Jerry, 681, 692

Sitz im Leben, 397, 410
Skinner, Tom, 474
Slavoj Žižek, 403
Smith, James K. A., 88–89, 108–23
Social Constructivism, 660
Social
 gospel, 465
 justice, 318, 319, 331, 374
 media, 309, 310, 311, 356
Socrates, 3, 409
Sodom and Gomorrah, 438, 636
sola scriptura, 589
solus Christus, 589
Songs of the Suffering Servant," 150
Sons of the Most High, 581
Sophia, 399
soul, 315, 315, 316, 317, 319, 320, 322, 373, 374
South Sudan, 604, 611–613
Southern Baptist Convention, 506
Southwest, 432
Spanish, 435
Specters of God, 100
speech-act theory, 299, 308
spirit as prevenient, 188
Spirit baptism, 289
spirit of antichrist, 725
 spirit of error, 725
Spirit of Christ, 270, 280, 281, 283, 284, 285, 287, 288, 293, 301, 303, 304, 305, 306, 312, 517
 of Creator, 440
 gifts of, 366
Spirit-Word-Community, 283, 284, 285, 287, 291, 292, 293
Sproul, R. C., 239, 722
Sri Lanka, 405
stars, manifestations of heavenly beings, 579–580
stewardship, 322, 325, 333, 342
Stolen Generation, 400
Structure, Sign and Play, 542
Structure of Scientific Revolutions, The (Kuhn), 84
Stuart, David, 588
Stuart, Douglas, 426
subjectivism, 311
 subjectivist hermeneutic, 310

Sudanese, 605, 617
Sugirtharajah, R. S., 402
Sun Dance, 437
sustainability, 318, 323–26
Sweat Lodge, 437
Sweet Honey in the Rock, 485
Sydney, 400
syncretism, 21–22
Syria, 683
Syrophoenician woman, 369, 372

Tacitus, 382
Taiwan, 403
Tamar, 504
Tan, Jonathan Y., 406
Tarsus, 440
Taylor, Charles, 127, 128, 161, 401
Taylor, Mark C., 30
Terrell, JoAnne Marie, 478
Tertullian, 204, 209, 483, 640, 644,
Tewa Pueblo, 431
Thailand, 405
Thandeka, 480
Theaetetus, 648
Theodore of Mopsuestia, 639
Theo-Drama (von Balthasar), 139
theology
 as never-finished task, 585
 conception of, 713
 post-colonial, 314
 theological boundaries, 715
 theological reflection, 716
Theology of Liberation, A (Gutiérrez), 447
Theology of the Social Gospel, A (Rauschenbusch), 466
Theophilus, 42
Theory after 'Theory' (Elliott), 71
Theravada Buddhism, 401
Thiselton, Anthony C., 414
Thomas, Christopher J., 283–84, 286, 290, 292
Thomas, Linda E., 478
Three-Self Churches, 405
Tiamat, 575
Tian, 409
Tibbey, Mandy, 400
Ticciati, Susannah, 65, 66

INDEX OF NAMES AND SUBJECTS

Tiglath-Hileser III, 536
Till, Emmett, 485
Tilling, Chris, 541
Time to Keep (Radner), 609
Tinker, George E. "Tink" (Osage), 437
Titus (book of), 387, 399
Tolton, Augustus, 467, 471
Torah, 531, 539
   and Psalms, and Prophets, 678
Torrance, Thomas, 249
Townes, Emilie, 487
Tracy, David, 94
traditional evangelicalism, service and evangelism, 728
traditional liturgies, 727
traditionalists, 714
traditions, Patristic, Catholic, and Anabaptist of, 721
Trail of Tears, 435
trauma, 682
   hermeneutics of, 681, 682, 686
   loss, 682
   questions, 687
   reality, 691
   suffering, 693
   traumatic experiences, 686
Treat, James (Muscogee/Cherokee), 436
Trickster, 432
Trinitarian, 552
   Trinitarian Incarnational Anthropology, 156–58
Trinity Evangelical Divinity School, 711
Trinity, 638
Troy, 392
Trueman, Carl, 205
Tsang, Sam, 403
Tubman, Harriet, 478
Turkey, 683
Turner, Henry McNeal, 465, 466
Turner, Nat, 466
Turtle Island, 429, 438
   hermeneutics of, 430–431, 434, 439–441
Twiss, Richard (Lakota), 436
Twitter, 406
Tyndale, William, 721

Ugaritic conception, 580
   literature, 581
Ukachukwu, 422, 427
ultimate narrator, 720
Umbrella Movement, 403
   Umbrella Square, 403
Underground Railroad, 469
UNESCO, 384
Union Theological Seminary, 478–79
Unitarian Universalist, 520
United Kingdom, 402, 519
United Nations, 512, 637
Universal Negro Improvement Association, 466
Upkong, Justin, 352, 357
Uriah the Hittite, 682

Vaka'uta, Nāsili, 352, 353–54, 357
Vanhoozer, Kevin J., 89–90
vegetarianism, 342
   meat consumption, 323–26
Vesey, Denmark, 466
Victorian, 605
Vietnam War, 400–401, 405
   Vietcong, 401
   Vietnamese, 400–401, 405
Vindication of the Rights of Woman, A (Wollestonecraft), 498
Virgil, 382, 391–392
Vitruvius, 387

Wakan tanka, 441
Walker, Alice, 477, 488
Walker, David, 465–66
Wallace, David Foster, 3–4, 6, 11
Warrior, Robert Allen (Osage), 435, 436
Watchman Nee, 611
Watson, David, 721
Weaver, Jace (Cherokee), 436–37
Wesleyans, 721
Western civilization, 607
Western Europe, 399
   Western Euro-Americans, 435
   Western, Euro-American Christians, 441
Westphal, Merold, 712

What Would Jesus Deconstruct? (Caputo), 30
Wheaton College, 714
White Jr, Lynn, 330, 332–33
White, Ellen G., 720
Who's Afraid of Relativism? (Smith), 88
Wilberforce University, 468
wilderness, 177, 243–44, 262, 432–44, 576–78, 629, 639, 724
Wildman, Terry 440
Wilkin, Robert, 639
Williams, Delores, 473, 478
Williams, James G.
Wilmore, Gayraud S., 472, 474
Wilson, Woodrow (president), 265
Wind Clan, 440
Winn, Adam, 45, 50, 54
Winslow, Karen Strand, 498–99, 502
Wirkungsgeschichte, 284
Wisse, Maarten, 597
Witch of En-Dor, 578
Wittgenstein, Ludwig, 5, 83–84
Wollstonecraft, Mary, 498
Wolterstorff, Nicholas, 692
Womanist theology, 473, 477–80
Woodley, Randy (Keetoowah), 433, 438
Woolston, Clarence Herbert, 385
Work, Telford, 719
World Health Organization (WHO), 697
World War II, 384, 399
world's coming of age, 127
Wounded Knee, 440
Wovoka, 439
Wright, N. T., 182, 331, 335
Writing and Difference (Derrida), 34
Wrogemann, Henning, 228

Xenophilia, 407

yada, 286, 288
Yahweh, 430, 531, 576–77, 580–82, 623, 626, 672–78
Yannaras, Christos, 163
Yeago, David, 725
Yeshua, 401
Yong, Amos, 284, 286, 696, 704, 708

Zacchaeus (undesirable shortness of size or stature), 704
Zechariah, 644
Zechariah (book of), 439, 624
Ziegler, Phillip G., 45, 47, 51, 58
Zimmerman, George, 484
Zimmermann, Jens, 64
Zion, 403, 637
Zipporah, 504
Žižek, Slavoj, 322
Zoe Ministry, 636

www.ingramcontent.com/pod-product-compliance
Lightning Source LLC
Chambersburg PA
CBHW021216300426
44111CB00007B/336